THE MAKING OF
MODERN SOUTH-EAST ASIA

VOLUME ONE
The European Conquest

Map of South-East Asia 1835

THE MAKING OF
MODERN SOUTH-EAST ASIA

VOLUME I
The European Conquest

REVISED EDITION

D.J.M. TATE

KUALA LUMPUR
OXFORD UNIVERSITY PRESS
OXFORD NEW YORK MELBOURNE

Oxford University Press

OXFORD LONDON GLASGOW

NEW YORK TORONTO MELBOURNE WELLINGTON

IBADAN NAIROBI DAR ES SALAAM LUSAKA CAPE TOWN

KUALA LUMPUR SINGAPORE JAKARTA HONG KONG TOKYO

DELHI BOMBAY CALCUTTA MADRAS KARACHI

● *Oxford University Press 1971*

First published 1971

Reprinted with corrections 1977

ISBN 0 19 580363 9 (*Boards*)

ISBN 0 19 580364 7 (*Limp*)

Printed in Singapore by Dainippon Tien Wah Printing (Pte) Ltd.
Published by Oxford University Press, 3, Jalan 13/3,
Petaling Jaya, Selangor, Malaysia

Preface

THIS is the first of a series of three volumes designed to serve as an introduction to the history of modern South-East Asia for students at pre-University level and beyond, as well as for the general reader. The series itself is presented not as a history of South-East Asia as a whole, but as a study of the modernization of South-East Asia as a result of its impact with the Western world. The series has been drawn up to deal with this theme in three parts. The first part—the present volume—is concerned with the way in which the Western powers came to assert their presence in South-East Asia and how they came to bring virtually the whole region under their sway. The narrative here is primarily concerned with the political story, starting with the arrival of the Portuguese pioneers and culminating with the last struggles of the old states of South-East Asia for their independence. The second volume deals with the consequences of the Western ascendancy, the economic and social impact and the changes that were produced. The third volume outlines the administrative and political superstructure which was built up and traces the evolution of the South-East Asian reaction to Western imperialism, or in other words, the rise and development of nationalism throughout the region with the ultimate achievement of a new independence by the various peoples concerned.

Although this book cannot claim to be any more free from bias than any other history, it is not written consciously either from a Euro-centric or Asian-centric point of view, nor is it designed either as an apology for Western colonialism or as a vindication of South-East Asian nationalism. The intention has been to try and present what has happened, bearing in mind the different points of view of all who were involved. However, since the book has been written in Malaysia, it tends to deal with events according to their immediacy for this country and her neighbours. As a result, more detail and emphasis have been given to those episodes and happenings which most concern the people of Malaysia, Singapore, Thailand and Indonesia. Furthermore, quite a large number of footnotes have been included. It is hoped that these will serve as a useful supplement to the main text, and not as a distraction; the idea here has been to present the main story as clearly and as succinctly as possible, providing more detailed background material for those who care to pursue the matter further.

In conclusion, it must be pointed out that this book can lay no claim to originality, for it is almost wholly derived from secondary sources and is in fact the fruit of the labours of many men with different backgrounds and differing outlooks. I gratefully acknowledge the great debt I owe to the writing and researches on South East-Asian history by a whole host of distinguished scholars, some of whose works are to be found quoted in the lists of books and articles at the end of each section.

Kuala Kangar   D.J.M. TATE
August 1969

Acknowledgements

IN the writing of the present volume, I must acknowledge my indebtedness to those who have given me encouragement and advice in its preparation. I am particularly grateful to my former mentors in the School of Oriental and African Studies, University of London; to Professor C.D. Cowan who went far out of his way to offer suggestions and advice on points of detail and on general structure; to Professor D.G.E. Hall and to Professor Hugh Tinker, both of whom were kind enough to read and comment on sections of my manuscript. I am grateful to Encik Abdul Aziz bin Ismail, once headmaster of the Malay College, Kuala Kangsar, for his advice and criticisms of what I have written. I also owe a special word of thanks to Almarhom Engku Muda Orang Kaya[2] Mahakurnia Raja Razman bin Raja Abdul Hamid, P.J.K. of Kuala Kangsar, Perak, for his help regarding the section on Perak. I owe a very great debt of gratitude to the publishers who have exercised both encouragement and no mean patience and restraint during the production of this book, and last but not least to a generation of Malaysian students who have provided the inspiration for this work.

Contents

Introduction

SOUTH EAST-ASIA AND EUROPE

SOUTH-EAST ASIA is probably one of the earliest homes of man. The origins of civilization in this region date back to over 2,500 years ago, the same period during which the foundations of Western civilization were being laid. Throughout their long history the peoples of South-East Asia have been constantly exposed to influences from outside, some of which have played a very important part in shaping the culture of South-East Asia itself. However, down the centuries they have also developed their own unique way of life which they have successfully preserved though absorbing new influences at the same time. Then within the space of barely 200 years the face of the region was transformed. At the beginning of the nineteenth century South-East Asians began to experience an economic, social and political revolution which was profoundly to affect every aspect of their lives. South-East Asians suddenly found themselves becoming an inextricable part of the international network of modern capitalism and industry which dominates the manner in which the world lives today. The great changes in South-East Asian life have their origins in Europe. The new nation-states of modern South-East Asia are in fact products of the history of the last 200 years, during which time the impact of the industrializing West exerted itself on the traditional forces in the region. In other words, the story of the making of modern South-East Asia is the story of the interaction of two civilizations and of two ways of life. As a prologue, therefore, it is necessary to introduce the two entities involved—the world of South-East Asia with its traditional background, and that of Europe from whence the Western impact has sprung.

Tables

Maps

Illustrations

I: SOUTH EAST ASIA: POLITICAL DIVISIONS, 1967

A.   **Sovereign States** (Arranged in order according to size of population)

State	Area sq. miles	Population	Date of Independence	Definition
Indonesia	736,469	104,500,000 (1965)	1945	Republic
Vietnam[1]	125,889	33,543,000 (1966)	1945	Republic
North South	59,933 65,951	17,000,000 16,543,000		
Philippines	115,708	33,477,000 (1966)	1946	Republic
Thailand	198,454	31,508,000 (1966)		Monarchy
Burma	261,760	25,246,000 (1966)	1948	Republic
Malaysia*	130,000	9,575,000 (1966)	1957[2]	Monarchy
Cambodia	66,610	6,250,000 (1966)	1953	Monarchy[3]
Laos	91,425	2,060,000 (1966)	1954	Monarchy
Singapore*	225	1,914,000 (1966)	1965[2]	Republic

B.   **Other Political Units**

Name	Area sq. miles	Population	Status
Portuguese Timor	5,768	500,000 (1960)	Portuguese colony
Brunai	2,226	101,000 (1966)	British protectorate

(Population figures from the *Far Eastern Economic Review Year Book*, 1968, Hong Kong)

1   Still divided, but reunification provided for by the Geneva Agreement of 1954.
2   Malaya independent in 1957; Malaysia, comprising Malaya, Sabah, Sarawak and Singapore, formed in 1963; Singapore seceded from the Federation in 1965.
3   At present the former monarch has abdicated and is acting as Head of State.
*   Members of the Commonwealth of Nations

1. *The South-East Asian Background*

Today South-East Asia in more than one sense stands between two worlds. Physically the region is placed at the crossroads between the Indian sub-continent, the Far East and the Antipodes. Politically it forms a pivot in the struggle for world supremacy between the Communist and anti-Communist powers. Socially, culturally and economically South-East Asia lies halfway between modernity and its ancient past.

In many respects South-East Asia is already enmeshed in the gigantic complex of international capital, production and trade that dominates the world today. About one-fifth of its 200 million people are concentrated in large cities and towns which are similar in detail to other such urban areas the world over and are part and parcel of the industrial age in which we live. Millions more earn their living on the plantations and mines and in the factories which form the sinews of our civilization. And yet in most of the rural areas, some remote, some not so, the bulk of the population of South-East Asia live their lives in the same manner that their fathers did and their fathers before them. Unlike their contemporaries in the towns and cities, on the great estates or mines, their way of life, beliefs and social organization remain the same today as they have been for centuries. However, the world of the towns, factories and businesses is new. Two hundred years ago Singapore, Rangoon, Bangkok and Saigon were names that no one had heard of, trivial fishing villages, not the thriving centres of trade and industry that we know today. Batavia (now Jakarta), probably the region's busiest port in the eighteenth century, had a population then of around 20,000, Manila half that figure, and in general the total population of South-East Asia as a whole stood at about 25 million in the 1830s. The rubber industry was unknown and the only uses of oil were for lamps and the preservation of wood and palm-leaf manuscripts. The average voyage between Java and Bengal took from five to eight weeks or from Malacca to Canton around four to six weeks.[1] Politically, only four of the sovereign states in South-East Asia today (Table 1) existed—namely Burma, Cambodia, Thailand (Siam) and Vietnam (Annam). The Philippines was a Spanish colony with no antecedents as a political unit of its own.[2] Indonesia, Malaysia and Singapore did not exist at all, not even as figments of the imagination. Instead Island South-East Asia was fragmented into a whole host of principalities and powers of varying sizes and strengths. In their midst, the Dutch lorded over Java and held a few outposts elsewhere in the archipelago.

Therefore the South-East Asia which we can see in the making around us today is a product of the events of the last two hundred years. The great changes that have taken place during this period are of course closely associated with the rise of Western imperialism and the spread of its control over the region. But the forces of Western imperialism themselves were transformed during the same period and became the agents for the expansion of the new industrial order. The real root for all the changes which we are experiencing today lies in the Industrial Revolution which first became manifest in eighteenth century Britain. Out of the new forces of production which this called into being, new wealth was formed, new needs arose

2: SOUTH EAST ASIA–DIMENSIONS AND POPULATION

	Population	Area (sq. miles)
Mainland South-East Asia (Burma, Cambodia, Laos, Thailand and Vietnam)	101,414,000 (1967)*	750,000**
Insular South-East Asia (Indonesia, Malaysia and Singapore)	112,311,000 (1967)*	747,000**
The Philippines	35,600,000 (1968)*	115,700**

The Islands	Area (sq. miles)	Population: density per sq. mile
Borneo (Kalimantan)	22 (1959)*	280,000*
Sumatra	80 (1969)*	184,000*
West New Guinea (Irian Barat)	6 (1955)*	160,000*
Celebes (Sulawesi)	93 (1959)*	73,000*
Java & Madura	1,168 (1959)*	51,000*
Luzon	260 (1958)*	40,422*
Mindanao	147 (1958)*	36,538*

* Figures taken from *Fisher, South-East Asia* (third edition), Methuen, London, 1968.

** Figures taken from *Far Eastern Economic Review Year Book*, 1969, Hong Kong.

and new values were created. The Industrial Revolution has transformed the West as much as it is transforming the East and has united or is in the process of uniting the two inexorably into a common mould. Now we are all part, to a lesser or greater degree, of the industrial age with its mass production, its mass markets and its international means of distribution and exchange.

South-East Asia's contacts with the West can be traced back to ancient times—at least as far back as to the days of the Roman Empire.[3] These contacts became significant with the expansion of Europe during the course of the fifteenth and sixteenth centuries, heralded by the so-called 'voyages of discovery'[4] and marked by the arrival in South-East Asian waters of the Portuguese and Spaniards in the first decades of the sixteenth century. Within a hundred years of their arrival, the Iberians were followed by the maritime nations of North-West Europe—the Danes, Dutch, English, French, Swedes—amongst whom the Dutch were to play the most prominent rôle. But, as we shall see, up till the beginning of the nineteenth century, this Western intrusion was of marginal significance to most of the peoples of South-East Asia. Although there were a couple of Portuguese and English outposts in the region, only the Spaniards in the Philippines and the Dutch in Java became local powers of consequence. Their presence did not upset the traditional balances of power or the normal lines of political development in the region as a whole. Economically the Westerners fitted into the prevailing system and indeed became part of it rather than acting as agents of change. The real transformation of South-East Asia was to start taking place in the nineteenth century when the impact of the Industrial Revolution began to make itself felt.

The South-East Asian background: a pattern of diversity
This transformation can only be understood against the background of South-East Asia itself. The most immediate impression that the region gives is one of great diversity. Politically South-East Asia has been likened to the Balkans of Europe, aptly enough in view of the number of small states between which the region is divided, together with the long record of jealousy, rivalry and mutual suspicion which has characterized their relationships with one another. Nor does South-East Asia share the cultural homogeneity of China, Europe or India, each of which is the seat of one particular culture whereas here four of the world's major cultures have taken root. Physically, too, the region presents an extremely variegated pattern. Covering a total land area of 1,613,000 square miles (Table 2) which is the equivalent of about twice the area of the United States of America, within South-East Asia there is a tremendous variety in relief and physical environment. The broad rice-bearing plains of the Irrawaddy, Menam Chao Phaya and Mekong are separated from one another by great tracts of jungle-covered mountain. The volcanic-rich valleys of Eastern Java[5] and the rich alluvial soils of the Mekong Delta and the Red River Valley in Tongking contrast sharply with the poor laterite soils generally prevalent in the region. While the unity of the mainland is broken up by swamp, jungle and mountain, the archipelago fans out into a pattern of islands, the great majority of which are either totally uninhabitable or because of their difficult terrain only able to support limited numbers. These general physical conditions help in turn to account for the great diversity in races and cultures which the region affords.

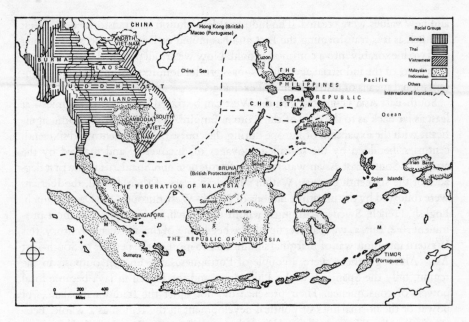

1. South-East Asia today, shewing national,
   racial and religious divisions

The racial background

In racial terms South-East Asia presents such a hotch-potch of peoples and tongues
that the region has been described as 'an anthropologist's paradise'.[a] There is not
one country in the entire region which can be described as racially homogeneous.
The most obvious example of the multi-racial society is that provided by Malaysia,
but even Thailand possesses considerable racial minorities.[b]

There are three main elements in the racial composition of modern South-East
Asia—the aborigines, who were either the original inhabitants of the region or its
first settlers; the later migrants, now forming the bulk of the indigenous population who settled in the region 2,000 to 4,000 years ago; and the most recent arrivals
who have made South-East Asia their home within the last hundred years or so.
The general trend of migration—until recent times—has been to use the peninsula
and islands of South-East Asia as a land bridge to Australia and beyond. Through
the centuries waves of migrants have gradually moved southwards, sometimes dis-
placing, sometimes intermingling and settling down with those they found
already established before them. In Mainland South-East Asia this has resulted in a
comparatively simple pattern by which the three major indigenous peoples—the

[a]D.G.E. Hall, *History of South-East Asia*, p. 5.
[b]See pp. 485–6.

Burmans, the Thais and the Vietnamese—have settled down in their present home-lands, either absorbing the earlier inhabitants or leaving them in isolated little pockets. In Burma where they form well over two-thirds of the present popula-tion, [a] the Burman infiltration appears to have begun sometime during the eighth century A.D. and the first Burman kingdom of consequence was founded three hundred years later. The Thai migration southwards was probably in process at around about the same time as that of the Burman but acquired its impetus and importance during the thirteenth century as a result of pressure from the Mongol conquerors of China.[b] The first Thai principalities in the region emerged in this century. The Vietnamese were already established in the valleys of the Red and Black Rivers in Tongking when history dawned in South-East Asia but their sub-sequent expansion southwards until they reached the Delta of the Mekong was stretched out over a period of sixteen centuries. There was a similar pattern in all these movements. They were not mass migrations but took place in the form of small groups of people moving down the great river lines from Tibet and south-west China. The Burmans and the Thais, as they moved south, encountered the Mon and Khmer while the Vietnamese moving down the coastline of Annam met the Cham and Khmer. By degrees these earlier established and more advanced races were conquered and absorbed or driven into the remote corners of their former homelands. Today the Khmer still maintain a national existence as repre-sented by the state of Cambodia, but only traces of the Mon and Cham peoples survive.[6]

In Indonesia, Malaysia and the Philippines today the racial pattern is far more complex and confused. Very broadly speaking the indigenous inhabitants of all three countries may be described as being of Malay, Malaysian or Indonesian stock, but these are very generalized terms which can cover a wide variety of ethnic strains and which have acquired several different uses.[c] The great complexity of the Malaysian-Indonesian racial pattern is a direct reflection of the fragmented nature of the archipelago in which these peoples have settled and also of the protracted manner in which the migrations took place. As a result large numbers of isolated and self-contained island communities grew up which were, however, always sub-ject to constant re-fusion by the arrival of new groups of migrants. The bulk of the region's present Malaysian-Indonesian population appears to have been settled within the archipelago by the end of the third century B.C. As far as it is possible to generalize on such matters, the indigenous population of the states of Malaysia and Indonesia can be said to be dominated by the Javanese and the Malays, and that of the Philippines Republic by the Tagalog and the Bisayan.[d]

In the meantime the aboriginal peoples of South-East Asia, about whose origins great uncertainty reigns, were either pushed south and eastwards by these great migrations till they ended up by becoming colonizers themselves in Micronesia, or withdrew deeper and deeper into the mountainous interiors of the mainland and the islands where they have preserved their own identity until this day.

[a]See p. 395.
[b]See p. 486.
[c]See p. 37, note 1.
[d]See p. 335.

As for the most recent arrivals, those who have migrated into South-East Asia within the last two hundred years—these are predominantly Chinese and Indians. The manner of their arrival has been totally different from that of the earlier migrants and belongs to the story of the emergence of modern South-East Asia itself.

Cultural diversity

The extreme racial diversity found in South-East Asia today is matched by its great variety of cultures. Indian influences expressed through various forms of Hinduism and Buddhism have left their mark. Today Hinduism is practised only on the island of Bali (though this does not take into account the Hinduism of recent Indian migrants into the region), but Buddhism is the official religion of 60 million Burmese, Cambodians and Thais (including Laotians)and is also followed by the majority of the 30 million Vietnamese.[7] Islam is practised by most of the indigenous peoples of Malaysia and Indonesia, amounting to some 110 millions. The Philippines has the distinction of being the only Christian nation in Asia but there are also important Christian minorities in Indonesia, Malaysia and Vietnam.[8] All these influences, however, must be considered in a cultural rather than a political sense, even where—as in the case of the West—political domination was also companion. Indian cultural influence affected all the peoples of the region, save for the Vietnamese who fell under that of China. In fact, Vietnam is the only South-East Asian country where Chinese cultural influence has predominated.

The underlying unity of South-East Asian life

Nevertheless, the wealth and strength of foreign cultures present in South-East Asia should not lead one to suppose that the peoples of the region have failed to evolve a cultural identity of their own. The current term 'South-East Asia' is of recent adoption[9], but it is evident from their chronicles that the Arabs, the Indians and the Chinese who had visited the region since ancient times regarded it as a distinct entity of its own. By the time that the first foreign influences started to make themselves felt in the early years of the Christian era, the peoples of South-East Asia had developed a distinctive way of life which was common to the region as a whole. According to Coedès,[a] this was characterized by wet-rice (sawah) cultivation, the domestication of the ox and the buffalo, the elementary use of metals (bronze and iron), the possession of navigational skills, matriarchy and the high social status of women, and a complex of beliefs which embraced animism, ancestor worship and reverence for high places. To this the Dutch scholar, N. J. Krom, adds (with reference to Java) the wayang kulit, the gamelan orchestra and batik work. All these presuppose considerable social organization and an advanced degree of technical progress.

This South-East Asian way of life provided the basis on which the kingdoms and empires of the future were to be built up. As the peoples of the region made contact with cultures from outside, they acquired new knowledge and new techniques. But there is nothing to suggest that they underwent political subjugation or that their culture became drowned by outside influences. To the contrary, the social organi-

[a]See G. Coedès, Les Etats Hindouisés d'Indochine et d'Indonésie.

zation of the region absorbed these influences and moulded them to its own purposes.

Land powers and sea powers in South-East Asia

The development of advanced techniques in rice cultivation and in navigation
underlines the two major directions along which the modes of life of the peoples of
South-East Asia moved in response to their environment.

Under the regime of the tropical monsoon,[10] the men who lived in the great
river plains and basins of the region had to learn to work together and control the
waters in order to grow their staple food, rice. This was true whether it was a matter
of water shortage as in the dry zone of Burma, or of abundance as in the region of
the Tonlé Sap in Cambodia, or merely of uncertain and irregular supplies as in
Central and Eastern Java. Analogous to what had happened on a grander scale
where the first civilizations of man grew up along the banks of the Nile, the Tigris-
Euphrates, the Indus and the Yellow River, the demands of water control gave rise
to the social organization from which kingdoms and empires were built. In this
way grew up one basic type of South-East Asian state; agrarian, based on the land
and the yield of the land, organized and controlled by a centralized hierarchy of officials, and headed by a ruler who was absolute and (in some cases) regarded as semi-
divine. Such was the nature of the first Mon kingdoms based on Lower Burma and
in the Menam Chao Phaya basin, of the early Burman empire of Pagan and its successors, of the rising and falling Thai dynasties. The foundations of Vietnamese
society were laid in the struggle to dam the waters of the Red and Black Rivers in
Tongking. Javanese agrarian power found expression in the kingdoms which
flowered in the Solo and Brantas valleys in the eastern part of the island—Mataram,
Kediri, Janggala, Singasari, Majapahit. The apogee of the agrarian state was
reached by the Khmer (or Cambodians) who from the splendours of their imperial
capitals in the district of Angkor dominated the Mekong Delta and the Menam
Chao Phaya basin for seven centuries.

The South-East Asian environment also gave rise to a second type of state whose
power was based on trade. Situated on the great east-west trade route, with its ac-
cessibility by sea and with again the rôle of the monsoons in providing their twice-
yearly pattern of contrary winds which served the needs of traders coming and
going,[11] the region was naturally destined as a half-way house for trade in transit.
Added to this, its own natural resources, its reputation for gold but more effectively
its fame as a source for spices made the region a goal for traders in its own right.
For some communities trade became the *sine qua non* of their existence and gave rise
to the sea power, centred on some estuary or on the lower reaches of a broad river
which provided safe anchorage and protection, and down whose waters came whatever produce the interior had to offer. Such powers were to grow up at strategic
points commanding the trade routes, like Sri Vijaya at Palembang on the Sumatran
side of the Straits of Malacca or Malacca itself on the shores of the Peninsula opposite, like Bantam commanding the Sunda Straits, the port states of North Java,
Brunai in north Borneo and Macassar in south Celebes. The rise and decline of such
states turned on their ability to control the trade route. Usually they were governed
by an aristocracy who built up and maintained their control by monopolizing some
staple article of trade such as pepper, rice or spices. This they achieved through the

indiscriminate use of naval power, imposing a monopoly in the area or simply by means that Europeans might term 'piracy'.[12] This type of state had its counterparts elsewhere in the ancient Greek and Phoenician city-colonies in the Mediterranean, or in city-empires like Carthage or later Venice and Genoa, or in trading aristocracies such as the Hanseatic League or in the port-states of Malabar.

On the periphery of these two types of power in the region, the land power with its agrarian base and the sea power founded on trade, flourished a whole host of smaller communities at various stages of development and with differing forms of political and social organization, usually self-sufficient and self-contained but influenced to a lesser or greater degree by their powerful neighbours. Such communities thrived transiently on the well-known trade routes before they were overwhelmed by some imperial power; typical of these were Langkasuka, P'an-p'an, Tambralinga and other small states which straddled the Isthmus of Kra before they fell before either Fu-nan or Sri Vijaya.[13] Similar also were the states of Sumatra and the Malay Peninsula which lived under a succession of stronger powers such as fourteenth century Majapahit, fifteenth century Malacca, or Acheh and Bantam in the seventeenth century. Other fringe societies flourished along the coasts of Borneo, on the islands of the Great East and in the Philippines. Meanwhile in the remote interiors of the region dwelt the older folk, the aborigines, who maintained fleeting contacts with the world without but who followed their own modes of life, little affected and little disturbed.

Trade and cultural assimilation

The importance of trade in the development of South-East Asian culture and civilization cannot be over-emphasized. Not only did the growth of overseas trade give rise to the typical sea power just described but it stimulated the growth and development of the agrarian powers as well. As elsewhere in the world, overseas trade acted as a vital agent for change. By promoting the accumulation of wealth in the hands of the ruling classes, it fostered economic and social development. It also brought the peoples of South-East Asia into contact with the cultures of their continental neighbours and led to the introduction of these outside influences into the region. In this way began the process of cultural assimilation which is such a marked feature of South-East Asia today.

The oldest influences from outside were those which came from India and China and which started to make themselves felt more or less simultaneously at the beginning of the Christian era. The influences from India were at first aristocratic and religious, expressed through various forms of Brahmanic Hinduism and Mahayana Buddhism,[14] but later these were to a great extent replaced by a more popular form of Buddhism which entered the region several centuries later.

The 'indianization' of South-East Asia

The extent of these Indian influences was so widespread, as is apparent from the evidence of inscriptions and stone temples and statuary, that the period during which they were paramount is known as the Hindu period or the period of 'indianization' in South-East Asian history. This period lasted from about the beginning of the first till the end of the twelfth century. During these 1,300 years the first historical states emerged, followed by the first empires.

The early Brahmanic-Hindu and Mahayanist-Buddhist influences were essentially aristocratic. They introduced into the region the concept of royalty and kingship according to the Hindu-Buddhist traditions of India, a code of laws[15] which were designed for the governance of the nobility not the masses, and a literature and mythology which were concerned with the struggles and exploits, not of ordinary people but of princes. Furthermore, the main sites of Hindu-Buddhist influence in South-East Asia are not to be found at the centres of trade in the region but at the seats of royal power, usually inland and far removed from the scene of commercial activity. These facts, together with the absence of any records from India of overseas conquests, the lack of regional evidence showing Indian racial admixtures amongst the indigenous peoples and the social barriers that existed between ordinary trader and landed nobility, appear to rule out all theories of conquest or of direct commercial proselytization. The initiative for the introduction of these Indian influences into the region seems to have come from local rulers themselves and had no direct connexion with trade or traders. The fame of the Brahmin and Buddhist priesthood for their magical powers was widespread. In very much the same way that in the West untutored Slav and German rulers who had carved out kingdoms for themselves from the remains of the Roman Empire turned to the prestigious and educated hierarchy of the Roman Catholic Church for aid in building up their new states, South-East Asian princes looked towards India. They summoned Brahmin priests and *savants* to their courts and probably artisans and soldiers of fortune as well, and employed them to sanctify their power and to organize their interests. In fact, apart from the Chola incursions of the eleventh century, and the interference of Bengal viceroys into the affairs of Arakan during the seventeenth century,[16] there is no concrete evidence of direct Indian intervention into the political affairs of South-East Asia at all. The spread of Indian culture in the region, therefore, must be dissociated from the idea of the extension of Indian political power. The process of 'indianization' was stimulated by local rulers and was bent to their local needs.[17] Knowing how the peoples of South-East Asia assimilated rather than adopted foreign cultures is essential to the understanding of traditional forms in the region.

The rôle of China

China's cultural influence, which began to exert itself at the same time as that of India, was confined to the Vietnamese, but unlike India, her political influence was wide. Chinese cultural influence itself amongst the Vietnamese was first implanted as the result of conquest[a] but survived Vietnamese liberation from Chinese dominion. This presumably was because the new Vietnamese ruling class, without any traditions of their own to fall back upon, needed to use the Chinese model of political and social organization to maintain their own power.

In general terms the presence of Chinese power has always been a factor of the greatest political significance in the politics of South-East Asia. This power has waxed and waned according to the conditions of unity and stability inside China itself but at its peak periods has always been felt throughout the region. From early historical times there are records of embassies from South-East Asian lands to the Chinese court—the number of similar embassies to India is very small by contrast:

aSee p. 434.

Chinese visitors were describing Fu-nan in the third century A.D.; Chinese pilgrims studied at Sri Vijaya's capital in the seventh century; Chinese armies under Mongol direction destroyed Pagan and unseated a Javanese dynasty in the thirteenth century; Chinese admirals protected Malacca from Thai raids in the fifteenth century. As late as the mid-nineteenth century both Burma and Vietnam acknowledged Chinese overlordship.[18] Although her cultural influence has been limited to Vietnam, China—apparently an outside power—through her political and commercial contacts has in fact been deeply involved in the region and its development. This involvement became intensified by the migration of large numbers of Chinese settlers into South-East Asian countries over the last two hundred years.

Hinayana Buddhism and Islam

The twelfth and thirteenth centuries saw the intensification of two other powerful influences in the region, profoundly modifying what had come before. These were Hinayana Buddhism, emanating from Ceylon and spreading over the states of mainland South-East Asia, and Islam which followed the trade routes and spread through the Malaysian world of the archipelago. Both the new religions had a more popular appeal than the old Brahmanic and Mahayanist cults which had preceded them. Hinayana Buddhism, purer, simpler and closer to the needs of the people spread through Burma into the Menam Chao Phaya basin where it was adopted by the incoming Thais and from there into the domains of the Khmer empire of Angkor where it helped to undermine the burdensome cult of the god-king. Islam, a revealed religion, expansionist and missionary, spread with similar effect amongst the peoples of the islands. Before these popular new forces the aristocratic cultures of the earlier 'indianized' states crumbled. In both cases accompanying political and economic factors played their part. The agrarian civilizations of the mainland, especially that of Angkor, had reached a period of crisis, with top-heavy superstructures and the pressure of migrant peoples;[a] in the archipelago a fortuitous combination of political circumstances rather than the influence of trade furthered the success of Islam. Muslim traders had penetrated the region for centuries prior to the age of conversion, but in the thirteenth and fourteenth centuries the doctrine became a weapon in the hands of local rulers. It could be turned against Hindu or Chinese traders or against a Hindu overlord. As Islam gained political mastery in India,[19] its influence was enhanced. The ruler of Malacca adopted it to gain backing for his newly-established port; the princes of the north Javanese port-states turned it against the fading Hindu empire of Majapahit; further east and a century later in the Celebes and Moluccas, Islam became the weapon of the local aristocracy in their struggle against the Christian European intruders.

The advent of the West

Such was the environment in which the influence of the West, the last and most recent of the influences from outside, was planted. From their point of view the Westerners in the fifteenth and sixteenth centuries were coming into a totally unfamiliar and exotic world. What they found was a region which had a strong and well-integrated culture of its own. They also found themselves irrupting into an

[a]See pp. 469-70.

ancient, complex and well-established system of international trade which linked South-East Asia with the world outside.

Against this background the culture of the West at first appeared like a grafted bud on the tree of indigenous civilization and it took slowly. But it also in time became irrevocably attached.[20] To see the nature of this Western graft and to understand its effects it is necessary to have a look at its own original environment in Europe.

2. The European Background

The term 'European' or even 'Westerner' is synonymous with the term 'white man', which in this connotation includes the Anglo-Saxon and Latin descendants of Europeans living in North and South America today. This, however, does not mean that all Europeans come from the same stock and race. In fact, Europeans can be divided into three broad categories[21] and each category in turn can be further sub-divided into several very self-conscious national groups. 'The races of Europe have always felt themselves to be different from one another, and have acted as if they were so.'[a] Indeed the history of Europe in many respects amounts to no more than a long catalogue of inter-racial and inter-nation strife. The origins of the First and Second World Wars lie largely in the quarrels and fears of rival European nationalisms, and the story of European imperialism in South-East Asia and elsewhere is likewise characterized by the bitter spirit of competition which has marked the relationships between the rival colonial powers.

One factor that does give all Europeans a common background is the Christian religion. Even if—as modern trends suggest—the influence of the Christian churches is pointedly on the wane, the attitudes and values of Europeans have been deeply influenced by Christian traditions. At the same time a study of European history will reveal that, superficially at least, Christianity or its pursuit has been as much a divisive force as a unifying one. Today there are three main branches of Christianity —Orthodox, Roman Catholic and Protestant. These divisions are the product of two major schisms which have taken place during the course of Christian history. The first occurred in the eleventh century over matters of doctrine and resulted in the Bishop of Rome establishing himself at the head of the break-away Catholic (Universal) Church.[22] His adherents were all to be found in Western Europe, while the traditionalists who maintained the Greek Orthodox Church peopled the greater part of Eastern Europe, including Russia. The second major schism took place in the early sixteenth century, this time within the Roman Catholic Church itself. A movement for reform, which became known as Protestantism, started in Germany and Switzerland and resulted in bringing into existence a whole galaxy of separatist churches.[22] As a consequence of this Reformation movement, the peoples of

[a]H.A.L. Fisher, *A History of Europe*, p. 6.

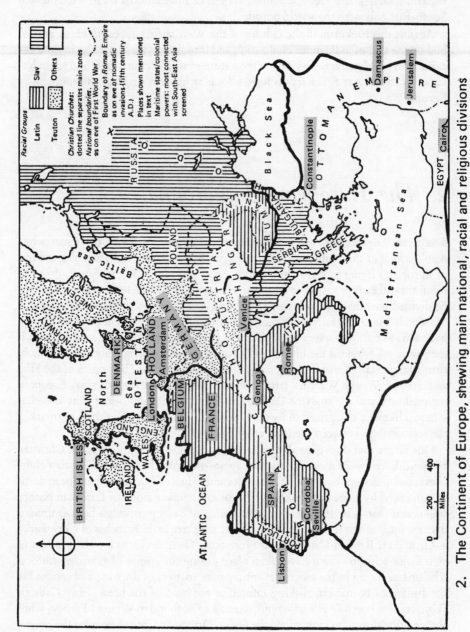

2. The Continent of Europe, shewing main national, racial and religious divisions

southern Europe have remained within the fold of Rome while the majority of those living in the north and north-west of the Continent have followed the Protestant persuasions. These religious dissensions inevitably had their political repercussions and gave rise to a long series of bitterly conducted persecutions and so-called wars of religion. These religious issues were also projected into the colonial policies and politics of the Europeans in South-East Asia.[23]

The fundamental unity underlying European civilization is cultural. As Fisher puts it, 'We Europeans are the children of Hellas'.[a] Hellas, the name for ancient Greece, was the cradle of European civilization and the ancient Greeks evolved those characteristics of thought and outlook which Europeans consider representative of their culture today. Salient amongst these is the emphasis on individual man as the basis for forming all value-judgments, which is humanism; the concept of man as 'a political animal'[24] who can only realize his personality to its fullest extent in conjunction with his fellow-men, in other words in society—and must be given the freedom to be able to do so—which leads to the assumptions on which the democratic system is based; and the sense that man is above all a reasoning being, free to use his mind to explore the world around him—which gives rise to the spirit of inquiry and to the systematic accumulation of knowledge which is science.

The main stages in European history

The period of Greek civilization which found its expression in a host of small, self-contained city-states both in Greece itself and along the shores of the Mediterranean Sea lasted from around the fifth until the third century B.C. The Age of Greece gave way to the Age of Rome. The Romans founded an empire which, lasting a thousand years, preserved the wisdom and values of the Greeks and spread these over the greater part of Europe. The Roman Empire also became the medium for the rise and spread of Christianity. Christianity's founder was executed on the orders of a Roman colonial governor but three hundred years later a Roman Emperor[25] made Christianity the official religion of the Empire. In the event the Christian religion came to be strongly influenced by the humanistic ideas of Greece but more significantly still, it came to be identified with European civilization and culture. In the long, dark years that followed the collapse of the Roman Empire in the West, the Christian Church became the sole custodian of civilized knowledge and values, and the only source of learning. In fact, Europe and Christendom became synonymous.

The Western Roman Empire collapsed in the middle of the fifth century A.D.[26] under the twin pressures of internal corruption and the incursions of nomadic peoples from the north and east which nearly extinguished European civilization altogether. A thousand years followed, known as the Middle Ages, during which time the modern nations of Europe began to take shape. A more primitive economic, social and political order—feudalism—took the place of the highly centralized and systematized administration of Roman times. Standards of living and culture dropped and only through the monasteries of the Roman Catholic Church was learning kept alive at all. The recovery and revival of Western Europe began towards the end of the eleventh century, stimulated to a large extent by increasing

[a]Fisher, *A History of Europe*, p. 1.

contacts with the ancient centres of civilization in the Middle East. These contacts were mainly renewed through the outbreak of a series of religious wars between Christian and Muslim powers. Starting with the First Crusade in 1056, they culminated 400 years later in the Portuguese searching for the kingdom of Prester John and finding the sea-route from Europe round southern Africa to India. The Christian powers of Europe aimed at recapturing their Holy Land of Palestine, with its sacred shrines at Bethlehem and Jerusalem,[27] from the Muslim Turks. Ultimately they did not succeed in this, but the Europeans were as a result reintroduced to the knowledge and learning of the Ancient World which formed the nucleus of the studies in the universities of Cairo, Baghdad and Damascus.[28] At the same time the equipping and maintenance of these Christian expeditions brought about a revival and fresh expansion of trade. (The important trade in spices was renewed between South-East Asia and Europe during this period.) The outcome of these contacts was to help restore prosperity to the peoples of Europe, more especially to those who had their homes on the shores of the Mediterranean Sea. The same contacts also helped to bring about the great intellectual revolution in European history called the Renaissance. The Age of the Renaissance, which began in Italy during the course of the fourteenth century, marked the emergence of Europe into the Modern Age.

The colonial powers of Europe in South-East Asia

When one speaks of Europeans, one should properly think of all Europeans, including Russians, Poles, Czechs, Hungarians and others from the central and eastern parts of the continent, as well as of west Europeans such as the Spaniards, Dutch, English, French and the like. However, in fact, most South-East Asian experience of Europeans is limited to those who come from the maritime states of west and north-west Europe.

Portugal and Spain

The two European nations which have had the longest association with South-East Asia are Portugal and Spain. The Portuguese and Spaniards, whose relationship to one another in race and language is somewhat analogous to that between the Malays and the Menangkabau, share the Iberian Peninsula between them as their homeland. The characters of both peoples were forged during the epic struggle in which they became engaged first to contain and then to expel the Muslim Berbers and Arabs of North Africa,[29] who invaded and overran the greater part of the Peninsula in the eighth century. This struggle which went on for five centuries, had two major consequences. In the first place, it imbued both the Portuguese and the Spaniards with a spirit of militarism and martial valour which expressed itself in the desire to reconquer the homeland from the Muslim invader, and which later transformed itself into the desire to conquer Muslim lands overseas. Secondly, it led them to regard themselves as the champions and vanguard of Roman Catholic Christianity. When in the fifteenth century, with their first conquests of territory in North Africa and armed with the new knowledge disseminated by the Renaissance, Portugal and Spain stood on the threshold of expansion into foreign lands, they carried with them not only the desire for great riches (which they most certainly had) but also the conviction that their mission was to spread the Christian religion. In this respect, they differed radically from the severely practical, business-minded Dutch and Englishmen who were to follow.

The accidents of geography also played their part in determining the expansionist course of Iberian history; that their position on the Altantic Ocean made them hardy and skilled seafarers; that their position on the Mediterranean (although here the Portuguese were only indirectly affected) kept them in touch with the latest commercial developments eastwards (from which, nevertheless, they were excluded); and that the West African coastline was adjacent for them to explore. Under the guidance of ambitious and nationalistic rulers who were deeply influenced by the spirit of the Renaissance, a Portuguese became the first European to explore the sea-route around the Cape of Good Hope into the Indian Ocean, and an Italian—but in Spanish pay—the first to cross the waters of the Atlantic and reveal the Americas.[30] These fifteenth-century voyages of exploration, which mark the beginnings of European expansion into the other continents of the globe, brought great wealth to Portugal and Spain, and made them the most powerful nations in Europe for the next one hundred years. But neither state had the human or material resources to defend empires of the dimensions they had founded once they were faced with a serious challenge, and after 1600 their possessions rapidly shrivelled in size and importance. As far as South-East Asia is concerned, with the exception of the Philippines, Portuguese and Spanish power was only of passing moment.[31]

Holland, Britain and France

The three European states which have played the largest rôle in the affairs of South-East Asia are Holland, Britain and France. They made their effective appearance on the scene at the beginning of the seventeenth century. Of these powers Holland was the most dominant for the first 200 years; Britain assumed the major rôle during the nineteenth century. France's interest in South-East Asia was spasmodic and less sustained.

Holland is and always has been a small country. The Dutch, who racially speaking are of Teutonic stock, have waged throughout their history a heroic struggle against the odds of nature which has taught them how to achieve much with few resources by dint of hard effort. To begin with, they wrested a good part of the land on which they live from the ever-threatening sea;[32] during the sixteenth century they wrested their political freedom from their powerful overlord, Spain. This, and their already well-established position as the carriers of northern Europe's trade[33] gave them the impetus which carried them past Lisbon into the Indian Ocean and beyond to Java and the Moluccas. The only explanation as to why the Dutch succeeded in establishing, and maintaining, for three and a half centuries a colonial empire nearly half way round the world, is that right from the very beginning they made a national effort. A considerable proportion of the capital resources of Holland were put into the first voyages sent out to Java on the eve of the seventeenth century. The Dutch East India Company when formed in 1602 was part of a great national enterprise, supported and backed by leading merchant families from the principal ports in the country and receiving the full authority of the state. Nevertheless, after the seventeenth century which as far as the European powers in South-East Asia were concerned was the Dutch century, plain facts and figures caught up with Holland. She could not hope to hold her own against the faster expanding and far greater resources of France and Britain. So gradually Holland sank to the rank of a second-rate power. All the same the Dutch managed to remain a leading colonial nation until the middle of the present century.

The British Isles are the homeland of four distinct races—the English, the Irish, the Scots and the Welsh. Divided by origin, race and language, it took time to achieve political unification and even to this day this is not complete.[34] However, English became established as the *lingua franca* by the twelfth century, and in matters of overseas colonization it became impossible to draw a distinction between the four racial groups. Although their position predisposed the islanders to become seafarers, the British Isles for long existed on the extremities of the civilized European world, and during Roman times formed a frontier province of the Empire. It was not until the latter part of the Middle Ages (by which period the islands had acquired their present racial composition and distribution), when English kings lost their feudal commitments on the European mainland, that the British started to develop as a trading nation. Their first main export was cloth, woven from the wool of English sheep. But it was the discovery of the Americas that transformed Britain and determined her destiny as a trading and imperial power. Now the British Isles were no longer on the outskirts of Europe but held the gateway to the Atlantic. As time went on, Britain's overseas connexions came to outweigh her European ones; the most important of these were her settlements in North America, her trading posts and growing possessions in India, and later on still her trade with China.[35] During the seventeenth century the British found themselves competing on roughly even terms with the Dutch and the French. A hundred years later the wealth they derived from their American and Indian possessions put them far ahead in the colonial race. Britain's rise was in no small part aided by her long duel with France. From very nearly the earliest days of their national existence the English were involved in hostilities with the French. During the Middle Ages this had centred on the feudal ambitions of English kings in France itself. After the sixteenth century the struggle turned on colonial rivalry, and Britain secured predominance in both North America and in India at the expense of France. However, the factor that gave Britain almost unchallengeable power during the nineteenth century and enabled her to establish a vast overseas empire in the four corners of the earth was the Industrial Revolution. This had its origins in England and gathered momentum during the course of the eighteenth century. Many forces combined to bring about this great change in the modes of production; one of the main forces was the growing pressure for more manufactured goods for the ever-expanding overseas markets. Britain's early start in industrialization gave a tremendous boost to her economic power and left her rivals so far behind that it took them nearly a century to catch up and overtake her. Britain's own natural resources were limited except for the coal and iron so necessary to power the new industries, but her established position in overseas markets and the technical skills and products she could provide offset this. London became the banker to the world, Britain its workshop; the world in return became Britain's source of raw materials.[36]

The Dutch and the British (except for the majority of Irishmen who are Roman Catholics) are both Protestant peoples and of Teutonic stock; the French on the other hand are closer to the Spaniards and Portuguese, being both Roman Catholic and of Latin origin. Until the second half of the nineteenth century when she was overshadowed by the creation of a united Germany, France was the strongest land power in Europe. Until the end of the eighteenth century when Britain started to garner the advantages of her lead in the Industrial Revolution, France was also one of the leading colonial powers. Occupying a rich and fertile land, with a large population, and under a dynasty—the Bourbons—who created the most brilliant court in Europe, France seemed cut out to play a great rôle in overseas expansion. That she failed to do so effectively or consistently was the consequence of her endemic entanglement in dynastic feuds and quarrels on the continent of Europe itself. The most serious and damaging of these was the feud with the powerful Habsburg family who at one stage held within their grasp the crowns of Spain and Austria and controlled most of Italy and Germany. Britain also got involved in these dynastic disputes but whereas the British participated in them to further their own national interests, French kings sought dynastic rather than national advantage. During the long series of dynastic wars which took place in the eighteenth century, Britain eliminated French competition in Asia and America while France fought all her wars on the European continent at little profit to herself. The economic burden of these wars, allied to other circumstances, contributed to the great French Revolution tion of 1789 which swept aside the old régime of Bourbon kings and did much to modernize the state. But it was not for another fifty years that the rulers of France succeeded sufficiently in overcoming their domestic problems so as to be able to resume colonization overseas.

Other colonial powers: the United States of America and Germany

In general the second half of the nineteenth century saw a great increase in the spirit of imperialism. This was to a large extent the result of the triumph of nationalism in Europe, symbolized by the achievement of unification for their nations by the peoples of Italy and Germany in the 1870s.[37] Old-established colonial powers found themselves challenged in their formerly secure preserves overseas by these new nation-states whose nationalism found expression in the demand for a place under the colonial sun. In addition to this, spreading industrialization over which Britain no longer commanded a monopoly or even predominance added to the pressures for overseas markets and colonies.

As far as South-East Asia is concerned two new Western powers made their presence felt during these years. The first of these was the United States of America which had developed an interest in the China trade in the last quarter of the eighteenth century and had become involved intermittently in South-East Asian affairs ever since.[a] The nucleus of the fifty states which make up the American Union today was formed by the thirteen English colonies founded during the seventeenth century along the Atlantic seaboard of North America. From this small federation which came into being when they broke away and declared their independence of Britain in 1776, the United States of America have expanded to control more than half the North American continent, stretching from the Atlantic to the Pacific Ocean. The first hundred years of her existence were taken up with this expansion, a process which involved the absorption of peoples from many other (but mainly

[a]See pp. 193; 200, note 79; 231; 369 et seq.

European) countries. By the middle of the nineteenth century the enormous potential of the United States with her huge area, vastly increasing population and apparently limitless material resources began to make itself felt. The establishment of
California as the thirty-first state of the Union in 1848 made the United States a
Pacific power.[38] In the 1850s she played a leading part in opening up Japan to Western trade and influence. At the end of the century she expelled Spain from the
Philippines and substituted her own rule there for that of the Spaniards.

The other Western power to become involved in South-East Asian affairs during
the last quarter of the nineteenth century was Germany. The Germans (also of
Teuton stock) as a race have dominated Central Europe for centuries, but they had
no existence as a united nation until as recently as 1871. Why this should have been
so lies beyond the scope of this book; it is sufficient to say that the eventual unification of Germany completely altered the existing balance of power among the states
of Europe. In terms of population the new Germany came next to Russia but was
far more efficiently administered; in terms of industrial output and potential, she
came next to Britain in 1871 and had overtaken her by the end of the century. Although Germany never obtained any colonial possession in South-East Asia itself,
she exerted a very strong influence, especially through her business houses which
were to be found in every large port and commercial centre in the region. The in-
visible German presence was keenly sensed by the older colonial powers.[a]

Reasons for Western interest in South-East Asia

From the foregoing it is obvious that the prime factor that attracted the colonial
powers to South-East Asia was trade. Alongside this were present various forms of
the idealism which in later years articulated itself as 'the white man's burden'—his
'civilizing' mission amongst the less fortunate and gifted peoples of the world; in
the case of the Catholic powers of Portugal and Spain—and to a much lesser degree,
of France—it showed itself as an unabashed attempt to Christianize heathen populations.

Asia in general has traditionally enjoyed amongst the peoples of Europe the reputation for great wealth and advanced civilization. This reputation was to a large
extent justified, but when the age of European expansion arrived it was the spice
trade which was the principle object of attention. Spices were in high demand everywhere and a market for them grew up in Europe during the period of the Crusades.
They had manifold uses as drugs, medicines and preservatives. The spice trade became the monopoly of the Arabs and Indians in western Asian and the Indian Ocean
and that of the Italians of Venice and Genoa in the Mediterranean. Because of this,
the scarcity of supply, and the difficulties of the long and hazardous journey
from the Spice Islands themselves, they fetched on arrival in Europe extremely high
prices. With colossal profits at stake it is not surprising that the Spaniards and Portuguese set out to pierce the spice monopoly and get it into their hands, nor that the
Dutch, English and French followed in their wake.

The spice trade in particular was the magnet which drew the Western powers to
South-East Asia, but it was not to be their mainstay. Once established, wider trading
interests developed. Finally, the development of the Industrial Revolution trans-

[a]See pp. 322–3.

formed the nature of these interests and created a demand for new raw materials—many of which South-East Asia could supply—and for new markets in which to sell manufactured goods, which in the process of time South-East Asia's population could partly satisfy.

[1]The period, of course, would vary with the type of sailing vessel involved as well as with the season of the year. The figures for Batavia and Manila quoted above refer to the population living within the walled cities, not to those living in the *kampongs* on the outskirts.

[2]The colony did not include the Muslim South (Mindanao and Sulu) which was ruled by two independent sultanates.

[3]Roman artefacts have been found at Oc Eo in the Mekong Delta, South Vietnam and at P'ong Tuk in Thailand; other similar discoveries in the Far East, and Chinese and Roman references to contacts with each other presuppose at least indirect contacts with South-East Asia as well. See Sir M. Wheeler, *Rome beyond the Imperial Frontiers*, London, 1955.

[4]A very Euro-centric conception. It could be argued that Europe needed to be 'discovered' by the rest of the world.

[5]There are 85 identified volcanoes in Java, of which 17 are active and 18 recently dormant; their debris has contributed greatly to the extreme fertility of the soil on the island.

[6]About 400,000 Mon survive in Lower Burma, and 120,000 Cham in the provinces of Binh Thuan and Ninh Thuan in South Vietnam and on the South Vietnam-Cambodian border.

[7]The Vietnamese style of Buddhism, however, is different; derived from China and Mahayanist in form. See note 14 below.

[8]There are about 2 million Christians in Indonesia (1.5 million Protestant; 0.5 million Roman Catholic), especially in North Sumatra and in Celebes. Vietnam's 1.5 Roman Catholics are the largest group of their kind in South-East Asia outside the Philippines.

[9]First coined by the Europeans and came into general use during the Second World War, especially after the setting up of South-East Asia Command (SEAC) for Allied operations against the Japanese in the region.

[10]Broadly speaking the whole of South-East Asia is affected by the south-west and north-east monsoons which produce alternate wet and dry seasons and facilitate a shuttle movement by sailing ships to and from the region. See note 11 below.

[11]The two monsoons blow as follows: a) the south-west monsoon—June till September; b) the north-east monsoon—October till March. But these vary considerably according to locality. Indonesia, especially south of the equator, receives the north-east monsoon largely as a westerly, while during the period of the south-west monsoon, it blows south-east from Australia. The mainland and islands of South-East Asia form a barrier to direct sailing between east and west, making it convenient for sailors to break their journey there and await the arrival of the contrary monsoon. Thus South-East Asia served as a natural meeting place for traders from either direction to exchange their wares.

[12]'Piracy was just as much a normal activity in Asian waters as in the Mediterranean at the time of Hellas' power and the time of the Berber harbour princes .... Relations in Oriental international trade should not be rendered in nineteenth century liberal concepts. Plundering fits completely into the historical picture of peddling trade on the one hand and on the other royal authority with personal trade, occasional trade, monopoly and naval power all for the benefit of the king's own treasury.' J.C. van Leur, *Indonesian Trade and Society*, p. 359, note 92.

[13]The main transhipment routes across the Isthmus of Kra were as follows: a) Takua Pa—Cha'iya; b) Kedah—Singgora (Songkhla); c) Tavoy—Three Pagodas Pass—P'ong Tuk—Pr'a Pathom and down the Kanburi river. Further to the north d) Moulmein via the Raheng (Tak) Pass to the Menam Basin. Another land route linked the Menam Basin with the Mekong via Korat and Si T'ep.

[14]Brahmanic Hinduism or Brahminism was that branch of Hinduism most closely associated with the teachings and practices of the Brahmin or priestly caste who claimed primacy and developed their doctrines along exclusive lines. Buddhism in or soon after the reign of Asoka (273–232 B.C.) divided into two main schools—Mahayana and Hinayana or Theravada. Mahayana Buddhism which aimed at liberalizing Buddhist teaching spread widely outside India, especially in China and Japan; it also spread inside India but became so closely linked to Brahminism that its identity was eventually lost. Hinayana Buddhism adhered more strictly to the original doctrines of Buddha, was purer and simpler in form and after the disappearance of Buddhism in India, it continued to thrive in Ceylon.

[15]Observance of the Dharma, a universal code of behaviour by which the individual cultivates virtue and religious merit; especially emphasized were the Manusamhita or Laws of Manu which were concerned with royal and priestly duties. They formed part of the Dharmasastras or law codes which were written some time between the first and fifth centuries A.D.

[16]Between A.D. 1000 and 1050 Lower Burma and the Straits of Malacca were subjected to a series of devastating raids carried out by the Tamil Chola kings of South India. They contributed greatly to the decline of Sri Vijaya's power. Regarding Arakan and the Viceroys of Bengal see pp. 405 et seq.

[17]A useful parallel can be drawn with Japan which during the eighth and ninth centuries A.D. borrowed heavily from and assimilated Chinese culture without at any stage submitting to Chinese political control.

[18]In Fu-nan the Chinese envoy K'ang Tai recorded the earliest account of a South-East Asian state in the third century A.D.; in the seventh century the Chinese Buddhist pilgrim, I-tsing, reported Sri Vijaya as the greatest centre of Buddhism in the region. For the other references see pp. 28–30.

[19]Mahmud of Ghazni (938–1030) was the first important Muslim conqueror of Indian territory. He was followed by Mohammad of Ghur who began the Muslim occupation of the country in 1191, bringing the important trading state of Gujerat under his control the next year. The Delhi Sultanate was established by one of his generals in 1206 and extended its power over the whole of north India. The Moghul Empire was established much later by Babur after the Battle of Panipat, 1526, and came to control nearly the whole sub-continent.

[20]'The engrafted slip of European outpost, at first of limited political significance, and practically without economic importance for the East, gradually grew irremovably fast to the tree of Asian civilization.' van Leur, op. cit. p. 149.

[21]That is Latin, Slav and Teuton: in fact these are linguistic rather than racial terms, but at the same time are closely identified with racial groups. The Latin or Mediterranean group tend to be short, narrow-headed, slightly built and dark; the Slavs (associated generally with those from Eastern Europe) broad-headed, stockish and fair; the Teuton or Nordic group, broad-headed, blue-eyed, tall and fair. As in South-East Asia, however, there has been great inter-mixture which makes generalizations misleading.

[22]The Bishop of Rome is the Pope: Roman Catholics form the largest and best organized of the Christian Churches, with a world-wide following of over 400 million which is nearly half the world total of Christians; the Orthodox Church is headed by a number of Patriarchs of whom the Patriarch of Constantinople is the most senior but the Patriarch of Moscow the most influential. The total number of Orthodox Christians totals some 142 millions. The sects of Protestantism are innumerable; the chief are the Baptists, Calvinists, Church of England (Anglicans), Lutherans, Methodists, Moravians, Presbyterians and Quakers. The total number of Protestants of all denominations stands around 226 million. 'Reformation' is the name given to the Protestant reform movement as a whole.

[23]That is, as reflected in the rivalries between the Roman Catholic Portuguese and Spaniards on the one hand and the Protestant Dutch during the seventeenth century, and between Roman Catholic and Protestant missionaries in more recent times.

[24]'Man is a political animal'—attributed to the Greek philosopher, Aristotle (384–322 B.C.).

[25]The Emperor Constantine (A.D. 306–37). The colonial governor was Pontius Pilate, Governor of Palestine.

[26]The eastern part of the Empire with its capital at Constantinople survived for another thousand years before it fell to the Ottoman Turks in 1453. The Byzantine Empire (as it was known) controlled the Balkan Peninsula and a large part of western Asia until the time of the rise of Islam.

[27]Officially there were eight crusades. The Portuguese struggle with the Muslims of Morocco, culminating in the expulsion of the latter from Portugal and the start of the Portuguese voyages of discovery to the East is sometimes referred to as 'The Last Crusade'. Bethlehem and Jerusalem were the scenes of the birth and death respectively of Jesus Christ.

[28]Also Cordoba in Spain (at a later date): Arab scholars knew of the writings of Ancient Greece long lost to the West, and inherited the scientific knowledge of the Egyptians and of the Mesopotamians. They developed medicine, optics, astronomy and geography in particular.

[29]Called 'Moors' (Moros) by the Spaniards and the Portuguese, a term which came to be applied to Muslims in general in South-East Asia by the Europeans. The Muslims of North Africa had an important cultural influence on the Iberian peoples, traces of which are still observable in the languages, literatures, art, music and architecture of both countries. Also the Muslim universities of Cordoba and Seville became great centres of learning for West European scholars.

[30]Namely Bartholomew Diaz who rounded the Cape in 1488: the Italian was Christopher Columbus of Genoa, who made his celebrated voyage in 1492. However, the Americas actually take their name from Amerigo Vespucci, who sailed across the Atlantic after Columbus but was the first to identify them as hitherto unknown continents.

[31]Spain held the Philippines until 1898 while Portugal retained her outposts at Goa, Diu, Daman and one or two other places on the Indian shore, at Macao, on Timor and on the coasts of Africa. The greatest Iberian stake was in Central and South (or Latin) America which remained in their hands until the nineteenth century.

[32]An old saying goes that God made the sea and the Dutch the land; half of Holland lies below sea-level and has been protected from the sea by an elaborate system of dykes and polders. The Dutch have also reclaimed about two million acres of their land from the sea by similar methods.

[33]The Dutch dominated the fishing industry of the North Sea; they also virtually monopolized the carrying trade between the ports of Portugal and Spain and those of north-west Europe, including Britain, Scandinavia and the Baltic. Amsterdam was the greatest port and banking centre in northern Europe during the sixteenth and seventeenth centuries.

[34]Wales was brought under the English Crown during the thirteenth century; the crowns of Scotland and England were united under one monarch in 1603 but the United Kingdom was not properly formed till 1707 when the parliaments of the two countries were merged. Ireland was the greatest problem. The English conquest started in the twelfth century but today the island is divided between Ulster or Northern Ireland which forms part of the United Kingdom, and the quite independent Irish Republic or Eire in the South. The existence of growing Scottish and Welsh nationalist movements today shows that the political unity of the United Kingdom should not be taken for granted.

[35]Newfoundland, Britain's oldest colony, was established in 1583, but the bulk of the early colonization of North America took place in the first half of the seventeenth century. The first English factory in India was founded at Surat in 1612. The development of the China trade dates from the end of the same century.

[36]Napoleon once rather unkindly described the English as a nation of shopkeepers; even more unkind were the comments of the English radical politician, John Bright, who remarked that the British colonies were a gigantic scheme of outdoor relief for the British aristocracy!

[37]Germany, which up till 1871 was made up of a loose confederation of thirty-nine states, was united under Prussian leadership through the statesmanship of Count Otto von Bismarck, the Prussian Chancellor. Similarly the various principalities of the Italian Peninsula were brought together into a united kingdom of Italy largely by the genius of Count Cavour, the prime minister of Sardinia, the most powerful of the Italian states. The kingdom of Italy was founded in 1862 and the process of unification completed in 1871.

[38]As new territories were peopled by European settlers, they were administered by Washington until they were sufficiently evolved to acquire statehood and be admitted as members of the American federal union. Today there are fifty states of the Union, most of them creations of the nineteenth century. The latest additions are Alaska and Hawaii, both in 1959.

BOOKS FOR FURTHER READING

Coedès, G., Les Etats Hindouisés d'Indochine et d'Indonésie, E.de Boccard, Paris, 1947.

Dobby, E.H.G., Monsoon Asia, University of London Press, 1961.

Fisher, C.A., South-East Asia, 3rd ed., Methuen & Co., London, 1968.

Fisher, H.A.L., History of Europe, 2nd ed., Eyre & Spottiswoode, London, 1957.

Hall, D.G.E., History of South-East Asia, 3rd ed., Macmillan & Co., London, 1964.

Harrison, Brian, South-East Asia, A Short History, Macmillan & Co., London, 1954.

Leur, J.C. van, Indonesian Trade and Society, Essays in Asian Social and Economic History, W. van Hoeve, The Hague, 1955.

Part One

ISLAND SOUTH-EAST ASIA

THE world of South-East Asia naturally divides into two parts, each with a character and dynamic of its own. To the north there is the land mass of Mainland South-East Asia which is dominated by the great river basins and valleys which have shaped its civilization: to the south lies the world of the archipelago—Island South-East Asia —where the dominating factor has been the sea which both unites and divides. Of the two parts, Island South-East Asia is by far the more complex, fragmented by its very nature yet bound together by certain basic strands. Today the Island region is comprised of the nation-states of Indonesia, Malaysia, the Philippines and Singapore, but none of these had any history as independent political units prior to 1945. In this sense they stand out in contrast to their long-established sister-states on the mainland which can trace their origins back long before the era of Western colonial control. In other words, Indonesia, Malaysia, the Philippines and Singapore are products of the period of European colonialism, a fact which tends to make a study of their historical antecedents confusing in the extreme. Before the spread of Western imperialisms, the region was a mosaic of political units in varying degrees of size, importance and development. These pre-colonial states bear very little resemblance to the new nations of today and modern frontiers have no meaning in terms of the past. However, beneath the political surface of the present, flow the basic historical currents which have shaped and still shape the destinies of the peoples of the region. The presence of these forces may not be immediately apparent when confronted by the plethora of today's Western technology and political forms but it is there all the same. The spirit of the peoples, their outlooks and attitudes, have been conditioned by their environment of sea-way and padi-field, of island and mountain. They have been conditioned by trade and the influences which have come along with it. They have absorbed much of these without losing their own identity. The last of these influences to establish itself before the arrival of the European was that of Islam, and this struck more deeply than the rest, to mould the average inhabitant of the archipelago today. In terms of political power also, certain basic factors emerge—the focal position of Java, so rich in manpower and fertile soils, and the never-ending duel between sea-power and the agrarian state. In short the world of Island South-East Asia has a life and rhythm of its own which has survived and operates to this very day.

Sculpture of an ancestor, Nias Island

1. INDONESIA, MALAYSIA AND SINGAPORE

1. The Malaysian World till 1500

The racial background

As we have already seen, the great majority of the peoples of Island South-East Asia may broadly speaking be classified as Malaysians or Indonesians.[1] There is still great speculation as to the origins, manner and time of arrival of the Malaysians/Indonesians, but nowadays it is generally accepted that the main waves of migration into the region took place during prehistoric times and were spread out over a number of centuries.[2] It is also generally agreed today that the peoples of the archipelago are all of the same basic Mongoloid stock. However, two factors have contributed to the profusion of races, dialects and cultures which thrive at present in the island world. One reflects the physical characteristics of the region itself which covers a vast area comprising six large islands[3] and over 2,000 smaller ones, all easily accessible by sea but with swampy, jungle-covered and mountainous interiors resulting in the growth of small, isolated self-contained communities. The second factor is the manner of the migrations themselves—small bands of men moving always southwards over the years, arriving amongst older-established communities, mixing with them, and passing on; the consequence has been a continuous and protracted process of inter-fusion and re-fusion of elements of the same fundamental stock and culture blending in different combinations and producing the motley racial and linguistic pattern of today. So we have the Malays, Menangkabau and Achinese of Sumatra[4] and the Peninsula; the Javanese, Sundanese and Madurese in Java and Madura; the Malays of Borneo;[5] the Macassarese, the Bugis and the men of Minahassa in the Celebes; and the Balinese who claim descent from Hindu Javanese refugees of the fifteenth and sixteenth centuries.

Of all these different groups, the three most dominant and widespread are the Javanese, Malays and Sundanese. The total number of Javanese in the 1950s was estimated to stand at around 50 million, that of the Malays around 13 million,[6] and that of the Sundanese around 11 million. The Javanese and Sundanese are mostly concentrated on the island of Java itself, although there are important colonies of Javanese elsewhere in the archipelago, especially in south Johore, south Sumatra, parts of Borneo and in the islands of the Great East. The Malays on the other hand have always been widely scattered, a natural outcome of their spirit of adventure and skill as sailors which has carried them the length and breadth of the archipelago and has made their language the lingua franca of the region. Today the Malays form the majority of the inhabitants in the Malay Peninsula, Sumatra and on the coasts of Borneo. They are also found in considerable numbers in the islands of the Great East.[7]

Nevertheless, 20 per cent of the population of Island South East Asia is made up of other races—mainly aboriginal—of non-Mongoloid stock. In the Malay Peninsula there are only about 40,000 such people. In Sumatra there are numerous small aborigine tribes but also over one million Bataks. In Borneo the Dayaks dominate the interior and form about one-third of the total population of Sarawak while there are several other important groups besides. In the Celebes there are the To-raja in the centre of the island and the To-aela of Minahassa;[8] the Bon-fia in the Moluccas, and the Papuans both in West Irian and on the nearby islands of the Lesser Sundas.

The pattern of diversity

Given the vastness of the region, the variety of peoples in it and the widely differing geographical circumstances which prevail, the absence of any political cohesion prior to modern times should not be at all surprising. Although, as we have seen, it is possible to speak of a basic Malaysian/Indonesian culture, nearly every conceivable form of political and social organization has developed amongst the peoples of the region. With the Menangkabau of West Sumatra, for instance, we find a matriarchal society based on the family, clan and village, while in Bali the social organization is patriarchal and patterned on the irrigation system. In Java society was hierarchical and bureaucratic, based on a closely worked out system of land tenure; in Ceram it was based on tribal groupings and in Timor simply on class. Monarchy was the traditional political form in the Malay states, oligarchy was the rule amongst the Bugis of South Celebes and republican forms were reflected in the government systems of the Menangkabau.[9] This wealth of political and social forms is matched by the incoherent nature of the region's political history. Unlike the mainland states of South-East Asia where a continuous line of political development is discernible behind the rise and fall of successive dynasties, the political

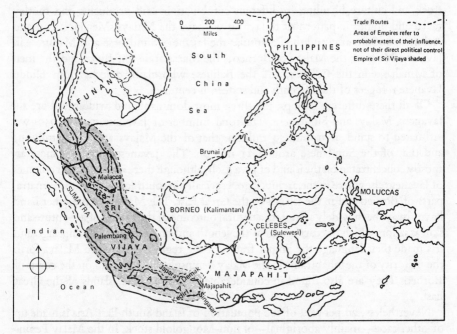

3. South-East Asia, illustrating early trade routes and the first Island Empires

history of the islands is full of the rise and fall of disparate states of varying strengths, extents and periods of time. However, within this bewildering kaleidoscope of events and régimes which have followed one upon the other, there are also certain basic elements to be found which give shape and meaning to the whole.

The rôle of the Javanese and the Malays

To begin with, two peoples can be seen to have played a predominant rôle in the shaping of events in the region. These are the Malays and the Javanese who, when the Portuguese arrived on the scene at the beginning of the sixteenth century, had the trade of the archipelago largely in their hands. In fact, at all the ports and transhipment centres throughout the islands, Malays or Javanese were dominant. The Malays were to be found on the coasts of North Borneo and in the ports of the Celebes and of the Great East, while Javanese settlements were concentrated in south and west Borneo and on such islands as Ternate, Hitu and Ambon in the Moluccas. There was also a sizeable Javanese population in Malacca.

Of the two, Javanese influence was the greater, both at the beginning of the sixteenth century and for the major part of earlier history. The superiority of Javanese influence is predicated by the great natural wealth of the island of Java itself, with its tropical vegetation, volcanic sub-soil and well-watered valleys—especially in the central and eastern parts of the island[10]—which have enabled a substantial population to live and flourish there. Although Java's population in the past never remotely approached the dense figures of today, in relation to the neighbouring islands it was always large and provided the source for Javanese political power. As a result, Java developed as the real centre of Indonesian culture and civilization, with Malay sea-powers based on the Straits of Malacca acting in a secondary and far more ephemeral role.

Land-powers and sea-powers

The profusion of states and the themes lying behind their rise and fall in the archipelago can be understood and simplified further by distinguishing between two basic patterns of development.[a] Conditions in Java favoured the evolution of the agrarian state, not so unlike those which rose up in the fertile flood-valleys and basins of the Irrawaddy, Menam Chao Phaya and Mekong on the mainland. In particular, in the fertile Brantas and Solo valleys and in the Madiun basin there arose this type of power which was based on a large settled peasant population, which could provide manpower and rice-tribute and which was administered by a hierarchic bureaucracy. The court of the ruler (the *kraton*) formed the centre of all power and authority in this type of kingdom and the royal capital was the political and military headquarters. As in the mainland monarchies, the sanctions for royal authority came increasingly from the sacred functions that the ruler assumed as the guardian of the state and the guarantor of its prosperity.

The earliest identifiable of such states is that of Mataram which was originally based in Central Java but later moved its capital eastwards into the Brantas Valley. The kings of Mataram were followed by the mysterious Shailendra dynasty[11] during the ninth century, which in turn gave way to the twin states of Kediri and

[a]Refer pp. 9-10.

Janggala. Kediri and Janggala were reunited as Singasari in 1222. Under its ruler, Kertanegara, Singasari became the first land-based Javanese power to extend its control overseas and it apparently established its sway in Sumatra.[12] However, in 1293, Kertanegara and his kingdom came to a sudden end, destroyed by a rebellion, and after a short hiatus the state of Majapahit rose up to take its place. With the rise of Majapahit, Indonesian history had reached a new stage in its evolution, for the new state became not only a land-power but a commercial empire as well.

Outside Java there arose the other basic pattern of polity, the sea-power whose strength was drawn from its control over the trade routes. Such powers were far more cosmopolitan in character than the agrarian states of Java and acquired at various periods great importance as diffusion centres for foreign cultures, such as was the case with Sri Vijaya in south-east Sumatra which became a great centre for Mahayana Buddhism during the eighth and ninth centuries, and then later Malacca which during the fifteenth century developed into the headquarters of Islamic missionary enterprise in the archipelago. The empires which these powers built up differed very considerably from the highly organized and centralized polity of the Javanese land-state. The empire consisted of the dominant trading port, the centre of royal authority, and a host of vassal ports which acknowledged the suzerainty of the imperial power, sent their tribute or trade to the capital and were left to govern themselves in their own way. Imperial authority was dependent on the royal fleets which could maraud and punish at will. Such states could rise and fall very swiftly, in response to local circumstances and events.

The first 'empire' of this type was not strictly speaking in Island South-East Asia at all. This was the empire of Fu-nan, based at the tip of what is today South Vietnam. Fu-nan probably reached its zenith during the third century A.D. when its sway extended down to the Isthmus of Kra and the northern part of the Malay Peninsula. Then as Fu-nan, beset with internal problems, declined in the early sixth century, her place was taken by the Sumatran power of Sri Vijaya. Sri Vijaya, the first Malay empire, was centred on Sumatra's east coast in the vicinity of modern Palembang. From this advantageous position, Sri Vijaya's control came to stretch southwards down the Sumatran coastline to the Straits of Sunda and Java beyond, and northwards across the water to the Malay Peninsula, touching as far as Ligor (Nakhornsrithamarat) in the Isthmus of Kra. At one period Sri Vijayan power appears to have been established over Central Java as well.[13]

Sri Vijaya lasted for over 400 years as the seat of commercial power in the Straits of Malacca before it eventually gave way to the Javanese empire of Majapahit which rose during the course of the fourteenth century. Majapahit reached the peak of its power and glory in the days of king Hayam Wuruk and of his even more celebrated chief minister, Gaja Mada. The actual extent of this empire is open to debate[14] but it is clear that whilst this Javanese power was effective, no port in the Straits of Malacca or elsewhere in the region could rise to a position of sufficient strength to challenge it. However, soon after Hayam Wuruk's death in 1389, Majapahit fell prey to internal feuds once more and started to lose its grip. Its decline was a long one and the empire did not finally disintegrate until over a hundred years later, by which time the Portuguese were already established at Malacca. But as early as 1400 Majapahit was no longer able to dominate the Straits of Malacca nor check the incursions of the raiding Thais from the north.

The last of the great Malay sea-powers to arise in the region before the coming of the Europeans was that of Malacca. The decline of Majapahit coupled with a timely resurgence of Chinese influence under the Ming dynasty,[15] which provided relief from Thai pressure, made its rise possible. A fugitive prince, bearing the Hindu title of Parameswara, from Sumatra or possibly from Majapahit itself, founded a new settlement at the mouth of the Malacca river on the west coast of the Malay Peninsula. The historical pattern then repeated itself. The new port-state filled the vacuum created by Majapahit's decline and waxed rich on its domination of the Straits. Within a generation Malacca had grown from a small village of aborigine fishermen to the largest port of call in all South-East Asia (or, as the Portuguese claimed, in all the world). By 1450 Malacca was strong enough to beat off Thai attacks unaided and to start acquiring an empire of her own.

In the circumstances of the region there was bound to be intercourse and conflict between these two types of power. As the material civilization and economy of each developed, they were thrown into increasing inter-dependence on one another, and at the same time became involved in a great struggle for hegemony in the region. The vague shadows of this conflict may be seen behind the mysterious story of the Shailendra dynasty; it emerges clearly with the rise of the Javanese states of Singasari and Majapahit and the decline of Sri Vijaya and Melayu.[16] There is evidence that Malacca was involved in the same pattern and that its sudden collapse before the ships of Portugal only served to forestall a probable Javanese conquest. Meanwhile the clash between maritime and land power was crystallized on Java itself with the struggle of the port-states of the island's north coast against dying Majapahit, and the subsequent rise of inland Mataram and its ultimate triumph. In fact this struggle between land and sea power continued as one of the major themes of Javanese history up till the eighteenth century.

Trade and 'indianization'

Another element which has drawn the peoples of the region together and has helped to determine the course of their development as well as mould their political pattern, is that of trade and the trade routes. Through the ages the peoples of the archipelago have been linked with the ports and marts of the world beyond by the 'gossamer, golden threads' of commerce.[a] The nature and importance of the rôle of the trade route in the historical evolution of the region are too obvious to need comment. Primarily, trade and the channels of trade have provided the paths along which foreign cultures have penetrated and influenced the region, although in this connexion it must be remembered that this was a two-way process. Not only did foreign traders come to the archipelago with their different techniques and skills, their values and their own ways of life; more significantly Malaysians/Indonesians visited countries outside the region and brought back their experience and evaluations of the cultures they had come into contact with.

However, to divine the exact nature of the part played by trade in the historical evolution of the archipelago it is essential to distinguish between modern patterns of trade and business and those of yesteryear. The patterns we know today of trade and commerce linked to centres of industrial production and serving markets of

[a]J.C. van Leur, *Indonesian Trade and Society*, p. 92.

millions are a development of the last hundred and fifty years. The nature of traditional trade in South-East Asia, in the Indian Ocean and indeed in the world at large
was totally different. It was a world of a pre-industrial economy, based on countless self-sufficient village communities scattered throughout the region. The old-
established trade which flourished was one in small quantities of rare and precious
commodities—goldware, nutmeg, mace, cloves, sandalwood, pepper, silks, porcelain—passing from market to market, not one of bulk imports for mass consumption linked to industrial centres of mass production.[17] Such trade confined itself to a
relatively small class of merchants and was of interest and importance to a ruling
aristocracy; it was not a trade in which the people, peasants and fishermen, partook
or about which they were concerned. Nor should it be supposed that the influences
which spread along with this trade were carried by the traders themselves. The
merchants formed small, self-contained communities of their own in the various
foreign ports where they did their business. They lived in their own quarters of the
town and were subjected to their own headmen and had little contact with their
neighbours beyond those with royal officials and in the market. The trade served
aristocratic tastes and aristocratic needs and what culture it carried was at the behest
of that aristocracy. It is only in this sense that the way the early Hindu and Buddhist
influences penetrated into the archipelago can be understood.

The presence of these Indian influences is evident, especially in Central and East
Java at the capitals of the old agrarian powers.[18] It is equally evident that the Hindu
and Buddhist influences imported were essentially aristocratic ones, They undoubt-
edly played a most important rôle in the consolidation of the administrative ap-
paratus which gave rise to the kingdoms and empires of later years, but they played
little part in the lives of the ordinary people and of their culture. As van Leur has
said, the period of indianization in the history of the islands left behind a 'thin, easily
flaking glaze on the massive body of indigenous civilization'.[a]

Trade and the coming of Islam

But the same cannot be said of the part played by Islam which was also brought
along the trade routes to become a major formative factor in the history of the
archipelago. In the first place the new religion stood out in strong contrast to its
predecessors. It was a religion of the people as well as of the individual, strongly
missionary, austere, yet simple and easy to follow. In contrast also to the manner in
which Hindu and Buddhist influences established themselves in the islands, the introduction of Islam was linked closely to the merchant community, for which it
had a natural appeal. In fact the spread of Islam in the region was linked with the
trade routes in a way which was not apparent with the spread of earlier Hindu and
Buddhist influences. The great centres of Hindu and Buddhist culture tended to be
associated with royal *kraton* which were far removed from the great emporia of
trade; Islam thrived first and foremost in the cosmopolitan ports of the Indies and
it is there that the religion is most strongly entrenched to this day.

However, Muslim traders had been in the region hundreds of years before the
age of conversion dawned. This is clear from that fact that there was a strong colony
of Muslim (Arab) merchants established at Canton as early as the seventh or eighth

[a]Van Leur, *Indonesian Trade and Society*, p. 169.

centuries A.D. According to Chinese sources, Arab merchants predominated in the carrying trade between China and India during the twelfth century. The earliest direct indication of the presence of Islam in the archipelago comes from an eleventh century inscription in Champa; in Java it dates from the Leran inscription of 1082, and there is also evidence of Muslim settlers in Majapahit and of Muslim authority in the Malay Peninsula at least half a century before the foundation of Malacca.[19] But Islam was not widely known nor a significant force in the region until the fifteenth century. The advent of Islam as a political factor was first noted by European travellers in the late thirteenth century[20] who reported Muslim states in north Sumatra. North Sumatra was to be the springboard from which the new religion jumped to Malacca just over a century later, and in turn Malacca was to act as the diffusion centre for Islam throughout the rest of the archipelago. From Malacca it spread effectively over the Malay Peninsula, back across the Straits to the pepper ports of Sumatra's east coast, and down south and east along the trade routes. By the end of the fifteenth century, Islam was firmly established in the Malay Peninsula and Sumatra, along the northern coasts of Java and at Brunai in north Borneo, and it was penetrating the Moluccas and the Sulu archipelago.[21] The most significant advance was the conversion of the port states of north Java. 'Java was converted in Malacca', as the saying goes, and the conversion of the north coast ports of the island sealed the fate of the tottering Hindu dynasties of the interior.

By the time of the Portuguese and the Spaniards' arrival on the scene, the process of islamization was by no means complete, and in the case of the Philippines, the Spaniards succeeded in checking the Muslim advance. Elsewhere, the Christians from the West lost the race and were forestalled in Java, the Moluccas, the Celebes and in other parts of the archipelago. The last important centre to embrace Islam was Macassar around the beginning of the seventeenth century. In the meanwhile the new centres of Muslim power extended the faith over the regions of their neighbours—the Achinese carried it to the Batak lands of the Sumatran interior and to the Menangkabau on the west coast; the new Javanese power of Mataram drove against the Hindus in the east; Brunai spread the Message along the shores of Borneo and Sulu and on to the island of Mindanao. By 1700 only Bali and Lombok remained as strongholds of the old Hindu-Buddhist faith and culture.

Islam and regional politics
Despite the very closely related links between trade, the trade route and the spread of Islam, its sudden efflorescence in the archipelago during the fifteenth century was also due to other factors. Foremost amongst these was a combination of political circumstances both within and outside the region which favoured its expansion in this period. In the outside world there was the swift rise of Muslim power in India which had such close trading ties with the archipelago. The incursions of Mahmud of Ghazni at the beginning of the eleventh century were followed by the invasions of Mohammad of Ghur who brought the whole of north-west India under his control and was instrumental in bringing into being the Delhi Sultanate. Later—in the first half of the sixteenth century—Muslim power was consolidated under the great Moghul dynasty which brought the greater part of the sub-continent under its control. With the rise of the Moghul power, Hinduism as a political force went into eclipse. Vijayanagar, the last Hindu kingdom of importance in the Indian south

disappeared in 1556, by which time the mantle of Islam had passed into the hands of Acheh and Johore in the Straits.

With the rise of Muslim power in India, South-East Asia was affected in several ways. In the first place the ancient sources of Hindu (and Buddhist) culture dried up.[22] Secondly, Muslim merchants in the archipelago could now reflect the influence of powerful Muslim potentates in India. Third and most significant of all was the conquest of Gujerat, which had taken place at the time of Mohammad of Ghur in 1292. Cambay, Ranir, Diu, Dhabol and Surat—all Gujerati ports—followed one another in swift succession as entrepôts for the goods of India, the West, of South-East Asia and beyond. Gujerati merchants were to be found by 1500 in all the important ports of the Indian Ocean and of the sea route to Canton. Meanwhile the new Muslim kingdom of Gujerat itself, after a period of vassalage to the Delhi Sultanate, established its independence in 1403 and thereafter grew into a strong and stable state under rulers who became renowned for their religious zeal and whose patronage of Islamic studies gave Gujerati religious teachers an unsurpassed reputation throughout the Muslim world. Gujerati influence was evident at the earliest stages of the Muslim penetration of north Sumatra,[23] and fifteenth-century Malacca had a settled colony of about 1,000 Gujerati traders. Their influence furthermore played an important part in the events which led to the Portuguese assault on Malacca in 1511.[a]

These external circumstances coincided with political changes within the archipelago which equally favoured the rise of Islam. By 1380 the Hindu-Javanese empire of Majapahit was beginning to decline. Sapped by debilitating feuds between members of the royal family, Majapahit was no longer able to exert its domination over the arteries of trade which were the source of its overseas power. This both enabled the rise of Malacca as a new trade emporium and seat of political power on the Straits and led within a short period to its adoption by Muslim merchants as a new centre for their trade and influence. The rulers of Malacca adopted Islam as a means to assert their power at the expense of Chinese, Thai and Hindu alike. When Islam was brought by the Javanese traders in Malacca back to their home ports on Java's north coast, they were also importing a political weapon which they used to assert their autonomy from the overlordship of Hindu Majapahit. Majapahit eventually succumbed, and its real successor, the inland state of Mataram, found it expedient to embrace the new religion itself in order to re-establish more effectively its suzerainty over the island.

The spread of Islam is therefore partly attributable to the rôle it played in the politics of the era. This political rôle was significantly increased at the beginning of the sixteenth century and thereafter with the appearance of the Europeans on the scene. The first two European peoples to arrive, the Portuguese and the Spaniards, came not only to grasp the monopoly of the spice trade but to spread Christianity to which they were also dedicated. In fact, their arrival in the region was in many respects an extension of the struggle which had already been going on in Europe for centuries between Christian and Muslim and now was carried into the Indian Ocean. Shortly after the Portuguese captured Malacca they sent their first missionaries to the Moluccas. The one and a half centuries which followed might be des-

[a]See p. 44.

cribed as a race between Islam and Christianity to convert the region. Everywhere, except in the Philippines, the Muslims won by a short head. Islam had the advantage of being established earlier, but political and economic motives became welded with the religious as Islam became identified with the struggle of the people of the archipelago to resist the European attempts at commercial domination. As we shall note, Portuguese and Spanish power in the region during the sixteenth century was severely limited; that of their successors, the Dutch, was not, and the challenge they presented to the political and commercial interests of the peoples of the archipelago during the seventeenth century was far more formidable. The Dutch were successful in imposing their control over the Spice Islands and Islam played a very important rôle in developing the spirit of resistance in those so-called 'free' ports, the centres of cosmopolitan trade, which lay beyond the Dutch monopoly. Acheh, Bantam, Macassar, Brunai—all became centres of missionary enterprise and fervour as well as centres of political and commercial defiance of the Dutch.

The impact of Islam

Nevertheless the spread of Islam was not just a matter of political expediency. Unlike its predecessors, Islam was a religion which struck deep into the societies of the region and profoundly modified their outlook and way of life. Such a penetration could not have been achieved as a result of political considerations alone. The islamization of Island South-East Asia was a process in which ruler, merchant and missionary all played their parts. The initial penetration concerned ruler and merchant, but the nature of Islam itself and the nature of the struggle which subsequently ensued between the Europeans and the peoples of the region over trade ensured that it did not become a court religion as Hinduism and Buddhism had been.

To understand the way in which the initial penetration must have taken place, the relationship between ruler and merchant must always be borne in mind. As was common throughout the countries of Asia, the South-East Asian prince was the chief merchant in his state. Without his permission, no foreign trader could do business in his territory; in addition the ruler controlled whatever produce or goods the country had to offer and had the first option on all trade which went through his ports. The goodwill of the ruler therefore was essential to any foreign merchant who hoped to do business in his domains. But the ruler and the ruling class also needed a link between themselves and the foreign traders who visited their ports. This link was usually provided by the *shahbandar*, more often than not a foreigner himself who owed his position to his ability as interpreter. A shahbandar enjoyed considerable influence and power, both at the court and outside. He could advise the ruler on matters of trade and overseas affairs and had control over the collection of taxes and imposts on the traders themselves. There is evidence to show that with the rise of Muslim power in India an increasing number of such officials in South-East Asian ports were Muslims; as such they became the channel for the introduction of Islam into court circles, as representatives or agents for powerful Muslim Indian potentates, through the introduction of Muslim financiers, technicians or teachers to the court, or even through intermarriage. Such men were influential in Bantam, Surabaya and other Indonesian ports[a] and the story of the Tamil-Muslim

[a] See pp. 63 et seq.

family that captured the office of Bendahara under the Malacca Sultanate affords a very graphic illustration of how these influences might work.

But the task of spreading Islam is the duty of every Muslim and we may suppose that many individual merchants acted as religious teachers and guides as well. In addition to this Muslim preachers and missionaries also accompanied the traders on their voyages and came to play an important part in spreading the religion amongst the people. The *Malay Annals* are full of stories about the missionaries who lived at Malacca which became a great centre of Muslim learning. Amongst these missionaries, the Sufi orders[24] played a prominent role. Sufi missionary orders predominated in the proselytization of the Malaysian–Indonesian world between the fourteenth and eighteenth centuries, and although concrete evidence is wanting, it seems reasonable to suppose that the individualistic and mystical approach of Sufism was peculiarly suitable to the traditions and way of life which prevailed in Island South-East Asia. In this respect, the absorption of the new religion was made all the easier.

There is considerable controversy among historians as to how far the peoples of the peninsula and the archipelago have become islamized, ranging from those who with van Leur think that it was as superficial as the adoption of the earlier Hindu-Buddhist influences, to those who think that the conversion of the peoples of the region was real and profound. In fact, it is clear that Islam has affected the peoples of the archipelago to different degrees. The earliest centres of Islam in the region were commercial centres—states like Acheh, Malacca, Brunai, Bantam, Macassar—and these became and have remained the strongest centres of Muslim activity up till modern times. In other areas Islam penetrated less profoundly and in some cases provoked severe social antagonisms.[25] In general, Islam was absorbed more completely in the cosmopolitan centres of trade or in the regions which lived by trade than in the centres of agrarian power.

In summing up, it can safely be said that Islam after the fifteenth century spread and became the way of life of many millions of people in the archipelago, fashioning their outlook and becoming a vital force in their social and political development. Furthermore, wherever Islam has taken root, it has never been dislodged.

Island South-East Asia on the eve of the Western intrusion
When the Portuguese and Spaniards arrived on the scene at the beginning of the sixteenth century, they came into a region which was in a state of transition. Islam was rapidly penetrating the archipelago while the older Hindu-Javanese order was crumbling and had nearly disappeared. Politically-speaking there were three main centres of power. The strongest and most apparent was that of Malacca whose control by 1500 was acknowledged in all the ports and harbours of the Malay Peninsula, in the pepper ports of the Sumatran coast opposite and in the Riau-Lingga archipelago to the south. But the real political centre of gravity still lay in Java. Javanese influence had suffered a temporary eclipse during the period of Malacca's rise as a result of the disintegration of Majapahit, which still survived but was on its last legs in the interior. Majapahit's heritage had fallen to the thrusting, fiercely competitive port principalities along the northern shores of the island, of which Tuban, Grisek and Surabaya were amongst the most prominent and where Demak (Japara) was nearest to establishing a local hegemony. The Javanese were well rep-

resented through their traders in the Great East, in south Borneo and in Malacca itself, and there were signs that Javanese influence was developing into a threat against Malacca's own continued authority in the region. By the same token, Javanese influence was also strong in the Great East where in the Moluccas the third centre of power lay, represented by the growing sultanates of Ternate and Tidore which divided control of the Spice Islands between them.

[1]The use of the terms 'Malay', 'Malaysian' and 'Indonesian' can give rise to great confusion. 'Malay' may refer to a) the Malays as a distinct race; b) Malay-speaking peoples; c) peoples in the region of the same basic ethnic stock. In this book the term is used in the strict sense of a). 'Malaysian' and 'Indonesian' were originally generic terms used to describe the ethnically-related peoples of Island and Mainland South-East Asia as a whole—in this sense 'Malaysian' has been used by Emerson and other writers. The term 'Indonesian' was introduced in 1881 for the same purpose, and was confirmed in this use by the German ethnographer, Adolph Bastian, in 1884. However, since the coming into being of Indonesia and Malaysia as political entities, these terms now refer to the nationals of these two respective countries. Throughout this book, unless otherwise indicated, the terms 'Malaysian' and 'Indonesian' are used in their original ethnic sense, and are regarded as interchangeable.

[2]That is, between 2,500 and 500 B.C. approximately. It used to be thought that there were two distinct migrationary waves associated with two distinct cultures (Stone Age and Metal) but nowadays it is believed that the cultural changes which took place within this period (the introduction of metals) were the result of increased trading contacts between China and Tongking on the one hand with the coastal areas further south on the other.

[3]That is, treating the Malay Peninsula as an island; the others being Irian/New Guinea and Borneo (the second and third largest islands in the world respectively), Sumatra, Java and Celebes.

[4]This leaves out of account other minor but distinct Malaysian racial groups as follows: Coastal Malays (from the East Coast and the Riau Archipelago); the Palembang Malays (claiming their origin from Malacca); the Serawayer (from Benkulen); the Rejang, Lebong, Pasemak, Ampat Lawang and Semanda (all from the West Coast); and the Orang Gunong, Orang Darat, and Orang Sekat (Bangka and Belitung).

[5]Here the term 'Malay' may refer to a) those who originated from Sumatra and Riau-Lingga (especially found in Brunai, Sambas and the West Coast); b) the Banjarese (mixture of Malay and Javanese) and the Bugis settled in Kutai and Banjarmassin; c) aborigines converted to Islam. Other related peoples include the Kedayan and Bajau (North Borneo and the Philippines).

[6]That, is including the Menangkabau of Sumatra—3 millions; Malays in Sumatra and other islands—6 millions; Peninsula Malays (including Menangkabaus)—4 millions.

[7]In the States of Malaya (the Malay Peninsula) Malays form 51 per cent of the total population (1960); they predominate in all the main centres of population in Indonesian Borneo and in Brunai; form 17 per cent of the population of Sarawak (1960) and are negligible in Sabah. In the Great East the Malays are thoroughly mixed with the Javanese, Macassarese and other elements.

[8]'Batak' is a collective term meaning 'heathen', applied by Malays to the peoples of the interior in the Lake Toba region. The Batak people fall into two main groups: a) the Da'iri, subdivided into the Karo and Pakpak tribes; b) the Toba. The Bataks are now divided between Hindu-animists, Muslims and Christians. The oldest (aborigine) inhabitants of Sumatra include the Orang Akit, Sakai, Utan, Rawar, Talang, Orang Mamak and Kubu—all from the eastern side of the island; the Lubu from Tapanuli district, and the O Nias, O Enggano and O Mentawai from the West Coast islands with those names. Amongst the aborigines of the Malay Peninsula are the Negrito, Semang, the Senoi and the Temiar. 'Sakai' is a general term applied by the Malays to all aborigines.

'Dayak' is also a collective term meaning 'highlander' or 'inlander' applied by the coastal peoples of Borneo to the tribes of the interior, and by early Dutch and English writers to all non-Malays on the island. The principal group is the Iban (Sea Dayak), now forming one-third of the total population of Sarawak; others include the Kadazan (Dusun) who form the largest single racial group in Sabah; the Land Dayaks, Kayan, Kelabit, Kenyah and Melanau (mostly in Sarawak); the Murut (mostly in Sabah); and the Punan/Penan, mostly living in the deep jungle.

'To-raja' is another collective term, originally applied by the Bugis to their subjects in Central Celebes, and by Europeans to all inland peoples on the island. 'To-' meaning 'man' is the prefix attached to the name of the river along which a particular tribe lives. There are three main groups: a) the Poso in east-central Celebes; b) the Sigi and allied tribes in central north-west Celebes; and c) the Sadan in the south-west.

[9]For a full discussion of the social and political forms in the archipelago, see van Leur, op. cit. Chapter 3.

[10]Those parts of Central and East Java watered by the Solo and Brantas rivers have soils made highly fertile by the erosion of volcanic materials and are rich in calcium, nitrogen and phosphorus. These conditions plus an adequate but not excessive rainfall have made possible intensive agriculture in the region.

[11]The Shailendra Dynasty apparently held sway in Central Java in the ninth century A.D. where it is associated with the great Buddhist monuments and shrines on the Kedu Plain near Jogjakarta—the most famous of which is the Borobudur. But the dynasty's origins and its fate remain a matter for speculation. To add to the mystery, its disappearance from Java in the middle of the ninth century coincides with its connexion with Sri Vijaya in Sumatra. For a full summing up of the present state of scholarship on this question, see Hall, *History of South-East Asia* (3rd edition), pp. 49-55.

[12]The nature of Kertanegara's influence in Sumatra is not clear. It might have been the result of outright conquest, but equally probably merely reflected the establishment of diplomatic relations and alliance.

[13]This refers to the Shailendra period in Javanese history during the ninth century A.D. What the precise relationship was between Sri Vijaya and the kingdoms of Central Java at this time has not yet been satisfactorily determined by scholars. Refer to note 11 above.

[14]According to a Javanese chronicle of the period, the *Nagarakertagama*, the empire of Majapahit embraced all Sumatra, many places in the Malay Peninsula, Brunai and parts of south Borneo, Bali, the Sundas, south Celebes and the Moluccas. Recently it has been suggested by the Dutch scholar, C.C. Berg, that these wide domains reflected the state of Javanese geographical knowledge at that period rather than their actual political power and that the available evidence confines Majapahit's control to Central and East Java, Madura and Bali. However, there is evidence of Javanese cultural influence in the islands further to the East.

[15]The Ming Dynasty came to power in China after overthrowing the Mongol Yuan dynasty in 1368, thereby marking a restoration of native Chinese rule. The new dynasty immediately embarked upon a policy of reasserting Chinese traditional claims and interests over her neighbours. One aspect of this was the series of naval and commercial expeditions sent out over a period of some thirty years at the turn of the fourteenth century to the islands of South-East Asia and beyond. Known as the Ming Voyages, the arrival of two of these expeditions at Malacca within the first decade of its foundation provided its prince with a much needed guarantee against Thai (and possibly Javanese) interference.

[16]Melayu/Malayu, a state based on Jambi in east Sumatra, had risen at the expense of Sri Vijaya during the thirteenth century. During the fourteenth century the centre of its power was transferred to the Menangkabau highlands near Padang on the west coast.

[17]'One needs to abandon here the idea of modern-capitalistic trade mobilizing mass quantities of goods and supplying raw materials for mechanized industries and industrial products in demand for everyday consumption. One should call to mind the old trade in valuable, high-quality products and hand-made craft products moving from market to market over routes lasting many months and years in a slow turnover through weigh-houses, treasuries and warehouses....' van Leur, op. cit. p. 189.

[18]That is, in the architecture and the cults it reflected of the Hindu and Buddhist shrines found near the centres of royal power in Central Java.

[19]In Champa inscriptions dated 1025/35 and 1039 have been found near Phan-rang (South Vietnam); the Leran inscription is in East Java; the earliest evidence from the Malay Peninsula comes from Kuala Brang in Trengganu with an inscription dated between 1303 and 1387. For a full discussion of the earliest evidence of Islam in the archipelago, see S.Q. Fatimi, *Islam comes to Malaysia*, Malayan Sociological Research Institute, Singapore 1963.

[20]The Polos returning from China through the Straits of Malacca in 1292 reported the presence of Islam at Perlak in north Sumatra.

[21]Dates of conversion of the principal centres in the region are as follows: Malacca—1405-25; North Java—1415-30; Brunai—1425-50; Moluccas—c. 1450; Sulu—1450-75; Banjarmassin —c. 1550; Macassar—c. 1600.

[22]Buddhism had in fact disappeared in India as a separate entity, re-absorbed by Hinduism, soon after the sixth century A.D.

[23]The tombstone of Sultan Malek al-Salleh, Pasai's first Muslim ruler, dated 1297, was of Gujerati origin. Gujerati influence spread from this region of north Sumatra to Malacca shortly after the latter's foundation.

[24]Sufism is the name given to a particular branch of Islam which developed from the eighth century A.D. onwards. Basically it was a movement of reaction from the dogmatic and scholastic approach of the ulamas and the schools of law and aimed to spread Islam by preaching directly and simply to the people. By the twelfth and thirteenth centuries Sufism as a movement had proliferated into numerous orders formed by famous teachers and their disciples. These Sufi orders played a most important role of the spread of Islam, and were particularly active as missionaries in India and later South-East Asia. There was always a tendency for Sufism to tolerate established local beliefs where this seemed to be advantageous for the spread of Islam, and it has been suggested that this tendency was exploited successfully in Island South-East Asia where Islam came into contact with the long-entrenched syncretic beliefs of the Javanese Hindu-Buddhist courts or the simpler tenets of the villager.

[25]Examples of this may be drawn from Central Java where a recent study (Clifford Geertz, *The Religion of Java*, Glencoe, 1960) brings out clearly the tensions which exist today between village communities following Muslim or more traditionalist patterns. The Padri wars of the first half of the nineteenth century in the Menangkabau lands of west Sumatra can also be viewed in the light of this basic antagonism between two elements of society.

Wayang-golek figures: Ardjuna and Prabu Gilling Wisi, Java

2. *The Malaysian World in Transition,* *1500–1800*

THE period of virtually 300 years which opens with the Portuguese conquest of Malacca in 1511 and closes with the establishment of a British settlement on the island of Penang in 1786 possesses well-defined characteristics of its own. It is the period marked by the intrusion of European powers into the archipelago, led by the Portuguese and the Spaniards and followed a century later by the Dutch and English, French, Danes, Swedes and others. It is the period in which the Western presence made itself felt without, however, producing many basic modifications in the traditional historical patterns. The Portuguese impact was slight and short-lived; the Spaniards remained on the periphery. The most spectacular achievement of the Portuguese was to bring to an end the Sultanate of Malacca; by then it was probably already on its last legs. Their efforts to capture the spice trade and spread their faith in the Moluccas if anything confirmed the already growing ascendancy of Javanese political influence and accelerated the diffusion of Islam. The Dutch impact was more substantial. Their first target was the Moluccas which they had brought effectively under their control within one generation; yet they shrewdly made their headquarters at the focal point of power in the archipelago, on the island of Java. Java was the base from which they extended their influence to other portions of the archipelago—effectively to Macassar and Malacca, which was also the work of a generation; with less effect to the shores of Borneo and Sumatra and the other islands. On Java itself the Dutch Company was transformed, as was its British counterpart in India, from merchant to landlord, becoming thereby the master of the island and the prime power in the region. But this power was strictly limited. The Dutch became the major power in the archipelago without being able to create new political forms or to bring about any degree of unity. Java was administered by the Company in the style of a Javanese prince. It modified the pattern of trade in the same way that any strong Malaysian power had modified the pattern of trade by creating a powerful monopoly of its own; but the Company was never strong enough to make that monopoly complete or to prevent its competitors from taking their share. Probably the most positive effect of the rise of Dutch power in the archipelago was to bring about the permanent fragmentation of the Malaysian states. As Majapahit, and presumably Sri Vijaya and Fu-nan in their day, the Dutch could quickly break the rise of any potential rival without, on the other hand, being able to go so far as to impose a political pattern of their own on the islands. In other words at the end of this period the outlines of modern Malaysia and Indonesia were still to be drawn.

The temptation in attempting to describe this period of 300 years is to view it entirely in terms of Western colonial history, as the period of the Portuguese and the Dutch. This is very easy to do because the activities of the Portuguese *fidalgos* and the rise of the Dutch East India Company in the archipelago form convenient themes around which the disparate events that took place in the region can be arranged. But it is also misleading, because it tends to give the impression that the history of Island South-East Asia after 1511 is only to be interpreted as an aspect or an extension of European colonial history. In fact, as has already been pointed out, the European presence in the region was only one of several factors operating during this period and was by no means the most dominant one. The evolution of society, above all in Java, was conditioned by forces much more deeply rooted in its historical background. Therefore in what follows a two-way approach has been taken. Firstly, a summary of the Western entry on to the South-East Asian stage and of its consequences is given so as to show the continuity and scope of European activities in the setting of Island South-East Asia. Then a brief survey of the fate of the principle Malaysian powers is given, one after the other, so that each can be seen as an integral unit with a dynamic of its own. The story of the spice sultanates of the Moluccas is given first, since they were the first to bear the full brunt of Western expansion, followed by the stories of Macassar, Bantam and Mataram. Mataram requires more space than any of the others since it was the most substantial Malaysian power involved. Acheh, which it could be argued, falls into the same category as the others as far as the course of its history during this period is concerned, has nevertheless been left out for a later section, since the story of its final demise belongs to the nineteenth century.

THE ENTRY OF THE WEST

The first Europeans

THE Portuguese were the first European people to obtain a foothold in Island South-East Asia and a century was to elapse before their position was challenged by a rival European power.[1] However, they were not the first European visitors to the region for their coming had been foreshadowed by earlier travellers from the West. The first known westerners to visit Island South-East Asia were the Polos, Italians from Venice. They stayed in Sumatra for five months in 1292–3 on their way back to Europe after a prolonged visit to Mongol China, and Marco Polo in his account of his travels gives us valuable witness to the spread of Islam in the north of that island.[a] During the course of the next hundred years, several Franciscan friars passed along the sea-route through the archipelago on their way to or from China, calling at places in Java and Sumatra as they went by. The most prominent of these was Friar Odoric of Pordenone in Italy, whose book, *Description of the East*, contains references to the Javanese monarch Kertanegara.[b] Then in the fifteenth century other Italians, but this time merchants, not missionaries, also journeyed through the region. One of them, Ludivico di Varthema, a merchant from the Italian city of Bologna, gave to Europeans their first description of Malacca which, he asserted, was the busiest port in the world.

The establishment of Portuguese power in South-East Asia was part of a much wider pattern. They irrupted into the Indian Ocean[2] with two major purposes

[a] Refer p. 38, note 20.
[b] Refer p. 30.

which went hand in hand. They were carrying on their centuries-old struggle against Islam by spreading Christianity into the East; at the same time they were interested in the spice trade and the rich returns it would bring, and the fact that this trade was virtually a monopoly in the hands of their Muslim opponents gave them a convenient justification for their policies. Under Alfonso d'Albuquerque, their second viceroy in the East, the Portuguese set out to achieve these twin aims by capturing a handful of strategic ports dominating the main routes of trade. Having destroyed a combined Turkish-Egyptian fleet off Diu in 1509, which gave them naval supremacy in the Indian Ocean for a century, the Portuguese began to put their policy into effect by seizing Goa from the Sultan of Bijapur and making it the capital of their maritime empire. They then launched assaults on Aden and Ormuz, the keys to the Red Sea and the Persian Gulf respectively,[3] and in 1511, in pursuit of the same objectives, appeared with a force to capture Malacca.

The Portuguese conquest

Although the conquest of Malacca was part of his overall design, Albuquerque had already been provided with a handsome pretext to attack the port by the treatment meted out to an earlier Portuguese mission there led by Lopez de Sequiera in 1509. On that occasion a number of the Portuguese had been arrested and imprisoned whilst on shore, apparently on the orders of the Bendahara, Tun Mutahir, but de Sequiera and his ships escaped back to Goa to tell the tale.[4] The subsequent fall of the city to Albuquerque's small force after two attacks spaced out over seventeen days marks the beginning of Western participation in the history of South-East Asia. Albuquerque arrived when the sultanate was torn by internal crisis, and his success was in no small measure due to the assistance which he received from the foreign merchants who were there at the time.[5] Sultan Mahmud abandoned his capital, apparently in the belief that the Portuguese had not come to stay. By the time that he had found out his mistake, the Portuguese had consolidated their position well enough to have become practically impregnable. Their first action was to build a fort which was to withstand sieges successfully for the next 130 years. Two years later (1513) they destroyed a Javanese fleet of 300 ships and slaughtered 8,000 men led by Patih Yunus of Demak[a] off Muar, after which their possession of Malacca was secure.[6] From Malacca, the Portuguese proceeded to expand their trading connexions and to spread the Christian religion in the new region opened before them. Their factors appeared in Thailand and Cambodia, China and Japan. Their first mission to the Moluccas in 1511-12 was a failure,[b] yet ten years later they had turned the rivalry between Ternate and Tidore to good account by obtaining a firm understanding with the ruler of Ternate. Subsequently they established posts at Ambon, Flores, Timor and Bantam besides.

The race with Islam

The dramatic appearance and spectacular successes of the Portuguese within the brief span of one decade tend to obscure the real effect of their arrival which was to carry the struggle between Christian and Muslim from Europe into the archipelago and stimulate the spread of Islam. The reaction of the Malacca Bendahara Tun

[a]Refer p. 36.   [b]See p. 56, note 6.

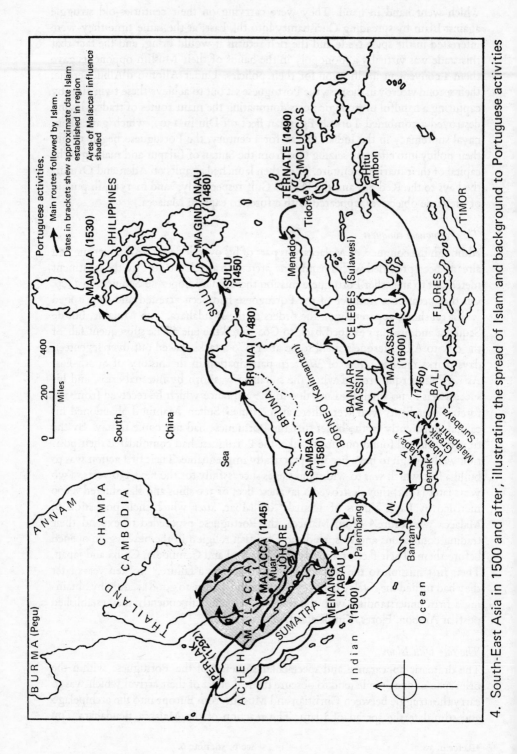

4. South-East Asia in 1500 and after, illustrating the spread of Islam and background to Portuguese activities

Mutahir, who was a Muslim of Tamil descent, to de Sequiera's expedition in 1509 was in fact a reflection of this struggle, for he had been instigated by Muslim Gujerati traders, of whom there was a large and influential colony at the port, and whose interests had been affected by Portuguese depredations off the Malabar coast of India. Portuguese activities off the Indian shore caused Muslim traders to avoid that area altogether and sail direct between Aden and South-East Asia via the Maldives, making it imperative in turn for the Portuguese to strike further east.

The immediate consequence of the Portuguese occupation of Malacca was to drive Muslim merchants to patronize Acheh, which within three decades rose to become the chief centre for West Asian and Indian Muslims in the archipelago and the strongest power in the Straits. As the Portuguese followed through their thrust against Islam in the region by sending missionaries to Malacca and beyond, so local rulers turned to Islam which became a rallying banner for all those who wished to destroy the commercial competition of the Portuguese. In Java the Portuguese cast around for alliances with the Hindu successors of Majapahit but were forestalled by the rising Muslim state of Demak.[a] They did succeed for a time, however, in prolonging the existence of the Hindu-Javanese kingdom of Panarukan in East Java before it fell to Pasaruan (Surabaya) around 1600. In the Moluccas and on the other islands of the Great East, a straight race developed between Christian and Muslim missionaries, as in north and south Celebes, on Solor, Ambon, Moro, Banda and Ceram, but the result of these activities was to provoke a reaction from Ternate, the strongest sultanate in the area. One of its rulers, Ba'abullah, drove the Portuguese off the island of Ternate itself and drastically curtailed their influence in the other islands.[b] From the impetus of his efforts Ternate was transformed from kingdom into empire during the last quarter of the sixteenth century.

The Portuguese impact

In all, the Portuguese position in the archipelago was even at the best of times precarious, and before the century closed they were beginning to lose what control they had obtained. The Portuguese in Malacca were subjected to constant attacks by the Johore Malays who had been disinherited and by the Achinese and Javanese who were the would-be inheritors.[7] In 1574 came their expulsion from Ternate and although they obtained a footing on rival Tidore, their power was greatly diminished. Despite these pressures, they maintained Malacca's position as an important centre of trade but in Island South-East Asia as a whole, they never became anything more than a new competitor in the old-existing pattern of political and commercial rivalry and power. This was hardly surprising. 'God gave the Portuguese a small country to be born in, but all the world to die in', as the Portuguese commentator wrote.[c] Portuguese techniques, resources and organization fell far short of what was required for cornering the spice trade or for dominating the carrying trade of the Indian Ocean, while the main effect of their missionary policy was to arouse still more local opposition against them. Portugal's monopolistic policies stimulated the spread of spice cultivation to areas beyond their reach, which in turn

[a]See p. 63. [b]See p. 52.
[c]Antonio Vieira, quoted by F. J. Moorhead, *History of Malaya and her Neighbours*, Vol. 1, p. 236.

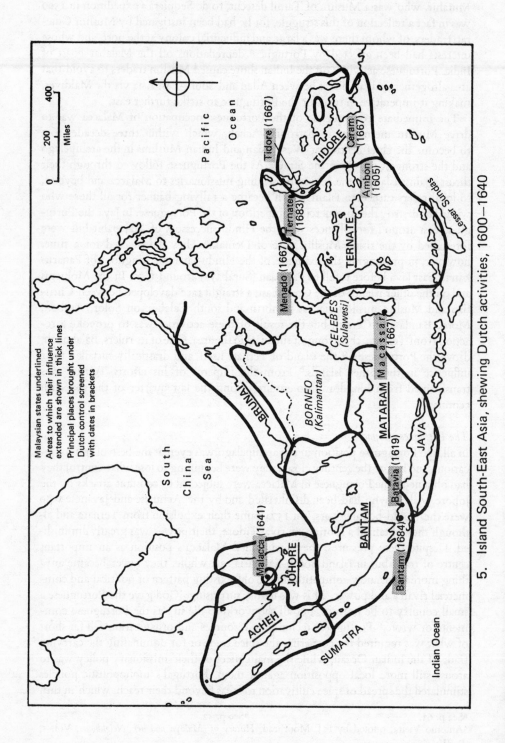

5.   Island South-East Asia, shewing Dutch activities, 1600–1640

promoted the rise of Ternate and Tidore and strengthened Javanese influence throughout the area. Far from changing the historical pattern, the Portuguese did much to further its development. The Europeans had arrived but the era of Western domination, political and economic, had not yet begun.

The arrival of the Dutch

At the end of the sixteenth century the Portuguese found their position challenged by new arrivals from Europe—the Dutch and the English. The newcomers confronted a different political situation from that which had faced the Portuguese pioneers in the archipelago. Three strong new Malaysian states had risen to fill the vacuum left by the fall of Malacca and the disappearance of Majapahit.

In the west of the archipelago stood Acheh, the closest heir to Malacca's *imperium*, which had gone a long way towards establishing an effective control over the Sumatran pepper market. On the island of Java the port-principalities of the north were succumbing to the power of the new inland state of Mataram.[a] To the East in the Moluccas, Ternate had emerged much the stronger for her hundred-year tussle with the Portuguese and Spaniards. Of lesser magnitude but to be reckoned with were Johore, whose rulers laid claim to the mantle of Malacca,[b] Bantam on the Straits of Sunda,[c] Brunai whose sway now stretched the length of the North Bornean coast and probed the Sulu archipelago,[d] and Tidore who maintained a fierce rivalry with Ternate for the control of the spice islands.[e] However, the Dutch (and the English) enjoyed one great advantage which enabled them quickly to establish a foothold in the most strategic parts of the archipelago right at the very beginning; they themselves came as the bitter rivals and enemies of the Portuguese. As such they were initially welcomed in Java and in the Moluccas by these Malaysian rulers who regarded the Portuguese as their most desperate foes.

The appearance of these two new trading powers spelt the end of Portugal's influence in the Indian Ocean. As far as Island South-East Asia.was concerned, the place of Portugal was taken by Holland, for the English soon found themselves obliged to give up their attempts to gain a share in the trade of the region in the face of the vigorous opposition of their powerful Dutch rivals. Fundamentally, the aims of the Dutch were identical with those of the Portuguese, with the major distinction that they did not come to spread Christianity.[8] The real difference between the two lay in the far greater thoroughness and efficiency of the Dutch. At first the Dutch traders came divided amongst rival merchant companies. In 1602 this was ended by the formation of the Dutch East India Company (VOC),[9] which converted Dutch trading activities in the East into something like a national enterprise. But the system of separate voyages under separate commanders continued until 1610 when the first governor-general (Pieter Both) was appointed. Having created a unity of command, the next step was to establish a headquarters in the region. Their choice fell on Jakarta, a vassal of the Sultan of Bantam.[10] Its capture by J.P. Coen[f] in 1619 formalized the establishment of Dutch power in the archipelago. The Company now ruthlessly and relentlessly pursued its goal of acquiring an absolute monopoly over the spice trade, regardless of friend and foe alike. The inhabitants

[a]See pp. 71 et seq.
[b]See pp. 115 et seq.
[c]See p. 63.
[d]See pp. 169–70.
[e]See p. 52.
[f]See pp. 64–5.

of the spice islands were brutally crushed between 1620 and 1650 and reduced to complete subjection. The English, despite a formal alliance signed in London in 1619, were pushed out of the spice trade altogether.[11] The Portuguese lost most of their outposts in the region within fifteen years (the main exception was their settlement on Timor which they retained up till the 1970s), and finally, after several attempts, the fortress of Malacca itself fell into Dutch hands in 1641.

The final stages of the struggle with the Portuguese were carried on by the Company outside South-East Asia during the 1640s, ending with a treaty signed at Goa in 1644 confirming the Dutch possession of all the Portuguese posts they had conquered in Ceylon.[12] Meanwhile in the archipelago, the Company survived successive challenges from the Javanese state of Mataram; Bantam and Macassar were subjugated and Acheh reduced to impotence. By the end of the seventeenth century the Dutch had established their hegemony on Java, although another generation of warfare was needed to confirm it, and they were indisputably the most powerful political force in Island South-East Asia.

The Dutch vanquished the Portuguese and drove off the English because of the superiority of the ships, weapons, organization and resources which they had at their disposal. The same factors explain why within fifty years of their arrival they had secured a predominant position in the archipelago and why, although their actual territorial dominion was mainly confined to the island of Java and those of the Moluccas, they were powerful enough to disrupt the prevailing system of trade and consequently cripple the rise and development of Malaysian states. After 1650 it might be said that the great indigenous states of yore withered away. The Dutch impact had its most immediate effect on the Moluccas which was their first target. Their subsequent conquest of Java placed them in the focal point of power in the whole archipelago.

[1]That is, Holland and England. This, however, is not to take into account the sister Iberian power of Spain, which for some years prior to the 1580s challenged Portugal's pretensions to the spice monopoly in the Moluccas, and established a foothold in the Philippines.

[2]The appearance of the Portuguese in South-East Asia was the fruit of their patient exploration of the African coast under the inspired direction of Prince Henry (the Navigator) (1394–1460), the brother of the king. In 1487 Bartholemew Diaz rounded the Cape of Good Hope; ten years later the first Portuguese expedition to the East under Vasco da Gama sailed beyond it into the Indian Ocean and arrived at the Malabar coast of India. This was followed by several more expeditions and the establishment of Portuguese power in the East. Their affairs in the East were put into the hands of viceroys, the first of whom was Francisco d'Almeida, and the second Alfonso d'Albuquerque. Albuquerque differed from Almeida as to the best tactics to follow in building up Portuguese power in the Indian Ocean, holding that sea power alone, without strategic bases commanding the trade routes, would be insufficient.

[3]Goa was captured in 1510. The attack launched on Aden in the same year was a failure, as were also the first two Portuguese assaults on Ormuz. The Portuguese never succeeded in capturing Aden although they occupied the island of Socotra nearby. Ormuz fell in 1512. The Mameluke rulers of Egypt and the Ottoman Turks had responded to the appeals of Aden and Gujerat for help against the Portuguese intruders first by protesting to the Pope in Rome and threatening to ravage the holy places of the Christians in Palestine if the Portuguese did not desist, and then by organizing naval leagues to oppose them.

[4]There is no more reason to suppose that de Sequiera was sent deliberately to provoke an incident with Malacca than there is to suppose that Albuquerque had any other purpose in mind other than to conquer the port. For a full discussion of this point, see D.K. Bassett, 'The Portuguese in Malaya', *Journal of the Historical Society*, University of Malaya, Vol. I, No. 3, 1962–3.

[5]It is clear that the Javanese, Indian and Chinese merchants in Malacca resented the exacting pressures of the Malay aristocracy on their trade, and that they lent ships, supplies, and provid-

ed valuable information about the defences to Albuquerque's men. The Javanese, in particular, may well have been planning for some time to seize the city for themselves.

[6]The Portuguese victory was a direct consequence of their superior fire-power. They possessed cannon and gunpowder whereas Patih Yunus did not, hence with a handful of ships they were able to put the Javanese to rout. Patih Yunus himself escaped, and in fact the whole episode seems to have helped him on his climb to power in Demak itself!

[7]The main attacks were as follows: by Acheh—1537, 1539, 1547, 1568, 1573, 1575, 1616 and 1639; by the Javanese—1513, 1535, 1551, 1574; by the Johore Malays—1551, 1586, 1606 and 1616.

[8]The coming of the Dutch to trade in the East sprang from their own struggle for independence from the Catholic power of Spain, which began in 1568. In 1580 Spain and Portugal were joined together in a dynastic union under Philip II of Spain, who fourteen years later closed the port of Lisbon to the shipping of his rebellious Dutch subjects. This severe blow to their carrying trade, for they distributed the spices which arrived at Lisbon all over north-west Europe, led the Dutch to endeavour to trade directly with the East on their own account. The first Dutch expedition to succeed in doing so was led by Cornelis van Houtman and reached the archipelago in 1596. This was followed by many others in the next few years, prior to the founding of the Dutch East India Company in 1602, promoted by well over fifty competing companies from rival Dutch ports. The English, whose East India Company was founded in 1600, were also the enemies of Spain, and their freebooters like Drake, Cavendish and Hawkins had already made their name pirating Spanish trade in the Americas. The first Englishman in Malaysian waters was James Lancaster, who plundered some Portuguese boats in the Straits of Malacca and put in at the uninhabited island of Penang in 1592.

[9]The *Vereenigde Oostindische Compagnie* or United East India Company was established by an act of the Dutch States-General on 20 March 1602. According to its charter which was valid for twenty-one years, the Company had exclusive rights for trade, shipping and the exercise of authority east of the Cape of Good Hope up to the Bering Straits and the meridian 100° E. of the Solomon Isles. The purpose in uniting the seventy-six existing companies was primarily political and not commercial—aiming at equipping the Netherlands with a political and military organization capable of waging war for Dutch interests in the East against the king of Spain. The management of the united Company was entrusted to a board of seventeen directors, among whom Amsterdam had the greatest number of representatives.

[10]The Dutch decision to found their headquarters at Jakarta was taken after rejecting Bantam, Malacca and Johore as alternatives. Jakarta was the weakest of these, a small, little-used port subject to the sultanate of Bantam.

[11]The English joined the Dutch in their attempts to wrest the control of the spice trade from the Portuguese and the Spaniards but Anglo-Dutch co-operation, desired by the two home governments in Europe, broke down because of the actions and attitudes of the men on the spot. Despite the London agreement of 1619 between the two countries to work together and share the trade and its costs in South-East Asia, Dutch resources were so much greater and their leaders in the region so determined, that the English East India Company decided that it would be more profitable to concentrate its efforts on India.

[12]In Ceylon the Dutch had captured Batticaloa (1638), Trincomalee (1639), Negombo (1640–subsequently lost and recaptured in 1644), Galle (1640) and Negapattnam (1642) but had failed to take Colombo, which did not fall till 1656. The Dutch company had also established itself at Pulicat (1610) and other places on the Coromandel coast, in Bengal at Hooghly (1634), in the west of India at Surat on a permanent basis in 1616, and had opened up trade with Persia, the Hadramaut, Aden and Mocha in the Red Sea.

THE SUBJUGATION OF THE MOLUCCAS

The sultanates of Ternate and Tidore

THE first Malaysian states to be conquered by the Dutch were the spice sultanates of Ternate and Tidore. Of the two, Ternate was the more powerful, exercising its authority over Ambon, the Bandas, Ceram and Buru, the northern part of Halmahera, the Uliassa Isles, and south down to the Lesser Sundas and west as far as Celebes to embrace Buton, Pose and the To-raja region. Tidore's dominions, on the other hand, were limited to southern Halmahera, the eastern part of Ceram and the

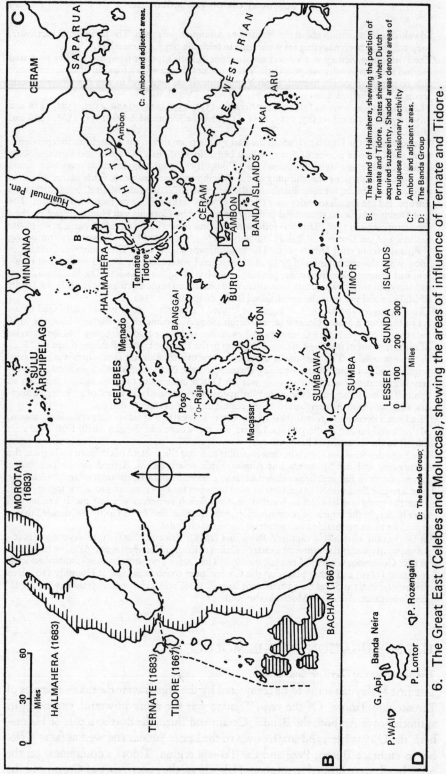

6. The Great East (Celebes and Moluccas), shewing the areas of influence of Ternate and Tidore.

B: The island of Halmahera, shewing the position of Ternate and Tidore. Dates shew when Dutch acquired suzereinty. Shaded areas denote areas of Portuguese missionary activity

C: Ambon and adjacent areas.

D: The Banda Group

coastline of West Irian. Ternate's greater strength was also reflected in its vigorous championship of Islam, while Tidore was more liberal in its policies.[1]

These two states embraced a total population of between a half to one million islanders[2] whose political organization varied considerably within the region. In the Bandas and on Ambon, a local aristocracy lorded it over a poor and subservient population of farmers and fishermen, deriving their power from a monopoly over the export of spices, a lion's share in the import trade, their slaves and their large estates. In Ternate and Tidore themselves, the system of government was monarchical, although the ruler was little more than the chief amongst his peers. But the exigencies of empire forced a degree of centralization on the monarchies of Ternate and Tidore. They exerted their sway through royal governors appointed to reside in the key spice islands where small colonies of their own men had also been planted; the chief functions of these governors were to levy tolls, collect the produce and control the ports under their authority. The royal power was also exerted by means of war fleets of long-planked outrigger *perahu*, manned by their conscripted subjects.[3] The politics of the region were infinitely complicated by the existence of rival tribal leagues and factions amongst the various islanders.

The spice trade itself, which was the magnet drawing Portuguese and Dutchman alike, had two main centres. In the south were the Bandas, the sole source for nutmeg and mace, and Ambon, famous for its cloves. In the north, on Ternate and Tidore and on the surrounding islands of Makian, Motir and Bachan, was another source of cloves.[4] One decisive fact which conditioned the political realities of the area was that the islanders were largely dependent on food imports for their survival, particularly with regard to rice and sago. The sago was brought from the Kai and Aru islands, Ceram, Sula and Banggai, while the rice came from Java and Bima. The rice trade gave the Javanese their entry into the islands and formed the basis of their political influence in the region. The Javanese were settled in colonies in various places, the most famous one of which was the Tuban colony on Hitu. The strength of Javanese influence was further enhanced with the spread of Islam[5] and promoted again later on by the intrusion of the Portuguese. The Javanese had a very large share in the exporting of the spices which in turn constituted a vital part in the general trade pattern in the archipelago, for they sold the spices to Indian merchants in exchange for precious stones, Coromandel batik, cottons and silks, to the Chinese for porcelain, gold, silk and silver coin. The north Javanese ports of Tuban, Jaratan, Grisek and Surabaya flourished on this spice trade.

The spice sultanates and the Portuguese

Both Ternate and Tidore were at an early stage of their growth when the first Portuguese arrived in 1513,[6] and the intense rivalry between them gave the European traders their opportunity to establish a foothold. Being evident from the start that it would be impossible to trade with both, the Portuguese chose the stronger Ternate, even though this implied a contradiction of their religious policies which was to cause them much trouble later on. So in 1521 the ruler of Ternate obtained Portuguese backing against Tidore and in return granted the Europeans the clove monopoly. However, Tidore soon acquired a friend of her own. As a result of Magellan's voyage,[a] Tidore was able to form links with Spain and in 1524 obtained

[a]See p. 338.

Spanish help against Ternate and the Portuguese. In the struggle which followed, it was Ternate and the Portuguese who gained the upper hand. As a result in 1530 the Portuguese exacted their due for the part they had played in the victory by converting the spice monopoly from being part of a bargain between equals into tribute from vassal to suzerain.

In fact, for the next generation the Portuguese behaved as if Ternate was their vassal and client state, a position which the lords of Ternate were not disposed to accept. Despite their efforts, the Portuguese had to continue sharing the spice trade of the islands with others—Chinese, Japanese, Thais, Arabs and Indians, let alone the Javanese, whose business exceeded many times that of the European newcomers. From their station on Ambon, where they had built a strong fort, the Portuguese tried to spread their influence by converting the islanders to Christianity. They achieved some local successes[7] but the main result was to stimulate local princes to counter-action by encouraging the spread of Islam. In Ternate itself, the activities of the Christian missionaries produced a strong reaction which first manifested itself clearly in the 1560s under Sultan Hairun, who extended his authority from Ambon to Mindanao and launched a wholesale campaign against the Christians. Matters came to a head soon after 1565 when the straits to which the Portuguese had been reduced by Hairun's pressure forced them to call for a special relief expedition from Goa. A little later the Sultan quarrelled with the Portuguese governor on the island over the division of the clove monopoly, which drove the Ternate ruler once more to arms. In the subsequent negotiations, he was treacherously murdered by the Portuguese. This provoked a general uprising on Ternate, led by Hairun's son and successor, Ba'abullah.

The new sultan proved a still more determined foe of the Europeans than his father had been. After a four-year resistance, the Portuguese garrison on the island was forced to capitulate and was massacred. Although soon after this the Portuguese were able to form a new base on rival Tidore, they never recovered their position in Ternate.

Under Sultan Ba'abullah, Ternate had recovered its full independence, and he proceeded to spread his power and Islam throughout the spice islands. Reputedly he brought seventy-two islands under his sway. In 1579 he played host to the Englishman, Francis Drake, on his voyage around the globe and welcomed him as a potential ally against the Portuguese. For the same reasons, when twenty years later the Dutch admiral, van Warwijck, anchored off Ternate, he received an equally warm welcome from Ba'abullah's successor, Sultan Said Din (Zaide). In the meantime the Portuguese had been able to get permission to build a fort on Tidore (1578) and they remained undisturbed on this island until 1605. In 1580 Portugal was united with the kingdom of Spain by dynastic union.[8] This resulted in the Spaniards of Manila launching a series of expeditions against Ternate which was lending powerful support to the rulers of Sulu, Spain's principal enemies in the Philippines.[a] There were three such expeditions. All of them failed.[9]

The Dutch impact; the conquest of Ambon, Ceram and the Bandas
With the arrival of the Dutch in 1599, it might have at first appeared to the islanders that their hour of deliverance had come, but events were soon to show that they

[a]See pp. 204 et seq.

were cruelly mistaken. The new arrivals proved to be more thorough and ruthless than the Portuguese or Spaniards had ever been. Within a decade both Ternate and Tidore had lost their real independence for ever.

The first area to receive the attention of the Dutch was that of the south Moluccas—Ambon and the Bandas, both of which were nominally at least within the domains of the Sultan of Ternate. Ambon in particular occupied an important position, and serving as a supply station on the way to Ternate and Tidore in the north and as a base from which the neighbouring Bandas to the south could be dominated, it was the key to the spice islands as a whole. Ambon and nearby Hitu were also the centres of the most powerful Javanese colony in the region. The initial Dutch penetration of Ambon and the Bandas was greatly facilitated by the fact that they came as enemies of the Portuguese. This made them very welcome to the islanders. The first to have relations with the Dutch were the Bandanese, who received Dutch factors in 1598, but Ambon was the first Malaysian country to sign a treaty with them and, later, to become annexed by Holland. In 1600 a Dutch fleet under Steven van der Haghen arrived at Ambon, intervened in the perennial feuds between the Muslim and Christian islanders and tried, in vain, to storm the Portuguese fort there. However, before he left, van der Haghen signed a treaty of alliance with the chiefs of Ambon against the Portuguese and built a fort of his own. Next year, a strong Portuguese force swept out the small Dutch garrison that had been left behind and restored their own domination of the island. But as part of their offensive sweep of 1605, the Dutch landed on Ambon again, captured the Portuguese fort and imposed a second treaty which acknowledged their overlordship and granted them the monopoly of trade. Freedom of worship was also guaranteed by the treaty (but this proved valid for only a few months) and a new Dutch fort was erected to 'protect' the islanders. In the same year Harmensz and van der Haghen concluded fresh agreements with the Banda chiefs by which they secured the nutmeg monopoly in exchange for promises of protection.[10]

The events of 1605 marked the end of the honeymoon period in the relationship between the Dutch and the islanders. Portuguese power to all intents and purposes was now successfully eliminated and the men of Ambon and the Bandas had to face up to the harsh realities of dealing with much more forceful and effective monopolists. The Dutch clearly intended to establish a complete monopoly over the exporting of cloves, nutmeg and mace from the islands, which in fact the islanders could not afford to let them do. They depended on the Javanese for their food supplies; without the rice from Java they must starve and the rice had to be paid for in kind. Therefore, with active Javanese encouragement,[11] the Ambonese and Bandanese resisted the Dutch attempts to impose their rigid monopoly. Faced with the physical presence of the Dutch ships and cannon, the chiefs signed whatever the Dutch wished them to sign, but as soon as they sailed away these agreements were broken. This is what happened the moment Harmensz and van der Haghen left the islands in 1605, and on subsequent occasions too. The islanders also received plenty of encouragement from other European traders, especially the Portuguese and the English, who offered them better prices for their crops.

Fifteen years of evasion, skirmishes, massacre and reprisal followed. The evasion of the monopoly terms of 1605 led to the visit of the Dutch admiral Verhoeff to the Bandas in 1609 in order to impose a new agreement. But as soon as this was signed, the Dutch admiral along with forty-six of his men was assassinated, and although within four months the Dutch had restored their position and imposed yet another treaty which confirmed their monopoly, annexed Banda Neira and placed the rest of the islands in the group under their suzerainty, they still failed to quell the islanders. Each year Dutch fleets appeared to collect the spices and attempt to enforce the monopoly. In 1616 and 1617 they successfully thwarted an English attempt to establish their sovereignty in the area,[12] but their goal of a water-tight monopoly remained as elusive as ever.

With the founding of their headquarters at Batavia in 1619,[a] the Dutch were ready to take decisive action in the Moluccas. In the words of Jan Pietersz Coen who had been a witness to the assassination of Verhoeff in 1609, 'Banda must be subjugated and we will have to dominate the scene there or it will not amount to anything either on Banda or Amboina'.[13] So in 1621 the violent conquest of the Bandas was begun. Coen arrived with a fleet of sixteen Dutch sail, twenty-six Javanese craft and 1,000 soldiers; on being refused the right to build a fort on any of the islands in the group, he attacked. Bandalontor and Pulau Run were ruthlessly overrun, forty-four chiefs taken as hostages were executed and another 160 notables died on Pulau Run while hundreds of others were deported. The action eliminated the indigenous population of the islands. The same treatment did not prove necessary on Ambon and Ceram, where Coen called together a meeting of the chiefs and reaffirmed Dutch overlordship and the Dutch monopoly. Nevertheless, two years later the English factory on Ambon was closed down after the trial and execution of its occupants on charges of conspiracy against the Dutch on the island.[14]

The reduction of Ternate and Tidore

While all this was going on in the south Moluccas, the Dutch had also brought about a complete ascendancy over the sultanates of Ternate and Tidore themselves. In 1599 Sultan Said Din had welcomed the Dutch with open arms as enemies of the Portuguese and Spaniards. He readily agreed to the establishment of a Dutch factory on the island in 1602 and the maintenance of close ties. But the new alliance speedily led him to disaster. In 1605 with Dutch support he launched an assault on Tidore. The attack was successful, the island was conquered and the Spanish garrison driven out. But the following year the Spanish counter-attack came. It was also a great success; Tidore was reconquered and the fleet of thirty-six ships and 3,000 men (half of whom were Spaniards) swept victoriously across to Ternate, stormed the capital and bore Sultan Said Din back to Manila to become a political exile and a convert to Christianity. These raids broke the power of both the sultanates. Hereafter they were the pawns of either the Spaniards or the Dutch, although Dutch power eventually predominated. In 1607 they re-established themselves on the northern part of Ternate, built a fort there and recognized a new sultan of their own while Sultan Said Din languished in his Manila captivity. The new Ternate ruler signed a treaty placing himself under Dutch protection and granting them the spice monopoly. The Spaniards remained in Tidore and south Ternate.

The sultanates of Ternate and Tidore survived as historical curiosities into the twentieth century[15] but the substance of their power vanished with the Spanish offensive of 1606. Nevertheless for the first half of the seventeenth century, while

[a]See pp. 64–5.

the Dutch relentlessly clamped down their control over the Moluccas, the sultanates, more particularly Ternate, attempted periodically to struggle against their fate. Naturally enough the Dutch measures to enforce an absolute monopoly over the spice trade of the region made them extremely unpopular as it struck directly at the livelihood of the islanders. Goaded to desperation by the threat of starvation, incited by other foreign traders running the Dutch monopoly who offered them better prices, and stirred up by religious propaganda from Java and Macassar, especially when the Dutch for political ends started to propagate Christianity themselves, the islanders found their rallying point in Islam.[16] In 1635 a general revolt throughout the islands broke out against the Dutch system after twenty restless years of smuggling and evasion. The movement had its centre on Ceram whose Malaysian governor was more influenced by the strongly Muslim Sultan Hassanuddin of Macassar than by his own overlord in Ternate. The movement was led by Kaki-ali from Hitu, long a Muslim and anti-Dutch stronghold. The visit of van Diemen with a fleet of seventeen sail in 1637 brought about a temporary lull but rebellion flared up anew as soon as he left. It finally came to an end in 1643 when Kaki-ali himself was killed in his sleep by a Spaniard after the blood-money. However, not long afterwards, trouble broke out again, under a new leader called Teluk-abessi, when the Dutch interfered with the traditional system of administration and placed it under their direct supervision.[17] Teluk-abessi's mountain redoubt of Kapaha was stormed in 1646 and fighting came to an end. The following year the Dutch made Sultan Mandar Shah cede west Ceram to them.

A second great revolt which swept through the Moluccas in the early 1650s came as a direct reaction against the institution of regular naval patrols known as *hongi-tochten*[18] around the islands to restrict spice production by burning and destroying unlicensed trees. Once again the centre of the rebellion was Ceram, which was the spice island nearest to the influence of anti-Dutch Macassar. Starting in 1650 under the leadership of a Malay called Saidi, it lasted for five years before it was mercilessly stamped out by the Dutch governor-general, de Flemingh van Oudshoorn. Saidi himself was eventually cornered in his mountain retreat on the Hualmual peninsula near Hitu, betrayed to the Dutch and killed by the hands of van Oudshoorn himself. By this time Ceram had become completely a Dutch possession since the Sultan of Tidore had ceded the eastern part of the island to them after their campaign of 1653. Ten years later, Tidore itself was exposed to the full blast of Dutch pressure when the Spaniards withdrew their garrisons from the area[19] in order to meet the Chinese threat to the Philippines from Formosa.[a] In 1666 the Sultan signed an agreement with the Company similar to that which Sultan Mandar Shah of Ternate had been forced to sign in the previous decade, by which for a pension he surrendered all his trading prerogatives. At the same time, the feud between the twin sultanates was formally brought to an end.

The twilight of the spice sultanates

Throughout this period the Dutch did their best to make the sultans of Ternate their accomplices. After the outbreak of the first general revolt in the islands in 1635, the Dutch governor-general van Diemen[20] paid a visit to Sultan Hamzah and tried to win him over to the Dutch side by offering their recognition of his

[a]See p. 206 and p. 217, note 17.

sovereignty over Ambon; but the ruler was not to be impressed by such empty gestures. In the 1650s, during the course of the second great wave of revolt through-out his domains, Sultan Mandar Shah fled to Batavia to escape a court faction led by a younger brother who considered him too pro-Dutch; nevertheless the Dutch rewarded his loyalty by restoring him only on condition that he accept their new policy of spice restriction.[21] In 1675 a new ruler raised the standard of rebellion and waged guerrilla warfare until he was captured and taken to Batavia. He returned to Ternate two years later, having agreed to become a vassal of the Company.

After this Ternate and Tidore continued as independent political entities in name only. The Moluccas were occupied by the British during the French Revolutionary and Napoleonic Wars (1793-1815), and so deep was feeling against the Dutch that a rebellion against the restoration of their rule broke out in the islands in 1817. Starting on Pulau Saparua with the assassination of the Dutch resident and his staff, it found a leader in Thomas Matua-lesi and spread to Ambon where the local Dutch forces were also overwhelmed. Only after a naval blocade and the arrival of reinforcements from Java was the uprising brought to an end. Later on, however, the Ambonese were to become the most loyal of all Holland's Indonesian subjects.[a]

[a]See Book III.

[1]Both states had close ties with Java. Ternate's conversion to Islam had taken place before 1497 through the influence of a Javanese noblewoman married to the Ternate ruler.

[2]Of these, the Bandas had a population of around 15,000, while Ambon and the north Moluccas had around 150,000.

[3]Known as *kora2*, they were usually more than 50 ft. in length and were paddled by more than a hundred rowers each.

[4]Spices in Europe were in demand both in the kitchen and by the druggist; not only were they used to give savour to winter food, but various concoctions of pepper, ginger, cinnamon, sugar, cloves and nutmeg were widely regarded as cure-alls for all manner of stomach, chest and head complaints.

[5]On Banda and Hitu, religious teachers were recruited from the Javanese traders who went there. The most important of the four headmen on Hitu was of Javanese descent, and 'Hitu is full of Moorish priests working much to spread their sect'. The *penambahan* of the *perdikan desa* of Giri—known in the islands as Raja Bukit—in Java was widely looked up to as the spiritual leader of the Muslims in the archipelago.

[6]Albuquerque sent Abreu and three ships to the Moluccas shortly after the fall of Malacca, but all were lost on the way. A second mission sent in 1513 was well received in both Ternate and Tidore.

[7]Especially under the famous St. Francis Xavier who was in the spice islands between 1546 and 1548. However St. Francis did not consider the Moluccas a fruitful region for his enterprise and decided to return to China and concentrate his efforts there.

[8]This union only lasted sixty years. In 1640 Portugal reasserted her independence.

[9]In 1582, 1585 and 1603. Another expedition (in 1593) never reached its destination as the Chinese crews mutinied on the way.

[10]This was the second Dutch attempt to secure the nutmeg monopoly in the Bandas by agreement. Harmensz had already made a similar agreement in 1602, which was, however, broken.

[11]As early as 1600 a Tuban fleet of thirteen junks and a 1,000 men harrassed the Dutch factors left behind at Banda.

[12]In 1616 English factors on the tiny Bandanese islands of Wai and Run persuaded the inhabitants to cede their territories to the English crown. This, however, did not deter the Dutch from attacking and overrunning Pulau Wai the same year, or from destroying an English vessel defending Pulau Run. The beleaguered English garrison on Run remained there, a source of incitement to the Bandanese to continue their defiance of the Dutch, until Coen's campaign of conquest in 1621.

[13]Jan Pietersz Coen: born 1586, at Hoorn, Holland; 1599, went to Rome, worked in the office of

a Dutch merchant there; became proficient in Italian book-keeping; 1605 (approx.), returned to Holland; 1607–10, first voyage to the Indies, sailing as V.O.C.'s second merchant in their fleet of 1607; 1612, second voyage—sailed as chief merchant in charge of two ships; appointed chief book-keeper and director of commerce at Bantam by Governor-General Both; 1618–23, first term as governor-general—founded Batavia, 1619; 1627–9, second term as governor-general—died of cholera in Batavia in 1629. Considered the founder of Dutch power in South-East Asia; pursued a forceful monopolistic policy and dreamed of achieving an ocean-wide commercial empire for Holland; ideas somewhat similar to those of Albuquerque. Coen's statement quoted by van Leur, op. cit. p. 392, n. 44.

[14]Those executed included 10 Englishmen, 9 Japanese and 1 Amboinese headman. The so-called 'massacre of Amboina' became a *cause célèbre* and embittered Anglo-Dutch relations for years to come. In practical terms, it had little significance since the English Company had already taken the decision to concentrate its efforts in India.

[15]The Dutch maintained the fiction of their continued sovereignty, even negotiating a treaty for the cession of Irian Barat with the Sultan of Tidore in 1898.

[16]Despite their frequent undertakings to the contrary, the Dutch Company encouraged (Protestant) Christian missionary activities in the Moluccas, especially on Ambon and Ceram, in an attempt to counter hostile Muslim influences.

[17]West Ceram consisted of a confederacy of seven self-governing tribes or 'ulis'. The Dutch reorganization not only brought them under direct Dutch control, but also led to their separation from one another.

[18]'*hongi-tochten*' comes from 'hongi', meaning a fleet of kora[2], and 'tocht', the Dutch word for voyage. Initiated by Oudshoorn in 1649, it consisted of fleets raised by Ternate's aristocrats and commanded by Dutch officers who cut down unlicensed spice trees on the islands. The policy was started because the Moluccas were producing too much for the world market— partly as a result of extended cultivation to escape the Dutch monopoly!

[19]That is, from Tidore, Ternate and Menado in Minahassa, north Celebes.

[20]Anthonie van Dieman; 1636–45, governor-general at Batavia; rated next to Coen as an empire-builder; during his governorship, he encouraged voyages of exploration which led to the discovery of the southern continent of Australia by Tasman in the 1640s.

[21]The Moluccans were to plant rice and sago in place of spices, and buy the excess they needed from Batavia; since Batavia's rice prices were higher than the islanders could afford, their ruin was accelerated. In return, the Sultan was granted an annual pension of 12,000 guilders.

THE RISE AND FALL OF MACASSAR

THE seventeenth century saw the rise and fall of a typical Malaysian sea-power, whose strength and politics were drawn from the currents of trade. This was the Gowa sultanate of Macassar whose course reflected both the traditional historical patterns and the factors introduced by the presence of the Europeans. The swift rise of Macassar at the beginning of the century was considerably influenced by the activities of the Dutch themselves. Its downfall at their hands over sixty years later was the outcome of its own success as a commercial·centre.

The rise of Macassar

Macassar's position made it a natural entrepôt for commerce. Situated on the main trade route between Java and the Moluccas, it was also well placed to dominate the neighbouring pepper fields of Banjarmassin in south Borneo, the islands of the Lesser Sundas—especially Timor with its sandalwood and Bima with its rice—and spread its influence over the spice islands as well, and to receive the shipping of China, the Sulu archipelago and the north. But circumstances did not permit the Macassarese to exploit these natural advantages until the sixteenth century. As long as the Malays of Malacca and Johore and the Javanese dominated the spice trade, Macassar remained a place of no significance. Then in 1511 the fall of the Malacca

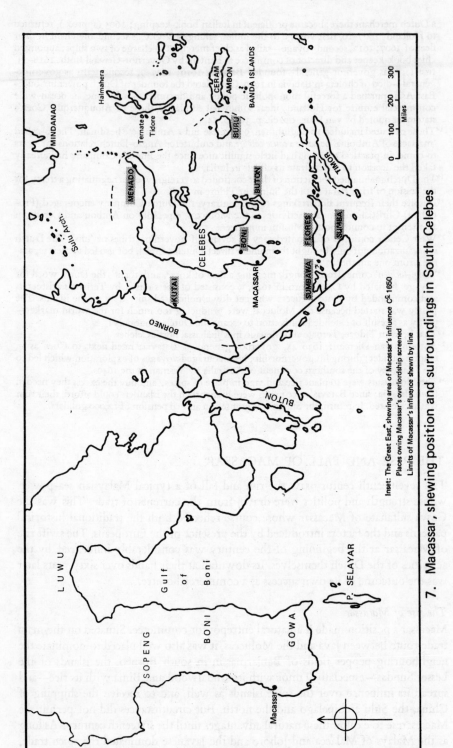

7. Macassar, shewing position and surroundings in South Celebes

sultanate to the Portuguese changed the whole picture. Soon Malays from Malacca, fleeing from a hostile Portuguese administration, were making Macassar their stapling port for the spice trade. The subsequent rise of Acheh in the Straits,[a] and the crippling of the successor empire of Johore by the raids of its kings accelerated Malay migration to Macassar. By 1600 there were 'many thousands' of them there and with the holds of their vessels crammed with cloths, porcelain, rice and silver coin they 'controlled most of the shipping in every direction'.[1]

However, it was not Malay patronage alone that put Macassar on the map. Under the wise policy of its rulers who encouraged foreign traders to settle down and trade free from onerous duties and imposts, Chinese, Indians, Arabs and Javanese, and later Portuguese, Englishmen and Danes made it their principal mart for the purchase of spices from the Great East. By the beginning of the seventeenth century Macassar was already a port of consequence. New political developments in the archipelago and the arrival of the Dutch favoured its growth still further. As the Dutch started to assert their power in the islands, driving all competitors out of the Moluccas, founding their headquarters on Java and shutting up the Portuguese in their fortress of Malacca, their rivals thronged to Macassar. In the 1620s there was a Portuguese colony there over 500 strong. The English made it the collecting centre for their spice trade after their expulsion from the Moluccas, followed by the Danes in 1625. The rise of the Javanese state of Mataram[b] during the same period also produced favourable repercussions for Macassar. While the stapling centres for rice and spices in north Java—Grisek, Tuban, Surabaya—fell before the advancing Sunan's power, Macassar took their place and also acquired the political influence in the Moluccas which went with it. The emasculation of Ternate and Tidore by the Dutch made it all the easier for the Macassarese to extend their power in this direction at the expense of the spice sultanates.

Another factor which played an important rôle in the rise of Macassar was its conversion to Islam. The conversion took place around the beginning of the seventeenth century[2] and its effect has been described as being 'at least as important as that of Java'.[c] The subsequent struggle with Holland for survival, though fundamentally economic, was dressed in religion. The Dutch conqueror van Goens reported in the 1660s that the ruler of Macassar 'does not fight us out of any enmity but only because of the Will of God, for the continuance of his religion and the protection of his fellow-believers'.[d] Though, perhaps, van Goens was unable to see the wood for the trees, Islam nevertheless played an important rôle in making Macassar into a new missionary centre and diffusion point which proselytized the region and provided a rationale and ideology for combating Dutch commercial imperialism.

At the beginning of the seventeenth century, the Macassarese ruling class still took very little direct part in the trade which passed through their hands. The ruler took the traditional rôle of first trader in the state and his consent and participation was required in all big rice deals, but his subjects were mainly farmers or traded

[a]See pp. 223 et seq.

[b]See p. 71.

[c]Van Leur, *Indonesian Trade and Society*, p. 150.

[d]Quoted by B. Schrieke, *Indonesian Sociological Studies*, Vol. 1, p. 74.

locally. Within the first decade of the new century, however, came signs of a greater interest taken by the aristocracy in trade. First they made use of the Portuguese
and other foreigners to trade on their account or to lend them money; then they
hired foreign bottoms and entered into the trade directly; finally they had their
own ships built in Java and using Portuguese pilots sailed straight to the Moluccas
themselves. By 1630 Macassar had grown into an empire. She could claim a general
overlordship over the whole of Celebes (at least of the coastal areas)[3] and her suzerainty extended as far east as Ceram and Buru and south to the Lesser Sundas—
Timor, Solor and Bima (west Sumbawa). Macassar could also boast of being able
to raise a force of 100,000 men, equipped with 4,000 fire-arms,[4] blowpipes and
poisoned arrows. In the words of a Dutch observer, they were 'quite well able to
handle fire-arms' and were 'good soldiers'.[a] Their skill as fighting men was to become only too familiar to the Javanese in the latter part of the century.

The conflict with the Dutch and its downfall

A clash between Batavia, intent on eliminating all competition from the spice trade,
and this rising Malaysian power whose *sine qua non* was its stake in the same trade
and its position as a free mart patronized by all those who wished to skirt the Dutch
monopoly, was ultimately inevitable. In 1625 the authorities in Batavia were requesting the Sultan not to let his subjects participate in the spice trade.[5] Nine years
later the Dutch attempted their first siege of the port, albeit to no avail since the
Macassarese simply unloaded their cargoes on the eastern side of the island and transported them overland. Two years later the Macassarese were signing an agreement
with the Dutch governor-general van Diemen to respect Dutch rights and their
position in the Moluccas, an agreement which was not kept. The fall of Malacca
in 1641 sufficiently impressed Macassar's rulers for them to abide by the Dutch
monopoly for a couple of years, but as Ternate disintegrated, Macassar filled the
vacuum and a collision between the two powers became all the more unavoidable.

Matters came to a head in the late 1650s. Sultan Hassanuddin of Macassar had
used the presence of the Portuguese and other Europeans in his city to acquire
supplies of arms and ammunition and to construct formidable defences. Then war
threatened between England and Holland in Europe[6] and the Dutch feared English
plans to lend their support to Macassar. By this time all resistance in the Moluccas
had been completely suppressed and Batavia felt ready to strike. In 1660 they sent
a naval expedition against the town which succeeded in capturing one of the forts,
whereupon the Sultan gave way and signed a new treaty. By this treaty Sultan
Hassanuddin promised to break off all contacts with the Moluccas, not to interfere
in either Buton or Menado[7] and to expel the Portuguese, of whom there were now
some 2,000, from the port. But as usual, when the Dutch sailed away none of these
terms was put into effect. The Portuguese continued to reside and trade at Macassar,
and spices continued to be smuggled in from the east. Furthermore Dutch shipping
was attacked and Sultan Hassanuddin broke his promise about Buton by sending a
large army to overwhelm that disobedient vassal. So in 1666 a second expedition
under the command of Cornelis van Speelman, consisting of twenty-one vessels
and 600 European soldiers and a large number of Bugis troops raised by the Aru

[a]Quoted by B. Schrieke, *Indonesian Sociological Studies*, Vol. I, p. 123.

Palaka of Boni who had a personal grudge against the Sultan, sailed against Macassar. First Buton was relieved from the pressure of Sultan Hassanuddin's besieging army, then the expedition sailed eastwards to impose a settlement on Tidore, and finally returned to Macassar to assault the city itself.

A four-month siege ensued which culminated in the capitulation of the Sultan and the signing of the Bongaya Contract. This agreement which was to form the basis of Dutch relations with all the states of South Celebes up till the twentieth century,[a] stipulated Dutch overlordship and imposed a Dutch monopoly over all trade. Macassar's forts were to be dismantled except for the main one which would be occupied by a Dutch garrison; all non-Dutch Europeans were to be expelled, and the Sultan was to pay a heavy indemnity.

Sultan Hassanuddin was defeated but not yet broken. In 1668 his attempts to evade carrying out the provisions of the treaty led to renewed fighting, the despatch of a third expedition in 1669, another prolonged siege (two months) and a final surrender. This time the Sultan was forced to abdicate and accept a pension while Macassar and its immediate environs were placed under the direct administration of a Dutch governor. The neighbouring Bugis principalities[8] were left to run their own affairs under a loose Dutch hegemony. The downfall of Macassar destroyed the prosperity of the inhabitants of the region, Macassarese and Bugis alike, and this led large numbers of them to seek their fortunes elsewhere. Some turned to piracy, some became good Dutch mercenaries; others found an opening in the politics of the Straits of Malacca and in the eighteenth century were to become the dominant force in the spent empire of Johore-Riau.[b]

[a]See pp. 311–13.
[b]See pp. 117–18.

[1]They traded much of their cloth on Buton in exchange for slaves whom they carried to Ambon. Quotation from Schrieke, *Indonesian Sociological Studies*, Vol. I, p. 66, taken from the account of an English merchant of the time.
[2]Formerly known as the *Batara*, the ruler of Macassar was converted either in 1603 (Schrieke) or in 1606 (van Leur).
[3]That is, including Menado, Boni and Selayar.
[4]Chiefly through the Portuguese who imported them from Europe, Japan and China.
[5]The Sultan, however, pointed out quite truthfully (at that time) that his own subjects were scarcely involved.
[6]During this period three wars were fought between the English and the Dutch; the first in 1652–4, the second in 1665–7, and the third in 1672–4.
[7]Both had become allies of the Dutch Company.
[8]The Bugis are distinct from the Macassarese of the Sultanate of Gowa; a related people, they lived in a series of village principalities on the western shores of the Gulf of Boni.

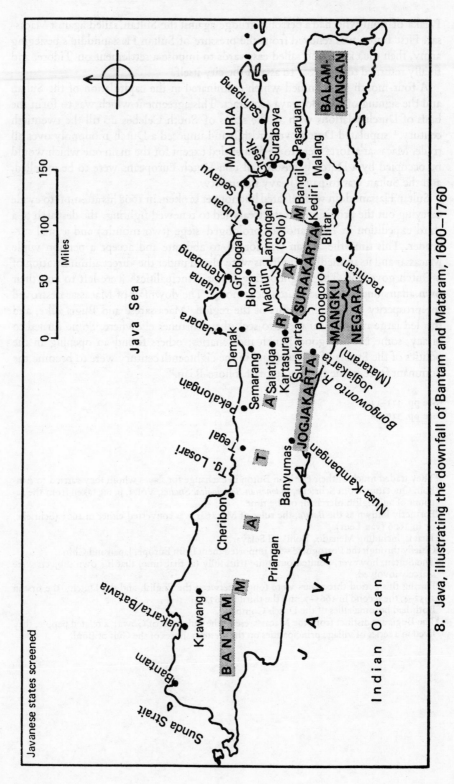

8.   Java, illustrating the downfall of Bantam and Mataram, 1600–1760

THE ECLIPSE OF BANTAM

THE same generation which saw the downfall of Macassar witnessed two other centres of Malaysian power crumble before the Dutch. The first of these was Acheh whose decline was more or less contemporaneous with that of Macassar itself,[a] and the other was the west Javanese sultanate of Bantam. Like Macassar, Bantam, which rose to power through its control over the pepper of south Sumatra, grew into a great centre of Muslim influence and of international trade, defiant of the Dutch attempts to establish a monopoly. These two alone were quite enough to guarantee eventual conflict with Batavia, but its strategic position on the Straits of Sunda was the factor which led to the sultanate's first contacts with Dutchmen. Bantam's earliest dealings with the Dutch date back to the original voyage of Cornelis van Houtman in 1596.

The origins of Bantam

Bantam's origins have their roots in the Muslim reaction to the fall of Malacca to the Portuguese. An insignificant fishing village in the domains of the Hindu-Sundanese kingdom of Pajajaran, it became, like Macassar again, a place of refuge for Malays escaping the unsympathetic rule of the Portuguese officials in Malacca. When in 1522 the Portuguese in pursuit of their campaign against the Muslim principalities of north Java formed an alliance with the king of Pajajaran and obtained permission to open a factory at neighbouring Sunda Kelapa (Jakarta), the Malay community at Bantam became alarmed and appealed to the rising Muslim state of Demak in the east for help. Five years later that help arrived in the shape of a force of Javanese led by a devout Muslim leader, Faletahan, who captured Sunda Kelapa, occupied Bantam and declared the whole area a Muslim state in the name of the ruler of Demak.[1] Some forty years later, Bantam's second ruler, Hassanuddin, took advantage of the turbulent politics of his time to assert his independence of Demak and in 1579 his son and successor, Pangeran Sedang Rana (Maulana Yusof), gave the death blow to the kingdom of Pajajaran.

Founded as a Muslim outpost in Hindu west Java against the threat of Christian Portugal, Bantam always served as a stronghold of Islam. Faletahan himself came from Pasai, one of the earliest centres of Islam in the archipelago. The links with Islam were strengthened at the beginning of the seventeenth century when for nearly twenty-five years the state was ruled by Pangeran Arya Ranamanggala, a haji, who was regent during the minority of Sultan Abdul Kadir (1595–1651). He encouraged the development of close relations between his court and Mecca and obtained from there the sanction for his sovereign to use the title of Sultan. Muslim influence reached its peak during the reign of Abdul Kadir's successor, Sultan Abdul Fatah (Sultan Agong 1651–82).

Meanwhile the rulers of Bantam were building up their economic and political power by extending their control over the pepper plantations and pepper ports of South Sumatra. In this way their authority spread out amongst the village federations of the Lampongs[b] and up the east and west coasts of Sumatra until it came into

[a]See pp. 225–6.
[b]See pp. 244–5.

conflict with the Achinese advancing from the north.[2] Bantam's importance as a market for pepper caused the Chinese to make it their southernmost stapling port in the archipelago.

The loss of Jakarta to the Dutch

Although Bantam was to become one of the last centres of cosmopolitan trade to fall to the Dutch, and survived into the last quarter of the seventeenth century, it was on Bantamese territory that the Dutch set up their headquarters and laid the foundations of their territorial power in Java. This took place in 1619 when the empire-building Jan Pietersz Coen arbitrarily annexed the small port of Jakarta (Sunda Kelapa).

The events at Jakarta in 1619 formed the culmination of twenty years of tension and intrigue which followed the coming of the Dutch and their English rivals to the sultanate. Dutch–Bantamese relations got off to a particularly bad start with the initial visit of the arrogant and intemperate van Houtman to Bantam in 1596, but the Bantamese were just as wary of the English who opened their first factory at the port eight years later.[3] Although there was a brief honeymoon period between the new arrivals and the Bantamese, which grew out of their mutual desire for trade and of a common dislike of the Portuguese, within a few years relations deteriorated. A complex situation arose in which Bantamese suspicions of the Europeans in general were entangled with the jealous intrigues of the Dutch and the English against one another. The Bantamese, whose main concern was to prevent the building by either the Dutch or the English of an impregnable fortress such as had been done by the Portuguese at Malacca, tried to exploit Anglo–Dutch rivalries and restrict their activities as much as they could. After 1608, when Pangeran Arya Ranamanggala emerged the victor in the struggle for the regency which followed the assassination of his predecessor, Bantamese pressure on the European traders increased considerably. This caused the Dutch to look around for an alternative base for their activities, and with the arrival of a new fleet under Governor Pieter Both in 1610, they obtained permission from the regent of Jakarta, Pangeran Vijaya Krama, to set up a factory there. Four years later, the English followed suit and opened their own factory at Jakarta.

What had been a three-sided affair now became a four-sided one. Pangeran Vijaya Krama who was nominally a vassal of Bantam but also had been a supporter of the murdered regent, welcomed the Europeans as bringing new prosperity to his port and providing him at the same time with a means of asserting his independence. Nevertheless he was unwilling to grant the Dutch request for permission to build a fort at Jakarta unless they were prepared to abandon their factory at Bantam altogether. Meanwhile Pangeran Arya Ranamanggala in Bantam resented the establishment of a Dutch foothold at Jakarta but did not wish to lose their custom at Bantam itself. The Dutch and the English tried to exploit the situation each to their own best advantage, the Dutch playing on Bantamese–Jakarta animosities to enhance their own position, and the English siding now with the regent of Bantam, now with the regent of Jakarta, in attempts to destroy Dutch influence. As Anglo–Dutch competition for the spice trade intensified after 1610, matters approached their climax. They came to a head during 1618 when the Dutch in Jakarta, on Coen's orders, started building a fort, despite the regent's objections, while the English seized a Dutch ship in Bantam harbour as a pledge for their demands for compensation for losses sustained at Dutch hands in the Moluccas. In retaliation for this, Coen, in December 1618, attacked and burned the English factory at Jakarta to the ground. But early the next year, the English, now in league with Vijaya Krama and taking advantage of Coen's absence on an expedition to the Moluccas, laid siege to the Dutch factory with their superior forces. At this juncture, Bantam decided to intervene. Just as the small Dutch garrison at Jakarta had negotiated its surrender and was about to evacuate its position, Pangeran Arya Ranamanggala arrived on the scene at the head of a large army to reassert his authority. In the confusion which followed, all parties lost out except the Dutch. The English refused to abandon their alliance with Vijaya Krama or go back on their pledges to the defeated Dutch, and rather than submit to the Bantamese demands, withdrew from Jakarta entirely. This left the Pangeran alone to cope with Vijaya Krama's men and the Dutchmen still entrenched in their factory, which he was unable to do, so that when Coen, a few weeks later, returned with reinforcements from the Moluccas, the Bantamese were forced to retire. Thereupon Coen declared Jakarta a Dutch possession, renamed it Batavia and established it as the Dutch headquarters in the East.[4]

All attempts made subsequently by the Bantamese to retake Jakarta or Batavia failed[5] but the Dutch, preoccupied by affairs in the Moluccas and the threat of Mataram, found themselves unable to take effective measures against Bantam either. Its pepper mart was closed to them and the sultanate's continued existence as an independent port represented a serious breach in the monopoly system that they were trying to establish in the Straits of Malacca. Once again the story of Bantam runs closely parallel to that of Macassar, for the more the Dutch advanced their power and monopoly in other parts of the archipelago, the greater Bantam's power and prosperity became.

The fall of Portuguese Malacca in 1641 which destroyed the commercial and political influence of Mataram in the Straits and presaged the commercial decline of Acheh had only favourable consequences for Bantam. By 1650 it was the only free pepper port in the region (that is beyond Dutch control) and as such attracted a very cosmopolitan trade.[6] The fall of Macassar in the 1660s diverted more trade and foreign traders to Bantam as well as strengthening Muslim influence there. Acheh's decline led to Bantam inheriting her Indian cloth trade, the monopoly of which rested in the hands of Tamil-Muslim and Gujerati merchants. They now made Bantam their headquarters in the archipelago, undercutting Batavia's own newly-risen cloth business and intensifying Muslim influences at the court.[7] The rise of Dutch power in the Straits after 1641 meant that Batavia acquired a larger share in the pepper trade but the presence of the English factory at Bantam enabled the sultanate to hold its own against Dutch competition.

Sultan Abdul Fatah and the Dutch

These developments reached their peak during the reign of the capable Sultan Abdul Fatah or Sultan Agong who came to the throne in 1651. He was a devout Muslim and resolutely opposed to the Dutch. The growth of Muslim influence in the state during his reign was reflected by the increasingly frequent contacts with Mecca[8] and by the presence of a large number of religious teachers at his court.

Under his patronage their hand was to be discerned behind the edicts passed against opium and tobacco addicts, the introduction of Arab dress and the stream of anti-European propaganda which was disseminated from west Java.

The Sultan pursued a deliberately aggressive and provocative policy towards the Dutch in Batavia. From 1655 till 1659 he made open war on Batavia until the Dutch blockade forced him to sue for peace. A decade later he sent raiding parties against the Dutch citadel and its environs whilst laying claim to Cheribon, despatched aid to the strongly orthodox and very anti-Dutch supporters of Trunojoyo[9] in his great Mataram revolt,[a] and co-operated with agents from Acheh in stirring up pan-Islamic and anti-Dutch movements amongst the pepper-growers on the Sumatran west coast, besides interfering in the politics of Palembang and Jambi as well. Under the influence of his religious advisers, Sultan Abdul Fatah declined to enter into any permanent peace settlement with the Dutch,[10] refused to return refugees from Dutch Batavia and forced their conversion to Islam. The ruler did all that he could to build up Bantam's commercial and military power. He bought arms from the Portuguese, English and Danes, corresponded with the Turks in the hope of securing their alliance, and promoted direct Bantamese participation in trade.[11] As surely as Acheh and Macassar had clashed with the Dutch, future conflict between Bantam and Batavia was unavoidable.

The Dutch bided their time. They were preoccupied by the affairs of Mataram (Trunojoyo's rebellion) and dared not launch an attack on the sultanate until circumstances favoured them. Such an opportunity was provided in the 1670s as the result of dissensions at the Bantamese court itself. They centred on a quarrel which arose between the Sultan and the heir apparent or Sultan Muda, Abu Nazar Abdul Kahar. Whilst the Sultan Muda was on his second pilgrimage to Mecca, Abdul Fatah transferred the succession to a younger son, the Pangeran Purbaya. When the Sultan Muda (or Sultan Haji, as he was now called) returned in 1676, he was naturally aggrieved by what had taken place and set up a court clique in opposition to his father. But Sultan Haji was unscrupulous and greedy for power, and in order to secure it was prepared to be friendly with the Dutch. So when war broke out against Batavia again in 1680,[12] he staged a palace revolt, and having seized power, made peace with the Dutch. Sultan Haji's pro-Dutch attitude alienated him from popular support, and two years later he was appealing for Dutch aid to maintain his position against his father. The Dutch gave Sultan Haji their support on conditions which spelt the end of Bantam's independence. Batavia demanded that he take effective measures against piracy, break off all relations with Mataram, renounce all pretensions to Cheribon and cease to harbour dissident foreign elements in the state. Sultan Haji accepted these terms and got their support, which resulted in the surrender of the old sultan the following year (1683) to end his days in Dutch confinement.[13]

Having won their victory, the Dutch then built a fort at Bantam in order to preserve their gains; they caused the English to abandon their factory for the Sumatran west coast, and then in 1684 imposed a definitive treaty on the state. The Treaty of 1684 converted Bantam in effect into a vassal of Batavia. Her port was closed to all foreign (non-Dutch) shipping; the Dutch took over the pepper monopoly, and also

[a]See pp. 74 et seq.

a monopoly over all manufactured imports (that is mainly cloth) in lieu of an indemnity to cover the costs of the campaign.

The great rebellion of 1750-3

Bantam retained its nominal independence for another seventy years until this was brought to an end by the great rebellion of 1750–3. During this period the Dutch used their position to extend their influence over Borneo's west coast, using the sultanate as their agent.[14]

The rebellion of 1750–3 had its origins in the misrule of the Arab consort of Sultan Ariffin (1733–53), the beautiful and ambitious Ratu Sharifah Fatimah, who completely dominated her husband and in fact governed the state. Unfortunately she governed solely in her own interests, and although a favourite in colonial circles in Batavia[15] the Ratu became very unpopular in Bantam itself because of her extortionate demands and her alliance with the Westerners. When her schemes reached to the setting aside of Pangeran Gusti, the heir apparent, for her own nominee,[16] he was provoked into revolt (1745). Beaten, Pangeran Gusti and his followers fled to Batavia, but the Dutch governor-general, van Imhoff, sided with the Ratu Fatimah, and in 1747, at the instance of the Sultan, recognized Fatimah's protégé as successor, while the Pangeran and his adherents were sent to exile in Ceylon. The following year the ambitious queen was able to persuade Batavia of her husband's insanity, which led to his deposition (he was sent to Ambon where he died) and to the naming of Fatimah herself as regent on behalf of the new Sultan who was still a minor.

These developments provoked the Great Rebellion which broke out in October 1750. The people of Bantam, tired of excessive taxes and calls on their labour, listened to the cries of Kyai Tapa, a hermit from Gunong Munara, for the overthrow of the Queen-Regent and the expulsion of Dutch influence. Under the leadership of Ratu Bagus Buang, another member of the Bantamese royal house whom they had declared Sultan, a large rebel force appeared at the gates of Bantam. The town was only saved by the combined efforts of Fatimah's men and soldiers rushed from Batavia. The new governor-general at Batavia, Jacob Mossel (van Imhoff had left earlier in the same year), quickly saw where the real source of the trouble lay, had Fatimah and the young sultan seized,[17] and appointed a younger brother of Sultan Ariffin, the Pangeran Adi Sandika, as regent in her stead. But these sound political moves came too late to take the heat out of the rebellion and in 1651 the Dutch in Batavia found themselves under the threat of siege for the first time in over a century. In 1752 Mossel took further steps. He declared Bantam to be a vassal state of the Company, brought back Pangeran Gusti from Ceylon to reinstate him as Crown Prince and imposed a harsh new treaty on the sultanate. Bantam was to cede the Lampongs outright,[a] pay an annual tribute of pepper, ban trade in coffee and restrict its sugar production. The immediate effect of this treaty was to prolong the rebellion still under the leadership of Kyai Tapa and Ratu Bagus Buang somewhere in the interior, which prompted Mossel to make Pangeran Gusti sultan (Sultan Abdul Nasar) in 1753. During the course of the next two or three years the

[a]See p. 244.

rebellion finally petered out, having achieved nothing but the total subjugation of the sultanate to the Dutch Company.

The last days of the Sultanate

The last chapter in the history of Bantam as a separate entity was written in the opening decades of the nineteenth century. The upheavals of this period bore directly on the principality.[18]

In 1808 Sultan Abdul Nasar (1804–8) found himself confronted with unprecedented demands from the new Dutch governor-general of Java, Marshal Daendels,[a] who was attempting to fortify the island against British invasion and centralize the administration at the expense of the Javanese rulers at the same time. Daendels wanted to fortify the Straits of Sunda. He ordered the Sultan to provide a labour force to work on the forts at Teluk Merah. Already alienated by the governor-general's regulations designed to reduce his status,[b] the Sultan and more particularly a clique at his court led by his chief minister, the Mangkubumi, were horrified by the high death rate amongst the labourers at Teluk Merah, caused by the unhealthy conditions there. The Sultan protested and threatened to withdraw the labour force. Daendels replied by an ultimatum demanding a thousand coolies, the dismissal of the Mangkubumi, and the transfer of the royal capital to Anyer. This ultimatum ensured the triumph of the anti-Dutch faction at the court, and Daendel's emissary to Bantam was murdered. The Marshal struck back swiftly and savagely. Bantam was occupied and annexed; the Mangkubumi executed and his body thrown into the sea; and Sultan Abdul Nasar hunted down, captured in flight, and exiled (1809).

Abdul Nasar's successor, Sultan Abdul Mufakhir Mohamad Alauddin II, put on the throne by Daendels, was not really a ruler at all, but a salaried official of the Dutch. A European officer called a prefect was put in charge of the administration and all revenues were sent to Batavia. The princes of Cheribon underwent a similar fate.[19]

The burden of Daendels' measures, strikingly reflected in the rapid decline in coffee production despite all his efforts to the contrary, led to further unrest in 1810. The Sultan, being suspected of complicity, was deposed and another relative, Mohamad Safu'iddin, found to put in his place. The new ruler was confined to the interior uplands of Sunda with his capital at Pandeglang, while the coastal areas remained under direct Dutch control. He was allowed, however, to collect all revenues apart from those on opium.

Meanwhile the British had started to move onto the scene[c] and under the guidance of Raffles, intrigued with the Pangeran Ahmad, a pretender to the throne. In 1811 the British came and took over the administration of the island.[d] Pangeran Ahmad was duly made Sultan of Bantam and Sultan Mohamad went into retirement. But Sultan Ahmad felt dissatisfied with the reward for his services, for Raffles did nothing to restore the powers or the boundaries of the sultanate. Restive and

[a]See p. 82.
[b]See p. 82.
[c]See p. 82.
[d]See p. 82.

anxious to increase his revenues, Sultan Ahmad started to intrigue against the British, was discovered and in 1813 deposed. Raffles' new nominee at Pandeglang (Sultan Much'iddin) found himself stripped of all authority and left only with his title and a pension of Sp. $10,000 a year.

After 1813 Bantam was a sultanate only in name. The Dutch restored Sultan Mohamad on their return in 1816[a] but they did not restore his power. Raffles' settlement remained in force. Finally in 1832 this ruler faced banishment to Surabaya, accused of being involved in a case of piracy. The sultanate was at an end, but for the greater part of the century there was periodic unrest—mainly incited by members of the Bantamese aristocracy whose own fortunes had been undermined as a consequence.[20]

[a]See p. 82.

3. THE RULERS OF BANTAM

1. Sunan Gunong-jati (Faletahan)	1526–±50*
2. Maulana Hassanuddin	±1550–70
3. Maulana Yusof	1570–80
4. Maulana Mohamad	1580–96
5. Sultan Abdul Kadir	1596–1651
6. Sultan Abdul Fatah (Sultan Agong)	1651–82
7. Sultan Abdul Kahar (Sultan Haji)	1682–7

[1]Faletahan is also known as Sunan Gunong-jati and is believed to have come from the strongly Muslim centre of Pasai in north Sumatra.

[2]Bantamese influence stretched up the Sumatran east coast as far as Palembang but fell short of Jambi where it vied with the Dutch and the Achinese; on the west coast, Bantamese authority reached as far north as Silebar, near Benkulen.

[3]Despite a good welcome, Houtman's arrogant behaviour led to him and some of his men being arrested and cast into prison. The Dutch ships thereupon bombarded the port and Houtman was eventually ransomed a month later. The English factory was founded in 1602 by the first voyage of the newly-formed English East India Company, under the command of James Lancaster.

[4]The name 'Batavia' is the Latin name for the Germanic tribes who lived in the area now forming the country of Holland. The tension between the English and the Dutch which irrupted into open fighting at Jakarta had as its background determined English attempts to challenge the Dutch spice monopoly in the Moluccas, especially after 1615. This had already led to clashes between the two parties in the Great East, which was the pretext for the English seizure of a Dutch ship in Bantam by way of compensation. The accidental burning of this ship occasioned Coen's decision to attack the English factory at Jakarta.

[5]In 1627 a group of Bantamese soldiers actually forced their way into Batavia's citadel before they were defeated.

[6]In the streets and at the market of Bantam were to be found Arabs, Persians, Turks, Abyssinians, Mons from Lower Burma (Pegu), Chinese and Indians, let alone Javanese and Malays.

[7]Before the Dutch had eliminated Portuguese competition and established themselves firmly in India, they were dependent upon the Indian Muslim merchants who traded at Acheh for

their supplies of cloth for sale throughout the archipelago. By 1650 this situation had altered; the Dutch could get their own cloth supplies direct while the Muslim merchants, driven from Acheh by the Company's ascendancy there, flocked to Bantam where they helped to undercut the Batavian cloth market. See Schrieke, op. cit. for a full discussion of the economics of the day; also van Leur, op. cit.

[8]Links between Mecca and Bantam were highlighted by the two pilgrimages of the Sultan Muda (Sultan Haji) in 1669–71 and 1674–6. Both Sultan Abdul Fatah and his predecessor had their claims to the status of sultan recognized by Mecca.

[9]Sultan Abdul Fatah fell increasingly under the influence of Sheikh Yusof of Macassar, who, a religious leader of repute and strongly anti-Dutch, did much to encourage Bantam to lend its support to Trunojoyo. After the Dutch intervention, Sheikh Yusof was exiled by them to the Cape of Good Hope.

[10]On the grounds that no Muslim should come to a permanent accommodation with a *kafir* power and even a truce should not exceed ten years.

[11]Sultan Abdul Fatah not only lent money to foreign merchants, which was a traditional rôle for the ruler of a Malaysian port-state, but possessed his own ships which he sent with partly English crews under Danish or English masters to Japan, Macao, Manila, Cambodia, Bengal, Coromandel and via Surat to Mocha and Ormuz.

[12]Over the detention of certain Bantamese traders as 'pirates' by the Batavian authorities. The question of 'piracy' and the rôle of Bantam as a refuge for escaped slaves, particularly Muslim ones, from Batavia, were amongst the chief issues which embittered the relations between the Dutch and the sultanate.

[13]Sultan Abdul Fatah died in Dutch captivity at Batavia in 1692.

[14]In 1698 Landak appealed to its suzerain, Bantam, for help against Sukadana. As a result, the following year a combined Dutch-Bantamese force attacked and conquered Sukadana. Subsequently Landak, Sukadana and Sambas all recognized Bantam's overlordship. In 1772 the founder of Pontianak voluntarily placed himself under Batavia's protection. Dutch interest in the region was largely stimulated by fears of English competition.

[15]Formerly the wife of a Malay lieutenant with the Batavia garrison, Fatimah was famous for her beauty, charm and conversation.

[16]The Pangeran Sharif Abdullah, a commoner who was married to one of the Sultan's daughters in exchange for a land cession.

[17]Fatimah,destined for exile on Saparua, died before she left; Sharif Abdullah was sent to Banda.

[18]Important political changes took place in Europe between 1789 and 1815 following the outbreak of the French Revolution. *Inter alia*, the Dutch East India Company was abolished, Holland was occupied by France and the Dutch colonies occupied by Britain. As a result of the general peace which followed 1815, Holland recovered her liberty and most of her overseas possessions.

[19]Cheribon had been a bone of contention since the early seventeenth century when it lay torn between the conflicting ambitions of Mataram and Bantam. On the whole Bantam got the upper hand, but suzerainty passed to Batavia after the defeat of the sultanate in 1683. Administered under three major chiefs, it was the scene of constant unrest, partly as a result of aristocratic feuds but increasingly because of the impoverishment of its population who were subjected to mounting demands for rice, coffee, pepper and sugar. A series of uprisings in the last 12 years of the eighteenth century (1788, 1793, 1796) culminated in the 'war' of 1802–6 when there was a general revolt against economic conditions. In 1809 Daendels characteristically annexed the territory, allowing the chiefs to retain their titles and serve as salaried officials of the Dutch administration.

[20]Most aristocratic opposition had come to an end by the 1850s; after that there were two other serious movements in the 1870s and more particularly in 1883 (when 57 villages were destroyed); which had their origins in social and economic factors.

MATARAM

THE last and greatest of the Malaysian states to succumb to Dutch pressure prior to the nineteenth century was the Javanese empire of Mataram. The significance of the collapse and disintegration of this state after three generations of struggle and confrontation with the Dutch far exceeds that of the downfall of Macassar, Acheh or even Bantam, because Mataram was much more than a commercial power blown up and deflated again by the fortunes of trade and monopoly. It was the only real land power in the archipelago, the direct heir of the Hindu-Javanese empire of Majapahit and of the earlier agrarian kingdoms of east Java. In fact, until the later stages, Mataram's development was only incidentally affected by the presence of the Dutch on the island. The course of its history was dictated by historical forces much more deeply entrenched. The main role of the Dutch Company was to prolong artificially the life of the ruling dynasty when the natural forces at play had already dictated its collapse.

The rise of Mataram

The basic dynamic in the rise of Mataram and in its subsequent career was the age-old struggle between the commercially-oriented port-states of the north Java coast and the agrarian kingdoms centred in the island's interior. The Hindu empire of Majapahit itself slowly crumbled before the rise of the north Javanese ports until it was finally given the *coup de grâce* by Patih Yunus of Demak around 1520.[1] For a season the struggle ebbed and flowed. Demak's hegemony was short-lived and agrarian power found a brief champion in Pengging[2], quickly to disappear in its turn. In the confused politics of the second half of the sixteenth century, Pengging re-emerged as Pajang, and in 1582 a court official at the Jogjakarta *kraton* called Senopati, took advantage of dynastic intrigue to usurp the throne for himself and found the state of Mataram. Political expediency made Muslim states out of Pengging, Pajang and Mataram, although the forms Islam adopted in the Javanese interior diverged considerably from the more orthodox version practised in the north-coast states.

Under Senopati and his successor, Penambahan Krapyak or Mas Julang (1601–13), Mataram consolidated its power in the interior of the island, bringing the princes and territorial chiefs from the borders of Cheribon in the west to the wilds of Balambangan in the east to acknowledge its sway. In 1603 the capture of the rice port of Japara gave Mataram its first access to the sea trade routes. But the great struggle with the port-states which began under Mas Julang was not brought to a successful conclusion until the reign of his successor, Chakrasuma Ngabdurrahman or Sultan Agong (1613–46) a decade later. The defeat of the northern ports was to a considerable extent their own fault. Divided by mutual jealousies,[3] they were unable to combine and co-operate until it was too late. One by one, Japara, Demak, Grisek and finally Jaratan in 1613 fell to Mataram. In 1615 Surabaya formed a league of port-states including Tuban and Madura to oppose the armies of Sultan Agong, but this was no longer of any avail. Pasaruan fell in 1617; Tuban—once Majapahit's greatest port and the largest city in all Java—was conquered two years later; the salt state of Pati was won over by marriage contract in 1624, Madura crushed the same year and finally in 1625 Surabaya itself was stormed at a terrible cost in life and property.[4] The sack of Surabaya left only Bantam (and the Dutch in Batavia) in the west and the remnants of Hindu kingdoms in the east of the island to deal with, and provided the occasion for Sultan Agong to assume the title of Susuhunan (Sunan), implying his suzerainty over the whole of Java.

The expansion of Mataram under Sunan Agong and the struggle with the Dutch
The new empire of Mataram was a formidable power. It had a population of over
2½ millions, by far the largest of any state in the region. Its wealth lay in its rice-fields
rather than in its merchant ships. 'I am not a merchant, as those (rulers) of Bantam
and Surabaya', Sultan Agong once observed.[a] Nevertheless the establishment of
Mataram's hegemony over Java meant that it had stepped into the shoes of Majapahit as a trading as well as a land power.

Rice, pepper and spices were the keys to the trade of the archipelago. Mataram
began with the rice, and having subdued the northern ports controlled the spices.
Portuguese Malacca, the Moluccas and the pepper ports of east and west Sumatra
depended on Javanese rice, which gave Mataram up till 1641, as far as the Straits of
Malacca were concerned, a political influence over the states of east Sumatra (Palembang and Jambi, in particular) which long outlasted her own dwindling share
in their pepper trade. Her manpower intimidated the petty states of south Borneo
and on occasion Bantam and Macassar as well. The need to secure the trade route
to the spice islands led to Mataram's expansion into Madura and to her attempts to
reduce Balambangan and Bali, the latter for its printed cloths which had such a
good market in the Moluccas.[5] In the west, Mataram was inevitably drawn into
conflict with Bantam who disputed her political and commercial aspirations in the
Straits of Malacca, and with the Dutch whose establishment of power at Jakarta in
1619 was a much more serious matter than their previous penetrations into the
Moluccas.

Having stabilized his position on Java by eliminating some of his chief rivals and
by confirming the vassalage of others,[6] and overseas by normalizing his relations
with such states as Palembang, Jambi, Banjarmassin, Acheh, and—to spite Batavia
—Portuguese Malacca, the Sunan now turned his attention to the problem of the
Dutch in west Java. Relations between Mataram and Batavia were broken off in
1626. In 1628 and 1629, the Javanese launched two assaults on the Dutch fortress.
They were ambitious attempts; padi-planters from east Java were settled in the Krawang district to produce food supplies for the 60,000 men who invested the city;[7]
elephants and cannon transported with incredible difficulty overland aided the besiegers. But the Sunan lacked the sea-power either to prevent supplies reaching the
embattled Dutch garrison or obtain sufficient stores to maintain his own armies.
Decimated by starvation and disease, his forces melted away and the campaigns
were a failure.

Unsuccessful in this direction, the Sunan turned to disputing the Priangan and
Cheribon with Bantam and to subjugating the east of the island. But the Dutch
were not forgotten. Unable to reduce Batavia, the Sunan saw the vital need to save
Portuguese Malacca from a Dutch conquest which would undermine Mataram's
commercial and political influence in the Straits of Malacca. He started to intrigue
with the English at Bantam and as early as 1633 sent an embassy to Goa to get
Portuguese co-operation. As Dutch preparations for the final assault became obvious, Mataram made feverish efforts to raise a league of Malaysian states in Malacca's defence. Palembang, Jambi and Banjarmassin all subscribed but it was too
late to bring in either Johore or Macassar. In 1641 Malacca fell into Dutch hands,

[a]Quoted from Coen by Schrieke, *Indonesian Sociological Studies*, Vol. I, p. 266, note 558.

and as Schrieke has said, 'this was the harbinger of the approaching end of Mataram's independence'.[a] Mataram's economic self-sufficiency was destroyed. Under the Dutch, Malacca could no longer serve as an outlet for Mataram's trade. The Dutch were also now in a position to dominate the pepper states of Sumatra's east coast (which they promptly proceeded to do, eliminating Mataram's influence there) and could in fact force the Javanese to conduct their export trade through Batavia. After 1641, Mataram became increasingly dependent on the Dutch Company for all its overseas trade.

The decisive factor in the Dutch favour was their command of the seas. This was the chief cause of the Sunan's failure to capture Batavia in 1628 and 1629 with his 60,000 men.[8] It was also the basis for their domination in the spice islands and their slow strangulation of the spice trade, and in 1641 it was the principle factor in their victory at Malacca, where the defenders were forced to surrender because of starvation.

Mataram at bay; the reign of Sultan Amangkurat I (1646-77)

The realities of the new situation brought into existence by the Dutch occupation of Malacca led Mataram to make its peace with Batavia. A few months after the death of Sultan Agong in 1646, the new Sunan, Amangkurat I (Sunan Tegalwangi), was signing a definitive peace treaty with the Dutch which emphasized the new state of affairs. Javanese ships were to be excluded from the Moluccas and they could trade with Malacca only under permits issued by Batavia; on the other hand, the Dutch were granted freedom of trade inside Mataram's domains. However, Mataram was not finished yet. By the same treaty (in which the Dutch governor-general was referred to as 'brother'), Batavia formally acknowledged Javanese suzerainty and agreed to send annual tribute-bearing missions to the Mataram court.

Amangkurat I entertained few doubts as to the dangers which his empire faced, and took a series of measures to try to overcome them. His master-stroke was to forbid the export of rice from his ports—a policy started by his father. By this means he hoped to compel traders, including the Dutch, to come to Mataram and in this way still evade the Company's monopoly. He also encouraged the growth of cotton in Java itself, to reduce dependence on Batavia as the cloth mart, and all trade was made a state monopoly.

The Sunan also set out to consolidate the administration of the state and to dispel for ever the ever-present threat of rebellion and disintegration by replacing the traditional hereditary rulers in the provinces with a hierachy of officials appointed and controlled by himself. He carried out these reforms ruthlessly. Whereas his father had been content to convert the landed aristocracy into a court nobility, Amangkurat determined to destroy them altogether.[9] He was 'a monster of cruelty whose atrocities were on so extravagant a scale as to be scarcely credible.'[b] What was at first done out of political expediency later became tinged with madness, but his measures were effective; by the end of his reign hardly a member of the old Javanese aristocracy still survived.

[a]Schrieke, *Indonesian Sociological Studies*, Vol. 1, p. 61.
[b]Hall, *History of South-East Asia*, p. 301.

Along with these measures went tax reform on a cash basis, which placed the profits of the provinces at the disposal of the royal court, although when these sources proved insufficient, the court farmed out certain revenues to its officials. Import and export duties, a separate department, were also farmed out. To complete the pattern of conformity and centralization, Amangkurat tried to stamp out the opposition of the orthodox religious teachers to the peculiar brand of Islam that had evolved in his court.[10] It is reckoned that over 2,000 religious teachers unsympathetic to his ways died under persecution.

The political breakdown of Mataram; Trunojoyo's rebellion

However, all these measures to preserve Mataram and the strength of the dynasty backfired. The Sunan's economic policies had the effect of destroying private Javanese commerce, while the Dutch soon found ways round the ban on rice exports without having recourse to Mataram's ports and by so doing enhanced Batavia's commanding position in the inter-Asian trade.[11] The decline in trade brought about by these policies impoverished the once flourishing ports of the north,[12] spreading popular dissatisfaction and discontent. Political persecution destroyed the loyalty of the ruling classes while Amangkurat's religious policies provoked a strong orthodox reaction. By the middle of the 1670s, Mataram was on the verge of an internal political breakdown and collapse.

The event which brought matters to a head was a revolt which broke out in 1674, led by a Madurese prince claiming descent from the rulers of Majapahit,[13] called Trunojoyo. Trunojoyo enjoyed the support of three elements—Bugis and Macassarese freebooters, violently anti-Dutch, who had turned to a life of buccaneering and adventure after the closing of the free port of Macassar in the previous decade; his own men of Madura who yearned to escape the oppression of Javanese officials; and the poverty-stricken, dispirited population of the northern coastal regions who no longer saw any hope of help from the dynasty against their peculant governors, burdensome taxes and a succession of harvest failures. The occasion for their despair was the sudden demand imposed by Amangkurat's court in 1674 on the four coastal regencies for the tolls and rents which had gone uncollected for fourteen years. Faced with these urgent and huge demands, the populace simply joined hands with the Macassarese who so frequently raided their shores. As the rebellion spread, the rebels received the aid of Sultan Abdul Fatah of Bantam who sniped at Batavia and stirred up trouble in the Priangan and Cheribon. The turmoil in the north prompted several royal pretenders to the throne to rise up and stake their claims, and finally the movement acquired a religious significance when it was joined by the followers of the eighty-year-old Penambahan of the *perdikan desa* of Giri.[14]

With his kingdom falling about his ears, Amangkurat invoked the 1646 treaty and appealed to Batavia for help. Seeing the formidable coalition of anti-Dutch elements ranged on the side of Trunojoyo against the Sunan, the Company decided, though reluctantly at first, to respond.[15] By the time that the Dutch took action in 1676, the whole of East Java and quite a large part of Central Java were in the hands of the rebels.[16] Despite a Dutch naval assault on Surabaya led by Speelman, followed up by a raid on Madura later the same year, in July 1677 Trunojoyo sacked the *kraton* at Plered, which in fact Amangkurat had abandoned without a fight, convinced that the days for his dynasty had run out.[17] Now a refugee making for Dutch territory, Amangkurat I died on the way, at Tegalwangi near Pekalongan. His dying injunctions to his son and heir were to continue to Batavia and confirm the alliance with the Dutch. This the new Sunan hastened to do, and there, in October 1677, signed a treaty which preserved his line but marked the end of his country's genuine independence.

The collapse of Trunojoyo's rebellion and its aftermath

This treaty by which the Dutch recognized the new ruler as Amangkurat II, completely reversed the relationship between the Javanese and the Dutch; the Dutch governor was now addressed as 'protector' and 'father' (later, 'grandfather') whereas in Amangkurat I's day he had been called 'brother'. The Dutch obtained the cession of the Priangan, Krawang and the port of Semarang. They were granted a monopoly over the importation to Mataram of opium and the cloths of India and Persia, Dutch currency became legal tender in Mataram, and all of Mataram's ports were closed to non-Dutch shipping. The Sunan had also got to meet the costs of the Dutch campaign in his aid.

Having made these sweeping concessions which were to add considerably to the opposition against him in his own domains, Amangkurat II now had full Dutch support.[18] For the first time in the history of the continent, a European army marched into the Asian interior. By August 1678, under the command of Captain Francois Tak, it had reached and seized Trunojoyo's capital at Kediri; at the end of the following year, Trunojoyo was hunted down and caught in the mountains of east Java by Ambonese and Bugis levies, to be treacherously slain at Amangkurat's court by the Sunan in person the next year. In 1680, the resistance of the Penambahan of Giri was brought to an end. By 1682 the Bugis mercenaries had eliminated all opposition in Madura and the rebellion was at an end. The symbolic end of Mataram's independence was also marked when in 1678 Tak, the Dutch commander at Kediri, crowned the Sunan himself in the presence of a scandalized court. And in the new capital of Kartasura, the Sunan's safety was guarded by the presence of a Dutch garrison.

The political consequence of Trunojoyo's upheaval was to pawn Mataram's independence to the Company. Nevertheless, the rebellion itself was not the product of Dutch action but of more traditional forces. Apart from the economic and social conditions that ignited the rebellion, the movement reflected old themes such as the tussle between coast and inland Java and the contest between two conflicting religious outlooks. Trunojoyo was in effect leading a league of coastal states against the agrarian hinterland. The Penambahan of Giri was continuing the struggle of orthodox Islam against the religious traditions of ancient Java, begun with the war against Hindu Majapahit and followed through with Demak's struggle against heterodox Pengging. And the rebellion provided the opportunity for the inherently divisive forces in Javanese society to assert themselves—in a land where the exercise of effective authority from the centre has always been hampered by regional self-sufficiency, poor communications and primitive means of waging war.

The Javanese Wars of Independence, 1705–55

The suppression of Trunojoyo's rebellion was a turning point in the history of the

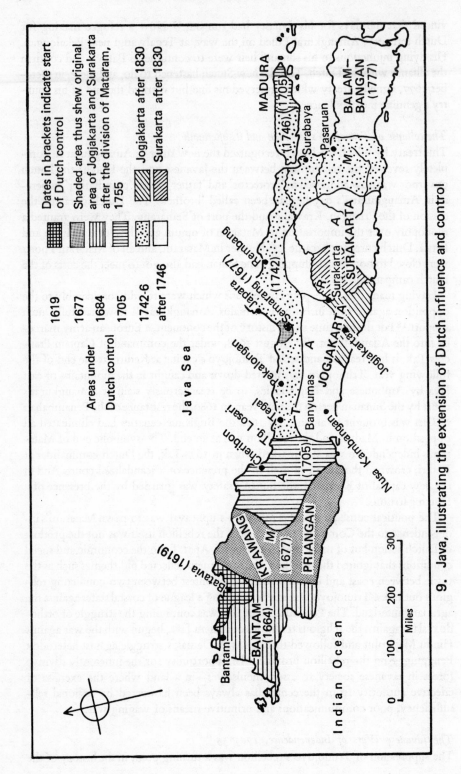

9.   Java, illustrating the extension of Dutch influence and control

Javanese struggle with the Dutch in as far as the ending of Mataram's real independence meant the start of the long Dutch hegemony in the archipelago. But its suppression did not bring peace to Java nor an end to Javanese resistance against Dutch domination. Trouble continued sporadically for the next hundred years, assuming the dimensions of a full-scale war on three occasions, with a final outburst during the first half of the nineteenth century.[a] The three wars are called by the Dutch the wars of the Javanese succession, but they could be more accurately described as the wars for Javanese independence, since in every case the Dutch were supporting a candidate for the throne of Mataram against those who sought to bring about an end of their power. Each war finished up with a Dutch victory and each peace treaty increased their political and economic stake in the island. Each treaty also saw a diminution in the lands of the sultanate until finally the former empire was split up into the twin principalities of Surakarta and Jogjakarta.

The first war (Surapati's war) broke out in 1705, two years after the death of Amangkurat II, but was the outcome of trouble which had been smouldering since the days of Trunojoyo. Surapati himself had a colourful background. Formerly a Balinese slave, he fled into the Priangan and became a bandit leader there. Then during Trunojoyo's rebellion, he entered into Dutch service where he distinguished himself. However he became involved in an incident which affected his pride and went back to the Priangan where he organized guerrilla war against the Dutch. With Dutch troops hot on his heels, in 1686 Surapati and his supporters fled to the Sunan's *kraton* at Kartasura where, already a hero, he was well received. When Major Tak, of Kediri fame, arrived from Batavia to demand Surapati's surrender, he and a large number of his escort were massacred on the spot. Batavia was in no position to exact revenge while Amangkurat II was happy to speed his guest on his way east, where Surapati now went to carve a kingdom for himself in Balambangan. Amangkurat II's son and successor, who came to the throne in 1703 as Amangkurat III (Sunan Mas), had been involved in these events and had openly sympathized with the anti-Dutch elements.[19] Once Sunan, he was resolved to put his anti-Dutch feelings into effect. He refused to renew his father's engagements with Batavia and actively intrigued with Surapati against the Dutch.

But Sunan Mas had also inherited something of his grandfather's (Sunan Tegalwangi) despotic disposition, and his autocratic and ruthless manners alienated several amongst the most powerful noblemen at the court, including his uncle, the ambitious and frustrated Pangeran Puger.[20] Fearing for his life, Pangeran Puger in 1704 fled to Dutch-held Semarang, and having obtained the support and recognition of the powerful regents of Surabaya and Sampang (in Madura) as the new Sunan with the title of Pakubuwana I, turned to Batavia for their aid to put him on the throne. It did not take the Dutch long to decide that their interests would best be served by backing Pangeran Puger, although his nephew, Sunan Mas, had a far better claim. The following year (1705) a Dutch force of 2,000 men marched on Kartasura, occupied it and installed Pangeran Puger as Susuhunan, all at the cost of one casualty.[21] Bloodless or no, the price which Pakubuwana I had to pay for his elevation to the throne was extremely high. The treaty which the Dutch now imposed on Mataram made them the unquestioned masters of Java. Mataram waived

[a] See pp. 83 et seq.

her claims to the Priangan and Cheribon, and acknowledged Dutch sovereignty over all lands west of Cape Losari in the north and of Nusa-kambangan in the south; Mataram also recognized as Dutch the eastern half of Madura (which in practice had acknowledged Dutch suzerainty since 1683). The economic terms were if anything more decisive since they laid the foundations of the system of 'contingencies' and 'forced deliveries'[a] which marked the first stage of the conversion of Java into a market garden for Dutch enterprise. The Dutch were granted complete control over Mataram's trade. In addition, to meet the costs of the war, Mataram had to provide Batavia with 800 koyans of rice annually for the next twenty-five years, and the Dutch were granted the right to demand produce from the territorial princes of the empire either free or for a nominal sum. To guarantee this settlement, the Dutch garrison at Kartasura was restored and another garrison established at Pasaruan.

In the meanwhile Sunan Mas had fled to the court of his ally, Surapati, in east Java. It took a three-year campaign to force them into submission. In 1706 the Dutch took Surabaya from the sea and overwhelmed the frontier fort of Bangil where Surapati was killed in the fighting. In 1708 Pasaruan was captured and Surapati's body was dug up and cast into the sea. In July the same year, Sunan Mas and Surapati's successors were forced to lay down their arms and were sent to exile in Ceylon. The Dutch then tried to reduce the power of the coastal lords for ever, by re-organizing the empire into forty-three regencies, each independent of the other and all of the same status.

The Second War of Independence

However, this did not bring peace to Java, for the followers of Surapati still continued their resistance and found increasing support from the princes of the coastal regions—especially in Jayeng Rana (Jangrana), the *adipati* of Surabaya, and in Chakraningrat III of Sampang in Madura—who resented the new commercial demands of the Dutch as well as the Dutch measures to reduce their authority. Jayeng Rana's murder at Kartasura in 1709 precipitated a fresh uprising led by his brothers, and sporadic fighting in the succeeding years merged in 1719 into a second struggle over the succession to the throne which began on the death of Pakubuwana I. In the highly confusing sequence of events that followed, the Dutch supported Pakubuwana's son, Sunan Prabhu (Amangkurat IV) against the claims of four of his brothers and an uncle besides.[22] Each claimant had his reasons but Sunan Prabhu, by relying on Dutch support, inevitably increased the general opposition to him. His rivals had been defeated by the time that he died in 1727 and he was succeeded by his sixteen-year-old son who took the title of Pakubuwana II. When the young prince came of age in 1733, the Dutch took the occasion to impose a fresh treaty on him in settlement for their support and in connexion with his debts to the Company. The deliveries of rice were increased to 1,000 koyan annually for a period of fifty years, and the Sunan also agreed to the suppression of coffee planting throughout Mataram as the Dutch supplies from the Priangan were already sufficient for the overseas markets.

The treaty of 1733 tightened the Company's economic grip over Mataram and

[a]See Book II.

alienated the Susuhunan still further from his subjects,[23] so much so that he became dependent on a Dutch garrison and non-Javanese mercenaries for his safety in his own capital.

The Chinese Rebellion and the Regent of Madura's Revolt

In 1740 a great massacre of Chinese took place in Batavia[a] which not only precipitated a general uprising of Chinese throughout Java against the Dutch but also set in motion the tangled train of events which led to the final disintegration and partitioning of Mataram fifteen years later. By this time the Sunan was regarded by his own people as little more than a Dutch puppet propped up by Dutch power, and he was opposed not only by anti-Dutch elements at the court of Kartasura but also by the ambitious regent of Madura, Chakraningrat IV, who believed that the downfall of the royal house of Mataram would give him the opportunity to create a kingdom for himself in east Java.

The Chinese revolt which spread along the northern coastline, engulfing Rembang and Juana and isolating Semarang, placed Pakubuwana II in a delicate situation. His own position depended on the Company but the Dutch themselves appeared to be fighting for survival. It was equally clear that the sympathies of his powerful officials in the north were on the side of the Chinese anti-Dutch movement. In order to secure the future, the Sunan gave his own surreptitious encouragement and support to the rebels. Such tactics gave Chakraningrat the chance he had been waiting for to strengthen his position at the expense of that of Kartasura. While the Sunan maintained his ambivalent attitude, the Madurese responded to the Dutch appeal for help, and in 1741 intervened decisively on their side.[24] The regents' forces crushed the centres of insurgency along the north-eastern coast and relieved the besieged Dutch garrison at Semarang.

Shocked by the Madurese challenge and their alliance with Batavia, Pakubuwana came out into the open and declared a holy war against the Dutch. The Dutch garrison at Kartasura was lured into a trap and massacred, but a Dutch victory at Semarang towards the end of the year quickly drained the Sunan's resolve. He made peace with the Dutch envoys from Batavia and by doing so, aroused the opposition of a large number of his own lords who wished to continue the struggle. In June 1742 the Sunan was driven out of his capital by the war party and took refuge at Madiun while they installed Mas Garendi, a grandson of Sunan Mas, in his stead.

Mas Garendi's tenure of power lasted only six months before he was forced out of his *kraton* by the troops of Chakraningrat of Madura. Chakraningrat was now literally where he aimed to be but, to his chagrin, his Dutch allies deprived him immediately of the fruits of his victory. They insisted on the restoration of Pakubuwana II with whom they had concluded a new treaty which officially made Mataram what it had long been in effect—a vassal of the Dutch Company. By this treaty of 1743, Mataram was made to cede all her northern coastline including Japara, Rembang, Surabaya and the land east of Pasaruan (meaning Balambangan) to the Company, which thereby gained exclusive control of all Java's seaports. Dutch garrisons

[a]See Book II.

were to be maintained at Mataram's expense and the Company also acquired the right to mint coins and to have the first option on all Mataram's produce.

These terms were naturally quite unacceptable to Chakraningrat of Madura who had gone to the aid of the Dutch against a promise of independence and in the hope of being at least part heir to Mataram's dominions.[25] So, recruiting men from Bali and Madura itself, the prince made war on the Company. After some initial successes he was driven back on to his island, and after a futile attempt to send for help from the English at Benkulen, he fled to Banjarmassin. There he fell into Dutch hands and was exiled to the Cape of Good Hope (1746). Resistance also came from other quarters, notably from Mas Brahim, a grandson of Surapati who held out in the districts of Pasaruan and Malang, and from Mas Said, a son of the Pangeran Mangkunegara exiled to Ceylon in 1733. Mas Said was still unsubdued when the agony of Mataram reached its final stage with the outbreak of the third Javanese war or the war of Mangkubumi and Mangkunegara in 1749.

The Third War of Independence and the partitioning of Mataram

This war began on the death of Pakubuwana II in 1749, but it was in effect a continuation of the earlier struggle. Reinstated by the Dutch in 1743, the Sunan transferred his *kraton* to Surakarta (Solo). Also, well aware of his dynasty's complete dependence on Dutch goodwill for its survival, he was prepared to pawn his power and sovereignty to an even greater extent to Batavia. Therefore in 1746 when the Sunan was visited at Surakarta by the new Dutch governor-general, van Imhoff, he was disposed to make a new and far-reaching treaty with the Company. In exchange for the cancellation of all his debts and for Dutch support of his nominee as successor, Pakubuwana II ceded Tegal and Pekalongan to the Company. The revenues of all the coastal districts were also handed over to the Company in return for an annual subsidy of 5,000 Spanish dollars. For the surrender of all rights of toll and taxation, including import and export duties and over the farming of birds' nests, tobacco and markets, the Sunan was to receive an additional 9,000 Spanish dollars, the Crown Prince 2,000 Spanish dollars, and the court 1,000 Spanish dollars.

These concessions which converted Mataram to all intents and purposes from a Dutch vassal into a Dutch province provoked strong resentment amongst the Javanese aristocracy. Their spokesman and leader was the Mangkubumi, a younger brother of the Sunan. The Mangkubumi's discontent was transformed into open hostility by the undiplomatic manner in which he was treated by van Imhoff during his visit.[26] He left Surakarta and joined Mas Said in the field. A couple of years later, Pakubuwana II, lying on his deathbed with Dutch envoys hovering anxiously in attendance, took the ultimate step and formally ceded the whole of Mataram to the Dutch Company, granting them the authority to appoint his successor as well. After his death, van Imhoff installed the Crown Prince as Pakubuwana III in the name of the Company (1749).

The late Sunan's cession produced an immediate reaction throughout Mataram and caused the Mangkubumi to have himself proclaimed Susuhunan at his headquarters of Jogjakarta. Seven long years of struggle followed, with the Dutch seeking to maintain their authority through their nominee on the one side, and the majority of the lords of Mataram opposing it on the other. The Mangkubumi and Mas Said were born fighters and leaders and made a formidable combination, while their guerrilla tactics and the wide popular support they enjoyed, led the Dutch to suffer several sharp reverses. The most notable of these was at the crossing of the Bogowonto river in Kedu at the end of 1751 when the Dutch commander was amongst those who fell.

However, the Javanese began to fall apart. The Mangkubumi quarrelled with Mas Said over the appointment of regents in the conquered region of Panaraga in 1752 and was subsequently driven out from there and from Madiun by his nephew. By 1754 everybody except Mas Said was ready to make peace. The Dutch were tired of a seemingly never-ending struggle to keep their puppet prince upon his throne, while the Mangkubumi felt that his position was compromised as a result of his quarrel with Mas Said. Talk of partition was in the air, as it had been on several occasions in the past,[27] and in that year Pakubuwana III agreed to the division of his kingdom. In 1755, in a treaty signed at Gianti by the Sunan, the Mangkubumi and the Dutch, the division was sealed. Mataram was divided into two roughly equal portions. Pakubuwana retained the title of Susuhunan and reigned in Surakarta; the Mangkubumi assumed the style of Sultan at Jogjakarta and took the title of Amangkubuwana I. Two years later, after winning a series of small but inconclusive skirmishes, Mas Said also made his peace. In an agreement signed at Salatiga with the Dutch, he was granted the fief of the Mangkunegorese at the expense of Surakarta and took the title of Pangeran Adipati Mangkunegara. Mataram was no more.

The successor states of Surakarta and Jogjakarta; Daendels and Raffles

The new realms of Surakarta and Jogjakarta with their ruling families survived as separate entities until the last days of Dutch rule. For three generations they were to retain a good deal of their autonomy before this was terminated with the episode of the Java War. Both remained centres of strong anti-Dutch feeling, and the royal house of Jogjakarta in particular was to play an important rôle in the struggle of the new-born nation of Indonesia after 1945.[28]

At first Dutch power sat lightly on the principalities and even on the new areas recently acquired by the Company. The Dutch at first made no effort to bring Surapati's old kingdom of Balambangan[a] in East Java under their control, although it had been ceded to them as part of the settlement of 1743. But twenty-five years later, when aroused by the activities of Chinese and English adventurers planting sugar there they began to take action. By this time the region had fallen under the Balinese and it was only brought under Batavia's effective authority in 1777 after ten years of hard campaigning.[29] In 1788 Pakubuwana III of Surakarta passed away and was succeeded peacefully as Sunan by his son, Pakubuwana IV. At Jogjakarta the Mangkubumi (Amangkubuwana I) died four years later and the throne passed equally quietly to his son and heir, Sepuh, who reigned as Amangkubuwana II.

However, the surface calm was broken by the upheavals affecting the Dutch themselves which came at the end of the century. In 1789 started in France the great Revolution which was to engulf the European continent and send its reverberations around the world. Four years later Holland itself was swept into the Revolutionary Wars to become first a client state and then a territory of France. As far as the Dutch colonies in South-East Asia were concerned, these events first reflected themselves

[a]Refer pp. 77 et seq.

in the collapse of the Dutch East India Company (1799) and in the introduction of the direct rule of the Dutch home government which followed in consequence.[30] But despite rumours of reform and pleas for freedom of trade, nothing was changed until the appointment in 1803 of Herman W. Daendels[31] as governor-general of Java on behalf of the French-controlled Batavian Republic. With Daendels came the first breath of the French Revolution and the first attempts to modernize the colonial administration of the island. Meanwhile the struggle for power between Britain and France had also reached the shores of the archipelago. In 1802 the British occupied the Moluccas. In 1806 and 1807, as a measure to forestall the French, Dutch naval power in the region was crippled by ships of the Royal Navy off Batavia and Grisek.

Then, in 1811, Daendels was recalled, leaving his successor (Jan W. Jannsens) to face a British invasion with hopelessly inadequate forces.[32] After a brief campaign the Dutch in Java surrendered and for five years (1811–16) the island was run as a British colony. For the greater part of this period, the British administration was in the talented and ambitious hands of Thomas Stamford Raffles[33] who made the fullest use of his position as governor for the English East India Company to introduce radical reforms and persuade his masters that Java should remain British. His efforts were nevertheless in vain, for in 1816 all Holland's possessions in South-East Asia that had been taken over by the British were restored to her.[34]

Under any circumstances such dramatic shifts in power would have presented a tempting opportunity to the rulers of the two Javanese principalities, especially in the case of the independent-minded Sultan Sepuh at Jogjakarta. The policies carried out, however, by Daendels and Raffles, both of whom aimed at consolidating the European hold over the island, ensured that the *status quo* would be disturbed.

It was the tactless and dictatorial manner in which Daendels conducted his relations with the two rulers (as was also the case with Bantam[a]) which aroused their antagonism and prompted them to turn the situation to their own advantage. Sultan Sepuh was the first to receive the reforming governor-general's attentions. The Sultan had always harboured strong anti-Dutch prejudices. These were now aggravated when in 1810 Daendels took steps to increase Dutch influence at his court. By means of new instructions on ceremonial and protocol Daendels elevated the status and authority of the Dutch Resident,[35] measures which he followed up by visiting Jogjakarta in person. Sultan Sepuh's answer was to take up the overtures of Raffles, who was already in Penang weaving his webs of intrigue amongst the princes of the archipelago as a prelude to the British invasion of Java. At the same time, the Sultan increased the number of his men under arms on the pretext of his quarrel with the Sunan at Solo. Alarmed, early in 1811, Daendels ordered the invasion of his territory, using as an excuse intrigue at the court, deposed Sultan Sepuh and placed his son, the Pangeran Adipati Anom, as Regent in his stead.[36]

Nevertheless Sepuh, who was still allowed to live on in his own palace, was not put out by this turn in events. He enjoyed, on account of his well-known hostility towards the Dutch, wide popular support and sympathy, which he made full use of to secure his restoration the moment that Daendels left the country. So when the

[a]Refer p. 68.

British assumed the administration of Java at the end of the year, they found the Sultan firmly seated back on his throne. Raffles, now governor, was at first chary of recognizing this restoration, well aware of the Sultan's independent pretensions which he himself had helped to foster, but all the same permitted the negotiation of a new treaty in 1812. By this agreement, in exchange for acknowledgement of British overlordship, the lands taken by Daendels were restored to Jogjakarta.[37] But Sultan Sepuh misinterpreted the treaty as a token of British weakness. He raised a new army and reinforced his *kraton*. Then, taking advantage of the departure of British troops for Palembang,[a] he prepared openly for war. His worst fears confirmed, Raffles' reaction was swift. A British force of 12,000 men marched on Jogjakarta. The Sultan was deposed for a second time, but this time banished, to begin with to Malacca, then Penang and then, after the Dutch restoration, to Ambon. Two million Spanish dollars from his treasury were confiscated as 'war booty', and his son was elevated to the throne once more, now as Sultan Amangkubuwana III (Sultan Rojo).[38] All these events took place in 1812.

Meanwhile Surakarta had been subjected to similar pressures. In 1811 Daendels also imposed a new treaty on the Sunan which tightened the Dutch hold on the principality by reducing his lands and his revenues.[39] This treaty was at first upheld by Raffles, but in 1812 the British negotiated a fresh agreement with the Sunan (Pakubuwana IV) which against a recognition of British overlordship and certain other conditions[40] restored to Surakarta the lands which Daendels had compelled him to surrender. Then came the Jogjakarta episode and in Sepuh's captured kraton the British found irrefutable evidence of Surakarta's involvement in the plans to overthrow British hegemony.[41] So Raffles sent his troops on to the Sunan's capital and imposed upon him another treaty which deprived him of his newly restored lands, cut down his army to the size of a private bodyguard and placed the appointment and dismissal of his chief minister (the *patih*) in British hands.

The outbreak of the Java War (1825–30)

The policy of systematically reducing the power and influence of the Javanese rulers and aristocracy in the principalities which was pursued by Daendels and Raffles in the name of modernization, was continued by the restored Dutch régime after 1816. It marked a real decline in the authority of the two rulers and a serious erosion of their political autonomy. The last vestiges of this were to be swept away as a result of the final upheaval of traditional Java against the domination of the West fifteen years later. In 1825 the Java War broke out. Lasting five years, its end brought about the reduction of the principalities to the status of puppet domains in the Dutch East Indian Empire.

The Java War centred around the personality of a prince of Jogjakarta called Dipo Negoro who was to become the focus of both aristocratic and popular discontent. The eldest son of Amangkubuwana III (Sultan Rojo), Dipo Negoro was born about 1785 and brought up in a strictly orthodox manner at Tegalrejo, near Jogjakarta, by his great-grandmother, the devout Ratu Ageng, the widow of Amangkubuwana I (Mangkubumi). This upbringing laid the foundations of the piety and religious mysticism for which later Dipo Negoro became celebrated and

[a]See p. 244.

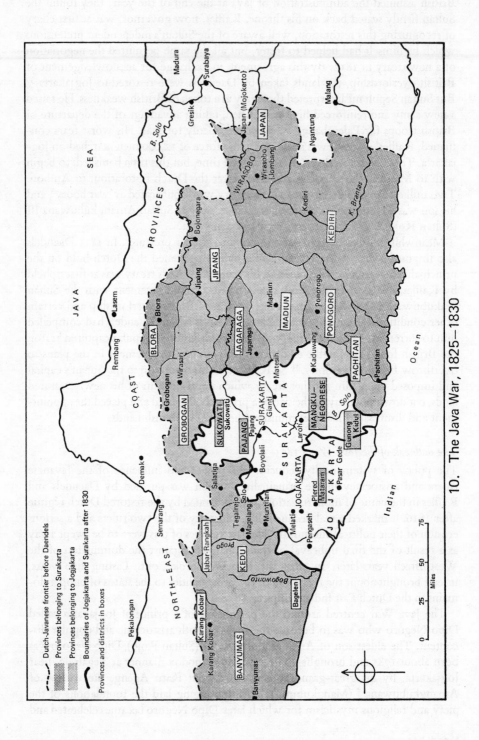

10. The Java War, 1825-1830

revered.[42] In 1814 his father died, but a younger son, Mas Jarut, whose mother was a queen of higher rank, was placed on the throne. This was done with British consent but Raffles allegedly promised Dipo Negoro the throne if his brother died. But in 1822 when Mas Jarut (Amangkubuwana IV) did die, the Dutch, either ignorant of or preferring to ignore Raffles' undertaking, placed the late ruler's two-year-old son, Menul, on the throne as Amangkubuwana V instead. At the same time, they made Dipo Negoro one of the four guardians of the new Sultan.[43] Thwarted personal ambition together with mounting concern at the encroachments on the power and privileges of the Javanese aristocracy in the principalities were probably the factors which conditioned Dipo Negoro's attitude in the years which followed. His dislike of things Dutch in particular and of Western influences in general became more pronounced. He resented the close relations which the dominating clique at court developed with the Dutch, the intrusion of Western dress and manners within the kraton, the drinking parties so beloved by Dutch officials, and the laziness and inefficiency of these administrators themselves.[44] His wrath was kindled still further by certain Dutch administrative actions and by their increasing failure to consult either himself or the Mangkubumi, another regent who abhorred the growth of Dutch influence, on such matters.[45]

Matters came to a head in 1825 over the issue of work on a road which ran through Dipo Negoro's lands. The road (from Jogjakarta to Magelang) was in the process of being widened without the prince having been consulted or informed. Insult was added to injury when Dipo Negoro discovered obstructions on the road near his seat at Tegalrejo and that even a *keramat* on his lands had been displaced. Furious, he ordered the arrest of the labourers concerned and the removal of the obstructions. When work was recommenced on the authority of the patih in Jogjakarta with the full backing of the Dutch resident, Smissaert, Dipo Negoro demanded that the Sultan's chief minister be dismissed from office. Smissaert, in his turn, commanded Dipo Negoro to come to Jogjakarta to explain his conduct; but Dipo Negoro, listening to rumours that the Dutch planned to arrest and deport him, refused to go. Smissaert next sent a detachment of troops to go and fetch the defiant prince from his estate. The troops went but on arrival at Tegalrejo were confronted by a large gathering of Dipo Negoro's supporters. In the sharp skirmish which followed, Dipo Negoro fled on horseback to Kalisoko, leaving his homestead in flames. A few days later he had returned to Selarong near Jogjakarta at the head of a large crowd of followers. The countryside flocked to his banners and thus at the end of July 1825 the Java War had begun.

The course of the War
For the first two of the five years of fighting which ensued, Dipo Negoro and his followers held the upper hand in the countryside. He was joined by the Mangkubumi and other aristocrats and received the support of the bulk of the peasantry, amongst whom he was widely regarded as the personification of the traditional saviour priest-king. Indeed one of Dipo Negoro's first acts once he had commited himself to rebellion was to have himself proclaimed sultan with the significant title of Abdul Hamid Eruchakra Kabirulmu'minim[46] before a gathering of *ulamas* and territorial chiefs at Selarong. Two other figures arose to play prominent parts by his side; one, Alibasa Sentot Prawiradirja, the son of the bupati of Madiun, who

became Dipo Negoro's principal commander in the field, and the other, Kyai Maja, a strongly religious leader from Surakarta, who was the prince's chief adviser and confidant on policy in the early years.

At the beginning, the foreigners (the Dutch and Chinese) in the principality of Jogjakarta found themselves completely isolated. Chinese toll houses were an immediate object of popular fury and were burned to the ground. Those who did not or could not make the safety of the Sultan's kraton were massacred. An early attempt by the Semarang garrison to relieve Jogjakarta was beaten back with heavy Dutch losses near Demak. Throughout July and until relief got through from Surakarta in mid-August, Jogjakarta itself was threatened by Dipo Negoro's forces, while uprisings broke out in Kedu, Demak, Pekalongan, Semarang, Banyumas and Madiun. However the Dutch moved fast. Although a considerable part of his forces were engaged in Palembang and South Celebes,[a] the Dutch commander de Kock rushed reinforcements to Surakarta to ensure the loyalty of the Sunan[47] and followed there in person as soon as he could. He persuaded the 'loyal' Javanese leaders to raise their own forces, but his stern measures of executing rebel prisoners and burning villages in reprisal were soon abandoned as proving totally ineffective. Tolls and customs were lifted and a new land policy introduced in an effort to ease popular discontent, but the Dutch found it necessary all the same to draft troops from Sumatra, the Celebes and Europe to meet the situation. By 1830 Dutch effectives numbered 23,000 men.

The early successes of Dipo Negoro were largely a result of the policy of waging guerrilla warfare and of avoiding pitched battles. Keeping his headquarters always on the move, the prince launched his men on ambushes of small Dutch detachments, the raiding of food columns and attacks on isolated outposts. His forces consisted of two groups—the regulars who were organized into units under commanders with prestigious titles and equipped with firearms, and the irregular bands who had to rely on their *keris* and sharpened bamboo staves.[48] Faced with such tactics and organization, the Dutch found that at the end of the first year of the war they had made very little progress. In September 1826 they tried a new political ploy by salving the aged ex-Sultan Sepuh from the obscurity of his Ambonese exile and restoring him ceremoniously in Jogjakarta. There Sultan Sepuh reigned a senile figurehead for the remaining one and a half years of his life; then the seven-year old Amangkubuwana V was restored to his former position without anything having been achieved. Equally in vain were letters of amnesty to the rebels, offers of rewards for capture dead or live of their leaders (Dipo Negoro had a price of 20,000 guilders on his head) and secret negotiations carried out through Arab and English intermediaries.

From 1827, however, Dipo Negoro's fortunes began to wane. In the first place, de Kock found an answer to the guerrilla tactics which so harassed his forces. In early 1828 he commenced the construction of a network of forts that were linked to one another by roads which could be patrolled by fast-moving columns of troops. He then divided his forces into three commands, each under the hand of an experienced general.[49] This new approach soon produced dividends. Although Dipo Negoro's men were threatening both Rembang and Lasem in the northern coastal

---

[a]See pp. 244 and 311 respectively.

districts before its effect began to be felt, by the end of the year his followers had been forced into a confined area between the Progo and Bogowonto rivers where they were being harried by ten mobile Dutch columns, while Dipo Negoro himself narrowly escaped capture in a surprise dawn attack on his headquarters. 1829 saw the virtual collapse of the rebellion as Dipo Negoro's lieutenants cracked under Dutch pressure. Pangeran Natadiningrat, the son of the Pangeran Mangkubumi, had been the first notable to surrender as early as April 1828. Within twelve months his seventy-year-old father followed suit. But the movement suffered an even severer loss with the capture of Kyai Maja in April 1829.[50] Desertion became more attractive as the Dutch showed generous treatment to those who surrendered and were prepared to go so far as to recognize the titles that Dipo Negoro himself had bestowed. The worst blow came in September 1829 with the surrender of Sentot, who with his men, was on the verge of starvation.[51] Confronted with the inevitable, Dipo Negoro reopened secret negotiations with the Dutch on the basis of his claim to be recognized officially as the spiritual leader of all Muslims in Java. In January 1830 the rebel prince was admitted to de Kock's headquarters at Magelang. Three months of fitful negotiations followed, but came to an abrupt end towards the end of March when, breaking his promise of safe-conduct, de Kock had Dipo Negoro summarily arrested and imprisoned. De Kock justified his action on the grounds that Dipo Negoro was using the protracted negotiations as a cover for regathering his forces to launch a surprise attack. Whatever the truth may be the arrest put a finish to everything. Dipo Negoro was exiled to Menado, and in 1834 transferred to Macassar where he died twenty years later.[52]

So ended the last great attempt to oust the Dutch by the leaders of the old order in Java. In terms of life and treasure, it was a costly affair all round. An estimated 200,000 Javanese died during the course of the war, although it is doubtful whether barely a tenth of these were actually killed in action. Far more effective as killers were famine and cholera which swept through the war-ravaged provinces and took a large proportion as well of the 15,000 Dutch soldiers who lost their lives.[53] Large tracts of country were laid waste, fields left untended and great coffee estates ruined. The war cost the Dutch about 20 million guilders and for the time being the economy of the island was completely undermined.

The causes of the War and its aftermath

Although the charismatic personality of Dipo Negoro was a leading factor in the great uprising, which owed its spread and duration in large measure to the awe which his name inspired amongst the peasantry of the principalities, the Java War arose out of a combination of circumstances that had been poisoning Javanese life for decades and which created the atmosphere of discontent and restlessness that the Jogjakarta prince was able to exploit. At the root lay an irremediable land problem which constricted Javanese aristocrat and peasant alike. Land in the principalities was at a premium. It was insufficient for the needs of a polygamous and fast-spawning ruling class of landowners. The *Pax Batavia* after 1757 made matters worse by closing the safety-valve of internal strife while the annexations of Daendels and Raffles merely compounded what had already become a serious economic and social problem. As the aristocracy multiplied, shortage of land meant smaller shares and reduced incomes all round. One solution was to lease lands to foreigners;

rich Chinese merchants or retired Company officials were prepared to pay hand-some prices. The rulers of Mataram before partition had long used this method in order to supplement their own incomes;[a] the process became more general during and after the time of governor-general Imhoff who farmed out large tracts to his Chinese and European friends.

The land problem in the principalities was in no way diminished by the departure of Raffles and the re-establishment of Dutch rule in 1816. The new administration, particularly after van der Capellen[54] had assumed sole charge, discouraged private European planters in those regions under its direct control for reasons of altruism and self-interest;[55] this made it all the more tempting for private speculators to in-vest in the principalities where the needs of the Javanese landlord made them wel-come. One of the Dutch residents at Jogjakarta, Nahuys, led the way by acquiring the land of Bedaya from its Javanese owner, and was quickly followed by other Europeans who obtained long-term leases and could afford the inflated prices demanded. For along with the land went the peasants on it and the landowner's feudal rights over them, enabling the new lessees to make large profits from the cash crops with which they replaced the padi.

At the receiving end of the whole process were the peasants who worked the land. They were slaves of feudal tradition and were bound by the feudal rights which their Javanese masters had transferred to the foreign lessees. The introduction by the foreigners of new cash crops like sugar, coffee and indigo imposed fresh burdens on the peasant-farmer, for they required more attention and time than the traditional padi crop had done. Overpopulation closed all avenues of escape and so the peasant sank into 'a kind of slavery'.[56] Living costs were made higher still by the ubiquitous toll houses, which, usually in the hands of Chinese farmers, levied dues on nearly all that could be carried.[57] When the Java War broke out, one of the first victims of the upheaval were the toll-farmers.

The plight of the Javanese peasant in the principalities ultimately came to the notice of Batavia, but the Dutch administration's attempts to remedy the situation became one of the immediate causes for the Java War. The problem came to the fore as a result of a tour of the principalities by van der Capellen in 1822. The abuses of the land lease system soon became apparent to his eye, and strengthened his dis-like of a system which went against the liberal principles he was trying to intro-duce and also offered serious competition to government enterprise in cash crop cultivation. On his return to Batavia, van der Capellen ordered that land-leasing in the principalities be brought to an end by 1824, the leases cancelled, the lands returned to their original owners and the lessees compensated for money advanced and for improvements effected on the properties. These well-intentioned measures precipitated a crisis which involved landowner, lessee and peasant, and finally rebounded on to the Dutch authorities themselves. To start with, most Javanese noblemen suddenly faced ruin. They had received large advances against long-term concessions; the money had been spent and they were now called upon to pay it back. Those who had speculated in land now found their investments worthless and their chances of adequate compensation minimal. Worst off of all were the peasants who faced a new set of increased demands and taxes as their for-mer landlords tried desperately to recoup their losses.

[a] See p. 91, note 23.

Batavia's clumsy efforts to alleviate the situation by other measures only aggravated the general discontent. In an attempt to reduce the burden of tolls, the Dutch government ordered the abolition of some against the cession of certain districts. Apart from worsening the land shortage, this revived Javanese fears that the Dutch were contemplating the annexation of the two principalities. These suspicions were heightened still further when Batavia offered to advance money to the Javanese landlords so that they could pay their compensation in return for the mortgage of their lands.[58] Against this background of aristocratic fears as to Dutch political motives and conditions of peasant misery and distress, the restless, troubled figure of Dipo Negoro emerged as the champion of aristocratic rights and as the deliverer of the people against the advances of the Dutch.

The Dutch retribution for the war once it was over bore as heavily on Surakarta as it did on Jogjakarta. The Javanese rulers had to hand over Banyumas, Bagelan, Madiun and Kediri to Batavia, which annexed them in exchange for some monetary compensation. In Jogjakarta only Mataram and Gunong Kidul remained under the direct administration of the Sultan; the other districts of the principality were ruled by Dutch officials in his name, while at the court itself the hierarchy was reorganized and placed under Dutch supervision.[59] The Sunan at Solo was told to make similar concessions on the grounds of contributing to the costs of his defence during the war. This was too much for Pakubuwana VI (Bangun Tapa) who had remained loyal to the Dutch throughout the whole period. After protesting to Batavia, the Sunan fled to the royal sanctuary at Imogiri in order to consult his forefathers on the crisis which faced his realm. He was pursued by Dutch troops, taken prisoner, accused of plotting rebellion and sent to exile in Ambon where he died in 1849. At Surakarta, his place was taken by a cousin, the Pangeran Purbaya, who reigned as Pakubuwana VII. The new ruler of course proved amenable to the treaty which the Dutch required him to sign, granting the cession of the territories Batavia wanted together with surrendering the administration of Manchonegoro to them in return for compensation amounting to 264,000 guilders. But unlike the Sultan, the Sunan was granted a say in the appointment of officials there.

After 1830 the two successor states remained autonomous in name only. They became museums of Javanese tradition, while the future came to rest in other hands.

4. THE RULERS OF MATARAM

1.	Senopati	±1582–1601
2.	Mas Julang (panembahan Krapyak)	1601–13
3.	Chakrasuma Ngabdurrahman/Sultan Sunan Agong	1613–45
4.	Amangkurat I (Sunan Tegalwangi)	1645–77
5.	Amangkurat II	1677–1703
6.	Amangkurat III (Sunan Mas)	1703–5
7.	Pakubuwana I (Sunan Puger)	1705–19
8.	Amangkurat IV	1719–27
9.	Pakubuwana II	1727–49
10.	Pakubuwana III – last ruler of Mataram and first Sultan of Jogjakarta	(1749–55) (1755–88)

[1]Demak, with its rice port of Japara and its command of the salt-fields of Pati, held the trump cards in the contest between the rising port-states of the north at the time. The date and story of Majapahit's end is traditional. The Majapahit regalia went to Demak and subsequently via Pajang to Mataram. Remnants of the Majapahit royal family fled east to Balambangan, Pasaruan and Panarukan where they survived till 1639. They then crossed over to Bali.

[2]Demak rapidly declined after the assassination of its ruler in 1546 as a result of dynastic intrigue. Pengging and its successor state of Pajang were both situated in the valley of the Pepe river, near Surakarta, in Central Java.

[3]The port-states were riven by commercial rivalry and conflicting overseas interests; for example, Tuban dominated the Bandas and Banjarmassin while Surabaya controlled Sukadana. Grisek, in the pursuit of its own interests, even went so far as to sign a treaty with the infidel Portuguese in 1532.

[4]To starve the city into submission, the surroundings of Surabaya were laid waste entirely. 40,000 Madurese were made prisoners of war and deported inland, while thousands of refugees fled overseas to south Borneo, Macassar and elsewhere.

[5]Balambangan was conquered in 1639 but Bali successfully defied all attempts at invasion.

[6]The Sunan pacified some of his vassals by dynastic marriages, and kept all attendant upon him at his court. He preserved the ruling families of Surabaya and Tuban but wiped out the line of Pati (which had revolted in 1627) and all the Madurese princes except the Sampang dynasty.

[7]Of these, some 600 bore firearms, but were not particularly adept at handling them.

[8]The bulk of the Sunan's supplies for his armies had to be brought by sea, as land routes were too difficult. Dutch naval superiority which resulted in 200 Javanese boats bringing rice being destroyed reduced this army to starvation even before the siege had begun.

[9]Large numbers of the old Javanese nobility perished in various plots and conspiracies, of which the most celebrated was that of Kajuran. The hierarchy of officials that took their place consisted of the following designations—*kyai, temenggong, ngabehi, rangga* and *kentol*.

[10]Under Sultan Agong, who himself is credited with the authorship of a treatise on philosophical mysticism, the study of traditional Javanese beliefs, myths and folk-lore was revived to justify the Mataram dynasty. The possession of the Majapahit regalia was used to emphasize Mataram's links with the pre-Islamic past. Seers and fortune-tellers in the Hindu-Javanese tradition of days gone by gained great prominence at the *kraton*. The religious teachers of the orthodox persuasion who suffered so severely at the hands of Amangkurat I are known as 'wali'.

[11]The Company started growing its own rice near Batavia and brought its supplies from wherever it could apart from Mataram, going to Burma and Thailand and even as far afield as India and Japan. The Sunan's measures (which were regarded as practical and wise from his point of view by the Dutch authorities in Batavia itself) forced the Company to conduct its trade directly through Batavia, to Batavia's own profit.

[12]For example, Tuban, once Java's largest seaport, was still 'only a hamlet' in the 1660s, over forty years after its sack at the hands of Sultan Agong in 1619. Grisek, formerly the leading stapling centre for the spices of the Moluccas, had lost its trade and that of Japara itself was severely reduced.

[13]Perhaps too much significance should not be attached to this claim, as it was virtually obligatory for every Javanese pretender to establish his credentials by proving his links with the past. For a full discussion of this problem, see Schrieke, op. cit. Vol. II, Chapter I.

[14]'Perdikan' means a district exempted from certain taxes and services but carrying with it certain duties or responsibilities. The perdikan desa of Giri, just outside Grisek, was a district whose ruler had briefly achieved paramount power in Java immediately after the fall of the Majapahit dynasty, and who subsequently enjoyed immense prestige as leader of Islam in the archipelago. His fame and influence stretched to the Moluccas and was sufficiently great for Sultan Agong himself to seek the legitimization of his rule at his hands—although the Sunan correctly regarded the *penambahan* as one of his most serious political rivals.

[15]The Dutch governor-general Maetsuycker (1653-78) strongly favoured a policy of strict nonintervention in Javanese affairs, fearing the expenses and complications that must follow. Several of his younger lieutenants, including the very able Rijcklof van Goens and Cornelis Speelman believed that the Company should exploit the internal dissensions of the Javanese states to strengthen the Company's position.

[16]Trunojoyo himself occupied Kediri and Surabaya. Pangeran Puger, a brother of the Sunan, was at Bagèlen. Pangeran2 Mertasama and Singasari held Kedu; Pangeran Rama, Kajuran in Central Java; and Sunan Tawang-alun who was allied to the Macassarese controlled the east of the island.

[17]It was an old Javanese tradition that no kraton or dynasty could survive more than one hundred years. Mataram was approaching this in 1677.

18One factor was that Maetsuycker died in this year and was succeeded by the activist, van Goens (1678–81).

19When still crown prince, Sunan Mas had given his open support to the Chinese during an anti-Dutch uprising in Semarang.

20Pangeran Puger had already made one attempt for the throne at the time of Amangkurat I's death in 1677; proclaimed Sunan in Kartasura, he was expelled by Dutch forces and subsequently (in 1680) made his peace with Amangkurat II.

21The main reason for this cheap victory was the connivance of Jayadiningrat, the commander of the armies of Sunan Mas. Jayadiningrat was actually in league with Pangeran Puger.

22Namely Blitar, Purbaya, Diponegoro, Dipasanta and uncle Pangeran Aria Mataram. Pangeran Aria Mataram surrendered to the V.O.C. and was exiled to Japara; the others gave up after waging sporadic guerrilla warfare in 1723, and were also exiled. The Dutch chose Sunan Prabu because he had never recognized Sunan Mas.

23In his attempts to raise money, the Sunan encouraged Chinese entrepreneurs to take over monopoly farms and land leases in Central Java. Their exactions and the economic demands of the Dutch under their treaty rights added to the burdens of the peasantry.

24The Dutch had offered to recognize his independence of Mataram as an inducement.

25Chakraningrat was occupying and intended to retain Blora, Jipang and Lamongan as well as obtaining the revenues of Grisek, Tuban and Sedayu. He also wanted Surabaya and the title of *penambahan*.

26The Mangkubumi was involved at the time in a dispute over the title to the district of Sukowati, with Pari Pringgalaya who had great influence at the court and had Dutch favour. Van Imhoff (governor-general 1743–50) publicly rebuked the Mangkubumi without even hearing his case.

27The idea of partition was not a Dutch innovation. Javanese history is full of precedents, including the famous division of the ancient kingdom of Kediri between his two sons by Erlangga (c. 1050) and the division of Majapahit in a similar manner by Hayam Wuruk on his death in 1389. The possibility of partitioning Mataram between the leading contestants for the throne had been discussed freely since the days of Trunojoyo's rebellion.

28Especially in the person of Sultan Amangkubuwana IX who came to the throne in 1940. Closely identified with the nationalist movement from his student days, the Sultan emerged as one of the leaders of the 1945 revolution; subsequently he served in several Cabinets during the Sukarno era and was put in charge of Economic and Financial Affairs in President Suharto's Ampera Cabinet in 1966.

29The Dutch campaign against Pangeran Singasari and the descendants of Surapati lasted from 1767 till 1772. The storming of the pirate stronghold on Nusa Bareng off the south-east coast finally brought the region under Batavia's control. The Dutch campaign was assisted by popular resentment against the Balinese domination.

30The affairs of the Company had been in a parlous state for over a generation and in 1791 with a debt of 96 million guilders, it was no longer possible to put off the question of reform. While a Dutch commission was studying the matter, the French invasion and occupation clinched it. The Board of Directors (the seventeen gentlemen) was replaced by a Committee for the Affairs of the East Indian Trade and Settlements, and when on 31 December 1799 the Company's charter expired, the government assumed complete control over its possessions and liabilities. During the eight years between 1791 and 1799, the Company's debt had mounted by a further 38 million guilders.

31Daendels, a provincial Dutch lawyer of radical persuasion, left Holland and joined the ranks of the French revolutionary armies in 1793. He so distinguished himself that he was created a Marshal (the highest rank available) by Napoleon. A great admirer of the latter, Daendels seemed to be an ideal appointment from the point of view of the francophile revolutionary authorities in Holland for the governorship of the valuable Dutch possessions in South-East Asia. On his return to Europe in 1811, the Marshall served in Napoleon's Moscow campaign (1812). He died in 1818 whilst serving as governor of the Dutch Gold Coast (present-day Ghana).

32During the period of the Revolutionary and Napoleonic Wars (1792–1815) in Europe, the traditional enmity between France and Britain was renewed. When Holland was overrun by the French in 1793, the Dutch ruler (the Stadhouder) fled to England, where from his place of residence at Kew Palace near London he issued orders (the Kew Letters) to all Dutch colonial governors, instructing them to permit a British occupation of their territories for the duration of the war, on the understanding that they would be restored to Holland afterwards. Not all the Dutch governors obeyed these instructions. In the case of Java, the British feared lest the

French should get a foothold there and gain control over the Dutch fleet in South-East Asian waters into the bargain. Napoleon's unilateral annexation of Holland itself in 1810 precipitated matters, and the British invaded Java to forestall the French. British forces numbered some 12,000 effectives; with a virtually empty treasury at Batavia, the Javanese princes completely alienated by Daendels (see below) and a French force rendered useless by its incompetent commander, Jannsen offered the best resistance he could against hopeless odds.

[33]Appointed Lt.-governor of Java and its dependencies (Madura, Macassar, Palembang and Banjarmassin) by the British governor-general in India, Lord Minto, in 1811; he was recalled in 1816 and succeeded by John Fendall. For the part played by Raffles in the foundation of a British settlement on Singapore Island a few years later and for biographical details, refer p. 120 and p. 143, note 16.

[34]Under the terms of an Anglo-Dutch Convention signed in London in 1814 as the Napoleonic era drew to a close. All Dutch possessions occupied by the British in South-East Asia were handed back, although elsewhere the British retained Ceylon and the Cape of Good Hope.

[35]The Dutch Resident was restyled 'Minister' and granted royal status; all ceremonial implying subservience to the Javanese rulers was discontinued.

[36]The intrigue in question centred on the attempts of the Ratu Kenchana Wulan, one of Sepuh's queens, to ensure the succession of one of her own sons to the throne. To achieve this, she stirred up trouble between Sepuh and the Crown Prince, the Pangeran Adipati Anom. Once installed as regent, the Pangeran Adipati Anom was made to pay Sp. $196,000 for the costs of the Dutch military operations in his favour, forego Dutch tribute for the coastal provinces, and exchange the districts of Kedu, Grobogan, Wirosari, Selo, Jipang and Jepun (Mojokerto) for Boyolali and Galoh in the Preanger on strategic grounds.

[37]Raffles also obtained direct jurisdiction over the Sultan's non-Javanese subjects and the right to supervise his correspondence. In addition, the Dutch system of contingencies and forced deliveries was discontinued, and the Sultan gave up his tolls, birds' nest monopolies and forest dues in exchange for compensation of Sp.$80,000. The British retained Pachitan for use as a port and Grobogan was given to the Pangeran Notokusumo who had been their staunch ally.

[38]Amangkubuwana III was made to surrender most of his dues in return for an annual pension. His chief minister was to be a nominee of Raffles. The Grobogan lands of the Pangeran Notokusumo were enlarged and he received the title of Pangeran Paku Alam. The British also took over the opium monopoly.

[39]Similarly to the Sultan, the Sunan had to forego Dutch tribute from the coastal regencies; north Kedu, parts of Blora and districts in Semarang, Salatiga, Demak and Japara were surrendered—on strategic grounds—in exchange for Malang and Ngantung.

[40]The other conditions were virtually the same as those imposed on the Sultan. The Sunan received Sp.$120,000 for surrendering his rights over specified tolls, dues and monopolies.

[41]The Pangeran Mangkubumi of Solo, a brother of the Sunan, had intrigued with the Indian sepoys to drive out the British, but the plot was discovered, the sepoys withdrawn and the Mangkubumi exiled to Ceylon.

[42]As a youth and later on in his life, Dipo Negoro was to spend much of his time in solitary meditation, particularly in the desolate caves of Langse on the Javanese south coast, where he had visions which brought him into contact with the legendary heroes of Java's past. During his period of wandering and self-communion Dipo Negoro was popularly known as Sheikh Ngadburahim or Sheikh Ngabdul-hamid.

[43]This whole episode of Menul's installation as sultan is obscure. The fact that the Dutch appointed Dipo Negoro as one of the guardians suggests that they were genuinely ignorant of Raffles' promise to him; on the other hand it could also have been a clever move both to conciliate him and at the same time restrict his power.

[44]A leading part in the introduction of Western modes into the Jogjakarta court was played by the Dutch Resident, Nahuys. His successors, de Salis and Smissaert, both offended Dipo Negoro with their arrogance and lack of courtesy towards him.

[45]De Salis and Smissaert clearly regarded both Dipo Negoro and the Mangkubumi as irreconcilable and together with the patih (prime minister) of Jogjakarta abandoned all pretence of consulting the two regents. Dipo Negoro was particularly incensed by their action in appointing a non-royal nominee to the post of penghulu of Danurejo.

[46]Eruchakra was the traditional title of the Javanese Messiah who was going to restore peace to earth (that is Java) and usher in a reign of order and contentment and plenty. Dipo Negoro was not the first to assume this title; it had been used by royal pretenders during Trunojoyo's rebellion and during the period of the first Javanese War (1705-08). For a full discussion of the concept of Eruchakra in Javanese history, see Schrieke, op. cit. Pt. II, 'Ruler and Realm in Early Java,' esp. pp. 81-83.

[47]The Sunan at this time was Pakubuwana VI (Bangun Tapa) who came to the throne in 1823. The old Sunan, Pakubuwana IV, had died in 1820. In the event, Pakubuwana VI led his forces personally against the rebels. The Mangku Negoro was another prominent figure at the court of Solo who raised a legion to fight by the side of the Dutch. Raffles' old friend, the Pangeran Paku Alam, also remained loyal to Batavia.

[48]The powder for the firearms of the regular units was produced in secret jungle factories. The only major occasion when Dipo Negoro departed from his policy of avoiding pitched engagements was at Plered in June 1826. It proved a costly failure. Amongst the headquarters made by the prince were Selarong (the first), Truchuk, Jumeneng, Dekso, Sejati, Breja, Bandut, Kesuran and Pengaseh.

[49]Namely van Geen, Cochius and de Kock himself. The new governor-general, du Bus de Gisignies, initially opposed the fort strategy on grounds of cost, although perhaps a clash of personalities was also involved.

[50]In fact, Kyai Maja's influence, which inclined to the visionary, had waned considerably since the early months of the war in measure as that of Sentot, the more practically-minded, increased. He was exiled to Menado.

[51]Not long after his surrender, Sentot was giving his services to the Dutch in their campaign against the Menangkabau Padri in Sumatra; see p. 154.

[52]Another controversial episode; de Kock's allegations may not have been groundless; on the other hand, as Sanusi Pane (*Sedjarah Indonesia*, Vol. II, pp. 71–73) suggests, de Kock, who was on the point of being recalled to Holland, had every reason to seize the prince and so end the war both to justify his policies and to satisfy his pride. In exile, Dipo Negoro wrote his version of events in the *Babad Dipo Negoro*.

[53]By Dutch here is meant all those serving in the Dutch regular forces whether they were Ambonese or Bugis levies or European; in fact just over half (8,000) the number who died were Europeans.

[54]Godert A.G.Ph., Baron van der Capellen, had originally come out to Java as one of the three Commissioners-General who took over the island from the British in 1816. When the other two commissioners returned home in 1818, van der Capellen stayed behind as the first governor-general of the restored regime. He was replaced by du Bus de Gisignies in 1826.

[55]Especially in the Preanger, where the competition offered by private planters to the government's own coffee-plantations was assuming considerable proportions; at the same time the cultivator in this region was fast falling into the hands of Western and Chinese speculators who advanced him cash so as to obtain his crops at a cheaper rate as the end-result.

[56]H.J. de Graaf, *Geschiedenis van Indonesië*, 's-Gravenhage, 1949.

[57]Tolls were levied on produce and all manner of transportable goods, even children in arms. Before the outbreak of the war, there were 300 such toll-farms in the principality; afterwards the Dutch abolished 25 out of 35 in Kediri alone.

[58]The case of the lands of Jaba-Rangkah and Karang-Kabar aroused particular resentment. These lands were initially acquired on lease for 30 years from the original European lessees in 1825; then the following year the Dutch government forced their outright cession. The general fear of the Javanese aristocracy in the principalities that the Dutch were bent on total annexation was further coloured by the widely-reported remarks of van der Capellan to the patih of Surakarta during his 1822 tour to the effect that he would like to see Jogjakarta and Surakarta like Bantam and Cheribon—under complete Dutch control.

[59]The administration of the territories of Jogjakarta under Dutch supervision involved the police, justice and the collection of revenue; at the same time, the boundary between the two principalities was also adjusted.

THE DUTCH IMPACT PRIOR TO THE NINETEENTH CENTURY

The reasons for Dutch success

By the middle of the eighteenth century, the Dutch were unquestionably the paramount rulers of Java. Two factors most obviously account for the Dutch success in attaining this position despite their limited numbers and resources. The first has already been mentioned[a] and is connected with the supremacy of the Dutch at sea.[1]

[a]Refer p. 48.

As we have seen, Malaysian empires were essentially sea powers, deriving their strength from their control over the trade routes. The successful establishment of Dutch power on Java, followed by the progressive strangulation of Malaysian centres of trade one by one led in turn to the region's one land power, Mataram, falling a pawn to the Company. The interaction of interests and events converted the Dutch from a purely maritime power themselves into a territorial state, and while during the eighteenth century circumstances elsewhere led to decline of their naval strength,[2] their influence as the paramount land power in Java actually increased. In the middle of the seventeenth century the profits of the Company were basically derived from the trade in spices; one hundred years later it was centred on coffee and sugar plantations—the produce of its new appanages in Java.

The other factor lies in the instability of the Malaysian states themselves. The circumstances of their environment and historical development created a pattern of events which made them very vulnerable to a strong outside power like the Dutch Company. The average Malaysian sea power thrived on a fortuitous set of circumstances beyond its control, quick profits and a succession of very able leaders. When one of these failed, its downfall was assured. The agrarian states of central and east Java were more stable, although no one expected a dynasty to last longer than a hundred years.[a] But they too were prey to the ambitions and whims of the sons of their own ruling families, and the court had always to contend with the pull towards regionalism and the perennial struggle with the commercially orientated districts of the northern coast. The rise of Dutch power in Java was not only brought about by the superiority of Dutch arms and men, however much this might be true of their activities along the trade routes. Batavia was drawn into the politics of Java, often against its better judgement, in order to protect its own interests. The exigencies of Javanese politics constantly provided openings and opportunities which the Dutch were able to turn to their own advantage. However, the government of the Company stood out in strong contrast to the Javanese administrations of the day, having a regularity of organization and policy which protected it against the caprices and weaknesses of individual governors-general. It was a contrast between the organization produced by the legalistic and bureaucratic trading systems of Europe, and the individualistic feudal pattern of society which existed in Island South-East Asia.

The limitations of Dutch power

However, even Dutch power had its limitations. Beyond the island of Java, the areas under direct Dutch control were limited to the Moluccas, Macassar and Menado in Celebes, Padang in West Sumatra and Malacca. Elsewhere their influence fluctuated according to local pressures and circumstances. Such was the case on the island of Borneo, in north Celebes, and in the greater part of Sumatra and the Peninsula. Throughout the other islands petty states flourished untouched by the Company.

In economic terms the Dutch were similarly circumscribed. Their trading organization was incomparably better than that of the Portuguese, and this enabled them

[a]Refer p. 90, note 17.

to maintain a firm hold over the Moluccas, consolidate their position in Java and keep their isolated possessions elsewhere. But outside Java and the Moluccas, the Dutch remained as competitors in the old-established system of trade. Chinese, Indians, Arabs and other traders from all over Asia, besides Malaysians themselves, traded virtually as freely with whom they pleased as they had always done. This was in spite of Dutch treaties and monopoly agreements imposed on unwilling rulers, their forts and their naval patrols. Furthermore, their European rivals were never entirely expelled from the archipelago. The Portuguese remained on Timor, the English established themselves at Benkulen and other points on the Sumatran west coast after their expulsion from Bantam in 1684, and privateers of all races[3] pierced the Dutch monopoly with increasing frequency and success as the eighteenth century wore on, and as the Dutch East India Company, overburdened and corrupt, sank in strength.

The nature of the Dutch impact

Although the Dutch presence did not alter the basic historical pattern of trade or forms of power in Island South-East Asia prior to 1800, it nevertheless brought about important modifications. To begin with, they stepped into the shoes of Sri Vijaya, Majapahit and Malacca and one of the most important consequences of their power was the prolonged fragmentation of the Malaysian states in the archipelago. Both the Malays and the Javanese lost their predominant positions as the carriers of the region's trade. In the case of the Malays, they were reduced to petty trade and to what Europeans described as 'piracy'; as for the Javanese, their influence overseas was suddenly cut off by the spread of Dutch monopoly and on Java itself they were reduced to the status of tenant-farmers of the Dutch. In specific areas like the south Celebes and the Moluccas, the ruthless application of the Dutch monopoly ruined the local inhabitants.

Yet, for all this, the important thing to remember about the world of Island South-East Asia as it stood at the end of the eighteenth century is the sharp contrast it offers to the conditions which developed in the 150 years that followed. Despite the presence of the Europeans, the age of Western colonial domination in its modern sense had not yet begun. A pre-industrial type of economy still prevailed, based on countless self-sufficient village communities scattered throughout the archipelago. The old-established trade which flourished was one in small quantities of rare and valuable commodities passing from market to market, not one of bulk imports for mass consumption linked to industrial centres of mass production. The old Dutch East India Company fitted into this pattern, and outside Java and the Moluccas was in fact engaged as an ordinary trader in the open market. Nowhere was there any evidence of an emergent Indonesia or an emergent Malaysia, for in fact the forces which were to lead to their creation were not yet operative. The forces that were to make possible the modern states of Malaysia and Indonesia today were those of the Industrial Revolution, for which the foundation of the small British settlement on the island of Penang, off the coast of Kedah, in 1786, served as an unsuspected harbinger.

5. THE MALAYSIAN WORLD IN TRANSITION (1500-1800): CHRONOLOGY OF MAIN EVENTS IN THE REGION AND IMPORTANT EVENTS RELEVANT TO THE REGION OUTSIDE

Year	The Moluccas	Bantam	Macassar	Mataram	General	Outside the region
1480–90	Conversion to Islam					
1497						Vasco da Gama at Calicut. Portuguese take Goa
1510						
1511					Portuguese take Malacca. Fall of Majapahit.	
1520+						
1521	Portuguese Foothold on Ternate				Magellan in the Philippines	
1524	Spanish alliance with Tidore					
1526						Rise of Moghul Empire
1527		Faletahan founds Bantam as Muslim outpost				
1530	Portuguese supreme in Ternate					
1537+					Rise of Acheh	
1546–8	St. Francis Xavier in the Moluccas					
1556						Fall of Vijayanagar
1563–70	Expansion of Ternate under S. Hairun				Spanish power established in Philippines	
1567		Bantam breaks away from Demak				
1570	Death of S. Hairun					
1574	Explusion of Portuguese from Ternate				Rise of Pajang	
1578	Portuguese build fort on Tidore					
1579	Drake at Ternate	Downfall of Pajajaran				
1580						Union of Portugal and Spain. Lisbon closed to Dutch
1582–1600				Foundation of Mataram. Mataram dominates Central and East Java		
1596		Van Houtman at Bantam				
1599	First Dutch traders in the Moluccas					
1600						Formation of English EIC.
1602		English factory at Bantam				Foundation of VOC
1603				Mataram conquers Japara		

Year	The Moluccas	Bantam	Macassar	Mataram	General	Outside the region
1603/6			Conversion to Islam			
1606	Spanish offensive in Moluccas. Ternate ruler captive in Manila					
1607	Dutch re-established on Ternate					
1608–24		Regency of Pn. Aria Ranamanggala				
1609	Death of Dutch Adm. Verhoeff on the Bandas					
1613			English factory opened. Start of hostilities with the Dutch	Jaratan falls to Mataram.		
1616–21	English attempt to gain sovereignty in the Moluccas					
1617				Pasaruan falls to Mataram:		
1619		Jakarta seized by the Dutch		Tuban falls to Mataram	Foundation of Batavia	
1620+			Expansion of Macassar			
1621	Coen's conquest of the Moluccas					
1624				Sultan Agong proclaims himself Sunan. Surabaya falls to Mataram		
1627		Bantam assault on Batavia				
1628–9				Mataram besieges Batavia		
1634			First Dutch blockade of Macassar			
1635–46	First general anti-Dutch revolt					
1636			Van Diemen's peace treaty with Macassar			
1639				The conquest of Balambangan		
1641					Dutch capture Malacca. Decline of Acheh	
1644						Manchu conquest of China
1646				Amang Kurat I signs peace treaty with Dutch		Treaty of Goa; Portuguese yields to VOC in Ceylon
1647	Ternate cedes West Ceram to Dutch					
1649	Start of the hongitochten.					
1650–6	Second general anti-Dutch revolt.					
1651		Accession of S. Abdul Fatah				
1652–4						First Anglo-Dutch War

Year	The Moluccas	Bantam	Macassar	Mataram	General	Outside the region
1653	Tidore cedes East Ceram to the Dutch					
1656						Dutch take Colombo
1656–9		Bantam wages war on Batavia				
1660			First Dutch expedition against Macassar			
1663					The Painan Contract	
1665–7						Second Anglo-Dutch War
1666	Spanish evacuate the Moluccas. Tidore accepts Dutch overlordship		Second Dutch expedition against Macassar			
1667			The Bongaya Treaty. Third Dutch expedition against Macassar. End of Sultanate			
1672–4						Third Anglo-Dutch War
1674–82				Trunojovo's rebellion		
1675	Rebellion of S. 'Amsterdam'					
1677				Cession of the Priangan, etc. to the Dutch		
1680		War with Batavia over Cheribon, etc.				
1682		Sultan Haji seizes power				
1683		Dutch intervention.				
1684		Bantam gives way to Dutch monopoly (treaty)				
1686				Assassination of Major Tak at Kartasura		
1705–8				First Javanese War Treaty: Mataram accepts Dutch trade monopoly, etc.		
1709				Assassination of Jangrana, regent of Surabaya at Kartasura		
1719–23				Second Javanese War Treaty; coffee-planting suppressed in Mataram.		
1733						
1740–1				The Chinese Revolt Treaty; Mataram accepts vassal status.		
1743						
1744–5				The Madurese War		
1746				Mataram surrenders revenues to the Company.		

Year	The Moluccas	Bantam	Macassar	Mataram	General	Outside the region
1749–57				Third Javanese War.		
1750–1		Gasti's revolt				
1753		Bantam made vassal of the Company				
1755				Treaty of Gianti; Mataram partitioned		
1757				Treaty of Salatiga		India; battle of Plassey.
1776						American War of Independence
1784						Treaty of Paris; Island South-East Asia opened to free trade
1789						Outbreak of French Revolution; Rev. and Napoleonic Wars
1793–1815						
1799						Abolition of VOC
1811–16	British occupation. of Java and all Dutch dependencies in region					
1815						Congress of Vienna
1824						Anglo-Dutch Treaty
1825–30				The Java War		
1832		Abolition of Sultanate				

[1]"The heart of the whole matter lies in its military aspect—the progress of Dutch power must be attributed not to more diplomatic insight, to greater courage and greater impetuosity, to greater economic reserves, but to the sturdier rigging and the greater speed of the ships, the more powerful cannon-royal, the greater mobility of armed troops.' van Leur, op. cit. p. 189.
[2]By the end of the seventeenth century the Dutch Republic was overshadowed by the greater resources of both Britain and France, with both of whom she had fought a series of wasteful and unprofitable wars. As a trading power, the eighteenth century was a period of decline for Holland, with the Company sinking into bankruptcy for want of efficiency in Europe and with the British obtaining a decisive advantage in the East by virtue of their seapower and their position in India. The final disaster for the Dutch was their participation in the American War of Independence against the British. By the Treaty of Paris of 1784, by which it was concluded they were forced to declare their South-East Asian preserves open to free trade.
[3]Especially Asian and European traders based on the Malabar and Coromandel coasts of India. Known as 'country traders' and trading under the Chinese of the English East India Company, one of the most celebrated of their number was Francis Light, the founder of the British settlement on Penang.

The Mosque at Fort de Kock, Bukit Tinggi, Menangkabau, Sumatra

3. The Dividing of the Malaysian World: the Fate of the Big Powers

DURING the course of the nineteenth century, the political pattern of the archipelago was completely revolutionized. The states of the region fell completely under the control (directly or indirectly) of either Holland or Britain, and from this division have evolved the sovereign powers of Indonesia, Malaysia and Singapore today. The manner in which this came about was a haphazard process, although not—as far as the Dutch and the British themselves were concerned—entirely unanticipated. The shape of things to come was foreshadowed by the Anglo-Dutch Treaty of 1824, which was signed in London, and which split the archipelago, politically speaking, into two spheres of influence .The treaty was also designed, *inter alia*, to prevent the intrusion of any third power. This agreement was confirmed by a second Anglo-Dutch Treaty nearly fifty years later. By 1909, all the formerly independent states in the Malaysian world had been subjected to either Dutch or British colonial power. In 1800, however, the picture was still very different. European power was very limited—the Portuguese on Timor and the British with their failing pepper port of Benkulen on the Sumatran west coast and their new settlement of Penang off the shores of Kedah. The Dutch were the only Western power with substantial holdings in the region and, as we have seen, these were basically confined to the island of Java with a few isolated outposts in the outer islands.

On the other hand, there still survived five major Malaysian states or polities which, though no doubt shadows of their former selves and totally incapable of measuring up to the pressures of a modern western power, were nevertheless factors to be taken into account. Probably the most effective of these was Acheh, with its strong Islamic traditions and advantageous geographical position; at the other end of the archipelago was the sultanate of Sulu—in Western eyes the stronghold of piracy but for all that a state which had successfully resisted Western (Spanish) encroachments for over three centuries. In between were the ancient empires of Brunai and Johore-Riau, and in central Sumatra and in the Malay Peninsula the incoherent but fiercely independent polity of the Menangkabau. All these units were visibly on the verge of disintegration, but still exercised nominal suzerainty over wide areas and some effective political influence within that. Outside of these remained a whole host of petty principalities, chieftainships and tribal societies, isolated from the main channels of influence and change, pursuing their own existences very little disturbed. The Johore-Riau empire was the first to succumb to Western pressure and its enforced partition in 1824 symbolized the processes which followed. Then came the turn of the Menangkabau whose last brave upsurge in defence of their liberty (at least in Sumatra) had been painfully crushed by 1840. The slow breaking-up of Brunai began at about this time and was completed by the end of the century. The downfall of the two sultanates of Acheh and Sulu took place almost simultaneously towards the end of the century. On the one

hand the Spaniards launched their final campaigns of conquest in the Sulu archipelago soon after the 1850s and the process was completed by the United States of
America within the first decade of the present century, while on the other the
Dutch started their war to subjugate Acheh in 1871 and had finally succeeded by
1908. As for the rest of the archipelago, it was absorbed piecemeal, as often as not
only after bitter struggle.

Once again, the process of disintegration and division may be approached in two
different ways. The story can be told in terms of the expansion of Western colonialism into the region, with the central theme provided by the activities of the Western powers themselves. Or it can be related in terms of the individual political units
involved. The latter approach has been preferred because that is how it actually
happened. Although time and again undercurrents of unity influencing the Malaysian states come to the surface, the polities concerned were essentially isolated from
one another and faced their fates alone. Acheh, at one extremity of the Malaysian
world, and Sulu at the other, for instance, had scarcely any mutual interest save a
common faith and a common enemy, and there was no significant political interaction between them. Brunai, Sulu's closest neighbour to the south, suffered partition at the hands of foreign adventurers without any noteworthy gesture coming
from Jolo. On a different scale, the same is true of the Malay states of the Peninsula.
It is no use treating Malaya as a political unit in the nineteenth century, because as
Metternich would have said, it was merely a geographic expression. While some of
the states in the Peninsula retained their ancient links with Johore, the Menangkabau remained closely bound to their Sumatran homeland and the northern states
fell clearly within the orbit of Thailand. So no attempt has been made to deal with
the Malay Peninsula as a political whole any more than this has been done in the
cases of Sumatra, Borneo or Celebes.

The story of the dividing of the Malaysian world has been broken up into two
sections, the first dealing with the collapse of the 'big' powers before the West
(Acheh, Brunai, Johore, Menangkabau and Sulu) and the second dealing with the
smaller units, generally on a more regional basis. However, the start is made with
one small state —that of Kedah—because the relations of that northern Malay sultanate with the British culminating in the loss of Penang, marked the beginning of
the whole process of partitioning between the British and the Dutch.

KEDAH AND PERLIS

THE starting point for the division of the Malaysian world came in 1786 when the
British occupied the Kedah-owned island of Penang.

Kedah is probably the most ancient state existing in the Malay Peninsula today,
and has a line of rulers who trace their ancestry back to the Hindu era.[1] Occupying
a rich rice-growing plain, possessing good harbours at Kuala Bahang (Kuala Kedah)
and at Kuala Merbok under the shadow of Gunong Jerai (Kedah Peak), and situated
on the direct course of the north-west monsoons from Coromandel—at one of the
main routes across the Peninsula—the country was destined to become a prosperous
centre for settlement and trade. But throughout its history, the rulers of Kedah have
found themselves faced with the problem of having to deal with more powerful
neighbours. In the seventh and eighth centuries A.D., Kedah was a vassal of Sri Vijaya.

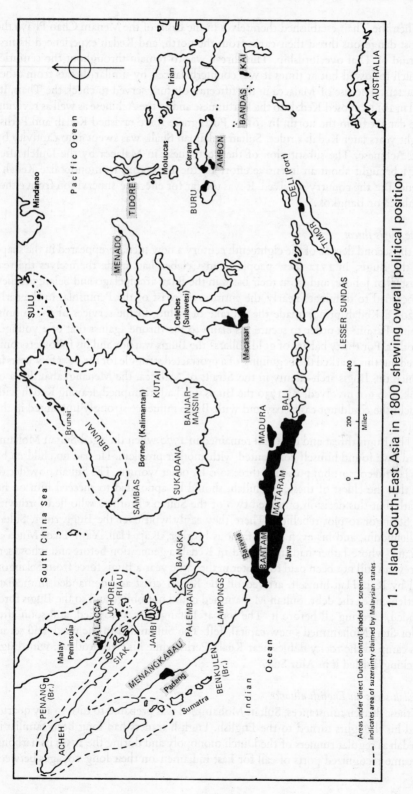

11. Island South-East Asia in 1800, shewing overall political position

Areas under direct Dutch control shaded or screened

- - - indicates area of suzerainty claimed by Malaysian states

When the Thais established themselves in the basin of the Menam Chao Phaya the most dangerous threat then came from the north, and Kedah experienced its first period of Thai overlordship. This threat was to remain throughout the centuries which followed but at times it was counterbalanced by similar threats from other quarters. The rise of Malacca in the fifteenth century served to check the Thais. Its fall in 1511 exposed Kedah to the Portuguese and to the Achinese as well as reviving the danger from the north. In 1611 a Portuguese force ravished Kedah and Perlis; eight years later Kedah's ruler, Sultan Sulaiman Shah, was swept into captivity by the Achinese. The substitution of the Portuguese in Malacca by the Dutch after 1641 brought about an intensive effort by the Europeans to monopolize Kedah's trade. But the country survived. It was too far for effective supervision from either Malacca or Bangkok.

The Bugis threat

In the second decade of the eighteenth century a new menace appeared in the shape of the Bugis. In 1722 these people from Celebes had made themselves the real masters of Johore, and from their bases in the Riau archipelago and Selangor, they proceeded to dominate nearly the entire west coast of the Peninsula. In the early 1720s, a Kedah prince made the mistake of calling in the services of the famous Daing Parani[2] in order to secure his claim to the throne against that of a younger brother. For thirty bahara of gold dollars[3] the Bugis warrior and his followers complied but this marked the beginning of a protracted struggle for the next few years in which the Bugis arch-enemy in the Straits of Malacca, the Menangkabau Raja of Siak, also got involved. By 1730 the Bugis side had triumphed, leaving Kedah with a debt she could not easily pay and with Bugis influence strongly implanted in the state.

The Bugis threat and debt still remained in 1770 when the aged Sultan Mohammed Jiwa found himself confronted with another problem. He had no children by his lawful consort but possessed three sons by other women. The Sultan now decided that the eldest of these, Abdullah, should be appointed to succeed him on his death, but this decision outraged two of the Sultan's brothers who fled forthwith to Selangor to plot rebellion. There they easily won over the Bugis ruler, Sultan Sallehuddin, and his even more famous brother, Raja Haji, Yam Tuan Muda at Riau,[4] whose father had intervened in Kedah a generation before and whose services had still not been paid for. Later in the same year a Bugis force from Selangor, led by Raja Haji himself, arrived off the Kedah coast and demanded immediate settlement of the debt. Sultan Mohammed could not oblige and so the Bugis force landed, carrying all before it. The fort at Batangan was stormed, and soon after Alor Star, Mohammed's new capital, fell. The Sultan fled to the north and set up his camp in the rocky defiles near Kuala Perlis while his two brothers, with Bugis backing, lorded it in Alor Star.

Kedah seeks an English alliance

In these dire circumstances, Sultan Mohammed was prepared to turn to any quarter and his thoughts turned to the English. English traders had long been familiar in Kedah as regular runners of the Dutch monopoly and during the 1750s its harbours became recognized ports of call for East Indiamen on their long voyages between

Bengal and Canton in China. Foreseeing the Bugis attack in early 1770, Sultan Mohammed had already taken the precaution of appealing to the officials of the English East India Company in Madras for military aid but had elicited nothing more than assurances of British friendship. Now, a year later, in his present plight he sent an emissary to Acheh where the presence of some English private traders had been reported. The result of this mission to Acheh was that Francis Light,[5] one of the traders in question, came to Perlis later in the year to discuss the Sultan's offer of trading facilities on the coast. The ruler's terms were as generous as his situation was precarious. Initially he had offered merely a trading post; now he was prepared to surrender Kuala Kedah to the English and meet half the expenses of their military assistance to him, as well as granting them a half share in its trade. Three months later he added the entire Kedah coastline from the Kuala to Penang to the bargain. Light's own firm showed little interest in these offers, but the East India Company's officials at Madras were sufficiently impressed by this and Light's own somewhat exaggerated account of the trading prospects that could be expected[6] to send an official mission. The mission was led by Edward Monkton, who arrived at Perlis in 1772 and was empowered to negotiate for the cession of Kuala Kedah and its port dues in exchange for *protection* against the Selangor Bugis. But Sultan Mohammed was not interested in defensive alliances. He wanted a sepoy force that could drive the Bugis and his brothers out of Alor Star and restore his kingdom, his treasure and his guns so, dismissing Monkton as 'that stuttering boy' and observing

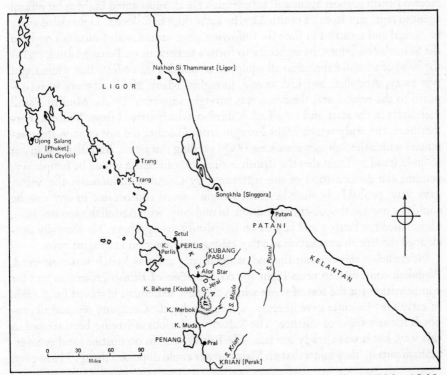

12. Kedah and Southern Thailand, illustrating the period 1700–1840

that the King of Siam had forbidden him to allow Europeans to settle in the country, negotiations were broken off.

Kedah had no more official dealings with the English for the next fourteen years, during which time several important developments in the region took place. In or around 1778 Sultan Mohammed Jiwa died and was succeeded by his eldest son, Abdullah. During the next few years the Bugis menace receded as a consequence of the severe trouncing they received at the hands of the Dutch admiral, van Braam, in 1784.[7] However, the diminishing threat from the south was replaced by a revived threat from the north as Thai power recouped against that of Burma.[a] In the meantime further British attempts to find a suitable site for a new base in Malaysian waters proved fruitless.[8]

The cession of Penang

This last development led to the re-appearance of Francis Light on the scene. Since 1772 he had been living and trading at Ujong Salang[9] from where he paid periodical visits to Kedah in pursuit of his own business activities, and became friends with the new ruler, Sultan Abdullah. In 1785 Light approached the Sultan with a new offer, this time in exchange for the island of Penang.

Sultan Abdullah, whose chief preoccupation was now centred on the imminent renewal of the struggle between the Thais and the Burmese which threatened to engulf his state, was prepared to strike a bargain. His terms, which Light conveyed by letter to the East India Company's officials in Calcutta, were that Kedah should receive British support against all his enemies. He also appointed Light as his official agent to represent Kedah's position to the authorities in Calcutta. Light sailed away to Bengal and returned in June the following year, armed with Calcutta's reply to the Sultan's conditions, its authority to form a settlement on Penang island, and at the head of a small expedition all equipped to put this into effect. But while Light was away, Abdullah had had second thoughts. Many of his advisers were opposed to the cession and their case was strongly supported by the Muslim Tamil merchants in the state and by a Dutch mission which arrived from Malacca. Furthermore, the reply which Light brought from Calcutta did not contain the guarantees which the Sultan was seeking.[10] On pressing this point, Abdullah was given to understand by Light that the British occupation of Penang would be temporary, pending the confirmation of the agreement by Calcutta. Reluctantly the Sultan gave way, probably because he trusted Light's word and because in any case he could not prevent the present expedition. In mid-July, with Abdullah's acquiescence, Light sailed for Penang and landed on the island two days later. He formally proclaimed the British annexation at a flag-raising ceremony on 11 August 1786.

Nevertheless this was not the end of the matter as far as Kedah was concerned. Abdullah continued to press Light for confirmation of British protection and for compensation for the loss of trade which the new settlement involved for Kedah. In early 1787 Calcutta gave its reply, which was that the Company rejected all proposals for any form of alliance. The Sultan was furious at having been treated in this way, but it was already too late. The British were in occupation, and as Swettenham puts it, 'they knew that no Malay power could dispossess them'.[11] However,

[a]See p. 499.

the enraged ruler made the attempt. According to Light, he sent letters to the French in Pondicherry and to the Dutch in Malacca but neither power was in a position to help.[12] Abdullah next turned to the Malay world and invited the assistance of a Lanun fleet from Sulu, reinforced with vessels from Riau, Selangor and Siak,[a] but although this force appeared in Kedah waters towards the end of 1790 it failed to carry out any attack on Penang because of dissensions amongst its commanders. Early next year the Sultan assembled an army of some 8,000 to 10,000 men at Prai, with the Lanun fleet standing by, but he was forestalled by Light who attacked first and destroyed a large number of his boats. After this defeat there was little to do but to bow to the inevitable and a couple of months later, Abdullah signed a treaty granting the formal cession of the island to Britain. By its terms, Penang became a British possession against an annual pension of $6,000 and *without* any promise of protection. In 1800 Sultan Dza'yuddin[13] signed a further treaty ceding the territory between the Muda and Krian rivers on the mainland opposite the island, which the British called Province Wellesley.[14] The ruler's annual pension was raised to $10,000, and the British undertook to protect the coast and not to harbour rebels. Beyond that they did not go.

Kedah after 1786

The cession of Penang to Britain sealed the fate of Kedah. Now without any bargaining factor and no one to turn to, she had to face the Thais of Bangkok alone. By 1800 Thailand had completely recovered from the Burmese invasions.[b] In 1803 the Thais 'suggested' that Sultan Dza'yuddin abdicate to make way for his nephew, Ahmad Tajuddin, whom they believed to be more tractable.[15] But this did not turn out to be the case. In 1810, Sultan Tajuddin took the opportunity presented by the visit to Penang of Lord Minto, the British governor-general in India, to send a long and reasoned appeal for a British alliance, but the only reply forthcoming was the instruction to the Company's officials in Penang *not* to protect Kedah from Thailand. In 1816 the Sultan was ordered to invade Perak and oblige its ruler to send the *bunga mas* to Bangkok.[16] This he carried out, but Sultan Tajuddin's obedience did not lead the Thais to overlook the fact that he himself had been remiss in sending tribute. This, together with the fact that the British had made it clear that they were not prepared to protect Kedah and the circumstance that the Sultan's own brother and other enemies in Kedah itself spread stories of his intriguing with Burma, resulted in Sultan Tajuddin being summoned to give an account of himself at Bangkok. The Sultan, who had few illusions as to what his fate would be if he went—and perhaps with a lingering belief that in the end the British would intervene on his behalf—ignored the demand. In mid-November 1821 a Thai war fleet under the command of the Chao Phaya Si Thammasokarat[17] approached Kuala Kedah, launched a surprise attack and wiped out the Malay garrison. Within a week Kedah was in Thai hands and its ruler a refugee in Penang.

Kedah revolts

Kedah never recovered its full independence. For over twenty years Sultan Tajud-

[a]See pp. 118 and 212.
[b]See p. 499.

din remained an exile on British territory before the Thais finally allowed him to return home as their vassal. In the meantime, the British refused to do more than to plead at Bangkok for his restoration, but finally in 1826 they recognized the Thai conquest and agreed to prevent the Sultan from using British territory as a base from which to attempt a comeback.[a]

Sultan Ahmad Tajuddin made three major attempts to drive out the Thais from his homeland during these years. The first came in early 1831 when 3,000 Malays crossed the border from Province Wellesley while a Malay fleet, gathered from Perak and the Sumatran east coast, attacked Kuala Kedah. The invasion was initially successful but ended in disaster when the Thai counter-attack came. By October of the same year it was all over, at a cost of 1,500 dead and 16,000 refugees in Province Wellesley. The collapse of this revolt was considerably hastened by the blockade of the Kedah coast which the British imposed in order to cut off supplies from Penang—action taken on the grounds of honouring the 1826 treaty with Thailand.[18] British action was entirely responsible for the failure of the second attempt in 1836 when the Sultan, on the pretext of going from Penang to Deli in east Sumatra, went to Bruas instead, and there started to assemble a war-fleet. Hearing of this and urged to action by the Thais, two British warships were sent to prevent further developments. A skirmish took place in which the Malay fleet was dispersed or destroyed, and the Sultan was taken to Malacca, his pension being reduced from $10,000 to $6,000 for his pains. The final attempt came in March 1838 when a Malay fleet under Wan Mat Ali defeated a Thai fleet off Kuala Merbok. This was followed by the landing of a force led by Tengku Mohammed Said, one of Sultan Tajuddin's nephews, which succeeded in stimulating a general uprising. As in 1831, at first all went well and a Malay army, 10,000 strong, marched through Perlis and Trang, reached the Patani river and was besieging Singgora (Songkla) at the end of three months. But when the Thais had had time to recover from their surprise and to re-gather their forces, the inevitable counter-blow came, Singgora was relieved and the Malays pressed back into Kedah. By early 1839 the Thais were once more in complete control of the state. As in 1831, the British blockade of the Kedah coast—imposed in response to 'treaty obligations'—was an important contributory factor to the failure of the uprising.

The restoration of indirect rule

Although it was a failure, the revolt of 1839 and the coincidental demise of the Chao Phaya Si Thammasokarat[19] during the course of the same year produced a change in the Thai attitude and helped to bring about the restoration of Sultan Ahmad Tajuddin. Bangkok was wearying of the constant troubles in the south which only resulted in a depopulated and impoverished province and decided that indirect rule through a Malay prince would probably be more conducive to peace and stability than direct rule through a Thai governor. However, to restore the Sultan himself seemed too bold a step at the time, so in 1840, a distant relative of his, Tengku Anom, was appointed governor (*chao phaya*) of Kedah, with Tengku Hassan to assist him. At the same time, Thai officials were withdrawn. A couple of years later, Sultan Tajuddin, who had also come to realize that the only sure way of re-

[a]See p. 505.

covering his throne was through negotiation, with British prompting appealed to Bangkok for pardon and his restoration. Bangkok relented and permitted the Sultan's return to the state as its ruler and their vassal. But his dominions were reduced by the creation of Setul, Kubang Pasu and Perlis as separate vassal principalities.[20]

Sultan Tajuddin had one more fling. The following year he seized the Krian district of north Perak, claiming it as part of Kedah,[a] but his successor was forced to hand it back again under heavy British pressure five years later.[21] From this time onwards until 1909, Kedah remained a vassal state of Thailand (together with Perlis) although in reality the state fell increasingly under the influence of the British in Penang. This was a natural result of the close trading links between the two territories while politically speaking the fact that the sultan was the recipient of a large annuity from the British (for Penang) both gave him more security and made him more amenable to British pressure. On occasion the British applied this pressure by stopping the annuity. They did so to settle the Krian affair in the 1840s, and again in the 1860s in order to secure a settlement of outstanding questions regarding the boundary with Penang territory (Province Wellesley) and the issue of local tariffs.[22] However, the treaty of 1869 which was the final outcome of the matter was negotiated between the British and the Thais and signed with Kedah's Sultan present as a helpless onlooker.

Kedah and the 1905 Agreement with Thailand

Nevertheless Kedah's rulers continued to enjoy virtually complete internal autonomy, for Bangkok made no further attempts to interfere with the Malay administration of the state. Kedah, like Trengganu, sent the bunga mas to Bangkok and, like Trengganu too, continued to regard this as a gesture of respect and friendship by a small state to its more powerful neighbour but not as a sign of vassaldom. However, towards the end of the century, new circumstances arose which indicated that the days of this twilight independence were numbered. Internal politics brought the Thais directly onto the scene once more while the development of British interests in the Peninsula attracted their attention increasingly to the state.[23]

During the reign of Sultan Abdul Hamid Halim Shah (1881–1943), Kedah's domestic politics centred more and more around a reform movement led by a progressive group of members of the royal family headed by the Raja Muda, Tengku Abdul Aziz, himself. But the reformers were opposed by another royal clique which was led by the Sultan. Sultan Abdul Hamid had sound reasons for opposing the measures proposed by the reform party, necessary though they were for the future development of the state, because they involved land and tax reform and would directly affect the sources of his own power and influence.[24] However, the ruler's position had been seriously undermined by the fact that he had suffered a serious illness shortly after his accession to the throne, as a result of which he was bed-ridden for the best part of the next twenty years. His subsequent indifference to affairs of state[25] was exploited by the reforming princes for their own purposes. As early as 1900 the Raja Muda appealed to Bangkok for the declaration of a regency on the grounds of his brother's unsuitability as a ruler, but the Thai commissioners sent to Alor Star to investigate did not find anything wrong. The reformers

[a]See p. 272.

were presented with another opportunity to restrict the Sultan with the financial crisis which arose as a consequence of the royal weddings of 1904.[26] With the state treasury facing bankruptcy and being pressed by its creditors, a group of senior officials headed by the Raja Muda petitioned Sultan Abdul Hamid for land reform and the abolition of *kerah* as the first steps back to solvency; but the ruler refused. This left no alternative but to retrench and seek a foreign loan. Accordingly, early in 1905 the Raja Muda was in Bangkok to get the loan and he took the opportunity to press for a regency once again. The Thais were still not prepared to regard the Sultan as unsuitable, but they granted the loan and stipulated the appointment of an adviser 'whose advice had to be accepted on all matters pertaining to finance'.[27] They also agreed to the Raja Muda's proposal to set up a Council of State to assist in the administration. In the same year the adviser, an Englishman named G.C. Hart, arrived and the State Council was instituted. Its president was the Raja Muda and it soon emerged as the stronghold of the reform party in the state.

The British take-over

During the negotiations in Bangkok in 1905, the British had been at work behind the scenes. They were fully informed on the progress of the talks and were consulted at every stage by the Thai government. When the idea of the appointment of an adviser was first mooted, the British wanted him to be appointed by the authorities in the Straits Settlements, but the Thais refused to agree and so the British settled for the appointment of a British subject in the employ of Bangkok as adviser and of a British consul in Alor Star to represent directly British interests there.

In fact, British interest in Kedah and the other northern Malay states had been growing ever since the Anglo-French agreement of 1896.[a] It was evidenced by the secret Anglo-Thai understanding signed the following year, and became even more explicit in the open agreement of 1902.[28] Not long after the appointment of Hart as adviser at Alor Star, the British government initiated new discussions with Thailand over the future of these states, including Kedah and Perlis. After more than twelve months of exhaustive negotiations, during which various courses of action were considered,[29] the definitive Anglo-Thai Treaty of 1909 was signed,[b] presenting the Malay rulers of all the states concerned with a *fait accompli*.[c]

But the treaty came as no surprise to Alor Star. As soon as the first rumours circulated about Anglo-Thai discussions in Bangkok regarding Kedah's future, the Malay government started to take energetic measures to forestall what was happening or to have a voice in the proceedings. Protests and memoranda, drafted by the State's Penang lawyers,[30] were depatched to Bangkok, and when those proved of no avail, similar ones were directed to London. Attempts were made by representatives of the Kedah government to interview Sir John Anderson the British High Commissioner in Singapore, and the Colonial Secretary and the Foreign Secretary in London, all of them without achieving any results. Kedah's sole success was to have a question asked in the British House of Commons in July 1909 (by which time the Bangkok Treaty had been signed and the transfer taken place) which pro-

[a]See pp. 291 and 519.
[b]See pp. 292 and 519–20.
[c]See pp. 291, 296.

duced the official assurance that as a result of Britain taking the place of Thailand, 'Kedah's integrity would be in no way affected'.

Kedah's status and the Treaty of 1923

The validity of this guarantee by the British government was quickly put to the test with the arrival in Alor Star of the first British Adviser appointed by the Colonial Office, who took up his post in mid-July 1909 in a ceremony where, as he himself described it, 'Malay dignity and courtesy were seen at their highest and best'.[a] The new man in question was W.G. Maxwell,[31] who by temperament and outlook was little suited to play the rôle of foreign adviser as it was conceived in Kedah or as it operated at Bangkok. Maxwell and his superior, Anderson, saw the British Adviser in Kedah as they saw the British Residents in the Federated Malay States[b]—the undisputed masters in their houses. But Sultan Abdul Hamid, Tengku Mahmud[32] and the State Council fastened on to the promises made by the British government that the status of Kedah was not changed, and who therefore interpreted the position of the new British Adviser as being exactly the same as that of the one appointed under the terms of the 1905 agreement with Thailand. Sooner or later these two conflicting views were bound to lead to some kind of clash. Maxwell's personality ensured that the first crisis was swift to arise. Within weeks of his arrival at Alor Star, he was issuing orders directly to government officials, ignoring Tengku Mahmud and the State Council and even by-passing heads of department as well. Within twelve months, he had reached a deadlock with the Tengku and the Council over the question of royal allowances, and referred the matter to the High Commissioner in Singapore.[33] The crisis finally broke when Anderson required Kedah's endorsement of Maxwell as British Adviser. Tengku Mahmud replied in a series of letters that Maxwell was not acceptable, alleging that he had exceeded his powers and accusing him of gross personal rudeness into the bargain. Alarmed by these developments, in July 1910 Anderson hastened up to Alor Star to investigate matters for himself. Having reprimanded Maxwell for, at the least, lack of diplomacy, the High Commissioner then met members of the State Council who refused to resume their functions unless Maxwell was dismissed. Anderson next won the Sultan over to his side by holding out the hope that the British would support him against the reformists, but Tengku Mahmud found a new issue by rejecting the instructions from the British resident-general of the Federated Malay States in Kuala Lumpur to carry out a census.[34] The Tengku forthwith resigned as President of the Council and the entire Kedah civil service went on strike. Although the strike lasted only forty-eight hours, it was an impressive demonstration of solidarity. But with the British adamant and the Sultan threatening to dismiss all the State Councillors from their posts and perquisites, the trouble blew over. Tengku Mahmud went diplomatically on leave, the State Council reconvened and Maxwell stayed in office.

The apparent outcome of this first crisis was victory for the British point of view, but in fact nothing was solved and by playing off the ruler against his own council, the British paved the way for what was to follow. For Sultan Abdul Hamid, en-

[a]Sir George Maxwell, 'Memories of the First British Adviser, Kedah', *Malaya in History*, IV. 2, 1958.
[b]See Book II.

couraged by the support he had received from Anderson and Maxwell during the affair, became bolder in his attitude towards the State Council and in 1912 precipitated a new crisis which resulted in the Council voting unanimously for the establishment of a Regency.[35] After some hesitation, during which time matters deteriorated in Alor Star, the British accepted this proposal forwarded by Tengku Mahmud, and in April 1913, the new regime was proclaimed, with the Sultan's eldest son, Tengku Ibrahim (Tengku Sulong), as Regent.[36]

However, the establishment of the Regency immediately provoked a second crisis with Britain over the old question of the status of Kedah and the powers of the British Adviser. This time the crisis centred on the position of the Regent and the chairmanship of the State Council. The British, led by the new High Commissioner (Sir Arthur Young) and Maxwell, maintained that the new Regent should assume the presidency of the State Council, as was the practice for rulers in the other Malay States under British protection, and that therefore the present incumbent, Tengku Mahmud, should step down. But although anticipated, this did not happen. Tengku Ibrahim refused to assume the chair and stopped attending meetings of the Council, while Tengku Mahmud carried on as before. A little later, the Regent appointed the State Auditor-General, Syed Shahbuddin, to represent him on the Council, but Young, in his turn, refused to confirm this nomination. Then the Regent appealed directly to the British Foreign Office in London, called upon the services of the State's Penang lawyers once again and caused more questions about Kedah's status to be asked in the British Parliament. But after a year of this confrontation, the Tengku backed down under the heavy threat of deposition made by Young (March 1915).

This second crisis settled the issue of Kedah's status which in fact had been a subject of debate between British and Kedah officials since 1907[37] clearly in favour of the British. Apart from Kedah's desire to preserve her independent status, there was also the well-founded suspicion amongst her leaders that the British were planning on forcing the state into the Kuala Lumpur-dominated Federated Malay States—which indeed had been the original British intention. On the other hand while Maxwell more or less correctly surmised the reasons for Tengku Ibrahim's stand, the High Commissioner, Young assumed that he was merely trying to consolidate his own power at the expense of that of his father, the Sultan. Nevertheless, although the Kedah government had to give way on the issue at stake, their own gain was perhaps greater in the end, for by the terms of the treaty which was eventually signed in 1923 regularizing the position of the Adviser, the Sultan was given the right of direct appeal to London should he object to the advice tendered to him on the spot. It also contained the important proviso that Kedah should not be combined with any other Malay state or with the Straits Settlements without the written consent of the ruler. Kedah had become part of the British Empire on slightly more advantageous terms than those of her neighbours. Perlis signed a treaty with Britain containing similar concessions in 1930.[38]

---

[1]The genealogy of Kedah's rulers is still incomplete and in places confused. According to one tradition, the first kings of Kedah were princes from Gumrun in Persia; see R.O. Winstedt, 'Notes on the History of Kedah', *J.M.B.R.A.S.*, Vol. XIV, p. 186; and J. Bastin, 'Problems of

Personality and the Reinterpretation of Modern Malayan History', p. 146, note 3, in *Malayan and Indonesian Studies*, London, 1966.

[2]Daing Parani was one of five famous warrior brothers associated with the rise of the Bugis power in the Straits of Malacca; sons of Upu Tenribong Daing Rilak, prince of Luwu, south Celebes. Daing Parani was killed *c.* 1723 whilst fighting against the followers of Raja Kechil of Siak in Kedah.

[3]6,000 lb. The Kedah prince only paid 3 baharas of this.

[4]Sultan Sallehuddin or Raja Lumu, and Raja Haji were sons of Daing Chelak, brother of Daing Parani and second Yam Tuan Muda in Riau. Raja Lumu was the first sultan of Selangor and Raja Haji became the fourth Yam Tuan Muda at Riau; Raja Haji was also, perhaps, the most famous of all the Bugis warrior leaders. He was killed at Teluk Ketapang, near Malacca, whilst besieging the Dutch in 1784.

[5]Francis Light; *c.* 1740, born in England; 1759-63, served as midshipman in the British navy; 1765, left England to make his fortune in India—joined Madras firm of Jourdain, Sullivan and de Souza; 1769, sent to Acheh with another Englishman to investigate trading prospects for his firm—whilst there met the envoy of Sultan Mohamed Jiwa of Kedah; spent the rest of his life in Malayan waters; died in Penang in 1794.

[6]Light gave the impression that Kedah was the emporium for virtually the whole archipelago and valued Kedah's trade at Sp. $4 million a year when in reality it was a fraction of this sum; see R. Bonney, 'Francis Light and Penang', *J.M.B.R.A.S.*, Vol. XXXVIII, Pt. I.

[7]Van Braam's fleet had been sent out from Europe to Batavia to strengthen Dutch power in the region and was diverted to Malacca to break Raja Haji's siege of the port; it then went on to establish Dutch control over Riau itself.

[8]In 1784 the English Company sent Kinloch to Acheh and Forrest to Riau; Kinloch went as British 'resident' as agreed to by an earlier mission in 1782, but after 15 months of trying to wear down the Sultan of Acheh's hostility, he left. Forrest, who had already visited the Mergui coast, Perak and Selangor, reached Riau to find the Dutch already in possession.

[9]Ujong Salang—modern Phuket; known to Europeans as 'Junk Ceylon', a corruption of the Malay name. Light retired there after the failure of Monkton's mission to Kedah and continued his pursuit of combining British strategic and commercial interests with those of his own.

[10]The Sultan's first condition was that the enemies of Kedah should be regarded as the enemies of the Company; Calcutta's reply was that 'This government will always keep an armed vessel stationed to guard the Island of Penang on the coast adjacent belonging to the Sultan of Kedah'. To his claim for compensation of $30,000 a year for loss of trade, the Company replied that they would take care 'that the King of Quedah shall not be a sufferer by an English settlement being formed on the Island of Penang'. His final condition that the Company provide military assistance if he were attacked was answered thus: 'This article will be referred for the orders of the English East India Company together with such parts of the King of Quedah's requests as cannot be complied with previous to their consent being obtained'.

[11]Frank Swettenham, *British Malaya*, London, 1948, p. 43. The whole question of how Penang was acquired by the British has become the subject of extensive controversy. That the Sultan of Kedah allowed a British settlement on the island, lured on by false assurances, seems beyond question. But who was the culprit? One school of British writers, mostly officials, including John Anderson and Swettenham, accuses the English Company of duplicity, while another school of thought led by the pro-Thai Crawfurd, Burney and James Low blames the Sultan for obscuring the nature of his relationship with Bangkok. Some modern historical opinion tends to find Light himself the most guilty party, misleading both the Sultan and the Company. See Bonney, op. cit. and D.K. Bassett, 'British Commercial and Strategic Interest in the Malay Peninsula during the late Eighteenth Century', *Malaysian and Indonesian Studies*, op. cit.

[12]Holland was by this time in alliance with Britain, fearful of French designs in Europe; France was increasingly involved in the domestic problems which led to the Revolution of 1789.

[13]Succeeded his brother, Abdullah, on the latter's death in 1798.

[14]Named after Arthur Wellesley, British governor-general in India at the time.

[15]Tajuddin had won the favourable opinion of the Thais by taking part in their campaigns against Burma, for which he had been awarded the rank and status of Chao Phaya.

[16]The *bunga mas* consisted of two plants with leaves and flowers modelled in gold and silver, and sent triennially to Bangkok; its value was around $8,500 (at values of 1924), L.A. Mills, 'British Malaya, 1824-67', *J.M.B.R.A.S..* Vol. III, Pt. 2. (Reprinted Kuala Lumpur 1961) The Thais regarded the tribute as a token of submission; the Malays as a token of alliance and friendship. Bangkok's motive in ordering the attack on Perak was in order to weaken both states.

[17]Known to the Malays and Europeans as the Raja of Ligor (Legur). He was the governor of the province of Nakhon Si Thammarat. He appointed one of his sons as governor (Chao Phaya) of Kedah.

[18]By Burney's Treaty, the British had undertaken to prevent Penang from being used as a base for launching attacks on the Thais in Kedah. But the Calcutta authorities pointed out to Ibbetson, the Governor in Penang, that the treaty did not require the British to give to Thais armed cooperation.

[19]The Chao Phaya had been the arch-enemy of Sultan Tajuddin; his death also gave Bangkok the opportunity of reducing the power of the family of one who had become an almost overmighty subject with ambitions of his own.

[20]The Sultan made his appeal with British approval although they were sceptical about his chances of success. Setul became part of Thailand in 1909. Kubang Pasu reverted to Kedah in 1864. Perlis remained separate from Kedah but was included in the transfer of 1909.

[21]Sultan Ahmad Tajuddin died in 1843; was succeeded by his son, Zainal Rashid (1843–54). British pressure took the form of stopping his annuity and threatening the use of force on the Perak boundary.

[22]Arising out of the Treaty of 1800 which defined the boundary and provided for duty-free food supplies into Penang. The boundary contained irregular salients which were difficult to police while the existence of gambling houses, liquor shops and opium dens immediately on the border was the source of frequent trouble in Province Wellesley. The provisions regarding duty-free food supplies had never been observed.

[23]British power in the Malay States of the Peninsula had been consolidated with the formation of the Federated Malay States consisting of Perak, Selangor, Pahang and Negri Sembilan in 1896. Kedah's proximity to British-occupied Penang, the development of railway communications and the sudden rise of the rubber industry were other factors.

[24]As things stood, the Sultan received directly the rent from all revenue farms as well as taxes in the state, and also had the authority to raise men for his defence through the system of *kerah* or compulsory labour. To do away with these things, therefore, would considerably reduce the ruler's personal influence and power.

[25]For the background to this episode, see Allen 'Anglo-Kedah relations, 1905–15', *J.M.B.R.A.S.* Vol. XLI, Pt. I, 1968.

[26]These were the marriages of Tengku Ibrahim (Tengku Sulong), the Sultan's eldest son, and four other royal children. The celebrations lasted for several weeks, costing at least $125,000. Adding to the state's existing debts, the treasury was unable to meet even the payment of civil servants' salaries!

[27]Thailand advanced a loan of $2,600,000 at the rate of 6 per cent per annum. The Adviser was to be withdrawn as soon as the loan was repaid in full. G. C. Hart was deputy to another Briton, W. F. J. Williamson, who was Financial Adviser to the Thai government and who supervised the initial arrangements concerning the loan in Kedah. The creation of the State Council was obviously a device by the Raja Muda to enable him to bypass the Sultan.

[28]By the secret agreement of 1897 Thailand promised not to cede, alienate or grant any special privileges in the Peninsula Malay States to any other government or national without the express consent of the British. The 1902 agreement more specifically related to Kelantan and Trengganu and recognized Thai control over these two states with the proviso that their foreign relations and the granting of concessions to foreigners would be strictly supervised by Bangkok.

[29]At various stages the British proposed leasing Kedah from Thailand and administering the state through a British consul; acquiring rights over all the territory south of the 7th Parallel (that is, up to the Songkhla region); and outright annexation.

[30]The firm of Adams and Allen, Penang.

[31]Maxwell was a grandson of Sir Peter Benson Maxwell, Recorder in the Straits Settlements from 1856 to 1871, and represented the third generation of the family in Malaya.

[32]Tengku Mahmud was a younger brother of Sultan Abdul Hamid, and became President of the State Council in 1907 on the sudden death of the Raja Muda, Tengku Abdul Aziz.

[33]The State Council had rejected Maxwell's proposal to reduce the allowances of all princes aged over 15. The brothers, half-brothers and sons of the Sultan who were thus affected numbered over 40 in 1913.

[34]Tengku Mahmud correctly interpreted the resident-general's move as the first stage in a British attempt to assimilate Kedah into the F.M.S.; hence his opposition.

[35]The occasion was provided by the Wan Mat Kulim affair. In 1912 Wan Mat Kulim, a friend of the Sultan, acquired by irregular means a concession from the ruler which he sold to a Penang Chinese. When the government found out, the Chinese was compensated, the land

re-acquired. Wan Mat Kulim was eventually tried and convicted for fraud and sentenced to 18 months jail, but was released on the orders of the Sultan (March 1913). Sultan Abdul Hamid also demonstrated his defiance of the State Council by giving Wan Mat Kulim possession of the keys to the state seals, which clearly created a very embarrassing situation for the government.

[36]The establishment of the Regency was delayed by the difficulty of deciding who the Regent should be; the Sultan accepted the move quietly, apparently because it was made in the name of his overlord, the King of England.

[37]In 1907, Dr. L.A. Hoops, the European doctor in the State, who was acting on behalf of Hart during his absence on leave, was accused by the Kedah government of exceeding his authority. The matter was referred to both Singapore and Bangkok but the return of Hart next year smoothed matters over, Hart accepting the Malay position. For a full discussion of the Kedah and British viewpoints, see Allen, 'Anglo Kedah Relations 1905–1915', op. cit.

[38]The Perlis Treaty came at a later date, since until the 1905 loan was paid, the services of a Financial Adviser were required. The final instalment of the loan was paid in 1930, making the Financial Adviser's presence no longer necessary. To the relief of the British, without any prompting, the Raja of Perlis himself requested a General Adviser to take his place.

THE JOHORE-RIAU EMPIRE

THE establishment of the British in Penang marked their return as an established power in the Malacca Straits,[1] and ushered in a fresh period of acute Anglo-Dutch rivalry in the region. Events in Europe gave the British a distinct advantage. The outbreak of the French Revolution and the rise of Napoleon plunged the continent into a long war, during which Holland itself was overrun by France.[2] The British as a consequence occupied the Dutch colonies which, in South-East Asia, meant the taking over of Java and all other Dutch possessions in the archipelago. When peace was finally restored, the British handed back these conquests, but the intervening period of some fifteen years had greatly increased the stake and scope of British trade and whetted the British appetite for a greater and more permanent share in the exploitation of the region. The first Malaysian power to feel the effects of this was Johore-Riau.

The rise and decline of the Johore Malays

The Johore-Riau Empire was the successor state to the Malay sultanate of Malacca, its first ruler being Sultan Mahmud who abandoned Malacca to the Portuguese in 1511 and who eventually made his headquarters on Bintang in the Riau archipelago. Mahmud and his successors never gave up their claim to Malacca and continued to demand homage from the vassals of their Malacca days. The prestige of their name was such and antipathy towards the new occupants of Malacca so great that this claim was accepted for generations to come by both the Peninsula and the Sumatran states which had acknowledged Malacca's suzerainty. But from their bases in the Riau archipelago and south Johore[3] the Malay rulers were never able to recreate a centre of power and commerce to simulate what they had lost. Although there were periods during the course of the first 150 years of Johore's history when she became a trading centre of some consequence, the political environment had altered. To the south she was overshadowed by rising Javanese power, first manifested in the port states led by Demak (Japara) and Surabaya, later

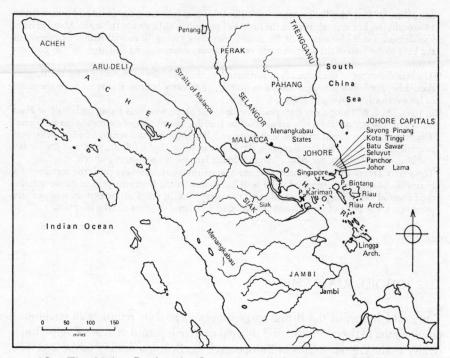

13. The Malay Peninsula, Sumatra and the Straits of Malacca, illustrating the decline of the Johore Empire

by Mataram and even more so Bantam which steadily gained control over the pepper plantations and markets of south Sumatra. In the Straits themselves the undisputed hegemony of the Malacca days had given way to the competition offered by the Achinese and the Portuguese in Malacca itself. By the end of the sixteenth century Johore's pepper vassals in north-east Sumatra as well as Perak had fallen into Acheh's hands. At the same time repeated attempts to drive the Portuguese out of Malacca proved fruitless. In the fierce triangular contest which dominated the politics of the Straits between 1511 and 1640, the Johore Malays gained a few notable victories, but on balance the struggle told against them.[4]

Johore's isolation in the three-cornered contest and the desire to win back Malacca at all costs led to an early alliance with the Dutch newcomers in 1603.[5] In this way began a relationship which was to continue for the next 200 years, at first full of promise but ultimately blighting the Malay power's existence. This became clear after the Dutch eventually captured Malacca from the Portuguese in 1641, an event which damned Johore's pretensions as much as it determined the decline of Acheh and undermined the strength of Mataram.[a] The disappearance of their rivals—Portuguese and Achinese—from the scene might have appeared to promise a new age of prosperity, but then the Johore Malays found they had to acquiesce in the establishment of a Dutch monopoly throughout their former dominions. They

[a]See p. 225 and refer p. 73.

had no say in the Dutch-Achinese agreements regarding Perak or the Sumatran pepper states in the 1640s and 1650s, and in the early 1660s they became involved in a disastrous war with Jambi which brought about an eclipse of their own power in the south of the Straits. The Jambi War led both to the intervention of the Bugis into Johore's politics and to the conclusion of the first of those one-sided treaties with the Dutch. In the 1670s Sultan Ibrahim, anxious to bring the Jambi affair to an end, called in the services of Bugis mercenaries from the Celebes.[a] The Bugis conquered Jambi but they also settled in the Riau archipelago and along the estuaries of the Selangor coast and could not be removed. In the meanwhile the Dutch were not slow to take advantage of the difficulties brought about by the Jambi War and the unpopularity of the Regent Laksamana to obtain two favourable treaties of their own (in 1684 and 1689), although in the event these proved inoperative.[6]

As far as the Johore Malays were concerned, at the end of the seventeenth century the main problem was that posed by the Bugis. The disturbed domestic politics which were the consequence of the assassination of the last direct descendant of the Malacca line at Kota Tinggi in 1699 brought about the circumstances which enabled the Bugis to become the real masters of the empire. When Sultan Sulaiman was placed on the throne with Bugis aid in 1722, he was virtually their prisoner. They created the new office of Yam Tuan Muda and it was the Bugis holders of this post who became the real rulers of Johore-Riau for the greater part of the century which followed.[7]

The ascendancy of the Bugis and their downfall

The consequences of the Bugis ascendancy were far-reaching. For fifty years, from their bases in Riau and Selangor they dominated the politics of the west coast states of the Peninsula but at the same time they were largely instrumental in bringing about the disintegration of the empire. Selangor became an independent Bugis sultanate in the middle of the century.[b] The Menangkabau colonies behind Malacca were driven to forming an independent confederation of their own in self-defence against Bugis pressure.[c] The rulers of Pahang and Trengganu, while nominally still officials and vassals of Johore, became *de facto* independent as well, and the ruler of Trengganu (Sultan Mansor) in particular played an active part in Riau politics by opposing Bugis ambition. Malay opposition to the Bugis in the Straits was initially led by the indomitable Menangkabau ruler of Siak, Raja Kechil,[8] while in the middle of the century Bugis activities and their scorn of the Dutch monopoly led them into direct conflict with Dutch Malacca.

Although the Dutch had been unable to prevent the rise of Bugis power over Johore, it was they who were to break it. The first Bugis-Dutch clash arose out of the affairs of Siak. The throne of Raja Kechil was disputed by his two sons, Raja Mohamed and Raja Alam, who were half-brothers. Sultan Sulaiman of Johore, who still claimed suzerainty over Siak, supported Raja Mohamed and at his bidding the Bugis Yam Tuan Muda, Daing Kemboja, had driven Raja Alam out of Siak to Borneo. But then Daing Kemboja attempted to turn the Siak conquest to his

[a]Refer p. 61.
[b]See p. 268.
[c]See p. 158.

own advantage at the expense of Johore,[a] and the outraged Sultan Sulaiman promptly turned to the Dutch for help. In 1745 a treaty of alliance was drawn up between the Sultan and the Dutch; in return for their help in driving Daing Kemboja from Siak, the Sultan agreed to cede the state to them and to grant a trading monopoly over such of his dominions as were in his grasp. Another treaty ten years later, also designed against the Bugis and aimed at restoring Johore's authority over Selangor, provided for a Johore regent to watch over Dutch interests in Siak and granted the Dutch a monopoly over Selangor's tin. These moves led to a fierce but inconclusive war between the Bugis and the Dutch, and to the temporary elimination of Bugis power in Riau itself. But in 1759, a year before Sultan Sulaiman's death, Daing Kemboja, by *force majeur*, re-established himself in the islands and chose the Sultan's successors.[9] The Bugis remained in control until the Dutch conquest of 1785.

So when Sultan Sulaiman died in 1760 the tottering empire was once more firmly under the thumb of the Bugis Yam Tuan Muda of Riau. Things might have stayed this way had it not been for the impetuous policies pursued by Raja Haji who became the fourth Yam Tuan Muda on the death of his cousin, Daing Kemboja, in 1777. The Bugis were now at peace with the Dutch but in 1782 Raja Haji quarrelled with them over the booty of an English ship they had captured off Riau.[10] War followed. The Bugis raided Dutch shipping in the Straits and after a Dutch attempt to blockade Riau itself had failed, Raja Haji took the offensive and launched a well-prepared siege of Malacca. But in March 1784, a strong Dutch force of six ships under Admiral Jacob Pieter van Braam came to the relief of the beleaguered port and Raja Haji himself was killed in the fighting which followed.[11] Van Braam then sailed on to Selangor, which he subdued, and Pahang, then arrived at Riau where he soon forced the expulsion of the Bugis. This was a blow from which they never recovered. Although circumstances enabled the Bugis to re-establish themselves in Riau after barely a decade, they were never a major force in the politics of the Straits of Malacca again.

Johore-Riau at the end of the eighteenth century

The Johore-Riau Empire was now on its last legs. The end of Bugis domination did not mean the restoration of Malay power as Sultan Mahmud who at first welcomed the Dutch intervention speedily found out. He soon discovered that he had simply changed masters. In the year that the British were settling in Penang, he was required to sign a treaty with the Dutch which provided for a Dutch Resident at Riau and which gave them a virtual monopoly and control over all his trade.[12] In his attempts to escape from this new dilemma, the Sultan was to play into the hands of an as yet absent third party, those of the British.

At first Sultan Mahmud intrigued with the men of Sulu, with the consequence that in May 1787, an Ilanun fleet chased the Dutch garrison from Riau. However the Dutch soon came back and it was the Sultan's turn to flee. The Dutch found out all the same that they needed the presence of the Sultan if Riau was to be restored as a centre of trade, and so became anxious to coax him back. Sultan Mahmud stated his terms—he would return only if the Dutch would give him full powers in Riau and prevent a Bugis restoration; for the latter condition he was prepared to

[a]See p. 248.

pay the sum of $60,000. In 1795 the Dutch accepted this offer but when the time came to implement it, they were no longer in a position to do so, because in that year the British occupied Malacca in the course of taking over Dutch possessions in South-East Asia.[13]

The British did not feel tied down by Mahmud's negotiations with the Dutch, and by disclaiming all political pretensions in the region, they gave the Bugis the chance to return to the islands (from where they had been banned since 1784) and so enabled them to restore their position in the Riau archipelago which in turn led to more trouble. The restored Bugis Yam Tuan Muda, Raja Ali, now was confronted by the hostility of the Malay Engku Muda who had arrogated himself the title after the Bugis defeat at Dutch hands in 1784. Skirmishes between the supporters of either side took place, and finally in 1803 Mahmud effected a compromise by confirming Raja Ali as Yam Tuan Muda and by conferring the office of Temenggong Sri Maharaja on Abdul Rahman, the nephew of the Engku Muda. Furthermore, Sultan Mahmud entrusted the upbringing of his elder son, Tengku Husain, to the Engku Muda as a prospective son-in-law, while his younger son, Tengku Abdul Rahman, was given to the care of Raja Ali. As is too often the way with compromises, this proved to be a most unsatisfactory decision, bringing further complications in its train, for by this action the Sultan had unwittingly created Malay and Bugis claimants for the throne when he died. This circumstance the English empire-builder, Stamford Raffles, was able to turn neatly to his advantage a couple of decades later.

Thus the Johore-Riau Empire was in an unenviable position at the turn of the century. Racked by internal dissensions, it was also at the mercy of more powerful forces from outside represented by the two rival colonial powers from Europe. This situation led within twenty-four years to the empire's dismemberment.

The cession of Singapore, 1819

The final crisis began in a muted way in 1812 when Sultan Mahmud died in Lingga. His eldest son, Tengku Husain, was away in Pahang at the time, and the Bugis faction in Riau were able to seize this opportunity to secure the installation of their protégé, Tengku Abdul Rahman, as the new sultan. At this.moment, the British who were the sole colonial power on the scene, as Holland was still in eclipse under French occupation, accepted the *fait accompli*. Temenggong Abdul Rahman and Bendahara Ali were disposed to help Husain but the British sent an envoy from Malacca to warn them against any action in Riau. Husain, therefore, without support from any quarter, was obliged to accept the situation and retired to one of the Riau islands where he spent the next few years living quietly in near penury.

A new situation was created in 1815 by the end of the wars in Europe and the restoration by Britain to Holland of her colonial possessions in the archipelago; as a result, intensified rivalry for trade and influence broke out afresh between the two powers. Johore-Riau was immediately involved. In 1818, Raja Ja'afar, the new Yam Tuan Muda, received a letter from Farquhar, the British Resident in Malacca,[14] warning him of Dutch designs to subjugate Johore and advising reliance on the British. This was followed up a month later by a visit in person, as a result of which, on 19 August, the Yam Tuan Muda was induced to sign a treaty with the British granting them freedom of trade throughout the empire and giving guarantees against the conclusion of one-sided agreements with any third power (meaning the Dutch). However, the effect of this engagement did not last long, because in November of the same year Raja Ja'afar had another visitor, this time a Dutch rear-admiral.[15] This visit produced another treaty, now with the Dutch, setting up Riau and Lingga as free ports but closing every other harbour in the empire to all but Dutch shipping. These sudden shifts in policy by the Bugis Yam Tuan Muda merely served to underline the fact that the initiative lay completely out of his hands, and that the Johore-Riau Empire stood at the mercy of the Dutch and the British. Shortly afterwards, a Dutch garrison occupied Riau which meant that as far as Raja Ja'afar and his client ruler, Sultan Abdul Rahman, were concerned, they had lost practically all freedom of action.

But other high officers of state still retained theirs. The Bendahara in Pahang and the Temenggong in mainland Johore were amongst these. It was Temenggong Abdul Rahman who was destined to play the next decisive part in the partitioning of the empire. On 29 January 1819 he received Stamford Raffles,[16] Holland's most persistent enemy in Malaysian waters, at his house on Singapore Island where the Englishman and a small party had landed 'either by accident or design' (as Swettenham puts it) the previous day. Raffles came with the authority of Lord Hastings the British governor-general in India, to find a suitable site for a new British base, in the region 'beyond Malacca, such as may command the southern entrance to those Straits'. On reaching Penang from Calcutta he had received news of how the Dutch had forestalled him in Riau, and leaving his other business in Acheh to one side,[a] decided to make straight for the south. Picking up Farquhar on the way, they both went down the Straits, called at Siak and the Karimun Isles, and rejecting them as suitable sites made for Singapore.

Temenggong Abdul Rahman was swift to agree to the terms which Raffles now offered him for permission to establish a trading base on Singapore. In return for allowing the British to set up their quarters on an island which contained barely 200 inhabitants[17] and produced nothing, he was to receive $3,000 a year, and more vital still, British protection. In this way the Temenggong was laying the foundations of the fortune of his own house. However all this was not—legally speaking—the Temenggong's to hold, for although Singapore fell within his fief of Johore, final sanction must come from his overlord.

But who was his overlord? If it was Sultan Abdul Rahman, recognized by the British in 1813 (and confirmed only six months previously by Farquhar) but now living under the shadow of a Dutch garrison in Riau, the prospects of getting that sanction were remote. However, there was also Husain, whose claim to the throne usurped in 1813 both Temenggong Abdul Rahman and the Bendahara had been prepared to defend at the time but for British interference.[b] The Temenggong and Raffles agreed that Husain must be called from his retirement in Riau and recognized as the lawful Sultan of Johore, and without further ado Raffles commissioned two Malay gentlemen for a fee of $500 to fetch the prince. Telling those that he left behind that he was going on a fishing trip, Husain sailed for Singapore and on 6

February, at a simple ceremony before the Temenggong's house, was proclaimed Sultan of Johore. The provisions of the preliminary treaty signed with the Temenggong were confirmed on the same day.

In fact, these acts marked the start of the British settlement on Singapore but at the time and for the next few years it was by no means certain that the island would remain a British possession. Predictably the Dutch reacted to the news by protesting vigorously and threatening military action, while the first reactions in Britain were to disown the whole affair. In these circumstances neither Husain nor the Temenggong felt secure of their positions and both wrote apologetic letters to Sultan Abdul Rahman and the Yam Tuan Muda in Riau and to the Dutch governor of Malacca, explaining that they found themselves in their present situation because of the pressure of the British.[18] However, these fears proved unjustified. The Dutch attack never came and Singapore flourished so spectacularly as a trading centre from the very beginning that this became the most effective argument for its retention by the British. So matters had to be regularized. This was done by a series of treaties and agreements during the next few years which added considerably to the compensation received by Husain and the Temenggong, and confirmed the British in their possession of the island. In June 1819 a new agreement dealing with administrative matters was signed. In 1823 Husain and the Temenggong signed another treaty with Raffles by which, in return for increased pensions, they surrendered their rights to trading dues and monopolies in the island, thereby bringing Singapore under complete British control. The following year Sultan Husain and the Temenggong signed a definitive treaty which ceded Singapore in perpetuity to Britain against a lump sum of $33,000 and a monthly pension of $1,300 for life to Husain, and $28,600, plus a monthly pension of $700 for life to the Temenggong. The Temenggong also granted trading privileges to Britain in mainland Johore and granted the British control over his external relations. This last treaty was made necessary by the signing of the Anglo-Dutch Treaty in London earlier in the same year.[a]

The dismemberment of the Johore-Riau Empire

The Anglo-Dutch Treaty signified the end of the old Johore-Riau Empire. The treaty sought to end the rivalry between the two powers in South-East Asia and came about partly through the issues raised by the British occupation of Singapore. Under its terms, Britain and Holland agreed to respect two spheres of influence on either side of the Straits of Malacca and north and south of a line south of Singapore. As part of the bargain British Benkulen and its dependencies on the Sumatran west coast were exchanged for Dutch Malacca. The dividing line south of Singapore meant that the Riau-Lingga archipelago was now cut off from the peninsula.

It took time for the Malay rulers concerned to adjust themselves to the realities of the new situation. Bendahara Ali in Pahang protested his loyalty to Sultan Abdul Rahman in Riau. Sultan Husain laid claim to and occupied the Karimun islands in the archipelago till he was expelled by Abdul Rahman and the Dutch in 1827. In the 1850s, one of Sultan Abdul Rahman's descendants was to revive the claim to the whole of the former empire.[19]

[a]See pp. 317–19.

14. The Riau-Lingga Archipelago

THE RIAU-LINGGA SULTANATE

As things stood, Sultan Abdul Rahman in Riau was already tied by treaty [20] to the
Dutch. In 1825 a new Treaty was negotiated by the Dutch official, van Angelbeek,
which recognized Abdul Rahman's authority over the Riau-Lingga archipelago as
the Sultan of Lingga in return for his acknowledgement of their suzerainty. He was
also compensated for the loss of his rights or claims over the territories in the British
north. A Dutch Resident continued to reside on Riau which the Dutch declared a
free port in 1829.

However Dutch pre-occupations in Java[a] meant that their control at first sat lightly upon Riau, and its Bugis and Malay rulers were able to run their own affairs largely unmolested. In the course of a short time the archipelago resumed its notoriety amongst foreign traders as a centre for piracy in which Sultan Abdul Rahman and his chiefs were either directly or indirectly involved, while Galang 'was a miniature Sulu, the Malays' principal market for the sale of slaves and booty'.[21] These activities were closely associated with the Lanuns[b] who were regular visitors to the islands and had a base of their own at Reteh on the Indragiri river in east Sumatra. Situated so close to Singapore and the main routes of commerce, British attention was inevitably attracted and this in turn led the Dutch to tighten their control so as to forestall any unilateral action by their rivals.

Thus in 1830 Sultan Abdul Rahman was required to sign a new treaty with the Dutch for the suppression of the pirates, which *inter alia* provided for the introduction of a pass system for local vessels carrying out lawful trade. But this led to no improvement and in 1833 a Dutch force raided pirate strongholds and destroyed the settlement of Eno on Lingga. In the meantime Abdul Rahman had died (in 1830) and was succeeded by Sultan Mohamed Shah who found himself the object of increasing Dutch and British attention. In 1836 the British authorities in Calcutta, nettled by constant complaints from the Straits Settlements, appointed two commissioners to inform local rulers of the new British policy on the pirate question, which was to hold the rulers themselves responsible for piratical acts emanating from their territories. This resulted in the visit of the commissioners in question in a British gunboat to the Riau archipelago. They failed to enlist the co-operation of the Dutch Resident who did his best to prevent them interviewing the Sultan and begged them not to take action without authority from Batavia, but the British bombarded the pirate mart of Galang just the same.[22] This action intensified Dutch efforts to assert their hold over the sultanate. A month after the bombardment of Galang, in July 1836, Sultan Mohamed Shah agreed to put a stop to his chiefs trading with the pirates. New chiefs were to be appointed to control the *orang laut* of the principal islands and all the Sultan's ships were to fly a black flag with a square in one corner as a sign of their business as authentic traders. In return, and in compensation for the loss in revenues incurred by the ruler and his chiefs, the Sultan was to be permitted to import 2,500 pikuls of gambier tax-free into Java each year. In 1837 these arrangements were confirmed but in place of the free import license on gambier, the Sultan was to receive an annual pension and his chiefs regular salaries.

The last bid of Sultan Mahmud Muzaffar Shah
Neither Sultan Abdul Rahman nor Sultan Mohamed Shah showed much disposition to reassert their ancient claims or to question Dutch authority, although Abdul Rahman (or rather his Bugis Yam Tuan Muda) secured the possession of the Karimun Isles from his half-brother, Husain, in 1827. But the successor to Mohamed Shah, who died in 1841, was of a different mould. Young, headstrong and ambitious, the new ruler, Sultan Mahmud Muzaffar Shah, dreamed of reviving his forefathers' authority over the whole of the former empire. Circumstances were

[a]Refer pp. 83 et seq.
[b]See p. 211.

not altogether unfavourable. Although the Temenggong of Johore[a] had identified himself closely with the British in Singapore and pursued an independent policy of his own in the Peninsula, both the Bendahara in Pahang and the Sultan of Trengganu tended to be more well-disposed towards Riau whose claims they were prepared to admit. A few years after his accession, the young ruler paid an official visit to Trengganu where he was grandly entertained by its newly established sultan, Baginda Omar.[23] This friendship was to last for several years and became an important factor in Mahmud's designs.

In the 1850s developments in Pahang led Mahmud to conspire for his recognition as ruler there, and when in 1857 civil war broke out between the new bendahara and his younger brother,[b] the Riau Sultan sided actively with the latter. However, by this time Mahmud had become thoroughly unpopular with the Dutch. According to them he was extravagant and dissolute, and his intrigues with his royal relations in the Peninsula alarmed them lest they too would become involved and thereby give the British the excuse of accusing them of contravening the terms of the Treaty of 1824. Matters came to a head during 1857 itself. The immediate issue which led to deadlock was a dispute between Mahmud and the Dutch over the vacant office of Yam Tuan Muda, either side championing different candidates. But of greater concern to the Dutch was the Sultan's proposed intervention in Pahang, so when despite their warnings Mahmud left the archipelago for Singapore and the north, they declared him deposed. Mahmud, now without any throne, stayed in Pahang canvassing for his recognition as its Sultan until, in October 1858, British pressure forced his departure.[c] From there he went to Trengganu and then to Bangkok where he solicited Thai support. The outcome of this journey was his reappearance in Trengganu in 1862 which culminated in the British bombardment of the capital.[d] The ex-Sultan once more withdrew to Thailand but was back in Pahang in 1864 where he died the same year. As for Riau, it was now ruled by Mahmud's half-brother, Sulaiman, who caused the Dutch no trouble. Shortly after Mahmud's deposition the Dutch eradicated the last remnants of his influence in the archipelago by raiding and destroying Reteh, the base of the Lanuns in Indragiri, who were strongly suspected of being involved in his larger schemes.

Sultan Sulaiman, who was the last direct male descendant of the Malay Johore-Riau line, died in 1883. In his place the Dutch installed Abdul Rahman Ma'adlum Shah, who was of the Bugis Yam Tuan Muda line on his father's side and was the great-grandson of Mahmud Muzaffar Shah through his mother. Sultan Abdul Rahman was the last sultan of Riau-Lingga, for in 1912, displeased with his pan-Islamic leanings and predilection for things English, the Dutch deposed him and he passed into exile in Singapore.

JOHORE

The fate of those portions of the Empire which fell into the British sphere by the Treaty of 1824 was more complex. Mainland Johore itself was the fief of the Temenggong while Raffles' Sultan, Husain, held the title and lived heavily in debt

[a]See p. 126.
[b]See pp. 134-5.
[c]See p. 135.
[d]See p. 295.

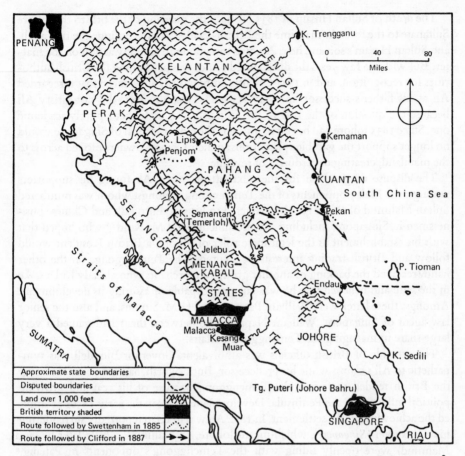

15. South Malaya during the nineteenth century, shewing Pahang and Johore

in Singapore. Pahang was ruled by the Bendahara who was inclined to regard the Sultan of Riau and not Sultan Husain as his overlord, while Trengganu—for long now independent of imperial Johore—enjoyed considerable autonomy under a loose Thai overlordship.[a]

The problem of the Johore succession

In Johore proper the first question to arise concerned that of the Johore succession. Whatever had been the original intention, the real ruler of Johore was the Temenggong. Temenggong Abdul Rahman died in 1825 and was succeeded by his second son, Ibrahim (Daing Ronggek). Ibrahim, who made a fortune for himself whilst living in Singapore out of his monopoly of gutta percha from the state, came to acquire considerable influence, both through his connexions with certain members of the business community in Singapore and through his relations with the rulers of the Peninsula states.

[a]See pp. 292 et seq.

The death of Sultan Husain in 1835 brought the question of the title to the Johore Sultanate to the fore. At that time the British decided not to continue the title at all, and Sultan Husain's son and heir, Ali, was too young to take any action on the matter. But within a few years the disinherited prince was petitioning the British authorities for recognition, and in 1841 Calcutta ambiguously announced that it regarded Ali as his father's successor 'in every respect'. This, however, did not satisfy Ali because the question of the title to the Sultanate was no longer a purely academic one. Since 1835 Johore had begun to prosper; the exhausted soil of Singapore would no longer support the gambier plantations so their Chinese owners moved across to the mainland, creating new sources of revenue.

The dispute dragged on for the next fifteen years. Ali found his supporters amongst the Malay opponents of the Temenggong, amongst whom was numbered Sultan Mahmud of Riau. He also attracted to his side European and Chinese businessmen in Singapore, including the prominent W.H.M. Read[24] who hoped that with his establishment as the legitimate ruler of Johore, a British Resident would follow and British trading interests be secured. The Temenggong, on the other hand, received the backing of another group of merchants who already had a stake in the state and believed that he was far more capable of assuring its development. Amongst these latter were William Paterson and H.M. Simons, and also the senior law agent of Singapore, William Napier, who between them had gained a very large share in managing the Temenggong's affairs.

The attitude of British officials was ambivalent. Governor Blundell was sympathetic to Ali's claims while his predecessor, Butterworth, had not been. However the British tended to favour the Temenggong because of his real and growing political influence in the Peninsula. Developments there in the early 1850s prompted the achievement of a settlement. In 1852 Ali was in Riau reportedly surrendering his rights over 'Singapore', which meant Johore, to Mahmud; a little later he (and Mahmud) were openly siding with the Temenggong's opponents in Pahang.[a] Finally, in 1855, after much wrangling, a final settlement was reached whereby Ali kept the title of Sultan, received $5,000 in cash, $500 per month as pension and the fief of the land between the Muar and Kesang rivers. In exchange he forfeited all his claims and rights over the state of Johore.[25]

Johore under the Temenggong Ibrahim and Sultan Abu Bakar

In the meantime Temenggong Ibrahim waxed prosperous as a result of his gutta percha monopoly and of the enterprise of the Chinese gambier and pepper planters in Johore,[26] and this prosperity was shared by the European and Chinese firms which ran his affairs. It was these interests which led to the Temenggong's intervention in the Pahang civil war on the side of Tun Mutahir in 1858 and which pressed for British intervention in favour of the Bendahara. But before the civil war was over, Ibrahim had died and was succeeded by his able and energetic son, Abu Bakar.

Temenggong Abu Bakar's accession was looked upon with enthusiasm by the British officials in Singapore for he was very anglicized and showed promise of deeper concern in running his state than his father had done. The new Temeng-

[a]See p. 134.

gong in fact was determined to strengthen his position as an independent ruler, and tried to loosen his dependence both on the commercial groups who had assisted his father and on the British authorities in Singapore. He did his utmost to avoid conflict with the latter by taking steps to prevent cases of maltreatment of British subjects and sternly hunting down and returning escaped convicts from the island. To the further relief of the British he removed his permanent residence from Singapore to his new capital at Tanjong Puteri (Johore Bahru) and instituted other modernizing measures.[a] The British authorities were very impressed. On the suggestion of Governor Cavenagh, Temenggong Abu Bakar visited England in 1866 and shortly after his return two years later was designated the Maharaja of Johore.

At the same time, Abu Bakar followed his father's forceful policy in the Peninsula. He did all that he could to uphold the cause of Tun Mutahir in Pahang but without success, so that the relations between Johore and the regime of the victorious Wan Ahmad, the new bendahara, remained clouded for several years to come. Johore also became involved in the politics of Selangor and the Menangkabau states during the late 1860s and early 1870s where, however, in both instances the Maharaja supported the losing side. Nevertheless the Maharaja's influence with Raja Mahdi of Selangor and with the Dato Bandar of Sungai Ujong proved useful to the British authorities in Singapore when they made their attempts to settle these affairs.

On the whole, Johore's policies in the Peninsula enjoyed the support and approval of Britain who welcomed a stable influence amidst the whirl and scurry of contemporary Malay politics; but in his relations with Pahang, Maharaja Abu Bakar became a hindrance to British attempts to establish their overlordship there. Johore's interest in Pahang grew as under the firm rule of Wan Ahmad that state recovered from its civil war. Apart from Johore itself, Pahang was by the 1870s the sole Malay country in the Peninsula which could claim to be free from the dominating influence of any outside power. Towards the end of the same decade there was increasing speculation about the wealth of Pahang's soil and mineral resources, and the Maharaja, whose extravagant ways had plunged him deeply into debt was as anxious as his Singapore backers to acquire new sources of revenue. In 1880 he succeeded in bringing about a reconciliation between himself and Wan Ahmad, and from henceforward was able to assume the rôle of Pahang's best friend and confidant regarding its relations with the British. During the next couple of years, Maharaja Abu Bakar obtained important land and mining concessions in the state.[b]

By 1883 it had become quite clear to Sir Frederick Weld, the energetic and expansionist-minded governor of the Straits Settlements, that the principal obstacle to the formation of a British protectorate over Pahang was the influence of the Maharaja of Johore.

The Anglo-Johore Treaty of 1885
Weld's own efforts to extend British authority in the Peninsula had already clashed with the Maharaja's interests elsewhere.[27] The Pahang question and a general tendency for the Maharaja to assert his independence of action in various other ways

[a] See Book II.
[b] See p. 136.

convinced the governor and his officials in Singapore that the relationship between Johore and the Colony should be redefined. A clash of personalities added fuel to the fires that Weld now set out to stoke up against the Malay ruler. Whilst on leave in London at the end of 1884, the governor urged upon the British Colonial Office the need for a closer control over Johore's affairs. He accused the Maharaja of mal-administration, of extravagance and of relying on bad advice from his private European lawyers, and pointed out the dangers of foreign intervention.[28] Hearing rumours of impending British moves against his sovereignty, Maharaja Abu Bakar himself repaired to London where he had several friends in influential circles.[29] The outcome was the signing of a new treaty between Britain and Johore in December 1885. To a large extent the new agreement represented a triumph for the Maharaja and a rebuff for Weld. While Johore was styled officially as a protectorate of Great Britain, and provision was made for 'joint defence'—which the original Treaty of 1824 had omitted—the Maharaja was now recognized as Sultan of 'the State and territory of Johore'. He was to accept a British Agent who would have 'functions similar to those of a consular officer', and was prohibited from inter-fering 'in the politics or administration of any native state' (a clause inserted at the express insistence of Weld) and was not to make 'any grant or concession to other than British subjects or British companies or persons of Chinese, Malay or other Oriental race' without British consent.[30]

Although Johore's relationship with Britain now stood closer defined, its inde-pendent status was also more explicitly acknowledged. In the remaining decade of his life and reign, Sultan Abu Bakar worked with considerable success to assert and maintain this position. A British Agent was never appointed, the Sultan indicating that he preferred to deal directly with the governor in Singapore, while Weld's attempt to implement the appointment was defeated by the unofficials in his own Legislative Council in 1877. [31]The Sultan also strengthened his influence in London by creating a Johore Advisory Board in 1876 on which sat powerful ex-colonial officials and which served as a means of direct communication with the Colonial Office, thereby by-passing the governor and his administration in Singapore.[32] The Board was to play an important rôle in defending Johore's integrity against British encroachments until its abolition in 1907. Sultan Abu Bakar took other steps to demonstrate his relative independence. He laid claim to the Natuna, Anambas and Tembelan Islands, created an Order of the Crown of Johore in direct imitation of European royal orders, rejected the offer of loans from the government of the Straits Settlements for fear of strings attached, turned down advice regarding Chinese affairs from the same source and successfully disputed Weld's unilateral award on a boundary issue affecting Johore, Jelebu and Pahang.[33] Sultan Abu Bakar's crowning effort was the passing of a constitution for the state in 1894, pro-bably on the advice of his astute secretary, Abdul Rahman bin Andak. This consti-tution, the most important clauses of which laid down the law of succession and provided for a Council of Ministers and a Council of State, did little more than confirm in writing the autocracy of the ruler himself, but it also underlined Johore's position as a Malay state with an identity and a legal framework of its own. When the Sultan died two years later (1895), Johore's special status was clearly accepted and recognized by the British and there seemed no immediate prospect that it would be changed.

Sultan Ibrahim's relations with the British: 1896–1906

Nevertheless within ten years Johore's quasi-independence, her special relationship with Great Britain and the advantages that this entailed had been all but lost. To a certain degree this came about as a result of the policies of the new ruler, Sultan Abu Bakar's son and heir, Sultan Ibrahim,[34] and of his attempts to secure and even further his independent position. It was also brought about, however, by the consolidation of British rule in the Peninsula—the Federated Malay States came into being the year of his accession and the northern Malay states were drawn into the British fold twelve years later[a]—and the relentless expansion of British economic interests which would no longer tolerate administrative or political non-conformities in the general pattern of British control and domination.

From the outset the new Sultan showed a disposition to seek his own counsel and follow his own interests, regardless of whatever the British in Singapore might desire. Official letters from the Colony to London were soon describing Sultan Ibrahim as 'headstrong' and 'reckless', and complaining of his extravagance and dissipations. Reports from various sources also came in of acts of despotism in his administration and even of violations of the constitution.[35] But what was far more serious in British eyes was the opposition the new ruler put up against Sir Frank Swettenham's (then resident-general of the new Federated Malay States) pet project for a trunk railway to run from the north to the south of British Malaya, a line which would link Penang with Singapore by way of the Federated Malay States themselves and Johore. Work on the project was started in 1898[b] and the following year Swettenham made his first proposals to Johore for the construction of the southern section of the line through the state. Swettenham's proposals were reasonable enough. He put forward two alternatives; either the line should be built by the F.M.S. government at a rate of 2 per cent interest on capital outlay while it would be worked by the F.M.S. until the section was giving a 5 per cent return on the original capital; or, Johore should finance the line while the F.M.S. government would be responsible for its actual construction. But after some initial wavering, the Sultan came out adamantly against these offers. To him a railway line built or financed and controlled by the government of the F.M.S. represented an undeniable threat to his independence and the first step towards Johore's incorporation into that federal set-up. So Swettenham's proposals were rejected, and while continuing to haggle over terms with London Sultan Ibrahim quietly opened negotiations with firms of his own choice for the construction of a line under the auspices of the Johore government itself.[36] This in turn provoked an angry and strong reaction from the British Colonial Office who threatened to withhold all co-operation if the Sultan persevered with his plans.[37] In 1902, the year in which Swettenham had originally hoped to start operations on the line but with no agreement in sight, he put forward new offers which contemplated the F.M.S. government financing half of the construction costs at a rate of 4 per cent of capital outlay. These terms were not found acceptable by Johore either and after another twelve months of fruitless bargaining the British Colonial Secretary (Sir Joseph Chamberlain) himself intervened and forced the issue by threatening to impose a British Agent as laid down by the Treaty

[a]See Book II.
[b]See Book II.

of 1885. This was sufficient to cause the Sultan to back down and in July 1904 the Railway Convention was signed.[38]

The idea of appointing a British Agent or Adviser to Johore had been raised at the time of Sultan Abu Bakar's death in 1896[39] and the Railway Question brought it up again. When British patience with the Sultan's procrastinations was wearing thin in 1903, Swettenham (now Governor of the Straits Settlements and High Commissioner of the Malay States) was ordered to conduct a survey of Johore's administration, but in his report he could find no serious fault,[40] so that there was no pretext for intervention in that direction. Two years later, Swettenham's successor, Sir John Anderson, argued against the appointment of a British Agent on the grounds that the Sultan's attitude in such a circumstance might lead to more problems than it would solve. And when the following year (1906), Anderson himself changed his tune and recommended the appointment of a British resident, the Colonial Office demurred, feeling that there were insufficient grounds for such action.

But in fact, since the signing of the Railway Convention of 1904, the Sultan's relations with the British authorities had been steadily growing worse. Aggrieved by his defeat over the railway issue and determined to strengthen his position and maintain his independence by fostering the economic development of his state, in 1905, the Sultan, in addition to granting generous concessions of land for rubber planting to Swettenham and others, entered into negotiations with Guthries of Singapore for the setting up of a 'developmental' company to be known as the Johore State Corporation. Holding virtually monopolistic rights for twenty years, the Corporation was to be made responsible for the development of Johore Bahru as the terminus of the Malayan railway into a port of consequence with its own facilities for handling trade; furthermore, an agricultural bank was to be set up, public works built, and mining operations were to be promoted.[41] This move once again raised the ire of the Colonial Office in London which foresaw that the task of bringing Johore into line with the other Peninsula Malay states would be all the more difficult if the deal were allowed to go through, and at the same time it resented the obvious threat to Singapore's interests that the scheme implied.

The Sultan's plans also brought him into collision with his own Advisory Board from whose chairman the Colonial Office had first learned of the affair.[42] Furious at this breach of confidence, the Sultan cut the Board's expenses, an action which led, as designed, to its resignation. The Board was then reconstituted more after his own fashion, with Rahman Andak, his mentor and confidential adviser, as its most prominent member. The Colonial Office thereupon retaliated by refusing to recognize or have any more dealings with the new Board, which of course destroyed the purpose of its existence. But matters did not rest there. By this time the Colonial Secretary (Lord Elgin) was sufficiently perturbed by the trend of events to decide that more decisive measures were necessary. Circumstances still did not appear to justify the drastic step of imposing a British Resident on the Sultan, so Elgin called him for an interview at the Colonial Office itself instead. There Sultan Ibrahim was informed in no uncertain terms where he stood as far as Britain was concerned. He was told that he was expected to 'conform' generally with the views of the British government, and in particular where concessions were concerned he should consult and follow the advice of the governor of Singapore. He was also told that he should spend more time in Johore and not leave the state without the prior consent of the Singapore authorities. If the Sultan did not pay heed to this warning, Lord Elgin continued, then Britain would be forced to make 'constitutional changes'. A couple of months later, a somewhat dejected ruler returned to his native land.[43]

The growth of British influence; 1906-14

The interview and ultimatum of April 1906 in London was a turning point in Anglo-Johore relations and marked the rapid increase of British influence at the expense of the Malay state. For the next three years, the Sultan acquiesced in the advice which he received from Sir John Anderson, Swettenham's successor in Singapore, and as he did so Johore's defences against British encroachments upon its sovereignty gave way. The Johore State Corporation project was abandoned at the behest of the Colonial Office. In 1907, Rahman Andak, the Dato' Sri Amar diraja and master-mind behind Johore's independent policies,[44] was pensioned off at the urging of the governor, and the Johore Advisory Board, once one of Johore's main lines of defence but admittedly paralysed since the crisis of 1905, was abolished. In early 1908, as part of important modifications to the 1904 Railway Convention, the F.M.S. were granted full control over the operation of the line.[45] In 1909, the Johore section itself was completed, opening the state to an intense boom of speculation in rubber land and to an influx of European planters. 'The planters who are now at work there will soon bring about what we want without any action of ours', observed Anderson in 1907; by 1909 the problems associated with the rapidly expanding plantation industry such as questions of land tenure, adequate surveys and stricter labour controls indeed justified his persuading the ruler to apply formally for a British Adviser.

The Adviser, who was called the General Adviser,[46] however, was still quite different in status and position to his counterparts in the Federated Malay States. He was, at least nominally, an official of the Johore government (although in practice responsible to Singapore) and his advice did not have to be followed, although it was no doubt politic for the Sultan to do so. According to his instructions, the General Adviser was to 'keep a close supervision over the different departments of the State with a view to bringing the administration up to something approaching the standard of the F.M.S.' The first man to fill the post, D.G. Campbell,[47] took up his duties in January 1910. He was made a member of the State Council, was put directly in charge of lands, mines and surveys and acted as judge for Europeans in the state. Campbell's appointment was soon followed by those of others, including a surveyor, a legal adviser, a commissioner of customs and collector of land revenue, besides an assistant to the General Adviser himself. In 1911 and 1912 other Europeans were recruited for the posts of Chief Engineer, Supreme Court Judge and Police Commissioner, all under the aegis of the General Adviser.

This influx of British influence and control was the natural corollary to the accelerated development of the State which followed the opening of the railway in 1909, but inevitably it grated upon the feelings of a man as proud and independent in outlook as Sultan Ibrahim. From 1912 onwards traces of friction began to show. In January that year, for example, he rejected the governor's (Sir Arthur Young) request that Johore should carry out all its official dealings through Kuala Lumpur rather than through Singapore.[48] In matters which the Sultan regarded as his own special preserve, such as the armed forces or prison administration, he steadfastly refused to give way to British attempts at interference. In 1913 he was being rebuked by the Colonial Office for trying to recruit his own teachers for the State through his London connexions. And in defiance of British wishes, the State Council doubled his allowances on the occasion of his fortieth birthday in that year. The Sultan gave further evidence of his feelings by absenting himself from meetings of the State Council, which caused delay or even cancellation in the carrying out of decisions, and by influencing his officials against the implementation of measures of which he did not approve. Sultan Ibrahim even vented his spleen on the British community in the State socially.[49]

By 1913, Campbell and his coterie of British officials in Johore were thoroughly dissatisfied with their position and started to agitate with Singapore and London for the imposition of a new treaty which would give them effective authority. They found ready support both with Young, the governor in Singapore, and with Anderson, who was now permanent under-secretary at the Colonial Office in London, for their designs. All that was necessary was a valid excuse for action. Such excuses were not hard to find. The Raja Ali affair which involved a relative of the Sultan who had fled from Dutch authority in Riau[50] had already aroused British official antagonism by the ruler's refusal to accept the governor's advice on the matter. The question of prison administration, however, was the issue which became the pretext for forcing full British control on the Sultan in 1914.

The Agreement of 1914

For over two years Campbell and his deputy, J.B. Elcum, had pressed Sultan Ibrahim for action regarding the persistent reports of maladministration in the Johore Bahru prison, which came under the direct supervision of the Sultan himself. But although Sultan Ibrahim promised to carry out some of the remedies suggested to him, nothing came of this. Finally in October 1913, on the insistence of the governor in Singapore (Young), the Sultan agreed to the setting up of an independent commission of enquiry into the prison administration at his capital.[51] The commission went into action straight away and early in 1914 produced its report, confirming the allegations, urging instant reforms and recommending as a basic first step that the powers of the General Adviser should be enlarged.

British concern on humanitarian grounds about the conditions in the Johore Bahru gaol was no doubt well justified, although it was odd that Swettenham had nothing adverse to say on the matter in the report of his inspection of 1903.[52] However by 1913 circumstances were already very different. The northern Malay States had been transferred from Thai to British control. The new Federated Malay States were consolidated under a bureaucracy at Kuala Lumpur, its government now controlled the railway which ran through Johore to link up with Singapore in the south, and Western interests in the State itself had rapidly increased with the rubber boom of 1910.[53] In 1913 Johore was the only peninsula Malay state where the British adviser had not the power to enforce his advice, and to British officials like Anderson, Young and Campbell this seemed increasingly intolerable. The 'prison scandal' provided Young with the pretext he needed for urging a new treaty relationship with Johore which would give the British official there the requisite authority. Together with an unfavourable report on the administration of justice compiled by M.H. Whitley, the State Legal Adviser, the Singapore governor was able to present a persuasive case for action to London.

At the Colonial Office, Anderson spoke for the deposition of the Sultan himself, but cooler counsels prevailed. In the event, Sultan Ibrahim was briefed beforehand about British intentions, and matters were arranged to preserve his dignity as much as possible. So the request for new arrangements with Britain officially came from the Sultan himself and was described in terms of a revision of the 1885 Treaty. Under the new agreement, the General Adviser was no longer an officer of the government of Johore but commissioned by and directly responsible to the governor in Singapore. The Adviser's powers were redefined by the now classical formula that his advice was to be accepted on all matters except those concerning Malay religion and custom, and he was put in direct charge of the collection and expenditure of revenue. The British desire to protect Sultan Ibrahim's prestige enabled him to gain one or two concessions that kept Johore still on a different footing from the other British-protected peninsula states. Malay as well as English was to be the official language; appointments to the civil service were to go by preference to educated Johore Malays and these were to be accorded equal status with their European counterparts. In the case of a dispute with the Adviser, the Sultan retained the right to refer the matter to the governor in Singapore. More symbolically, the adviser was still called the General Adviser; European officials had to wear the uniforms of the Johore State civil service, and all official correspondence from the State was to be transmitted via Singapore and not Kuala Lumpur.

Nevertheless, these concessions made by Britain to the susceptibilities of Johore formed the shadow of the Treaty of 1914. In its substance it ended the quasi-independence of Johore which she had enjoyed for so long under the shadow of British Singapore. It would appear that Sultan Ibrahim had come to regard such an outcome as inevitable for when the moment of truth came, he accepted the British demands 'with much dignity and even cordiality'.[a] The Sultan continued to sit on his throne, and as has been the way with certain other rulers who accepted the realities of British power, he eventually became so identified with it that he was one of its foremost champions when it was challenged by the new forces of nationalism which broke loose after the Second World War.[54] However, in the new era which dawned after 1945 there was no place for the old Johore-Riau empire. Riau was irrevocably linked with the emergent Republic of Indonesia; the mainland provinces formed part of the new Federation of Malaya; while Singapore was ultimately to emerge as an independent city-state on its own.

PAHANG

The rulers of Pahang were able to take advantage of the conditions created by the Anglo-Dutch Treaty of 1824 to make themselves virtually independent for the best

[a]Governor Sir Arthur Young, quoted by Keith Sinclair, 'The British Advance in Johore', *JMBRAS*, XL(1), 1967.

part of the next sixty years before circumstances led to the loss of that independence in 1888.

The ruler of Pahang at the time of the Treaty was the Bendahara Ali[55] who had been installed by Sultan Mahmud, the last emperor of Johore-Riau, in 1806. Ali's first reaction to the news of Raffles' recognition of Sultan Husain at Singapore in 1819 was to play for safety. He addressed a letter to the Dutch governor at Malacca, Timmerman Thyssen, expressing his amazement at a fate which separated father from son, brother from brother, and friend from friend. He also declared that he continued to recognize Sultan Abdul Rahman of Riau as his overlord, and his seal diplomatically styled him as the representative of the late Sultan Mahmud! In the same year he refused to allow the British flag to be raised in Pahang. Later, as the situation became clearer, Bendahara Ali modified his attitude and apparently accorded his recognition to Sultan Husain as well, and in 1841 Husain's son and heir asked to come to Pahang to be installed as the new sultan by the Bendahara.[56] In 1853 the Bendahara felt sufficiently sure of his position to have himself proclaimed an independent ruler, although the fiction of Johore's sovereignty was allowed to continue up till 1864.

The Pahang Civil War, 1858-63

The first serious threat to Pahang's sovereignty came on the death of Bendahara Ali in 1857. His eldest son and heir was Wan Mutahir; but the late Bendahara had also prescribed in a will of 1856 that the revenues of the rich districts of Kuantan and Endau should go to a favourite younger son, Wan Ahmad. Wan Mutahir, now Bendahara, claimed ignorance of the will. Wan Ahmad, who was present at his dying father's bedside to receive his last injunctions, claimed that these districts were for him to rule. Neither party was interested in compromise, and hardly had his father been laid in his grave before Wan Ahmad took himself and his followers off to Singapore to raise money and support to contest the inheritance by arms.

In fact, both sides had their supporters outside the country. Wan Ahmad secured the backing of Baginda Omar, the sovereign of Trengganu, of Sultan Mahmud of Riau-Lingga, and more remotely that of Thailand as well. Mahmud, as we have seen,[a] was in search of a throne; he had sounded out Wan Sultan Mutahir about his pretensions to be recognized as the Sultan of Pahang, and meeting with no response from that quarter sided with the new Bendahara's rival brother. Baginda Omar of Trengganu saw in Wan Ahmad a useful counterfoil to the ambitions and designs of Temenggong Ibrahim of Johore, behind whom the Trengganu ruler fancied that he discerned the hand of Britain. Temenggong Ibrahim, on the other hand, with good reason regarded Sultan Mahmud as the most serious obstacle to his own schemes of hegemony, and wished to establish his control over the aging Wan Mutahir whose weak, opium-eating sons would be easy to handle. The Temenggong, furthermore, enjoyed the backing and confidence of wealthy commercial interests in Singapore.

It was these commercial influences which tried to sway the attitude of the British authorities. Blundell, and his successor as governor, Cavenagh, were both reluctant to become involved on either side because the main British interest was to prevent the outbreak of inter-state disturbances in the Peninsula which could only disrupt

[a] Refer p. 124.

trade and create fresh political complications.[57] It was official British policy to localize conflicts where they occurred and as far as possible forestall possible outside intervention.

With this in mind and also concerned about Thai intentions, the British tried to mediate and to check the far-reaching designs of ex-Sultan Mahmud. In May 1858 Blundell made the voyage to Pahang and also Trengganu where he persuaded Baginda Omar to remove Wan Ahmad from his base of operations at Kemaman, but Wan Ahmad returned there immediately after the departure of the British governor. Later in the same year, when the ex-Sultan Mahmud reappeared in Pahang, the Temenggong successfully aroused British influence to secure his removal. In June 1861, perturbed by the fighting at Endau and Kuantan,[58] Cavenagh sailed to Pahang and attempted mediation on the basis of the 1856 will, but Wan Ahmad refused to accept this arbitration. British attention was next drawn northwards to Trengganu where ex-Sultan Mahmud was attempting to stage his last comeback with Thai backing. This culminated in the bombardment of Kuala Trengganu in 1862.[a]

However, none of this deterred Wan Ahmad who in the August of the same year launched his third and this time successful invasion of Pahang by the land route through Ulu Pahang. Wan Mutahir had already handed over the administration of the state to his weak-minded and ineffective son, the Engku Muda, Koris. As Wan Ahmad advanced he won over most of the chiefs to his side, and despite all that the Temenggong could do[59] his arms carried the day. By May 1863 Wan Ahmad was in Pekan, and Mutahir and Koris were exiles in Johore where both died within a couple of weeks of each other at Kuala Sedili.

Pahang under Wan Ahmad

Wan Ahmad was now in control of Pahang and was to remain its ruler until his death in 1914. He had a strong character and personality which were very necessary for he had a turbulent state to control; in a short time after the end of the civil war he succeeded in making himself its undisputed master.[60] Nevertheless, after twenty years of personal rule and independence, he found himself obliged to yield to British power and accept British overlordship.

Wan Ahmad was fully aware of the threat of this power and the danger that it represented, and although the British had tended to favour Mutahir in the recent civil war, the new Bendahara hastened to establish correct relations with the British authorities in Singapore. In 1863 he informed Singapore of his victory and was accorded de facto recognition. Thereafter he kept Singapore fully informed of the progress of his dispute with Johore over the possession of Pulau Tioman and adjacent islands and showed willingness to accept British mediation. The British did mediate and in 1868 the British governor, Ord, arrived at Pekan with Maharaja Abu Bakar of Johore to announce his award.[61] In the early 1870s, on being invited to intervene in the civil war in Selangor on the side of Tengku Kudin,[b] the Bendahara sought and obtained British approval first.

This decade saw the start of the British forward movement in the Malay Penin-

[a]See pp. 294-5.
[b]See p. 286.

sula and Wan Ahmad trod delicately but firmly to avoid British pressure. In 1874 the initiator of the new British policy, Sir Andrew Clarke, came to Pekan to mediate in a new dispute with Johore over the Endau boundary, and took the opportunity to offer his advice and assistance in governing the country. The offer was firmly declined. The following year, Jervois, Clarke's successor, paid a visit in July and suggested British advice and assistance in the development of Pahang's natural resources, and received an evasive reply. Complications in the west coast states[a] caused the British to drop their advances for the next few years.

Pahang, Johore and the awakening of outside interest

The 1880s, however, brought new factors to the fore which contributed to the ending of Pahang's isolated independence. The first of these was the fresh initiative taken by the Maharaja of Johore to establish friendly relations with Wan Ahmad. As one of his main opponents during his struggle for power, Wan Ahmad had little reason to like the ruler of Johore.[62] However, since the 1870s, the Maharaja had adopted a conciliatory approach towards Pahang. The boundary disputes were reasonably settled and the issues closed. By 1880 sufficient time had elapsed for old wounds to have healed and in that year Maharaja Abu Bakar paid an official visit to Pahang and cemented a new friendship. Towards the end of the same year, Bendahara Ahmad paid a return visit to Singapore and Johore which lasted for five months.

Johore's new interest in Pahang was closely related to the Maharaja's own problems and ambitions. Pahang was the only state left in the Peninsula where Johore could still freely pursue its own interests. What precisely these interests were soon emerged. The visit of the Bendahara to Singapore and Johore in 1880-1 stimulated a new interest in the resources of Pahang amongst the business and trading community. The price of tin was high and rumour soon had it that the Maharaja himself was seeking concessions, which in fact was the case. In 1882 William Cameron, a fellow of the Geographical Society, returned from a survey of Ulu Pahang with an encouraging report. Something like a little land-rush was the result. The first concessions—on extremely favourable and loose terms[63]—were granted in 1883, including one to a Chinese from Billiton with his Singapore associates which comprised nearly one-fifth of the state! Other often large concessions followed in the next few years, granted with scant regard for the rights of the chiefs whose ancestral lands were involved or for the complications that might follow. But they formed a source of great profit to the Sultan[64] and his coterie of favourites at Pekan. Amongst the concessionaries, one of the largest sponsors was the Maharaja who had now found a cheap way of rewarding his own sundry creditors[65] and circumventing his own pressing financial problems. As a consequence Maharaja Abu Bakar acquired a great influence with the court at Pekan and this influence was to play a decisive part in the events to come.

Another development in 1880 of which Wan Ahmad soon became aware was the arrival of a new governor in Singapore, Sir Frederick Weld.[66] Weld was a capable and forcible man with a reputation for getting things done. Now in his new post as governor of the Straits Settlements he fully intended to expand British in-

[a]See section 4(c), pp. 266 et seq.

fluence throughout the Peninsula, and Pahang was one of his targets. Sultan Ahmad met Weld for the first time during his visit to Singapore in 1880. On his second visit in November 1881, Weld made his first advance, suggesting the settlement of the question of the succession to the throne, and a treaty of friendship into the bargain. Wan Ahmad gave back one of his characteristically evasive replies. Undeterred, Weld followed this up in the following year by announcing an impending visit to Pahang, to which the Sultan responded by pleading for its postponement on the grounds that the special reception hall being prepared for distinguished visitors was not yet ready. It was clear that the ruler of Pahang was not interested in talking terms.

Realizing this, Weld now sought excuses for British intervention. In the beginning of 1883 he was considering the case of Syed Salim bin Akil,[67] and later in the year an opening seemed to be provided by the quarrel between the Sultan and his brother, Wan Mansor, over the succession to the throne. In what Winstedt describes as a 'rash moment',[68] Wan Ahmad had promised the throne to Mansor instead of to his own son, Mahmud, and now regretted his decision. In 1883 Wan Mansor wrote to W.H.M. Read[a] in Singapore imploring his influence to secure British intervention in the settlement of his dispute with his brother; he was prepared to receive a British Resident and said so to the governor, who interviewed him in Singapore. Wan Mansor then attempted to invade Pahang from the west but was prevented from doing so by the British.[69]

This prompted Wan Ahmad, fearful of British intervention, to send three emissaries to Singapore, who in April 1885 signed a document recognizing Mansor as the Raja Muda with an allowance of $200 per month. Weld now decided that the moment had come to act, and sent Swettenham into Pahang to settle outstanding questions such as the fate of Wan Mansor, a dispute over the Pahang-Jelebu boundary, and above all to persuade Wan Ahmad to sign a treaty with the British. Swettenham, who took the overland route (the first recorded European to do so), reached Pekan on 6 May 1885, to find the Sultan 'ill with anxiety'. He was also very unwilling to negotiate and was only induced to meet Swettenham after the latter had sent several very strongly-worded letters. Regarding the boundary dispute and reconciliation with Wan Mansor, the Sultan was prepared to give way, but he declined to give a ready answer to the idea of a treaty; he said he would have to consult his chiefs and would send his reply later. The reply, when it came in July, stated that while he and his children were living his chiefs 'had not the heart to have an officer of the Government', that is, a British Resident, in Pahang.

Wan Ahmad yields to Britain

Several factors account for the failure of Swettenham's mission of 1885. Wan Ahmad himself had little to gain and much to lose by the introduction of British agents into the state; Swettenham, whose visit to Pahang convinced him of the desirability of bringing it under British control, was also partly to blame with his overbearing attitude, for he spoke 'plainly and tactlessly' to the ruler. However, the decisive factor was the influence of Johore. Tuan Hitam, the Johore agent at Pekan, cabled Maharaja Abu Bakar in protest against the pressure Swettenham was

[a]See p. 143, note 24.

attempting to put on the Sultan. The Maharaja did not want a British protectorate in Pahang which would interfere with his own speculations there: a similar attitude governed the minds of other speculators and land-hunters who knew that a British Resident would soon tighten up conditions under which leases were granted.[70]

Johore's attitude dictated the course of events that followed. In 1886 Weld went to Pekan in person, only to meet with failure for the same reason; all that he elicited was the usual response that the chiefs must first be consulted and that the reply would follow later. At the beginning of 1887, Weld, who was now near exasperation point, entrusted this time one final mission to his nephew, Hugh Clifford. Clifford arrived at Pekan by the overland route in March 1887, collecting plenty of evidence of the discontent being created by the policy of land-leases on the way.[a] At first it seemed that his mission was going to meet with failure like those of his predecessors and at the end of ten days his position appeared hopeless. But all this changed at the end of the month with the unexpected arrival of the Dato Mentri of Johore and Syed Alsagoff.[b] They now intervened in favour of Britain, and by 10 April Clifford was on his way to Singapore with a letter from Sultan Ahmad requesting a treaty.

The reasons for Johore's change of policy were probably connected with the realization of Sultan Abu Bakar that he stood in need of the good will of the British government, while the concessionaries also began to see that their concessions once obtained would be more secure under British protection than without it.[71]

However, the end was not yet in sight. Clifford returned to Pekan to negotiate the terms of the treaty (which was to be based on that of 1885 between Britain and Johore) but when Weld arrived to sign it in August of the same year, Sultan Ahmad had changed his mind and wished to add impossible new conditions, including the right to appoint and dismiss the British agent, the recognition of his son, Mahmud, as heir, and his complete control over land-leases. Weld in reply put up his own terms, demanding greater powers for the British Agent.[72] The final deadlock ensued over an alteration in the original treaty regarding the defence of Pahang, and Weld sailed back from Pekan with the agreement unsigned. Once more, Johore came to the rescue, prompting a letter from Sultan Ahmad to the governor apologizing for 'his mistake and folly'. Clifford and the Dato Mentri of Johore went again to Pekan, were received royally, and two days after their arrival, on 8 October, the treaty was signed. By its terms, the Sultan accepted a British Agent, 'having functions similar to those of a consular officer' and British protection. Britain was to control Pahang's foreign relations and recognized Ahmad's position as Sultan.

The consolidation of British control

However, these new arrangements soon proved unsatisfactory. Clifford, the new Agent, did not possess enough power to force the ruler to accept his reforms, and the ruler was reluctant to be advised. Nothing short of residential status would fulfill British requirements, so they began once more to look for excuses to foist their authority on the country. Such a pretext was offered in February 1888, when a

aSee p. 146, note 63.
bSee p. 146, note 65.

Chinese of alleged British citizenship, called Go Hui (Chan You Wee), was stabbed
in the mouth near the precincts of the *istana* in Pekan. Clifford immediately declared that justice must be done if people were to believe that security of life and pro-

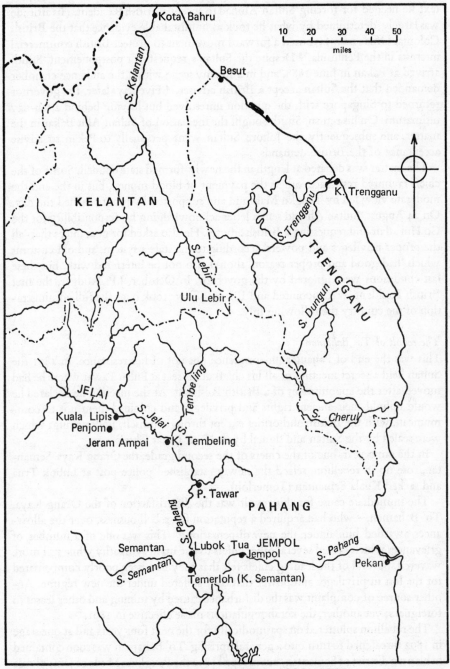

16. The Pahang Rebellion, 1890–1895

perty existed in the state, and half-hearted measures were ordered by the Sultan to arrest the culprits. But when Clifford was away the following month, Sultan Ahmad had Go's wife forcibly detained while the victim himself succumbed to his injuries.

Sir Cecil Smith, now governor in Singapore, decided that he had got the pretext he needed for forcing Sultan Ahmad to accept a British Resident. His attitude was largely determined by what he took as unmistakable evidence that the British Colonial Office now favoured a forward movement to protect British commercial interests in the Peninsula.[73] Despite the Sultan's requests for postponement, Smith arrived at Pekan in June 1888, and in a stormy scene within the audience chamber demanded that the Sultan accept a British adviser.[74] Five days later, the governor returned to Singapore with the question unresolved but leaving behind a ten-day ultimatum. On his return, Smith sought the mediation of Sultan Abu Bakar in the matter, and subsequently the Johore Sultan went personally to Pekan to advise acceptance of the British demands.

The matter was debated at length in the newly-formed state council. Some of the chiefs favoured resistance, others the payment of blood money, but in the end the moderate view led by Tengku Mahmud and supported by Johore carried the day. On 24 August, Sultan Ahmad sent a letter acknowledging his responsibility for the Go Hui affair and requesting a British adviser. He also asked for guarantees that 'all the proper privileges and powers' according to the state's system, and old customs which 'had good and proper reason' should also not be interfered with, but these last conditions were ignored by the governor. In October, J.P. Rodger, the first British Resident, was appointed and British officers took over the full administration of the country the following July.

The revolt of To' Bahaman

This was the end of Pahang's independence but not of her resistance. In 1891 the Sultan held a secret meeting of all his chiefs at his seat at Pulau Tawar where he had moved after the appointment of a British Resident. At the meeting he declared he would uphold their ancient rights and privileges and enjoined them not to communicate with the British authorities except through himself, undertakings which were sealed by the Sultan and signed by the Four Great Chiefs.

In the same year, one of the chiefs of the second grade, the Orang Kaya Semantan, rose up in rebellion, seized the newly established police post at Lubok Trua and sacked Kuala Semantan (Temerloh).

The immediate cause for this revolt was the dissatisfaction of the Orang Kaya, To' Bahaman,[75] who had acquired a reputation for rebelliousness, over the allowances awarded him under the new dispensation.[76] This was one of a number of grievances which caused several other chiefs to rise up in sympathy while still more wavered. Several of the leading chiefs felt that they had been poorly compensated for the loss in privileges and power that they suffered under the new régime. Another source of complaint was the disturbance caused by mining and other leases to foreigners; yet another, the kerah regulations made effective in 1891.

The rebellion spluttered on spasmodically for the next four years and at one stage in 1892 threatened to turn into a general uprising. To' Bahaman was soon contained in his own district of Semantan, but in April 1892 the Panglima Muda of Jempol rose up, killed two Europeans of the Pahang Exploration Company and threw the small

European community in Pekan into a panic. In the same month Mat Kilau, son of To' Gajah, favourite of the Sultan and one of the most influential Pahang chiefs, looted Kuala Lipis, while another powerful chief, the Maharaja Purba (Dato Jelai) was on the point of joining the rebellion. At the last moment, however, the last-mentioned chief was restrained from doing so by a special envoy from the Sultan whose own attitude towards events was at one period quite equivocal.

In the meantime the British sent forces from Singapore, Perak and Selangor and three warships patrolled off Pekan. By August 1892, they had got the upper hand, and the rebels now joined by To' Gajah himself, were refugees in Kelantan. In October, at a conference between the governor and the sultans of Pahang and Johore it was agreed to offer a general amnesty except for To' Bahaman and To' Gajah; at the same time efforts were to be made to persuade these two leaders to return to Pahang and give themselves up. To this end negotiations were conducted by the Maharaja Purba with the rebels in their Kelantan hideout which continued throughout 1893 but neither Bahaman nor Rasu[77] could be drawn to allay their suspicions as to their fate should they surrender.

Early in 1894 these two fell under the influence of Engku Syed of Paloh of Trengganu, who had acquired a great reputation locally for his magical powers. He now inspired To' Bahaman and Rasu to renew their sacred struggle against the infidel and gave them charms and raised a fighting force of one hundred from Besut and Ulu Lebir for the purpose. In July 1894 the rebels swept down the Tembeling, enlisting support as they went. They overran the police post at Kuala Tembeling and then took up positions at Jeram Ampai, a few miles upstream. About a week later detachments of the Colonial, Perak and Selangor police arrived to reinforce the Malay supporters of the Maharaja Purba already entrenched nearby. At the end of the month Jeram Ampai was attacked and stormed. Forty of the rebels were reputedly killed, the British force lost five.

Clifford and a force of police pursued the rebels to the Trengganu border but were called back on the orders of the governor. In 1895, having secured the permission of the Thai authorities, Clifford led an expedition into Kelantan and Trengganu to hunt down the rebels. He was not very successful as the ruler of Trengganu gave as much help and cover to the fugitives as he dared. A detachment under Duff[a] went to Besut and found the population uniformly hostile. Eventually Clifford and Duff succeeded in driving a body of the rebels to Kuala Trengganu, but there they escaped owing to the Sultan's assistance. In June Clifford withdrew from these states, acting on orders from Singapore. In November six rebel survivors, including To' Bahaman himself, surrendered to the Thai authorities and were removed to Thailand. Mat Kilau and his father reportedly died in Kelantan.[b]

So ended the revolt of To' Bahaman. From the British point of view it never represented more than a nuisance value which nevertheless further impoverished Pahang and influenced the development of their policy towards the protected states.[c] However, although the rebellion was on a small scale and never involved

[a]See p. 295 and p. 305, note 109.
[b]In December, 1969, in the Mosque at Pulau Tawar, Pahang, Mat Kilau publicly revealed himself to be still alive. His claim was officially recognized in August 1970. He died shortly afterwards.
[c]See Book II.

more than a few hundred men at any one time, its significance lies in its marking the last resistance of the old order to the new. With it died the remnants of the old Johore-Riau Empire.

[1]The British settlements on Sumatra's west coast (Benkulen Presidency) were too far off the beaten track to be taken into account.

[2]The French Revolutionary and Napoleonic Wars commenced in 1793 and lasted virtually without a break until 1815, Holland was overrun in 1795.

[3]The vicissitudes of war led to frequent changes of the Johore capital which was usually located on the Johore river or in the Riau archipelago. Amongst the sites of Johore capitals were Riau (Bintang), Johore Lama, Panchor, Seluyut, Batu Sawar, Kota Tinggi and Sayong Pinang.

[4]The Johore Malays (and their allies) inflicted heavy reverses on the Achinese in 1540 (off Aru/ Deli), 1582 (in Johore), 1589 (Aru), and 1601 (at Batu Sawar). The Achinese, on the other hand, controlled Johore's former vassals of Aru, Siak, Kedah, Perak and Pahang for the greater part of this period (up till 1641); razed the Johore capital and killed, captured or drove out the Johore ruler on three occasions—1564 (Johore Lama—Sultan Ala'uddin); 1613 (Batu Sawar— Raja Bongsu); 1623 (Lingga—Sultan Abdullah, former Raja Bongsu).

[5]This was the start of the long Dutch connexion with Johore. A second treaty was concluded in 1606 with the Dutch admiral, Matelief: the Dutch promised to help the Sultan recapture Malacca from the Portuguese but did not recognize his claim to the town; he was to have all the guns captured and half the loot. In return the Dutch were granted the duty-free monopoly of trade with Johore. Prior to 1641, the Dutch made two unsuccessful attempts on Malacca; in 1605 and 1607.

[6]The quarrel with Jambi originated when the ambitious and influential Laksamana of Johore who had an eye on the sultanate, married his daughter to Raja Ibrahim, heir to the Johore throne, thereby causing the cancellation of Ibrahim's engagement to a daughter of the Pange-ran of Jambi. The Laksamana absorbed most authority into his hands when Raja Ibrahim came to the throne in 1677 and completely dominated the scene when Ibrahim died in 1685 and was succeeded by his son, Mahmud, a minor. Already highly unpopular amongst his brother chiefs, the Laksamana sought to buttress his own position by allying with the Dutch but was driven into a Trengganu exile all the same in 1688. The Jambi war provided the occasion for Siak to assert its independence.

[7]Sultan Mahmud (1685–99) turned out to be an autocratic ruler. Assassinated at Kota Tinggi without any issue, the throne was taken by Abdul Jalil Riayat Shah, Bendahara and direct descendant of the line of Malacca Bendaharas. The new ruler was more concerned with reli-gion than government and left the management of affairs in the hands of his younger brother, the Raja Muda, who was both arrogant and unscrupulous. A group of rebellious Johore chiefs invited Raja Kechil of Siak to take over the throne. Despite an agreement with the Bugis for their aid, in 1718 Raja Kechil seized the throne by himself. The Bugis-Siak Menangkabau quarrel which followed culminated in Daing Parani driving Raja Kechil from Johore by a stratagem in 1722. The Bugis then made Raja Sulaiman, a younger son of Sultan Abdul Jalil (who had been killed by agents of Raja Kechil in Pahang), the Sultan.

[8]Raja Kechil continued to oppose the Bugis in the Straits till the 1730s, when worn out and lovelorn he retired from the scene. Failing to retake Johore after 1722, he combatted the Bugis in the Peninsula Menangkabau states, Perak and Kedah but was ultimately worsted in every case.

[9]Daing Kemboja simply sent his nephew, Raja Haji, past the muzzles of the Malay guns to Sultan Sulaiman's palace in Riau and demanded his reinstatement. In the absence of the vigo-rous leader of opposition to the Bugis, Sultan Mansor of Trengganu, Sultan Sulaiman gave way. After his death, the old Johore-Riau Empire knew three rulers—Abdul Jalil Muazzam Shah (1761); Ahmad Riayat Shah (1761); and Mahmud Shah (1761–1812). Abdul Jalil died mysteriously in Selangor; Ahmad, his son and successor, a minor, shortly afterwards. The Bugis then proclaimed Sulaiman's one-year-old grandson, Mahmud, as Sultan despite Malay protests in favour of a younger brother of Sulaiman's.

[10]The Dutch refused to admit Raja Haji's claim to a share of the booty—1,154 chests of opium.

[11]Van Braam's fleet had been sent out from Europe to restore Holland's shaky position in South-East Asian waters after her conflict with Britain during the American War of Independence (1776-83).

[12]Riau's trade had grown greatly in volume and importance since the 1750s, and it had become a key entrepôt for British ships engaged in the China trade. (See Bassett, *British Commercial Interests*, op. cit. pp. 137-8.)

[13]France had occupied Holland in January 1795: the British acted on the authority of the Dutch Stadthouder (the Kew Letters) who was a refugee in England.

[14]Shortly before he handed the town back to the Dutch as agreed by treaty in 1814.

[15]C. J. Wolterbeek, the leader of the Dutch expedition to reoccupy Malacca and its dependencies.

[16]Thomas Stamford Raffles: son of a sea-captain in the West Indian trade, born at sea in 1781: 1795, joined East India Company as clerk in London: 1805, sent to Penang as Assistant Secretary— learning Malay on the voyage out: 1808, at Malacca—prevented total destruction of fort and abandonment of settlement: 1810, appointed by Minto British Agent to Malay Rajas to prepare way for invasion of Java: 1811, accompanied expedition, left behind in Java as Lt.-Governor till 1816: 1818, Lt.-Governor of Benkulen: sought Hasting's approval for new British settlement: 1826, died of apoplexy in England.

[17]Although Raffles and Munshi Abdullah only mention Malays, there is evidence of Chinese settlement on the island—probably more than the 30 mentioned by Newbold.

[18]On hearing of these letters, Farquhar, now administering Singapore, made both Sultan Husain and the Temenggong sign statements of disavowal.

[19]The following excerpt from a letter from the Bendahara of Pahang (Wan Mutahir) to Sultan Mahmud of Riau-Lingga in 1855 reveals the way in which a Malay prince viewed the European settlement of their domains: 'Thirdly, Your Highness enquires of me about the division of territory between the English and the Dutch; I admit ignorance in this matter as I am not directly involved. What I know is that, the people before our time have made it such that whoever is Ruler, to him belongs the empire of Johore and the nine islands and no one is entitled to them except with the Ruler's consent.' Quoted from 'A Conqueror's Correspondence A Century Ago', related by Ungku Pengiran Anum (Ungku Syed Abdul Kadir of Kuala Trengganu), *Malaysia in History*, Vol. 6, No. 2, 1961.

[20]The treaty of 1784, renewed by Wolterbeek in 1818.

[21]Mills, op. cit. p. 26. As for the pirates, strong suspicions attached to Sultan Husain and to the Temenggong of Johore as well.

[22]The British burnt three kampongs, 14 large perahus, 30 to 40 smaller ones and many fast rowing boats. There was little resistance and few casualties on either side.

[23]Baginda Omar was the uncle of the Riau Sultan by the marriage of his sister to Mahmud's father, Sultan Mohamed Shah.

[24]W.H.M. Read, head of one of Singapore's leading commercial firms, A.L. Johnstone & Co: born, 1819: came to Singapore in 1841: resided there till 1887: acquired great influence and played important rôle in extending British interests in Johore, Pahang, Selangor, Sungai Ujong and Perak: also had close relations with King Mongkut of Thailand: was Dutch Consul-General in Singapore from 1857-85: appointed first unofficial member of Legislative Council in 1867: died in England in 1900.

[25]This agreement did not end the pretensions or the intrigues of Sultan Ali to gain a share in Johore's development—with the encouragement of Read and other backers. When Sultan Ali died in 1877 the title was disputed again, but this time by his own descendants. The outcome was that the territory was annexed by the Maharaja, the title lapsed, but the successors were still given the pension!

[26]The Temenggong's income was reckoned at 100,000 Spanish dollars per annum by Governor Blundell in 1857.

[27]That is, Weld's attempt to undermine the treaties of 1876 and 1877 which gave Johore a stake in the Sri Menanti Confederation annoyed the Maharaja. Abu Bakar's reliance on his Singapore lawyers, Rodyk and Davidson, rather than on the governor for advice, particularly after 1880, riled Weld.

[28]In particular, the Maharaja's concession of over 100,000 acres of land together with various sweeping rights, including that of issuing banknotes in Johore, to the Malay Peninsula Agency in 1884. Rumour soon spread abroad that French financial backing was involved. Weld pointed out that after he had been 'rescued' by the British from an unwise concession a few years previously, the Maharaja had promised to seek the advice of Singapore before making any fresh deals of that sort.

[29]Maharaja Abu Bakar was personally on good terms with Queen Victoria and well-known in British court circles; he was first received by the British monarch on his tour of 1866.

[30]Amongst other terms of the treaty were provisions regarding the succession which would be recognized by Britain as 'lawfully succeeding according to Malay custom'; extradition rights; trade and transit arrangements between Singapore and Pahang; and an agreement regarding the validity of Straits coinage in Johore. The point about the title of the Sultan as 'ruler of the State and territory of Johore' was to preclude any possible claim by him to the Riau archipelago. The independent status of Johore subsequent to the Treaty was upheld by the Colonial Office which declared in the Mighell v. Sultan of Johore case of 1893 that Johore's relations with Britain were 'of alliance and not of suzerainty and dependence'. For a full treatment of this period see Thio, 'British Policy towards Johore: from advice to control' and Sinclair, 'The British Advance in Johore, 1885–1914', both in *J.M.B.R.A.S.*, Vol. XL, Pt. 1, 1967.

[31]The occasion was the presentation of the estimates for that year, in which Weld had earmarked $3,600 for the costs of installing a British Agent. His grounds were that this was necessary for dealing with questions of immigration, extradition and general relations between the state and the colony. Opposed by all the unofficials on the Legislative Council, they were led by their senior member, Thomas Shelford, the representative of the Chambers of Commerce and a partner in Paterson, Simons & Co., who were the Sultan's agents in Johore. The unofficials with justification suspected Weld's motives and feared that official interference would impede their private interests. A similar attitude governed the merchant and business community of Singapore towards British policy in Pahang at this period, refer p. 138.

[32]The Board was to advise the Sultan on all important matters and sat in London. Comprising a chairman, vice-chairman and four other members, both Abu Bakar and his son, Ibrahim, were careful to appoint prominent ex-colonial officials or others with close connexions with leaders of the British government. The chairmen of the Board during its brief existence were: 1. Lt.-General W. Fielding (1886–95)—cousin of Sir Robert Herbert, then Permanent Under-Secretary at the Colonial Office; 2. Sir Robert Herbert (1895–1905)—on his retirement from the Colonial Office; 3. Sir Cecil Clementi Smith (1905–6)—former governor of the Straits Settlements (1887–93) and appointed to the Board as vice-chairman in 1899.

[33]For example, in 1886 he laid claim to the islands when Britain had already formally conceded sovereignty over them to the Dutch; in 1891, the Sultan refused to suppress Chinese Secret Societies in Johore as a measure to keep in line with recent Colony legislation, maintaining that they provided the only effective means for controlling the Chinese and that in any case there was only one—the Ghee Hin; similarly, he declined to suppress the *Wai Seng* lotteries arguing that to do so would be an exercise in futility.

[34]Aged 22 at his accession, Sultan Ibrahim had had little formal schooling; was commissioned a Second Lieutenant in the Johore Military Forces and became A.D.C. to his father; proclaimed Tengku Mahkota in 1891; made first overseas visit in that year. Not given much chance to participate in state affairs by his father, the young prince devoted his energies to becoming a keen sportsman, hunter and horse-racer.

[35]The *Straits Budget* in 1897 complained of his 'oriental despotism'; his uncle, Tengku Khalid, complained to the British governor in 1898 about the Sultan's unconstitutional acts, but he had axes of his own to grind. For more details, refer Sinclair, op. cit. p. 91.

[36]The English firms of Pauling & Co. as contractors, and Barrie & Leslie as engineers. He also raised a loan at less favourable rates for its construction from private financiers.

[37]Swettenham informed the Sultan that the FMS government would refuse to connect the two lines if Sultan Ibrahim acted independently.

[38]By the terms of the convention, the railway was to be jointly controlled by the F.M.S. and Johore governments through a Railway Board; ownership was formally vested in the state of Johore and the Sultan's private contractors and engineers were to receive compensation; active construction work was to be carried out by the F.M.S. government, and Johore was to pay interest on the capital costs. According to Chai Hon-chan the detailed terms of the Convention are not known. See Chai Hon-chan, *The Development of British Malaya, 1896–1909*, Kuala Lumpur, 1960, especially Ch. V.

[39]Frank Swettenham, Pickering (Protector of Chinese in the Straits Settlements) and others in the Colony argued that the demise of the Sultan provided an ideal moment for doing so, but the Colonial Office rejected such proposals as 'ungenerous' and as a 'breach of faith' towards the late ruler.

[40]Swettenham had been told to pay special attention to the police, prison, schools, hospital, etc. Although Swettenham criticized various aspects, he apparently regarded Johore's administration as the best possible under the existing circumstances.

[41]Under the terms of the concession, the Johore government was to guarantee a 5 per cent dividend on all preference shares. An initial capital of £10,000 was raised for the Corporation in London.

[42]The Advisory Board, dominated as it was by colonial ex-officials, clearly would not promote activities detrimental to British interests, but at the same time its members felt obliged to campaign for the best terms they could get for the state. During the railway crisis, for example, the Board strove hard to achieve a reasonable bargain between both parties and in the last resort backed the Sultan in his own interest against the proposals of the Colonial Office which, they considered, placed too heavy a burden on Johore.

[43]The interview was held in the presence of the High Commissioner, Sir John Anderson, the Johore State Secretary, Abdul Rahman Andak and two Colonial Office officials.

[44]Abdul Rahman bin Andak played an important role in shaping Johore's policy from the time of his appointment as confidential secretary to Sultan Abu Bakar in 1885. A nephew of the ruler, he was promoted Secretary to the Johore government in 1893; also made Dato' Seri Amar di-Raja and appointed on to the Johore Council of State. Described variously by British officials as 'astute', 'a clever, little fellow' and 'an evil genius', they suspected that he lay largely behind Sultan Abu Bakar's attempts to assert his independence after 1885 and that he dominated the young Sultan Ibrahim. His command of English and his long experience of Europe and European society made him well equipped for handling Johore's relations with British officialdom in Singapore and London. Anderson clashed with Abdul Rahman specifically in 1907 over the granting of the Johore opium and spirit farms to a Chinese of whom the governor disapproved. Abdul Rahman retired to Europe with his German wife on a pension of £1,000 a year.

[45]In 1911 the line was leased to the F.M.S. government and eventually it passed completely from Johore's control.

[46]General Adviser was the term usually applied to designate European officers employed by the Thai government in Bangkok, where their advisory as opposed to executive capacities were rigorously defined.

[47]Douglas G. Campbell had previously been the British Resident in Negri Sembilan and was considered one 'of the best officers of the S.S. and F.M.S. service' (quoted by Thio, 'British Policy towards Johore', p. 33).

[48]As was the case with the leaders of Kedah (refer p. 111), Sultan Ibrahim felt that to deal through the High Commissioner for the Malay States, even though he was the same person as the governor of the Straits Settlements, was to admit the inferiority of his position and would be the first step to subordination to the F.M.S. government in Kuala Lumpur.

[49]In 1912 Campbell officially informed Ibrahim that no European officials would attend his birthday celebrations in view of the inferior status accorded to them at other state functions.

[50]Raja Ali was a brother of Sultan Abdul Rahman of Riau who was deposed by the Dutch in 1911 (refer p. 124). Implicated in the alleged plot against Dutch sovereignty, Raja Ali fled to Johore where he was granted asylum and appointed Ketua Ugama despite the protests of governor Young that he was a threat to 'the peace and order of a neighbouring state'. However, he was made to leave Johore on the insistence of Young, as part of the settlement of 1914.

[51]The main complaints were that the convicts were kept in irons, warders carried canes and abused their authority, medical facilities were inadequate and convicts were also compelled to work on the Sultan's estates.

[52]In 1903 Swettenham had described the prison as 'most creditable in every respect'.

[53]250,000 acres were taken up for rubber during the first half of 1910. The same year saw the peak of the boom in rubber prices.

[54]Sultan Ibrahim died in 1959. He was entitled to have been elected as the first Yang di-Pertuan Agong of Malaya in 1957 but declined the post.

[55]Appointed when aged around 25: descendant of the Malacca Bendahara line who succeeded to the throne of the Johore-Riau Empire on the assassination of Sultan Mahmud at Kota Tinggi, 1699.

[56]This was a ruse to gain the Bendahara's support for Ali's claims: the Bendahara did not oblige.

[57]In 1858, governor Blundell thwarted a scheme of two European adventurers to raise a force of European sailors and Bugis warriors to drive Wan Ahmad out of Pahang—much to the annoyance of the Temenggong and his faction.

[58]Wan Ahmad launched two invasions of Pahang by sea. The first (the war of the Kemaman men), lasting from November 1857 till February 1858, was a failure. The second attempt came in March 1861, but was also unsuccessful and he withdrew to Endau where he engaged the forces of Wan Mutahir and the Temenggong with better fortune—March to May 1861.

[59]In 1861 the Temenggong signed a treaty of mutual alliance with Bendahara Mutahir: subsequently he kept Mutahir's forces in supplies, put pressure on Perak and Trengganu not to intervene on Wan Ahmad's side, financed raids into Pahang and offered $500 for Wan Ahmad's head.

[60]Clifford described Wan Ahmad's influence in the state as follows: 'Thereafter, for more than a quarter of a century, he ruled a turbulent people in such wise that no man in all that lawless state dared think above a whisper without his leave. He so impressed his will upon his subjects that for them his lightest word, his merest whim, his hinted desire were law, and though.... he governed selfishly using his "high place as a perch for low ambition and a vantage-ground for pleasure", his was a personality, a force, that kindled the imagination and claimed the tribute of a reluctant admiration'. From his *Bush-whacking and other Asiatic Tales and Memories*, quoted by Thio, 'The Extension of British control to Pahang', *J.M.B.R.A.S.*, Vol. XXX, Pt. 1, p. 57.

[61]Pulau Tioman and islands north of latitude 2° went to Pahang; those south of the line to Johore: the dispute arose out of the cession of these islands by Wan Mutahir in the treaty of 1861 with the Temenggong which Wan Ahmad refused to recognize. The 1868 compromise was not finalized till 1897.

[62]Wan Ahmad rightly suspected the Temenggong's complicity in the attempted invasions of Pahang in 1868 and 1870 by the sons of Wan Mutahir.

[63]The usual conditions for these concessions were a 50 to 99 year lease, with a royalty for the Sultan of 10 per cent on all minerals exported; grace of 12 months to 3 years was granted for mining operations to commence. The consequences that could occur from granting such vague conditions are well illustrated by the concession at Penjom, near Raub, granted in April 1885 to two Malays and a European. The vaguely-worded concession gave rights over land worked by old-established Malay and Chinese mines. Chinese miners at Jalis were expelled with meagre compensation; the Malay gold-miners in the lands of the Orang Kaya Lipis were expropriated without any compensation at all. The future of whole villages was at stake. When Clifford arrived on his Pekan journey of 1887 he found both Malays and Chinese in great agitation, and a Chinese attack on the concession's offices was restrained with great difficulty by the Orang Kaya Lipis.

[64]Wan Ahmad assumed the title of Sultan in 1882, on the advice of Abu Bakar of Johore; was proclaimed as such by his chiefs in 1884 and his title recognized by the British in 1887.

[65]Principal amongst these was the Singapore merchant, Syed Alsagoff; his Legal Advisors, Rodyk and Davidson, Johore's commercial agents in Singapore, Paterson, Simon & Co, and his private secretary, William Hole, were all involved in the Pahang concessions. The Johore ruler reportedly owed £140,000 ($1,200,000) in London alone.

[66]Frederick Aloysius Weld: born in England 1824, migrated to New Zealand 1844, became Prime Minister of New Zealand 1864: appointed Governor of Western Australia, 1867: of Tasmania, 1874: Governor of the Straits Settlements, 1880–87.

[67]An Arab, born in Penang, therefore a British subject; died of suspected poisoning after intriguing with a lady of Wan Ahmad's household. Inconclusive evidence led to the matter being dropped.

[68]R.O. Winstedt, *A History of Malaya*, p. 233.

[69]In fact, it is possible that before doing so, the British actually encouraged Wan Mansor as a means of putting pressure on Wan Ahmad. See Thio, 'The Extension of British Control to Pahang', pp. 54–55.

[70]For example, William Fraser, whose brother helped found Fraser & Neaves, one of the land speculators in Pahang at the time, spoke of his opposition to the imposition of an 'obnoxious Resident'. Quoted by Thio, 'The Extension of British Control to Pahang', p. 61.

[71]Abu Bakar was hoping for official British support to help overcome his financial embarrassments.

[72]Wan Ahmad's change of front was occasioned by false rumours about British plans to annex the state spread by concessionaires in Kuantan antagonized by Clifford's efforts to curb their leases.

[73]Connected with the affair of the Pahang Corporation, formed by William Fraser on the basis of a 2,000 square mile concession, he and his associates acquired from the original lessee in 1888; the Corporation become involved in a dispute arising out of the rectification of the Pahang-Jelebu boundary and appealed when the Singapore authorities' findings were not in its favour: the Colonial Office supported the Corporation's appeal.

[74]Swettenham who witnessed the scene says: 'The more vehement was the Governor in his demands, the more obstinate was the Raja in refusing them.' Quoted by Thio, 'The Extension of British Control to Pahang', p. 71.

[75]Partly Jakun, of humble origins: first employed as menial servant in the Bendahara's household: distinguished himself fighting for Wan Ahmad in the Pahang Civil War; rewarded with second grade rank of Dato' Setia Perkasa Pahlawan of Semantan: took part in Selangor campaign: influence in Temerloh increased on death of its territorial chief whose vacancy was not filled; ambitious and independent, once defied Wan Ahmad's order not to collect taxes—

but was pardoned: described as a born fighter and probably had the best knowledge of jungle-lore in the Peninsula.

[76] Allowances were fixed at the second meeting of the new State Council in January 1890. To' Bahaman was one of seven leading chiefs who expressed their dissatisfaction at the sums awarded and who sent an ultimatum to Rodger, stating that they would refuse to recognize the laws of 'your council' unless the allowances were reviewed; the British Resident replied that only the Council could alter its own decisions, that the Government was responsible for fixing allowances and that he would entertain no further complaints unless more courteously addressed. The reply was not addressed to To' Bahaman because he was considered of inferior rank.

[77] To' Gajah's original name: he was deprived of his titles in August 1892.

---

6. THE JOHORE-RIAU EMPIRE: CHRONOLOGY

A. 1511–1824

1511	Portuguese conquest of Malacca
1513	Sultan Mahmud founds new base in Riau archipelago
1513–1640	Triangular contest with Portuguese and Achinese for control of the Straits of Malacca
1603–41	Alliance with Dutch against Portuguese Malacca
1660–75	The Jambi quarrel; start of Bugis ascendancy
1684–89	Treaties with the Dutch granting monopoly rights
1699	Assassination of Sultan Mahmud; end of direct Malacca Line
1706–22	Menangkabau (Siak)-Bugis struggle over Johore
1722–45	First period of Bugis ascendancy at Riau
1745–60	Dutch-Johore alliance; the Siak crisis
1760–84	Second period of Bugis ascendancy
1784	Dutch expel Bugis from Riau; establish garrison there (1785)
1787	Lanuns (invited by S. Mahmud) drive out Dutch from Riau
1788	Dutch return to Riau. S. Mahmud flees
1795	S. Mahmud reinstated (by the British); Bugis immigration permitted again
1812	Death of Sultan Mahmud. Succession dispute. Bugis favourite, Abdul Rahman becomes ruler
1818	Farquhar's treaty with Sultan Abdul Rahman
	Dutch re-establish themselves in Riau
1819	British occupy Singapore and recognize Sultan Husain
1824	Anglo-Dutch Treaty. Empire divided between islands and mainland

B. The Riau-Lingga Sultanate

1825	Treaty with Dutch establishing new sultanate
1830	New Treaty with Dutch concerning suppression of piracy
1836	British destroy pirate haunt of Galang

1837	Third treaty with Dutch regulating Sultan's position
1841	Accession of Sultan Mahmud Muzaffar Shah
1857	Sultan Mahmud deposed by Dutch
1911	Sultanate abolished by the Dutch

C. The Sultanate of Johore

1824	Treaty with Britain providing for cession of Singapore island
1835–55	Johore title succession dispute
1858	Temenggong Ibrahim intervenes in Pahang civil war
1862	Accession of Temenggong Abu Bakar
1868	Abu Bakar becomes Maharaja
1885	Treaty with Britain defining relations; Abu Bakar becomes Sultan
1895	Promulgation of Johore constitution Death of Sultan Abu Bakar; accession of Sultan Ibrahim
1914	Johore forced to accept a General Adviser (British)

D. The Sultanate of Pahang

1853	Bendahara Ali assumes status of independent ruler
1857	Death of Ali; accession of Wan Mutahir
1858–63	Pahang Civil War
1863	Triumph of Wan Ahmad
1868	Pahang accepts British mediation over Pulau Tioman problem
1880	Reconciliation of Johore and Pahang
1882	Wan Ahmad assumes the title of Sultan
1883+	Land speculation in Pahang
1885	Swettenham's mission to Pekan
1886	Weld's mission to Pahang
1887	Clifford's mission to Pahang; Wan Ahmad accepts British agent
1888	Pahang receives British Resident
1891–5	To' Bahaman's rebellion

E. The Malacca Line

1. Mahmud, last Sultan of Malacca, 1511–29
2. Ala'uddin Riayat Shah I, son of (1); died at Acheh, 1529–64
3. Muzaffar, son of (2), 1564–80
4. Abdul Jalil Shah I, nephew of (3), 1580
5. Ali Jalla Abdul Jalil Riayat Shah, father of (4), 1580–97
6. Ala'uddin Riayat Shah II, son of (5) & half brother of (4), 1597–1613
7. Abdullah Ma'ayat Shah, brother of (6), 1613–23

8. Abdul Jalil Shah II, son of (6), 1623–77
9. Ibrahim Shah, son of (7), 1677–85
10. Mahmud Shah, son of (9); assassinated at Kota Tinggi, 1685–99

F. The Bendahara Line

1. Abdul Jalil Riayat Shah, descended from Tun Mutahir, Bendahara. of Malacca; assassinated in Pahang 1699–1720
2. Sulaiman, restored with Bugis help, 1720–60
3. Abdul Jalil Muazzam Shah, 1760–1
4. Ahmad Riayat Shah, 1761
5. Mahmud, 1761–1812

G. The Sultanate of Riau-Lingga

1. Abdul Rahman, as ruler of Johore-Riau till 1819, 1812–30
2. Mohamed Shah, 1832–42
3. Mahmud Muzaffar Shah, deposed by Dutch, 1842–57
4. Sulaiman, 1857–83
5. Abdul Rahman, deposed by Dutch and Sultanate abolished, 1883–1911

H. Johore

1. Abdul Rahman, Temenggong; acceded 1806, 1819–25
2. Ibrahim, Temenggong, 1825–62
3. Abu Bakar, Temenggong: Maharaja (1868); Sultan (1885) 1862–95
4. Ibrahim, Sultan, 1895–1959
5. Ismail, Sultan, 1959

I. Pahang

1. Ali, Bendahara, 1806–57
2. Wan Mutahir, Bendahara, 1857–63
3. Wan Ahmad, Bendahara; Sultan (1882), 1863–1914
4. Mahmud, Sultan, 1914–17
5. Abdullah, Sultan, 1917–32
6. Abu Bakar, Sultan, 1932

THE MENANGKABAU LANDS

RAFFLES describing an expedition which he made into Menangkabau territory in 1818, spoke with surprise of 'the wreck of a great empire,' with 'a cultivation highly advanced, and manners, customs and productions in a great degree new and un-described'.[1] Indeed, Menangkabau civilization was little known to the outside world in the nineteenth century and the manner in which this ancient people came to lose their independence and to be divided between two colonial powers during this period attracted very little attention.

The Menangkabau state of Melayu was probably the cradle of Malay culture and civilization. Situated in the hills of the Padang Highlands, Menangkabau power was at its greatest extent and influence in the years that followed the decline of Sri Vijaya during the twelfth and thirteenth centuries.[a] With the rise of Javanese power the empire began to go into eclipse. By the time of the rise of the Sultanate of Malacca, Menangkabau had already become an inland agricultural state of peasant-farmers which played little direct part in the politics of the Straits.

However, the development of Malacca in the middle of the fifteenth century led to Menangkabau migration to the Peninsula on a large scale for the first time. This process was accelerated during the Portuguese period in Malacca that followed. Furthermore during the eighteenth century, Menangkabau influence also made it-self felt through the activities of Raja Kechil, the Menangkabau ruler of the east Sumatran state of Siak. By 1800, there were two main areas of Menangkabau settle-ment and influence—both inland; one the original homeland above Padang on Sumatra's west coast, and the other the more recent settlements in the Malay Penin-sula behind Malacca, a collection of small, autonomous chieftainships forming what is now Negri Sembilan.

SUMATRAN MENANGKABAU

Menangkabau proper, at the time of Raffles' visit, had long been in a state of poli-tical obscurity. A population of some one and a half millions lived in the hills of the interior, farming and trading down the rivers which flowed to the west and east coasts; but their political influence had long since vanished from the lowlands. There was a traditional monarchy, that of the shadowy maharajas of Pagar Ruyong whose heartland was in Tanah Datar near Padang Panjang; but this royalty which once claimed suzerainty over the whole of Sumatra, had been stripped of virtually all its temporal powers which were now distributed amongst territorial chiefs, and it survived primarily as a religious symbol over a land whose government was largely regional and autonomous. Nevertheless the prestige of the princes of Pagar Ruyong was such that the Menangkabau colonists across the water in the Peninsula sent for its scions to become their overlords.[2]

The Menangkabau lands were famed for their gold and for their pepper which led, after the fall of the Malacca sultanate, to the domination of the ports along the west and east coasts through which these articles of trade passed, by the Achinese and Bantamese, and subsequently by the Dutch. By the middle of the sixteenth century the Achinese were claiming the pepper monopoly on the west coast as far south as Benkulen and Silebar, whilst their effective control ran as far as Barus. With Acheh's rapid decline after 1640[b] the Dutch began to take their place. Ex-ploiting the resentment of the Menangkabau planters at the Achinese monopolists,

[a]Refer pp. 30 and 31.
[b]Refer pp. 225-6.

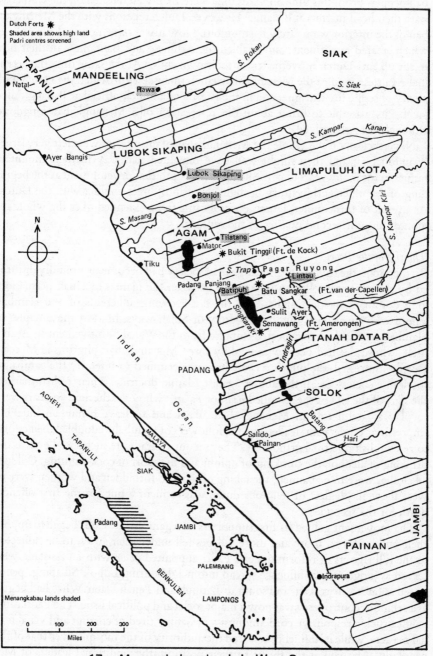

Dutch Forts ✳
Shaded area shows high land
Padri centres screened

TAPANULI

MANDEELING

Natal

Rawa

SIAK

S. Rokan

S. Siak

Ayer Bangis

LUBOK SIKAPING

Lubok Sikaping

LIMAPULUH KOTA

S. Kampar   Kanan

Bonjol

N

S. Masang

AGAM

Tilatang

Mator

✳ Bukit Tinggi (Ft. de Kock)

Tiku

S. Trap   Pagar Ruyong

Padang Panjang

Batipuh

Lintau

Batu Sangkar   (Ft. van der-Capellen)

Sulit Ayer

Semawang   (Ft. Ameronqen)

S. Singkarak!

S. Kampar Kiri

TANAH DATAR

Indian

PADANG

SOLOK

S. Indragiri

Ocean

Batang

Hari

Salido

Painan

ACHEH

TAPANULI

MALAYA

SIAK

Padang

JAMBI

JAMBI

PAINAN

Menangkabau lands shaded

BENKULEN

PALEMBANG

Indrapura

LAMPONGS

0   100   200   300

Miles

17. Menangkabau lands in West Sumatra

in 1663 the Dutch were able to bring about the closing of the Painan Contract with the chiefs of Indrapura, Tiku and Padang, the main outlets for the best Menangkabau pepper. From this time onwards they were firmly established on the west coast with their headquarters at Padang.[3] However, Dutch relations with the Menangkabau of the interior were rarely harmonious. Now it was *their* monopolistic policies which created resentment, and enabled the Achinese and Bantamese in their turn to stir up anti-Dutch movements for their own ends.[4] At the same time the perennial rivalries amongst the Menangkabau chiefs themselves provided the Dutch with plenty of scope for intrigue, and in the late 1660s a Dutch official at Padang called Jacob Pits was able to bring about the re-creation of a Menangkabau kingdom, although very shortlived.[5]

Nevertheless, on the whole the Menangkabau of the interior were left very largely untouched, and they might well have remained that way in their mountain fastnesses for many years to come had not a new internal development at the beginning of the nineteenth century brought them into direct conflict with the Dutch. As a result of this conflict, Dutch control came to be extended over the whole region during the second quarter of the century.

The rise of the Padri

By the 1800s, the rhythm of Menangkabau society had become profoundly disturbed by the growing religious contention between the ulamas of Shiah persuasion, long dominant in local affairs, and the fast-growing adherents of the Hambali school who questioned the unorthodoxy of Shiah ways. In 1803 the disciples of Hambali received an unexpected impulse from the Wahabbi movement in Arabia itself, whose rise had been witnessed by three Menangkabau pilgrims in Mecca.[6] Deeply impressed, the pilgrims came home determined to intensify the campaign to cleanse society of all the abuses against Islamic doctrine. Their return marked the start of the rise of the so-called *padri* or *pidari*,[7] who over the next 30 years were to play a fateful role in Menangkabau affairs and to leave behind an indelible impression. Under padri leadership, the followers of Hambali redoubled their efforts to re-establish doctrinal orthodoxy. They set out to eradicate such social evils as the drinking of alcohol, the smoking of opium and the sport of cock-fighting. Coloured clothes were to be banned, the taking of tobacco forbidden and women were to wear the veil. Neglect of religious duties was to incur a fine for the first offence, death for the second.

The movement gained its first supporters in Agam. As the Padri began to impose their will by force, more and more villages fell under their sway, to be subjected to the full rigours of reform under a Padri-appointed *imam* with an assistant who served as judge. Their influence spread into neighbouring Lubok Sikaping, penetrated as far north as Rau, and south to Batipuh and Tanah Datar. What had begun as a religious controversy was now a major social and political issue. The Padri campaign struck a responsive cord amongst a peasantry tired of corrupt and venal feudal masters, while its influence restored the authority of the mosque over that of the penghulu. Alarmed at the threat to their position, the traditional leaders of Menangkabau society rallied to their side all those who, for one reason or another, were opposed to the Padri. As a result, the Padri found ranged against them under penghulu leadership all those elements who felt the need to defend their traditional rights and privileges. The stage was set for civil war. Fighting broke out in Agam, causing a Padri withdrawal to the north, where they established their headquarters and main stronghold at Bonjol, under the captaincy of the Tuanku Imam. The heart of the movement nevertheless remained in Agam. In Tanah Datar the Padri met with the most spirited opposition for this was the heartland of the Menangkabau aristocracy and contained the seat of royal power at Pagar Ruyong. But under Tuanku Pasaman, who came from this district, the Padri gained a foothold and in 1809, under circumstances which remain obscure,[8] succeeded in eliminating the royal house altogether.

Dutch intervention and the First Padri War

However, matters had already come to a head around 1819, just at the moment that the British were handing back to the Dutch their possessions on the west coast.[9] It was to the Dutch that in despair some of the aristocratic opponents of the Padri, now refugees in Padang, turned for assistance. Raffles whilst still at Padang, had stationed a small garrison at Semawang on the banks of Lake Singkarak in order to protect the district from Padri attacks. Now this was withdrawn and the Tuanku Suruasu and several *penghulu* appealed to the Dutch for its replacement. The Dutch sent a small detachment, then withdrew it, for at this period they were anxious to avoid the further extension of territory. Nevertheless, the Menangkabau supporters of *adat* continued to press for Dutch intervention, and in the end succeeded. The advantages for the Dutch were obvious. At one and the same time they could crush the Padri who spoilt their pepper trade by dealing with the British and put paid to the intrigues of Raffles, still British governor at Benkulen, in the Menangkabau world.[10] The result was an agreement signed in early 1822 by the Dutch Resident and 14 fugitive penghulu from Menangkabau, by which in effect the latter vicariously handed over Menangkabau sovereignty in exchange for Dutch aid against the Padri. This done, the Dutch reoccupied Semawang at once and a couple of weeks later were attacking the Padri stronghold at nearby Sulit Air. The fort fell after some days of sharp fighting and the first of the Padri Wars had begun.

During the first phase of the struggle which lasted till 1825, the Dutch tried to establish their control over the Padri and protect their allies by setting up a series of strong-points in the region. A force under Lt.-Col. Raaffe, who had seen service with Napoleon in Europe, was sent from Batavia for this purpose. After the reoccupation of the fort at Semawang in 1821, another one was set up close to Pagar Ruyong itself, at Batu Sangkar, in the same year. (This fort was known by the Dutch as Fort van der Capellen.) However, Raaffe's troops encountered stiff resistance and his attempts to occupy Padri positions in Agam were repelled. Fighting spread throughout the region without the Dutch being able to get the upper hand and on occasion suffering severe reverses such as when they attempted to force the pass to Lintau (1822) and take Bukit Marapalam (1823).

Raaffe was called back to Java for consultations and on his return as military and civil governor of Padang at the end of 1823 he sought to negotiate a settlement. On 22 January 1824 an agreement was signed at Masang between the Padri leaders and the Dutch which defined the limits of Padri influence and by which the Padri agreed to conduct their trade through Dutch-held ports only. But a couple of months later, the Dutch broke the agreement by attacking and seizing the Padri stronghold of Pandai Sikat. The death of the exhausted Raaffe at Padang in April and several minor reverses suffered by Dutch troops brought about a resurgence of Padri power and when in 1825 the Java War[a] broke out the Dutch began to look again for the means of a settlement with the Padri. The new Dutch commander in Padang, Col. de Stuers, founded Fort de Kock (Bukit Tinggi) then reduced his forces in the region. Finally, through the mediation of an Arab trader, he succeeded in making a truce with some of the Padri leaders (nan Rencheh and Pasaman) by which both parties agreed to give up attacking one another. The truce was signed at Padang in November 1825.

The resurgence of the Padri and the Second Padri War

During the next few years the Padri got the upper hand once again. The Padang truce notwithstanding, they were able to take advantage of Dutch pre-occupations in Java to extend their influence over more Menangkabau districts, and this influence also spread along the coast from Tiku up to Ayer Bangis and into the Tapanuli region. There were increasing numbers of incidents involving the Dutch and in 1831 the Padri mounted an assault on Padang itself which was, however, defeated.

But by that year the Java War was over and the Dutch were able to turn their full attention once more on to West Sumatra. Under a new Resident and Commander, Elout, the Dutch veteran Major Michiels led an offensive along the coast, forcing the Padri to retire to the hills. The Padri threat to Natal and Ayer Bangis was removed and Katiagan, which they had used as their principal port, was captured and sacked. Another Dutch force penetrated the highlands and occupied key villages such as Tilatang and Kamang. The following year (1832) fresh reinforcements arrived, led by Ali Basah Prawirodirjo (better known as Sentot),[11] now serving as a Dutch mercenary. His Bugis followers entered Lintau. Some months later, the Padri leaders of Bonjol, Tuanku Imam and Tuanku Muda, were defeated and sued for peace. Meanwhile in Rau and Mandeeling the local population, tired of puritanism, rose up against Padri domination and chased their adherents away. After this the Dutch succeeded in bringing about a general pacification. They reoccupied Bonjol and garrisoned it and appointed anti-Padri chiefs like the Yang di-Pertuan of Rau and Raja Gedombang from Mandeeling as their agents in charge of districts. Raja Alam Muning Shah was also reinstated in his own district of Pagar Ruyong. The second Padri War had come to an end. The Padri had been defeated not only by the efforts of the Dutch but through the co-operation of the Menangkabau supporters of *adat* as well.

The anti-Dutch uprising and the Menangkabau War

However, Padri power was not yet broken and soon general anti-Dutch feeling spread in Menangkabau as a result of the Dutch occupation. Local feelings were outraged by the use of mosques to quarter 'infidel' colonial troops by the requisitioning of houses for their officers and by the imposition of forced labour. The general attitude of the occupying soldiers was high-handed and cruel. Another potent source of dissatisfaction was the new duties imposed on market produce and cockfights, the imposition of forced labour for the needs of the army and the creation of opium farms, the main effect of which was to raise the price of opium. Within six months of their defeat, Padri influence had become stronger than ever before and they had little difficulty in posing as the champions of the people against Dutch oppression.

Consequently, at the beginning of 1833 a popular uprising—Padri-inspired—broke out in Menangkabau. Tuanku Imam, the Bonjol Padri, had issued letters appointing 11 January as the date for the rising but in fact fighting broke out before this when the Dutch commander at Fort van der Capellen, sensing the impending danger, withdrew his garrison to Sipisang. There he was promptly besieged and forced to make a further withdrawal, this time to Bukit Koriri in Agam. On 11 January the people of Bonjol itself rose up and slew the entire Dutch garrison quartered in the mosque there. Several chiefs, who up to this point had opposed the Padri, now changed side and gave them their support, including the Yang di-Pertuan of Rau who besieged the Dutch garrison at Fort Amerongen. Sentot himself became involved in the anti-Dutch intrigue, conspiring with the hitherto anti-Padri Raja Alam Muning Shah of Pagar Ruyong to expel the foreigner. Tuanku Alam, yet another strong anti-Padri leader, also changed side.

The Dutch reacted swiftly. Sentot was sent back to Batavia on the pretext of raising more troops, was arrested on arrival and sent to exile in Benkulen. Raja Alam Muning Shah along with several other Menangkabau chiefs was tricked into captivity and exiled.[12] In the case of Tuanku Alam, the Dutch decided to make an example of him and had him beheaded for all to see.

But these measures did not prevent the spread of the uprising into a general outbreak all over the country by April. Soon afterwards it was joined by a new figure, one Pakeh Salleh, a *guru* from Tambusai, who, taking the title of Tuanku Tambusai, gathered a force of adherents and invaded Mandeeling. The seriousness of the new war led the Dutch governor-general, the capable and energetic Johannes van den Bosch,[13] to take a personal hand in the campaign which followed. In June 1833, fresh Dutch forces under General Riesz landed at Padang to launch a counter-attack. They advanced into the highlands and captured Kamang. In the following month van den Bosch arrived on the west coast.

In the meantime several of the Menangkabau leaders had been captured or had given themselves up, fifteen of whom were executed in July, including the veteran Tuanku Mansiangan. The Padri were once more obliged to retreat into their mountain strongholds, of which as before Bonjol remained the main centre. Van den Bosch gave orders that Bonjol be captured by mid-September but a Dutch force was checked on the way at Matur and obliged to retreat. Fresh outbreaks at Pagar Ruyong forced the Dutch to abandon their offensive against Bonjol completely for the time being.

The defeat of the Padri

Faced with widespread and stubborn resistance van den Bosch formulated new principles on which the administration of the region was to be based. Published by the Resident of Padang in October 1833, they consisted of seven points and became known as the 'Plakaat Panjang'.[14] The declaration set out to remove the principal grievances of the Menangkabau and thereby the principal causes of the resistance movement. Burdensome dues and taxes were withdrawn immediately, forced labour abolished, and modifications made in the prevailing system of import duties and of the salt and opium farms. Local chiefs were to be paid a fixed salary according to their status, influence and ability; local administration was to be left largely in local hands, but the Dutch had the right to intervene in disputes and keep the peace. Civil government was to replace military government as soon as possible and the coffee culture[a] prices were fixed at a fair rate for the growers.

But the war went on. Tuanku Tambusai and his insurgents raided the Mandeeling district again and the Dutch garrison at Fort Amerongen was obliged to abandon the fort. In 1834 the Dutch were more successful; they succeeded in repelling Tuanku Tambusai in Mandeeling and in regaining control of the Agam and Tanah Datar districts; they also advanced on Bonjol but their attempts to reach there were again a failure. Their principal Menangkabau ally, Raja Gedombang of Agam, was killed during the course of this expedition.

Nevertheless by 1836 the Padri movement was limited to the Bonjol region where it held out against the Dutch for another eighteen months. At the end of the year, African and Bugis mercenaries fighting for the Dutch were severely repulsed in an attempt to storm Bonjol. Early in 1837 General Cochius was sent from Batavia to make a report on the situation. He recommended taking a different approach route to the Padri stronghold, a change of tactics which led to Dutch success in August of the same year. At long last and after careful preparation, a Dutch force led by Michiels stormed into this last centre of Padri resistance.

The fall of Bonjol marked the collapse of the Padri movement. The 64-year old Tuanku Imam, the prime spirit behind Bonjol's resistance, was tricked into surrender by the Dutch three months later. He was sent into exile, first to Batavia, then to Ambon, and finally to Minahassa where he died in 1864. Only Tuanku Tambusai remained; driven back to his home district, in December 1838 his stronghold at Dalu-Dalu was stormed and he disappeared from the scene.[15]

The final outcome of the Padri movement, therefore, was the ending of Menangkabau independence in Sumatra. It is doubtful whether the Dutch would have advanced their control into the Padang Highlands during this period had they not feared the threat which the Padri appeared to pose to their settlements and trade on the west coast and to the opportunities opened to British intervention by the restlessness in the Padang Highlands.

PENINSULA MENANGKABAU

The Menangkabau of the Peninsula likewise lost their independence during the nineteenth century because of internal dissensions which originated, however, in different factors. Futhermore the Peninsula Menangkabau became involved with the colonial power because of economic circumstances which were not operative in the 1820s and 1830s on Sumatra's west coast.

The formation of Negri Sembilan

The problem of the Menangkabau colonists in the Peninsula was how to achieve political unity. As things stood, they were divided up into a number of little chieftaincies, each quite independent of the other.[16] The manner of their settlement in the hinterland of Malacca, the traditions of local autonomy which they brought with them from their home districts in Sumatra and the nature of the territory they

[a] See Book II.

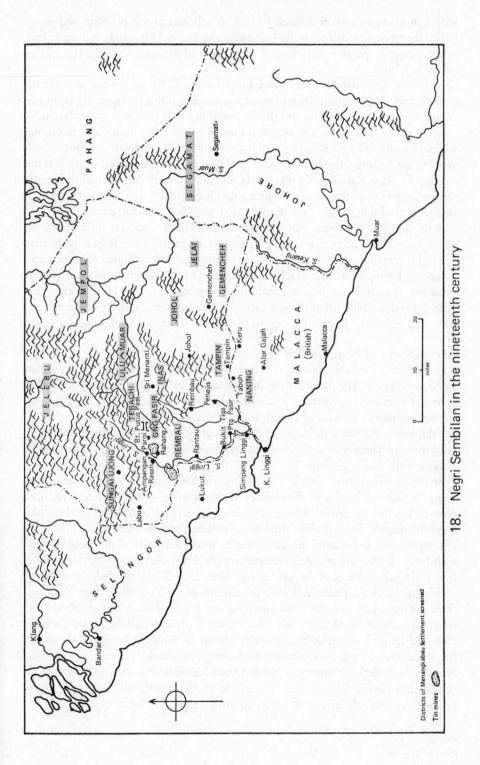

18. Negri Sembilan in the nineteenth century

Districts of Menangkabau settlement screened

Tin mines

settled in made an answer difficult to find. A solution to this problem was post-poned for two and a half centuries because in any case the Menangkabau chiefs had to recognize the paramountcy first of the Sultans of Malacca, and then that of the rulers of Johore.

However, the decline of the Johore Empire towards the end of the seventeenth century and the growth of Bugis power and the Bugis threat, especially from Se-langor,[17] altered the situation and the first steps towards the formation of an inde-pendent entity took place. The colonists turned towards their homeland and to the ancient royalty of Pagar Ruyong, and in the early 1730s a deputation of four chiefs went to the Padang Highlands to secure a prince to lead them. The result was the coming of Raja Kasah to the Peninsula, but he was unable to establish himself against Bugis opposition. A second pretender, Raja Adil,[18] with Bugis connexions, was unsuccessful in securing the support of all the Menangkabau chiefs.

A third prince succeeded where the others had failed. This was Raja Mahmud, better known as Raja Melewar who, having overcome his rival, Raja Khatib, won general acceptance amongst the chiefs, was recognized by the Sultan of Johore, and according to tradition was installed as the first Yang di-Pertuan Besar of Negri Sembilan at a ceremony held at Penajis near Rembau in 1773.[19] He then chose the strategic and secluded site of Sri Menanti as his headquarters, carefully avoiding con-flict with either the Bugis or the powerful chiefs of Sungai Ujong and Rembau.

The constitution of Negri Sembilan

Raja Melewar probably drafted the constitution on which Menangkabau politics came to be based. The post of Yang di-Pertuan Besar was elective; it carried with it royal rights and prerogatives, made its holder the head of Islam in the state and the final authority in cases of appeal under *adat*. But, as was the position with the royal house in Sumatra, the office of head of state gave the prince direct authority only over the lands around Sri Menanti and gave him no powers of taxation over the rest of the Menangkabau.

So the Menangkabau confederation, known as the Negri Sembilan,[20] came into being. It was a reflection of the realities of the situation—the constituent districts were far too independent to submit to a strong central government but on the other hand the outside threat (by this time much reduced) and the need for an arbiter in settling rivalries and dissensions, gave validity to the authority of the Yang di-Per-tuan Besar. By the end of the eighteenth century this confederation consisted of the four main principalities of Sungai Ujong, Rembau, Jelebu and Johol, the rulers of which were styled Undang and were the electors of the Yang di-Pertuan Besar; of these Sungai Ujong was the most powerful and senior. Then grouped around the royal demesne of Sri Menanti were the territories of Terachi, Ulu Muar, Gunong Pasir and Jempol, all under their own chieftains. In Sungai Ujong was the small Bugis enclave of Linggi, subject to the Undang's overlordship; attached to Rem-bau was the turbulent territory of Naning,[a] and linked with Johol the chieftainships of Inas and Gemencheh. During the course of the nineteenth century, Tampin broke away from the rest of Rembau to form a separate district of its own.[b]

[a]See pp. 159–60.
[b]See p. 167, 25.

The question of succession

Raja Melewar's constitution could only be effective with a strong Yang di-Pertuan Besar. He himself filled this role well and the problem of succession was resolved reasonably smoothly on his death in 1795, when the Undangs invited another Pagar Ruyong prince to take his place. This was Raja Hitam who married judiciously and reigned uneventfully till his death in 1808. His successor, Raja Lenggang, also allegedly of royal Menangkabau stock, ruled in Negri Sembilan till he died in 1824.

However, all attempts to make the office of the Yang di-Pertuan Besar hereditary met with opposition from the four Undang, particularly from the Undang of Sungai Ujong who feared the growth of an established dynastic authority. For this reason, Raja Melewar's attempts to get his son, Raja Tokoh, elected as his successor came to nought in 1795, and Raja Lenggang's attempt in favour of his son, Raja Nasaruddin (Raja Radin) also failed in 1824.

This second failure had serious consequences. Dato Kawal, the Dato Klana and Undang of Sungai Ujong, in his anxiety to prevent the creation of a hereditary Sri Menanti line, sent his soldiers into the district and drove out Raja Radin and his supporters, installing an adventurer and freebooter of doubtful character called Raja Kerjan to hold the position until a successor from Sumatra could be provided. Two years later (1826), this successor arrived in the person of Raja Laboh (Yam Tuan Sati) who assumed the royal title. Raja Laboh, unpopular as the patron of Raja Kerjan and widely regarded as a usurper, never won the acceptance of the majority of the Negri Sembilan chiefs. He owed and maintained his position solely because of the support of the powerful Dato Klana. However, in 1830 Raja Laboh was foolish enough to alienate that support and as a result the office of Yang di-Pertuan Besar was once again open to dispute.[21] The supporters of Raja Radin, knowing that Sungai Ujong would no longer protect Raja Laboh, drove him and the detested Raja Kerjan from Sri Menanti. But Raja Radin still faced rival claimants, no fewer than four in number.[22] Of these the most serious was the ambitious Yam Tuan Muda of Rembau, Raja Ali.

Raja Ali of Rembau and the Naning War

This succession dispute threatened to bring the British into Menangkabau politics. The British in Malacca[a] could not fail to be affected by events in the neighbouring Negri Sembilan and in particular they were concerned when the feuds and quarrels of the chiefs hindered the trade in tin and jungle produce which flowed down the rivers to the coast, or which threatened the security of the settlement in other ways.

In the early 1830s Raja Ali of Rembau exploited the British involvement with Naning to boost his own position. Naning, under its chief, Dato Abdul Said (Dol Said), had been embroiled with the British authorities in Malacca for several years. The quarrel revolved around the status of Naning and its obligations to Malacca. As understood by the British authorities, Naning was supposed to pay tithes on its rice and fruit harvests each year under agreements concluded long before under the Dutch.[23] The true position was not clearly understood in Malacca and the British

[a]Refer p. 121.

governor in Penang felt that British rights in Naning must be maintained if Dato Abdul Said's refusal to pay his dues was not to be copied by Malays living in Malacca territory itself. Attempts to collect revenue and conduct a census in the late 1820s failed, and finally in 1831, under pressure from Calcutta, governor Ibbetson ordered a small force of 150 sepoys and two 25-pounders to bring the Dato to reason. The little expedition was an ignominious failure and it was obliged to withdraw, having accomplished nothing.

These developments were watched with misgiving by Raja Ali and his son-in-law from Malacca, Syed Shaaban, who feared that British intervention in Naning would lead to British interference in Rembau itself, and so at first they encouraged Dato Abdul Said in his resistance. The British on the other hand, who wanted to avoid added complications in the Menangkabau states, were as anxious to reassure Rembau that there was nothing to be feared. Thus in late 1830 and again in early 1831 the British signed agreements with Rembau of 'perpetual friendship and alliance', renounced all monopoly rights they had acquired when they took over Malacca from the Dutch, and secured the promise of Raja Ali's support against Naning. In 1832 the British launched a second and larger expedition which culminated in a surprise attack on and the capture of the Dato's kampong of Tabor in June. In this campaign Raja Ali and Syed Shaaban played an invaluable part on the side of the British.[24]

Immediately after the conclusion of the Naning affair, Raja Ali, strong in his British connexion, felt emboldened to proclaim himself the Yang di-Pertuan Besar, and he appointed his son-in-law Yam Tuan Muda of Rembau in his stead. It was a short-lived triumph. A few months later, Syed Shaaban quarrelled with the Bugis Dato Muda of Linggi, which precipitated a civil war in Rembau. Raja Ali and Syed Shaaban were worsted and in 1833, Raja Radin was proclaimed the Yang di-Pertuan Besar with the general acquiescence of the Menangkabau chiefs.[25] This long succession dispute, besides demonstrating the frailty of the Negri Sembilan constitution, brought about one significant innovation—the Yang di-Pertuan Besar could be a local-born.

Menangkabau politics and Sungai Ujong

The question of the succession continued to present problems. When Raja Radin died in 1861 after a successful tenure of power, he was followed by his brother Raja Ulin (Yam Tuan Imam); this was the wish of Raja Radin himself, probably a product of his own unfortunate experience. However, when Raja Ulin died eight years later, there were two claimants for the succession—Tengku Antah, one of Raja Radin's own sons, and Tengku Ahmad Tunggal, a son of Raja Ulin. Another long succession crisis ensued which this time brought in its train British intervention and the loss of Menangkabau independence.

The decisive rôle in the new crisis was again played by Sungai Ujong. This principality, always the strongest in the confederation, had acquired a new importance over the preceding fifty years as a centre of tin-mining.[a] In 1825 the first Chinese miners were invited into the district. By 1828 they numbered over 1,000. By 1860

ªSee Book II.

there were 5,000 and within the next fourteen years they were to rise to 15,000. The rise of the tin industry had two important consequences. It aroused the interest of the merchants and businessmen of the Straits Settlements, especially those in Malacca who were financially involved, in the politics of Sungai Ujong; and it contributed greatly to the historic enmity between the Dato Klana and his rival, the Dato Bandar, on the one hand, and to the struggle to control the Linggi river—the main highway for tin from the interior—on the other.[26] It was these quarrels which had largely distracted the Dato Klana as Undang from the politics of Sri Menanti, and which by the same token had enabled Raja Radin as Yang di-Pertuan Besar to increase his own influence and authority by virtue of judicious arbitration.

The key issue was the struggle to control the Linggi river. Not only was passage of this waterway disputed between the Dato Klana and the Dato Bandar, but there were also the Undang of Rembau and the Dato Muda of Linggi itself to be considered, not to mention the freebooters who set up stockades and tried to levy tolls on their own account. The freeing of the Linggi river to trade became the constant theme of the British authorities in Malacca after 1840.[27] But neither the Dato Klana nor any other chieftain was powerful enough to impose a unilateral solution.

Matters came to a head during the early 1870s. In the first place the control of the Linggi river now became a matter of vital concern to the protagonists in the Selangor Civil War,[a] for it formed a useful route for the bringing of men or supplies from outside. In fact, in the middle of 1872 it became the route by which Raja Mahdi[b] passed from Johore on his way to renew the campaign against Yap Ah-loy's forces near Kuala Lumpur, which caused the Selangor viceroy, Tengku Kudin,[c] to take immediate steps to close the river to his enemies.[28] Earlier in that same year Dato Klana Sending had granted an important mining concession to a Dutch Eurasian from Malacca called Velge, who thereupon formed the Sungai Ujong Tin Mining Company.[29] Sending's concession no doubt promised to bring in handsome dividends but it was also provocative because it totally excluded the Dato Bandar as well as the Yam Tuan *fainéant*, Tengku Antah, and other lesser Linggi chiefs from what they would naturally consider their share of the dues. In the certainty that implementing the terms of the concession would arouse local opposition and now confronted by Tengku Kudin's pressure to close the river altogether, in September the Dato Klana turned to Singapore for help. British officials, harassed by Straits commercial interests, and Tengku Kudin were equally as anxious for a settlement, so that a few weeks later a meeting took place at Kuala Linggi between Dato Sending, Tengku Kudin and the British governor, Harry Ord. There a compromise formula was found; the Dato Klana agreed to close the Linggi to Raja Mahdi and his followers provided that the passage of his own trade down the river was not interfered with. The Dato Bandar, who was a supporter of Raja Mahdi, was not consulted.

The Dato Klana of Sungai Ujong seeks British protection

The crisis evolved still further a month later when both Dato Klana Sending and Dato Akhir, Penghulu of Rembau, died. The death of Dato Akhir precipitated a

[a]See pp. 281 et seq.
[b]See p. 286.
[c]See pp. 285 et seq.

struggle for the succession between Haji Sahil, the Dato Purba, and Haji Mustapha, bringing all trade on the Linggi to a standstill and provoking in the first half of 1873 a new series of appeals for British action from the merchants of the Straits Settlements.[30] Dato Sending's successor as Dato Klana in Sungai Ujong was Syed Abdul Rahman. He was young, westernized and a shrewd diplomat. He was also an outsider (his father was an Arab from Acheh who had married the daughter of a former Dato Klana) and was better known in Malacca where he had been brought up than Sungai Ujong where he was never to enjoy much popular support. However, Dato Abdul Rahman's Malacca connexions were to stand him in good stead in dealing with the problems which he now inherited. Principal amongst these arising out of his predecessor's concession was the presence in Sungai Ujong of a large influx of Chinese tin-miners who were extremely difficult to control, and the difficulties which he faced in fulfilling his obligation to keep the Linggi route open. This forced his attention on to the Rembau civil war, and with the approval of his backers in Malacca the new Dato Klana gave his support to Haji Mustapha. But Tengku Kudin, and therefore the British administration in Singapore, supported the Dato Purba.[31] Faced with two petitions, Ord in July 1873 acted and made a vain attempt to arbitrate between the two factions. Only the Dato Klana took advantage of this opportunity to present his case to the governor in Singapore, the outcome of which was that he was persuaded to transfer his support to the Dato Purba on the understanding that he could reach agreement with Tengku Kudin over the Linggi river. Towards the end of the year the matter was clinched by the victory of the Dato Purba over his adversary and his establishment as the *de facto* ruler of Rembau.

However, Dato Syed Abdul Rahman's position remained precarious. In none of his doings had he consulted and sought the approval of the aged but formidable Dato Bandar[32] who admittedly would have been very unlikely to have given it in any case. So when early the next year (in 1874) the British under the innovating Sir Andrew Clarke[a] made fresh moves to end the disturbances on the Linggi river—for the Dato Purba's victory had not given him control over his own supporters—he responded readily, and willingly made clear his desire to be identified with British policies. In February 1874, at a meeting arranged in Malacca with the Dato Purba, a provisional agreement was reached to clear the stockades on the river. In April the Dato Klana and the Dato Muda of Linggi were the only two Menangkabau chiefs to go in person to Singapore in response to Clarke's request for a meeting of all the parties involved in the dispute—the others merely sent representatives. The result of this visit was a treaty signed on 21 April, which the Dato Muda of Linggi also signed, recognizing Dato Syed Abdul Rahman as the paramount ruler of Sungai Ujong and granting him the 'moral and *material* guarantee and protection of the British government' against his promise to safeguard trade on the Linggi river. The treaty also ceded control of the river from Simpang Linggi to Permatang Pasir to the British.

This was followed early the next month by a second attempt by Clarke to impose, Pangkor-style, an agreement on all the warring chiefs of the Menangkabau states. But only the Dato Klana appeared at either of the meetings summoned at

[a]See pp. 278–9 and 288.

Kuala Linggi. After this fruitless endeavour he accompanied the British governor up the river, destroying the stockades of the Dato Purba at Bukit Tiga and others further upstream. Then, acknowledging officially the Dato Purba as ruler of Rembau, Clarke returned to Singapore, and Syed Abdul Rahman to Sungai Ujong.

Menangkabau opposition to foreign control

Dato Klana Syed Abdul Rahman had thus thrown himself into the arms of the British. The legality of his actions was highly questionable, for they had all been done on his own initiative without taking into consultation any other Menangkabau chief. On the other hand the Dato Klana had shrewdly insured his own position by obtaining a written assurance of British support and he intended to use this advantage against his enemies to consolidate his power.

Dato Syed Abdul Rahman's reliance on foreign support, on the other hand, also served to consolidate the opposition against him. In Sungai Ujong itself popular feeling strengthened the position of the Dato Bandar whose claims to parity with the Dato Klana had been set aside without his even having been invited to the negotiations.[33] The Dato Klana's moves also gave Tengku Antah a new basis on which to establish his claim for recognition as the Yang di-Pertuan Besar since his rival, Tengku Ahmad Tunggal, was already compromised by seeking the friendship and support of Dato Syed Abdul Rahman. All the same at first no one moved, and the Dato Bandar himself, confronted with the reality of British action in destroying the Linggi stockades and in the happenings in Selangor and Perak, was inclined to acquiesce in the new situation. But, in July 1874, his courage was restored by the arrival in Sungai Ujong of Raja Mahdi and Raja Mahmud, refugees from Selangor,[34] and he then came out in open opposition to the Dato Klana. When Dato Syed Abdul Rahman attempted to claim British protection by raising the Union Jack in front of his istana, the Dato Bandar's men warned him not to do so. The Dato Klana now realized that he needed more than paper agreements to maintain his position. Early in August he asked for a British Resident and in September for British troops. The British forces arrived early the following month in the shape of a small police party from Malacca, accompanied by W.A. Pickering, Chinese interpreter to the Straits government,[a] whose main duty was to forestall intervention by the Chinese tin-miners in the area on either side in the dispute.

However, the Dato Bandar refused to recognize Dato Syed Abdul Rahman's treaty with Britain and refused to give way to Pickering when he came to negotiate with him. He prepared for war, and Raja Mahmud, whose fame and prowess as a warrior caused the greater part of the Dato Klana's followers to desert, he made commander in-chief. But Pickering's presence also gave new heart to Dato Syed Abdul Rahman who felt bold enough first to raise the British flag in front of his residence despite the Dato Bandar, and then, one month later, to launch a surprise night attack on the Dato Bandar's position. Initial success turned within twenty-four hours to rout with the Dato Klana's soldiery fleeing in terrified disarray on the appearance of Raja Mahmud. Pickering saved the day for Dato Syed Abdul Rahman, and sent for more help. This came at the end of November when 150 British troops arrived along with 20 artillerymen, but by then Pickering and the

[a] See Book II.

local forces had already captured Rahang and Rasa, and soon after the eighty-year old chief together with Raja Mahmud and Raja Mahdi were in full flight.

The Dato Bandar and Raja Mahmud fled to Selangor and placed themselves at the mercy of Sultan Abdul Samad. There they met Swettenham and were persuaded by him to go to Singapore and make their submission to the governor, which they did in the third week of December. Both were made to live in Singapore for a year, and the Dato Bandar was given a pension and a house where he stayed until his death.[35] Meanwhile in Sungai Ujong he was replaced by Haji Ahmad bin Mohamed Ali, a friend and supporter of the Dato Klana. Raja Mahdi escaped to Johore where he placed himself at the disposal of Maharaja Abu Bakar. Towards the close of the year (1874), Captain W.T. Tatham took up his appointment as Assistant Resident, Sungai Ujong.

Sri Menanti and the British

These developments were watched with resentment and dismay from Sri Menanti where Tengku Antah, now recognized as Yam Tuan Besar by most of the Menangkabau chiefs, stood at the head of an anti-Dato Klana and anti-British coalition. A direct clash between the two sides followed late the next year. In November 1875 a small British force which entered the disputed territory of Terachi[36] on a scouting mission, was attacked by Tengku Antah's men and forced to withdraw. Following up this advantage, Tengku Antah then invaded Sungai Ujong, overwhelmed the police post at Paroi and on 4 December occupied Ampangan, opposite the residence of the Dato Klana.

The British counter-attack was swift in coming. A stream of reinforcements came in from Malacca. Tengku Antah was forced to abandon his position at Ampangan and on 11 December a British force of about 180 men attacked the stockade at Paroi, and after a bloody skirmish,[37] forced Tengku Antah's soldiers into retreat back to the Bukit Putus Pass. A few days after this, the rearguard of the reinforcements arrived at Rasa, led by Colonel Anson, the British lieutenant-governor in the Straits, in person, who now found that he had over 500 men at his disposal. Even though the activities of Tengku Antah and his supporters had precipitated wild rumour and near panic in Malacca, they were no match against such a force. On the morning of 20 December the Malays were surprised at their stockades on the Bukit Putus Pass and easily routed. By the end of the month, the British were in possession of Terachi and Tengku Antah and his followers had gone into hiding.

The last days of Menangkabau independence

The last days of Menangkabau independence were at hand. In May 1876, Tengku Antah turned up in Klang and placed himself in the hands of the Sultan of Selangor, and from there went to Johore where the Maharaja took the opportunity to try and revive Johore's ancient overlordship over Negri Sembilan. By an agreement of the same year Tengku Antah was recognized as the Yang di-Pertuan Besar of Sri Menanti, and all disputes were to be referred to Johore.[38] The following year Rembau and Jelebu signed similar treaties, giving Johore authority to intervene in disputes, but these were quickly repudiated as illegal by their people.

In the 1880s the progress achieved by Sungai Ujong under British protection brought a change in Yam Tuan Antah's attitude towards the Johore connexion, and British protection now seemed more desirable. Accordingly he responded more favourably to the process of bringing the Menangkabau confederacy under direct British influence which had been initiated under the empire-building governor, Sir Frederick Weld.[a] He began by accepting the loans offered for the construction of bridle paths to encourage trade between Sri Menanti and Malacca territory. In 1886 he received Weld in person at Sri Menanti, with the result that he agreed to accept a British official to help in the collection of revenues. The success of that experiment—the Yam Tuan's revenues quadrupled within twelve months—persuaded him to sign a new treaty in June 1887, placing the Sri Menanti Confederation under British protection.

This left Rembau, Tampin and Jelebu still outside the British fold. In July 1889, with British prompting, the rulers of Rembau and Tampin agreed to federate with Sri Menanti, creating thereby what was called 'Old Negri Sembilan'. Rembau and Jelebu had already signed agreements with the British in Singapore which made the British governor their arbiter in domestic problems, and Jelebu accepted a British collector in 1883.[39]

With still further British prompting, the states of Old Negri Sembilan were brought into an administrative union with Sungai Ujong in June 1895, when the new Yam Tuan Muhammad (who had succeeded his father, Yam Tuan Antah, on his death in 1887) together with the four Undang signed a treaty creating a new confederation of six states under British protection and with a British Resident.[40] The process of shaping the Negri Sembilan of today was completed three years later when the four Undang and the Dato Bandar of Sungai Ujong agreed to accept Yam Tuan Muhammad of Sri Menanti as the holder of the hereditary office of Yang di-Pertuan Besar of Negri Sembilan.

The extinction of the independence of the Peninsula Menangkabau was no doubt inevitable in the circumstances of British power established as it was in the Malay Peninsula by the second half of the nineteenth century. It was hastened by the complications produced by the rise of the tin-mining industry in Sungai Ujong and by the already long-existing political contradictions in Menangkabau society. However, the ironies of history were to ensure that it was a descendant of the ancient line of Pagar Ruyong who through the Yam Tuans of Negri Sembilan became the first ruler of an independent Malaya.

[a]Refer p. 146, note 66.

[1]The expedition was in order to conclude a treaty with the Menangkabau ruler of Pagar Ruyong recognizing full British sovereignty over the districts of the west coast; agreement signed in July 1818.

[2]The origins of Menangkabau's monarchy are wrapped in obscurity, but probably began with the prince, Adityavarnam, who founded the state of Malayu in the fourteenth century,

contemporaneous with Majapahit. The earliest Muslim Menangkabau ruler known to us by name was Raja Alam Alif. After his death early in the seventeenth century royal authority was split into three segments, namely the Raja Adat, the Raja Ibata and the (most senior) Raja Alam, while real power came to rest in the hands of the penghulus.

³The Dutch got their first foothold in the trade of the west coast in 1638 when they obtained a share in the pepper trade. In 1641 the Achinese granted them further concessions which were converted into a formal contract in 1649. These arrangements were reconfirmed in 1659 and in that year the Dutch placed a factor at Padang for the gold trade.

⁴The Achinese and the Bantamese were behind the sporadic anti-Christian movements which sprang up amongst the Menangkabaus during this period.

⁵The Menangkabau 'king' in exchange ceded to the Dutch a small district at Salido near Padang, reputedly rich in gold; the gold mines never proved sufficiently profitable and were eventually abandoned.

⁶TheWahhabi sect was started in Central Arabia by Mohd. ibn Abd-al-Wahhab around 1744. A thoroughgoing and puritanical reform movement, it received the military support of the local emirate, whose ruler overran east Arabia and then captured Mecca itself in 1806. The political power of theWahhabi movement was finally broken by Pasha Mehmet Ali of Egypt in 1818, but its influence as a religious force remained profound. The three pilgrims were Hj. Miskin from Agam, Hj. Sumanik from Limapuluh Kota and Hj. Piabang from Tanah Datar.

⁷The origin of the term 'padri' used to describe this religious movement is not certain. According to one version it derives from the Malay word 'padri', meaning a Christian priest or missionary (from the Portuguese 'padre'), and was wrongly applied by European writers to the Muslim hajis. Another variant of the term is 'pidari', more commonly used by Indonesian writers, which may be derived from Pedir, an important Islamic centre in Acheh particularly associated as a port of departure for the Haj. See Pane, *Sedjarah Indonesia*, Vol. II, p. 84.

⁸Although some historians assert that the story of the royal massacre was merely a fabrication to blacken the Padri name, there seems no reason to doubt that it did in fact take place. See *Sedjarah Menangkabau*, Drs M.D. Mansoer et al., Bhratara, Jakarta, 1970; p. 66 and p.124.

⁹As had occurred in Malacca, Riau, Borneo, the Moluccas and in Java itself, Padang and other Dutch settlements on the Sumatran west coast had been occupied by the British on the authority of the Kew letters after 1795: the west coast settlements were handed back to the Dutch in 1819.

¹⁰The Dutch had every reason to be suspicious of Raffles who, well aware that Padang was soon to be returned to them, treated with the Menangkabau rulers in 1818 not only to confirm the position of the British possessions on the west coast but to get himself appointed as the Menangkabau representative and agent in all the Malay states. This last stipulation was annulled by the governors of the East India Company in London. Holland's reluctance to get involved in extensions of territory at this time was due to her own precarious economic position after the Napoleonic Wars.

¹¹He was nephew of Dipo Negoro, and one of the most prominent of the Javanese leaders against the Dutch in the JavaWar (1825–30). A brilliant guerrilla fighter, he went over to the Dutch when his uncle's cause became hopeless after 1828.

¹²By this time Raja Alam Muning Shah had assumed the title of Sultan Alam Bagagar Shah.He was first imprisoned in Padang and then taken to Batavia. He had been arrested whilst paying a visit to the residence of Elout, together with several followers.

¹³The man who proposed the Culture System and was responsible for its introduction into Java. Refer Book II.

¹⁴In English, 'The Long Declaration'.

¹⁵The fate of Tuanku Tambusai is not known. Some writers believe he was mortally wounded whilst escaping by boat after the affray at Dalu-Dalu and died subsequently in the jungle: others say he went to Bila and from there became an adventurer at the head of a small band of followers.

¹⁶Menangkabau settlers were originally to be found in an arc from Klang in Selangor to the Muar river in Johore, stretching inland as far as the borders of Pahang.

¹⁷In the 1720s, a Bugis force led by Daing Kemboja seized Kuala Linggi and some years later the Bugis brought about a change in the style of the ruling chief of Sungai Ujong from Penghulu Mentri to Dato Klana Putra, a Bugis title (about 1760). Bugis influence in Sungai Ujong remained dominant for the greater part of the eighteenth century.

¹⁸Raja Adil subsequently settled in Rembau where he was given authority to rule by Tengku Abdul Jalil, heir apparent in Johore. Raja Adil's successor, Raja Asil, arrogated to himself the title of Yam Tuan Muda in 1798.

¹⁹Supposedly carried out before the chiefs of Sungai Ujong, Jelebu, Johol and Rembau, it seems

unlikely that either the Dato Klana—who, if not a Bugis himself, was under strong Bugis influence—or the chief of Johol whose own position was still in dispute in his district, would have attended. Winstedt suggests that the four chiefs might not have installed Raja Melewar and that he merely extended his authority from Ulu Muar. In fact it is highly doubtful whether Raja Melewar or his successors were kinsmen of Pagar Ruyong royalty at all.

20 Why the confederation became known as the Nine States is not known. Possibly Raja Melewar conceived the name from the treaty which was signed between the Dutch and the chief of Rembau and eight lesser chiefs in 1759 (see Sheppard, op. cit.). According to Winstedt (*J. M. B. R. A. S.* Vol. XII, Pt. III, 1934, p. 41) the 'usual' list is Klang, S. Ujong, Naning, Rembau, Jelai, Ulu Pahang, Jelebu, Johol and Segamat: these all had Menangkabau settlers but in fact only S. Ujong, Rembau, Jelebu and Johol are part of the Negri Sembilan today.

21 The Yam Tuan outraged the Dato Klana by demanding a 2.5 per cent commission on the latter's winnings on a cockfight at Sri Menanti. The Dato Klana forthwith left the istana and went to see the Penghulu of Ulu Muar, encouraging him to dethrone the Yam Tuan.

22 The deposed Yam Tuan Sati, Raja Kerjan, Raja Ali—the Yam Tuan Muda of Rembau (nephew and successor of Raja Asil), and Raja Radin's own self-appointed guardian, Raja Beringin.

23 The territory of Naning comprised the greater part of the modern district of Alor Gajah. According to tradition the earliest Menangkabau settlement there was founded by one Perpateh Pinang Sa-batang, who took the title of Orang Kaya Sri Maharaja Merah, Dato Naning. In 1641, the Dutch, newly established in Malacca, obliged Naning's chief to sign an agreement accepting Dutch overlordship by which Dutch approval and confirmation were necessary for each successor to the chieftainship, and an annual tithe was required on all produce and other items besides. Similar to previous agreements between Naning and the Portuguese, the Dutch, however, insisted on its observance, but because of the districts' poverty, later commuted the tithes into a nominal annual tribute of rice. This situation prevailed when the British took over Malacca for the first time in 1796 and was confirmed by a treaty in 1801. However, when the British returned to Malacca in 1824 under the terms of the Treaty of London, a British official called Lewis insisted that Naning was British territory and that the tithes should be paid in full. The refusal of the Dato to comply led to the quarrel. Abdul Said was the ninth Dato and his accession in 1802 had been confirmed in the same year by the British.

24 Consisting of over 1,000 men, it progressed at the rate of 3 to 4 miles a month, hacking a 600 ft. wide path as it went. This force, which was opposed by barely 100 Malays, took four months to reach its destination. The actual capture of Tabor was carried out by a small force under Syed Shaaban from Rembau. Naning was annexed. Dato Abdul Said surrendered in 1834 on guarantee of a pardon. He was obliged to live in Malacca where he was given a house and $100 a month. In 1849, with a reputation as a *dukun*, he was allowed to return to Naning where he died later in the same year.

25 Syed Shaaban and Dato Muda Katas of Linggi were personal enemies of long standing. Syed Shaaban's attempts to send a force to assassinate the Undang of Rembau for not coming to his aid led to the intervention of Dato Klana Kawal and all Rembau on the side of the Undang. As a result of the civil war which followed, Raja Ali retired to Keru near Tampin, where he died in 1850. Finally, Tampin was detached from the rest of Rembau and became an independent district with Syed Shaaban as its Tengku Besar. Syed Shaaban continued to intrigue against the Undang till his death in 1872.

26 The offices of Dato Klana (formerly Penghulu Mentri) and Dato Shahbandar had been created by Dato Scudai of Johore during the seventeenth century. The hostility between the two chiefs developed when the Dato Klana fell under Bugis influence nearly a hundred years later. The key position of the Dato Bandars on the lower reaches of the Linggi river down which the tin from Rasah had to pass, enabled them to assert their independence and claim equality in the state. The conflict between the two chiefs came to a climax during the period of Dato Klana Sending (1848–72) and Dato Bandar Tunggal, resulting in a prolonged civil war. In 1849 Yam Tuan Radin intervened, achieving a compromise by which the Dato Klana was allotted a fixed share of the tin revenues on Linggi, and the Dato Bandar was recognized as of equal status; but this settlement did not in fact end the fighting between the two parties.

27 The British governors in Singapore were in constant communication with the Menangkabau chiefs at this time over the affairs of the Linggi river. In November 1855 the British government issued a proclamation forbidding the erection of stockades on the Ujong and Linggi rivers and a gunboat visited Kuala Linggi the following year, but to little effect.

28 Already in 1870, foreseeing the need, Tengku Kudin had signed an agreement with the Penghulu of Rembau over Simpang Linggi, promising the Penghulu his support in securing control of it. However, the Penghulu had not succeeded in establishing his authority there and now Tengku Kudin pressed for its outright cession to Selangor.

[29]That is, granting Setoh, Sempadan and Rajang for tin-mining or for any other purpose: Velge's agents were to receive protection and only imports of opium were to be taxable: in return, Velge was to pay $4.25 on each bahar exported, and collect a tithe on the profits, one-third of which would be retained by him and the remaining two-thirds to go to the Dato Klana. The Dato Klana also undertook to make a cart road from Linggi to Setoh, thereby by-passing would-be toll collectors on the Linggi rivur, above Bukit Tiga. The company Velge floated then had the backing of such people as Whampoa (Ho Ah-kay) and his associates in Singapore.

[30]In March and April 1873. The first was a general petition from the Chinese merchants in the Straits Settlements which showed signs of European inspiration; the second was from 65 merchants and traders at Malacca complaining of illegal exactions on the Linggi river at Bukit Tiga—Dato Purba's stockade. For a full discussion of the background of these petitions, see Parkinson, British Intervention in Malaya, p. 109. and Cowan Nineteenth Century Malaya, pp. 125–43.

[31]Syed Abdul Rahman also enjoyed the support of the British Commissioner in Malacca, Capt. Shaw, who was closest to the scene and probably the best informed. But the British administration in the Straits had already committed itself on the side of Tengku Kudin in the Selangor imbroglio. The Dato Klana's support for Haji Mustapha was probably inspired by his fear that Tengku Kudin would annex Simpang Linggi.

[32]'The Dato' Bandar was passing old, as Malays go, and also passing wicked, even for his age and times; but he had far more character than his younger joint-chief, and declined absolutely either to change his ways, give up any of the privileges he claimed, or come to terms.' Swettenham, op. cit. p. 187.

[33]Apart from the basic rivalry between them, the Dato Bandar sympathized with Raja Mahdi, Tengku Kudin's chief opponent in Selangor, while the Dato Klana aimed at coming to a friendly deal with the Selangor viceroy.

[34]They fled from there in July as the result of a British expedition against Labu following another piratical incident off Kuala Langat. The Dato Bandar welcomed them with open arms.

[35]Raja Mahmud eventually returned to live in Selangor; he accompanied Swettenham in the Perak campaign following the assassination of Birch in 1875.

[36]Terachi was disputed by the Dato Klana and Tengku Antah but the latter's claim was more justifiable in that the territory lay on the Sri Menanti side of the Bukit Putus Pass. The British Assistant Resident in Sungei Ujong (Murray) led a small party into Terachi to investigate the dispute and left behind a survey group which was subsequently attacked.

[37]The Malay defenders were estimated to have suffered 280 casualties, of whom 80 at least were killed. On the British side, there were 42 casualties, including 11 killed.

[38]The agreement was reached through the mediation of the British governor, Jervois, and recognized by the British government in London in February 1877. The states involved were Sri Menanti, Ulu Muar, Jempol and Johol, along with the districts of Terachi, Gunong Pasir and Inas.

[39]Agreements made in March and August 1883 respectively.

[40]Namely S. Ujong, Jelebu, Rembau, Sri Menanti, Johol and Tampin.

THE SULTANATE OF BRUNAI

WHILE Malay power was crumbling in the western part of the archipelago, a similar process had begun in the East. The course of the nineteenth century saw the disintegration and partitioning of the old-established sultanate of Brunai and the overwhelming of its eastern neighbour, the sultanate of Sulu.

The rise and decline of Brunai

Brunai became established as a Muslim sultanate some time during the fifteenth century, probably through its Malacca connexions.[1] Already a flourishing commercial centre for generations along a route used by traders from China, the Moluccas and the West, it reached its zenith in the century following the fall of Malacca

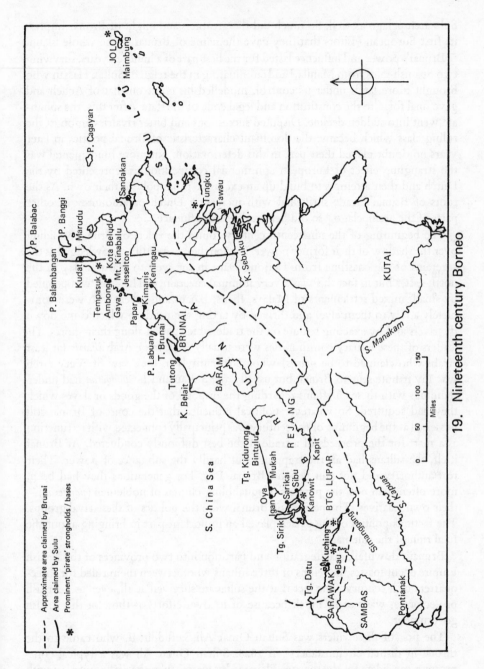

19. Nineteenth century Borneo

and was at the height of its power when it received its first European visitors. One of these[2] described the size and splendour of the Brunai court and town which he estimated contained around 125,000 people—certainly the most populous Malay mart of its day. The ruler he described was probably Sultan Bolkiah who laid the foundations of Brunai's empire. Under him and his successors, Brunai came to cover the whole of what today is Eastern Malaysia, and its sway extended over the

Sulu archipelago as well. So much did the greatness and might of Brunai impress its first European visitors that they gave the name of Brunai to the whole island.

Brunai's power and influence lasted for the best part of a hundred years, surviving two Spanish raids from Manila,[3] and culminating in the reign of Sultan Hassan who brought more lands under its control, modelled his court on that of Acheh and gave final form to the constitution and legal code of the state. After this, the sultanate went into sudden decline. Disputed successions and bitter rivalries amongst the ruling class which became the dominant characteristic of Brunai politics in later years no doubt played their part in this deterioration, but more fundamental was the strangling effect of European commercial competition as represented by the Dutch and their attempts to build up an exclusive monopoly of their own. As the roots of Brunai's trade shrivelled with increasing Dutch paramountcy in other parts of the archipelago,[a] so did her wealth and influence.

The beginning of the nineteenth century found the rulers of Brunai presiding over the shadow of their former power. In 1800 they were still acknowledged as the suzerains of the coastline from Tanjong Datu in the west to Marudu Bay in the north-east,[4] but in fact this was a very nominal suzerainty. The coast was peopled by small, mixed settlements of Malays, Ibans, Bajaus and others who were completely a law to themselves and thrived by taxing the produce which came down the rivers and by exacting tribute on the trade which passed along their shores. The leaders of these estuary communities were usually Malays or Arab *sharifs* (at least, Arabs who claimed to be *sharifs*) who acted entirely as they saw fit. Very rarely was any tribute sent to Brunai but usually the Sultan and his *pangeran* had understandings with these chieftains regarding the disposal of the goods or slaves which they had acquired. So whatever political influence that the court of Brunai still possessed at the beginning of the century was principally connected with its function as a mart for the proceeds of a trade at the best dubiously conducted. At Brunai itself, the sultans had all the trappings but hardly the substance of power. Their real authority did not run beyond Brunai Bay. For generations they had been, more often than not, the puppets of squabbling cliques of noblemen (*pangeran*)— their own relatives. The politics of Brunai were the politics of these rival groups. The factious politics of the palace played an important part in bringing about the final ruin of the sultanate.

Brunai's downfall, disintegration and partition into two provinces of the British Empire encompasses the reigns of three sultans who between them ruled for three-quarters of a century. The fact that the sultanate survived at all, even as a British protectorate, was not so much because of its own efforts as those of the British government.

The first of these rulers was Sultan Omar Ali Saifuddin II, who came to the throne in dismal circumstances[5] in 1828. Sultan Omar Ali was a typical compromise candidate for the throne. Elevated by his mother, the real power lay with his relations, one of whom, his uncle Hassim, he had to appoint as Raja Muda. He was physically deformed, suffered from cancer of the mouth and was widely believed to be half-deranged; he had no control over his relatives who formed his court. It was to be Sultan Omar Ali's lot to witness the loss of his province of Sarawak to a British adventurer who set himself up there as an independent *raja*, and to have to grant the cession of the island of Labuan in Brunai Bay to the British government as a British Crown Colony. These two events were to determine the course of Brunai's history to the present day.

The loss of Sarawak

The loss of Sarawak was due in the first instance to the activities and schemes of another of the Sultan's uncles, *Pangeran* Usop. One of Raja Muda Hassim's chief rivals at court, he had been expelled from Brunai. In 1835, Usop raised a rebellion against the governor of Sarawak, another Brunai nobleman called Pangeran Makota. This was not very hard to do since the Pangeran Makota's rule was harsh and extortionary in the extreme and affected not only the passive Land Dayaks but also the proud local Malay aristocracy as well. However, Usop's motives were not so much concerned with the welfare of the inhabitants of Sarawak as with his own private advantage. Sarawak, which then only comprised the area around Kuching, was emerging during the second and third decades of the nineteenth century from an obscure and ignored district into a province of some importance. It began to develop largely as a consequence of the foundation of Singapore. With its easy crossings into neighbouring Sambas, it became well known as a convenient route for smuggling contraband goods like salt and opium into that Dutch-controlled territory; furthermore it was building up a small but profitable trade in antimony with Singapore. In short, Sarawak's value was enhanced and this led Pangeran Usop to intrigue with a brother of the Sultan of Sambas for the detachment of the province from Brunai to Sambas in return for a suitable reward for himself. Then, exploiting the simmering discontent and promise of aid from Sambas, Usop incited the rebellion. Pangeran Makota proved quite unable to suppress the uprising and finally, in 1838, Raja Muda Hassim went to Sarawak himself to handle matters.

Raja Muda Hassim's presence in Sarawak was the principal cause of the arrival on the scene of an English adventurer called James Brooke[6] in August of the following year. The Raja Muda was known to and well thought of by the British authorities in Singapore[7] and when Brooke passed through Singapore on his way to explore the Bornean coastline, its governor, Bonham, took the opportunity to ask him to call at Sarawak first to contact the prince. Bonham was anxious for a restoration of the antimony trade which the troubles in Sarawak had interrupted. The Raja Muda received Brooke well and although he did not say so[8] welcomed the moral support against the rebels implied by Brooke's visit. But Brooke had other plans and sailed away to the east to visit Marudu Bay and the Celebes. On his return almost exactly twelve months later he found the same state of affairs as before. The rebellion remained uncrushed. This time Hassim was eager for Brooke's assistance to finish off the affair. Brooke agreed to help but after two months of trying to stir Hassim's soldiery to more aggressive action, threatened to abandon his attempts. In desperation, Hassim, who well knew that without the decisive advantage offered by Brooke's guns and men he could never hope to pacify Sarawak, now offered Brooke the governorship of the province as an inducement to stay. From the point of view of the interests of Brunai this was a disastrous mistake, because Brooke was no ordinary adventurer. Romantic and idealistic, James Brooke was a latter-day Raffles with dreams of extending British influence

throughout the whole archipelago.[9] He did so without any official backing whatever and he had no precise plans when he landed at Kuching. After proper hesitation, Brooke accepted this unparallelled opportunity. Within a short time, as much
by diplomacy as by warfare, Brooke brought about the submission of the rebels and
the restoration of peace.

The Raja Muda now found himself in an awkward situation. He had no authority to offer Brooke the governorship of a Brunai province in the first place and now
the Englishman was pressing him to implement his promise. Naturally enough,
opposition also came from Pangeran Makota, the actual governor, who had no
desire to surrender his fief to a foreigner and who had not been consulted anyway.
In February 1841, Hassim compromised by naming Brooke as 'resident of Sarawak'
but since this only allowed him to live 'for profit' in Kuching and said nothing
about a transfer of powers, Brooke was not satisfied. After further prevarications
and delays, Brooke forced the matter. Taking advantage of the chance arrival of a
British man o'war at Kuching[10] and finding an apt pretext for action in an attempt
by the Pangeran Makota to have him poisoned, Brooke trained his guns on the
town and delivered an ultimatum. Makota's supporters deserted him while 200
Ibans rallied to Brooke's support. The Raja Muda gave way and as Brooke himself
described it: 'after this demonstration affairs proceeded cheerily to a conclusion.
The Raja was active in settling; the agreement was drawn out, sealed, and signed:
guns fired, flags waved; and on September 24th, 1841 I became the governor of
Sarawak with the fullest powers'.

However, these powers needed confirming by the Sultan himself. The next year,
Hassim, who had now committed himself irrevocably to the Brooke cause, brought
the Englishman to Brunai where he appeared before the Sultan. Sultan Omar Ali
confirmed the agreement with a wave of the hand but his approval meant nothing without that of the Majlis Pangeran Brunai. This was secured through the good
offices of Pangeran Usop who was perhaps pleased to see his enemy, Pangeran Makota, worsted. So James Brooke became the governor of Sarawak 'with all its
revenue and dependencies' in return for an annual tribute of $2,500 and on condi-
tion that religion and custom should not be touched nor the province alienated
without the Sultan's consent.

The implications of allowing a British subject to become the ruler of a Brunai
province soon showed themselves when the following year Brooke returned to
Brunai, but this time with a squadron of five ships of the British navy under the
command of Capt. Sir Edward Belcher.[11] Overawed by the sight of this miniature
fleet which contained the first steamship he had ever set his eyes on, Sultan Omar
Ali signed a new treaty, in this case with the British government. Described as a
preliminary agreement, by this treaty the Sultan professed his friendship for Britain,
promised to foster trade, suppress piracy and avoid all alliances with foreign
powers. He also granted the cession of Sarawak in perpetuity to James Brooke
and his successors.

Brunai politics and Brooke policies

Despite the outward show, these developments were not welcome at Brunai. Not
only was James Brooke a foreigner and an infidel but he harboured dangerous
schemes. It was part of his belief and policy that in the general context of extending

British trade and influence, the people of Brunai should also recover their past glory and prosperity. In order to do this the ramshackle empire had to be reformed. The system of toll and tribute by which greater and lesser chieftains lived would have to be replaced by a system of regular taxation. Law and order would have to be substituted for the present violence and piracy. The results of all this would be the expansion of Brunai's trade with Singapore to the mutual benefit of both—and beyond this lay dreams of wider expansion into the interior and to Kutai beyond. To achieve these things James Brooke planned to use the Raja Muda as the instrument of his purpose in Brunai, while leading the way with the example he set by his own administration in Sarawak. Viewed from the court of Brunai, this programme had little that was attractive to offer. As far as most of the pangeran were concerned it was bad enough that the Raja Muda had strengthened his position and weakened theirs by relying so completely on Brooke. The policy of suppressing piracy which Brooke immediately engaged upon also struck at one of the Court's principal sources of revenue. Finally, no one welcomed a policy which encouraged the chances of British intervention. The unhappiness of the Brunai Court was shared even more strongly by the numerous self-governing chiefs along the coast who were to be the first to feel the effect of the new presence in Kuching. Inevitably a strong clique opposed to the Raja Muda and to Brooke quickly developed at Brunai with its ramifications stretching out along the entire coast. Its leader at Brunai was Usop who now held the post of Chief Minister in the stead of the absent Raja Muda.

In these circumstances Hassim's reluctance to leave Sarawak for Brunai is very understandable. At Kuching he could wait securely in the background, ready to take over if need be; at Brunai he would be in the midst of a hostile and intriguing court. However, Brooke found the Raja Muda's presence in Kuching an encumbrance to his administration and wanted him to return to Brunai where Brooke's own schemes were to be furthered. It was not till 1844 that the Raja Muda could be persuaded to go back. In October of that year, accompanied by Brooke and Belcher in two British warships, the voyage was made. They were well received, although noticeably not so well as the previous year, and once again the Sultan acquiesced in all that was demanded of him. Pangeran Usop was to be removed from the position of Chief Minister and the Raja Muda reinstated. The treaty of friendship between Brunai and Britain was reaffirmed and Brooke persuaded the Sultan to write a letter to the Queen of England offering to cede the island of Labuan.[12]

In the meantime Brooke had already taken vigorous steps to secure his position against the piratical chiefs who lived either within or on the borders of his new territory.[13] The most immediate problem was that of the Saribas Ibans who had answered the governor's call to abandon piracy by suspending a basket from a high tree to await his head and now were receiving active encouragement from Pangeran Makota. In June 1843 a British naval expedition under the command of Admiral Henry Keppel gave Brooke its support by raiding and destroying their strongholds at Padeh, Paku and Rimbas. The following year another British naval force, once again under Keppel's command, moved against the Ibans of Skrang, whose leader Sharif Sahab had established himself with Pangeran Makota at Patusan, not far from modern Simanggang, on the Batang Lupar. This stronghold was also destroy-

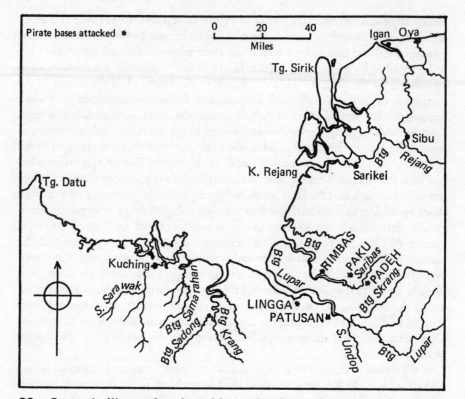

20. Sarawak, illustrating the raids on the Ibans of Skrang and Saribas,
    1843–1846

ed, making 'a glorious blaze' which lasted for three days: the expedition then went
on to wipe out all other pirate stockades along the Batang Lupar and its tributaries,
turning Pangeran Makota, Sharif Sahab and his brother, Sharif Mullar, into jungle
fugitives.[14]

   This disposed of the pirate problem in the west for the time being, and in 1845
British naval forces acting on the inspiration of Brooke and on the urgent appeals of
Hassim next launched an assault on the Illanun base in Marudu Bay. The Illanun
pirates of Marudu Bay were under Sharif Osman, who was not only threatening
to sack Brunai Town but was also in league with Usop, the leader of the
anti-Hassim, anti-Brooke faction at court. It was this fact which gave Hassim's (and
for the time the Sultan's) appeal its urgency when Brooke called at Brunai early in
1845 to announce his appointment as British Confidential Agent in Borneo.[a] 'The
pirates are exceedingly displeased we have made an alliance with the English and we
would strongly recommend an attack upon Marudu.'[15] Consequently in August of
that year a British naval squadron of eight ships sailed into the Bay, landed its force
of marines (of whom there were over 500) and forthwith completely destroyed
Sharif Osman's base at Langkon. Osman himself died of his wounds after the battle.
As Brooke put it, 'Marudu has ceased to exist'.

[a]See p. 200, note 70.

The blow against Sharif Osman was a blow against Pangeran Usop; but he had already been forced to flee the Brunai Court and go into open rebellion before the raid took place. On the way to Marudu, the commander of the British squadron, Sir Thomas Cochrane, called at Brunai to demand redress for the illegal detention of two shipwrecked British sailors some time before.[16] Sultan Omar Ali correctly laid the blame for the incident at the feet of Usop, who having had his house destroyed by the British for refusing to parley, fled into the jungle. When the British sailed away, Usop tried to seize Brunai Town but was defeated by one of the Raja Muda's brothers. Usop then retired to his lands at Kimanis where he was assassinated at the end of the year by agents of the Raja Muda.

The Brunai Palace Revolt and the cession of Labuan, 1846
Despite the defeat of the Iban and Illanun pirates, the flight of Pangeran Makota and the elimination of Pangeran Usop, the faction at the Brunai Court opposed to the Raja Muda, Brooke and all that they stood for remained strong. Usop was soon replaced by a new leader, Haji Seman, a man of humble origins. Haji Seman gained the ear of the Sultan and skilfully exploited the ruler's own grievances and resentments against the Raja Muda.[17] The outcome was that at the beginning of 1846 the Sultan gave his sanction to a plot to kill Hassim and all the pro-British pangeran on grounds of high treason. The plot was put into effect one January night when Haji Seman and his followers slew the Raja Muda and twelve of his principal supporters. The anti-foreign faction was now supreme.

It took three months for the news to reach Kuching;[18] Brooke, shocked and outraged, appealed at once for British naval support. In response, Admiral Cochrane in his 14-gun flagship with six other warships sailed from Singapore in June, picked up Brooke at Kuching and arrived in Brunai Bay in the first week of July. The forts guarding the approaches were quickly reduced and the fleet sailed up to Brunai Town which was also heavily bombarded. Marines were then landed only to find that the Sultan and his court had fled into the jungle. Two of the 'very few surviving pro-British chiefs' were placed in control of affairs, and Brooke and Cochrane then left, leaving behind a proclamation promising pardon on condition that piracy was abandoned and agreements with the British government honoured. The Sultan took some time to be persuaded that it was safe to re-emerge from his jungle hide-out, but when Brooke paid a second visit in August, the ruler was there to receive him.

All that now followed was decided under the lee of British guns. The court of Brunai was thoroughly cowed—and helpless—before British naval might and the ambitious James Brooke. Nothing could be done except to give in. Sultan Omar Ali asked Brooke for pardon and reconfirmed all his existing agreements with both Brooke and the British government. He also agreed to forego his annual tribute from Sarawak which meant that Brooke could now be considered a fully independent ruler, and recognized all territory between Tanjong Datu and Sungai Samarahan as the domains of the white raja. The appearance of another British warship later in the same month under the command of Capt. Mundy made the Sultan and his court retreat into the jungle for a second time but they felt composed enough to receive the British commander on his return visit three weeks later. Mundy had come to re-establish relations and the Sultan intimated that he was prepared to submit to any proposals put to him.[19] In December Mundy returned to Brunai to negotiate the cession of Labuan. At first the Sultan was inclined to bargain but demands for compensation were easily brushed aside, for, as Mundy described it: 'The boats in line of battle in front of the palace, and the marines with fixed bayonets on the threshold of the audience hall, though a picturesque group, were by no means calculated to encourage any act of violence'—or haggling, for that matter. A short treaty of cession was drawn up and signed, by which both parties also agreed to co-operate in the suppression of piracy. Six days later, in a simple ceremony on Labuan itself before the assembled pangeran of Brunai,[20] Mundy formally annexed the island in the name of the British Crown.

Brunai was now all but a British satellite. The process was carried one stage further in May the next year when James Brooke, in his new capacity (since February)[a] of 'Commissioner and Consul-General to the Sultan and Independent Chiefs of Borneo' dictated the terms of a second treaty between Britain and the sultanate. Brunai was to give Britain certain trading privileges, including free access to all her ports, and the Sultan undertook not to make 'any cession of an island or of any settlement on the mainland in any part of his dominions to any other nation, or to the subjects or citizens thereof, without the consent of her Britannic Majesty'. This last clause was one which James Brooke, who in January 1848 was appointed Governor of Labuan by the British Government, would live to regret.[b]

Brunai after 1846

The events of 1846 form a turning point in the history of the sultanate. After this it could hardly follow an independent policy of its own, faced with the growing power of its former vassal, Sarawak, and with a British base on its doorstep. Sarawak was the main problem. Although the palace revolt of January 1846 ultimately brought disaster to Brunai, it also marked the destruction of Brooke's policy of reforming the empire from within. His agent and supporter, Hassim, was dead and there was no one to take his place. From henceforth Sarawak would have to rely on its own resources, and it became Brooke policy to absorb the Brunai empire instead of reforming it. This policy was followed relentlessly during the second half of the nineteenth century until Brunai was reduced to its present proportions. It would probably have disappeared altogether had not the rulers of Brunai found unexpected champions in the British colonial governors of Labuan who followed Brooke. However, these were problems to concern Sultan Omar Ali's successor. The old Sultan made one last significant gesture of independence in 1850 by signing a commercial treaty with the United States, granting the Americans the most favoured nation treatment. Two years later he died and was succeeded by Abdul Mumin, his brother-in-law and distant relation.[21]

Sultan Mumin was to reign for the next thirty-three years. He was probably more competent than his predecessor but he was handicapped by the same circumstances—he had no control either over the principal pangeran, his relatives, at court, and still less over the numerous datos, sharifs and lesser chiefs along the shores of his dominions. He was also impoverished and was forced to bargain away his king-

[a]See p. 200, note 70.
[b]See p. 179.

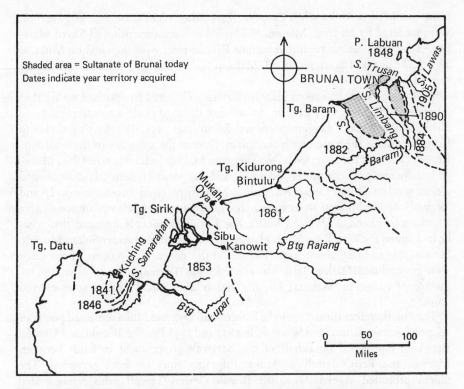

Shaded area = Sultanate of Brunai today
Dates indicate year territory acquired

P. Labuan 1848

S. Trusan

S./Lawas

1905

BRUNAI TOWN

Tg. Baram

S. Limbang

1890

1884

1882

Baram

Tg. Kidurong
Bintulu

Mukah

Oya

Tg. Sirik

1861

Tg. Datu

Sibu
Kanowit

Btg Rajang

Kuching

S. Samarahan

1853

1841

1846

Btg Lupar

0   50   100

Miles

21. Sarawak and Brunai, illustrating the growth of Sarawak's territory under the Brookes at the expense of the Sultans of Brunai

dom in concession after concession which further reduced its chances of recovery. The first of these was made within a year of his mounting the throne, when Brooke successfully bargained for the extension of Sarawak's frontier to the Rejang basin (to include Kanowit and Tanjong Sirik) in return for an annual tribute of $1,500. Brooke's intention was to curb the piratical activities of the Skrang and Saribas Ibans who had found a new leader in Rentab,[a] by building forts in the area and cutting off their access to the sea. Since Sultan Mumin did not have effective control over the districts concerned nor derive any revenue from them, the bargain seemed a good one.

The Muka crisis and Baram

Sarawak's next demand was for the territory between the Rejang and Tanjong Kidurong, beyond Bintulu. In this case the politics were more involved and centred on Oya and Muka, which were producers of sago. The sago trade which was carried on between these districts and Singapore via Kuching formed an important element in Sarawak's economy and so the political stability of the region was important to Brooke. However, the region was far from stable, being the stage for the rivalries of local chiefs, over whom as usual Brunai had no control. In 1855 matters

[a]See pp. 187–8.

came to a head at Muka when Pangeran Ersat, the Sultan's nominee as governor, was murdered by his rival, Matusin.[22] This led to the intervention of Sharif Masahor,[a] a Sarawak subject rebellious against Brooke rule, who marched on Muka to avenge the death of Ersat, his friend. Matusin fled to Kuching where he sought the help of James Brooke.

Since these events had taken place on Brunai soil, James Brooke had no right to interfere, but he was very keen to do so since the sago trade was interrupted and Sharif Masahor was a dangerous enemy. So in June 1855, Brooke paid a visit to Brunai to discuss the matter with the Sultan. Despite the existence of the usual anti-Brooke faction at the court led by the Pangeran Makota (who was now Chief Minister but discreetly absent on this occasion) and Pangeran Hashim Jalal,[b] an alleged son of the late Sultan Omar Ali, Sultan Mumin received Brooke cordially and 'begged' the Englishman to reorganize his government. He also promised to give Brooke a free hand at Oya and Muka. For a brief moment it appeared that what he had aimed for with Raja Muda Hassim had been attained under Sultan Mumin. He was able to bring about some changes at the court. The powers of the datos were revived and Hashim Jalal was created Dato Temenggong to offset the influence of Pangeran Makota; but the rest of the Sultan's offers soon proved illusory.[23]

The visit therefore turned out to be fruitless and Oya and Muka remained points of friction between Brunai and Sarawak. In 1857 and 1858 Brooke Brooke and Charles Brooke[24] intervened on behalf of the Sarawak government in feuds between Matusin and Ersat's family at Muka, imposing fines on both occasions. The Sultan protested vigorously to the British Consul-General who remonstrated with Kuching: the Sarawak government admitted its mistake and returned the fines. The position became more complex and serious in 1860 when an impostor named Tunjang proclaimed that he was the Dato Temenggong of Brunai and plotted with Sharif Masahor and others to drive all the Westerners out of Borneo altogether.[25] The plans miscarried. Tunjang was surrounded and captured by Dutch troops when he invaded the Kapuas basin while Sharif Masahor, forced to abandon his plans to assault Kuching, eventually turned up a fugitive in Muka which once again fell under his control. From Muka Masahor approached the British governor of Labuan, the Hon. G.W. Edwardes, and found a ready audience for his propaganda that he was a victim of Brooke imperialism.[26] The outcome was that when Brooke Brooke and Charles Brooke appeared at Muka at the beginning of 1861 to find out whether the port was really open to trade again as the Sultan had informed them, they found their way barred by Pangeran Nipah, Ersat's successor as governor, backed up by Sharif Masahor, and were prevented from taking counter-action by a British Navy gun-boat! Edwardes was on board, and he ordered the Brooke brothers to return to Kuching, which they did under protest.

The spectacle of the British governor of Labuan protecting Brunai from the advances of Sarawak was too good to be true, and although Sultan Mumin and his court were elated, they could only continue to remain the spectators that they had been throughout the whole affair. Disillusionment soon came. The Sarawak government protested to London, Edwardes was reprimanded and dismissed and in April

[a]See p. 188.
[b]See p. 184.

James arrived in Brunai to negotiate the cession of the coast as far as Tanjong Kidurong. At first this was not easy as some pangeran still pinned their hopes on British opposition to Sarawak, but in the end Brooke persuaded the Sultan that the
cession of the land for a rental of $4,500 a year was a good recompense for the
trouble that Muka and Oya caused him. The cession was confirmed on a second
visit in August. In the meantime, Muka had been occupied by a force of 200 British
marines sent from Singapore, and soon after Sharif Masahor went into exile forever.[a]

For the next few years after this episode, Brunai's attitude towards Sarawak stiffened. This was partly the result of encouragement from Labuan whose governors
looked upon the Brooke advance as a threat to the colony's own commercial interests, and partly because Sultan Mumin did not like Charles Brooke, James' new
heir apparent, who now ran Sarawak affairs. The Sultan's pride had been upset by
Charles' high-handed actions at Muka in 1861 and a new quarrel arose over a
matter of protocol in 1867[27] which resulted in Sarawak holding back two-thirds of
the annual tribute money owing to Brunai. Therefore, when shortly before James'
death in 1868, Charles requested the cession of another hundred miles of coastline
up to the Baram river in exchange for the usual annual payment, the Sultan refused
and appealed to the British governor of Labuan for protection against Brooke's
aggression. Labuan responded favourably and on its advice the British Foreign
Office warned Brooke that according to the Treaty of 1847 the Sultan was not allowed to make any cession of territory without the approval of the British government. Sultan Mumin's attitude had the support, of course, of those pangeran who
had property in the region.

The main reason for Sarawak's interest in Baram was connected with the Kayans.
The Kayans of the newly-acquired districts of the Upper Rejang proved impossible
to control while their kinsmen in Baram remained free. However, in 1870, goaded
by excessive taxation, the Baram Kayans became restless and finally in 1874 broke
out in open revolt against the Sultan's authority. This development altered Sultan
Mumin's attitude and he became prepared to negotiate the cession of the territory.
But still acting on the advice of Labuan,[28] the British Foreign Office forbade any
such negotiations and at the same time rejected out of hand Charles' own proposal
that either Britain or Sarawak should place Brunai under its protection. It also
turned down Charles' suggestion of two years later that in the case of Sarawak the
territorial alienation clause of the 1847 Treaty should be waived by Britain.

The creation of British North Borneo
Nevertheless, although Britain used the 1847 Treaty to check the Sarawak advance
she did nothing about a most far-reaching concession obtained by a certain Charles
Lee Moses[29] from the Brunai government in 1865. In July of that year Moses presented himself in Brunai as the American consul, a post provided for by the treaty
of 1850.[b] Within a month of his arrival and by making the maximum use of his
official position, Moses secured from the Sultan and the Temenggong a personal
ten-year lease over the greater part of north-east Borneo, including the islands of

[a]See p. 188.
[b]Refer p. 176.

Banggi, Balabac and Palawan, for an annual rental of $9,500. He then went to Hong Kong and sold his rights to an American businessman there called Joseph Torrey who, entering into partnership with three others,[30] formed the American Trading Company. In November of that year Moses returned to Brunai with Torrey, who was installed as 'Raja of Ambong and Marudu and Supreme Ruler of the whole of the North portion of Borneo'. This was followed by the organization of a small plantation and trading settlement at Kimanis Bay, consisting of ten Americans and eighty Chinese labourers—all financed by advances from Chinese businessmen in Labuan. The settlement lasted barely one year before it went bankrupt. Torrey fled back to Hong Kong hotly pursued by one of his Labuan creditors, while Moses, who had broken with him, desperately tried to recoup his losses by other methods.[31]

As far as the Sultan and the Temenggong were concerned (neither of whom had realized a single dollar out of the whole transaction so far), this was the end of the matter until one day ten years later, when Torrey reappeared accompanied by a German adventurer with an Austrian title, called Baron Gustavus von Overbeck.[32] Von Overbeck was one of several who had learned about the Moses-Torrey concession, and in the beginning of 1875 bought out Torrey's rights in the American Trading Company for $15,000. He now came to renew the concession, due to expire. Temenggong Hashim, improvident and hard up, was quite prepared to renew the lease for another ten years and signed an agreement to that effect on 21 June for $1,000. However Sultan Mumin, now very old, proved stubborn. He refused to endorse the Temenggong's agreement. He mistrusted Torrey and was influenced by Hugh Low, the British governor of Labuan, who regarded the whole deal as a dangerous threat to British interests.

Undismayed, Overbeck left for Europe to acquire capital for his venture. In London he met Alfred Dent, a rich British businessman with interests in Hong Kong,[33] who entered into partnership with him to exploit the Borneo concession. Dent now became the master-mind behind the whole operation. In 1877 Overbeck and Torrey returned to Brunai, leaving Dent in Singapore, to reopen negotiations with the Brunai Court. This time Sultan Mumin's reception was very different. There was a new British governor in Labuan, the young W.H. Treacher. Treacher saw in Overbeck's offers great opportunities for Britain (and probably for himself) and so he advised the Sultan to grant the concession subject to certain restrictive clauses ensuring that it remained under British control. The leading Chinese merchants of Brunai also interceded in Overbeck's favour and Sultan Mumin himself, overwhelmed by the sight of the ready cash Overbeck brought with him, gave way. On 29 December 1877 the Sultan and the Temenggong signed an agreement with Overbeck and Dent which granted the foreigners the cession of 'all territories, rivers, lands and provinces' lying between Kimanis Bay and the Sebuku river; Overbeck was created 'Maharaja of Sabah and Raja of Gaya and Sandakan', with powers of life and death over the ceded areas, absolute ownership of all agricultural animal and mineral products of the country, the right to make laws, coin money, create an army and navy, and levy customs duties and taxes, with 'all other powers and rights usually exercised by and belonging to sovereign rulers'. All this was in exchange for an annual tribute of $12,000 for the Sultan and $3,000 for the Temenggong, with the provision that the lease would lapse if the tribute was not paid for three consecutive years. There were no safeguards for British interests as desired by Treacher. In this way Sabah was detached from Brunai and the foundations were laid for the modern state of today.

The concessionaries, accompanied by Treacher who went to keep a watching brief for Britain, then went to Sulu where they signed a similar treaty with Sultan Jamal-al Alam[a] so that they could have undisputed claim to the whole of the northeastern portion of Borneo. Then, leaving new officials at Sandakan Bay, Papar and Tempasuk,[34] Overbeck and his friends sailed away.

Having obtained their concessions, Dent and Overbeck now required either to sell them or acquire the necessary financial and political backing to run them. Overbeck failed to interest the capitalists of Vienna and in 1880 sold out his stake in the venture to Dent. Dent, who earlier had thought of selling *his* share to Overbeck, now had to go on and get what backing he could in England. He succeeded in interesting a number of rich and prominent Englishmen who had connexions in the Far East, and between them they brought about the formation of the British North Borneo Company to run the concessions.[35] This body was granted a Royal Charter by the British Parliament in November 1881. The Company, like the East India Company of yore, was granted sovereign powers over Dent's concessions provided that it always remained 'British in character and domicile', that it did not alienate territories or concessions without the British government's approval, and that it took all practicable steps to abolish slavery, adhered to local religion and custom and administered justice with due regard for native law. The Company's principal representative in Borneo must have the prior approval of Britain. Britain was to control the territory's foreign relations, and its harbours were to be at the free disposal of the British Navy. However, Britain did not undertake to protect the territory, a commitment which was not entered into until all the North Borneo territories were placed under British protection in 1888. The British North Borneo Company administered Sabah (under the name of British North Borneo) until the Japanese invasion of 1941.

The 'Scramble for Brunai'

The stage was now set for the 'Scramble for Brunai'. The Sultanate had called into existence two states more powerful than itself. Sarawak under Raja Charles remained committed to a policy of unrelenting expansion and the absorption of what remained of Brunai, a policy intensified by mortification at the establishment of British North Borneo. The British North Borneo Company was anxious to round off its own acquisitions which were not co-terminous but separated by river valleys still under the control of independent chiefs or vassals of Brunai. The Sultan's own misgoverned subjects were increasingly attracted to the stable conditions provided by Brooke or Company rule, with the consequence that revolts became more and more frequent.

Firstly pressure was renewed by Sarawak for Baram. Charles, infuriated by reports of the concession granted to Overbeck and Dent, appeared in Brunai in early 1878 to protest to the Sultan, angrily interviewed Treacher in Labuan,[36] and sent vigorous objections to London. Sultan Mumin by this time was quite ready to hand over Baram to Sarawak as he had lost all hope of restoring his Kayan subjects to his

[a]See p. 214.

22. British North Borneo, shewing concessions after the purchase of the Overbeck-Dent Concession of 1877–1878

allegiance, and in December came to an agreement with Charles for its cession against an annual payment of $4,200, subject to the approval of the British government. This was still not forthcoming, for although the Colonial Office was sympathetic to Charles, the Foreign Office was influenced by Treacher against allowing the concession. Sultan Mumin took full advantage of these circumstances to procrastinate in the hope of raising the price, but Charles, quick to sense these tactics, broke off negotiations altogether. However, when in 1881 the British government granted a charter to Dent and his associates it no longer had valid grounds for objecting to the cession of Baram. The objection was withdrawn and in 1882 Baram was transferred to Sarawak for the original offer of $4,200 a year.

The cession of Baram in 1882 helped inspire the inhabitants of Limbang to rise in revolt against Brunai two years later. Like the people of Baram, they were exasperated by the exactions of the uncontrollable Brunai pangeran and compared their own sorry state with that of Baram, now benefiting from Brooke rule. The revolt was serious. There were no more Kayan subjects to turn on to the rebels, as had been the practice on such occasions in the past, and in the end the Sultan was reduced to the expedient of borrowing rifles from Labuan to defend his palace from the insurgents. This rebellion was probably spontaneous although Treacher was convinced that Charles' agents were behind it. Nevertheless, he admitted in his report that the people of Limbang were ready to accept anybody's rule rather than be replaced under the government of Brunai. By the end of the year, through his intervention, a truce was patched up, but Brunai authority was not restored in the territory.

In the meantime both the Company and Brooke were busy coveting other bits of Brunai. Treacher, now governor of North Borneo, 'quietly annexed' the uninhabited island of Balambangan[a] in the early 1880s; he purchased the Pangalat river for $300 a year in 1883, and the Putatan district from the late Raja Muda Hassim's impoverished son, Damit, for $1,000 annual rental the following year. Treacher and Brooke both competed for control of the Padas-Klias peninsula during 1884, a territory of some 4,000 square miles. Treacher won, because his agent, the west coast resident, Davies, effectively bribed members of the royal harem to overcome Sarawak pretensions. The peninsula passed to the Company for $3,000 a year.[37] Sarawak was compensated for this advance of her rival by securing the cession of Trusan at the end of the same year on the pretext of the murder of Sarawak traders by some Murut tribesmen. Obliged to admit that he could not bring the murderers to justice and confronted with a demand for $22,000 as compensation for the incident, the Sultan found it preferable to accept the alternative suggestion that he offer the district to Charles for an annual rental of $4,500, to go to Temenggong Hashim, the owner. As was remarked by a Colonial Office official a few months later, 'If something is not done soon to cool the exasperation of Messrs. Brooke and Treacher, there will not be a pangeran left in Brunai'.[38]

Brunai becomes a British Protectorate

Early in 1885, with the 'scramble' in full swing, Sultan Abdul Mumin, who was nearly a hundred years old, died. Faced with the prospect of the extinction of his

[a]See pp. 209–10.

kingdom by the combined efforts of his rapacious neighbours and his own greedy pangeran, his last act was to make the latter take a solemn oath that no more districts under the sway of Brunai should be leased to foreign nations or individuals. This engagement did not have much effect. The instability of the regime was further increased on the accession of the Temenggong as Sultan Hashim Jalal-al Alam Akamudin, for many of the Brunai pangeran refused to accept him as the son of Sultan Omar Ali that he claimed to be, and withheld their recognition of his sovereignty.

The Company's advance continued. Treacher annexed the Mantanini Isles in 1885, and later in the same year secured the Kawang river despite Sarawak's opposition.[39] In November the Limbang problem blew up again when the people rebelled for a second time and threatened Brunai Town. This development provoked a crisis over the continued survival of the sultanate itself, and culminated in Brunai becoming a British protectorate. Sultan Hashim's first reaction was to appeal to Charles of Sarawak for aid. The appeal was rejected on the grounds that Sarawak did not wish to help in the restoration of Brunai misrule, and Charles sent his agent to Limbang to encourage its inhabitants to believe in a Sarawak deliverance. This did nothing to improve the relations between Sarawak and Brunai and the murder of a Sarawak pangeran in Brunai Town early in 1886, whose perpetrators the Sultan refused to arrest, made them worse. This time, however, Sultan Hashim found that he could no longer rely on the traditional support of the British in Labuan. Dr. Leys, the new British consul-general, supported Sarawak in its claims to Limbang as the best means to restore peace and order, a solution acceptable to the pangeran holding land there (it offered hope of securing their rents) and one which would probably have been received in the end by the Sultan himself. But he now found an unsolicited champion in Treacher, who was determined to prevent at all costs the cession of Limbang to Sarawak and the eventual absorption of the sultanate by Charles. He had questions asked in the British Parliament and launched a campaign in government circles against both Charles and Dr. Leys.

The outcome was that in 1887 Weld, the Governor of the Straits Settlements, was appointed to inquire into the whole situation. In Brunai Weld, who fancied his own ability at handling the Malay rulers of the Peninsula, found the Sultan determined to retain Limbang and apparently anxious to receive a British official as adviser. The Sultan liked Weld who listened to all that he had to say, and was prepared completely to override Leys and his policies. Weld reported that things should stay as they were; Brunai should have a British Resident who would administer Limbang in the name of the Sultan. He added later from Singapore that Brunai should also be placed under British protection. Dr. Leys, humiliated by Weld, still campaigned for Sarawak and reported at the end of the year that the Sultan was willing to cede Limbang for $20,000, while Charles himself still encouraged the inhabitants of the district to place their hopes on him. Weld retorted by accusing both Charles and Dr. Leys of putting pressure on the Sultan, and persuaded the Foreign Office to forbid the cession. Alcock of the British North Borneo Company[40] then entered a desperate plea that Brunai be placed under British protection as the only way to save it from Brooke rapacity. This, and other considerations,[a] led to the final decision to make Brunai a British Protectorate, together with

[a] See p. 323.

Sarawak and British North Borneo. Weld negotiated the terms with the Sultan who was content to accept the protectorate because it was the best guarantee for the preservation of his own dynasty and sovereignty. However, Hashim rejected the British proposal for the appointment of an Adviser on the model of those in the Peninsula states, and for reasons of economy the British government accepted this rejection. Brunai came under British protection in September 1888.

The partitioning of Brunai—the last phase
Nevertheless, British protection did not prevent the sultanate from losing still more territory. In 1889 it lost its nominal control over Padas Damit.[a] In 1890 the people of Limbang rose up for a third time and declared for annexation by Sarawak. Charles went there in person in March and in a proclamation took over the government of the district 'unless Her Majesty the Queen of England may see fit otherwise'. After the British Consul at Labuan had ascertained that this was what the inhabitants really wanted, Britain in 1891 recognized the annexation—on condition that the Sultan received an annual rental of $6,000. Sultan Hashim refused to accept this unilateral solution, wired Queen Victoria, rejected the indemnity and continued protesting until in 1895 he was told by the Foreign Office that the matter was closed.[41] In 1898, as a consequence of the Mat Salleh revolt,[b] the Company purchased the Inanam, Mengkabong, Menggatal, Api Api, Simbulan and Nafas Tambalang rivers. The Sultan sold his sovereign rights for $1,200 a year while the chiefs sold their personal rights[42] for payments which ranged from $2,500 to $200 a year. The Company made these purchases since these little enclaves in the middle of its domains served as places of refuge for rebels and law breakers, and were ideal marts for the sale of guns and child-slaves.

In 1897 Kinarut was acquired when its inhabitants drove out the agent of the absentee Brunai pangeran who was its landlord because of his excessive impositions and placed themselves under the protection of the Company. In 1899 there was a rebellion in Belait and Tutong, again the result of unbearable exactions by the Brunai nobility whose sources of income were now so reduced. The rebels appealed to be placed under Sarawak, but Charles declined the prospect of another long drawn-out tussle with Brunai, North Borneo and the British government. The situation was exploited by various pangeran while the palace remained helpless. In 1902 Lawas, another great mart where Murut children were traded for guns and ammunition, was purchased by the Company, paying the Sultan $600 for his sovereign rights while the pangeran accepted annual payments to a total value of $4,475 a year. But this led to a dispute between the absentee landowners at Brunai and the actual occupant of the land, a pangeran called Abu Bakar, who swore he would yield his territory only to Sarawak. The matter was submitted to Swettenham[43] for arbitration, who, solomon-wise, upheld both the legality of the lease to the Company and the claim of Abu Bakar. After trying the expedient of inviting a nephew to administer the territory, which did not work out well, the Company decided to offer the land to Sarawak. A bargain was struck which came into effect

[a]See pp. 190–1.
[b]See pp. 191–2.

in 1905. Charles renounced some shadowy claims of his to mining concessions in north-west Borneo and Lawas became part of Sarawak. This was Sarawak's last accretion of territory. North Borneo made its last acquisition at the expense of Brunai in 1903 with the purchase of the Membakut river for $2,400.

Meanwhile Charles had not yet given up hope of absorbing the rest of Brunai. In 1903 he proposed annexing all Brunai except Brunai Town. The Sultan and his heirs would still receive all the cession money due to them besides an annual pension of $1,900 during the Sultan's own lifetime and $500 for his successors. In addition to this the sultan was to receive a down payment of $10,000 and all honours due to him. Similar provisions were offered to the Pangeran Bendahara and Pangeran Pemancha, the two chief noblemen. Neither Sultan Hashim nor the British Foreign Office committed themselves to this proposal but at about the same time the Sultan showed where his true feelings lay when he appealed vainly to the Sultan of Turkey for help, offering to surrender all his possessions (including Limbang) to him. At last, in 1906, having long been urged to do so by men like Weld, Swettenham and Ernest Birch, the British government decided to impose a British Resident on Brunai. Sultan Hashim, who at the last moment appeared to prefer Charles' terms to a British official at his court, was obliged to sign an agreement accepting a British official whose advice had to be taken on all matters except religion and custom. His own income and that of the principal pangeran were guaranteed by the British government.

This was the last act of Sultan Hashim Jalal-al Alam Akumudin. He died a few months later and his successor, Sultan Mohamed Jamal-al Alam, began his reign in a state now fully under British control.

Sarawak: Iban resistance to Brooke rule
Although James and Charles Brooke were highly successful in their dealings with the rulers of Brunai, it took them many years to bring all their own subjects under effective control. The first twenty years of Brooke rule were taken up by constant campaigns against rebels and unsubmissive chieftains. Resistance came from two main groups—the Ibans of Skrang and Saribas on the one hand, and the followers of Sharif Masahor, the undeclared ruler of the Lower Rejang, on the other. The Ibans of Skrang and Saribas were the first to offer resistance since they were the first affected by the policy of suppressing piracy. Under a succession of leaders they opposed Brooke domination. First it was Sharif Sahap of Sadong, his brother, Sharif Mullar from Undop, Sharif Ahmad from Lingga and Linggir from Saribas, aided and abetted after 1842 by Pangeran Makota, who were James' main enemies. They could put a force of 20,000 warriors into the field, tough, skilled sailors, adept at jungle warfare and sea-fighting alike. As we have already seen,[a] Brooke, with the aid of the British navy had to make two strong raids on their strongholds on the tributaries of the Batang Lupar in 1843 and 1844 to break their power. After these assaults, Sharif Sahab escaped to Pontianak where he died shortly afterwards. Sharif Mullar became an exile for many years but was eventually allowed to return and die in his homeland. Pangeran Makota was captured but allowed to return to

[a]Refer p. 173.

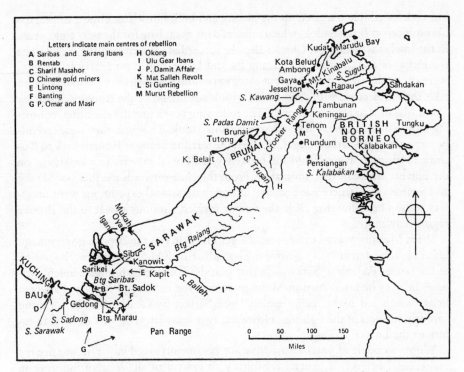

23. North Borneo, illustrating rebellions and centres of resistance to British control

Brunai where he continued to act as a nucleus of opposition to Brooke power but never directly interfered in Sarawak again.[44]

The place of these men was taken by a Malay who was simply known as the Laksamana. His activities in late 1848 and early 1849 raiding the Sadong, killing scores of Malays, driving the Melanau in droves to Kuching, and threatening Gedong, led to the so-called 'battle' of Batang Marau in July of that year. At Batang Marau, at the entrance to Batang Skrang, a flotilla of British naval vessels and 2,500 Iban auxilliaries led by Brooke's personal war perahu, encountered a large Saribas Iban pirate fleet on its way back from a raid along the Rejang. In the slaughter which followed over 800 Ibans lost their lives and 88 perahus were destroyed: the British force suffered 'two natives killed and about six wounded'. This action eliminated the Laksamana, Linggir and many other notable Saribas and Skrang chiefs. It was the most devastating blow they had ever suffered.[45]

But it was not the end of Iban resistance. One survivor from Batang Marau was an Iban chief called Rentab, who swore that he would never submit to Brooke control. He lay quiet until 1853 when he made preparations to attack the Ibans of Skrang, now in Brooke territory.[a] Forewarned, Brooke's officials were able to thwart the expedition in an engagement fought on the Skrang river from which, after both sides had suffered heavy losses, Rentab was able to withdraw, checked

[a]Refer p. 177.

but undefeated. He retreated up the Skrang and built himself an almost impregnable position on Bukit Sadok, which remained his main base for the next eight years. In the lowlands at Lingga, Charles Brooke succeeded in pacifying the area despite the intrigues and opposition of Dang Isa and Dang Ajar, two Malay ladies who were the principal landowners, but three expeditions sent against Rentab failed to take their objective.[46] In 1860 Rentab took advantage of the troubles caused by Sharif Masahor to resume his raids. The following year a fourth expedition, consisting mostly of Ibans, was led by Charles against Sadok. This time they were carefully prepared, reached their target, stormed the fort and brought Rentab back to Kuching in triumph. Rentab, old and broken, was allowed to retire to a longhouse on the Entabai where he died soon after. From this time onwards the Ibans of Skrang and Saribas were largely pacified, and although occasional expeditions were necessary to stop head-hunting raids they never formed a serious threat to the Brooke régime any more.

Sharif Masahor was an even more dangerous enemy of the Brooke government. Until 1853, his territory lay outside the bounds of Brooke authority but the cession of the Lower Rejang to Sarawak in that year did not change his independent attitude. In 1855 he intervened in Muka to avenge the murder of his ally, Pangeran Ersat, which led to his being exiled from Sarikei by Charles Brooke for using Sarawak subjects in the fighting. However, two years later, he was allowed to return to the Lower Rejang.[47]

Within a couple of years Sharif Masahor became involved in—if he was not the mastermind behind—a general conspiracy to get rid of all Western influence in Borneo. His principal accomplices were Tunjang, who claimed to be the Pangeran Temenggong of Brunai, and Abdul Gapur, the Datu Pa' Tinggi of Sarawak,[48] who was already a long-established opponent of James Brooke. The first signs of trouble came when two European officials at the fort at Kanowit were murdered by the Iban tribesmen there. Sharif Masahor's involvement in these happenings was deeply suspected in Kuching, although he acted very correctly and there was no concrete evidence. However, he showed his hand next year when he openly associated himself with Tunjang and joined in the general plan to seize Kuching. The grand scheme miscarried, Sharif Masahor's own part in it was exposed, and he fled to Muka, from where he succeeded in embroiling Labuan against the Brookes.[49] His downfall came when Sultan Mumin ceded the coastline up to Tanjong Kidurong to James Brooke, and a force of British marines occupied Muka. He fled to Brunai where, an embarrassment to the court, he was handed by the Sultan over to the British who exiled him to Singapore. There he lived out the rest of his days, intriguing fitfully but with his power broken; he eked out his small pension from the Sarawak government by shipbuilding. He died in 1890.

Sarawak: The Chinese Rising of 1857

In 1857 the Brooke régime faced another rebellion which took it entirely by surprise and which came nearer than any other to extinguishing its rule. This was in February of that year, when the Chinese kongsi working the gold mines at Bau rose up in insurrection, sailed downstream to Kuching and occupied the town for the best part of a week. Their intention was to kill James, overthrow his government and set up one of their own in its stead. James escaped by a hair's breadth and fled downstream. Several of his closest associates were killed, the town and istana were burned, and the initiative fell completely into the hands of the Chinese. But the goldminers could not hope to succeed for long, since once the element of surprise had been taken advantage of, the odds were against them. Even had they killed James, his nephew, Charles, was at Skrang with 10,000 loyal Ibans behind him to exact revenge. The insurgents numbered barely one thousand. Moreover, the Malay population was wholly behind Brooke and merely waiting for the moment to strike back. The kongsi leaders decided on retreat, leaving a party behind to oppose the return of James and his supporters. Meanwhile James himself was waiting at the mouth of the Sarawak river for aid to come. It arrived in the shape of the regular steamship from Singapore, followed shortly afterwards by Charles and his Ibans. With these forces James was able to re-possess his capital. The Chinese goldminers retreated or were driven across the border into Sambas and Dutch territory. About a thousand of them died. Another 2,500 fled the country. The great kongsi of Bau was no more, to the audible relief of the other Chinese inhabitants of the country.

This uprising which Spencer St. John[50] described as 'the most absurd and causeless rebellion that ever occurred' had its roots in the great autonomy enjoyed by the goldmining kongsi at Bau, which like its counterparts in Sambas,[a] was accustomed to conducting its affairs like an independent state. All attempts by the Kuching government to control or interfere with its activities were resented. During the early 1850s the number of the Chinese miners at Bau increased; the events in Sambas[51] brought in a large number of refugees so that by 1857 the population was estimated to stand at around 4,000. During the same period there was also increasing interference on the part of the Kuching authorities. In 1852 the Bau kongsi was forced to hand up a secret society member wanted by the police for criminal activities, but he was only surrendered after a show of force. In 1856 Kuching, noting that while the mining population was larger, the revenue from opium, a government monopoly, was less, imposed a fine of £150 on the kongsi for smuggling. This fine was paid with the greatest show of resentment in January the next year. This, the damage suffered by James' reputation by the trial in Singapore, and the general wave of anti-British feeling sweeping the Chinese world of South-East Asia as a result of the start of the Second Anglo-Chinese (Opium) War[52] all contributed to the sudden insurrection of February. After this single episode the Chinese never rose up against Brooke rule again.

Other Sarawak rebels
After the submission of Sharif Masahor, the Brooke family had only to face a small number of other rebellions in the years ahead, led by natural leaders, which caused great inconvenience but did not seriously challenge their hegemony. Charles brought about the submission of the Kayans of the Baram in 1863. In the 1870s the Ibans of Kanowit found a leader in Lintong, who in May 1870, attempted to capture the fort at Sibu. In the punitive expedition which followed, Lintong was cap-

[a]See pp. 259–61.

tured and made to live in Kuching where he became a loyal supporter of the régime. Some of the Ibans of Kanowit, however, continued their resistance, and only after several more expeditions and the resettlement of some tribes in more accessible areas were they brought under control.

The last of the great rebels was an Iban called Banting, who although of humble origins, made himself the leader of the Ibans of the middle Batang Lupar in the 1890s. For the next eighteen years he was a source of concern to Kuching. Expeditions sent against him to end his raids in 1894 and 1897 had no lasting results. In 1902 the largest force Sarawak had ever seen was assembled under the leadership of the Raja Muda, Vyner Brooke,[53] and moved up the Batang Lupar. But the expedition was ravaged by cholera which claimed over a thousand victims, and it was forced to withdraw. However, determined attempts in 1903 against the rebels in the Pan Range and up the Engkari river caused most of their chiefs to submit. But Banting, and his ally Ngumbang[54] remained elusive. They offered to give themselves up in 1906, and then changed their minds. In 1907, with the numbers of their supporters falling, they attended a great peace meeting at Kapit where, in the presence of Charles and Vyner, Banting, Ngumbang and the Ibans of Ulu Ai agreed to make their peace with the Ibans of the Lower Batang Lupar. But at the last moment, Banting reneged and took to the hills once more. Finally, in 1908, a destructive expedition led by Bailey, the District Officer at Simanggang, forced Banting to submission and order.

After this there was no more fighting in the First and Second Divisions of Sarawak except for the minor affairs of Pangeran Omar and Masir in 1908 and 1909 respectively.[55] Further east, Okong, a chief of Trusan, rose in rebellion in 1900, which was eventually quelled. In the Third Division there was trouble on the upper reaches of the Sungai Balleh and its tributaries amongst a group of Iban tribesmen there between 1915 and 1919.[56] But essentially Brooke rule remained unchallenged until 1941.

Sabah: The Padas Damit Affair

In the new dominions of the British North Borneo Company, the resistance to the establishment of its authority was sporadic and isolated, and apart from a couple of instances not serious. However, the resources of the Company were at first so limited and the area under its jurisdiction so large that even a small uprising could be a grave matter.

The first serious incident concerned the Padas-Klias Peninsula. When this was ceded in 1884, the valley of the Padas Damit river was not included. Immediately there arose a boundary dispute. Padas Damit was administered by the Pangeran Shahbandar on behalf of his sister. He claimed that his territory extended to the right bank of the neighbouring stream: his neighbours nevertheless claimed otherwise and said that the boundary lay along the watershed dividing the two valleys. The matter was as simple as that, and after mounting tension on both sides with the Shahbandar's neighbours staking out their claims with white flags and his men raiding into their valley, in February 1887 the matter was referred to the Sultan of Brunai. The Sultan decided in favour of the watershed as the proper boundary, a decision rejected by the Shahbandar. His raids continued. Hugh Low, newly arrived in Brunai, offered his mediation but this was turned down by the independent-minded chief. The British Foreign Office refused to intervene and after warnings had been issued on all sides, the Company decided that it must act. In October 1888 the acting Resident on the west coast, D. Daly, sent an ultimatum to the Shahbandar, demanding the release of four notorious criminals known to be taking refuge in the valley. There was no reply. Next month Daly invaded Padas Damit, heading a small force which included Ibans recruited from Sarawak (without permission). He met with determined resistance and the campaign was badly managed.[57] In December two guns from Singapore came as reinforcements followed in early January 1889 by a hundred Perak Sikhs. The following month the main fort was captured and in March the Pangeran Shahbandar surrendered his charge on the intervention of Hamilton, the governor of Labuan, who insisted that he should be amply compensated.[58]

Sabah: The Mat Salleh Revolt

The chief characteristic of the Padas Damit affair was the clumsy way in which it was handled. Even clumsier still was the handling of a chieftain of mixed Sulu-Bajau descent called Mat Salleh which provoked the most serious and prolonged rebellion against its authority which the Company was to experience.

Mat Salleh, who was a chieftain from the upper reaches of the Sungai Sugut, first came to the attention of the Company's officials in 1894 as a refractory chief who tended to ignore the dictates of the police and of the law courts.[59] In August 1895, he appeared at Sandakan at the head of a considerable armed following, demanding to see the Resident with grievances of his own. Obtaining no satisfaction, he retired and apart from sending a letter inquiring why his village had been burned,[60] was not heard of again. All attempts to contact him having failed, in July 1896 he was declared an outlaw and a police party was sent to capture him. This was also a miserable failure and at the end of the year Mat Salleh was offered a free pardon— and exile. Mat Salleh's reply came in the following July (1897), when with a force of Bajaus recruited from Brunai enclaves[61] he swept down upon the settlement at Gaya and sacked it. In November, he launched another attack with a mixed group of a hundred Bajaus, Sulus and Kadazans, this time on Ambong, seizing the residency but not capturing the village. By this time Mat Salleh had the whole of the west coast in a state of high alarm. He then withdrew to Ranau in the hinterland where he had constructed a formidable fortress.[62] At the end of that year, while British Navy gunboats patrolled the coastline, a government expedition made its laborious way to Ranau where the fort was finally stormed at a cost of twenty-two lives. Mat Salleh escaped and became a rebel fugitive with a remnant pack of bandits and outlaws.

However, the prospect of a long game of hide-and-seek with Mat Salleh was more than the Company with its slender resources was prepared to contemplate, so early in 1898, W.C. Cowie,[63] its Managing Director, came out from England and at a pre-arranged meeting with Mat Salleh struck a bargain: Mat Salleh and his followers were all to receive free pardons and be allowed to settle and govern themselves in the Tambunan Valley free from Company interference if he would submit and abandon his activities. Mat Salleh accepted these very generous terms, but immediately cries of bad faith rang out from all sides. The written agreement set out after the verbal agreement at the meeting was different.[64] The Tambunan Valley was not the Company's to offer for they had never occupied it and its Kadazan inhabitants had not been consulted. Numerous Company officials resigned in protest against Cowie's policy.[65] Mat Salleh defied the Company and Cowie quarrelled with his fellow directors as to whether they should follow a policy of conciliation or war. The net outcome was that Mat Salleh occupied the Tambunan Valley, using the Tegaas Kadazans to build a network of forts and fortified villages at one end, and raiding the Tambunan Kadazans at the other. He recruited Bajaus, obtained arms and ammunition from the Brunai enclaves and awaited the inevitable assault by the Company.

In the meantime, in early 1899, the Tambunan Kadazans had appealed to Fraser at Keningau, the nearest Company outpost, for protection. Beaufort, the governor, decided that a government post must be set up in the valley, and an expedition to clear Mat Salleh out of his redoubt started on its way at the end of the year. In February 1900 the Company's forces were launching their attacks on the main fort and Mat Salleh was killed by a stray shot.

However, his death did not mark the end of the rebellion which spluttered on under his lieutenants for the next three years. The chief of them, Mat Sator, led 300 Bajaus, Lanun and Kadazan to raid Kudat in April 1900. They captured the town but bungled their own opportunities and in the ensuing confusion both Mat Sator and two of his principal followers were killed. The capable and energetic Clifford,[66] seasoned by his Pahang experiences, was now governor, and in an expedition to track down the raiders captured thirty of them. But others continued and for two more years the west coast was prey to lightning raids made by bands of rebels led by Kamunta, Langkap and others. 1901 saw increasing police activity and the construction of Kota Belud in the heart of Bajau country played a decisive part in pacification. More and more rebels were captured or surrendered; most were eventually pardoned but some were shot.[67] By June 1901 there were fifty left—only six months after Jesselton (Kota Kinabalu) itself had been thrown into panic by rumours of an impending attack. By January 1902 sixteen remained. In April Kamunta was wounded and all but captured in a sea fight off the west coast, and gave himself up the following month—to be shot by the firing squad. In 1903 the last of the rebel leaders, Langkap, was captured and executed.

Sabah: other rebels

Apart from these two episodes, the Company's rule was established and accepted without undue friction. Shortly after his arrival in Sandakan Bay in 1878, Pryer secured the help of a British gunboat to destroy the Illanun pirate base at Tungku, which had a decisive effect on the east coast. There was trouble in Kawang in 1885, largely connected with Sarawak's interest and intrigues in the district, which cost the lives of four officials but did not lead to an uprising[a]. There was an ugly massacre of over a hundred people at Kalabakan in 1891 as a result of a megalomaniac police officer's desire for revenge.[68] A Kadazan from Mumus on Marudu

[a]See p. 198, note 39.

Bay called Si Gunting defied government from the slopes of Mount Kinabalu for ten years before he gave himself up in 1905.[69] And in 1915 the individualistic Muruts astonished everybody by combining under the leadership of a certain Antanum to rebel against the pressures of western civilization which impinged upon their ancient pursuits of slave-trading and head-hunting. This rebellion which was centred on Rundum in the country between Tenom and Pensiangan, met its end before a police party which besieged the rebel stronghold at Selangit on the Tagul river. The death of Antanum during this siege destroyed their unity and their resistance evaporated. Like Sarawak, the next challenge faced by the Company came from Japan.

The problem of Sarawak's status

Both Sarawak and British North Borneo faced certain international difficulties in establishing their status and their boundaries. James Brooke spent the whole of his career as ruler of Sarawak in an attempt to obtain annexation, protection or recognition by the British government. At first, James hoped that he could induce the British government to take over Sarawak as a Crown Colony, but although he secured the annexation of Labuan and between 1845 and 1853 held official appointments under the British Crown,[70] it was evident by the 1850s that he was not going to be successful. In 1850 Sarawak signed a commercial treaty with the United States which two years later James used as one of the foundations for his claim to be recognized as an independent ruler by Britain. But in 1855, when a new British Consul-General to Borneo was appointed, the British government refused to make that appointment dependent on the approval of the Kuching government, as James demanded. In 1858 and 1859, he submitted to successive British governments proposals that Britain take over Sarawak as a colony or protectorate, subject to certain conditions,[71] but nothing came of these attempts for the next five years. This failure led James to turn, with similar results, to Holland, France and Belgium.[72]

In 1862, the British Foreign Secretary, Lord Palmerston, who was sympathetic towards James, got Cabinet approval for the appointment of a British Consul specifically to Kuching, who was to be issued with an *exequatur* from the Raja of Sarawak. The appointment took effect in 1864 but at the last moment even this recognition was rendered ambiguous since the Consul's instructions spoke vaguely of getting the acceptance of the 'local authorities'. In 1866, two years before his death, James made another offer to cede Sarawak, which was rebuffed as before. So the position rested until 1888, the year in which Britain extended her protection over Sarawak, thereby acknowledging her existence as an independent state.

Charles, the Second Raja, was no more successful than James, in obtaining any form of British recognition prior to this, largely on account of his embroilment with Labuan and Brunai over the extension of his territories.

Dutch and Spanish claims in Borneo

The establishment of British power in North Borneo, whether through the efforts of private individuals like James Brooke, or in the form of Crown colonies like Labuan or chartered companies like that which governed British North Borneo, met with resentment and opposition from Holland. The first news of James

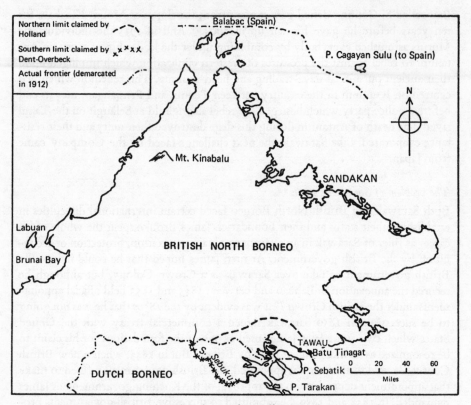

24. North Borneo, shewing boundary disputes between the British, Dutch and Spaniards

Brooke's expedition, gathered in the Hague in 1838, caused considerable consternation in government circles. His establishment as ruler of Sarawak in 1841 aroused still more alarm amongst Dutch officials and the Dutch governor-general in Batavia informed the Hague of his intention of setting up a Dutch agency in Brunai. But the Dutch Colonial Secretary of the day, Baud, advised that no action be taken. The Kutai affair of 1844,[73] when another British adventurer called Erskine Murray was killed, caused the Dutch to warn Britain against any naval demonstration in the area, to review their own Borneo policy, and to re-examine Brooke's activities more closely. In 1845 and 1846 they presented new protests in London about Brooke and his new official status, now developing the argument that the British presence in Borneo was an infringement of the Treaty of 1824.[74] This was to remain the main Dutch case for many years.

The diplomatic battle continued for the next two decades, fluctuating in intensity with the shifts in the strains and stresses of the European scene. In the early 1850s it was Dutch policy to acquiesce in British activities on the northern shores of Borneo. In the 1860s, anticipating the demise of James, it became the Dutch purpose to persuade the British government to abandon any commitments in the north of the island. In any event, Dutch pressure had no effect on British policy.

Dutch reaction to the British acquisition of Sabah, however, did not confine itself to diplomatic channels. Whilst repeating the argument of infringement of the 1824 Treaty of London, the Dutch authorities in the East sent a gunboat to raise the flag at Batu Tinagat, near Tawau, in September 1879. Dutch anxiety, nevertheless, was centred not so much on the cession itself as on the question of the boundary between the new British and Dutch Borneo. The matter had not been carefully thought about before; now it had become urgent.[75] The problem remained unsettled for many years to come. At first local officials of either side occupied themselves by organizing symbolic demonstrations of sovereignty. In response to the Dutch action at Batu Tinagat the preceding September, Pryer delivered a formal protest to the Dutch authorities in July 1880. In 1883 a Dutch *controlleur* set himself up in Tawau and Dutch naval vessels based on Tarakan commenced regular patrols of the coastline. In retaliation, Treacher[76] sailed to the Sebuku river in September, raised the North Borneo flag on its south bank and set a boundary mark. Both were removed by the Dutch immediately on his departure.

At last, in 1884, by which time the Dutch had been obliged to recognize the *fait accompli* of the British North Borneo Company's existence,[77] both parties agreed to the setting up of a joint boundary commission. The Commission convened and started its work in 1889 and the fruits of its labours were to be seen in the Anglo-Dutch Frontier Convention of 1891 which struck a judicious compromise between the extreme claims of both sides. Nevertheless it was not until 1912 that the present Malaysian-Indonèsia border was fixed in detail by an Anglo-Dutch survey team. Its decisions were confirmed by the agreement signed between the two powers in September 1915.

Spain also reacted sharply against the establishment of British power in North Borneo. The Spaniards laid claim to the eastern part of the cession on the grounds that it was part of the Sultanate of Sulu, and therefore Spanish by right of conquest. It was to forestall this claim that Overbeck, Dent and Treacher had sailed to Sulu in January 1878,[a] to sign a treaty with the Sultan, confirming the cession already made by Sultan Abdul Mumin of Brunai. The treaty was not signed at Jolo, the Sulu capital, since this was already in Spanish hands, but at Maimbung on the other side of the island. Within six months of signing away his Borneo possessions, Sultan Jamal-ul Alam had to bend to Spanish power, and in articles of pacification and capitulation acknowledged Spanish sovereignty over all his dominions—including those just ceded in Borneo. The Spaniards followed this up quickly by sending a gunboat two months later to Sandakan Bay to lay claim to north-east Borneo. There they found Pryer[b] who calmly refused to give way to Spanish threats. The gun-boats departed and the matter was taken up at diplomatic level. The outcome was the Protocol of 7 March 1885, signed by Spain, Germany[78] and Britain. Amongst other things the Protocol stated that Spain waived all her claims in Borneo, whilst Britain and Germany recognized Spain's undisputed authority over the entire Sulu archipelago, including the islands of Cagayan and Balabac.[79]

In assessing the factors which led to the downfall of the Brunai sultanate, it is clear that the lack of political insight or principle on the part of her rulers played a

[a]Refer p. 181.
[b]See p. 198, note 34.

very important part. More important still was the absence of a sound economic base on which a firmer social and political structure could be built up. The foundations of Brunai's power and prosperity had been corroded by the spread of European commercial enterprise. On the other hand, it is equally true that individuals of great character, courage and idealism like James Brooke, of initiative and foresight like Overbeck and Dent, played a great role in the establishment of British control. But behind them all lay the realities of British power. Without the British Navy, James Brooke would never have quelled the Ibán pirates or established his influence over the court of Brunai. The enterprise of Overbeck and Dent would have shared the fate of that of Moses and Torrey unless, for reasons of its own, the British government had not chosen to give them its backing.

[1] According to the *Brunai Annuals* (*Selesilah Raja2 Brunai*), the first Muslim ruler of Brunai was Alak Bertata (Aduk/Ahlok Batatar), who took the style of Sultan Mohamed. See H.R. Hughes-Hallett, 'A Sketch of the History of Brunei', *JMBRAS*, Vol. XVIII No. 2, 1940, p. 25.

[2] Antonio Pigafetta, an Italian knight who accompanied Magellan on his voyage round the world and was the chronicler of the voyage. He was at Brunai in 1521.

[3] In 1578 and 1580, representing Spanish attempts to weaken the Muslim threat to their own position by exploiting internal dissensions. The effects of both raids were shortlived.

[4] Brunai territory to the east of Marudu Bay had been ceded in 1674–5 to Sulu (or seized) in return for their support of the winning side in a succession dispute.

[5] As the result of a palace revolution led by his mother against the sadistic Mohamed Alam (Raja Api), one of his uncles. The story goes that whilst awaiting death, Mohamed Alam told the witnesses to see which way his body fell on strangulation—to the left would be a bad omen for Brunai. It fell to the left.

[6] James Brooke: born in Benares, 1803; fifth child of East India Company High Court Judge; sent to school in England in 1815; 1819, joined army of the Company as ensign; 1821, promoted lieutenant; 1825, wounded in action near Rungpore, Assam, in the First Anglo-Burmese War; invalided out and returned to England to convalesce; 1829, left Company's service; 1830, made first voyage to China, passing through Malaysian archipelago—'deeply impressed with its beauty and the devastation wrought by piracy and internecine warfare'; 1834, made second voyage to China; 1835, on death of father inherited large landed property and £30,000; 1836; bought the yacht, *The Royalist*; 1838, made preparations for expedition to the east, published prospectus entitled *Expedition to Borneo*: 16 December—sailed for the East; May 1839, arrived at Singapore; 27 July, sailed for North Borneo; 15 August, anchored off Kuching.

[7] In 1838 the Raja Muda had helped the survivors of a British ship wrecked at the mouth of the Sarawak river, housed and fed them and sent them back to Singapore at his own expense. He had an eye on British friendship as a counter to the approaches made to the Dutch by the rebels. The Raja Muda had also impressed an English missionary, Tradescent Lay, whom he had met in Brunai in 1837, as being 'an enlightened prince'.

[8] When Brooke enquired at their first meeting about the progress of the rebellion, the Raja Muda replied that 'there was no war but merely some child's play among his subjects'.

[9] Brooke's intentions are clearly set out both in the prospectus of his expedition and in his numerous letters and journals.

[10] The Company's steamship *Diana*, especially equipped to combat piracy; she called at Kuching to enquire into reports of shipwrecked British sailors held at Brunai.

[11] Belcher's instructions from the Admiralty on leaving England earlier in the year were to ascertain Brooke's position in Sarawak and investigate the coal deposits of Brunai; both objectives had been inspired by Brooke's agent in London, Henry Wise.

[12] This would be in the Sultan's own interests if he was going to follow British policy, as an insurance against pirate reprisals.

[13] The two main tribes, the Ibans of Saribas and the Ibans of Skrang, had their bases within a 50 mile radius of Kuching, mainly between the Sadong and Rejang rivers, and especially on the Sadong itself, the Batang Lupar and its tributaries (including the Lingga, Undop and Batang Skrang), the Batang Saribas and the Kalaka.

[14] These raids were devastating: the destruction and subjugation of the Saribas strongholds in 1843 took ten days, greatly aided by a force of 800 Ibans led by Sharif Ja'afar from Lingga; in 1844 at Patusan, 56 guns, 1.5 tons of gunpowder and 'vast quantities of ammunition' as well as over 200 warboats were captured.

[15] Sultan Omar Ali Saifuddin to Bethune, British naval officer who accompanied Brooke on this occasion in March 1845. Quoted by Irwin, *Nineteenth Century Borneo*, p. 90.

[16] The *Sultana* affair of 1841; struck by lightning off Palawan—the vessel was pirated and two lascars made prisoner.

[17] The Sultan was vexed in particular over the reinstatement of Raja Muda Hassim, since he hoped to gain the succession for his own son.

[18] The news first reached Brooke through a slave-boy of Pangeran Badruddin, a younger brother of the Raja Muda and also a victim of the *coup*. The boy, Ja'afar, took the chance provided by a British warship running aground in Brunai Bay to escape the town, and to fulfill his master's dying injunctions to inform Brooke.

[19] Mundy's description of this meeting suggests why the Sultan was so compliant: 'The Sultan received me at the entrance to the audience-hall, and the marines who were drawn up in a position directly enfilading the divan, presented arms as I stepped over the threshold, and made their pieces tell well together. I observed the old monarch tremble in his slippers.' Quoted by Irwin, op. cit. p. 122.

[20] The Sultan himself, however, was not present, pleading that he was a bad sailor and could not make the journey.

[21] A former Chief Minister succeeded as the most acceptable to all concerned. No one believed in the legitimacy of Sultan Omar Ali Saifuddin's son.

[22] Matusin was a cousin of Ersat but local-born, and popular champion against Ersat's exactions. Matusin went amok and killed Ersat after having being insulted by him in public.

[23] In fact, while promising Brooke a free hand in the government of Muka on the one hand, he placed it in the hands of Pangeran Makota.

[24] Brooke Brooke—John Brooke Johnson, James Brooke's nephew; joined Sarawak service in 1848; changed name by deed poll from Johnson to Brooke as prospective heir; 1861, installed as Raja Muda; 1863, disinherited: Charles Brooke—Charles Johnson, nephew of James and younger brother of Brooke Brooke; joined Sarawak service in 1857 and known as Tuan Muda; changed name by deed poll to Brooke in 1863; appointed heir in 1865; became the second Raja in 1868.

[25] Tunjang's scheme was for the Malay chiefs to forgather on the Sadong; one force would then march down the Kapuas and enlist the Malays of Pontianak, massacre the Dutch and then turn back on Kuching. In the meanwhile, Sharif Masahor would lead a second force up the Sarawak river to aid in the attack.

[26] Also at this time acting Consul-General to the Borneo chiefs. 'He strongly disapproved of Sarawak and the Rajah.' Runciman, *The White Rajahs*, p. 144. He was also on good terms with Sultan Abdul Mumin, and hoped to improve Labuan's trading prospects by winning over the pangeran of Brunai.

[27] The quarrel concerned some letters addressed to the Sarawak government, whose seals had been carelessly or improperly closed. The Sarawak State Council read this as a deliberate insult, leading to the decision to withhold the money.

[28] Henry Bulwer, the governor of Labuan, was behind the pressure. His successor, H. J. Ussher, revealed to the Foreign Office in 1876 that Charles was holding back $3,000 due to the Sultan because of bad debts of Brunai pangeran in Kuching, and was using this as a means of putting pressure to gain his demands.

[29] Moses was a cashiered seaman from the U.S. Navy: how he acquired his papers to be the U.S. consul in Brunai is not known. He had to borrow money in Singapore for his passage to Brunai.

[30] Torrey's partners were Thos. B. Harris, Lee Ah Sing, Pong Am Pong and also Wo Hang who withdrew. Harris joined the Kimanis settlement and died there in 1866 after exploring the Crocker Range. Conditions attached by Moses to the sale of his rights were the colony to be under the protection of the U.S. flag, U.S. laws to be adopted and one-third of the profits to go to Moses himself.

[31] Having failed to get compensation from Torrey, Moses brought a party of sixteen German adventurers from Hong Kong to see Kimanis Bay—they were not interested. In 1867 penniless in Brunai, Moses set fire to his attap consulate and demanded compensation from the Sultan. A U.S. gunboat sent to investigate the case did not support him; he moved to Labuan and was later drowned at sea on way back to the U.S.A.

[32] Gustavus von Overbeck—'a large man ... of courage and ability', Tregonning, *A History of Modern Sabah*, p. 9. Born 1831, in Lippe-Detmold, Germany, migrated to the United States,

spent time whaling in the Behring Sea with base at Honolulu, then settled in Hong Kong as local manager of Dent & Co; became Austrian Consul-General and Baron; after withdrawal from the Borneo scheme, eventually went to the U.S.A. where he married an admiral's daughter and speculated in railways.

33Alfred Dent: son of founder and now head of Dent & Co., firm of opium dealers in Hong Kong; born, 1842; advanced £6,000 out of £10,000 total capital on condition he had chief control and management of the enterprise; helped by his younger brother. 'Neither was to be more than a normal, obscure, rather insignificant London businessman for the rest of his life; yet in this enterprise they were to work enthusiastically, courageously, and most tenaciously to accomplish great things.' Tregonning, op. cit. p. 12.

34Namely, William Pryer in Sandakan, H.L. Leicester at Papar, and William Pretyman at Tempasuk.

35Dent's associates included Richard Biddulph Martin M.P.., 'the prominent banker'; Admiral Sir Henry Keppel; Sir Rutherford Alcock, 'a retired diplomat with long experience in the Far East'. Alcock had the ear of the Legal Adviser and later Permanent Under-Secretary to the Foreign Office, Sir Julian Pauncefote, who played the key rôle in getting the royal charter approved. The first step was the formation of the British North Borneo Provisional Association which acquired Dent's interest for £12,000; those involved were Dent, Martin, Alcock, Rear-admiral R.C. Mayne and W.H.M. Read. When the Charter was granted, the Association transferred its assets to the British North Borneo Company in May 1882.

36According to Treacher, Charles lost his temper and threatened to stir up the people against Overbeck: this was the start of a personal feud between the two men which influenced all Treacher's subsequent attitudes.

37This did not end the matter. Much of the land in the concession was owned by Pangeran Karim, a Sarawak subject, who was expelled from the territory. The dispute was referred to the pro-Sarawak British Consul-General, Dr. Leys, who advised the headman not to pay poll tax; the matter finally went to London which decided in the Company's favour in 1885.

38Quoted by Irwin, op. cit. p. 213.

39This gave rise to another dispute involving the local landowner. Sarawak supported the claims of Pangeran Raup against those of his rivals. However, the Sultan upheld the Company when the matter was brought before him. A short time after this, the supporters of Pangeran Raup were responsible for the killing of two European officials and two policemen of the Company. Refer p. 192.

40First chairman of the Company.

41The Sultan privately explained that his refusal of the $6,000 rental was not out of pride but to punish two recalcitrant pangeran, the Pangeran Bendahara and Di Gedong, who would have been its recipients. In 1895 the Foreign Office instructed Sarawak to spend the money on the development of the district. The question of Limbang was raised in 1906 and in 1941 the Sarawak government offered to pay $20,000 compensation and $1,000 rental a year. This offer was accepted by Brunai but disallowed by the British Agent.

42Ownership in Brunai was of three kinds: 1. kerajaan—state land from which the Sultan derived revenue but could not alienate; 2. kuripan—lands belonging to ministers of state during their lifetime but reverting to the ruler on their death; 3. tulen—land which was the personal property of the landowner, although sovereignty was vested in the Sultan. In these concessions, tulen rights were concerned.

43Now the High Commissioner for the Malay States and Governor of the Straits Settlements.

44Pangeran Makota was eventually killed whilst on an expedition abducting Bisayan girls for his harem in November 1858.

45300 pirates were killed outright, 500 more died of their wounds whilst fleeing through the jungle later—this number would have been even greater, had not Brooke forbidden pursuit. British losses: '2 natives killed and about 6 wounded'. 'The Albatross Affair' as the Batang Marau incident was termed by the British press gave fresh ammunition to those people who were attempting to have Brooke impeached for cruelty against innocent inhabitants of Borneo, and they succeeded in having an official committee of enquiry set up to investigate these charges, which held its sittings in Singapore in 1854. However, Brooke was exonerated of all the charges.

46In 1854, led by James; in 1857 and 1858, both led by Charles.

47This was a gesture of gratitude by James for Malay loyalty during the Chinese uprising of 1857.

48Abdul Gapur: Pa' Tinggi of Sarawak; one of the three principal Malay noblemen of Sarawak (others were the Dato Bendahara and Dato Temenggong); one of the leaders in the 1835–40 rebellion against Makota; restored from exile to his former office on the insistence of James in 1842; alienated from the Brooke regime because traditional right to buy and sell Iban goods arbitrarily replaced by fixed salary; also because of attempted interference by James in the marriage of his daughter to Sharif Bujang, a brother of Sharif Masahor; 1854, started intriguing to overthrow Brooke; discovered, and after a showdown concerning his authority in Kuching, made the pilgrimage to Mecca on the advice of James (hereafter known as Pa' Haji); on return, continued to be hostile to Brooke—exiled to Malacca; 1857, allowed to return, at same time as Masahor and for same reasons—see previous note; 1859, joined forces with Masahor—then went to Lundu to plan seizure of Kuching and extirpation of all Europeans; plot betrayed and arrested on arrival at Kuching; exiled to Singapore; 1860, escaped, went to Pontianak in the hope of joining up with Tunjang—arrested on arrival by the Dutch and sent a prisoner to Batavia.

[49]Whilst on his way to attack Kuching, Masahor met Charles coming downstream; realizing all had failed, he followed Charles to Semunjan on the Sadong where his own complicity was revealed. Charles attacked his forces but Masahor escaped via Sarikei to Muka. All his houses and property at Sarikei and Igan either burned or confiscated.

[50]St. John, Sir Spenser: 1848, became private secretary to James Brooke; 1855–61, British Consul-General to the Borneo states; 1890, published a life of James Brooke.

[51]Referring to the suppression of the Chinese kongsis by the Dutch, 1850–4. See p. 259.

[52]The impression created by the Committee of Enquiry in Singapore regarding James and the suppression of piracy was that he was out of favour with the British government, and also that he was only a vassal of the Sultan of Brunai. Trouble between the British and the Chinese had been simmering ever since the conclusion of the First Anglo-Chinese War in 1842. As the second war broke out in 1856, Imperial Commissioner Yeh at Canton offered $30 per head for every Englishman, an offer which reverberated throughout the Chinese world in South-East Asia.

[53]Brooke, Sir Charles Vyner; born 1874; fourth but eldest surviving child of Charles, the second Raja; acceded as third Raja in 1917.

[54]A chief of the Batang Lupar Ibans, and associated with Banting since 1893.

[55]Pangeran Omar and Masir were both bomohs who spread their influence of disaffection against authority by the sale of magic charms. Pangeran Omar, who operated on the borders of the First Division with Sambas was arrested by the Dutch, and his handful of followers punished by a small expedition from Kuching up the Sadok. Masir stirred the Lingga Iban to ambush the Resident but the attack failed and he was caught and punished.

[56]Led by a group of young Ibans who revived head-hunting—of their neighbours and unwary Chinese traders. A strong punitive expedition in 1915 curbed these activities, but a hard core retreated to Ulu Gaat where they defied authority for the next few years. Fresh outbreaks in 1919 led to a new expedition which caused the rebels to flee to Dutch territory where the ringleaders were captured and handed over to Kuching. Their followers were resettled on the Igan river.

[57]The ammunition ran out and much of it was useless anyway; only four out of one hundred police could handle the mountain guns.

[58]Pangeran Shahbandar was advised to litigate by Raja Charles, but he made the pilgrimage instead, leaving his children in a Singapore school.

[59]Mat Salleh first aroused suspicion when two Iban traders were murdered in his village, although his guilt was never established. Then there were complaints of his ignoring police posts and of harbouring known fugitives from justice. He was married to a sister of the Sultan of Sulu.

[60]After Mat Salleh and his force had safely withdrawn from Sandakan, a small police party was sent in pursuit and burned his deserted village. See Tregonning, op. cit. p. 201.

[61]River valleys like Inanam and Mengkabong, still belonging to Brunai chiefs.

[62]It took two years to build and had walls two feet thick. It was completely destroyed by government forces after its capture.

[63]William Clarke Cowie: had long connexions with North Borneo; claimed to be primarily responsible for the British concession—in fact, did his best at first to oppose it; began his career in the Far East in the employ of Carl Schomburgk and Co. of Singapore; engaged in running the Sulu blockade imposed by Spain; 1872, secured permission from the Sultan of Sulu to found transhipment centre in Sandakan Bay; started Labuan Trading Company in partnership with Schomburgk and Capt. Ross, another seasoned trader—the Company's sole purpose was the smuggling of guns and ammunition, opium, tobacco and other contraband goods to Sulu; 1876, whilst in Hong Kong with a Borneo cargo, received demand for 10 per cent export duties from Torrey—wanted to buy Torrey out but Schomburgk and Ross refused; Labuan Trading Company came to an end; bought ship and traded on own account; 1877–8, used influence with Sultan of Sulu to help Overbeck obtain his treaty but failed to conclude a

commercial deal with the Baron—subsequently tried to force Pryer out of Sandakan Bay with Sulu backing; failed—granted a subsidy by Overbeck and Dent and withdrew; acquired concession in Muara Peninsula from Sultan of Brunai (coal)—sold to Sarawak in 1888 (Sarawak handed it back to Brunai in 1931); 1894, nominated to Court of Directors of British North Borneo Company; 1897–1905, Managing Director; 1905–1910, Chairman; 1910, died. His claim to have been responsible for Overbeck-Dent cession not borne out by the facts.

[64]This meeting with Mat Salleh was arranged through the Sultan of Sulu who secretly urged the rebel to continue his resistance: Cowie promised when they met that all his supporters should be pardoned. The written agreement limited the pardon to those who were not escaped convicts.

[65]As one of them put it, Cowie's policy was one of sacrificing 'the interests and risking the lives of the loyal natives in order to propitiate the disloyal ones.' Quoted by Tregonning, op. cit. p. 205.

[66]Subsequently Clifford wrote two novels: *Sally, A Study*, published in 1904, and *Saleh, A Sequel*, published in 1908. But neither of these have anything to do with Mat Salleh.

[67]Santara, Timus and Sarah were amongst those shot.

[68]The officer in question was Raffles Flint, a descendant of Raffles. His action, perpetrated with the aid of Iban policemen, was taken to avenge the murder of his brother in that area.

[69]He was later pardoned and became a model chief and supporter of the administration.

[70]1845, Confidential Agent of the British government in Borneo (unpaid); 1847, Commissioner and Consul-General to the Sultan and Independent Chiefs of Borneo at £500 a year: 1848, Governor of Labuan at £2,000 a year: 1852, dismissed as Governor (not in disgrace): 1854, resigned the Consul-Generalship.

[71]The 1858 conditions were that he and his staff be allowed to continue as administrators for the time being; that his money spent on development be refunded and that he receive compensation for the value of the state revenues surrendered. These proposals failed owing to the defeat of Palmerston's Liberal government two weeks after they were received. The 1859 offer to Lord Derby's Cabinet was Sarawak as a protectorate with an option on annexation later; Britain should also assume responsibility for the State debt. These new moves were made as a consequence of the Chinese rebellion of 1857, which revealed the weaknesses of his position.

[72]The negotiations with these countries were carried out half-heartedly and never carried through—probably chiefly aimed at arousing a suitable reaction from the British government. James' backer and admirer, the rich heiress and philanthropist Angela Burdett-Coutts, diverted his attention from the negotiations with Napoleon III of France by presenting him with a new steamer, *The Rainbow*, for Sarawak. It was she who made the half-serious suggestion that James seek Greek protection, to which he replied: 'Sarawak could protect Greece as much as Greece protect Sarawak.' Quoted by Runciman, op. cit. p. 151.

[73]Murray arrived at Kutai in February 1844, with the aim of opening trade and establishing a permanent settlement. At first he was well received, then probably due to Bugis influence his two ships were lured into a trap on the S. Mahakam from which they escaped with the loss of three lives, including Murray's. The tightening and extension of Dutch control over the south-west and east coasts of Borneo was an immediate consequence of this incident. See p. 263–4.

[74]The Dutch contended that Borneo was included by the clause of the treaty stating that the formation of new settlements by the British in the Karimun islands, the Riau archipelago 'or any other islands south of the Straits of Singapore' was prohibited. The British maintained that Borneo had been deliberately excluded. For a full discussion of the treaty, its implications and background, see Irwin, op. cit. Ch. III, and Tarling, *Anglo-Dutch Rivalry in the Malay World 1780–1824*, Ch. V.

[75]In fact, the Dutch themselves were not clear as to where the boundary lay between their territory and the domains of the Sultan of Sulu. The Decree of 28 February 1846 defined it as south of latitude 3° 20' N. (that is up to S. Kayan) while a Cabinet decision of March 1850 located it on a line south of latitude 4° 20' N. (Pulau Sebatik), although this was not made public. Up till 1879 Dutch atlases likewise showed conflicting boundaries.

[76]Now governor of North Borneo (from 1881 till 1887).

[77]In response to its diplomatic pressure, the Dutch government was kept fully informed of all the stages in the evolution of the Chartered Company. The Dutch objected to the terms of the Charter when sent to them in July 1881, but these objections were ignored.

[78]Germany's interest was due to the fact that between them British and German traders virtually monopolized the Sulu trade.

[79]The United States also lodged a protest over the establishment of the British Company, sending a warship in 1880 to deliver it formally to Sultan Mumin and W.H. Read; but the grounds were so flimsy that the matter was dropped.

7. THE SULTANATE OF BRUNAI

A. Chronology of Main Events in the Nineteenth Century	
1828	Accession of Sultan Omar Ali Saifuddin II
1835–41	Pangeran Usop's rebellion in Sarawak
1838	Raja Muda Hassim takes charge in Sarawak.
1839	James Brooke's first visit to Sarawak
1840	Brooke's second visit to Sarawak; accepts Raja Muda's invitation to crush rebellion
1841	Brooke appointed governor of Sarawak
1842	Brunai court confirms Brooke's appointment
1843	Brunai signs treaty of friendship with Britain First expedition; (with Keppel) against the Saribas Ibans
1844	Second expedition; (with Keppel) against the Skrang Ibans Return of Raja Muda Hassim to Brunai
1845	Pangeran Usop flees Brunai court
	British destroy Lanun base in Marudu Bay
1846	Brunai court coup d'état; Raja Muda Hassim and supporters killed; British bombardment of Brunai Town
	Relations restored with Sultan; Labuan ceded; Sarawak fully independent.
1847	Second treaty between Britain and Brunai; Brooke British Commissioner to Brunai
1849	The battle of Batang Marau; destruction of Iban strength
1850	Brunai signs commercial treaty with the USA
1852	Death of Sultan Omar Ali Saifuddin; succeeded by Sultan Mumin
1853	Cession of the Rejang Basin to Brooke
1853–61	Rentab's rebellion against Brooke rule
1855–61	The Muka Crisis
1857	The Chinese Rebellion in Sarawak
1861	Brunai cedes Oya and Muka to Brooke
1865	Lee Moses obtains concession in North Borneo
1865–6	The Kimanis Bay settlement
1868	Death of James Brooke; succeeded by Charles
1870	Lintong's revolt at Sibu
1874	Kayan revolt in Baram
1875	Overbeck acquires Moses-Torrey concession
1877	Sultan Mumin grants concession to Overbeck and Dent in North Borneo
1878	The Sultan of Sulu grants similar concession
1879	Start of British-Dutch border tension at Tawau
1881	Founding of the Chartered Company of British North Borneo.
1882	Baram ceded to Brooke
1882–8	The 'scramble for Brunai'

1885	Death of Sultan Mumin. The Sulu Protocol (Spain, Germany, Britain)
1888	British Protectorate declared over Brunai, Sarawak and British North Borneo
1889	The Padas Damit affair
1890	Limbang revolt; Sarawak acquires Limbang
1891	Anglo-Dutch Frontier Convention, settling boundary disputes in Borneo
1894–1908	Banting's rebellion (Sarawak)
1895–1903	The Mat Salleh Revolt (British North Borneo)
1899	Rebellion in Tutong and Belait
1905	Lawas ceded to Sarawak
1906	Brunai accepts British Resident.

B. Nineteenth Century Rulers of Brunai

1796–1809	Mohamad Tajuddin II
1809–28	Khanzul Alam
1828	Mohamad Alam
1828–52	Omar Ali Saifuddin II
1852–85	Abdul Mumin
1885–1906	Hashim Jalal

SULU AND MAGINDANAU

THE partitioning of Brunai, as we have just seen, also involved at one stage her neighbour in the east, the sultanate of Sulu.[a] Sulu, with its sister sultanate of Magindanau in southern Mindanao, stood like Acheh, their counterpart in the west, at an extremity of the Malay world of Islam. The history of both sultanates is bound up with the rise of Islam in the region and with their three hundred year struggle with the Christian power of Spain centred on Luzon and the Visayas in the Philippines. Today, both Sulu and Magindanau form an integral part of the Philippine Republic, but their history and culture bind them more closely to their Muslim cousins of Borneo and the islands of the Great East rather than to their Christianized brothers in the Philippines.

The formation of the sultanates of Sulu and Magindanau
Islam was well established in the Sulu archipelago and was spreading northwards from southern Mindanao when the first Portuguese arrived in the Spice Islands.[1] In 1521 the Portuguese explorer Magellan 'discovered' the Philippines for the King of Spain, marking the beginning of the European connexion there.[b] By the time that Spanish colonization began in earnest with the arrival of Legazpi's expedition some

[a]Refer p. 181.
[b]See p. 338.

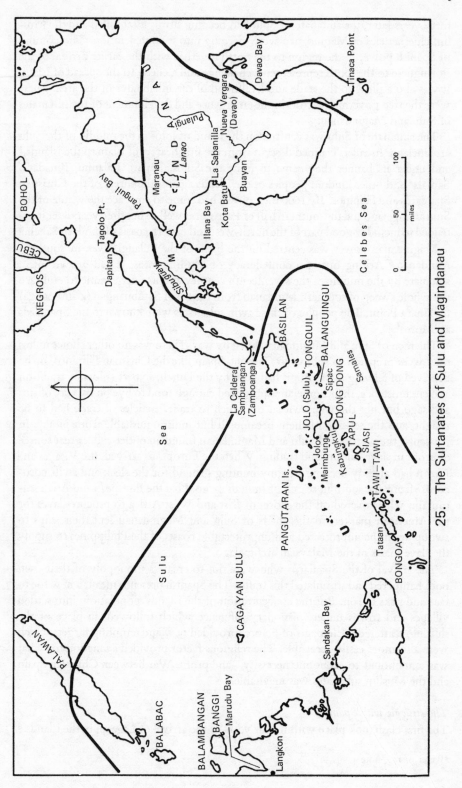

25. The Sultanates of Sulu and Magindanau

forty years later, the sultanate of Sulu had become firmly established and the Muslim chieftaincies of Magindanau were merging into a confederation. The coming of Spanish power in the region to the north together with the earlier arrival of the Portuguese to the south represented a challenge and a check to the spread of Islam. It was also a blow to the trade and livelihood of the inhabitants of the area. These were the two governing factors in the emergence and development of the sultanates of Sulu and Magindanau.

The sultanate of Sulu was centred on the island of Jolo[2] in the middle of the Sulu archipelago. Its rulers claimed descent from the first bearers of Islam to the islands,[3] and under its banner they came to unite the Sulus, Bajaus, Balanini, Binadans, Samals[4] and other kindred peoples of the islands against the threat of the Christian Spaniards and Filipinos. By 1600 their power had come to embrace the whole of the Sulu archipelago and the southern half of Palawan as well. A hundred years later it extended to include a good part of the north-west and eastern coasts of modern Sabah.[a]

Magindanau power was centred on the basin of the Pulangi river in southern Mindanao.[5] Arising out of a confederacy of Muslim datos, it had grown into a sultanate by the middle of the seventeenth century and its power came to embrace the whole sweep of southern Mindanao from the tip of Sambuangan (Zamboanga) to Tinaca Point. The peoples of these twin sultanates were known to the Spaniards as 'Moros'.[6]

The men of Sulu and Magindanau lived by war. There was no other choice unless they were prepared to submit to Catholic Spain like the Christian Filipinos, or be deprived of a living as the Bugis had been by the Dutch. Expert sailors by tradition and circumstance, their homelands produced enough food to live on by way of rice and sago but not the wherewithal by which to trade. Articles of trade had to be sought, and the seeking of them became all but indistinguishable from piracy. In particular the warriors of Sulu and Magindanau found an outlet and a great source of profit in slave-raiding and trading. When the Europeans arrived, the Visayas and Luzon had already become a happy hunting ground for the sleek and swift coro-coros[7] from the south in search of human cargo. Like the European and Asian sea-captains who hovered off the shores of East and West Africa to procure slaves for the American market, so the chiefs of Sulu and Magindanau sent their ships to swoop upon the unprotected and unprotectable coasts of the Philippines to supply the slave marts of the Malaysian archipelago.

The arrival of the Spaniards who were out to create a monopoly of their own both hampered and stimulated this traffic. The Spanish presence meant a new foe to face and risks to run. But the concentration of the islands' populations into settled villages and towns under missionary influence which followed, in place of the shifting, scattered settlements of before, provided new and tempting targets which were also more easily accessible. The religious factor provided a sanction for what was tantamount to economic necessity—and profit. War between Christian Spain and the Muslim sultanates was inevitable.

The struggle with Spain
The first clash took place within four years of the arrival of Legazpi in the islands.[8]

[a]Refer p. 196, note 4.

The conflict began in earnest nearly twenty years later, in 1578, when a flotilla under Esteban Rodriguez de Figueroa assaulted and captured Jolo, and followed this up with a far less successful foray against Magindanau.[9] At Jolo, however, where Sultan Pangiran, the sixth of his line, surrendered and signed a treaty with Figueroa by which he acknowledged 'himself and his descendants vassals of His Majesty Don Felipe, King of Castile and Leon...' and presented twelve pearls and thirty-five tahil of gold as token of his good faith and loyalty, the Spanish triumph was short-lived. Hardly had Figueroa's sails disappeared over the horizon than Sultan Pangiran declared a *jihad* against the Spaniards and launched his people on a struggle that was to last for generations. Together with their co-religionists in Magindanau, the Muslims of Sulu waged a relentless campaign not merely to defend their own homeland and faith but to drive the Spaniards out of the Philippines if possible. This goal was never achieved nor even, perhaps, nearly approached but their attacks placed a very serious strain on Spanish resources and greatly hampered the work of the Christian missionaries in the islands.

On the other hand, the Spaniards too wreaked havoc on the Muslims, and more fundamentally still stunted the development of their civilization. The Spanish presence and power made it impossible for Sulu and Magindanau to evolve peaceful trading economies, even if other circumstances had been favourable. With the new China trade to the Americas being filtered through Manila, and the Spice Islands to the south falling firstly under the domination of the Portuguese and then under the much more effective control of the Dutch, the avenues for the development of a legitimate commerce were blocked.

The three-hundred year war between the Muslims and the Spaniards was a see-saw affair, largely made up of raids and counter-raids by either side. There were brief periods of Spanish ascendancy, followed by much longer spells when the vessels of Sulu and Magindanau burned and plundered the Philippine shore more or less at will. For the first forty years the initiative rested with the Muslims. At first, Magindanau, still a confederacy of dato's, found three intrepid leaders[10] who conducted a series of devastating raids on the Visayas which threatened to destroy Spanish rule in the region. These raids followed the failure of a second attempt by Figueroa in 1596 to conquer Magindanau. Between 1599 and 1609 the three led six major expeditions against the Philippines, enslaving at least 3,000 people and doing untold damage in the process. In 1603, Bwisan came near to inciting the chiefs of Leyte into a general insurrection against Spain. However, in 1609, the Magindanau men met a severe reverse when they were trapped by a Spanish flotilla in Panguil Bay. The sudden disappearance of the three datos from the scene after this date may have been brought about by that event, although internal dissensions are a more likely cause. There was recrudescence of Magindanau activity in 1613, after a visit by the Dutch urging action against Spain the previous year; an expedition led by a chief called Pagdalanun raided the Visayas and returned with over a thousand captives. After this there was a lull in Magindanau activity which lasted for twenty years. During this lull their place was taken by the men of Sulu who found in Sultan Bongsu a man determined to oppose and end the Spanish menace.[11] In 1634 Magindanau rejoined Sulu in its attacks on the Philippines, presenting a threat to the Spaniards which they could not ignore.

However, the revival of Magindanau activity coincided with the arrival in Manila in 1635 of a new and energetic governor who was to earn the title of 'the last Conquistador'.[12] Governor Sebastian Hurtado de Corcuera was determined to crush the Muslims once and for all. In 1637 he launched an all-out attack on the newly established sultanate of Magindanau[13], whose ruler, Sultan Kudrat, was forced to take to the hills while his nephew, Mongkai of Buayan, played for time by accepting Spanish terms for the time being. The following year Corcuera attacked and captured Jolo itself with a force of 80 sail, 600 Spanish and 3,000 Filipino troops. Sultan Bongsu fled to Tawi Tawi from where he sent emissaries to the south to seek Dutch help. For a second time, the Spanish triumph was shortlived. In Magindanau, Sultan Kudrat's supporters soon surrounded and besieged the new Spanish garrisons at Buayan and La Sabanilla (Polloc Harbour), while Spanish attempts to reduce the Maranau[14] met with complete failure. In 1642 Corcuera gave his reluctant sanction to the evacuation of the Spanish positions in Magindanau and within the next two years Kudrat completely re-established his influence throughout Southern Mindanao.

The Spanish garrison at Jolo held on, but it was useless and isolated in territory which was uniformly hostile and subject to Dutch attack. Fajardo, Corcuera's successor, came to the conclusion that with the Dutch threat to be taken into account as well, it would be best to come to terms with the Muslims, and so in 1644, having just taken over, he set out to achieve this. The fruits of the new policy were peace treaties negotiated by Jesuit brothers with both Kudrat and Bongsu in 1645 and 1646 respectively.[15] The truce lasted for about ten years. By 1655 Sultan Kudrat could restrain his impatient warriors no longer while Spanish activities in Mindanao itself provided him with an excuse for action.[16] Sulu was not long to follow.

For the next generation the advantage lay with the Muslims. Spanish counter-attacks were ineffective and in 1662 they felt obliged to abandon the strategic fort of Sambuangan because of the threat of Coxinga[17] in Formosa. By doing this, the 'Spaniards had removed the stopper from a bottle and released a malignant djinn'.[18] Up till the 1730s the Spanish Philippines remained on the defensive against Muslim attacks. These became virtually an annual affair, starting with the south-west monsoon, pouncing unexpectedly on Bisayan fishing villages, mission stations, shipyards and occasionally even garrison towns on Luzon itself, carrying away Filipinos as slaves and Europeans as hostages.

An attempt at reform: Sultan Alimuddin I of Sulu
In the meantime changes and developments had taken place in both Sulu and Magindanau society. While the institution of the sultanate was now unquestioned in either state, its incumbents found their authority severely curtailed by their datos, the most powerful and independent of whom were those who claimed relationship with the royal house itself. The sultans exercised their power through councils known as the *rumah bichara*, and could not act alone. More important they often could not control the activities of individual chiefs either.[19] By the beginning of the eighteenth century there were signs that the sultans were finding this hedged-in situation increasingly irksome and that they were looking for means by which to centralize and increase their own powers.

This was a trend which the Spaniards were only too pleased to encourage as a way of securing stability and an end to the Muslim raids. In 1718 they reoccupied Sambuangan and in the next few years sent out a number of fruitless expeditions against Jolo. In 1725 Sultan Badruddin I signed a peace treaty with them and ceded the island of Basilan. This treaty, however, was not a mere surrender to Spanish pressure. The Sultan, on the contrary, was out to secure Spanish friendship and support. Under circumstances which are not clear, in 1735, whilst in retirement, he succeeded in putting his son, Mohd. Alimuddin, on the throne in place of the elder born Nasaruddin, 'to bring his plans to fruition and realise his ideas'.[20]

Sultan Alimuddin I, the most remarkable of the rulers of Sulu, at once embarked on a well-defined policy of centralization. He started to organize an army and a navy under his own command, thereby freeing himself from dependence on feudal levies. He coined money with the aim of establishing a uniform currency, re-codified the laws—both Islamic and customary—and attempted to standardize forms of worship.

Such centralizing policies were bound to provoke opposition and the Sultan sought to insure himself against this by establishing firm bonds with Manila. In 1737 he sent two ambassadors there who successfully negotiated a treaty of peace and alliance. This was put to the test a few years later when in 1742 (the year King Philip V of Spain ratified the Treaty) Sultan Alimuddin secured the support of the Spanish garrison at Sambuangan to put down a conspiracy led by a dato called Sabdula. A couple of years after this, the ruler returned the favour by accompanying a Spanish expedition against the Orang Tedong[21] of North Borneo. In the same year the Sultan demonstrated his wide horizons by sending a trade mission to China.

Nevertheless the policy of befriending the Spaniards carried with it one very serious drawback; those who did so exposed themselves to Christian missionary fervour. Just as one hundred years later Raja Muda Hassim of Brunai[a] found himself increasingly dependent on James Brooke to maintain his own position, in a similar fashion Sultan Alimuddin was perforce more and more obliged to lean on the Spaniards to carry through his policies of centralization and reform. When in 1747 the King of Spain sent a formal request for permission to proselytize in Jolo, the Sultan—probably against his better judgement—gave his consent. As a result a Jesuit mission arrived there the next year but right from the start it was clear that this was a very unpopular move amongst the people of Sulu. Very soon after their arrival, Sultan Alimuddin was forced to keep the missionaries in the royal compound to protect their lives—an arrangement satisfactory to neither side. He forbade his son, Mohd. Israel, to receive instruction from them and made other gestures to show his loyalty to Islam to his people. But he did not send the Jesuits back and the mounting opposition in Jolo led by his brother, Bantilan, culminated in an attempt on his life. Thereupon, either at his own volition or at the behest of Bantilan and his supporters the Sultan decided to leave the island. Leaving behind a council of regency[22] and the Jesuits, he sailed for Basilan where, on hearing that the regents of their own accord had resigned and proclaimed Bantilan as the new Sultan (Mohd. Mu'izzuddin), he continued his voyage to Sambuangan, and from there to exile in Manila.

Similar trends took place in Magindanau. In the 1730s the sultanate was wracked

aRefer pp. 172 et seq.

by dynastic disputes and the Spaniards intervened unsuccessfully on the losing side. In the early 1740s, Sultan Pakir Maulana Kamzah, no doubt in an attempt to strengthen his own position, signed an identical treaty to that signed between Jolo and Manila in 1737. In 1744 the Sultan received a request from the Spanish King to allow Jesuit missionaries in his territories, and three years later he gave his consent. In the same year Sultan Kamzah died and his successor, Sultan Mohd. Amiruddin, found his throne disputed by a rival claimant. Manila and the Jesuits sped help to Amiruddin but the new sultan correctly saw Spanish support as the death warrant for his cause as far as his subjects were concerned. So rejecting his father's engagements, he forced the Spanish missionaries to withdraw.

These mid-eighteenth century episodes marked the only occasion when Spanish influence came close to being established in the Muslim south by peaceful means. After the flight of Sultan Alimuddin from Jolo, and the rebuff by Sultan Amiruddin in Magindanau, the relations between Manila and the Muslim sultanates relapsed into their customary state of warfare.

Relations with other colonial powers: Sulu and the British

One of the factors behind the survival of both Sulu and Magindanau up to this point and in the years to come against the pressure of Spanish power was the intermittent but invaluable assistance they received from other western colonial powers. During the seventeenth century the Dutch were useful allies, especially during the first half when they went all out to extinguish Spanish rule in the Philippines.[a] Even more welcome than the Dutch were the British about whom 'the admirable thing was,' as de la Costa puts it, 'that they were interested neither in conquest nor conversion but only in trade'[b] This interest, however, nearly led to the establishment of British dominion in the Sulu archipelago, which was also another consequence in part of the imaginative but somewhat reckless policies of Sultan Alimuddin.

When Alimuddin appeared in Manila as a fugitive in 1749, his first move was to ask to become a Christian. Whatever the motives behind this request were, he went through with his conversion, obtaining the appropriate collaboration of the Spanish authorities,[23] and to the joy of Catholic Manila was baptized a Christian prince with the name Fernando three months later. The next thing was to restore him to his throne, and for this purpose he left Manila with a Spanish expedition to recover his kingdom in May 1751. Then things went wrong. Alimuddin's own vessel was held up for repairs at Calapan while the rest of the fleet sailed on to cow the datos of Jolo into submission. When two months later, the Sultan arrived at Sambuangan, he aroused the suspicions of the Spanish governor[24] and the outcome was that he was arrested along with the other 217 persons in his retinue, and sent back a prisoner to Manila. There he remained, a prisoner of state in liberal captivity, until the British occupied Manila in October 1762.

In the meantime Jolo under Sultan Mu' izzuddin had already received an English visitor. This was Alexander Dalrymple, whose stay there in 1759 convinced him of the suitability of Sulu as a new outpost of the English East India Company for its

[a]See p. 350.
[b]H. J. de la Costa, *Readings in Philippine History*, p. 198.

trade with China.[25] He returned to India where he got the approval of the Madras Council for his schemes and reappeared in Jolo in 1761. This time he negotiated a treaty with Sultan Mu'izzuddin and trading agreements with the datos.[26] By the treaty the British obtained exclusive trading rights in Sulu (that is, exclusive to all other European powers), the right to acquire land for a factory wherever suitable, and in return committed themselves to an alliance with the sultanate. Dalrymple then departed once more in order to get ratification of these terms in India; he came back in August the next year, having chosen the island of Balambangan as the site for the Company's settlement. He signed a second treaty with Sultan Mu' izzuddin in September by which the island was ceded to Britain.

Sultan Mu'izzuddin's policy clearly was to get British backing against the Spanish threat, but matters became complicated when Spanish power suddenly vanished with the British capture of Manila only one month later.[a] This brought Alimuddin back into the picture. After the fall of the city,[27] he contacted the new British authorities to get their recognition as Sultan. He was well received and in February 1763 he signed a treaty with Dawson Drake, the British governor, confirming all previous agreements made between Dalrymple and Sultan Mu'izzuddin, and granting land to the Company on Jolo itself for good measure. His son, Mohd. Israel, was sent back to Jolo to prepare the way for his return. In May 1763, Israel was able to report that the embarrassing problem of Sultan Mu'izzuddin had been solved by his demise, and that although the rumah bicara had chosen the late Sultan's three sons to take over the government, they were prepared to include him as a fourth and to receive back Alimuddin as their ruler.

Nevertheless, by now a highly complex situation had arisen, which became even more complex as events unfolded. In September 1763, Dalrymple was back in Jolo from Madras to find that the regency of four had given way to the rule of the eldest of Mu'izzuddin's sons who had assumed the title of Sultan Alimuddin II. In addition there was a Chinese from Batavia trying hard to get an exclusive trade agreement for the Dutch.[28] Fortunately for Dalrymple, Sultan Alimuddin II had come to the conclusion that his own position was dependent on British recognition and support, so he was easily persuaded to sign yet another treaty with the English Company, on this occasion ceding all Sulu's dominions in north Borneo and on southern Palawan, as well as Balambangan. These cessions were accepted by the three sons of Alimuddin I in Jolo, namely Israel, Sharifuddin and Ja'afar.

This situation was soon reversed by the news that in Europe a peace treaty had been signed restoring the Philippines to Spanish rule.[29] This meant that the Spaniards, who claimed to have reached a prior agreement with Alimuddin I in Manila, might have grounds to dispute the concessions signed by his nephew, Sultan Alimuddin II, and Dalrymple in Sulu.[30] Dalrymple decided on a *volte-face*. Alimuddin II was now required to make way for his uncle, Alimuddin I, who would then make a fresh treaty with the Company confirming all previous cessions. The plan was successfully put into effect despite all Spanish efforts to prevent it. In May 1764, as the British withdrew their forces from Manila, Alimuddin I left with them and was transported back to Jolo. There the following month, Alimuddin II and his followers having withdrawn to another part of the island, the rumah bichara

[a]See p. 350.

restored him officially as Sultan and at the end of the same month the old ruler signed a new treaty with the British, identical to that signed by his nephew the previous year but stipulating his cessions as a sale.

On paper at any rate, the British had thus acquired a new empire in the south of the Sulu archipelago. Dalrymple dreamed of a British protected sultanate of North Borneo[31] with Sulu as a buffer state in between it and the Spanish Philippines. In fact, it all came to nothing. In the year that Sultan Alimuddin I, old in years, abdicated in favour of his son, Mohd. Israel, the British established a settlement on Balambangan. But the British presence was resented as much as the Spanish one by the independent-minded datos of Sulu and two years later, in 1775, the settlement was attacked by a force led by Dato Taiteng which led to its abandonment.[32] Another attempt by the British to found a settlement on the island took place in 1803 but was given up two years afterwards.

There were two subsequent British attempts to establish their influence in the Sulu archipelago. The first was inspired by the indefatigable Raffles who sent John Hunt to Jolo in 1814 to negotiate the posting of a British agent there. The Sultan, Mohd. Abidin Shakirullah, was willing to agree but the principal datos said no, telling the British envoy that 'Even though we are pirates, the British have no right to interfere'.[33] Hunt finally succeeded in signing a treaty with the Sultan, possibly without the datos' knowledge, which confirmed Dalrymple's old treaty of 1764; but the mission itself incurred such great expense for so little visible return that nothing came of it. The second attempt was made by James Brooke in 1849, but although he signed a treaty of friendship and trade it was never ratified in the face of Spanish protests.

Magindanau and rival colonial powers
Magindanau's relations with the Dutch and British followed a similar pattern to those of Sulu. The Dutch were active in inciting Magindanau rulers against the Spaniards or in getting Magindanau support for their own attacks in the seventeenth century. Later they and the British competed, both in vain,[34] to obtain commercial treaties and privileges from Magindanau rulers. The British occupation of Balambangan in 1773, however, excited lively interest in Magindanau and caused Sultan Amiruddin to send an embassy there to offer an island of his own for British settlement. He was attracted by the thought of finding a bulwark against the Spaniards. Thirty years later (in 1809) Sultan Mohamed Shah Anwaruddin wanted a British alliance against his own unruly subjects and appealed to Lord Minto, the British governor-general in India, but without success.[35] This appeal was one of the factors which encouraged Raffles to send Hunt to Magindanau in 1814 where he was accorded a far more enthusiastic welcome than in Jolo. The outcome was a treaty which provided for the establishment of a British agent in Magindanau with extra-territorial rights in his compound, exclusive trading privileges and half a share in perpetuity of all the Sultan's revenues, duties and imposts. But as we have already seen, Hunt's mission proved such a commercial failure that this opening was never followed up.

The age of piracy
There are two main reasons which account for the failure of Great Britain or any

other western power other than Spain to establish itself in Sulu or Magindanau prior to the nineteenth century. In the first place, the trading prospects were never sufficiently attractive to induce the authorities concerned to mount the costly expeditions necessary to impose their will. Secondly, it is clear that the rulers of Sulu and Maginadanau more often than not had barely nominal control over the datos and chiefs who lorded it over the communities scattered along the southern shores of Magindanau and amongst the islands of the archipelago.

With the increasing domination of the Europeans along the avenues of trade throughout South-East Asian waters towards the end of the eighteenth century and during the course of the nineteenth, the opportunities for legitimate commerce by the inhabitants of the region diminished still further. The consequence was a great increase in what the Europeans called piracy. The great bay of Mindanao (Moro Gulf) and certain of the islands became notorious amongst peaceful traders as the homes of pirate communities whose activities stretched from the Indian Ocean to the Pacific. Although these pirates were not actually the henchmen of the Sultans of either Sulu and Magindanau, Jolo in particular became the greatest mart in all island South-East Asia for the disposal of their gains.[36] And in the same way that the sultan and pangeran of Brunai had to live by patronizing the operations of the sharif-led Ibans and Malays of the estuaries along the north coast of Borneo, so a similar relationship developed between the rulers and datos of Magindanau and Sulu on the one hand and these pirate communities on the other.

Two groups especially struck terror in the hearts of those who heard their name —the Lanun and the Balanini. The Lanun or Ilanun took their name from their bases along Ilana Bay in Southern Mindanao, and were made up of a mixture of Malays, Bajaus and Samals.[37] By the beginning of the nineteenth century they had also established strongholds in north Borneo (at Tempasuk, Pandasan, Langkon-Marudu and Tungku), at Tantoli in the Celebes, and in Sumatra at Selangut off Lingga and on the Indragiri river at Reteh. The Balanini took their name from the island of Balanguingui in the Samales group due east of Jolo itself, and had settlements on Tawi Tawi, Binadan and Tongquil, and later on at Dongdong and Kabungkul on Jolo. The Lanun and Balanini became known and feared throughout the whole of the Malaysian archipelago on account of their regular and well-planned voyages. When the appropiate winds blew they set out from their bases in Sulu and Magindanau for Tempasuk in north-west Borneo and there divided up into some four or five squadrons to cover all the Eastern seas. One group would circumnavigate the island of Borneo itself and ravage New Guinea and the Celebes on the way back. A second visited the Gulf of Siam and passed along Malaya's east coast. Another sailed through the Riau archipelago and the Straits of Malacca penetrating as far north as Burma; a fourth swept down to the northern shores of Java and then westwards into the Bay of Bengal. One squadron was left to ravage the Philippines. The regularity of these sweeps led the British authorities in the Straits Settlements to refer to the months of August, September and October as the 'Lanun' season.[38]

These Sulu and Magindanau sea-warriors played a political role as well. As we have seen, Sultan Mahmud of Johore-Riau called in the Lanun to drive out the Dutch in 1787[a] and a few years later secured their co-operation in a grand scheme

[a]Refer p. 118.

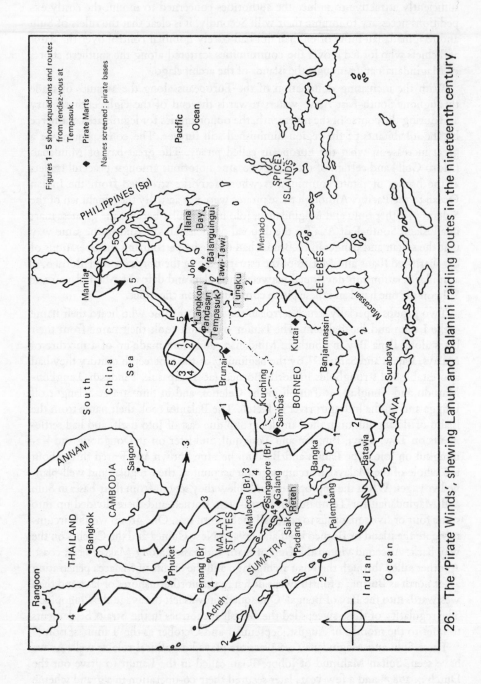

26. The 'Pirate Winds', shewing Lanun and Balanini raiding routes in the nineteenth century

to sweep not only the Dutch from Malacca but also the newly-established British from Penang at the behest of the Sultan of Kedah.[a] In the 1840s Sultan Mahmud Muzzaffar Shah of Riau had a close understanding with the Lanun of Reteh, as indeed did both Baginda Omar of Trengganu and Bendahara Ali of Pahang. The men of Sulu and Magindanau also had friends in the court of Brunai.[b]

Western intervention and the Spanish conquest

Inevitably the activities of the Lanun and Balanini during the first half of the nineteenth century attracted the unfavourable attention of the various western colonial powers who were busy establishing and extending their empires in the region, and provided them with ample excuse to intervene in Sulu or Magindanau affairs to their own advantage. The Dutch destroyed the Lanun colony at Reteh in 1858[c] after they had already (ineffectively) bombarded Jolo itself ten years previously.[39] In 1844 the French made an attempt to seize the island of Basilan. Having lost some men on the island and failing to take satisfactory reprisals, the head of the French mission, Lagrené, succeeded in signing a treaty with Sultan Mohd. Pulalun in February 1845, whereby Basilan was ceded to France for $100,000.[40] But for various reasons, this cession was not followed up.

The real threat to Sulu's independence still came from Manila. In 1837 Sultan Jamal-ul Kiram I signed a commercial treaty with the Spanish governor, Salazar, who hoped thereby to encourage legitimate trade and discourage piracy. From that point of view the treaty remained a dead letter. But the signing of this treaty was not merely the result of Spanish pressure. By the mid-nineteenth century Sulu politics was dominated by two factions amongst the datos, one of which favoured ties with and the protection of a western power (not necessarily Spain) and the other which opposed for fear of loss of the pirate trade. Jamal-ul Kiram's successor, Sultan Pulalun, faced mounting Spanish pressure which was precipitated by the moves of other colonial powers. Spain had always laid claim to suzerainty over the archipelago even though she had never been able to substantiate it. Manila protested against Dutch, French and British contacts with Sulu. In 1848 the Spanish governor, Narciso Claveria, sent an expedition which raided the island of Balanguingui and stormed the chief Balanini fortress of Sipac.[41] This attack marked the writing on the wall for Sulu, for it owed its success principally to the presence of three steam warships recently bought in England. In the decade which followed, this small steam fleet was increased and gave the Spaniards a means of overawing Sulu which hitherto they had never possessed. Following up this advantage, Claveria's successor, Urbiztondo, in 1851 bombarded and captured Jolo, forcing Sultan Pulalun into flight. Since the only way to regain possession of his capital was by making peace, the Sultan and his principal datos came to terms. The Sultan recognized Spanish sovereignty, agreed to fly the Spanish flag, to suppress piracy and not to sign any treaties with foreign powers. In return the Spaniards promised to pay regular allowances to the Sultan and the leading datos, to respect the practice of Islam, and to guarantee the succession to the throne.

This surrender was shortlived. As soon as the Spaniards withdrew, these terms

[a]Refer p. 107.
[b]Refer p. 174.
[c]Refer p. 124.

were forgotten and the ancient state of warfare was resumed. Knowing his situation to be desperate, Sultan Pulalun spent the remaining years of his reign trying to get support from some other power. He particularly directed his attention to Britain but in response to his appeals in the 1860s, after Manila had declared Jolo to be closed to all 'foreign' trade, the British government replied that it could not allow itself to become involved in a quarrel with Spain. However, private adventurers were able to exploit the situation and make handsome profits by running guns and ammunition to Sulu in defiance of the Spanish blockade. Amongst the handful of Germans, Englishmen and adventurers of other nationalities who indulged in this traffic was W.C. Cowie, who sufficiently won the confidence of the Sultan as to get his permission to set up a depot in Sandakan Bay for his gun-running activities.[a]

Ten years after declaring Jolo closed to outside trade, the Spaniards launched an all-out campaign to reduce the sultanate once and for all. In 1871 Jolo was bombarded and Tawi-Tawi raided. Two years later they imposed a tight blockade of all the islands. In February 1876, Pulalun's successor, Sultan Jamal-ul Alam, found his capital confronted by a combined Spanish-Filipino force of 9,000 men, supported by a fleet of gun-boats. After a fierce struggle, Jamal-ul Alam had to flee the capital, and set up his headquarters at Maimbang on the other side of the island. Here, early in 1878, he grasped at what appeared to be his last chance of gaining outside support by signing a treaty with Overbeck and Dent, two European speculators, ceding them his territories in North Borneo for an annual tribute of $5,000 a year.[b] But although this treaty received British recognition,[42] it did not result in any British backing for his resistance against Spanish encroachments. Six months later the Sultan could withstand Spanish pressure no longer and put his signature to articles of 'pacification and capitulation', offering his complete submission.

Formally speaking, this marked the end of Sulu independence, a fact which received international recognition in 1885 with the signing of the Sulu Protocol by which both Britain and Germany acknowledged Spain's undisputed authority over the whole of the Sulu archipelago.[c] However, that authority continued to be disputed by the Sulus themselves for the remaining quarter century of Spanish rule. While a Spanish governor and garrison remained at Jolo, the other islands resisted the imposition of Spanish authority. The Sultan's ability to control affairs was weakened by his own position of subservience to the Spaniards, and also by the fact that his datos exploited the situation to intrigue for the sultanate or to disregard it altogether. Succession disputes followed the death of Sultan Badruddin II in 1884 which prompted Spanish intervention and further weakened the authority of the sultanate. In the meanwhile guerrilla warfare flared up spasmodically throughout the archipelago as the Spaniards extended their control. In 1882 they occupied Siasi, Tataan on Tawi Tawi, and the island of Bongao at its tip. In the following decade Sulu guerrillas killed over 300 Christian soldiers. When Spanish rule came to an end in 1899, the Sulu archipelago had still not been completely subdued.

The Spanish forward movement in the archipelago was accompanied by a parallel movement in southern Mindanao. The first step came in 1847 when a Basque

aRefer p. 191 and p. 199, note 63.
bRefer p. 181.   cRefer p. 195.

called Oyanguren obtained the permission of the Manila authorities to organize the conquest of the land round Davao Bay.[43] The acquisition of steam warships spelt doom for Magindanau as much as it did for Sulu. These and modern field artillery enabled the Spaniards to set up a new chain of fortified posts along the Magindanau shore during the 1850s and 1860s. In 1885 they started on a definitive campaign to conquer Magindanau itself. But despite initial successes the Spaniards were unable to overcome the Magindanau resistance inland. In 1891, despite a change in command, the Spaniards found themselves forced to withdraw to Sambuangan. In 1895 they launched a drive into the Maranau country around Lake Lanao for the first time in 250 years,[a] but retreated after campaigning for three months. A fresh campaign against Magindanau launched in 1898 had made little progress by the time that the writ of Spanish authority expired just over twelve months later.

The American conquest

The final phase in the struggle of Sulu and Magindanau to maintain their independence came with the arrival of the Americans.[b] In May 1899 two American battalions arrived at Jolo to replace the Spanish garrison there. By this time the sultanate was at its lowest ebb and the Sultan, Jamal-ul Kiram II, could exercise scarcely any control over his datos.[44] Nevertheless he was still the palladium of sovereignty and the American military commander, General John C. Bates, hastened to conclude an agreement with him. The result was the Bates Treaty of August 1899. Signed by the Sultan and four principal datos, it defined Sulu as an American protectorate, enjoined the Sultan to suppress piracy and control the importation of firearms, and forbade him to prevent a slave from seeking his freedom or to alienate any of his territory to a third power. In return, the Americans promised to safeguard the worship of Islam and assured the Sultan and his datos of regular allowances.

The Sultan accepted these terms without making any difficulty but although he had acquired an American income he was, as he well knew, in no way able to enforce the provisions of the agreement. Most of the datos on the other islands or even on Jolo itself were as unwilling to acknowledge the suzerainty of the United States of America as they had been to accept that of Spain, and an increasing number of incidents took place against the American presence in the archipelago.

In mid-1903 the Sulu archipelago, Sambuangan, Kota Batu, Lanau and Davao were constituted into the Moro province by the Americans and placed under the control of an American governor. The first holder of this post was General Leonard Wood who soon came to the conclusion that the Bates Agreement should be torn up since it meant 'the payment of salaries to a large number of people who have never been loyal to the United States, and who... interpret this agreement as indicating that they are a people of great importance and that we are willing to pay them to be good'.[45] Several other American officials felt the same way and finally, in early 1904, the treaty was abrogated by Congress.[46]

For obvious reasons, the abrogation of the Bates Treaty was not well received at the court of Sultan Jamal-ul Kiram, and only increased the general restlessness in the

[a]Refer to p. 206.
[b]See pp. 379-80.

islands. During the next few years resistance intensified. More and more guerrilla attacks were made on U.S. posts and there were several instances where the struggle took the tragic form of mass suicide, when large bodies of men, women and children deliberately hurled themselves to a certain death against the unwilling bayonets of American soldiers. Such tragedies occurred twice on a large-scale on Jolo; the first took place in the crater of the extinct volcano of Bud Dajo in 1906 when 600 people perished in this way; the second occasion was in 1913 on Mount Bagsak when 300 lost their lives. But American arms and organization were far superior to those of Spain, and as the years went by and the more notable leaders of the resistance were killed or captured,[47] opposition began to fade away.

A great change in the situation came about with the appointment of the first civilian, Frank W. Carpenter, as governor in 1913. He believed in a policy of conciliation and tolerance in place of the more uncompromising attitudes of his predecessors. Travelling unarmed and even without escort through the islands he sought out the hostile datos and tried to win them over to the new order of things by fair words and the offer of friendship. The measure of his success was made two years later when in March 1915, he negotiated a new treaty with the aged sultan Jamal-ul Kiram II. By this agreement the Sultan renounced all his political authority, was granted a life pension of Ps. 12,000 a year as well as land, and was officially recognized by the Americans as the spiritual leader of all Filipino Muslims. By this time Magindanau had been completely pacified, and under American aegis the two last independent sultanates of the Malaysian world accepted their destiny to become welded to the emergent Filipino nation.

[1] An expedition of three ships under Francisco Serra(n)o and Antonio de Abreu was despatched by Alfonso d'Albuquerque after the fall of Malacca in 1511 to explore the Moluccas. During the course of his wanderings Serrano became the first known European to reach the Philippines.

[2] Jolo is the Spanish rendering of Sulu.

[3] According to Sulu tradition—as given in the *Tarsila Sulu*—Islam was introduced to the islands around 1380 by a 'makhdum' (he who serves) from Arabia. Shortly afterwards, a Menangkabau prince known as Raja Baginda conquered Jolo. Meanwhile an Arab sharif, Abu Bakar el-Hashimi, was continuing the work of spreading Islam. He married Raja Baginda's daughter and became ruler on the death of his father-in-law. Abu Bakar el-Hashimi is considered the founder of the line of Sulu sultans.

[4] Also known as *Lutaus* or men of the sea.

[5] Known to the Spaniards as the Rio Grande (Great River).

[6] Or Moor; a term applied by the Spaniards and Portuguese to all Muslims. The name is derived from the Arab-led Muslim tribesmen from Morocco in North Africa who overran and occupied the Iberian Peninsula in the seventh century and after.

[7] Or 'caracao': 'A corocoro is a vessel generally fitted with outriggers, with a high arched stem and stern, like the point of a half-moon.... They have them from a very small size to above ten tons' burthen; and on the cross-pieces which support the outriggers, there are often put fore-and-aft planks, on which the people sit and paddle, beside those who sit in the vessel on each gunnel. In smooth water they can be paddled very fast, as many hands may be employed in different ranks or rows.... When they are high out of the water they use oars, but on the outriggers they always use paddles.' Description by Captain Forrest, a British naval officer who visited Magindanau in 1775. Quoted by de la Costa, *The Jesuits in the Philippines*, p. 294.

[8] In 1569 off Cebu when a small squadron under Martin de Goiti drove off some Sulu vessels raiding Bisayan villages.

[9] When Figueroa arrived in Magindanau he found the coast and villages deserted. Unable to make contact or obtain provisions he was forced to withdraw. He was eventually killed in 1596 leading his own privately-equipped expedition to subdue the country.

[10]The three leaders were Raja Mura (Muda), the titular head of the Confederacy; Sirongan from Buayan (Bwayan), its most powerful chief; and Bwisan of Magindanau whose son Kudrat was to become Magindanau's first sultan.

[11]Sultan Muwallil Wasit Bongsu succeeded to the throne around 1625 after a civil war involving his predecessor. His policy in fighting the Spaniards was to secure Dutch support. When he was driven from Jolo in 1638 he managed to get Dutch assistance, resulting in their attacks on Spanish-held Jolo in 1645 and 1646.

[12]A title given to the Spanish pioneers who won new lands for Spain, especially in the Americas.

[13]The renewal of Magindanau activity seems to have come about as the result of the consolidation of the country under a sultanate.

[14]The Maranau were a pagan race living around the shores of Lake Lanao, whose chiefs had embraced Islam and were linked by marriage with the aristocracy of Magindanau. In Corcuera's time their number was estimated at some 8,000, concentrated in four large towns and about fifty villages. The Spanish failure was largely brought about by aid given by Kudrat.

[15]The principal terms of the treaty negotiated between Bongsu and Father Alejandro Lopez at Lipir included provision for a defensive and offensive alliance; a recognition of Sulu's authority from Tawi-Tawi to Tutup and Bagahak with Spain having a free hand in Tapul, Balangu-ingui, Siasi and Pangaturan; a yearly tribute of three jaongs of rice to Sambuangan and the withdrawal of the Spanish garrison from Jolo. It was also agreed to conduct a joint expedition against the Orang Tedong with fair division of spoils and that Jesuit missionaries should have freedom to preach in Sulu. At first Bongsu's two sons refused to accept the treaty but after Raja Paktian Baktial, the heir apparent, had been defeated by a Spanish flotilla off Sambuang-an, they gave way. Kudrat's treaty signed at Simuai the previous year was similar. His dominions were recognized as comprising the area between the Ino river (in the interior), Tagolo Bay (near Dapitan in the west) and the Sibuguey river (also in the west), Kota Batu and Magolabon.

[16]Sultan Kudrat had been antagonized by the activities of the commander of the Spanish garrison at Caraga who pursued rebels into his territory. In 1650 and 1653 Manila sent emissaries to Simuai in an effort to preserve the peace. The murder of the Spanish envoy, Father Lopez, on a third mission in 1655, precipitated the renewal of hostilities.

[17]Coxinga was the Spanish rendering of Cheng Ch'eng-kung, a Chinese rebel leader and adventurer who drove the Dutch out of Formosa and made himself master of the island.

[18]De la Costa, op. cit. pp. 281-2. Actually in the quotation given here de la Costa is referring to the removal of the Spanish garrison from La Caldera in 1599, but the effect of the withdrawal from Sambuangan sixty years later had precisely the same effect.

[19]There are many instances of datos refusing to accept the provisions of treaties entered into by the Sultan, as happened in 1638, 1705 and in 1878. See Cesar Abdul Majid, Political and Historical Notes on the Old Sulu Sultanate , J.M.B.R.A.S., Vol. 38, No. 1, 1965.

[20]Francisco Jose de Ovando by Solis, Marquis of Ovando, Governor of the Philippines, 1750-44. Quoted by De la Costa, 'Muhammad Alimuddin I, Sultan of Sulu, 1735-73', J.M.B.R.A.S, Vol. 38, No. 1, 1965. Alimuddin had had experience of the outside world before his accession; lived in the Arab quarter of Batavia; knew Arabic and Malay; knowledge of Islamic studies entitled him to the honorific title of 'pandita'.

[21]A people settled in North Borneo and Palawan—known as Orang Tedong in Borneo; the Spaniards called them Camucones. They were pagan and their repute as ruthless raiders was greater even than that of the Malays.

[22]Comprising two leading datos, Salleh Kala and Memancha, and Bantilan himself.

[23]In fact there was fierce controversy amongst the Catholic prelates of the Philippines as to Alimuddin's sincerity. The Acting-Governor and Bishop of Nueva Segovia, Juan de Areche-derra, took Alimuddin at face value and accepted his conversion as genuine, despite the protests of the Sultan's own Jesuit instructors and those of the Archbishop of Manila, Pedro Martinez de Arizala. As a result, Alimuddin was officially baptized in Pangasinan, outside the jurisdiction of the Archbishop. See de la Costa, The Jesuits, op. cit. pp. 547-8.

[24]The governor had already been told that on the voyage Alimuddin had not conducted himself as a Christian should: he also discovered from the translation of an official letter from Alimuddin to Sultan Amiruddin of Magindanau exhorting him to accept Spanish protection that Alimuddin had added a postscript indicating that he was not a free agent: finally the arrival of an exceptionally large group of Sulu chiefs and followers at Sambuangan to escort the Sultan back on the last of his voyage home and the subsequent discovery of caches of weapons on board their vessels sealed the matter.

[25]Alexander Dalrymple—official of the English East India Company at Madras, who had considerable experience of trading in South-East Asian waters. Dalrymple saw Sulu as a new mart

for importing British and Indian goods into North China, thereby circumventing the Co-hong. His views were put down in *A Plan for Extending the Commerce of this Kingdom and of the East India Company.*

²⁶His agreements with the datos were purely commercial ones. The datos were to buy Indian piece goods at double their value which they would pay for in local produce having a market in China. The Company would tranship these goods for disposal in China, the profit or the loss being sustained by the dato's themselves. The scheme foundered at the very start since when Dalrymple arrived at Jolo he found several of the original signatories dead from small-pox. On top of that two of his own vessels were forced to avoid Sulu and sail straight for Canton, owing to bad weather.

²⁷Alimuddin actually took an active part in the defence of Manila, being seriously wounded in the process. Escaping to Tayabas, he was refused permission to return to his homeland by the acting Spanish governor, Anda, but ordered north to Pangasinan to help quell the disturbances there. Detained by an accident at Pasig, near Manila, on his way, he made overtures to the British and allowed himself to be captured there when the town was occupied by British forces.

²⁸The Dutch had already been forestalled by a matter of weeks by Dalrymple in 1761.

²⁹The Treaty of Paris, ending the Seven Years War between Britain and her allies with Spain and France—which had been the occasion for the British occupation of Manila. The war itself was essentially a conflict involving Anglo-French colonial rivalries (in India and in North America) and dynastic rivalries in Europe. The Philippines were a pawn in the game.

³⁰This was because Alimuddin I had already signed a provisional treaty with the Spanish government of the Philippines prior to the British invasion; its terms ceded much the same area that his nephew, Alimuddin II, now gave to Dalrymple. Unless Alimuddin I could be removed from Manila and restored as ruler in Sulu, the Spaniards could claim that their agree-ment with him was valid. Therefore Alimuddin II was required to step down and enable his uncle to resume his status as an independent ruler who would repudiate all his former engage-ments and conclude a new treaty with the British. See de la Costa, 'Muhammed Alimuddin I, Sultan of Sulu', op. cit.

³¹Dalrymple was able to win Alimuddin I's consent to his schemes by promising that one of the ruler's own sons, Sharifuddin, should become the ruler of the ceded territory. The English East India Company actually confirmed this arrangement in 1764. To please the Spaniards, Dalrymple also shrewdly proposed to permit Jesuit evangelization in the new sultanate.

³²Apart from the Sulu attack, the settlement had been so badly mismanaged by its governor, John Herbert, that it was already on the point of collapse. Subsequent to the Sulu raid, Herbert tried to found a settlement on Labuan but this, too, proved a failure.

³³Quoted from John Hunt's account of his mission by John Bastin, 'Raffles and British Policy in the Indian Archipelago, 1811-1816', *J.M.B.R.A.S.*, Vol. 27, No. 1, 1954, pp. 100-4.

³⁴For example, the Dutch mission of 1689 to obtain permission to establish a factory and a fort in Magindanau was turned down; a similar British mission in 1694 met with the same response.

³⁵In the end the Sultan did the unthinkable and appealed to Manila in 1812, and obtained the help he needed.

³⁶Hunt described Jolo as 'the greatest slave-mart and thieves' market in the whole East Indian islands. Here the pirate fleets returned after their long cruises to sell their slaves and booty and buy supplies from the Chinese and Bugis merchants who came to it'. He also reported that Jolo datos equipped the expeditions and received 25 per cent of the booty. During his six months' stay on the island in 1814, Hunt heard of the capture of 28 ships, including a Spanish brig and the kidnapping of a thousand inhabitants of the Philippines. Quoted by Mills, 'Bri-tish Malaya 1824-67', *J.M.B.R.A.S.*, Vol. 33, No. 3, 1960.

³⁷According to the information gathered by a British naval captain called Blake, who visited Manila to find out about the pirate question in 1838, the Lanun main base in the bay was situa-ted between a lake and the shore: 'here they build and repair their praus, which they convey to and from the sea by means of ways or platforms constructed of bamboo and ratan placed to the unsolid surface of the mangrove roots and branches, over which their praus are hauled to and fro. On this lake, too, they have their wives or females in the praus in which they live; and in short they carry on all intercourse with each other, as an isolated and distinct community; born and bred in a life of piracy, they look on it merely as a means of living, and not as a cri-minal occupation....' Quoted by Tarling, *Piracy and Politics in the Malay World*, p. 153.

³⁸The average galley in a Lanun fleet varied from 40 to 100 tons burden and carried between 40 to 60 men. The British admiral Hunter, who once in 1847 went on a Lanun voyage disguised as a Malay, described the flagship on which he sailed as being 95 ft. long, with 90 oars, double-banked, 56 fighting men, 12 lelas and one Spanish 18-pounder. See Mills, op. cit. p. 258.

[39]The bombardment of 1848 was the outcome of a Dutch expedition sent to Jolo to demand satisfaction for pirate depredations in the Moluccas and the Riau archipelago. Receiving only evasive assurances from the Sultan, they opened fire on the town but were themselves damaged by the return fire from the Jolo forts, and so the Dutch sailed away, having achieved nothing.

[40]This was part of a conscious French attempt under the July Monarchy to increase French influence in the Far East, by founding a suitable naval base there. See de la Costa, *Readings in Philippine History*, pp. 206–7.

[41]This attack came as a reaction to the French attempts to establish themselves on Basilan.

[42]The British governor of Labuan, W.H. Treacher, was present at the signing to protect British interests. On his insistence it was stipulated that the ceded territory was not transferable without the approval of the British government, and that disputes between the concessionaires and the sultanate must be submitted to British arbitration.

[43]The settlement was founded in the same year, and after two years of hard fighting, firmly established. Oyanguren founded Nueva Vergara, now Davao City. In 1853 the concession was cancelled and the territory taken over by the Manila government; the region was organized as the province of Nueva Guipuzcoa. The Basques are a people whose home stretches from northern Spain at the western end of the Pyrenees into south-west France.

[44]Cesar Abdul Majid (op. cit. p. 42) cites as an example of the low prestige of the sultanate by 1900 Sultan Jamal-ul Kiram II's request to the American military governor for the recovery of some of his horses stolen by one of his datos.

[45]Quoted by Grunder and Livezey, *The Philippines and the United States*, p. 41.

[46]Since under the American Constitution, foreign relations are subject to the control of the Senate, its sanction was necessary for abrogation. In fact, the treaty never came before the Senate for approval.

[47]Amongst prominent Sulu leaders killed during the course of the struggle against the Americans were Dato Ali in 1905, Jikiri in 1909, Nakib Amil and Jami in 1913, and Saipul, Bunglu and Sallehuddin in 1914.

8. SULU AND MAGINDANAU: CHRONOLOGY OF MAIN EVENTS

A. Spanish attacks

	Sulu	*Magindanau*
1578	*Jolo captured by Figueroa.* Sultan signed treaty of submission	Figueroa's attack unsuccessful
1596		Figueroa's second expedition; killed
1599	Pacho's expedition repulsed at Jolo	
1602	Gallinato's force besieges Jolo for three months; retires unsuccessful	
1609		Gallinato surprises and defeats Magindanau fleet in Pangil Bay
1614	Spanish outpost established at Caraga	
1628	Lugo's expedition fails to take Jolo	

	Sulu	*Magindanau*
1630	Olaso's expedition fails to take Jolo	
1635	Spaniards found Zamboanga and build fort there	
1636		Spaniards ambush Magindanau fleet off Panoan; severe defeats for Muslims
1637		*Governor Corcuera conquers and occupies Magindanau*
1638	*Governor Corcuera attacks and captures Jolo and occupies it*	
1639		Corcuera's second expedition against Magindanau; Maranau territory subdued; fort built at Illigan; garrisons at Sabanilla and Buayan
1642		Spaniards withdraw from Buayan and Sabanilla
1643		Third expedition against Magindanau without results
1645		Peace Treaty with Magindanau; Spanish withdrawal
1646	Spaniards abandon Jolo	
1658		Spanish expedition against Magindanau ineffective
1663–1718	Spaniards abandon Zamboanga because of Formosan threat	
1721	Rojas' expedition; failure	
1722–3	Garcia's expedition; failure	
1723	De la Mesa's expedition; failure	
1731	Iriberri's expendition; failure	
1753	Spanish assault on Jolo repulsed	
1754		Maranau defeated near Iligan Spanish raids in Ilanun Bay
1824	Martinez' expedition against Jolo and Magindanau; unsuccessful. Spanish attack on Jolo repulsed; Lanun bases raided	
1848	Governor Urbiztondo bombards Sipac; town captured	
1851	*Jolo captured by Urbiztondo; Sulu signs peace treaty accepting Spanish overlordship*	
1871–8	*Spanish conquest of Sulu. Jolo occupied permanently (1876)*	

	Sulu	*Magindanau*
1878	Guerrilla warfare against Spaniards	
1882	Spaniards occupy Bangao & Siasi; also Tata'an on Tawi[2]	
1886		Start of Spanish campaign of of conquest on Magindanau
1891		General Weyler takes over campaign; forced to withdraw to Zamboanga
1895		Campaign resumed under General Blanco; abandoned after three months
1898		Campaign started again under General Baille

B. Muslim Attacks

1. Initial skirmishes with Legazpi off Cebu	1569
2. Magindanau raids under the three dato's (Salleh, Sirongan, Bwisan)	1599–1609
3. Sulu raids, in league with the Dutch and especially under Raja Bongsu (1625–38)	1614–38
4. Revival of Magindanau under Sultan Kudrat (1630+–63); raids	1605–63
5. Period of frequent Sulu and Magindanau raids	1656–1735
6. Height of Muslim incursions from Sulu and Magindanau	1764–1800

C. Treaty Relations with Western Powers

Sulu		*Magindanau*	
1578	Spain	1605	Spain
1646	Spain	1637	Spain
1725	Spain	1645	Spain
1737	Spain	1743	Spain
1761*	Britain	1814	Britain
1764*	Britain		
1769*	Britain		
1805	Spain		
1837	Spain		
1842	USA		
1843	France		
1845	France		
1849	Britain		
1851	Spain		
1878	Overbeck and Dent		

Sulu	Magindanau
1878 Spain	
1899 USA	
1915 USA	
* *The Balambangan Affair*	

D. Treaties with Britain

1. Sultan Mu'izzuddin and Dalrymple — Alliance—land on Jolo for British factory (28 January 1761)

2. Sultan Mu'izzuddin and Dalrymple — Cession of Balambangan (12 September 1762)

3. Alimuddin I/Israel and Dalrymple — Confirming first treaty above (23 February 1763)

4. Alimuddin II and Dalrymple — Confirming existing agreements and ceding all territories in North Borneo and Sulu Peninsula (September 19, 1763)

5. Alimuddin I and Dawson Drake — Confirming all previous cessions (19 June 1764)

E. The American Conquest

1899	US forces land at Jolo
	The Bates Treaty
1903	Sulu, Lanao, Kotabatu, Davao and Zamboanga created the Moro province
1904	US Senate abrogates the Bates Treaty
1906	Battle of Bud Dajo, Jolo
1913	Battle of Mt. Bagsak, Jolo
1915	The Carpenter Agreement

F. Rulers of Sulu in the Nineteenth Century

Died 1808	Alauddin
1808–23	Sharik'ullah
1823–44	Jamalul Kiram I
1844–62	Mohamad Pulalun
1862–81	Jamalul Alam
1881–4	Badruddin II
1886–94	Harun
1894–1915	Jamalul Kiram II

ACHEH

ACHEH was the Sulu of the west. Traditionally the first home of Islam in the Malaysian archipelago,[1] the Achinese to this day pride themselves on being the champions and defenders of the faith in the Malay world, while Acheh for long has remained an important centre for Islamic studies and the diffusion of the religion. Like the men of Sulu and Magindanau, the Achinese found their faith and political independence challenged from the very outset by the European, and like the eastern sultanates, Acheh's rise and decline was to a large extent shaped by the struggle which ensued.

The rise of Acheh and the struggle for the control of the Straits
Acheh's rise was the direct consequence of the fall of Malacca to the Portuguese in 1511. Malacca's downfall was Acheh's gain. Muslim traders from India and the Near East flocked to Acheh in preference to the port of Malacca, now under the rule of their commercial rivals and religious antagonists, the Christian Portuguese. Not only Muslim traders but merchants from Coromandel, Ceylon, Bengal and Pegu also came to Acheh to avoid the high Portuguese imposts of Malacca. This sudden accession of trade brought with it wealth and power, and within a short time Acheh's rulers were able to extend their control over their pepper-producing neighbours along the eastern and western coastlines and turn Acheh into the greatest pepper mart in the region. This brought them into conflict not only with the Portuguese, out to establish their own monopoly, but also with the new power of Johore to the south, which laid claim to Malacca's heritage.[2] However, Acheh was able to rise to the occasion. Under a succession of forceful rulers,[3] she played a dominant role in the next hundred and fifty years of triangular struggle which now began for the control of the trade of the Straits of Malacca.

The prime enemy of the Achinese was Portuguese Malacca. Considerations of religion as well as of trade made this conflict inevitable.[4] By 1537, Sultan Ala'uddin Riayat Shah, new on the throne, felt that his forces were strong enough to launch a frontal assault on the Portuguese bastion which he attacked with over 3,000 men. The attack was beaten off with heavy losses, but this was the prelude to a century of Achinese assaults. Amongst the half dozen or more expeditions hurled against Portuguese Malacca,[5] the one which came nearest to success was in 1568 when, led by the Sultan himself, 300 Achinese war-boats carrying 15,000 soldiers, 400 Turkish artillerymen and 200 bronze cannon, besieged the fortress. In 1587 internal troubles caused the Sultan (Alauddin of Perak) to sign a truce with the Portuguese, but it was shortlived. The last serious Achinese attack on the Portuguese in Malacca came in 1639.

One reason for the survival of the Portuguese during those years was the enmity between Acheh and Johore. The course of the struggle with Johore fluctuated, although on balance the honours remained with Acheh. When Sultan Ala'uddin Riayat Shah conquered the Johore vassal state of Aru (Deli) in 1539, he was badly defeated the following year by the combined fleets of Johore, Siak and Perak.[6] This was a severe blow from which the Achinese took some time to recover. Nevertheless Sultan Ala'uddin had his revenge some twenty years later when in 1564 an Achinese fleet sailed down the Straits and up the Johore river to his rival's capital at Johor Lama, sacked the town and carried his namesake, Sultan Ala'uddin of Johore, back to Acheh as a prisoner, where he later died or was murdered. By 1591 Johore had in turn recovered sufficiently to annihilate a second Achinese fleet off Aru, but underwent a second drubbing in 1613 when the most famous of Acheh's

Limits of Johore power
at its greatest extent ⌐⌐

Limits of Achinese power
southwards at its greatest
extent ——

Pasai
Kota
Raja
Samudra
Pedir
Merudu
Samalanga
ACHEH
KEDAH
Penang
Susuh
Aru
Deli
Langkat
PERAK
Tumpat
Tuan
PAHANG
Singkel
Barus
Asahan
P.
Nias
Tapanuli
Malacca
JOHORE
Batu Sawar
Johor Lama
Siak
Kampar
Tiku
Priaman
Padang
Salido
Indragiri
Painan
Indrapura
Jambi
Benkulen
Palembang

0   100   200
Miles

27. Acheh in the sixteenth, seventeenth and eighteenth centuries

rulers, Sultan Iskandar Muda,[7] struck at the new capital of Batu Sawar and carried off the heir apparent to the Johore throne. In the meantime Acheh extended her dominion both in Sumatra and on the peninsular mainland opposite. On Sumatra their power came to reach as far south as Padang where they forced the shadowy rulers of Pagar Ruyong[a] to acknowledge their overlordship along the coastal plain and its pepper ports, while on the other side of the island their rule came to embrace

[a]Refer p. 150.

Deli, Siak, Kampar and Indragiri and was poised threateningly over Jambi. In the Peninsula, Perak was first raided in 1575 when an Achinese force sacked the capital, killed the sultan and carried off one of his sons back to Acheh,[a] along with thousands of his subjects.[8]

Iskandar Muda launched a second wave of conquest, aimed at consolidating the Achinese pepper monopoly and at eliminating the competition of rivals. After the reduction of Johore in 1613 and again two years later, Pahang was conquered in 1618, Kedah raided and its pepper plantations destroyed in 1619 and Perak made a vassal for the rest of the century in 1620. The rulers and large numbers of the inhabitants of these states were swept away into captivity. However, in 1629 the Achinese suffered another devastating naval defeat, this time at the hands of the combined fleets of Portugal, Johore and Patani near Malacca. This battle marked a turning point in Acheh's history. For a variety of reasons it proved to be a blow from which she was never able to make a full recovery.

The Dutch and the decline of Acheh

Perhaps the most important single factor which brought about the sudden Achinese decline was the arrival of a new power on the scene with the presence of the Dutch.[b] At first Acheh was not inclined to treat the Dutch any differently from the Portuguese, and Achinese-Dutch relations got off to a bad start with the murder of Cornelis van Houtman at Kota Raja in 1599.[9] However, the realities of the situation soon convinced Acheh's rulers that a Dutch alliance was politic to meet the existing threat from both the Portuguese and Johore. In 1607 the Sultan signed Acheh's first treaty with the Dutch in order to ward off an expected Portuguese attack.[10] But after this, as Iskandar extended his power and the Dutch were still engaged in their struggle to oust the Portuguese from Malacca, the relations between the two powers remained distant. The Dutch did not dare challenge Achinese pretensions, and to avoid possible friction limited their trade with Acheh as far as possible.

However, as the Dutch consolidated their position in South-East Asian waters, it was clear that rivalry between the two powers must grow. In 1639 Sultan Iskandar Thani[11] signed the first of a series of ineffectual agreements with the Dutch concerning the tin trade of his vassal, Perak.[12] The fall of Malacca into Dutch hands two years later transformed the political situation in the archipelago[c] and gave them a decisive advantage over their rivals. In the same year, Sultan Iskandar Thani died, and was succeeded by his widow, Zaqiyat-uddin Taj-al Alam, the first of four women who were to reign over the sultanate for the next sixty years. The indisputable paramountcy of the Dutch in South-East Asian waters and the disappearance of firm rule from Kota Raja that these two events signified consigned Acheh to a swift decline.

During the next twenty years the Achinese conducted a losing struggle to dispute Dutch encroachments into the field of their two basic trade monopolies—Perak tin and Sumatran pepper. In 1641 the Dutch followed up their agreement with the sultanate regarding Perak's tin of 1639 by blockading Kuala Perak and trying to force the Perak ruler into an exclusive monopoly agreement. Not succeeding in

[a]See p. 268.
[b]Refer p. 47.
[c]Refer pp. 72-3.

securing a firm engagement they eventually approached the Achinese court direct and compelled Sultana Zaqiyat-uddin in 1650 to sign a treaty sharing the Perak monopoly on a fifty-fifty basis. This agreement seriously interfered with the prosperous trade in Indian piece-goods between Surat and Acheh as well as antagonizing the Perak chiefs. The following year the Dutch factory at Surat itself was attacked and plundered while their factory in Perak was stormed with Achinese connivance at a cost of nine Dutch lives. Although Sultan Muzaffar II of Perak promised redress in 1653, nothing came of it, nor did a further agreement between the Perak ruler and the Dutch company signed in the presence of Achinese envoys in 1655 produce any better results. Open war followed. To put pressure on Perak and Acheh, the Dutch blockaded both Kuala Perak and Acheh Roads. The Achinese retaliated by destroying the new Dutch factories at Priaman, Tiku and Salido. In 1659 a new compromise was reached by which Acheh was to have one-third and the Dutch a two-thirds monopoly of Perak's tin.[13] In effect, after this date, the Achinese ceased to obtain any significant share in Perak's trade simply because the process of internal disintegration had gone too far. For the same reasons the sultanate could do little but acquiesce in the Painan Contract of 1663, a few years later,[14] by which most of the pepper states of western Sumatra fell under the Dutch monopoly system. Thus deprived of her monopolies, Acheh's hopes of revival as an imperial power were destroyed.

Nevertheless the Achinese maintained their independence despite—particularly during the eighteenth century—constant internal upheavals and the substitution of a Bugis line of rulers.[15] The Dutch found it unprofitable to keep their factors either in Acheh or Perak, and attempts by the English and other European powers to establish permanent bases on Achinese soil all proved fruitless.[16]

Acheh falls under British influence
By the beginning of the nineteenth century the sultanate of Acheh was in a sorry state. Its rulers no longer lorded over the northern waters of the Straits of Malacca or dominated the peninsula states opposite; their influence was confined to the immediate northern tip of the island, in particular the Acheh valley, while they exercised a much vaguer suzerainty over the territorial chiefs of the west and east coasts until they met their challenge with Siak or in the Dutch presence south of Tapanuli.

Achinese politics after 1641 centred on the tug-of-war between the court and the territorial chiefs. The sultan's officials became a hereditary aristocracy determined to prevent any repetition of the tyranny of Iskandar Muda; the placing of female rulers on the throne was their first ploy. The sultanate survived, acknowledged by all Achinese but retaining effective authority only over the capital and its port. The autonomy of the territorial chiefs was further enhanced by the development of the pepper trade in their own districts. In 1737 Lebai Dapa, the chief of Susuh, pioneered a pepper contract with a merchant from British Benkulen. Others followed and the West coast districts opened up a profitable trade with mostly American buyers. The struggle between the court and the chiefs now acquired a new aspect; the sultans demanded a complete monopoly over customs dues and the control of all trade through the capital; the chiefs much preferred to operate on their own account, as indeed did their customers who wanted direct dealings with the local producer.

The instability inherent in this situation was greatly aggravated at the same time by the establishment of the British settlement on Penang which developed a brisk trade with the pepper districts. The net result was to strengthen the position of the chiefs, weaken the sultanate and broaden the scope for intrigue and intervention by interested parties outside.

This was the background to British intervention in Achinese affairs within the first twenty years of the new century, which nearly brought the sultanate under British protection and control. The trouble began in 1802 when Sultan Jauhar al-Alam Shah came of age and assumed full powers on the throne which he had ascended seven years before. From the outset Lebai Dapa of Susuh refused to share the control over the pepper trade of his district with Kota Raja, and was soon joined in this posture by the chiefs of Acheh Besar and Pedir. Jauhar al-Alam, on the other hand, who spoke English well and employed European advisers, yearned for a British alliance which would enable him to reassert his authority over his dominions. He turned towards Penang but the merchants of that settlement were too involved in trading with his rebellious subjects to wish to listen. These were the circumstances which provided the opportunity for Syed Husain,[17] a trader who had settled and made his fortune in Penang, to pursue his own ambitions in Acheh. His wealth gave him considerable influence in the British colony, while his interest in the sultanate sprang from a flourishing trade, both on his own account and as an agent for several European trading houses, and from his connexions with the Achinese royal house. In fact Syed Husain's ambition was to secure the Achinese throne for himself. Spending generously amongst the rebellious factions in the sultanate, he finally succeeded in getting the most powerful of them, the chiefs of Acheh Besar,[18] to rise in revolt and to adopt his son, Saif al-Alam, as the rival claimant for the throne. This took place in 1813, while the actual proclamation of Saif al-Alam was made at Pedir two years later. The result was civil war. Sultan Jauhar al-Alam, still secure at Kota Raja, crossed to Penang to solicit British help, but once again returned empty-handed.

Up to this point the British had observed an attitude of strict neutrality although opinion in Penang generally supported Syed Husain's faction. The desultory struggle which followed aroused increasing consternation in the British colony because the chief victims appeared to be innocent traders going about their affairs, which hit local business badly. However, nothing decisive was done about it until it came to the ears of Raffles in Benkulen that in desperation Sultan Jauhar was thinking of turning to the Dutch for aid. To forestall this, Raffles obtained sanction from the supreme government in India to go to Acheh, investigate the situation and conclude a firm agreement with one of the rivals. He arrived there in March 1819, immediately after having finished his affairs in Singapore[a]. Overriding the opposition of his colleague,[19] Raffles took the part of Sultan Jauhar and signed a treaty with him recognizing him as the legitimate ruler, concluding a defensive alliance, and providing for a British agent to reside at Kota Raja. Furthermore all Acheh's ports were opened to British trade, all monopolies within the state (that is by individual chiefs) forbidden, and neither Europeans nor Americans were to be permitted permanent settlement nor any treaty to be signed with any other foreign power with-

[a]Refer p. 120.

out British consent. The pretender, Saif al-Alam was removed to Calcutta in 1820 where he lived on a pension of $500 a month.[20]

However, this very dangerous agreement was a dead letter from the very start. Sultan Jauhar found it quite impossible to restore his authority against his opponents once Raffles had departed, and the British authorities in Penang did not follow up his initiative. After 1823 when Jauhar al-Alam died without ever re-entering his capital, the royal line continued under Sultan Mohamad Shah, one of Jauhar al-Alam's illegitimate sons but firmly under the control of the territorial chiefs.

Acheh under the Anglo-Dutch Treaty: 1824–71

Having so nearly fallen under the British aegis as a result of the schemes of Raffles, after 1824 Acheh was to find its life and independence guaranteed for the next fifty years as the consequence of a new development in British policy. In that year the Anglo-Dutch Treaty was signed in London.[a] Amongst its provisions it was stated that while Britain disavowed all her previous political connexions with Acheh (that is those established by Raffles), the Dutch would respect Achinese integrity and not interfere with British trade there although they were responsible for containing piracy off Sumatra's shores. The Penang interest had secured these terms.

With this guarantee of British support against Dutch intrusion, the Achinese could rest secure, but it did nothing to solve the problem of internal stability. The territorial chiefs, particularly those of the coastal pepper areas, retained their autonomy, although as a result of the events of Jauhar al-Alam's reign no ruler attempted to levy duties on the pepper trade of the districts, but were content with an annual tribute instead. By this time Acheh was producing more than half the world's pepper supply, and as the trade flourished new pepper centres sprang up.[21] After 1830 the main centre of production shifted northwards towards Meulaboh, and in the 1850s a new pepper-growing area developed between Lubok Samoy and Tamiang. The weakness of the sultanate was welcome to Western traders, who found dealing with the autonomous chieftains of the pepper ports far more profitable than having to cope with a royal monopoly. But such unstable conditions in the 1830s and 1840s also gave rise to various incidents where Western crews were murdered or their ships plundered.[22] In Penang or Batavia such incidents were regarded as piratical and often resulted in reprisals in the form of gunboat bombardments of the offending coast; but they often sprang from the unscrupulous practices of Western traders themselves.[23] In any case such incidents never posed a real threat to Achinese sovereignty, since Western traders preferred things to stay as they were. However after the 1850s conditions improved under the capable and firm rule of Sultan Ali Alauddin Mansor Shah (Tuanku Ibrahim) who succeeded in asserting his own authority over his factious chiefs and in extending it as far south as Langkat, Deli and Serdang. In so doing Acheh came into direct confrontation with the Dutch. The Achinese had watched with growing apprehension (as indeed had the British) as Dutch power started creeping up the east and west coasts, particularly after the

[a]See pp. 317–19.

subjugation of Menangkabau in 1837. In 1838 Indragiri acknowledged Dutch sovereignty and in the same year, Michiels, the conqueror of the Padri, wanted to move against Acheh itself.[24] However it was the Dutch occupation of Siak[b] in 1857 which brought matters to a head, since Siak laid claim to suzerainty over Langkat, Asahan, Deli and Serdang, the petty states immediately to her north. Only 3 years before Tuanku Ibrahim had confirmed Achinese authority over this area and was outraged when visits by Netscher, the Dutch Resident in Riau, in 1863 supported Siak's claims. Acheh protested and the ruler of Asahan appealed to the British in Penang without success. A Dutch expedition in 1865 quelled Tamiang, another Achinese outpost, and confirmed Dutch power on the coast beyond all doubt, although it was not until 1870 that Asahan was finally pacified. The Achinese, without British backing, could do nothing but give way and equally as helplessly they watched the Dutch annexation of Nias, off the Tapanuli shore, in 1863.

Up to this point the British government in London had insisted on a strict adherence to the 1824 treaty with regard to Sumatra and Acheh in its dealings with the Dutch. But by the 1860s circumstances had changed. Not only were the Dutch pushing northwards, but other colonial powers such as France and the United States were becoming increasingly active in the region. As much as local trading interests in the Straits Settlements cried out against Dutch encroachments on their preserves, London saw the need to reach a *modus vivendi* with the Dutch, even if this meant recognizing Dutch paramountcy in Sumatra, rather than see another and stronger colonial rival establish itself on the island.[25] The preservation of Acheh's integrity for the benefit of Penang's trade was proving more trouble than it was worth, but the complaints of Straits Settlements traders provided at the same time a useful bargaining counter. In the negotiations which developed out of the Dutch occupation of Siak, and its dependencies,[26] a package deal gradually evolved between the British and Dutch home governments. Acheh's independence was to be bartered for the cession of the Dutch Gold Coast and for permission to recruit Indian labourers for employment in the Dutch West Indies. The outcome was the triple agreements of 1871[27] of which the one concerning Sumatra withdrew the British restriction on Dutch action against Acheh.

The outbreak of the Achinese War, 1873
The Achinese themselves had already been preparing for an eventual showdown with Holland. At first they relied on the British, in particular on the British traders in the Straits Settlements who themselves were perturbed by the Dutch advance. In 1857, for example, the Sultan only signed the treaty the Dutch wished to make with him after having consulted the British governor in Singapore and receiving his advice to do so. In the meantime, like the Burmese,[c] the Achinese looked around for help from other quarters. In 1850 Tuanku Ibrahim sent an embassy to Constantinople and placed his country under the protection of the Porte, the doyen of Muslim powers. In 1868, not long after the conclusion of the Siak affair, Acheh again

[a]Refer pp. 155–6.
[b]See pp. 249–50.
[c]See p. 415.

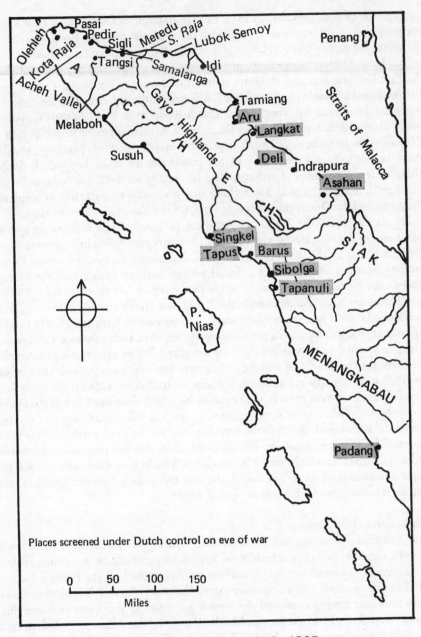

Places screened under Dutch control on eve of war

0   50   100   150
Miles

28. The Acheh War, 1873–1905

sought Turkish protection. However, neither these nor approaches to the French produced results.[28] In 1871, after the signing of the new Sumatra Treaty and whilst on Dutch insistence they were engaged in fresh negotiations over trade and piracy, the Achinese turned in desperation to the Italians and Americans through their representatives in Singapore. The Italian consul made no response but the Americans showed sufficient interest to draw up a draft commercial agreement which was however quickly repudiated after Dutch protests.[29] In Dutch eyes these Achinese moves were 'traitorous' and only served to hasten the Dutch to action before it was too late. Recurrent incidents of piracy provided convenient pretexts for interference. In early 1873 a member of the Dutch Council of the Indies, Nieuwenhuizen, sailed for Kota Raja. On arrival, he demanded an explanation from the new ruler, Sultan Mahmud Shah, about the Achinese moves in Singapore. Not receiving a satisfactory reply, the Dutch bombarded the shore and early the next month launched their assault on Acheh. The subjugation of Acheh took thirty years. The first assault proved a disaster. The 3,000 men under General Koehler who landed at Olehleh in April 1873 were back in their ships sailing to Batavia three weeks later, having failed to storm the Sultan's stockade and with Koehler himself killed. A larger and better equipped expedition of 8,500 men with cavalry and artillery detachments and some 6,000 auxiliaries and reserves landed under General van Swieten at the end of the same year, to face still more determined opposition, since the Achinese had had time to organize themselves. However by April 1874 the Dutch had gained full possession of Kota Raja and its environs, and convinced that the bulk of the resistance was broken, van Swieten then withdrew half of his troops, leaving the rest behind to serve as a garrison.

The Thirty Years Struggle

However, the war had hardly begun. Sultan Mahmud Shah died in January 1874 of cholera, a victim of the epidemic which swept both sides; his successor, whom the Dutch refused to recognize, was in no position to negotiate with them. But the real resistance to the Dutch was now led by the *ulamas* and territorial chiefs who rather than the palace possessed real power and influence over the people. As the Dutch forces were reduced in numbers, a general uprising took place conceived in terms of a Holy War to defend Islam and expel the foreigner. There were many leaders. Sometimes they co-operated with one another; sometimes they fought lone battles. Amongst the two most prominent were Panglima Polem and Teuku Uma,[30] neither of whom were finally forced into defeat until the beginning of the new century. Teuku Muda Ba'et, the Imam of Lueng Bata and the former *perdana mentri*, Nabib Abdul Rahman were others who at various stages and in various ways played major roles in fighting the Dutch.[31] In their early days the Achinese also received support from their compatriots in Penang who formed a body known as the Council of Eight, headed by Tengku Ibrahim.[32]

The Dutch reacted to this resistance by extending their control along the coast between Kruing Raba in the west and Sungai Raja in the east, hoping in this way to cut the defenders off from the sea and their sources of supply. This was achieved; the Dutch occupied Pedir, Pasai, Perlak and extended their occupation as far south as Melaboh on the west coast and Idi and Tamiang on the east. But the cost was high. The Dutch commander-in-chief, General Pel, died suddenly in 1876, and the war was costing more than one and a half million rupiahs a month. This caused the Dutch governor-general, van Lansberge, to come all the way from Batavia to see the situation on the spot for himself at the end of the next year. As a result of his visit, a new commander, General Karel van der Heijden, was appointed, and at the beginning of 1878 he launched a new offensive designed to conquer the Acheh Valley and regain the upper hand along the coast.

By 1880 it appeared that these objectives had been secured. Yielding to the pressure of the overwhelming Dutch strength, chief after chief laid down his arms, including—*inter alia*—those in Samalanga, long a centre of bitter resistance, and such figures as Habib Abdul Rahman, Teuku Muda Ba'et, and Sheikh Marabahan, a man of very wide influence. Encouraged, the Dutch authorities decided to set up civil government, but fighting broke out again. Dutch garrisons all along the coast were attacked and there were sharp engagements at Sigli, Idi and Silang. Guerrilla warfare became the order of the day.

In the opinion of the Dutch governor, three courses of action were left open: to continue fighting as at present; to restore the sultanate; or to withdraw behind a strongly defended perimeter protecting Kota Raja and the northern coastal strip. It was decided to take the third course—a policy known as 'concentration'—the theory being that within the perimeter peace and order would be established which would act as a magnet on the troubled districts outside. In 1885 the new process of concentration was begun. A defensive line protected by sixteen forts was drawn between the east and west coasts. A light railway was also built to join up the line, and Dutch troops were withdrawn behind it. This tactic did not work either. The Achinese regarded the Dutch withdrawal as a sign of weakness and as therefore a great victory for themselves; attacks increased instead of decreasing, Dutch morale suffered, and disease and desertions weakened their forces.

For the next twelve years the Dutch floundered from one expedient to another, vacillating from harshness to leniency and back to harshness again. Governor Demmeni lifted the naval blockade (which was ineffective anyway). His successor reimposed it and forced some more chiefs into submission; but he could not stop the attacks on coastal shipping nor the guerrilla attacks on his troops. Governor Pompe van Meerdervoert switched back to milder measures, attempting to win over the chiefs with gifts, but in vain. His successor, Col. Deijkerhoff, hit on the idea of setting Achinese against Achinese and hoped to win over some influential chieftains to his side. He thought he had succeeded when in 1893 Teuku Uma placed himself at the disposal of the Dutch authorities. Trusting him, the Dutch gave him a small force of 250 men and a free hand to fight his compatriots. Teuku Uma waged a successful campaign to win back several districts, which were thereupon reoccupied by the Dutch. But by 1896, the chief had decided that he had had enough and rejoined his people in their struggle, giving new impetus to their resistance.[33]

The last phase: Snouck Hurgronje and van Heutsz
However by now a turning point had been reached. The Dutch had gained enough experience to change their tactics; they switched from defensive manoeuvres to offensive ones. A special jungle squad was set up to hunt down the Achinese guerrilla bands in the jungles and mountains. During 1896 and 1897 General Vetter reconquered the areas lost to Teuku Uma and Teuku Uma himself fled to the west coast.

The real architects of the Dutch victory took over command in the following year. They were General J.B. van Heutsz, who became governor in 1898 and Dr.

Snouck Hurgronje[34] who was made his adviser on native affairs. Their policy was a combination of what had gone before. Stern measures were to be taken against the resistance movement; a pass system was to be set up and the possession of all fire-arms forbidden; shift culture and living in the highlands were to be made illegal. At the same time a methodical campaign to reduce the east coast districts was to be undertaken, accompanied by heavy fines in pepper to defray expenses. Politically it was decided to abandon all attempts to restore the sultanate,[35] and to take vigorous measures to crush the ulamas who were in fact the war party. Welfare measures on a wide scale were to be taken to win over the populace to the side of the Dutch government. Along with all this, the Dutch also hoped to placate Muslim opinion by establishing regular consular relations with Mecca and by encouraging Achinese to make the pilgrimage. An Indonesian vice-consul was appointed to represent Batavia in Mecca for this purpose.

Heutsz and Hurgronje had been advocating such measures for nearly eight years. Now they had a chance to put their ideas into practice. The new policies soon showed dividends. An offensive was launched against Pedir, the chief centre of resistance and the headquarters of Panglima Polem and Teuku Uma who were now in alliance. Dutch headquarters were set up at Indrapura and other sub-bases at Lhok Nga and Jut Menjang. The defenders were forced out and driven either to the Gayo Highlands or to the west coast. The spirited resistance of Tengku Tapa from Gayo around Idi was overcome. Acheh Proper was brought firmly under Dutch control. During the next couple of years the principal leaders of Achinese resistance were brought to their knees. Teuku Uma was killed in February 1899 in an ambush near Melaboh, his home territory. Action by lightly-armoured flying columns took the place of large-scale operations. In 1900 the stronghold of Tangsi was taken, in 1901 the mountain redoubt of Batu Ileh. Early in 1903, Sultan Mohamed Daud gave himself up at Sigli; in September of the same year Panglima Polem followed suit at Lubok Semoy. Acheh's resistance had been crushed.

Nevertheless, it was not quite the end. The victories of Japan over Russia[36] encouraged many Achinese in the belief that the Dutch might yet be overcome. Sultan Mohamed Daud and some of the ulamas tried secretly to contact Japanese representatives in Singapore. Sporadic outbreaks took place, some of which were quite serious, such as the attempted assault on Kota Raja itself in 1906. Following this incident, the Sultan was sent to Batavia and from there to exile on Ambon. Another reason for the continued unrest was the very harsh nature of the Dutch administration. Military government was restored in 1908 but van Heutsz, now governor-general, visited Acheh the next year and insisted on introducing a milder regime. The practice of taking women and children as hostages in order to bring about the surrender of Achinese guerrillas was, for instance, discontinued. The milder policies and exhaustion from such a prolonged struggle finally brought peace,[37] and the last independent state in what had now become the Dutch East Indies was no more.

The epic resistance of the Achinese created a great stir in the world of Islam[a] at the time and became a great source of inspiration to future Indonesian nationalists. This prolonged resistance was no doubt the result of the great bravery and devotion

[a]See Book III.

to the cause of faith and freedom that inspired the Achinese. However, it was also due to a considerable degree to Dutch concern about British reactions to their activities in North Sumatra and its effects on British commerce in the Straits Settlements. That and a general ignorance of the people against whom they were fighting accounts for the constant fluctuations in their policies.

[1]The first Muslim states in the archipelago recognized by historians were at Samudra and Pasai in north Sumatra, as evidenced by the remarks of Marco Polo who voyaged through the Straits of Malacca in 1292 and the tombstone of a Sultan Malik Salleh, dated 1297, probably Samudra's first Muslim ruler. However, there is evidence of Muslim settlement elsewhere, both in Java and in the Malay Peninsula, antedating the Sumatran sultanates.

[2]The founder of the new Johore-Riau Empire was Sultan Mahmud, the vanquished ruler of Malacca. As such, he and his successors styled themselves kings of Johore and Malacca and laid their claim to suzerainty over all Malacca's former vassals.

[3]The origins of the Achinese sultanate are obscure. Probably the first ruler was Sultan Ali Riayat Shah who freed Acheh from Samudra's domination around about the end of the fifteenth century.

[4]Two incidents marked the start of Achinese-Portuguese hostilities: the first was when the Portuguese sea-captain, Jorge de Brito, visited Acheh in 1521 and tempted by tales of treasure in the great mosque tried—unsuccessfully—to seize the town. Later the same year the Portuguese obtained permission from the ruler of Pasai to build a fort there and monopolize the pepper trade, after which they tried to get similar concessions from Pedir. The Achinese thereupon attacked Pedir (1521) and Pasai (1524), annexing both and driving the Portuguese away.

[5]The principal Achinese assaults on Malacca took place in the following years: 1537, 1547, 1568, 1573, 1575, 1616, 1629, and 1639. Acheh placed herself voluntarily under Turkish suzerainty in the 1560s.

[6]On this occasion the losses reputedly sustained by Acheh were 13,500 men and 146 out of a fleet of 160 ships. Sultan Alauddin Riayat Shah al-Kahar (1537–68) was the first of the great Achinese conquerors, who came to the throne by deposing his cousin, Sultan Salleh-uddin, 'who neglected affairs of state'.

[7]Iskandar Muda (1607–36) who received the posthumous title of Mahkota Alam was the most powerful of the Achinese sultans; he succeeded his uncle, Sultan Ali Riayat Shah.

[8]The murdered Sultan (Mansur) of Perak's son or nephew married the daughter of his captor and mounted the Achinese throne as Sultan Alauddin (Mansur) Shah in 1577. He was assassinated by an Achinese nobleman around about 1586.

[9]Cornelis van Houtman, the leader of the first Dutch expedition to South-East Asia, arrived in Acheh Roads on a second visit in 1599. His assassination there appears to have been the result of his own insulting behaviour, for which he had become notorious during his first voyage. The Achinese held prisoner his brother and other members of the Dutch ships for two years and then released them as a gesture to obtain Dutch support against Portugal.

[10]By the terms of the treaty the Dutch were granted a monopoly of Acheh's trade and the right to build a fort. The terms were never put into effect.

[11]Iskandar Thani Alauddin Riayat Shah (1636–41) was the son-in-law of Iskandar Muda, and son of Sultan Ahmad of Pahang who was made captive in the raid of 1618. Iskandar Muda had his own son killed for his cruelties. Iskandar Thani was the last of the strong rulers.

[12]The agreement simply granted the Dutch the right to participate in Perak's tin trade.

[13]According to Winstedt, History of Malaya, op. cit. p. 129 the bargain struck was half shares each, but Hall favours the Dutch historian, Stapel's version as the more acceptable.

[14]In fact in order to free themselves from Achinese control, Indrapura, Tiku and Padang placed themselves under Dutch protection, in exchange for which they granted the Dutch an absolute monopoly over their trade. Padang became the Dutch headquarters on the Sumatran west coast. An Achinese attempt to stir up trouble in 1667 was foiled by a Dutch expedition led by Abraham Verspreet and resulted in the total elimination of their influence from the region.

[15]With the accession of Sultan Alauddin Ahmad Shah (1727–35). See Sanusi Pane, op. cit. p. 186. The institution of an Arab dynasty in 1699 ended the series of female rulers.

¹⁶The first English dealings with Acheh were in 1602 when Sir James Lancaster concluded the earliest British treaty with a Malay ruler. In 1615 a short-lived English factory was set up. A mission led by Ord and Cawley in 1684 to re-establish a permanent British settlement was rebuffed, leading indirectly to the foundation of the British post at Benkulen the following year. In the 1770s and 1780s for strategic as well as commercial reasons the British renewed their efforts to obtain a settlement at Acheh (1771—Holloway; 1772—Desvoeux; 1782—Botham) but all were fruitless, although on Botham's mission the Achinese agreed to a British resident 'to live under the government of Acheh': I.Y. Kinloch, who was sent there stayed for only a few months in 1784. The Achinese attitude was conditioned by fear of the possible reaction of other European powers as well as by internal politics.

¹⁷Syed Husain Idid, grandson of an Arab trader of Acheh who settled there around 1700 and married one of the daughters of Sultana Kamalat Shah (1688–99); born in Acheh, moved to Kuala Selangor whilst still young; c.1790 moved to Penang, made his fortune and became one of the richest merchants in the community; because of royal connexions traded duty-free with Acheh till this right abrogated by Jauhar al-Alam in 1809; still continued trade with rebellious chiefs. Conscious of his wealth and influence, he once asked Light for authority to be in charge of all social and religious matters amongst the Malays and Arabs.

¹⁸Acheh Besar was divided into three Segi or districts known by the number of mukims which each contained (i.e. the 22, the 26 and the 25 mukims), each under a Panglima who had become hereditary chieftain in their own districts. The Panglima Polem (=elder brother) of the 22 mukims was the most powerful, and his district the most populous.

¹⁹Capt. J.M. Coombs. Coombs had already paid a visit to Acheh in 1818 on behalf of the Penang government, and recommended that Saif al-Alam's claim should be supported. Raffles and Coombs were appointed as joint commissioners by Calcutta to reach a firm decision on Acheh.

²⁰Syed Saif al-Alam eventually died in Penang in 1828.

²¹Amongst the principal pepper ports which traded on their own account in defiance of the Sultan's authority were Batu, Pedir, Samalanga, Kuala Klewang, Kuala Batu, Bukit Batu, Teluk Samoy (Lhokseumawe), Serdang, Deli, Asahan, Langkat, Kerti, Geegin and Meredu.

²²Two typical incidents involving British vessels were the case of the brig Tay, owned by the Raja Muda, in 1827, and the Bagiana incident of 1836. The incident involving the Raja Muda's ship was the outcome of his attempts to enforce the collection of customs dues from recalcitrant chiefs. His efforts involved the detention of a Penang-registered junk off Samalanga, whose Chinese owner raised the matter before the Straits authorities. In this case no action was taken, but the Bagiana incident was more serious since a British vessel was plundered and subsequently a pilgrim ship seized as a pledge for compensation. The British sent Chads, a naval officer, to Kota Raja in 1837 to settle this and other outstanding matters. In fact Chads was one of the two commissioners appointed by the British authorities in Calcutta in 1836 to implement their new policy against piracy of holding local rulers responsible for incidents that took place off their shores. British vessels were involved in skirmishes in the 1840s off Pedir and Meredu and in 1851 Lambert, the 'combustible Commodore' of Burma fame, called at Kota Raja to investigate incidents that had taken place.

²³The Western traders could operate with almost no restraint as they were only dealing with petty local chieftains, but in times of low prices their excesses tended to become unbearable and would result in retaliatory attacks and plundering of vessels or murders of crewmen. The Americans who had a large share in the pepper trade of the West coast up till mid-century bombarded Kuala Batu in 1832 as a reprisal for the seizure of the Friendship the previous year by local inhabitants who claimed that they had been cheated by its crew. They bombarded Tumpat Tuan and Muki under similar pretexts in 1838. Muki was shelled by the French the next year and the French also bombarded Dahia (on behalf of the Italians) in 1851.

²⁴He was prevented from doing so, however, on orders from The Hague. Around this time, the Dutch also extended their control over Barus (1839), Tapus and Singkel(1840).

²⁵For a full discussion of British and Dutch policy towards Sumatra in this period, see Anthony Reid, The Contest for North Sumatra, Oxford University Press, Kuala Lumpur, 1969, esp. Chapter 1.

²⁶The sudden success of Jacobus Nienhuys and other tobacco planters around Deli in the early 1860s completely changed the nature of Dutch interest in the dependencies of Siak; it was no longer purely strategical.

²⁷For reasons of party and parliamentary politics in Holland, the Dutch government wished to present the agreements as separate items.

²⁸The approach to Turkey signified a revival of the contacts first established in the 1850s (see

note 5 above). Although the Achinese embassy of 1850 was well received and evinced a *firman* declaring Ottoman protection, it proved a dead letter. The second approach was quite unsuccessful; the Porte had its own problems caused by great power rivalry over control of the Dardanelles and the Bosphorus.

[29]The contacts were established by Tengku Ariffin, a member of the Achinese delegation negotiating in Riau with the Dutch .The Italian consul rejected the overtures on the spot, but the American, Major Studer—probably reflecting current anti-Dutch feeling amongst Singapore's commercial circles—showed more interest. His moves were taken entirely on his own initiative and completely disavowed by Washington. A part in these events was played by W.H.M. Read who, as Dutch Consul-General in Singapore, was responsible for sending somewhat exaggerated reports of these developments to the Dutch government. Tengku Ariffin, 'a young man of excellent manners, very intelligent, who speaks and writes excellent English' (Reid, op.cit. p.91) was a Menangkabau from Sumatra's West Coast and related by marriage to the rulers of Acheh and Trengganu. At the time of the negotiations he was in the entourage of the Sultan of Johore.

[30]The Panglima Polem was the most powerful territorial chief in Acheh (see note 5 above) and the three men who held the title during this period all served as the main foci of resistance against the Dutch—i.e. Polem Chut Banta (1845–79); Polem Kuala Raja (1879–91) and Polem Muhammad Daud (1891–1940). For Teuku Uma refer to note 35 below.

[31]Although holding a religious title, the Imam of Lueng Bata was a secular chief of equal status to the Uleebalang (Hulubalang) of Acheh; Teuku Muda Baet was one of the most influential of the Achinese leaders up till his death in 1901. Nabib Abdul Rahman (Syed Abdul Rahman bin Mohamad Al-Zahir)was an Arab from the Madramaut, well educated and travelled, who entered into the employ of the Maharaja of Johore in 1862 and came to Acheh two years later. In Acheh he quickly made his mark on account of his experience and scholarship and played a major role in internal politics until he retired from the Achinese War with a Dutch pension in 1878. He died in Mecca in 1896.

[32]The prolonged war excited great interest and feeling in neighbouring Malay lands and gave rise—as was the case with Sulu—to a brisk smuggling traffic in arms, ammunition and other war supplies between Acheh and the ports of the Peninsula. Penang, as the nearest port to Acheh and the centre of a small colony of Achinese traders, was the natural focal point for these activities and for anti-Dutch propaganda which the Council of Eight stimulated. For further details of this council and its members, refer Reid, op. cit. pp.129-33.

[33]Teuku Uma was a born leader and warrior from Meulaboh. His role in the AchineseWar was highly controversial. In the eyes of the Dutch he was a traitor who double-crossed them twice (i.e. in 1884 and again in 1896). He was certainly an adventurer and used the Dutch to strengthen his own position. But at no stage was he prepared to wage war against the most important Achinese leaders and never obstructed the religious propaganda against the Dutch. He probably changed sides for the last time in 1896 when he realized that supporting the Dutch was no longer compatible with holding the respect of his own people. For Teuku Uma's role, see Reid, op.cit. p.237 and pp.273-4.

[34]Christian Snouck Hurgronje: born 1857; studied Arabic at the universities of Leyden and Strasbourg; returned to become Professor of Islamic Law and Religion at Leyden; 1884-5, spent six months in Mecca as Abdul Gaffar; studied Islamic studies and Indonesian hajis; 1890, went to Batavia as adviser to the colonial government on Muslim affairs; 1891, lived seven months at Kota Raja, studying ways of the Achinese; 1893, published the classical work *De Atjehers* which advocated strong measures—abandon the sultanate, crush the ulamas and restore confidence through social welfare; believed—correctly—that support of local aristocracy could be won against the ulamas who had largely usurped their authority. Joannes Benedictus van Heutsz: born 1851; joined army and sent to Acheh at outbreak of war as 2nd lieutenant; served in Acheh 1874-6, 1879-81, and 1889-91; 1889 appointed Chief of Staff under General van Teijn; 1895 appointed regional commander Sumatran East Coast; 1896, column-commander at Indrapuri; 1898-1904, governor of Acheh; 1904-1909, governor-general of Dutch East Indies; largely responsible for extension of Dutch forward movement throughout the archipelago; died 1924.

[35]At first the Dutch had not recognized Sultan Mahmud Shah's successor, who was a minor at the time. But when the Achinese installed him at the mosque in Indrapuri in 1880 as Sultan Mohamed Daud, the Dutch decided to recognize and win him over. They were not successful.

[36]The Russo-Japanese War of 1904-5. The Japanese victory in this war had repercussions throughout Asia.

[37]There were however outbreaks in 1912 and 1915, and 'before 1940 the flame (of defiance) was still sufficient to cause an occasional fanatic to attack a police post in an attempt to merit admission to the paradise of Allah', Robequain, *Malaya, Indonesia, Borneo and the Philippines* p.151.

9. ACHEH

A. Chronology of Main Events 1500–1908

1500	Foundation of the Sultanate
1526–1629	Period of struggle with Portuguese and Johore
1599	Cornelis van Houtman killed at Acheh
1601	First Dutch factory
1639–63	Dutch-Achinese struggle over pepper and tin
1663	The Painan Contract
1727	Start of Bugis dynasty in Acheh
1771–84	British attempts to open up relations with Acheh
1815–24	Dispute around the Acheh throne; British interference
1824	Anglo-Dutch treaty guaranteeing Acheh's independence
1832	Americans bombard Kuala Batu
1838	Americans bombard Tumpat Tuan: Dutch protectorate over Indragiri
1839	French bombard Muki; Dutch extend control to Barus
1840	Dutch extend control over Tapus and Singkel
1851	French bombard Dahia
1857	Siak placed under Dutch protection
1852–65	Dutch control extended over Asahan, Deli and Serdang
1871	Anglo-Dutch treaty (The Sumatra Treaty) giving the Dutch a free hand
1871–3	Achinese-Dutch negotiations
1873–1908	The Achinese War

B. Achinese Treaty Relations with Western Powers

	Holland	Portugal	Britain
1587		peace treaty	
1602			Lancaster
1607	commercial		
1639	over Perak		
1641	pepper trade		
1650	over Perak		
1655	qver Perak		
1659	over Perak		
1782			Botham
1819			Raffles
1857	commercial and piracy		

C. The Rulers of Acheh 1496–1903

1. Ali Mughayat (Riayat) Shah		± 1496–1528
2. Sallehuddin	(son of 1)	1528–37
3. Alauddin Al-Kahar	(son of 1)	1537–68
4. Husain		1568–75
5. Sultan Muda		1575
6. Sri Alam		1575–6
7. Zainal Abidin		1576–7
8. Alauddin	(or Mansur Shah of Perak)	1577–89 (?)
9. Buang		(?) 1589–96
10. Alauddin Riayat Shah		1596–1604
11. Ali Riayat Shah		1604–7
12. Iskandar Shah (Mahkota Alam)		1607–36
13. Iskandar Thani	(from Pahang)	1636–41
14. Safiyatuddin Taj al-Alam*	(widow of Iskandar Thani)	1641–75
15. Naqiyatuddin Nur al-Alam*		1675–8
16. Zaqiyatuddin Inayat Shah*		1678–88
17. Kamalat Shah Zinatuddin*		1688–99
18. Badr-al-Alam Sharif Hashim Jamaluddin		1699–1702
19. Perkara Alam Sharif Lamtui		1702–3
20. Jamalul Alam Badr-al-Munir		1703–26
21. Jauhar al-Alam Aminuddin		1726
22. Shamsul Alam		1726–7
23. Alauddin Ahmad Shah	(Bugis dynasty)	1727–35

24.	Alauddin Johan Shah		1735–60
25.	Mahmud Shah		1760–81
26.	Badruddin	(interregnum)	1764–5
27.	Sulaiman Shah		1775
28.	Alauddin Mohamad		1781–1802
29.	Jauhar al-Alam		1802–15
30.	Sharif Saif al-Alam		1815–19
31.	Jauhar al-Alam	(i.e. Jauhar al-Alam	1819–24
32.	Mohamad Shah	restored)	1824–38
33.	Sulaiman		1838–57
34.	Ali Ala'uddin Mansur (Ibrahim)		1857–70
35.	Mahmud Shah	1870–	1870–4
36.	Mohamad Daud Shah		1874–1903

Mountain temple at Besakih, Gegel, Bali

4. *The Dividing of the Malaysian World: the Absorption of the Lesser States*

APART from the five main centres of Malaysian power in the archipelago whose collapse before the pressure of the West we have been discussing, there were in addition well over 400 other Malaysian countries of lesser and varying sizes and importance. During the course of the nineteenth century or during the first decade of the twentieth, these smaller units fell inexorably under the sway of the Western colonial powers as circumstances haphazardly dictated. Many of them did not succumb without offering fierce resistance. In most cases these smaller states had been theoretically under Dutch or British overlordship right from the very start of the period, but the theory was turned into practice only as the century wore on. In dealing with the story of these lesser states, it must be borne in mind that they had very little power or political significance. They do not bear comparison with the monarchies of the South-East Asian mainland which were politically well-developed and substantial nations with considerable resources and large populations. The states of the archipelago, by contrast, were very backward and undeveloped and owed whatever importance they had to their position as local centres of trade, usually under the lee of a larger power, or to their possession of a particular commodity in demand on the world market, such as tin, tobacco, oil or pepper. The numbers of their inhabitants, with the exception of Bali, were to be reckoned in thousands and hundreds of thousands, not in millions, and their eventual absorption by either Britain or Holland was in any case a foregone conclusion. So in terms of balance of power and world politics the British occupation of the Malay states of the Peninsula or the extension of Dutch authority over the various island communities in Sumatra, Borneo, the Celebes or the Sundas was of no consequence. These events did not make the headlines in Europe. Their significance lies within the region itself. The way in which the fifty individual states of the American union came to form part of the United States of America is possibly of limited interest to the outside world, but it is a matter of great importance to the history and character of the United States themselves. Similarly the evolution of modern Malaysia has been conditioned by the manner in which the British established their control over the territories which form its component parts during the course of the nineteenth and early twentieth centuries. And likewise the pattern of modern Indonesian politics has been to a large extent determined by the way in which the Dutch brought the smaller territories of the archipelago under their sway.

DUTCH SUMATRA

AT the beginning of the nineteenth century nearly all the principalities of Sumatra apart from Acheh and Menangkabau acknowledged in theory the overlordship of the Dutch, whose main settlement was at Padang on the west coast. In fact, most of the rulers in the island had things their own way during the first decades of the century, particularly those on the east coast between Acheh and the Lampongs. Led by Siak who tried to assert her dominance over some of them, they flourished with the development of trade in the Straits centred on Penang.

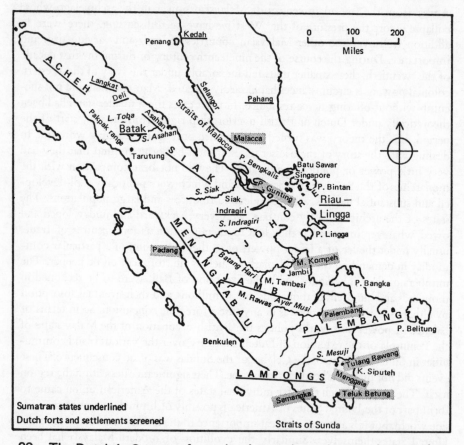

29. The Dutch in Sumatra from the sixteenth to nineteenth centuries

PALEMBANG

The first of these states to fall under direct Dutch control was Palembang. Situated over fifty miles up the Ayer Musi, its capital occupied a site near the centre of the ancient empire of Sri Vijaya; but Palembang never came near to recapturing Sri Vijaya's glory or power. In fact, after the downfall of Sri Vijaya, the region was fated to become subject to the sway and influence of more powerful neighbours, especially those based on Java. In the thirteenth century Palembang was subjected to the pressure of Singasari under Kertanegara. Aria Damar, a representative of a Majapahit ruler, was sent there to rule during the fourteenth century. Towards the end of the same century Palembang achieved notoriety as the lair of Chinese pirates who were sufficiently dangerous to provoke raids from Java and bring down the wrath of the Ming admirals on their heads.[1] During the fifteenth century Palembang fell under the sway of the expanding Malacca Sultanate and received its first Muslim missionaries. By 1500, however, Java's influence as the main rice-granary in the archipelago was replacing the power of Malacca and Palembang was under Japara's (Demak) dominance. The fall of Malacca to the Portuguese in 1511 exposed Palembang to the pressures of the swift-rising states of Acheh, Bantam and Johore which were struggling to control Sumatran pepper.[2] Mataram now replaced Japara as Palembang's suzerain[3] but her increasing prosperity as a pepper-port attracted the Dutch. On the eve of capturing Malacca the Dutch got their first opportunity to gain a foothold in Palembang when her ruler unwisely sought their assistance against Bantam. He had cause to regret this when the following year (1641) Portuguese Malacca fell into Dutch hands, making them the arbiters of the destinies of the Straits. In 1642 the Dutch came to Palembang again, this time not as sought-after allies but as monopolists out to drive a hard bargain. Van Vliet, the Dutch commander, with a force of seven ships, arrived at the port and 'brought the king —who had conducted himself rather strangely—to reason and made a terse contract with him, fulfilled more out of respect than love'.[4] The 'terse contract' gave the Dutch the pepper monopoly they wanted and a treaty for mutual defence. In this way began the long, uneasy Dutch connexion.

Until the beginning of the nineteenth century Palembang's rulers maintained their twilight existence of semi-independence under the shadow of Dutch power. Indeed during the second half of the seventeenth century Palembang succeeded in asserting herself to a certain extent. Her growing pepper trade combined with the influence of the still independent sultanates of Macassar and Bantam inspired the men of Palembang in the late 1650s to an attempt to cast off the bonds of the Dutch treaty. In 1658 the Dutch factory at Palembang was seized and sacked, following the plundering of two Dutch ships the previous year. The inevitable Dutch retaliation came in 1661 with the bombardment of the town and the imposition of a new treaty restoring the old monopoly. The Dutch also built a fort there. After this the Dutch presence remained but it was restricted to matters of trade and did not prevent Palembang's rulers from pursuing their own politics in the island. In 1662 a new ruler came to the throne called Ki Mas Hindi. Three years later he assumed the style of Sultan with the name Jamaluddin Chadri Walang or Abdul Rahman. During his long reign Islam is said to have become firmly established amongst the people and the system of government properly organized. Sultan Abdul Rahman was forced to sign new contracts with the Dutch in the year of his accession, in 1678, and again in 1681 when in return for their aid against Jambi he conceded to them the monopoly over opium and control over all foreigners. In 1722 the Dutch intervened in a succession dispute and gained a monopoly over Bangka's tin, an arrangement confirmed in 1755. In 1738, on the other hand, they built a fort at Tulang Bawang in the Lampongs as a protection against Palembang incursions.

The end of the century and the collapse of Dutch power during the Revolutionary and Napoleonic wars in Europe gave Palembang an opportunity to make a bid for its complete freedom. In 1811, with British encouragement, Sultan Mohamed Badruddin rose up and massacred the Dutch garrison and residents in the town and declared his independence.[5] When three British commissioners sent by Raffles, now the lieutenant-governor of Java,[6] arrived at Palembang later in the year in order to conclude a treaty with the Sultan, they learned for the first time of these events. They also discovered that the Sultan had no intention of sacrificing his newly-won freedom by allowing the British to step into the Dutch shoes. This went further than the British had intended and so Raffles despatched an expedition to punish the ruler, which arrived at Palembang in April 1812. The town was captured, Sultan Badruddin fled, and the British installed Najmuddin, the Pangeran Adipati, his younger brother, in his stead. Najmuddin then signed away the tin-rich islands of Bangka and Billiton to the British as compensation for the massacre![7] When the Dutch returned in 1818 they made the best of a bad job; they divided the power between Badruddin who was restored as Sultan and Najmuddin who was made Sultan Muda and promised the succession, and annexed a third portion of the sultanate for themselves. Najmuddin was not prepared to accept this dispensation and the following year appealed to the British. Raffles, now at Benkulen, was swift to send a small force overland in his support; but it was promptly arrested by the Dutch authorities on arriving at Palembang, and Raffles' action was completely disavowed in London. It was now Badruddin's turn to revolt. In 1820 he drove the Dutch out of Palembang while an insurrection also broke out at the same time on Bangka. In due course the Dutch suppressed this uprising. In 1821 Badruddin was exiled to Ternate. In his place the Dutch put Najmuddin's son on the throne as Sultan Najmuddin II, while Najmuddin himself was given a fancy title and no authority. However, not satisfied with this arrangement and probably fearing British intrigue, in 1823 the Dutch forced the new ruler to cede all his sovereign rights in exchange for a pension. Thereupon Sultan Najmuddin II also rebelled, but was captured and sent to Batavia where he died in 1825. His father (Najmuddin I) was captured in the same year and exiled to Menado. These events determined the Dutch to abolish the sultanate and place Palembang under their direct rule.

In the hinterland supporters of the royal family defied Dutch authority for many years. In 1849 the Dutch abolished the post of *perdana mentri* as the result of a large-scale rebellion inland. However sporadic troubles lasted until the 1880s.

THE LAMPONGS

To the south of Palembang and divided from that state by the line of the Sungai Mesuji lies the great plain which constitutes the greater part of the districts known as the Lampongs. Inhabited by a mixture of peoples from the interior together with immigrants from Sunda and organized into village polities, the Lampongs were famous for their pepper. For this reason the Dutch showed an early interest in the region but although they established a fort at Menggala on the Tulang Bawang river in 1738 and officially annexed it in 1753,[8] the Lampongs was not destined to fall under their effective control until the middle of the nineteenth century.

Before the ascendancy of the Dutch, the Lampongs had formed a dependency of Bantam which had brought the region under its power early in the sixteenth century and established a jealous control over its pepper holdings. From Menggala the Dutch presence did not give real effect to their claims to overlordship after 1753.

Forty years later the pressure of external events[9] led to the Dutch abandonment of their post at Semangka and the fort at Menggala itself. From this date onwards until his death in 1828, the real power in the land was a Javanese called Raden Intan who owed his elevation largely to Sulu support.[10] In 1805 the Dutch opened negotiations with the prince and then when these failed launched an attack with equally unsuccessful results. These disturbances destroyed the Lampong pepper culture for the time being with the result that during the period of the British occupation of Java, Raffles did not take active measures to interfere in the region.[11]

In 1817 the returning Dutch established a fort at Teluk Betong at the head of Lampong Bay but their efforts to induce Raden Intan to accept an annual allowance and acknowledge their authority were again unsuccessful. The following year Raffles, in pursuit of his aim to dispute the re-establishment of Dutch authority wherever possible, set up a small British post at Kalambajang in the neighbouring Semangka Bay, but the British government ordered its evacuation early in 1819. Saved from this danger the Dutch made fresh attempts to reduce the power of Raden Intan but they still failed to meet with success. In 1828 Raden Intan died and was succeeded by Raden Imba Kasuma. Four years later the Sultanate of Bantam was finally suppressed.[12] This led to campaigns against Imba Kasuma. The first two expeditions got nowhere but the third, in 1834, forced Raden Imba Kasuma to flee to Lingga, where he was subsequently captured and exiled to Timor. After this the Lampongs became quieter and accepted Dutch jurisdiction. However, the periodic upheavals in Bantam spread across the Straits of Sunda from time to time. There was a serious uprising in the Teluk Betong district in 1846 and disturbances in coastal districts (connected with Bantam) in the 1850s.

JAMBI

After the Lampongs south of Palembang, it was the turn of Jambi to the north. This state became a dependency of the Dutch in 1833 but it was not until the beginning of the twentieth century that resistance to their authority was finally eliminated.

Jambi was a sister-state of Palembang and as the centre of Melayu of yore[13] had been the real heir to the Sri Vijayan Empire in Sumatra. The principality owed its importance to its position on the Batang Hari which flows eastwards from the Menangkabau highlands and down which came the pepper and gold which gave Jambi its life. Because it had no products of its own and owed its wealth to its function as an outlet for Menangkabau trade, the politics of Jambi tended to be drawn inland rather than onto the Straits. It was the goodwill of the Menangkabau chiefs upstream that mattered; the Straits had to be left to look after themselves. Jambi therefore tended to remain on the fringe of Straits politics. She was touched by Kertanegara,[a] acknowledged the sway of Malacca, then of Japara (Demak), then at the beginning of the sixteenth century of Mataram, during which period she acquired her royal line of rulers founded by the legendary Dato Berhala from Turkey.[14]

It was also during this period that Jambi rose up as the principal pepper-port on Sumatra's east coast, far surpassing her neighbour, Palembang, in importance. This pre-eminence after the fall of the Malacca Sultanate exposed Jambi to the ambitions

[a]Refer p. 30.

of Acheh, Johore and Bantam but her rulers managed to avoid conquest by any one of them largely by the connivance of appropriate alliances at the right time and perhaps to a degree by the conflicting ambitions of the powers involved.[15] It was Jambi's survival as virtually the only independent pepper port in Sumatra by the middle of the seventeenth century that heightened her importance and prosperity. Both the Dutch and the English established factories there in 1615[16] but it was not until 1643, resulting from their conquest of Malacca, that the Dutch were able to impose one of their commercial agreements and were permitted to set up a post at Muara Kompeh. Even then their trading concession was not an exclusive one. In fact, despite the Dutch presence, Jambi retained its trade and prosperity for another generation. Then its ruler was dragged into a long-drawn-out war with his former suzerain Johore. This struggle, which began in the 1660s and lasted for thirteen years had disastrous consequences for Jambi, although it was equally disastrous for Johore.[17] By 1680, defeated with Bugis help and with her pepper trade dislocated, Jambi never recovered her position as the prime centre of trade on the east coast. However, Jambi's sultans[18] maintained their independence and in 1724 even succeeded in bringing about a withdrawal of the Dutch after the Company's post at Muara Kompeh had been attacked.

But Jambi was now quite insignificant. This insignificance meant that the great events of the first two decades of the nineteenth century passed her by; but there was a revival of foreign interest as a result of the upsurge of British activity in the Straits following their establishment at Penang and Singapore. In 1821 a British mission from Penang whose chief aim was to explore means of excluding the Dutch visited the state. In 1833 Jambi precipitated Dutch intervention by very unwisely invading the Rawas district of Palembang, now under Dutch control.[a] The Dutch jumped at this excuse for extending their own paramountcy and excluding that of the British by forcing the Sultan to sign a treaty converting his domains into a Dutch dependency. The ruler was obliged to grant the Dutch control over all duties as well as over the salt monopoly in return for an annual pension of 8,000 guilders a year. The Dutch also reinstalled themselves at Muara Kompeh where they built a fort. This action angered the traders of the British Straits Settlements and was one of the issues which became the subject of protracted correspondence between the British and Dutch governments during the course of the next few years.[19]

Awareness of the existence of British and other foreign sympathies in opposition to Dutch control acted as a source of encouragement to Jambi's royal family and chiefs.[20] In 1855 the young and newly elevated Sultan Taha decided to throw off the Dutch yoke. Although this only resulted in his own expulsion and flight, it marked the beginning of a prolonged defiance of Dutch authority which only ended when he was killed by a colonialist bullet fifty years later. The Dutch installed his uncle, Nazaruddin, in his stead but the ex-Sultan still possessed the royal regalia which he had taken with him into the jungle. In 1858, alarmed by the occurrences in Siak,[b] the Dutch imposed a new treaty on Sultan Nazaruddin. Sultan Nazaruddin reigned till 1881.[21] His successor, the heir apparent, Mahiluddin, was only prepared to become the new ruler on condition that he was free to live outside the capital

[a]Refer p. 244.
[b]See pp. 249–50.

and that a cousin of Taha's should be his successor. In 1882, the Dutch accepted this compromise. Three years later, Sultan Mahiluddin died but his nominated successor was only prepared to become sultan provided that one of Taha's own sons became the new heir-apparent. Renewed attacks by the ex-Sultan himself persuaded the Dutch that it was worthwhile to accept this bargain as well in the hope that the ex-ruler and his supporters would at last be pacified. So in 1888 Taha's cousin was installed as Sultan Ahmad Zainuddin and Taha's son became the heir apparent. By the same agreement, the Dutch tightened their grip on Jambi. While leaving the Sultan with full autonomy in internal affairs, they gained the right to build forts wherever they chose and secured the appointment of a Dutch adviser.

But opposition continued. There were recurrent incidents between Taha's men and state officials. In 1899 the Dutch deposed Sultan Ahmad Zainuddin on the grounds that he had failed to co-operate with them in the task of pacifying the country. But neither the heir apparent nor Mahiluddin's son accepted Dutch offers of the sultanate which included the proviso that the ex-Sultan and his lieutenant, Dipanegara, give themselves up. At the same time the Dutch rejected the nominee for sultan put forward by Taha himself and a number of Jambi chiefs. Having reached a complete stalemate and already engaged on a general forward movement throughout the archipelago the Dutch now took the final steps to erase Jambi's independence. The state was placed under the direct administration of the Resident in Palembang and then a campaign was launched to eliminate Taha and his followers. The Dutch occupied Muara Tambesi in the ex-Sultan's country and in 1904 they succeeded in locating the old ruler in his own stronghold. Taha was killed in its defence, and his principal ally, Dipanegara, perished soon afterwards. The heir apparent then took up arms in order to continue the resistance, having in his employ a Hungarian ex-colonel of the Turkish army. But he was captured in 1905 and exiled to Parigi in North Celebes. In the same year the sultanate was officially abolished and the year after the last hero of Jambi's resistance, Mat Tahir, also met his end.

The subjugation of Jambi was small beer compared to the scale of the struggle of the Achinese and the Balinese against Dutch rule.[a] The numbers involved on either side were small and the issue of a Dutch victory was never in doubt. But it provides proof of the spirit of independence which the Dutch had so many times to face and overcome as they extended their dominion throughout the archipelago.

SIAK

To the north of Jambi lies Siak which after Indragiri became in the middle of the nineteenth century the next east coast Sumatran state to fall under direct Dutch control. With a predominantly Menangkabau population, Siak emerges into history as a pepper province subservient to its more powerful neighbours. During the expansion of the Malacca Sultanate under Mansur Shah (1456–77) Siak was raided, its raja killed and his son carried away to Malacca itself where he was married to one of Mansur's daughters and was returned to his homeland, sultan and vassal. The fall of Malacca to the Portuguese exposed Siak to Achinese imperialism,[22] but Mahmud—ex-Sultan of Malacca and now Sultan of Johore—maintained his claims

[a]Refer pp. 231 et seq. and see pp. 309–11.

to suzerainty; in effect Siak acknowledged Johore's overlordship and control for the next 150 years. The sack of the Johore capital of Batu Sawar by Jambi in 1673 was the signal for Siak's ruler to shake off his allegiance to his suzerain, although Johore still kept up the fiction of her claims till the middle of the next century.

In the meantime Siak developed as a centre for the pepper trade, taking over the role of Jambi weakened by her quarrel with Johore.[a] This and the discovery of tin deposits attracted the Dutch who in the 1680s made Johore sign its first treaty giving them a monopoly over Siak's trade.[23] But it was another three-quarters of a century before the Dutch intervened actively in Siak's internal affairs and tried to gain a tighter control, a period during which under an energetic and capable ruler, Raja Kechil, Siak played an active role in promoting Menangkabau interests and forming the vanguard of the opposition in the Straits to the spread of Bugis influence.[b] The confused politics of the Menangkabau-Bugis struggle and the attempts of Sultan Sulaiman of Johore to escape from the Bugis mesh which enveloped him gave the Dutch their next opportunity for intervention in the middle of the eighteenth century. The old Raja Kechil favoured the succession of Raja Mohamed, his son by his favourite wife, but this was opposed by Mohamed's half-brother, Raja Alam. Sultan Sulaiman of Johore gave his support to Raja Mohamed, and Daing Kemboja, the Bugis Yam Tuan Muda of Johore, then drove Raja Alam from the state. But then the Bugis chief tried to turn Siak into an appanage of his own by marrying his sister to Raja Mohamed and alienating the ruler from Johore by insinuating that Sulaiman planned to hand Siak over to the Dutch. Outraged by this double-play by Daing Kemboja, that is precisely what Sulaiman now proceeded to do. In 1745 he signed a treaty with the Dutch governor-general, van Imhoff, ceding the state to the Dutch and promising them the trade monopoly in his dominions (when he could control them) in return for their help against the Bugis. Raja Mohamed apparently acquiesced in this as in the previous arrangements, presumably since he had little choice, but in 1753 he was driven from his throne by Raja Alam who immediately started to wage war on Dutch shipping in the Straits. The Dutch retaliated two years later by sending an expedition which deposed Raja Alam and restored Raja Mohamed. They then signed a new agreement with Johore (1756) and established a fort on Pulau Gunting in the Siak river. In the new Johore treaty, they and the Johore Malays became equal partners in the Siak cloth trade while a Johore representative would watch over Dutch interests in the principality. This arrangement did not please Sultan Mohamed, so he brought about a reconciliation between himself and Raja Alam, who now enjoyed Bugis support,[24] and then massacred the Dutch garrison on Pulau Gunting. Sultan Mohamed died before the inevitable reprisal raid came in 1761 which sacked Siak. Then, making the best of a bad business, the Dutch recognized Raja Alam as the new ruler and imposed a new treaty on him. Nevertheless, four years later, the Dutch abandoned their post on Pulau Gunting as profitless, and sailed away, leaving Siak whose trade and importance had declined as a result of these disturbances in peace for the rest of the century.

Siak became a focus of attention again during the second decade of the nineteenth century. By this time the state had acquired a new importance and prosperity on

[a]Refer pp. 117 and 246.
[b]Refer pp. 117 and 150.

account of the development of a flourishing trade in timber with the British settlement on Penang. This brought about a revival of Siak's political influence which
extended northwards to embrace the new pepper districts of Asahan, Langkat and
Deli. The dominant figure on the political scene was the Tengku Pangeran, king-
maker, timber merchant and a former agent for Raffles who had far-ranging connexions, in particular with Johore and Kedah.[25] Siak's new-found prosperity and its
links with Penang made it the centre of attention of the British in Penang itself, who
wanted to keep the state outside the Dutch sphere of influence, of the Dutch who
wanted to keep out all foreign competitors, above all the British, and of the
Achinese who also claimed overlordship in Asahan, Langkat and Deli. Of these
three the Achinese were in the weakest position and their only hope lay in British
backing, which was not forthcoming. Siak's rulers also looked to Penang for support against the most serious threat which was that presented by the Dutch. With
regard to this problem Penang was at first very willing to help. In 1818 Farquhar
visited Siak and signed a treaty with the ruler[26] whilst on his voyage down the
Straits of Malacca to forestall the Dutch,[a] and in 1823 Anderson, also from Penang,
signed an anti-pirate convention there. On the other hand a Dutch treaty of 1822
was nullified by Batavia itself.[27] All the same, the Dutch had the last say. The
Anglo-Dutch Treaty of 1824 stipulated that Sumatra lay within the Dutch sphere
of influence, and despite all British attempts to achieve the contrary, Batavia henceforward regarded the treaties of 1818 and 1823 as superseded. When Indragiri was
brought under their direct control in 1838, the Dutch became Siak's next-door
neighbour.

Siak's internal politics continued turbulent and resulted in recurrent incidents involving trading vessels from the Straits Settlements as well as from Dutch ports. In
1827 the Tengku Pangeran staged another of his palace revolutions, placing Ismail,
a minor and a grandson of the reigning sultan, on the throne. In 1840 Sultan Ismail
assumed full powers, but was immediately confronted by a rebellion which he only
managed to survive with the help of a younger brother, the Tengku Putera, who
thereafter became the real power in the land as Raja Muda. Relations between the
Sultan and his deputy were never easy, and matters came to a head in 1854 when
Acheh exacted homage from all the pepper principalities nominally under Siak suzerainty as far down as Serdang. In 1856 Sultan Ismail went to Singapore to seek
the help of his kinsman, Temenggong Ibrahim of Johore. It was through the Temenggong that Sultan Ismail met Adam Wilson[28] whose subsequent intrusion into
Siak's affairs led to Dutch intervention and control. Governor Blundell, bound by
the Anglo-Dutch Treaty of 1824, had to turn a deaf ear to Ismail's pleas for help,
but Wilson readily made himself available. The Sultan returned to Siak and later the
same year Wilson followed with a Bugis force raised in Singapore which quickly
established Ismail's supremacy in the state. Wilson, who no doubt saw himself as a
Sumatran James Brooke, then exploited his position to the utmost to gain concessions for himself. Faced with this situation, the Sultan fled to Riau and like the
Tengku Putera who had arrived before him, implored Dutch aid. The Dutch without delay (1857) sent a gunboat to Bengkalis where Wilson had made his head-

[a]Refer p. 119 and see p. 320.

quarters — he styled himself 'raja' claiming Sultan Ismail had ceded the island to him — and drove the English adventurer to flight. The Dutch received such a shock from all this that the following year they set out to bring Siak under their direct control. Sultan Ismail signed a treaty acknowledging Dutch sovereignty and accepting a Dutch resident. Also, to supplement his revenues, he pledged his rights over Asahan, Langkat and Deli.[29] A few years later, despite vigorous protests from Acheh and Britain,[a] the Dutch extended their administration over these districts. At this time (1864) they also deposed Sultan Ismail on the grounds of insanity and placed his brother Sharif Kasuma in his position as Sultan Kassim. Twenty years later (1884) this ruler gave up his sovereign rights and claims over Asahan and Deli for 40,000 guilders a year.[30]

A strong anti-Dutch spirit amongst the royal family and chiefs of Siak manifested itself for years to come. In 1888 the Dutch felt that Sultan Kassim should retire on account of his age and appointed the Tengku Muda to act as his representative. But the Tengku Muda evinced a very un-cooperative and hostile attitude towards Dutch officials. Believing him to be under the influence of the powerful Tengku Putera, they banished the latter to Bengkalis—but the Tengku Muda's attitude did not change. The Dutch then made the council of chiefs depose the Tengku Muda, but Tengku Bagus, a younger brother chosen to take his place proved no different. Finally Tengku Ngah, the youngest brother, was persuaded to act as chief of the council although he was not appointed the Sultan's representative. Then the following year Sultan Kassim died. Tengku Muda and Tengku Bagus tried to seize power but were thwarted and exiled—Tengku Bagus to Bengkalis and the Tengku Muda to Riau. The next year (1890) Tengku Ngah was installed as Sultan with the style and name of Yang di-Pertuan Besar, Sherif Hashim Abdul Jalil Saifuddin. The last Sumatran state of any consequence, apart from Acheh, was now completely under Dutch power.

THE BATAK LANDS

By the last quarter of the nineteenth century there only remained one considerable area in Sumatra not yet under Dutch rule. This was the Batak Highlands. In this region, especially around Lake Toba and between the Lake and the west coast the Batak peoples[b] still maintained their independent tribal existence, constantly warring with one another, but despite their ancient and time-worn trading connexions with the Achinese and the Menangkabau, undisturbed and largely unknown by the outside world. The Dutch intrusion came about through the activities of German Christian missionaries[31] who started to move into the region in the 1860s. Within a short time the missionaries were calling for Dutch help against anti-Christian Batak chiefs led by the Singa Mangaraja[32] of Bakara. In 1877 following Dutch mediation in local quarrels, the Tapanuli Residency was formed to govern the region. However the hostility of the Singa Mangaraja of Bakara continued and to counteract this the Dutch established fortified posts at Sipuhulon and Tarutung. During the 1880s there were several clashes between Batak tribes and the Dutch

[a]Refer p. 229.
[b]Refer p. 37, note 8.

on the shores of Lake Toba. In 1904 under van Dalen and in 1907 under Christoffel determined campaigns by the Dutch to pacify the region were undertaken. The last of the Singa Mangaraja was killed near Pakpak in 1907 and final pacification brought about in the Batak Highlands within the next two years.

[1]1377—Majapahit raid on Palembang; 1407—the Ming admiral Cheng Ho, forewarned of an impending attack by the pirate-settlers, arrested their leader and appointed a new man in his stead. The Ming Chinese made another raid on the pirate-base in 1415.

[2]During this period Palembang became the main port for exporting the pepper of both Jambi, and Tulang Bawang to the south.

[3]Gedeng Sura, a princely refugee from Japara (Demak), arrived at Palembang at this time and became the founder of the Palembang royal house.

[4]Quoted by Schrieke, *Indonesian Sociological Studies*, Part I, p. 62

[5]The Sultan acted in the knowledge of the collapse of Dutch rule on Java to the British and had been instigated by a series of letters from Raffles urging him 'to get rid of all the Dutch and the Resident, making a complete job of it'. The entire garrison and all the members of the factory—24 Europeans and 63 Javanese—were killed. For a full discussion of the controversy around Raffles' responsibility for this tragedy, see Bastin, 'Palembang in 1811 and 1812', *Essays on Indonesian and Malayan History*, op. cit.

[6]Raffles was the brains behind all British moves in the region between 1811 and 1816, first as the British agent responsible for gaining the support of the Malay world for the projected invasion of Java, and then as the chief British authority in Java itself from the time of its occupation till his recall in 1816.

[7]Najmuddin's reign under British auspices was not all smooth sailing. Robison, the British Resident at Palembang, faced the task of overcoming the opposition of Sultan Badruddin who had entrenched himself at Muara Rawas. Robison persuaded himself of Badruddin's innocence in the affair of the massacre and decided to reinstate him (1813). Raffles, however, countermanded his action and Najmuddin ruled once again till the coming of the Dutch.

[8]This was the outcome of the great Bantam rebellion on 1750-1 which at one stage threatened Batavia itself. When the rebellion was crushed, the Dutch declared Bantam their vassal and annexed the Lampongs outright (Treaty of 1753). Menggala was the official residence of the representative of the Sultan of Bantam in the Lampongs.

[9]In 1793 Holland was overrun by France at the start of the French Revolutionary Wars. The post at Semangka had been founded in 1763 to counter the influence of the British at Benkulen.

[10]The men of Sulu were established at Kuala Siputeh.

[11]When the British took over Java neither the Lampongs nor Bantam itself was producing a pound of pepper. The Napoleonic embargo on British-borne goods in Europe under the Continental System, however, resulted in large stocks of unsaleable pepper accumulating in the East India Company's godowns, so that Raffles had no need to press for more of this commodity.

[12]The Sultan was arrested and banished to Surabaya on the grounds that he was involved in piracy.

[13]Melayu asserted her independence of Sri Vijaya around A.D. 1100 and developed into the most powerful Sumatran state during the next hundred years.

[14]Or Paduka Berhala. This is to follow Jambi tradition but Sanusi Pane (op. cit. pp. 242-3) points out that this claim to Turkish ancestry may be only a device to raise the prestige of the Jambi royal house by its chroniclers.

[15]For instance, the alliance of 1615 directed against Acheh, consisting of Jambi, Siak, Indragiri and Palembang and led by Johore. Jambi's rulers also encouraged Dutch and English traders, knowing that Acheh was anxious to avoid direct conflict with them whilst the Portuguese in Malacca remained uncrushed.

[16]The English maintained their factory till 1679, in which year it was sacked by the Malays. They withdrew from the Jambi trade altogether two years later.

[17]This war arose initially over a broken dynastic marriage pledge involving the heir to Johore and the daughter of the pangeran of Jambi. Johore was in the wrong. As a result of the struggle, during which the Johore capital itself was raided and sacked (1673), Sultan Ibrahim of Johore summoned the help of Bugis mercenaries. They sacked Jambi and then settled in his dominions, marking the start of their influence and rise to power. Another consequence was

Siak's breakaway from Johore vassalage which in turn brought with it trouble for both Johore and Jambi in the years that followed.

[18]In the 1670s during the course of the struggle with Johore, the Jambi pangeran assumed this title.

[19]The principal point at stake concerned the imposition by the Dutch of tariffs which discriminated against British ships and goods, this being—the British claimed—an infringement of the Anglo-Dutch Treaty of 1824. To calm British objections, the Dutch actually withdrew the post in 1841 for 15 years.

[20]In 1851 an American sea-captain called Gibson was arrested by the Dutch authorities on charges of instigating the Sultan of Jambi to revolt.

[21]In 1879 a meeting took place between ex-Sultan Taha and Nazaruddin, but Taha still refused to acknowledge Dutch sovereignty.

[22]In 1613 Siak was raided and subdued by Acheh but two years later joined Johore and neighbouring states in a league against the Achinese—refer Note 15 above. Achinese claims to suzerainty over Siak date from this time.

[23]According to the Dutch historian, Stapel, the agreement proved 'very profitable' to the Dutch who were able to strengthen·their position there, but Winstedt describes the agreement as 'futile'. Winstedt is probably right.

[24]By virtue of the fact that he was an enemy of the Dutch.

[25]The Tengku Pangeran dominated Siak politics for about a generation. He put his brother-in-law on the throne in 1810, co-operated actively with Raffles when the latter was preparing the way for the British occupation of Java by soliciting the support of Malay rulers. His right hand man was Tengku Long Puteh whom the British regarded as 'a desperate pirate' but who was related to Sultan Ahmad Tajuddin of Kedah by marriage. Through Long Puteh, the Tengku Pangeran had links with Nakhoda Udin and contributed to the Malay attempts to expel the Thais from Kedah in the 1830s.

[26]The treaty, similar to the one Farquhar signed with Raja Ja'afar of Riau, primarily guaranteed that British trade should not be excluded from Siak through agreement with another power.

[27]The Dutch treaty prohibited Siak from allowing any other foreign power to establish a settlement in its territory in return for freedom of trade and a guarantee of protection. Batavia objected to the last provision but a mission sent in 1823 to obtain a modification of the original terms was a failure.

[28]At this time Adam Wilson was the chief clerk of the firm of Martin, Dyce and Company. The fact that this company was closely connected with Temenggong Ibrahim of Johore during this period may indicate that Wilson was initially recommended to Ismail by the Temenggong himself. After the collapse of his enterprise, Wilson became secretary to the Singapore Exchange as well as a broker and auctioneer. The British authorities in the Straits Settlements completely disassociated themselves from Wilson's activities.

[29]The Dutch occupied Deli and Langkat in 1862 and consolidated their position in Asahan three years later. By this time the success of tobacco as a commercial crop was already assured and hence the Dutch moves.

[30]In fact, although European planters had long been running the local administration de facto, the Dutch faced some difficulty in getting the local rulers to acknowledge Siak's sovereignty or their own. The Dutch commissioner Netscher secured the allegiance of Deli and Langkat in 1863, Serdang and Batu Bara quickly submitted before a Dutch show of force in 1865 but it was not until 1870 that Asahan was finally pacified. The Dutch moves were the subject of bitter protests by Acheh and merchants in the Straits Settlements.

[31]These missionaries were Lutherans. The first European to reach the shores of Lake Toba was a Dutchman, Dr. A. Neubronner van der Tunk in 1863, who soon had to withdraw in face of Batak hostility.

[32]Singa Mangaraja was a traditional title of the rulers of Bakara.

DUTCH BORNEO

On the island of Borneo, apart from the sultanates of Brunai and Sulu in the north, there were three other states of consequence and numerous other principalities of little or no significance at the beginning of the nineteenth century. The three states whose rulers could lay claim to an extensive jurisdiction and influence were Banjarmassin in the south-east of the island, and Pontianak and Sambas on the west coast.

On the eastern side of Borneo, subject to the conflicting claims of the rulers of
Banjarmassin and Sulu but on the whole left largely to themselves were a number
of small principalities, the largest and best known of which was Kutai.

The Borneo states and the Western powers before the nineteenth century

Banjarmassin, Pontianak and Sambas all owed their origins and rise to outsiders.
Banjarmassin, the largest and strongest of these sultanates, had close links with Java
and a predominantly Javanese population. Pontianak and Sambas were centres of
Malay power and Sambas in particular traditionally had strong ties with Peninsula
Johore.

Banjarmassin's rise to importance took place during the first half of the seventeenth century under the aegis of the Javanese port-state of Demak (Japara),[1] and
resulted from the growth of pepper planting by Chinese immigrants, its convenient
position between Java, Macassar and the Spice Islands, and its growing fame as a
shipbuilding centre. Banjarmassin's development was largely determined by its
close Javanese connexions. Demak gave way to Mataram as suzerain in the 1620s,[2]

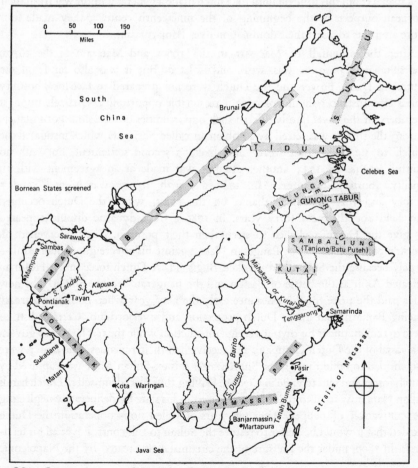

30. General map of Borneo illustrating the historical background

and after Mataram's decline with the fall of Malacca to the Dutch,[a] Banjarmassin established close relations with Macassar which became the principal mart for its pepper. During this period Banjarmassin's rulers extended their own sway westwards to Kota Waringin up to Sukadana (Tanjongpura), Landak, and possibly as far as Sambas as well. Banjarmassin's pepper, her principal source of wealth, acted as a magnet to the Dutch who made their first attempt (along with the English)[3] to establish a factory there during the reign of Sultan Inayat-ullah in the early 1600s but withdrew after some years in the face of Javanese-inspired hostility.[4] As a result, the rulers of Banjarmassin eschewed the Dutch for some time until, in 1635, fears of an impending attack from Mataram caused the Sultan to look to Batavia for help. The outcome was that in that year the Dutch were able to conclude their first treaty with Banjarmassin by which they obtained the pepper monopoly, and in 1636 they set up a factory at Martapura. But these good relations were short-lived. The danger from Mataram receded, making the Dutch as allies valueless and as monopolists oppressive. Resentful and wishing to restore their freedom of trade the Banjarese provoked war in 1638 by massacring the Dutch garrison at Martapura to a man.[5] From this time on until the Dutch made a general withdrawal from their Bornean outposts at the beginning of the nineteenth century, they made four more attempts to assert their domination over Banjarmassin.

After the downfall of Macassar in the 1660s and Mataram in the 1670s, the sultanate's position was weak and isolated. But it was also far from the centres of Dutch power and the Dutch were not prepared to face local hostility unless circumstances should provide a reasonable opportunity. Quarrels amongst members of the royal family offered such opportunities on occasion. For instance, in 1663 the throne was seized by a nobleman called Surianata which instigated the Dutch to sign a second treaty and make a second settlement, but with no fruitful results. In 1733 another attempt was made at an agreement with an equally abortive outcome.[6] In 1747 a fourth treaty was signed[7] and a factory and fort built at Tabanio on the coast, which the Dutch occupied and held for the next forty years. In 1786 a fresh dynastic dispute appeared to give the Dutch a chance to strengthen their position. They intervened on the side of the *mentri besar*, Pangeran Nata, against his sovereign, Sultan Amir—largely because the Sultan had invoked Bugis aid. A Dutch force under Hoffman defeated Amir at the battle of Basson and the pangeran became Sultan. The new ruler paid the price for this assistance early the next year when he signed a treaty placing Banjarmassin under Dutch protection and overlordship. Certain districts were to remain under his own sovereign jurisdiction while the rest he was to govern as a vassal of the Dutch Company and receive half their revenues. The Dutch were also entitled to build more forts. Shortly after this ex-Sultan Amir was captured by Dutch forces and sent to exile in Ceylon. Having thus placed himself in Dutch hands Sultan Nata now tried to reduce their interest in his state by deliberately neglecting the cultivation of pepper. After ten years of veiled non-cooperation the Dutch decided that it would be better to restore the Sultan to full control over all his territories. In 1809, under the pressure of the circumstances created by the Napoleonic

[a]Refer p. 73.

Wars and the imminent British assault on Java,[a] they withdrew from Banjarmassin altogether.

Sambas first appeared as a centre of power at the end of the sixteenth century when it was under an overlordship exercised by Brunai but disputed by Johore. After the decline of both these powers the Sultans of Sambas[8] maintained a quasi-independence, acknowledging the suzerainty of the far more powerful Sukadana to the south, and when Sukadana succumbed to Bantam, that of Bantam. Famous for its gold and diamonds Sambas early attracted traders, including the Dutch. The occupants of their first factory there, however, were massacred in 1610 and the Dutch never returned to assert their power or to impose their monopoly, but were content in the eighteenth century to regard Sambas as a vassal through the claims of their client state of Bantam. By the beginning of the nineteenth century, Sambas's chief claim to fame was its reputation as the chief base for the Lanun on the Bornean west coast.

The chief rival of Sambas for control of the west coast was its neighbour, Pontianak, which was a recent creation, founded by an Arab sharif called Abdul Rahman in 1772.[9] Abdul Rahman and Pontianak rose up entirely by virtue of the Dutch and Dutch power. He accepted Dutch overlordship, granted the Dutch Company a monopoly and permission to build a fort by a treaty of 1779 and in return was recognized by them as Sultan and obtained their aid to destroy his neighbouring rivals. As a result of this policy, a combined Dutch-Pontianak expedition destroyed Sukadana in 1786 for failing to acknowledge Pontianak's overlordship[10] and the next year meted the same treatment to the Bugis settlement at Mampawa. Four years after this, nevertheless, the Dutch abandoned their Pontianak factory because of the effects of the Treaty of Paris of 1784[11] leaving the port to thrive as a favourite resort for free traders and to become the principal outlet for the precious stones of the interior. In fact, Pontianak's prosperity at the beginning of the nineteenth century was due in no small measure to the security she offered to legitimate trade by contrast with the pirate stronghold of Sambas.

The Borneo states and Raffles

The Dutch withdrawal from Borneo[12] at the turn of the new century brought about by economic and political pressures in Europe and South-East Asia left the Bornean states with a new freedom to conduct their own affairs. But it was short-lived because the Dutch vacuum was soon filled by the British who, under Raffles' inspiration, set out to establish and maintain themselves in the new regions opened by the collapse of their rivals. Banjarmassin, Pontianak and Sambas all soon felt the effects of the forward policy adopted by Raffles.

Banjarmassin by virtue of its position, influence and trade was the state most affected, and because of its ruler the first to be so. When the Dutch withdrew from Banjarmassin, Sultan Sulaiman, a son of Sultan Nata, was on the throne. Sultan Sulaiman did not view the Dutch withdrawal with equanimity. Banjarmassin's own influence over south and east Borneo was a direct consequence of Dutch support and their sudden departure exposed the sultanate more openly to the raids of the Lanun; furthermore Sulaiman's own position in the state was still challenged by the enem-

[a]Refer p. 82.

ies of his father. So as the Dutch left, the Sultan set out to contact the British and in-vite their presence. He sent letters to an English trader known to him called Ale-xander Hare[13] and followed this up by despatching an embassy to Penang. The first mission did not produce any British response, but the second through Hare's good offices met Raffles in Malacca, and a little later a third embassy was presented to Minto, the British governor-general of India himself. Minto gave his sanction to the Banjarese request for British protection and a British resident, while Raffles gladly grasped this opportunity to make Banjarmassin the keystone in his plans to establish a British foothold in the archipelago.[a] He decided to make Hare his agent for this purpose and so in 1812 Hare went to Banjarmassin as the first British Resi-dent to establish the British protectorate there. Sultan Sulaiman received him well and Hare had no difficulty in securing a treaty which granted Britain full sovereign rights over the former Dutch forts at Tatas and Tabanio, the Dayak provinces of south Borneo and over all the petty principalities and districts to which Banjar-massin laid—more often than not theoretical—claim to overlordship. The rest of the treaty sounded very similar to previous agreements with the Dutch. In return for British protection against his enemies 'as well European as Asiatic', the Sultan consented to divide any revenue surplus equally with the British authorities in Batavia, to maintain the pepper monopoly, to authorize logging and mining throughout his dominions, and agreed not to raise new taxes or duties without con-sulting the British resident or to appoint a chief minister without the approval of the British governor of Java. By this treaty it was also stated that the Sultan, no longer standing under any obligation to the Dutch, negotiated as an indepen-dent ruler, and that the agreement with Britain was distinct from the British oc-cupation of Dutch possessions in the rest of the archipelago.[14]

The British occupation of Banjarmassin lasted for four years. During that time an ambitious scheme was launched to make the sultanate a prosperous concern for the English East India Company by developing the cultivation of pepper and by exploiting the mines. But the whole scheme turned out to be a disaster. Whether or not through the mismanagement of Hare, who certainly complicated matters by obtaining a large private concession for himself[15] and failing to draw a clear line between official and personal revenues and investments, by 1816 when the decision to restore the Dutch colonies in the archipelago was about to be put into effect, things were approaching a critical state. Instead of increasing, Banjarmassin's trade had declined. Pepper and rice production had almost stopped entirely and the im-portation of large numbers of Javanese labourers[16] to open up the country had cre-ated a serious problem because of the difficulty of feeding, clothing and housing them. Whatever Hare[17] and Raffles thought about it, the English East India Com-pany's officials were happy to conclude their Banjarmassin adventure, and Sultan Sulaiman was doubtless as relieved to see them go. But as negotiations between the British and Dutch took place regarding the future of his kingdom, the Sultan let it be known that he wished to run his own affairs 'as the Rajahs of Pontianak, Kedah and Acheen do'.[18] But the ruler did not persist long in this attitude, probably because as before he realized that he needed European protection for his own position. He refused to allow the Javanese immigrants to stay (on the grounds that he could not

[a]See pp. 320-1.

feed them) but signed readily enough a new treaty with the Dutch at the beginning of 1817 which granted them substantially what he had granted earlier to the British. The districts which remained under his direct authority were confined to the Barito Basin but they constituted the most populous part of his dominions; furthermore he was given guarantees of full Dutch support against any foe, whether from within or without, and retained complete autonomy over domestic affairs. In 1825 Sultan Sulaiman died and was succeeded by his son, Adam, who confirmed this agreement. On these terms Banjarese relations with the Dutch stood until the middle of the century.

The British impact on Sambas and Pontianak was more abrupt and limited. In October 1812 a small British naval expedition appeared off Sambas in order to reduce the town which was notorious amongst European traders as a pirate centre. This action was part of the unfolding of Raffles' general plans for suppressing piracy and extending British influence in the archipelago. But the British force encountered a Lanun fleet in Kuala Sambas and at the same time came under the heavy fire of shore batteries. Unprepared for such lively opposition, the British withdrew. At this time the reigning Sultan was in his dotage and the real power rested in the hands of an illegitimate son, Pangeran Anom, who was in league with the Lanun. Nine months later a second and more powerful British expedition arrived which demanded the ending of piracy and the handing over of Pangeran Anom. Receiving no response, the British attacked and in a thirty minute battle destroyed the town and killed 150 of its defenders as against eight casualties of their own. The Sultan and the Pangeran fled into the jungle. Later in the same year (1813) a British envoy came and opened talks with the Sambas chiefs. The outcome was the signing in October of a treaty which restored the Sultan and established a British protectorate. A British resident was to be appointed who would have the power to control revenue and trade, and the British were also to have the right to alter the succession to the sultanate—aimed, of course, at ensuring that Pangeran Anom never mounted the throne. This treaty was never followed up.[19] The next year the old sultan died, just after the British had announced their pardon of Pangeran Anom. In the uncertainty which followed, the Sambas regent appealed for a British Resident, but Raffles was no longer able to oblige, and soon afterwards Pangeran Anom was installed as the new ruler. Sultan Anom also decided in view of the growing problem of the Chinese goldminers of the interior to secure European protection, and early in 1817 wrote to Semarang for that purpose. The Dutch responded to this and a similar request from Pontianak by sending an expedition the next year under van Boekholtz[20] to reassert Dutch sovereignty. Van Boekholtz landed at Sambas in September 1818, just as the Sultan was setting out to raid his rivals in Pontianak. The raid was cancelled and Sultan Anom signed a treaty instead, acknowledging Dutch sovereignty and accepting a Dutch resident. A couple of weeks later the first Dutch official, Mueller, arrived to take up that post.

Pontianak had also received an envoy from Raffles shortly before Sambas was attacked in 1812, but unlike the rulers of Sambas, the Sultan, a son of Abdul Rahman, welcomed British protection enthusiastically as the best form of guarantee for the continuance of his trade. In 1813 the Englishman, John Hunt,[a] was therefore sent there as a commercial agent and later in the same year a British resident was

[a]Refer to p. 210.

31. Kongsi Wars in Pontianak and Sambas in mid-nineteenth century

appointed. However, barely two years later, in consonance with general British policy,[a] the resident was withdrawn and Pontianak left to its own devices. Facing the same problem of the Chinese goldminers as his neighbour, the Sultan followed the example of Anom in Sambas and appealed for Dutch protection, Van Boekholtz and a Dutch garrison made up of Ambonese arrived in 1818 and established themselves in Pontianak prior to sending a detachment to Sambas.[21]

In this way Dutch influence was re-established on the west coast of Borneo. These moves were bitterly resented by the British in Penang, whose governor, Banner-

[a]See p. 320.

man, sent Farquhar in 1818 to conclude commercial treaties with Pontianak and possibly Sambas as well. But when he arrived at Pontianak he found van Boekholtz already there. His efforts therefore were in vain and he returned to Penang empty-handed. This rebuff led to much antagonism between the local Dutch and British authorities and the matter was not finally settled until the signing of the Treaty of 1824 which apparently assigned Borneo to the Dutch sphere of influence.[a]

The absorption of the Borneo states: Sambas

The states of south and west Borneo continued running their own affairs with very little Dutch interference until the middle of the century when a series of circumstances and events brought about Dutch intervention and the institution of closer control.

The first to be affected were Sambas and Pontianak where the presence of autonomous Chinese kongsis mining gold gave rise to a serious problem. The first Chinese miners had come into the region probably at the behest of the Penambahan of Mampawa between 1740 and 1745 from Brunai, and others were soon afterwards encouraged by the ruler of Sambas to mine the gold of the interior. Their numbers grew rapidly and amounted to several thousands by 1770 when they massacred the Dayak supervisors appointed to control them by the Sultan of Sambas; after this, they became to all intents and purposes quite independent of Malay authority. By 1812 they numbered over 30,000 and were steadily increasing.[22] The miners were spread out over an area in the foothills stretching from the Sambas basin in the north down to Landak and the Kapuas valley. They were organized into kongsis which fell into three main groups. The largest and most powerful of these was a federation of kongsis known as the Tai Kong, whose mines were in the heart of the gold fields in the Monterado-Larah area of Sambas. To their south was the Lan Fong kongsi situated at Mandor which was in Pontianak territory, while the third group was the Sin Ta Kiou kongsi located at Sepang, Seminis and Pemangkat overlooking the Sambas valley.[23] These kongsis made their own laws, levied their own taxes and administered their own justice. They ignored the Malay rulers of Sambas and Pontianak and paid an insignificant poll tax to the Dutch.[24] The presence of these Chinese miners was irksome in the extreme to the Malay rulers. Not only was their undeclared independence an affront to the rulers' dignity and a bad example for their subjects but it also represented a considerable loss in potential revenue.[25] To make matters worse, the miners were involved in the profitable contraband trade which had sprung up with Singapore at the expense of the royal customs at Sambas and Pontianak, and even made extensive use of a port of their own at Sinkawang whose existence was not marked on the maps of the day.

The sultans of Sambas and Pontianak had asked for Dutch help against the kongsis in 1818 but several Dutch expeditions against the Chinese failed to gain permanent control, being defeated by such tactics as poisoning the water supplies. The outbreak of the Java War[b] in 1825 led to the abandonment of all Dutch attempts to subjugate the kongsis for several years. Things started coming to a head again with mounting disorders amongst the kongsis themselves. Always bitter rivals of

[a]See p. 319.
[b]Refer pp. 83 et seq.

one another, in the 1830s they were faced with the rapid exhaustion of the gold-mines which provoked fierce squabbles over those that remained. In 1837 there were pitched battles in the gold-mines. Some kongsis turned to agriculture while smuggling and banditry became more rife. It was this situation, reminiscent of similar conditions developing in the tin states of Malaya's west coast[a] at around the same time, that led the Dutch—with Malay support—to look for an opportunity to intervene. The Dutch were also concerned at James Brooke's successful rise to power in neighbouring Sarawak which threatened to undermine local loyalties in Sambas. An opportunity presented itself in 1850 when a Chinese vessel smuggling opium from Singapore was apprehended by the men of the Pangeran Ratu of Sambas, who was the opium farmer of the state, as it entered the mouth of the Sadow river. But the Chinese crew refused to surrender their cargo. Dutch demands for the surrender of the guilty party by the kongsi officials involved also brought no results and a Dutch frigate sent to chastise the culprits failed miserably in its task.[26] These events encouraged the Tai Kong kongsi to make war on the Dutch and endeavour to drive them out of Sambas altogether. To do this, the Tai Kong men had to pass through Sin Ta Kiou country; the latter resisted but in August 1850 their post at Pemangkat was stormed, and the great majority of them fled overland to Sarawak.[b] This was followed by a sharp clash at the same place the following month between the Tai Kong warriors and a military force rushed there by the Dutch.[27] Another indecisive encounter took place in October and then the monsoon rains prevented further action.

The Tai Kong move on Sambas had been checked but this was as much due to internal dissensions in the Tai Kong camp as to any other factor.[28] The leaders of the kongsi were divided as to which was the best policy to pursue. The upshot was that suddenly in December the kongsi offered its unconditional submission to Willer, the Dutch resident at Sambas. The provisional agreement which both parties then signed laid down that the kongsi was to pay an indemnity and an annual tax in gold, refrain from sedition and submit to Dutch control over its internal affairs. But these terms were rejected by Batavia because they did not cater for the interests of the Sambas Malays, the Dayaks or of the loyal kongsis who had sided with the Dutch authorities, and it was now suggested that the kongsis be disbanded completely. This was easier said than done. In 1851 Willer appointed Cheng Hung, a leader of the pro-Dutch faction in the Tai Kong kongsi as kapitan of the Chinese in the Tai Kong district. In 1852 military measures were lifted, Cheng Hung's position confirmed and general measures passed to protect the interests of Malays and Dayaks in the mining districts and to control taxation. Beyond this the Tai Kong kongsi was left largely in charge of its own affairs. However Willer soon found out that the Chinese miners would not tolerate any attempt to change their traditional way of doing things. Cheng Hung and his faction rapidly lost their influence and by the end of the year a complete deadlock had been reached. This situation led Batavia to change from Willer's policy of backing up Cheng Hung's faction to one of repression and reprisals. A Major Andresen was put in charge of political and military affairs in Sambas, all Chinese immigration was prohibited, and in April

[a]Refer p. 161 and see pp. 274–6, 283 and 285–6.
[b]Refer p. 189.

1853 the kongsi was declared to be in a state of rebellion. These moves produced a real rebellion and the Dutch found it necessary in 1854 to send a strong military expedition of 2,000 men to restore order. The arrival of this force brought about an abrupt (but temporary) collapse of Chinese resistance. To prevent any recurrence of trouble all the kongsis were brought under direct Dutch administration,[29] all fortifications and stockades were systematically broken down and Dutch troops stationed at strategic points. An assistant residency of Monterado was created in the charge of Dutch officials who had Chinese headmen and the Pangeran Temenggong of Sambas as advisers.

In the meantime the Sultan of Sambas himself had become alarmed at the new trend of events. While he welcomed the suppression of the Chinese goldminers, he had not bargained for the curtailment of his own internal autonomy which came about as a result. In the same year (1854) he was deposed by the Dutch for intriguing against them with the Chinese![30] In the months that followed there was sporadic Chinese and Malay resistance in the gold-fields but by 1856 all opposition had been brought to an end, and Sambas, together with Pontianak, came under close Dutch supervision.

The Banjarmassin War

A few years after this Banjarmassin suffered the same fate. The cause of Banjarmassin's final subjugation as a sultanate was the discovery of coal, especially at Pengaron (in the district of Martapura itself) in the dominions of the Sultan, and the reluctance of Sultan Adam and his chiefs to permit its exploitation by foreigners. By the middle of the nineteenth century, the possibility of possessing resources of coal in the midst of her South-East Asian dominions meant much to Holland who possessed none of her own. The age of steamships had arrived, the sugar industry of Java—the backbone of the Culture System[a]—was being mechanized, and in the future lay railway development. In 1846 the Dutch managed to secure their first mining concession at Pengaron and one or two others elsewhere shortly after,[31] but the difficulties involved caused the Dutch governor-general Rochussen in Batavia to express the desire that 'the coals lie in Government (that is Dutch) territory and that Martapura is part of that territory. Perhaps,' he continued, 'the uncertainty which surrounds the succession will provide an opportunity of bringing these districts under government rule....'[32]

During the next few years the Dutch looked hopefully for an opportunity to exploit this uncertainty. Their chance came in 1852 when the Sultan Muda (heir apparent to the throne) died, leaving behind several sons, two of whom were instant rivals for the throne. The elder of the two was Tamjid-ullah, whose mother was Chinese, and the other was his half-brother, Hidayat-ullah, who was of royal descent. Popular opinion favoured Hidayat-ullah, while another prince, Prabu Anom, an uncle to them both, also enjoyed a considerable following. Tamjid-ullah, well aware of his poor chances, decided to canvass for Dutch support by letting it be known that he would be willing to make any concessions that they might require. The Dutch Resident at Banjarmassin accepted these assurances and persuaded Batavia to recognize him as the new Sultan Muda. When unrest in Banjarmassin and

[a]See Book II.

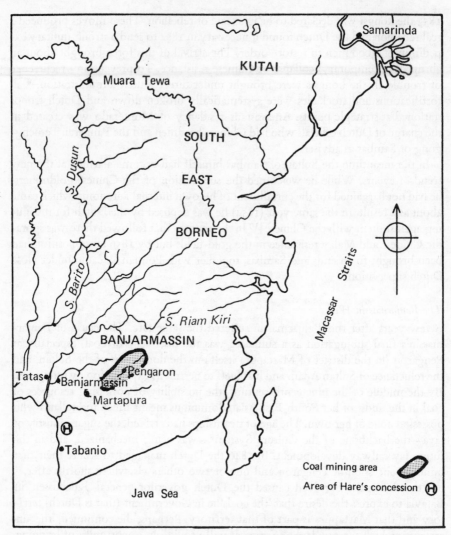

32. Banjarmassin in the nineteenth century

Sultan Adam's public support for Hidayat-ullah revealed the flaws in Tamjid-ullah's position, Batavia regretted its decision and recalled the Resident. But the Dutch did not withdraw their support from Tamjid-ullah and sent a gunboat to Banjarmassin to persuade the old Sultan to accept the man of their choice. In return they granted the Sultan's request that Hidayat-ullah be appointed the chief minister in the state. As for Prabu Anom, he was made to move from the capital and live at Banjarmassin.

When Sultan Adam died in 1857 trouble inevitably followed. In defiance of the Dutch Resident's orders, Prabu Anom went to Martapura to attend the royal obsequies. Tamjid-ullah was duly installed as sultan under Dutch auspices but Hidayat-ullah refused to execute the Dutch command to arrest Prabu Anom except on the condition that he be allowed to continue living in Banjarmassin as before, restricted but not a prisoner. The Dutch agreed to this condition but once the prince was in their hands they banished him to Java. In disgust Hidayat-ullah resigned his post of chief minister.

The next development came in March of the same year (1857), when Antasari, a descendant of the Sultan Amir who was exiled to Ceylon in the previous century,[a] raised the standard of rebellion, which resulted in the Dutch mining concessions being attacked. Sultan Tamjid-ullah decided to turn this to his advantage by implicating Hidayat-ullah in the unrest. Hidayat-ullah, on his way to suppress the revolt, found out about this stratagem and abandoned his mission. The Dutch now had a fine excuse for suppressing the sultanate altogether. In 1859 they deposed Sultan Tamjid-ullah for his scheming and after Hidayat-ullah predictably had refused to mount the throne merely to become a Dutch puppet, they declared in 1860 that the sultanate had 'lapsed', and placed it under their direct administration.

This was the signal for the start of the Banjarmassin War which lasted officially for the next seven years. The Dutch were harassed everywhere. Hidayat-ullah went over to the forces opposing them. The Dutch steamer *Onrust* was sunk by Surapati, a relation of Antasari's, off the mouth of the Barito. Antasari himself dominated its waters upstream. Hidayat-ullah was captured and released twice before he made his final surrender in 1862, when he was sent, an exile, to Chianjur in west Java. After Hidayat-ullah's surrender the Dutch got the upper hand, at least in the lowlands and along the coastal areas. Upstream Antasari, Surapati and their followers remained unassailable. Antasari died of the plague in 1863 and his place was taken by his son, Mohamed Suman, who carried on the struggle. Twenty years later the leadership of the resistance movement was in the hands of a refugee from Acheh[b] until he was defeated at Muara Tewa in 1883. But the next year a Dutch force suffered a sharp reverse in the same Ulu Dusun area. It was not until 1905 that the last of the Banjarese pretenders was forced into submission by the redoubtable Dutch military commander, Christoffel.

The subjugation of Kutai and the East Coast

The subjugation of Kutai and the smaller sultanates of the east coast in the 1850s was a direct consequence of the activities of British adventurers in North Borneo. Kutai[33] was the most important of these states and was ruled over by a line of rajas of probably Dayak ancestry; by the nineteenth century, however, the sultanate was dominated by Bugis traders. Kutai had been left largely to itself during the first half of the nineteenth century[34] but attracted Dutch attention with the establishment of James Brooke in Sarawak, whose larger schemes for extending British influence he made no secret of.[c] However the event that really stirred the Dutch to action was the Erskine Murray affair. Murray, another Britisher (he was actually a Scotsman) who hoped perhaps to emulate Brooke himself, arrived with two vessels at the Kutai port of Samarinda in 1853 and requested permission to trade. The Sultan (Mohamed Sulaiman) welcomed Murray's trade but firmly rejected his additional request for permission to form a permanent settlement with an eye to establishing

[a]Refer p. 254.
[b]Refer pp. 231 et seq.
[c]Refer p. 173.

a protectorate over the state. Despite this rebuff Murray allowed himself to be lured twenty-five miles up the Sungai Mahakam to Tenggarong where he suddenly found himself cut off from the sea by the Sultan's shore batteries. Having failed to terrorize Tenggarong with the threat of bombardment, Murray's vessels had to force their way downstream again, but having done so ran into a Bugis war fleet at the mouth of the river. In the ensuing engagement Murray himself was killed although his two vessels got away.

The Sultan, doubtless with Bugis prompting, had demonstrated his desire for independence but in the Dutch view where one Britisher had failed another might succeed and Batavia also feared British counter-measures. So early the next year (1854) a Dutch expedition went to Kutai and obliged the Sultan to sign a treaty acknowledging Dutch sovereignty and promising to turn away the nationals of any other European power. Similar treaties were then imposed on the neighbouring princes of Pasir, Sambaliung, Gunong Tabor and Bulungan. But the Dutch had another shock when they learned that two months after their departure from Sambaliung and Gunong Tabor, the British naval captain, Belcher,[a] had signed provisional treaties of friendship with the self-same rulers.[35] Obviously paper arrangements were not enough; in 1846 a permanent Dutch administrator was stationed at Kutai, with his main function the securing of an acknowledgement of Dutch sovereignty from all the chiefs along that coast. By 1850 this official—van Dewall— had completed his task and all the most important rulers of the Bornean west coast had accepted Dutch suzerainty.

[a]Refer p. 172.

[1]The founder of the Banjarese royal house is traditionally a Majapahit prince called Raden Putera or Surianata. The first ruler to embrace Islam was Surian Shah in about 1550.

[2]The rise of Mataram at the expense of the port-states of North Java led to an influx of Javanese refugees between 1625 and 1640.

[3]The English had a factory at Banjarmassin on three separate occasions before the nineteenth century; namely—1615-55 (intermittently); 1700-7; and 1737-47. The fortunes of the English factors there were very similar to those of the Dutch.

[4]The Dutch factory was established in 1603. In 1612 the Dutch raided and sacked Banjarmassin as a reprisal for the maltreatment of their factors there. As a result of this attack, Inayat-ullah moved his capital to Martapura which remained the seat of Banjarmassin's rulers until 1860.

[5]64 Dutchmen and 21 Javanese mercenaries lost their lives. In retaliation the Dutch disfigured 27 Banjarese captives and sent them to the Sultan. The Sultan offered compensation in 1641.

[6]The treaty was signed as between equals. The Dutch were to help the Sultan against his enemies and in return be allowed to build a new factory and have the pepper monopoly. But after waiting for five successive years for delivery of the pepper the Dutch gave up the attempt. The factory was not built.

[7]The terms were similar to those of the 1733 engagement but the Dutch were no longer obliged to assist the Sultan against internal threats.

[8]The Malay rulers of Sambas, whose origins were from Johore, embraced Islam sometime between 1580 and 1600.

[9]Sharif Abdul Rahman was the son of an Arab ulama and a Matan princess. He married a daughter of the Raja of Mampawa and established himself at Pontianak, then a small village at the mouth of the Landak river. He secured Dutch support against his suzerain, the Raja of Landak, and relied on their backing to build up his own power.

[10]After this Sukadana disappeared as a state from the map. Sukadana had a long history as the most powerful sultanate on the west coast. With a predominantly Javanese population, during the seventeenth century it was a vassal first of Surabaya, then after 1622 of Mataram. Around 1650 it asserted its own independence and extended its power northwards to include

Sambas. In 1699 a combined Dutch-Bantamese expedition came to the aid of Landak and sacked Sukadana. From this time onwards Bantam claimed overlordship over the whole west coast but in fact Bugis influence was greater. In 1778 Bantam handed over her suzerain claims to the Dutch, which Sukadana refused to recognize. This was the cause of the Dutch-Pontianak expedition of 1786.

11By this treaty which concluded the American War of Independence in which Holland had sided with the American colonists against Britain, the Malaysian-Indonesian archipelago was declared open to the trade of all nations, thus ending the exclusive commercial monopoly which the Dutch had tried to maintain and on which their prosperity was based.

12The only exception was the Dutch position at Tatas, opposite Banjarmassin town.

13Alexander Hare, born between 1780 and 1785 in London, the eldest son of a watchmaker, is one of the more colourful and controversial characters of his age in the region. First employed as a clerk in a Lisbon commercial house, he then went to Calcutta and then to Malacca where he was established running his own business by at least 1807. There he made the acquaintance of Raffles in 1808. Through his trading contracts, Hare had already acquired an extensive knowledge of persons and conditions in the archipelago. John Clunies Ross, who was biased against Hare, described as him being 'superficially clever, but vacillating and indecisive in character, and his greatest feature was his licentiousness in regard to all bodily indulgences' (quoted by Irwin, op. cit. p. 18). Be that as it may, his standing with the Sultan of Banjarmassin was such as to safeguard his life on a dangerous journey to Kutai in 1812, and he evidently was of great help to Raffles in formulating his plans for the archipelago. After the Banjarmassin fiasco and his expulsion from Java in 1820, Hare lived first in Cape Colony (South Africa), then in the Cocos Isles from 1827. Having quarrelled over their ownership with John Clunies Ross, the founder of the British settlement there and his own former employee, Hare was ejected from the islands in 1831. He went to Benkulen and died either there or on a journey into the interior a few years later. For full details and discussion on Alexander Hare and his background, see C.A. Gibson-Hill, 'Documents relating to John Clunies Ross, Alexander Hare, etc.', *J.M.B.R.A.S.*, Vol. 25, Pts. 4 & 5, 1952, p. 138.

14Raffles' object here was to establish that Banjarmassin did not form part of the Dutch Empire in South-East Asia at the time of the British occupation, and therefore was not liable to be handed back to the Dutch when the time came for the British withdrawal.

15In October 1812, by a private agreement with Sultan Sulaiman, Hare acquired 1400 square miles of land south of the capital between the Martapura and Tabanio rivers 'in full sovereignty and for ever'. Hare had been granted the right to engage in private trade when he was appointed British Resident at Banjarmassin, and Raffles approved his concession on the condition that he would be prepared to transfer his rights to the British government against fair compensation if required.

16To carry out his plans, Hare had obtained Raffles' approval to import convicted felons, banishees, vagrants and general undesirables as well as free emigrants from Java. Banjarmassin was declared a penal settlement for the purpose and 3,200 such immigrants were transported there at a cost to the government of 25 rupees a head. This arrangement and indeed the whole episode of Hare's concession became a favourite target of Raffles' English and Dutch critics after 1815. In the period 1812–16 the Banjarmassin venture cost Rs. 649,685 against a total revenue of Rs 92,915!

17When the Dutch reoccupied Banjarmassin, Hare refused to give up his concessions or let the Dutch enter them, arguing that they had been ceded to him by Sultan Sulaiman as an independent ruler and therefore remained British territory. Raffles supported this stand. Hare's agent, John Clunies Ross, fortified the main settlement at Moluko and hoisted the British flag. However, the higher British authorities disowned him and his lands were taken over by an armed Dutch expedition in 1818. Hare himself now lived in Java near Batavia where he continued to wage a campaign for the recognition of his claims. The Dutch authorities issued the order for his expulsion in 1819 and he left for South Africa the following year.

18Quoted by Irwin, op. cit. p. 37.

19Consequent on the instructions of Lord Moira, new British governor-general in India, who disavowed Raffles' forward policy in the archipelago on grounds of expediency and moral obligation towards the Dutch. He 'grudgingly' allowed the Banjarmassin settlement to continue.

20Jacob d'Arnaud van Boekholtz, appointed in 1816 as Commissioner for Borneo with the responsibility of restoring Dutch authority on the island.

21The value of the restored Dutch connexion soon proved itself when the Dutch sent their troops to crush a rebellion in the Tayan district up the Kapuas river the same year.

22The rate of increase has been estimated at 3,000 a year, until the 1820s when the Dutch established a firm control of the coast. By 1834 an English trader, Earl, calculated the Chinese kongsi population to be around 90,000. At this period the fighting strength of the main kongsis was estimated to be as follows: Tai Kong—10,000 men; Lan Fong—6,000; Sin Ta Kiou—5,000.

23There were also smaller kongsis, especially at Buduk and Lumar, which were also under Tai Kong control.

24By an agreement reached in the 1820s the kongsis paid the Dutch government 5,600 guilders a year, which represented a poll tax of 20 duit per head of the Chinese residents in Sambas.

25The annual gold production of the kongsis was evaluated at 80,000 tahil by the Pangeran Ratu of Sambas in the 1820s. The Chinese also largely by-passed or ignored the royal monopoly in salt, the opium farm (held by the Pangeran Ratu himself) and they imported gunpowder which was prohibited.

26The chief cause of the failure of the Dutch gunboat to take effective action was the disagreement between the boat's commander and the Sambas Resident about the best tactics to follow.

27Although the Dutch got the better of the fray, their commander was killed.

28The kongsi was divided into two factions: those who enjoyed voting powers by virtue of holding shares in the mines, and those who did not. The leadership was also confined to the China-born. The traditional leaders who represented the first and wealthier group favoured conciliation with the Dutch since they had much to lose. The second group saw in conflict a chance to improve their own position.

29The Lan Fong kongsi at Mandor was exempted on account of its friendly attitude during the troubles. However, when its headman, Liou/Lin Ah-sin died in 1884, the Dutch took over direct control. This was followed by a serious uprising which took four years to crush.

30The Sultan was exiled to Java but was allowed to return to his throne in 1879.

31Between 1840 and 1860 there were only two government and one privately-owned mining concessions in operation, namely 1. the Hoop on the Sungai Riam Kiri (1846–8); 2. the Oranje-Nassau (1848–84)—both government owned; and 3. the Julia Hermina mine at Pengaron (1849–59). This last mine came to an abrupt end with the Banjarmassin War when it was completely destroyed and all its employees massacred.

32Quoted by Irwin, op. cit. p. 165.

33The political divisions of east Borneo in the middle of the nineteenth century were broadly as follows: 1. Kutai—the oldest, largest and most powerful sultanate, controlling the Mahakam river; 2. Pasir to the south; 3. Tidong, Bulungan, Gunong Tabor and Sambaliung. All these had formerly been part of the Sultanate of Berau, which fragmented in 1770 after a civil war. Tidong was nominally subject to the rulers of Bulungan but consisted in effect of eight independent chieftaincies. Sambaliung was usually known as Tanjong between 1770 and 1834 and as Batu Puteh after that date. All four territories of the ancient Berau sultanate were claimed by both Sulu and Banjarmassin. Banjarmassin's actual dominions extended to include Tanah Bumbu south of Pasir.

34The Dutch visited the east coast only twice between 1817 and 1844. In 1825 Mueller negotiated a treaty with the Sultan of Kutai, which was never ratified, and in 1834 a Dutch naval expedition bombarded a Sulu sharif's base in Batu Puteh for piracy and secured the nominal submission of the princes of Gunong Tabor and Sambaliung.

35Belcher's treaties were never confirmed. Belcher's visit was part of his anti-pirate sweep based on Brunai waters. Refer p. 172.

BRITISH MALAYA

IN the Peninsula it was the British and not the Dutch who by virtue of the Treaty of 1824 were to end the independence of the Malay States. We have already seen the fate of the old Johore Empire, of Kedah and of the Peninsula Menangkabau principalities. Of the remainder, Perak and Selangor survived up till the last quarter of the nineteenth century, poised uncertainly between the Thais to the north and the British themselves in the Straits Settlements. Kelantan and Trengganu, the other two, fell more or less within the Thai orbit until the 1900s when they became the last countries in the Malay Peninsula to fall into British hands.

33. The Malay Peninsula during the first quarter of the nineteenth century

PERAK AND SELANGOR

If Kelantan and Trengganu were the last Malaysian states to come under British rule, Perak and Selangor were the last states in the Peninsula which could regard themselves as truly independent prior to 1874. Their prolonged independence during the first three-quarters of the nineteenth century was itself the result of British policy to keep others out while avoiding entanglements themselves. Tin, the principal factor in bringing about a change to this policy, was also the determining factor throughout the history of these two states.

Of the two Perak was the older, the more prestigious and populous, and also the weaker. It emerged as an independent state after the fall of Malacca to the Portuguese in 1511, its rulers enjoying their high prestige as direct descendants of the Malacca royal house.[1] But this independence was always in jeopardy because of the tin which gave the state its name. During the sixteenth and seventeenth centuries Perak was the prey of the Portuguese, the Achinese and the Dutch. Amongst these, the Achinese had the greatest success and wrought the greatest influence. Between 1575 and 1675 four Perak sultans[2] were carried away, along with thousands of their subjects as captives to die in Acheh, while apart from altering the royal line of succession the Achinese made Perak their vassal for the greater part of this time. As the Achinese gave way to the Dutch,[a] Dutch interference and influence increased in Perak but without lasting results. The first Dutch factory was established near the mouth of the Perak river in 1641 but was withdrawn shortly afterwards. A second settlement a few years later ended in the massacre of all its occupants inside twelve months. Despite treaties with Perak's overlord, Acheh,[b] and with the Perak rulers themselves, new trading posts, blockades and a fort on Pangkor Island,[3] the Dutch never gained the effective monopoly of Perak's trade that they desired. When the Dutch garrison at Tanjong Putus surrendered to a small British force from Malacca in 1795, their influence was nominal.

In fact, despite the Dutch presence, the real threat to Perak's independence during the course of the eighteenth century came from her Bugis neighbours to the south in Selangor. The first Bugis invasion came in the 1720s led by Daing Mere-wah during the reign of Sultan Alauddin Riayat Shah. In 1742 Sultan Muzzafar Shah III, who probably owed his throne to Bugis support in the first place, was punished for changing sides by undergoing a second Bugis assault, this time led by Daing Chelak. From this time onwards the destinies of the two states became close-ly linked, so that 'there was one coverlet for them both, that night in Perak should be night in Selangor, sickness in Perak be sickness in Selangor and the demise of a ruler of either state be announced to the other state'.[4] According to tradition the Sultan of Perak formally installed the first sultan of Selangor in 1769 and Perak rulers were required to attend the installation of their brother rulers in Selangor thereafter. It is clear that the forging of these links was done by the Bugis side.

The state of Selangor was indeed a Bugis creation. Bugis settlers were established along the Selangor estuaries by the 1680s and within fifty years had welded five river valleys[5] into political unity. The sultanate itself was formed around 1742 by a son of Daing Chelak, known as Raja Lumu, who took the title of Sultan Sallehud-din and made his capital at Kuala Selangor.[6] Of Bugis origin the sultanate of Selan-gor forms an integral part of the story of Bugis politics and their rise to power in the Straits of Malacca. The Bugis of Selangor faced many foes. They were opposed by the Malays of Johore-Riau who claimed Selangor as part of their legacy.[c] They confronted the emnity of the Sumatran Menangkabau who under the leadership of Raja Kechil of Siak contested the general Bugis upsurge in the region. Finally they aroused the hostility of the Dutch, jealous for Selangor's tin and out to reassert their monopoly.

The struggle with the Menangkabau which ranged from Kedah to Riau was largely over and won by the time the sultanate was established. This left Johore-

[a]Refer p. 225–6.
[b]Refer p. 226.
[c]Refer p. 118.

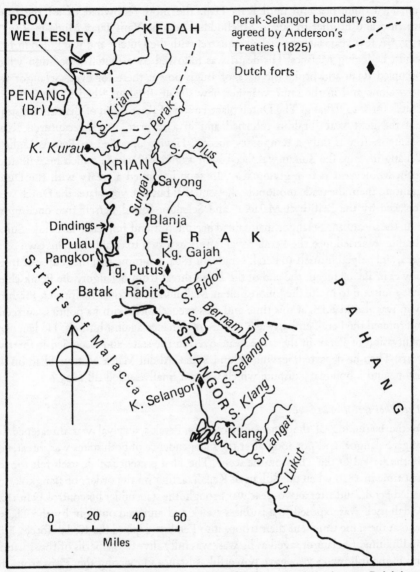

34. Perak and Selangor in the nineteenth century prior to British intervention in 1874

Riau and the Dutch who joined forces to curb Bugis power. In 1745 Sultan Sulaiman of Johore recognized in a treaty with the Dutch that he had lost control over his Selangor fief. In 1756 he made another treaty with them, promising the monopoly of Selangor's tin in return for Dutch aid in restoring his own authority there. This led to a short, bitter war between the Dutch and the Selangor Bugis which ended with the Dutch capture of Kuala Linggi in 1757 and a treaty by which the Bugis accepted the Dutch commercial demands. After this Dutch-Bugis relations remained quite peaceful until Raja Haji, the most renowned of all the Bugis warriors and brother to Sultan Sallehuddin, became Yam Tuan Muda in Riau in 1777.[a] A few years later he picked a quarrel with the Dutch[7] and was killed in 1784 whilst besieging Malacca. His death was followed by a Dutch expedition which occupied Riau and broke the back of Bugis power there for ever. Selangor was now alone and in the same year her new sultan, Ibrahim,[8] had to flee before a Dutch force to Pahang. The Dutch placed a son of Raja Alam of Siak[b] in his stead, but the next year Ibrahim returned and in a surprise attack recaptured Kuala Selangor. It was only a temporary success. Having appealed to Francis Light in Penang in vain, the Sultan was faced with a Dutch blockade which he withstood for a whole year before giving way. In 1790 he signed a treaty with the Dutch granting them the trade monopoly they sought; but five years later the Dutch were replaced by the British at Malacca[c] and Selangor found herself free once more.

In the meantime Selangor maintained her interest and influence in Perak. Sultan Ibrahim married into the Perak royal family as a step to establishing his own pedigree, and helped himself to Perak's trade. In 1804, assuming that the eclipse of Bugis power in Riau[d] meant the end of the Bugis threat from Selangor, the Perak chiefs sent a mission to invite the Johore Sultan, Mahmud, to become their ruler. Ibrahim, who was also in Riau at this time and was preoccupied with its politics, correctly interpreted the Perak embassy as a gesture of defiance against himself. He launched an invasion of Perak in the same year, overran the state and occupied it for two years. Then he departed, leaving behind Sultan Abdul Malek Mansur Shah on the throne and a boundary dispute which was not finally settled till 1825.[9]

The Thai threat: 1816–26

At the beginning of the nineteenth century Perak's survival was threatened by Bugis Selangor, and not long after the independence of both states was threatened by the arrival of the Thais on the scene. The Thai presence made itself felt for the first time in 1816 when the Sultan of Kedah, acting on the orders of Bangkok, invaded Perak, and after a two-year war brought the state under his control.[10] In 1821 Kedah itself was exposed to a ruthless attack and annexed outright by the Thais,[e] who at the same time sent their troops into Perak to replace the Kedah forces. Sultan Ibrahim of Selangor, aged as he was, was fully alive to the perils of the situation and in the following year gave powerful assistance in evicting the Thais from the state. Perak was made to pay a high price. By a treaty signed in 1823 she had to share her tin revenues with Selangor, and admit Selangor traders without taxing them.

The fact that Perak did not become a permanent vassal of Selangor and that neither state became a dependency of Bangkok during the first quarter of the new century was solely due to the presence of a new third force in the region in the shape

[a]Refer p. 118.
[b]Refer p. 248.
[c]Refer p. 119.
[d]Refer pp. 118–19.
[e]Refer p. 107.

of the British now settled on Penang. At this period the chief British concern was to keep open the tin trade upon which Penang's prosperity appeared largely to depend. This meant resisting Thai attempts to bring Perak under their domination and at the same time to pacify Selangor so that her dispute with Perak would not become the occasion for either Thai (or for that matter, Dutch) intervention. However the British did not do anything about the Bugis invasion of 1804—which was before the Thai threat had definitely materialized—nor did they respond immediately to Sultan Abdul Malek's appeal for assistance against Kedah in 1816.[11] But in 1818 they sent a mission to both Perak and Selangor to make agreements for the security of British trade.[12] Cracroft, the leader of the mission, also offered British arbitration in the Perak-Kedah war which the Sultan and his court were not willing to accept, while in Selangor on the other hand he had to turn down Sultan Ibrahim's offers to place his country under the British flag. The ruler feared the Dutch, newly restored to Malacca, who indeed hastened the following year to reimpose their treaty of 1790 on Selangor. In the absence of British support this the Sultan was obliged to accept. In Perak, after the failure of a Dutch attempt to re-establish their fort on Pangkor Island at the same time, the British opened negotiations for the cession of the Dindings as a counter to Dutch influence but without results.[13]

With the appointment of Fullerton[14] as the new governor of Penang in 1824 British policy became more positive, and within the next two years the Penang authorities had taken steps which fully restored Perak's independence and provided both Perak and Selangor with firm guarantees for the future. At the time of his arrival Perak was facing renewed pressure from the Thai governor of Ligor[a] who pressured Abdul Malek into asking for Thai help against Bugis aggression. The next stage in this ploy was for the governor to assemble a war fleet at Kuala Trang with the avowed object of delivering Perak from Selangor but in reality to subject them both. Fullerton acted decisively. In May 1825, learning that the Thai fleet was about to set sail, he sent the gunboats at Penang to the mouth of the Trang river in a feint.[15] These tactics succeeded in preventing the Thai force from leaving the estuary. He followed up this success with diplomatic measures. In July of the same year, Burney, an East India Company official stationed at Penang, made a preliminary agreement with the Thai governor by which both sides agreed not to interfere in Perak, and dissuaded the Thais from sending a 3,000 man force into the state. This agreement was confirmed in a treaty between the Company and the Thais negotiated by Burney at Bangkok the following year.[16] In the meantime Fullerton had sent Anderson, another of his officials, to Selangor and Perak in the second half of 1825 to end the border dispute between them. This mission was also successful, and by almost identical treaties signed by him and the rulers of the two states the Bernam river was fixed as their common frontier. It was also agreed that Selangor's agent in Perak, Raja Hassan, should return to his own country.[17]

These activities meant in effect the restoration of Perak's independence and so delighted the new Sultan, Abdullah Muazzam Shah, who came to the throne in 1825, that he invited the British to annex his state. Nevertheless the Thai threat was not yet at an end. Despite the agreement he had himself signed with Burney in 1825 and

[a]Refer pp. 107-8.

the subsequent treaty in Bangkok, the governor of Ligor still schemed to extend Thai control. Early in 1826 he sent a small force of some 300 soldiers in the guise of an 'embassy' to 'advise' the Sultan. In fact the Thais came to bribe the Perak chiefs to oppose the Sultan and support the Thai presence. These methods won over the Raja Muda and several other chiefs, so Sultan Abdullah appealed to Penang. After protests to Ligor had proved futile, Fullerton in September sent Captain James Low with a gunboat and forty sepoys up the Perak river to the Sultan's court to see things for himself. The appearance of the British frightened away the Thai troops but Low found it necessary to affirm British support for the Sultan lest they return. The only means of doing this was by treaty, which Sultan Abdullah was very willing to enter into. The agreement which was signed not only recognized Perak's right to independence but promised British support against any intruder—a condition which directly opposed the British policy of the day and led to Low's suspension from all political duties for two years.[18] In a second document signed at the same time there were provisions for British trade and the Sultan ceded Pangkor Island and the Dindings to Britain. Although these treaties were apparently never ratified on the British side, they were recognized and formed the basis of Anglo-Perak relations for the next fifty years.[19]

One more event in the same year confirmed Perak's freedom from Thai encroachments. This occurred in November when Low, once again on orders from Fullerton and with the consent of the Sultan, bombarded the stockade of Nakhoda Udin at Kuala Kurau and destroyed it. The Nakhoda[20] who had been appointed Raja of Kurau by the governor of Ligor and was an agent of Thai designs as well as a pirate who made frequent slaving-raids in Penang harbour itself, was caught two years later in the streets of Penang and sent to Ligor for trial. His removal eliminated the last Thai ruse against Perak. After this there was only one occasion when Perak was seriously disturbed by her northern neighbour. In 1842 the restored Sultan of Kedah[a] seized the Krian district of Perak. Two years later Sultan Shahbudin Riayat Shah appealed to Penang, and Penang approached Bangkok and Kedah itself for the return of the district. However, it was not until 1848 when the British threatened the use of force that Kedah gave way and returned the district to Perak.

The events of 1826 resulted in the preservation of the independence of Perak and Selangor for another fifty years. But the very force—the British in the Straits Settlements—which saved these two states also helped to bring about their internal disintegration and final absorption into the British Empire. The Straits Settlements became the powerhouse for the introduction of new elements into the Peninsula which led to economic and political revolution.

Perak: the Rajas of Larut and the Perak chiefs

These new elements were connected with the rise of the tin industry.[b] The Industrial Revolution in Europe and the development of the canning industry created a new demand for tin which European sources alone could not meet. This demand led to an influx of Chinese tin miners, financed by Straits Settlements capitalists, in-

[a]Refer p. 109.
[b]See Book II.

to Perak, Selangor and Sungai Ujong. They revolutionized tin mining, produced great wealth, and at the same time helped to bring into being a new kind of Malay territorial chief, much richer and more powerful than any of his traditional peers in the state. The rulers of Perak and Selangor soon found that they could not control these chiefs and, alas, the tin chiefs themselves found that they could not control the activities of the Chinese tin miners. The ensuing anarchy led to British involvement, interference and control.

In the case of Perak the main scene of action was Larut. Separated from the traditional centre of political and economic power along the Perak river by the Bintang Range, this district together with neighbouring Matang and Selama was a desolate, sparsely populated region of low-lying jungle and swamp until the 1840s when rich tin deposits were found there. This circumstance led to the swift rise of Long Ja'afar, the son of a minor chief, who had settled near modern Taiping as a collector of dues for the Dato' Panglima Bukit Gantang.[21] Skilfully exploiting his opportunity Long Ja'afar sponsored the entry of Chinese tin miners from Penang to work the tin and soon became the wealthiest Malay in the state. He was also able to take advantage of the faction-ridden politics of the Perak river chiefs to secure recognition of his position as territorial chief in Larut; he obtained two grants making him responsible for the development of the district, the first in 1850 and the second six years later.[22] Already Long Ja'afar was virtually beyond the Sultan of Perak's control. In 1857 he died and was succeeded by one of his sons, Ngah Ibrahim. Ngah Ibrahim continued his father's policies with even greater success. He obtained confirmation of his position from the new Sultan (Ja'afar) in 1858, receiving nearly sovereign rights.[23] At the same time Larut tin continued to increase the family fortune, so much so that by the early 1860s Ngah Ibrahim was receiving an annual income of some $200,000 a year. In addition he owned a European style bungalow at Matang and a town residence in Penang, had two steam yachts and retained a prominent Penang lawyer, while his brother chiefs, including the Sultan himself, lived in much simpler style in their kampongs along the banks of the Perak river. The wealth and power of the Raja of Larut were strikingly demonstrated in 1862 when on behalf of the Sultan he paid up over $17,000 in compensation for losses incurred during Chinese tin miners' disturbances in his district.[a] Sultan Ja'afar rewarded Ngah Ibrahim for this good service the following year by investing him as Mantri of Perak, one of the four great offices of state.[24]

Ngah Ibrahim probably now stood at the height of his influence and prestige, and was to exercise a powerful and on the whole disastrous effect over the course of events in Perak during the next few years. He was an ambitious man and had his eyes on the sultanate. Under prevailing conditions this was not an impracticable goal. The sultanate was getting involved in an ever-deepening crisis. In Perak the Sultans were traditionally weak and the territorial chiefs strong—to be expected in a country of considerable expanse and distended river-lines of communication. Furthermore there was in existence an elaborate and ingenious constitution which has been aptly described as being in practice a kind of spoils system[25] ensuring that the great offices of state and the perquisites which went with them were shared on a roughly even basis between the main branches of the royal family. Nevertheless

aSee pp. 274 et seq.

the system gave rise to many inconsistencies and quarrels. None of the sultans who came to the throne in the nineteenth century enjoyed an undisputed succession. In 1851 when Sultan Abdullah Mohamed ascended the throne it was the signal for the outbreak of a civil war along the Perak river, laying the seeds for the more famous dispute of 1871 which provided the pretext for British intervention. Abdullah Mohamed made at least two appeals for British aid but both these were rejected.[26] When he died in 1857 after a reign in which he had hardly exercised any authority at all, the chiefs of Perak made the first of their alterations to the normal order of succession which was to cause so much trouble later on. The Raja Muda Ja'afar became Sultan as of right, Bendahara Ali became Raja Muda, but the new bendahara was not Raja Yusof, Sultan Abdullah's eldest son, as he should have been, for he was a strong personality and had alienated all the other chiefs by his efforts for his father during the previous reign. Instead they chose for the post Raja Ismail of Siak, who was barely of the blood royal at all, and Raja Yusof was by-passed.[27] In 1865 Sultan Ja'afar died, and was duly succeeded by the Raja Muda Ali. But because Bendahara Ismail was an outsider he was not promoted to become Raja Muda; this post was given to another Raja Abdullah, a son of Sultan Ja'afar. Ismail remained as Bendahara and Yusof remained out of the running altogether. As a result of these developments on the death of Sultan Ali in 1871 there were three persons with strong claims to the sultanate; those of Raja Abdullah as the incumbent Raja Muda, of Ismail as the eldest and once passed over Bendahara, and of Yusof whose rights had been completely set aside. Under the weak rule of Sultan Ali jockeying for the succession began in earnest. From 1865 onwards it became clear that the Mantri favoured Raja Ismail; in 1869 the unpopular Raja Yusof wrote to Singapore putting forward his rights to the succession; in 1870 the Raja Muda Abdullah emerged as the clear rival of Raja Ismail and the enemy of the Mantri.[28]

The Larut Wars

With his wealth and power, the Mantri was obviously in a position to play a decisive role in the evolution of the succession problem but this position was completely undermined by his own inability to control the 40,000 odd Chinese miners who were now in his home territory of Larut. The disturbances amongst the tin miners which resulted in the $17,000 cc mpensation he paid in 1862 marked the first phase in a twelve-year struggle to con rol the Larut mines between the two rival Chinese factions—the predominantly Cantonese Ghee Hin and the predominantly Hokkien Hai San.[29] Rivalry between the two groups, which reflected their general rivalry elsewhere, had existed ever since the first mines had been opened in the district in the early 1850s. Long Ja'afar and Ngah Ibrahim had hitherto managed this situation by skilfully playing one side off against the other. But in the disturbances which broke out in 1861 this policy no longer proved feasible. Starting with a quarrel over water rights, the Hai San, who enjoyed a local superiority in numbers, drove the Ghee Hin miners out completely and caused them to appear as refugees in Penang. Either Ngah Ibrahim was already in collusion with the Hai San or seeing that they were the stronger subsequently took their side. However expedient this decision might have seemed at the time, it was to prove fatal for the Mantri's capacity to master events. The expelled Ghee Hin, many of whom claimed to be British subjects from Penang, appealed to the British, and under strong pressure from com-

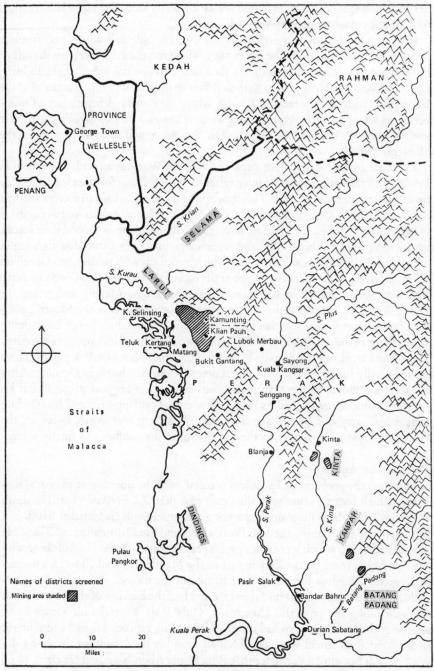

35. Map illustrating British intervention in Perak

mercial interests the governor, Cavenagh, ordered a gunboat to blockade the Larut river until satisfaction for Ghee Hin claims to compensation were met. The manner in which these debts were settled we have already seen. The Ghee Hin returned to their mines and the tension revived.

However the Mantri was now committed to one side and when fresh troubles between the two factions broke out in 1865,[30] he intervened decisively on the side of the Hai San. In this second outbreak the Ghee Hin got the worst of the fighting again and were unable to return to their mines until the following year. In 1867 the Ghee Hin transferred the feud to Penang where they enjoyed superiority of numbers, and set upon their rivals causing riots at the end of July which lasted over several weeks.[31] These events left the Hai San weakened and the prestige of the Mantri impaired.

The final and most desperate stage of the Larut Wars began with an incident in February 1872,[32] and continued intermittently with varying fortunes for either side up till the end of the next year. This time it was the Hai San turn to receive the first defeat. By March 1872 they had been driven out of Larut and arrived as fugitives in Penang. In October, the Hai San, having regathered and re-equipped their forces, set sail secretly from the island[33] and regained control over Larut after fighting in which hundreds of lives were lost and which ended up with some 2,000 Ghee Hin refugees fleeing back to Penang. Then at the end of the same year, a Ghee Hin force landed at Sungai Limau in Krian, marched overland to Matang and seized the village. These vicissitudes completely exposed the weaknesses of the Mantri's position. His support for the Hai San in the first place was an admission of his inability to be arbiter in the struggle. Their defeat in March destroyed his position altogether. The Mantri tried to save himself by befriending the Ghee Hin,[34] a policy which proved totally bankrupt with their own defeat at Hai San hands in October. After this second catastrophe the Mantri switched back to his original protégés but his power to influence events had by now almost entirely disappeared and his standing with either party had been reduced to nil. For what it was worth, however, the Mantri now gave his support to the Hai San until the conflict was finally solved.

The succession dispute

By this time the problem of Larut had merged with the question of the royal succession which became acute with the death of Sultan Ali in May 1871. His death found the Perak chiefs quite divided amongst themselves. Raja Ismail at Blanja had the support of the Mantri, the Ulu Perak chiefs and the Dato Panglima Kinta. He was old and weak, which were amongst his principal assets in the view of those who supported him, more particularly in that of the Mantri who had all to gain in establishing the precedent for an outsider to mount the throne. Raja Abdullah controlled the strategic lower part of the river and had the backing of the Lower Perak chiefs including the powerful Laksamana. Only Raja Yusof, in his kampong of Senggang above Blanja, who had the best claim of all, remained feared and solitary. In the event Raja Ismail was elected Sultan, possibly by default, probably by design.[35] It was not until a year later that Raja Muda Abdullah stated his claim to be Sultan before a mission sent by the British governor, Ord, to ascertain who in fact the ruler of Perak was.[36] From this moment onwards the die was cast. The contest was in reality between Abdullah on the one hand, and the Mantri, Ngah Ibrahim, on the other, for Ismail was the Mantri's man. Both gathered to their side influential forces to support them in their claims. Abdullah's first move was to secure the backing of Raja Yusof by appointing him the Raja Muda. He then negotiated with the Hai San, at that time (July 1872) the ousted party in Penang deserted by the Mantri, but later became the ally of the Ghee Hin.[37] Abdullah also enjoyed the friendship of Tengku Kudin of Selangor[a] and through him acquired important connexions with wealthy commercial interests in the Straits Settlements. The Mantri's allies, apart from Sultan Ismail and the Ulu Perak chiefs, were most of the time the Hai San and their connexions.

However, the see-saw contest going on in Larut at the end of 1872 without either of them being able to take an effective part opened the eyes of both Abdullah and the Mantri to the fact that the Chinese might well come to a decision quite independently and establish the same kind of kongsi republics that the goldminers of Sambas had done years previously[b]. This realization brought both men to a temporary reconciliation at the beginning of 1873. In January the Mantri moved his family and himself from Matang to Krian to be out of the way of the Chinese struggles, coming to an area where Abdullah's influence was already established.[38] Shortly afterwards he made an agreement recognizing Abdullah as Sultan in return for Abdullah's confirmation of his title and concession, and then both went to Penang in an unsuccessful attempt to reconcile the two warring Chinese factions. But although Abdullah confirmed this agreement once more in April, the two fell out soon afterwards—probably over the Krian revenues. In February Abdullah had already entered into a fresh alliance with the Ghee Hin, promising them men and money in order to restore their position. In June the Mantri went one better and struck a bargain with Penang's superintendent of police, T.C.S. Speedy,[39] who forthwith resigned his post to enter the Mantri's service. This act brought about a formal break between Abdullah and the Mantri. Abdullah, furious at this new development, declared the Mantri deposed in a proclamation of mid-August, while the Mantri himself replied a few days later by declaring the Hai San legal occupants of the Larut mines and by sending supplies to the beleaguered miners around Klian Pauh (Taiping).

The British intervene

However the shaping of events no longer remained in the power of the Malays. The British authorities in the Straits Settlements, harassed as they were by the persistent protests and outcries of the merchant community,[40] could not ignore a situation which cut off Penang's valuable tin trade with Perak, led to increasing acts of piracy in the Straits and had spread to the streets of Penang itself. As late as March 1873 the British were still refusing to take the part of either side but when the Mantri appealed for British help in July, the governor, Ord, suggested that as a first step he realign himself with one of the Chinese factions. The consequence of this was the renewal of his alliance with the Hai San and the procurement of the services of Speedy who was despatched to India to recruit a small military force to restore his authority in Larut. In August Anson, the British lieut.-governor of Penang, made a

[a]See p. 285.
[b]Refer pp. 259-60.

strong attempt to bring about an armistice between the two factions. At a meeting held at Penang at the beginning of that month both sides agreed to an armistice pending arbitration by the British themselves. But Abdullah who had volunteered with Ghee Hin support to put the armistice into effect in Larut failed completely in his task,[41] and the deadlock continued. This prompted the British decision to give their full backing to the Mantri and the Hai San. On 3 September Ord issued a proclamation recognizing the Mantri as the *independent* ruler of Larut. A couple of days later he partially lifted the arms embargo imposed since February so as to allow the Hai San to receive munitions. In the middle of the month a British vessel was involved in an incident with Ghee Hin junks and this became the pretext for the bombardment and capture of the Ghee Hin stockades at Matang and Kuala Selinsing.[42] Finally at the end of September Speedy passed with British blessings through Penang on his way back from India to Larut with a flotilla of two steamers and fifteen small sailing craft bearing 110 Indian soldiers (Pathans and Sikhs) and some Krupps guns to restore authority to the Mantri and to secure the undisputed possession of the mines to the Hai San. During November Speedy and his men captured Bukit Gantang, reopening communications between Larut and the Mantri's ally, Sultan Ismail, in the Perak River valley, and squeezed the Ghee Hin in between the mines and the sea where the guns of hostile British gunboats lay in wait.

In the meanwhile Abdullah and the Ghee Hin had not been idle. Their immediate response to the British recognition of the Mantri as ruler of Larut came in mid-September when they blew up his Penang residence, but not killing him. Then a week later Abdullah, on his way from Krian to Kuala Perak to raise men for the cause, was arrested at sea and taken to Penang a prisoner by the very ships which had just bombarded Matang and Kuala Selinsing.[43] Released in Penang but forbidden to go to Perak, Abdullah went to Singapore instead, accompanied by Raja Dris,[44] the Shahbandar and a Penang lawyer in order to get help from the Ghee Hin fraternity there. This mission brought Abdullah to the home of the powerful Tan Kim Cheng,[45] the recognized leader of the Ghee Hin on the island. Tan Kim Cheng and Abdullah soon entered into an agreement whereby Abdullah made the towkay the collector of the Larut revenues for a period of ten years provided that he obtained British recognition as Sultan. To help bring this about, Kim Cheng introduced Abdullah to W.H.M. Read and J.G. Davidson,[46] with whom his friendship with Tengku Kudin counted much in his favour. Read in turn introduced Abdullah to Ord on the eve of his retirement, and drafted a letter on his behalf to the new governor, Sir Andrew Clarke, in which the Perak prince requested his recognition as ruler, British protection and 'for a man of sufficient abilities to live with us in Perak... and show us a good system of government for our dominions...'. This letter was dated 30 December but did not reach the hands of Clarke until 9 January, by which time he had already taken the first steps towards bringing Perak under British control.

The Pangkor Engagement and after

The new governor's instructions from London required him to investigate and report whether anything could be done—including the appointment of a British agent—to end the anarchy in the west coast tin states. Clarke decided soon after his arrival that he could not afford to wait for a report to be made and sent to London for decision but that he must act at once and report afterwards. There was deadlock in Larut with Speedy apparently concentrating on reopening the mines, leaving the Ghee Hin pinned down on the coast and resorting to piracy in order to stay alive.[47] No end was in sight. So he sent Pickering to Penang to open fresh negotiations between the Chinese factions. Pickering was quickly successful. The Ghee Hin who were quite war-weary and had sustained heavy financial losses were prepared to lay down arms against a guarantee of impartial arbitration.[48] Their leader, Ah Yam, and the Hai San leader, Chung Ah Kwee, agreed to meet at Pangkor for this purpose. But impartial arbitration meant that the policy of recognizing the Mantri as sovereign ruler of Larut had to be abandoned since he was committed to the Hai San cause. Not to recognize the independence of Larut meant that the Larut problem could not be solved without obtaining the approval of the Sultan of Perak. But who was the Sultan of Perak? To solve this problem Clarke decided to invite the chiefs of Perak to the Pangkor meeting as well. Thus Abdullah's appeal for recognition was not responsible for the new policy nor even for the meeting at Pangkor. But it provided Clarke with a handy justification for his moves and probably decided him to give his recognition to Abdullah.[49]

The result of Clarke's initiative was the Pangkor Engagement signed in a British vessel off the island on 20 January 1874. There were in fact two distinct agreements. The first one, which had been ready for over a week prior to the signing, concerned Larut and provided for a settlement between the Hai San and Ghee Hin which both sides respected and carried out satisfactorily.[50] The second agreement concerned the succession dispute around the Perak throne and was unsatisfactory from the very beginning. In the first place only one of the pretenders was present, namely Abdullah. Sultan Ismail refused to come while Raja Yusof, whose existence the British did not appear to be aware of, received no invitation at all. The agreement signed recognized Abdullah as Sultan, relegated Ismail to the status of Sultan Muda with a pension, and provided for 'a British officer called Resident... whose advice must be asked for and acted upon on all questions other than those touching Malay Religion and Custom'.[51]

The Mantri's position in Larut as granted by Sultan Ja'afar and confirmed by Sultan Ali was recognized. However only Sultan Abdullah and his supporters could be pleased with these new arrangements, and even they do not seem to have grasped the significance of what they had done. The Mantri could not avoid being present since the affairs of Larut were being discussed, albeit over his head, and his own interests were directly involved. But the new British policy contradicted those interests both regarding Larut and his ambitions towards the sultanate, and he accepted the inevitable with bad grace. As for those chiefs of Perak who were not at the meeting at all, their attitude was that it had no point since the question of the succession had been settled three years before with the election of Sultan Ismail. Furthermore the British fait accompli was not perfect. They might proclaim Abdullah Sultan but his accession would not be valid in Malay eyes if he was not in possession of the regalia. The regalia was in the hands of Sultan Ismail and all attempts which were now made to persuade him to hand it over failed.[52] In short, contrary to what Clarke believed, as far as Perak was concerned the Pangkor Engagement had settled nothing. It took the assassination of the first British Resident and a military campaign to establish the fact that Perak had lost its independence to Britain.

The assassination of Birch and the Perak War

When J.W.W. Birch[53] took up his appointment as first British Resident in Perak in November 1874, the odds were already against his being able to implant the British presence without arousing active opposition. When he arrived he only had the grudging support of Sultan Abdullah and the Lower Perak chiefs. Within two months he had alienated even that support. The issue which became the prime source of friction concerned taxation. According to the Pangkor Engagement the revenues of the country were to be collected in the name of the Sultan. Birch quickly made it clear that this meant he and his officials were going to do the collecting and that the old system by which the chiefs lived off the revenues from their own districts and surrendered merely a portion of them to the Sultan was coming to an end. This was too much for Sultan Abdullah and the Lower Perak chiefs to swallow. By January 1875 Abdullah had secretly joined the Mantri in urging Ismail not to surrender the regalia[54] and then proceeded to put off signing the proclamations containing the new taxation proposals. On top of this there were other vexations. The new Resident was earnest, overbearing and self-righteous. He took no heed of offending influential chiefs and thought nothing of upbraiding high personages such as the Laksamana, the Mantri and even the Sultan himself in public and in front of their followers. To add insult to injury Birch permitted or actively encouraged debt-slaves to seek refuge in his compound and let them be smuggled to British ships and asylum in the Straits Settlements.[55]

During the first nine months of 1875 matters moved inexorably to their climax. In February Abdullah, with the backing of the Laksamana and the Mantri, declined to sign the taxation proposals for the first time. In March they proved unacceptable to the Lower Perak chiefs, the Maharaja Lela started to fortify his kampong of Pasir Salak, and the Mantri moved his family for safety to Larut. In May Abdullah sent a delegation led by Raja Dris to Singapore pleading for the governor's intervention to restrain or remove Birch.[56] In June Abdullah declined to sign the taxation proposals for a second time whereupon Birch threatened to dethrone him if he did not do so by the end of the month. Abdullah had this ultimatum extended to 20 July but at a meeting of all the Perak chiefs (or their representatives) except Raja Yusof, held at Durian Sabatang (Telok Anson) on 21 July the decision was taken to kill Birch and to drive the British out of the country. This decision made, Sultan Abdullah made a show of compliance with British wishes. On the 24th he signed a proclamation authorizing the collection of taxes and the appointment of officials by the Resident and the Shahbandar, but at the same time laid plans to assault the Residency, sent money to Penang for the purchase of arms and ammunition and sought the services of a Penang lawyer to bring about Birch's removal.

The difficulties Birch encountered both over taxation and the regalia led Jervois,[57] the new governor, to pay a visit to Perak in person during September. He brought with him a new scheme by which the Sultan and the chiefs would be given pensions and the state would be ruled directly by British officials styled Queen's Commissioners in the Sultan's name. At Senggang he met Raja Yusof who was strongly in favour;[58] at Blanja Ismail who, well under the influence of the Mantri and the Ulu chiefs, refused to give any answer to Jervois' proposals on the spot but later rejected them by letter; and lastly at Bandar Bahru Sultan Abdullah who was granted fifteen days in which to make up his mind. On 2 October he was browbeaten by Birch into accepting the British terms,[59] and Swettenham went to Singapore to see to the drafting and printing of the appropriate proclamations. By the time he returned on 27 October, the plot to assassinate Birch had been finalized. On 12 October Ismail and the Ulu chiefs gave their support to Sultan Abdullah's plans and a little while later the Maharaja Lela received the royal authority to put them into effect. For the first time in a generation, the chiefs of Perak were of one mind.

Birch was killed at Pasir Salak on Hari Raya Puasa (which fell in 1874 on 1 November) by the men of the Maharaja Lela, as he stopped there to post proclamations regarding the British annexation. The inevitable consequence was the launching of a military campaign by the British to avenge the Resident's death and to crush all opposition. It lasted six months. The first British attempt to occupy Pasir Salak within a week of Birch's death was rebuffed with the loss of four lives. But reinforcements from overseas soon poured in.[60] In the end two columns made their way into the heart of Perak. One consisting of fifty boats and some 310 soldiers and sailors advanced up the Perak River to Blanja and thence to Kinta. The other column of some 300 men moved overland from Larut to Kuala Kangsar and then downstream to Blanja. Sultan Ismail fled via Kinta to the north and was eventually captured in Kedah (March 1876). The Maharaja Lela gave himself up the following July. By this time most of the active leaders of resistance had been captured or killed. From the testimony they gave the involvement of Sultan Abdullah and the Mantri was made clear. It August they were both called to Singapore to stand trial; they were sentenced to banishment and sent to the Seychelles. Perak was now part of the British Empire.[61]

The origins of the Selangor Civil War

The disintegration of the Selangor sultanate followed in several respects the pattern of events in Perak. As in Perak the balance of Selangor politics was upset by the rise of a 'tin chief', and the feuds of rival Chinese factions became intertwined with the politics of the Malay ruling class. And as in Perak the Sultan was regarded more as a first amongst equals than as an absolute ruler.

However, Selangor's stability was more susceptible to upset for other reasons. Unlike most other Peninsula states, Selangor was not formed around one great river system but comprised five separate river valleys. The first two Bugis rulers were strong enough to impose a political unity over these by virtue of their own abilities and because of the ever-present threat from outside presented by Menangkabau, Malay, Dutch and Thai. By 1826 both these props to internal unity had been removed. Sultan Ibrahim died in 1825 and was succeeded by his son, Raja Muda Mohamed, about whom very little is known except that he did not possess the qualities of his father and failed to command the obedience of the Selangor chiefs.[62] At the same time the Anglo–Dutch Treaty of 1824[a] and British diplomacy at

[a] See p. 319.

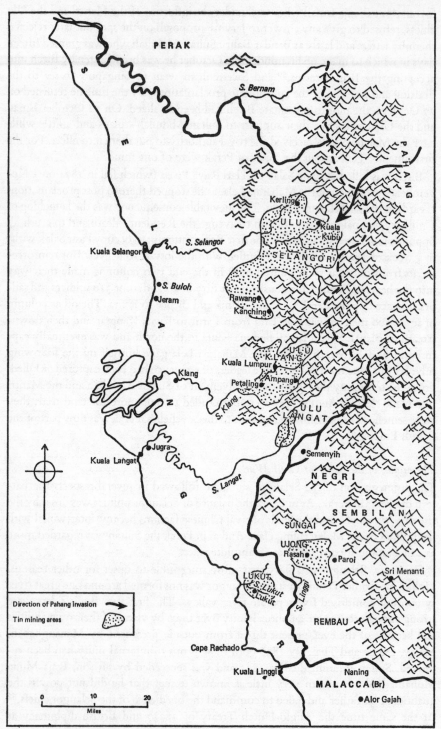

36. Selangor at the time of the Civil War, 1866–1873

Bangkok had brought the Dutch and Thai threats to an end. Sultan Mohamed was left therefore with only internal problems to cope with in the shape of a proliferation of royal progeny for whom some form of livelihood had to be found, and of the development of tin mining which brought with it the rise of over-mighty subjects.

The Larut of Selangor was the district of Lukut. By as early as 1824 it had started to become a centre of tin mining and although the district suffered a severe setback ten years later as a result of clashes between the Chinese miners and the local Malays,[63] it quickly recovered through the efforts of a Bugis nobleman from Riau called Raja Ja'afar.[64] In this way Raja Ja'afar laid the foundations for the rise of his family, which were ably built upon by his son and successor, Raja Juma'at. By the 1850s Juma'at had become the wealthiest and the most powerful chief in Selangor. Not only had he set up a model administration in Lukut with an enlightened taxation policy which attracted 2,000 Chinese miners and was bringing him in a return of around $120,000 a year, but he had established for himself a strong hold over the ruler as well.[65] He had been recognized as territorial chief of Lukut, been bestowed with the titles of Raja Tua and Mantri, and had married a daughter of Sultan Mohamed. Raja Juma'at's rise to power inevitably excited envy and jealousy amongst the other chiefs. He was a foreigner.[66] Furthermore he made new enemies by securing the Klang valley for his brother, Raja Abdullah, instead of letting the chieftainship lapse to Raja Mahdi, the son of the incumbent who died in 1854.[67] New controversy was created on the death of the Sultan himself in 1857. The late ruler's son was still a minor, and Raja Juma'at eventually succeeded in getting the chiefs to nominate Raja Abdul Samad, a nephew of Sultan Mohamed and a protégé of his own, instead. Raja Juma'at was well aware of the problems being created by his own policies and by the tensions brought about by the uneven distribution of wealth which was the consequence of the spread of tin mining. At the meeting in 1857 when the problem of the succession was discussed he made radical proposals—that there should be uniform duties on tin and other products throughout the state, that they should be collected into a central treasury, and that the chiefs should receive allowances from these revenues. But besides being too advanced for the chiefs of Selangor at that time, these ideas were overshadowed by the question of the succession, and matters were allowed to rest where they were. The seeds of future conflict had been sown but they were not allowed to bear fruit until Raja Juma'at himself had died in 1864.

There were other causes of conflict in Selangor besides those created by the rise of the Rajas of Lukut. These were also to be found centred on the Klang valley which at the end of the 1850s superseded Lukut itself as the richest tin mining area of the state. By 1860 the Lukut mines were already practically worked out and in that year much of the remaining mining force was scared away by the bloodshed resulting from a Chinese faction feud. In the meantime Juma'at and his brother, Abdullah of Klang, financed the opening of new mines at Ampang in Ulu Klang, not far from the site of modern Kuala Lumpur.[68] Within ten years (that is, by 1866) these mines were employing between 5,000 and 10,000 labourers and were already producing five times as much tin as was obtained from the whole of Selangor in the 1840s. But the new mines at Ampang and Kuala Lumpur which were worked by Hai San men soon found themselves embroiled with their older-established Ghee Hin neighbours at Kanching in Ulu Selangor, barely twelve miles away.[69]

This became another source of serious friction. However, Chinese were not the only miners and traders in the Klang valley; there were also a number of Sumatrans, mostly Menangkabau men, who formed a self-contained community of their own under their leader, the Dato Dagang, who was directly responsible to the Sultan. These Sumatrans had little love for the Bugis rulers of the state.[70]

The start of the Selangor civil war:

In 1856 this network of rivalries and tensions snapped as the result of an incident in the Klang valley which unleashed a civil war lasting for seven years before it was cut short by British intervention. Right from the beginning interests in the Straits Settlements were involved, and in fact the prolongation of the struggle was largely due to the support which either side could obtain from the British colony. At the same time the fighting and the dislocation of trade and general lawlessness that it brought about also closely affected the interests and the security of the Straits Settlements and formed a powerful reason for the change of policy initiated by Clarke in 1874.

Unlike in Perak the heart of the struggle was not around the succession to the throne itself. Sultan Abdul Samad did not actually participate in the civil war at all. The fact that it started in the first place is adequate comment on the limitations of his own authority. The Sultan owed his position to the Rajas of Lukut and had little or no influence with their rivals. He was in his late fifties and his main interest was in his own survival. So when the struggle began to reach serious proportions he withdrew from the Klang valley altogether and retired to Jugra near Kuala Langat, from which place he distributed judicious favours to either side as the situation appeared to dictate.[71]

The trouble began in 1866 when Raja Abdullah of Klang granted the tax farm of the Klang valley to two very prominent Singapore businessmen, Tan Kim Cheng and W.H.M. Read.[72] The new tax-farmers then proceeded to levy their taxes on all and sundry, including the Selangor rajas themselves who were traditionally exempt from such duties. When Raja Mahdi was presented with a demand to pay duty on some opium he was importing for the miners of Kuala Lumpur, he was provided with an excuse for taking affront and for contesting by force of arms what he considered to be a lost inheritance, which no blandishments by Abdullah had made him forget. So Raja Mahdi rose up in rebellion. He was in a strong position because the Sumatrans in the Klang valley had just been antagonized by Raja Abdullah[73] and flocked to his side. Klang was blockaded by Raja Mahdi's men. After a siege of several months and one abortive attempt at its relief, Abdullah's Klang garrison elected flight to starvation with the result that by the end of the year Raja Mahdi had become master of Klang and its valley.

By virtue of his victory and of his control over the richest tin field in Selangor Raja Mahdi was now one of the strongest chiefs in the state. His position was strengthened still further when Sultan Abdul Samad acquiesced in the new situation provided that Raja Mahdi paid his tribute of $500 per month. The Sumatrans were his allies and the miners of Kuala Lumpur would do a deal, as they must, with whosoever was master downstream at Klang. Nevertheless within two years Raja Mahdi had thrown all these advantages away and had opened the path for his feud with Raja Abdullah and his sons to lead into a full scale civil war.

In the first place Raja Mahdi lost the friendship of the Sumatrans who found him just as oppressive as Abdullah had ever been. Next he irked the Sultan by defaulting on his monthly tribute. This was to prove a costly mistake. At first Sultan Abdul Samad did nothing more drastic than to break off his daughter's engagement to the Raja. But early in 1868 this same princess was wedded to a younger brother of Sultan Ahmad Tajuddin al-Mukarram Shah of Kedah, called Tengku Dzia'uddin (or Kudin). The new son-in-law, westernized in his upbringing and tastes, intelligent and energetic, sought a place in Selangor politics. The Sultan could think of nothing better than to put his country into his hands as viceroy—together with Langat as his fief. It was the Sultan's wish that Tengku Kudin should arbitrate in the Klang affair, but the new viceroy soon found that he was quite unacceptable, as a foreigner, to the Selangor rajas (including the Sultan's own sons), least of all to Raja Mahdi. When Tengku Kudin left the state to attend the funeral of his mother towards the end of 1868, he also went to arrange credit and supplies from a Chinese merchant in Malacca. It was clear that a fresh campaign was about to open in Selangor.

Tengku Kudin intervenes

The intervention of Tengku Kudin into Selangor politics marked the enlargement of the Klang feud into a widespread civil war which engaged nearly everyone of consequence in the state and many others outside as well. Tengku Kudin had influential connexions in the Straits Settlements which he made full use of and which tried to make full use of him.[74] Having been sharply rebuffed by Raja Mahdi in his offer to arbitrate, he now came to give his full support to Raja Ismail, Abdullah's son and heir,[75] in his efforts to recapture Klang. Raja Ismail started to besiege Klang with a motley force of Lanun and Bugis from Sumatra, having carried the approach forts by a surprise attack in August 1869. In October Kudin joined the besiegers with a force of 250 Kedah Malays and a European gunnery officer.[76] The Sumatrans, Raja Mahdi's erstwhile allies, also joined in the fray on the side of the attackers. After a desperate defence which lasted six months, the defenders surrendered while Raja Mahdi himself fled north to the shelter of the friendly chiefs of Sungai Buloh and Jeram. Klang and the Klang valley had changed hands for the second time. They were to remain in the hands of Tengku Kudin and his allies for the rest of the war.

The pattern of the war and of the two opposing sides now became well-defined. Based on the Klang valley were Tengku Kudin and his supporters. Based on the Selangor River basin was the coalition of chiefs led by Raja Mahdi. Both sides gained new adherents. Soon after the fall of Klang, the new Capitan China of the Hai San Chinese at Kuala Lumpur, Yap Tek-loy (Yap Ah-loy), met Tengku Kudin at Jugra and not long after that formed an alliance with him. By doing so he was deserting Raja Mahdi who had installed him as Capitan China at Kuala Lumpur the previous year, but circumstances determined the new combination which was essential to both sides.[77] At about the same time Tengku Kudin acquired the services of J.G. Davidson.[a] Davidson probably lent the viceroy much of the money for his campaign and certainly formed along with his friends a powerful pressure group in Kudin's interest in Singapore itself. On the other side Raja Mahdi already

[a]Refer p. 278.

enjoyed the backing of most of the Selangor rajas, disgruntled with a foreign viceroy, and in particular of Raja Mahmud[78] who was to play a prominent part in the fighting. By virtue of Yap Ah-loy's alliance with Kudin, he also got the support of the Ghee Hin men of Ulu Selangor, led by Chong Chong. Soon after his flight from Klang Raja Mahdi acquired another useful ally, a former lieutenant in the pay of Kudin, called Syed Mashhur, who had fallen out with his master.[79] More remotely Raja Mahdi appeared to enjoy the favour of the Maharaja of Johore and through him of another group of influential Europeans in Singapore.[80]

What followed were four years of annual campaigning. In 1870 and 1871 Raja Mahdi and his allies, having secured Kuala Selangor as a base for their supplies and as an outlet for their tin, made two unsuccessful attempts to capture Kuala Lumpur and Ampang. In 1871 and 1872 Yap Ah-loy made two equally unsuccessful attempts to drive Raja Mahdi, Syed Mashhur and Chong Chong out of Ulu Selangor, being thrown back on both occasions at Kuala Kubu. In the middle of 1871 Tengku Kudin was able to recover Kuala Selangor as the consequence of a British naval bombardment, but the mixed garrison of Kedah Malays and Sikhs under the command of an ex-British army sergeant he left behind was overwhelmed the next year by a surprise attack by Raja Mahdi, aided by treachery. The middle of 1872 proved a bad time for Yap Ah-loy, too. Falling back on Rawang after his second failure at Kuala Kubu, Yap and his Kuala Lumpur men suddenly found themselves threatened from all sides. His Sumatran allies were won over by Syed Mashhur[81] and blocked the way down the Klang valley; Raja Mahdi appeared from Sungai Ujong in the south and he was being pressed by Syed Mashhur and Raja Mahmud from Rawang. By the middle of June Kuala Lumpur was virtually surrounded and cut off. Waking up one morning to find that his European-led garrison of sepoys had decamped,[82] Ah-loy had no choice but to abandon Kuala Lumpur himself. He and his followers managed to escape and make their way down to Klang but of his 2,000 Chinese only 300 reportedly survived.

The fall of Kuala Lumpur marked the peak of Raja Mahdi's fortunes and the nadir of those of Tengku Kudin, whose power was now restricted to the Klang estuary. But although the British governor, Jervois, on a visit to Kuala Langat, suggested that the viceroy might be well advised to withdraw, he declined to do so. He had one trump card up his sleeve, that was the support of Pahang. Pahang had already sent troops to his aid in 1872 but owing to defective advice or communications they were not able to save Kuala Lumpur. But early next year the same troops joined in a pincer movement with forces from Klang and recaptured Kuala Lumpur from Raja Mahdi. By the middle of 1873 Ah-loy was victoriously driving Syed Mashhur out of Ulu Selangor and in November a force of 500 men from Pahang led by the Imam Prang Mahkota Raja assaulted Kuala Selangor from the sea and restored it to the hands of Tengku Kudin. Within the same month another Pahang force regained control of Kuala Kubu. With Raja Mahdi a refugee at Lukut, Syed Mashhur a fugitive at the court of Raja Abdullah in Perak and Chong Chong disappeared from the scene, Tengku Kudin obviously now had the upper hand. But there was no guarantee that Raja Mahdi and his allies, having secured fresh backing and fresh supplies, would not return. That they were not given the chance to do so was the result of British intervention which took place on the initiative of governor Clarke at the beginning of 1874.

The bombardment of Kuala Selangor

In fact the British had already intervened. Despite appeals for help from the Sultan himself and other interested parties, the British made no move till 1871 when a case of piracy which was traced to Kuala Selangor attracted their attention.[83] What began on this occasion as an attempt to punish the pirates in question developed into active intervention in the civil war in favour of Tengku Kudin. Raja Mahdi's men who held Kuala Selangor at the time opposed the attempts of a British landing party to search for the suspected pirates. As a consequence a British warship, H.M.S. *Rinaldo*, bombarded the town and fort, causing Raja Mahdi and his followers to flee into the jungle. When the British subsequently withdrew, Tengku Kudin was able to reoccupy the place without any opposition. But that was not the end of the matter. The acting British governor, Anson, who had sanctioned these moves decided to follow up his advantage by pressing Sultan Abdul Samad for guarantees against further outrages by ensuring that Kuala Selangor remained in the hands of a reliable chief, and by bringing about a settlement of the civil war itself if possible. The mission sent in mid-July to Jugra to achieve this was headed by the Colonial Secretary, J.W.W. Birch.[a] What followed has been described as 'as good an example of "diplomacy by gunboat" as any to be found in the story of the European penetration of Asia'.[84] Birch exceeded his instructions. Not only did he persuade the Sultan to proclaim Rajas Madhi and Mahmud and Syed Mashhur outlaws but to confirm the plenary powers of Tengku Kudin as well. When Sultan Abdul Samad proposed that Raja Bot and Raja Yahya should share the vice-regal powers, Birch peremptorily threatened him with a twenty-four hour ultimatum.[85] Since all this took place within the shadow of a British gunboat, the Sultan gave way; Birch then toured the Selangor coast spreading the news of the Sultan's agreements and sailed back to Singapore satisfied that he has settled the affairs of Selangor. Of course he had not, for Sultan Abdul Samad was quite unable to give effect to his promises even if he had wished to. However the immediate effect of the visit was to confirm the impression that Tengku Kudin enjoyed British support while Raja Mahdi was held in disfavour.

British actions during the next few months strengthened this impression. Early in 1872, Ord, back in Singapore, obtained Dutch help in frustrating an attempt by Raja Mahdi, now in Sumatra, to raise a fleet there with which to resume the struggle. A couple of months later the governor tried to induce Mahdi through the Maharaja to settle down in Johore with a pension of $350 a month which Tengku Kudin would pay. Raja Mahdi was not interested. The governor would like to have had Mahdi arrested and put on trial but his Singapore supporters successfully advised the governor that such action would be of doubtful legality.[86] The result was that no steps were taken against Raja Mahdi who, in July 1872, was able to leave his Johore asylum and make his way back into Selangor by way of the Linggi river and Sungai Ujong, and resume the war. British policy still favoured Tengku Kudin but the failure to restrain Raja Mahdi suggested the opposite, which had unfortunate repercussions for the viceroy in the Klang valley.[b] However, in the meantime

[a]Refer p. 280.
[b]Refer p. 286.

Ord had visited Pekan and encouraged Bendahara Wan Ahmad to give his support to Kudin.[87] In October 1872 he was at Kuala Linggi where the Dato Klana promised not to let any war supplies go through to Raja Mahdi,[a] and at the beginning of November he visited Sultan Abdul Samad who despite earlier complaints about his viceroy[88] confirmed Tengku Kudin's position and his faith in him. After this the British let things take their own course in Selangor, which in the ensuing months turned out well for the viceroy.

The establishment of British control

In the middle of 1873 pressure for British intervention began to mount once again. In March 1873, Tengku Kudin granted a very large and generous concession for tin mining in the state to Davidson and a certain Dutch count from Java, no doubt in return for the help which he had received from these quarters.[89] On the basis of this concession Davidson brought about the formation of the Selangor Tin Mining Company with a capital of £10,000, while his friends in London started pressing the Colonial Office for British protection. One of them went so far as to suggest that without British help Kudin might well turn to another European power. How decisive an effect this suggestion had on the British government is not known but when the new governor, Sir Andrew Clarke, landed in Singapore towards the end of the year he had instructions to look into the question of extending British control. His attention was first taken up by Perak[b] but when another act of piracy occurred, this time just off the Sultan's own Kuala Langat in November, he was furnished with the excuse he needed for taking action in Selangor. Two other small piratical incidents during the next two months further strengthened his hand.[90]

In February 1874, having settled Perak affairs at Pangkor, Clarke took advantage of the presence of a British naval squadron in the Straits to pay a visit, escorted by six warships, to Sultan Abdul Samad at Jugra. The Sultan, fearful for his throne, was relieved to find that all the British governor wanted was justice to be done to those implicated in the Kuala Langat piracy, which included one of his sons. He readily agreed to a commission of six[91] being set up for this purpose, paid up compensation in $5,000 bahars of tin on the spot and expedited the execution of those found guilty of piracy in the trial which the commissioners held. All this was done under the lee of British guns once more but there is nothing to suppose that the Sultan was not pleased to have the problem of his squabbling chiefs taken care of by the British while his own position was made secure and improved at the same time.

The effect of Clarke's action was to bring the civil war to an end in Tengku Kudin's favour. British support for the viceroy was confirmed[92] and it was made clear that Raja Mahdi would not be permitted to stage a comeback. Raja Mahmud and Syed Mashhur both placed themselves in the hands of the British authorities and although Raja Mahdi made one more attempt to stir up trouble in Ulu Langat in 1875, he too in the end accepted his fate and lived in retirement in Johore.[93] Meanwhile in August 1874 Frank Swettenham was left at Jugra with twenty sepoys to act as British Agent with the Sultan. He so completely won the old ruler's esteem

[a]Refer p. 161.
[b]Refer pp. 278–9.

37. Map to illustrate the Northern Malay States especially Kelantan, Trengganu and Patani, 1826–1919

that Sultan Abdul Samad was soon writing to Singapore offering to pay him a salary of $1,000 a month if he would stay as adviser. Swettenham was actually confirmed in the post of assistant British resident in December while Davidson was appointed resident to work with Tengku Kudin. In this way Selangor became part of British Malaya.

TRENGGANU AND KELANTAN

In a treaty signed at Bangkok on 10 March 1909 Thailand agreed to surrender her 'suzerainty, protection, administration and control whatsoever they possess' over the two north-eastern states of Kelantan and Trengganu to the British government. The operative words were 'and control whatsoever they possess', for although the Treaty of 1909 established beyond shadow of doubt Britain's acquisition of Thai rights over the two states concerned, what these rights actually amounted to had been in doubt throughout the whole of the preceding century. In fact, the Anglo-Thai Treaty of 1909 replaced the Anglo-Thai (Burney's) Treaty of 1826 which contained the ambiguous clause that 'Siam shall not go and obstruct or interrupt commerce in the states of Tringano and Calantan. English merchants and subjects shall have trade and intercourse in future with the same facility as they have heretofore had... and the English shall not go and molest, attack or disturb those states upon any pretence whatsoever'. The rulers of both Kelantan and Trengganu maintained that they *were* independent right throughout this period, and for the greater part of it their claims had the support of British officials in the Peninsula. Of the two, Trengganu's claim had some substance in reality. Kelantan, weaker and situated next door to Thai power, was in effect much more subject to Thai influence.

The northern states and the colonial powers

However, throughout the course of the nineteenth century, the fate of Kelantan and Trengganu rested on the nature of the relationship between the British and Bangkok, and this in its turn was closely connected with French colonial activities in South-East Asia. Until the 1850s British policy towards Thailand was dictated by the Calcutta government's desire[94] to develop trade with Bangkok and to avoid expensive commitments in the Malay Peninsula. Such was the background to Burney's treaty.[a] After 1850 there arose the spectre of rising French colonial power in the region,[b] and for the rest of the century British diplomacy was occupied in finding ways and means of containing it. The French presence caused the British to adopt a very cautious attitude to Thailand as far as the northern Malay states were concerned and in an attempt to avoid driving the Thais into the arms of the French, there was an increasing tendency to affirm Bangkok's claims in the Peninsula. The bombardment of Kuala Trengganu by British warships in 1862 in order to discourage Thai encroachments on the state stands out strongly in contrast to the policy of acknowledging and even encouraging the extension of Thai suzerainty which followed. For when in 1869, the Sultan of Trengganu sent his envoys direct to Britain to ask for British protection, the British Foreign Office (acting on the

[a]See p. 321
[b]See pp. 442 et seq.

advice of Ord, the governor of the Straits Settlements) made its reply through Bangkok, thereby conceding for the first time the Thai claim to overlordship. The previous year Kelantan was the victim of a similar gesture by Ord when he appealed for Bangkok's assistance in persuading the ruler (Raja Mulut Merah) to adopt a more liberal policy towards Straits traders.[95] In 1895 the presence of Toh Bahaman and his supporters from Pahang[a] as refugees in Kelantan and Trengganu caused the British to seek permission from Thailand to pursue them there, and the expedition which was sent was accompanied by Thai commissioners expressly assigned for the purpose.

Nevertheless, by this time circumstances had changed and British policy was informed by new motives. In 1896, in the aftermath of Paknam[b] and Mong Sing,[c] France and Britain came to an important understanding with one another over the future of Thailand itself, which established the Menam Chao Phaya basin as a buffer region between their colonial empires.[d] This was the first step to a general rapprochement between the two powers which found its ultimate expression in the Entente Cordiale of 1904.[96] The new understanding in Europe enabled Britain to play a bolder hand with respect to the Thai-protected Malay states. At the same time British power in the Peninsula itself had consolidated with the extension of the Residential System to Pahang in 1888 and with the formation of the Federated Malay States in 1896, while in general the mounting fever of activity by private speculators and adventurers in this peak age of European colonial rivalry and expansion[97] created new uncertainties for both London and Bangkok.

The British reaction to these new developments was at first to continue the policy of recognizing and confirming Thai authority in the north of the Peninsula as the surest means of keeping others out, but later as the situation evolved, they sought gradually to replace it. This process, whereby the Thai authorities were transformed into agents for Britain, became clearly marked in the series of agreements between the British and Bangkok regarding the northern Malay states after 1896. One year after the Anglo-French Agreement of that year, a secret convention was signed between the British and the Thais which laid down the principle that Thailand would not 'cede or alienate to any other power any of the rights over any portion of the territories or islands lying to the south of the Muong Bang Tapan' or grant to any foreigners 'any special privilege whether as regards land or trade' in the region without specific written consent from the British government. In return Britain promised to help Thailand resist any attempts by any other power to obtain such concessions. This convention remained a secret not only to the world at large but also to the rulers of Kelantan and Trengganu. The Pahang-Trengganu boundary agreement of 1899 was likewise signed above the heads of the Malay rulers concerned and served to confirm British recognition of Thai suzerainty over the northern states. The next step was the Anglo-Thai Agreement of 1902, not secret this time, whereby Britain formally recognized Bangkok's right to supervise the foreign

[a]Refer p. 141.
[b]See pp. 516–17.
[c]See p. 518.
[d]See p. 519.

relations of Kelantan and Trengganu and which provided for the appointment by the Thai government of advisers to those states whose advice was to be followed, according to the same formula as used for the British residents in the protected states of the Peninsula. By a secret annexe to this agreement, it was stipulated that the advisers appointed should be of British nationality and that their selection and removal should have the prior approval of the British government.[98] This agreement which had been hastened by the activities of a British speculator in Kelantan called Duff, marked the first stage in the British takeover. In 1909, after negotiations which had begun several years earlier, this process was completed with the signing of the Treaty of Bangkok,[a] by which Kelantan and Trengganu, together with Kedah and Perlis but not Patani nor Setul, were transferred to British overlordship.

The background of Patani, Kelantan and Trengganu

The attention which the west coast tin states of Malaya naturally attracted during the nineteenth century on account of their location, their resources and the fact that they were the scene for the start of the British forward movement into the Peninsula, tends to obscure the fact that at this period the bulk of the Malay population was to be found concentrated in the Malay states under Thai domination. Between them, Kedah, Kelantan, Patani and Trengganu contained more than half the total Malay population of the Peninsula.[99] However, politically they were weak and economically backward.

Patani lost its independence altogether in 1790 and after an abortive uprising in 1808 was broken up into seven small principalities.[100] The present dynasty of Kelantan was founded at the end of the eighteenth century but its rulers were only able to maintain a nominal independence against Thai pressures.[101] Raja Mohamad II (better known as Raja Senik or Raja Mulut Merah) who came to the throne in 1837 was probably the strongest of his line, but even he owed his position to the active intervention of the powerful Thai governor (the Chao Phaya) of Nakhorn Si Thammarat[b] who came to his aid in the civil war of 1838–9.[102] As a consequence, Raja Mulut Merah sent the triennial 'bunga mas' to Bangkok, while under his successors, Thai influence greatly increased.

Trengganu, on the other hand, with the advantage of distance, was more independent, and its rulers, despite their close ties with Johore-Riau, were able to follow successfully a policy of isolation.[103] Nevertheless, it was during the reign of the long-lived and capable Sultan Mansor Shah (1740–93) that Trengganu also sent the 'bunga mas' to Bangkok for the first time. Although the Thais accepted this as a sign of submission, it was never admitted in this sense by the rulers of Trengganu. Sultan Mansor Shah purportedly sent the 'bunga mas' in 1782 as a gesture of gratitude.[104] All the same, its despatch coincided with the founding of the powerful Chakri dynasty at Bangkok which quickly brought about Thailand's recovery from the Burmese invasions, and enabled her to resume the traditional policy of southward expansion. A few years later Mansor Shah was appealing to the British

[a]See pp. 519–20.
[b]Refer p. 107.

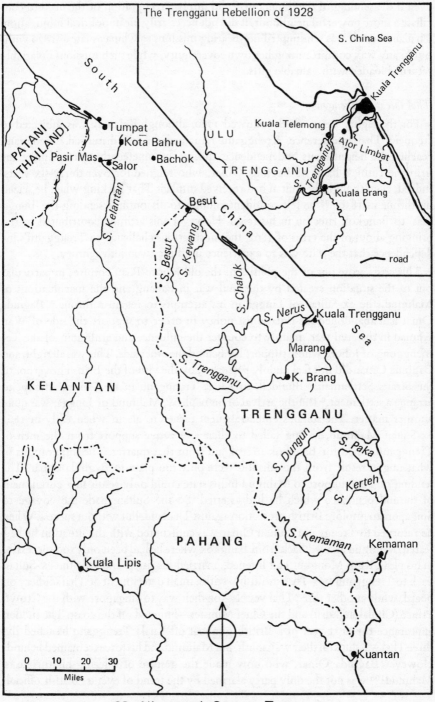

38. Nineteenth Century Trengganu

in Penang for help against Thai demands for submission and tribute. However, even if the sending of the 'bunga mas' did imply a recognition of the need to conciliate a more powerful neighbour, it did not necessarily mean political subjugation. Thailand herself was sending tribute-bearing missions to China as late as 1820 without in any way compromising her own sovereignty, while such missions invariably returned loaded with valuable gifts.

Thai threat to Trengganu

For the eighty years which followed 1790, although Kelantan was subjected to frequent Thai interference, Trengganu remained far less disturbed. Trengganu reached the height of its 'independence' during the nineteenth century under the firm and ruthless hand of Baginda Omar, who reigned for over thirty-six years. Indeed, even though the Sultan had received implicit Thai backing when he seized his throne in 1839,[105] he felt confident enough to discontinue sending the 'bunga mas' to Bangkok later on in his reign. However this attitude contributed to the bringing about of the crisis of 1862, the most serious challenge to Trengganu's independence that the state was to experience until the twentieth century.

This crisis arose out of the politics of the old Johore-Riau empire; in particular out of the situation created by the civil war in Pahang and the machinations of Mahmud, the ex-Sultan of Lingga in his attempts to regain a throne.[a] Baginda Omar had abandoned his isolationist policy in order to support the side of Wan Ahmad in the civil war, mainly to counter the influence and ambitions of the Temenggong of Johore whose support lay behind the other side. This was all right, and Baginda Omar did not feel unduly perturbed by the visit of the British governor of the Straits Settlements, Blundell, to Kuala Trengganu in 1858 in an attempt to arrange a settlement.[b] But the arrival of his nephew, Mahmud of Lingga, was quite another matter. The sultan's embarrassment turned to alarm when early in 1861 ex-Sultan Mahmud, having failed to elicit any active support from the men of Trengganu, sailed for Bangkok to seek aid from that quarter. The implications of what might result from this mission were only too plain to Baginda Omar. The sending of Thai support to Mahmud in his state could only result in a curtailment of the independence which he had asserted. So the Sultan made the voyage to Singapore to implore British protection against Thailand, but without success. When he returned to Trengganu, Sultan Omar was confronted with the situation he had feared. Mahmud arrived back from Bangkok where he had been only too successful in his pleas. King Mongkut had listened, married his sister, and sent the ex-Sultan back to Trengganu in a Thai steamship with a small detachment of Thai soldiery on board, while another three Thai vessels—on their way to Singapore with the Crown Prince (Chulalongkorn) and the Chief Minister—lingered off the coast. The sudden appearance the next year of a British gunboat off Kuala Trengganu hastened the three Thai warships on their way south, but Mahmud and his forces remained behind. However Baginda Omar, who now made the gesture of offering his throne to Mahmud[106] was not the only party alarmed by the trend of events. British officials

[a]Refer p. 124 and p. 134.
[b]Refer p. 135.

in Singapore and Bangkok, fearing an extension of Thai influence southwards into Pahang, were following developments closely, but diplomatic pressure to get the Thais to remove Mahmud from Kuala Trengganu only produced promises without action. Realizing that the Thais were gambling on the monsoon to stymie any effective British action for a vital six months,[107] the British governor in Singapore, Cavenagh, decided to force the issue by sending two more gunboats to Kuala Trengganu. There in November, they delivered a forty-eight hour ultimatum to Mahmud, demanding that he be taken on board to Bangkok. Receiving no response, the two ships proceeded to shell the royal fort, killing twenty people.[108]

This demonstration produced no visible effects but it ultimately achieved what it was supposed to do. On the delivery of the ultimatum, Baginda Omar quarrelled with his nephew, and then withdrew from the town out of range of the guns. Having undergone bombardment, Mahmud joined him and agreed to accept the good advice to leave the state. He then made his way to Besut where a few weeks later he was picked up by a Thai ship and taken back to Bangkok. After this episode, Baginda Omar was not troubled by any more serious pressure from either Bangkok or Singapore for the rest of his reign.

Kelantan submits; the Duff concession

As far as Kelantan was concerned the pressures brought about by the changed circumstances of the end of the nineteenth century began to become apparent during the reign of Raja Mohamed IV (1899–1918), a great-grandson of Raja Mulut Merah. New on the throne, the Raja found himself being subjected to mounting Thai interference which had started in 1897 with the appointment of a new and able governor of Songkhla (Chau Phaya Sukhom) under whose jurisdiction Kelantan lay. Within the space of three years, prompted by Clifford's pursuit of the Pahang rebels into the state, the Chau Phaya had established a resident commissioner, set up a postal agency and installed a gunboat and a garrison under a Danish commander at Kota Bahru as measures to tighten Thai control.

In these circumstances, the appearance at his court of a British speculator called R.W. Duff[109] at the beginning of October 1900, seemed most opportune. Duff was to offer £2,000 cash down and 2,000 shares in the company he was floating in exchange for a concession of 3,000 square miles (about a third of the total area of the state) together with broad powers of administration and 'sole commercial rights of every description'.[110] Despite the fact that the Thais were breathing down his neck[111] and that there was no formal assurance of official British backing, Mohamad IV clearly thought that the risk was worth taking, for within ten days he put his signature to the agreement which was to cost Kelantan so dear in the years to come.[112]

The immediate result of the concession was to create a crisis in cameo. Bangkok was furious, for Duff had already been there and been refused permission to obtain the concession. In London, the British Foreign Office was alarmed by the thought of possible Thai reactions, of the exposure of the secret convention of 1897 and of countersteps by rival imperialist powers. And in Singapore, the supporters of a British forward movement in the northern Malay states found their champion in Swettenham, the new British Governor and High Commissioner (1901–4), who exploited the situation Duff had created for all that it was worth. He strongly supported Duff's claim that Kelantan was entitled to make land concessions on its own account and that the sole prerogative to do so did not rest with Bangkok. During the course of the following twelve months while Thai diplomacy faltered and the British in London prevaricated,[113] the High Commissioner resolutely intrigued with the rajas of the Patani states, and when in February 1902 Bangkok reacted to all this by arresting one of them, Raja Abdul Kadir of Patani itself, Swettenham received with exaggerated marks of honour Raja Mohamad IV (who was the detained raja's nephew), when he came to Singapore from Kelantan to implore British protection. The British Foreign Office received Bangkok's protests about Swettenham's activities but by this time had reached the conclusion that the least dangerous course was to establish British interest in the northern states beyond any further doubt.[114] The result was the Anglo-Thai Agreement of 1902. When Swettenham went to Kota Bahru to get the Raja's signature, he encountered no difficulties, and next year two Englishmen in the employ of the Thai government came to take up their posts.[115] Six years later the Treaty of Bangkok was also signed, and although not well received in Kelantan, the arrival of the first British Resident, J.S. Mason, later in the same year took place without incident.

In 1910, a new treaty was signed between Kelantan and the British, by which Raja Mohamad IV was recognized as Sultan while he accepted a British Adviser according to the usual terms.[116] With this, British control over Kelantan was an established fact. In 1915 there was a short-lived rebellion centred on Pasir Puteh led by one To' Janggut, and supported by the Ungku Besar. With its roots in extreme poverty and springing out of protest against the new land code, it represented the first and last open opposition to the new order.[117]

Trengganu under Sultan Zainal Abidin III

In the meantime Trengganu's reaction to the changing circumstances of the early 1900s was very different. When Swettenham made his voyage to Kuala Trengganu in 1902 to obtain the Sultan's acceptance of the Anglo-Thai Agreement of that year, the ruler, Sultan Zainal Abidin III, refused to sign, for he would not acknowledge his allegiance to Thailand! After a second attempt by Swettenham a few months later had also failed, the British left Trengganu undisturbed any further until 1909. When the British implemented the Treaty of Bangkok in that year, the Sultan bowed to the inevitable and, although 'visibly distressed', received the new British representative, W.L. Conlay, well. However Sultan Zainal Abidin refused to accept the letter from King Chulalongkorn of Thailand announcing the transfer and had Conlay return to Singapore with letters about the treaty for the British High Commissioner, Anderson. In April 1910 a new treaty between Trengganu and Britain was signed, according to Trengganu a far greater deal of autonomy than Kelantan had been permitted to enjoy. In place of a British Adviser, the Sultan was to receive a British Agent with the functions and powers of a consular official. The treaty provided for mutual help, the extradition of criminals, British protection and control over the state's foreign relations, and restrictions on the Sultan's authority to grant concessions to foreigners.[118] Trengganu's comparative freedom lasted for another eight years.

The man chiefly responsible for this state of affairs was the Sultan himself. Although frequently pictured by British officials as an indolent and self-indulgent religious recluse with little concern for affairs of state, the opposite would appear to have been the case. He shared two things with his great-uncle, Baginda Omar—a long period on the throne and a passion to preserve his country's independence.

Sultan Zainal Abidin's reign began under disadvantageous circumstances. Only seventeen years old on becoming ruler, he was subject at once to the pressures of powerful relatives and the menacing presence of the Thais. But although he had to make initial concessions to these forces,[119] as his reign progressed the ruler knew how to reassert his position. Within the state a combination of skilful marriage alliances, well-designed patronage and a deliberate policy of allowing titles to lapse helped to recentralize authority.[120] At the same time, the Sultan became distinguished for his religious learning and was able to identify himself with the strong religious establishment in Trengganu.[121] In his dealings with Thailand, Sultan Zainal Abidin was equally as shrewd and as successful. Although he revived the practice of sending the 'bunga mas' to Bangkok early on in his reign and had to play host in person to King Chulalongkorn on two occasions as the Thai monarch made his way to and fro on his visit to Singapore in the 1880s, the Sultan firmly withstood further attempts at encroachment. In 1892 he turned down a Thai request to open a post-office at Kuala Trengganu which would sell Thai stamps, and although he paid a visit to Bangkok in 1896, he equally firmly rejected the Thai offer of a loan of $2 million, despite the added inducement of $500,000 to be paid in advance. In 1898 the Sultan visited Singapore in a Thai warship but nevertheless was not prepared to admit Thailands' suzerainty in 1902.

The twilight years of Trengganu's independence, 1909–1919

For the rest of Sultan Zainal Abidin's reign, there was no change in the status of Trengganu, but the traditional administration started to deteriorate as the problems connected with the growing British presence accumulated. There was increasing interest by private speculators in the state and the accompanying need for a stable land settlement, efficient justice and currency reform which only a more elaborate administration could procure. But Trengganu, despite its population, was poor and its resources could not easily support an expansion in government. In 1911 the Sultan gave the state its first written constitution,[122] probably in an attempt to get more power into his own hands, but at first at any rate it did not function very well.

One reason for this was the steadily worsening financial situation, which was considerably aggravated by the costs of the Sultan's attempted pilgrimage in 1913.[123] Another factor was the existence of a considerable faction of Trengganu noblemen who were deeply opposed to the introduction of British influence. They found a leader in the young Yam Tuan Muda, Tengku Mohamad, who played an increasingly prominent part in state affairs and dominated the new state council.[124] The underlying atmosphere of resentment and frustration created by these circumstances was no doubt a cause of the Sino-Arab riots in Kuala Trengganu in 1914, and only the outbreak of the First World War and British fears of a Muslim reaction against them[125] prevented their taking more positive action. With little progress in the direction of reform and modernization achieved and fewer prospects in sight, the British High Commissioner, Young, formally warned the Yam Tuan Muda in 1916 that he would be deposed if he continued to be 'obstructive'. The discovery of wolfram in the state, urgent for Britain's war needs, heightened British impatience at their lack of effective control over policy, and Young, who had already imposed a British adviser on the prestigious ruler of Johore,[a] decided in 1918 that the time had come to do the same thing in Trengganu. Excuses for action were not hard to come by, and in July that year an unwilling Sultan was summoned to Singapore to discuss charges of maladministration in his state.[126] Zainal Abidin was able to rebut Young's allegations on several points and declined to accept the High Commissioner's proposal for a commission of enquiry to be set up without prior consultation with his State Council. Although Young was tempted to prevent the Sultan's return, Zainal Abidin was allowed to go back and politically enough, the State Council agreed to the appointment of a commission, which, however, was to confine itself to the investigation of three specific issues. The Bucknill Commission was appointed in September 1918.[127] One month later Sultan Zainal Abidin III died.

Trengganu; the establishment of British control

All that followed was predictable enough. The Yam Tuan Muda who now succeeded his father as Sultan Mohamad did not undergo any change of heart or come to like the British more on account of his accession. Early in 1919 Sultan Mohamad was informed of the inevitable conclusion of the Bucknill Commission that only the appointment of a British Adviser would enable Trengganu to put its house in order. At first he refused to go to Singapore to negotiate a new treaty with the British, and when he changed his mind, the ruler took with him a hand-picked team of anti-British counsellors. At last, after protracted and bitter bargaining, the new treaty was signed in May.

After this, the Sultan's relations with the British remained strained. The first act of the new British Adviser was to cause the ruler's emoluments to be cut by two-thirds.[128] Sultan Mohamad retaliated by releasing the former Chief Judge of Trengganu who had been jailed for corruption in 1912 and making him his chief minister instead of Haji Ngah, who had served his father.[129] He also cut the regular allowances to his relatives and dependants, tried to place himself at the head of the religious party in the state and to exploit anti-British sentiment aroused amongst district chiefs by the abolition of debt slavery. The situation was impossible and soon the following year Sultan Mohamad chose abdication as his way out. He was succeeded by his brother, Sulaiman, who never 'gave a moment's anxiety to his British Adviser and the High Commissioner'.[130]

There was only one more moment of anxiety for the British, or one more serious expression of protest against the new regime in Trengganu. Sometimes called the Trengganu rebellion, it broke out in 1928 and was an affair involving some 2,000 villagers which lasted one week. Led by Lebai Abdul Rahman (also known as Toh Janggut) of Alor Limbat and Syed Alsagof (Sagap) in Ulu Trengganu, the movement spread in a district which was desperately poor in reaction against the new land tax and forest laws in the state. Its aim was to march on Kuala Trengganu, expel the British and restore the old Malay government. Attempts by Malay officials and Sultan Sulaiman himself to reason with the insurgents failed, and near Kuala Telemong, with Kuala Brang already in their hands, a force of about 1,000

[a]Refer pp. 132–3.

peasants came into a head-on clash with a small police detachment. In the brief engagement which followed eleven of the villagers were killed. The movement had already collapsed by the time that reinforcements from Kuala Lumpur had arrived, and its ring-leaders—some twelve people—were arrested and sent to Singapore for imprisonment. Lebai or Haji Abdul Rahman was also sent to Singapore, and then to Mecca, where he died in 1929.[131] The last of the Malay states had laid down its arms.

[1]Muzzafar Shah, the founder of the ruling Perak dynasty, was the eldest son of Mahmud, the last Malay ruler of Malacca.

[2]Namely: Mansur Shah (1549–77), Mukaddam Shah (1603–19), Mansur Shah (1619–27), and Sallehuddin (1630–5): the seizure of the last-named brought to an end the direct male line and the substitution by the Achinese of a collateral branch of the family from Siak.

[3]The Dutch signed treaties with Acheh and/or Perak in 1639(A), 1645(A), 1650(A), 1653(P), 1655(A), 1659(A), 1747(P), 1765(P). The first Dutch fort on Pangkor was built in 1670 and abandoned in 1690, reoccupied in 1745 and abandoned in favour of Tanjong Putus three years later. Tanjong Putus was occupied with a brief gap in the 1780s until the British came as a result of the Kew Letters.

[4]As quoted by Winstedt from a letter by the Sultan of Selangor to the Sultan of Perak in 1804 (*J.M.B.R.A.S.*, Vol. 12, No. 1, 1934, p. 64).

[5]Namely, the Bernam, Selangor, Klang, Langat and Lukut rivers.

[6]Daing Chelak, one of the famous five Bugis warriors, sons of Upu Tenribong Daing Rilak of Lakkai in the Celebes. He was the second Yam Tuan Muda of Riau (1728–45). The date of Raja Lumu's accession is not altogether certain.

[7]At issue was the disposal of the loot from a British trading vessel captured at Riau in 1782, whilst the Dutch were at war with Britain (the American War of Independence).

[8]Succeeded to the throne of the death of his father, Sultan Sallehuddin, around 1780.

[9]On withdrawal from Perak, Selangor originally demanded the land on the right bank of the Perak river as far as the Sungai Plus; later modified this claim to as far as Sungai Bidor. The matter was settled by Anderson's treaty in 1825—see below.

[10]The Sultan's authority was set aside and the state administered for Kedah by the Raja Muda and the Bendahara.

[11]On this occasion the Sultan asked for two warships, 2,000 troops (of whom half should be European) and offered in exchange the monopoly of Perak tin and rattans for $2,000 a year.

[12]Cracroft's mission was part of the general policy initiated from Penang of trying to forestall the returning Dutch by securing British trading rights with local rulers, like Farquhar in Riau. The terms of Cracroft's treaties included most favoured nation status for both parties and a promise by the Malay rulers not to revive monopolistic agreements with other powers (that is the Dutch) which excluded British trade.

[13]Kedah, now in control, feared the Thai reaction to such a cession; Perak wanted a money payment.

[14]Hon. Robert Fullerton, 'able and energetic'; governor of Penang presidency (1824–30); formerly a civil servant in Madras and a member of the Madras Council. Retired in 1830 and died 1831.

[15]In fact Fullerton had no authority to threaten a Thai governor with war and would have earned a severe reprimand from Calcutta if his action had been known at the time.

[16]By the clauses regarding Perak and Selangor, Thailand promised not to 'go and molest, attack or disturb' these two states; the English Company promised likewise regarding Perak and also not to allow Selangor to attack Perak. The Sultan of Perak was to be permitted to send the 'bunga mas' 'should he desire', and embassies of forty to fifty men between Perak and Ligor were permissible.

[17]Raja Hassan/Hussein, a son of Sultan Ibrahim, had operated in Perak since 1806, using Pangkor as his base from which to enforce the terms of the 1823 treaty.

[18]Low had gone far beyond his original instructions by concluding the treaty. He was an officer of the Madras Native Infantry transferred to Penang in 1818. 1823–40, in charge of Province Wellesley (Saberang Kurau); 1840–50, Assistant Resident, Singapore; 1850, retired to Europe.

[19]However, the British did not occupy the Dindings or do anything about them until Anson raised the issue in 1867. They became part of the Straits Settlements in 1874 but were handed back to Perak in 1935.

[20]Nakhoda Udin was actually appointed at Kurau by Tengku Long Puteh of Siak who was brother-in-law to the Sultan of Kedah. Instead of being put on trial when he reached Ligor he was rewarded and later reappeared as the commander of a Thai fleet sent to co-operate with the British in 1830 in a sweep against pirates off the Kedah coast!

[21]Long Ja'afar: a Perak Malay, son of Dato Paduka Setia (of Lubok Merbau) and grandson of Dato Johan, both minor chiefs; related through the marriage of his brother to the daughter of the Panglima Bukit Gantang, one of the Big Eight Chiefs of Perak, and warden of the passes leading from the Perak River Valley to Larut; settled near Taiping (then Klian Pauh); c. 1840, appointed as collector of tenths of rice and other dues in Krian, Kurau and Larut.

[22]First title granted on 6 November 1850 by Raja Muda Ja'afar on behalf of the Sultan plus five other chiefs, including Panglima Bukit Gantang, with powers to administer and develop Larut; confirmed by the Raja Muda in 1856.

[23]Dated 24 May 1858, granted by Sultan Ja'afar, the Raja Muda and the Raja Bendahara; the grant states 'we bestow a province of this country of Perak upon Ngah Ibrahim bin Ja'afar to be governed by him and to become his property .... Therefore we endow Ngah Ibrahim with the power of legislation and give him authority to correspond and to settle matters with other countries and with the British Government without reference to us three or to anyone who may hold sovereignty in Perak'. Quoted by Winstedt, op. cit. p. 79.

[24]Mantri of Perak and *not* Mantri of Larut as many Western writers have tended to suppose. The office of Mantri was originally held by the descendants of Syed Husain al-Faradz from the previous century; the line was in decline in 1862.

[25]As stated by Cowan, op. cit. p. 43. The offices of state involved were those of Sultan, Raja Muda, Raja Bendahara and Raja di-Hilir. The Sultan and the other office-bearers were elected by the great chiefs; on the death of the Sultan, the Raja Muda normally succeeded and the others moved up one position. The Raja di-Hilir was normally the chosen son of the reigning Sultan.

[26]In 1851 and 1853; on the grounds of Low's treaty, but the British maintained that its terms did not cover internal rebellion. In 1854 the British governor, Blundell, came to Perak to meet the chiefs in a vain attempt to solve the dispute.

[27]Raja Ismail, a favourite of Sultan Ja'afar, was descended from the Perak royal line on his mother's side; his father was Raja Abdul Rahman of Siak. When appointed, it was understood that he was not eligible for the throne; he was there to keep Raja Yusof out.

[28]In 1870 Abdullah granted a 15-year lease for $15,000 a year to a Eurasian called Bacon in the Krian district, which formed part of Larut; thus Ngah Ibrahim regarded the concession a direct challenge to his position. One of the last acts of Sultan Ali was to annul the concession.

[29]The Larut tin miners were divided into the Si-Kuan (Four Districts) and the Go-Kuan (Five Districts), divisions of Kwangtung province, south China. The Si-Kuan miners were members of the Ghee Hin secret society, mostly Cantonese and Teochew; the Go-Kuan were members of the Hakka Hai San and the Hokkien Toh Peh Kong societies (they formally allied in 1863). The enmity between the two groups in Larut centred over land and water rights but also reflected the rivalry between Ghee Hin and Hai San in Ujong Salang, Selangor, Penang, Singapore and Kwangtung itself where there was warfare between 1855 and 1868. The Larut troubles were a continuation of conflict between Ghee Hin and Toh Peh Kong members in Ujong Salang in 1859 which spread to Penang. The first mine in Larut was opened by Ghee Hin men in 1849.

[30]Over a gambling incident; 13 Ghee Hin were killed in the affray which followed the death of a Hai San, and as the rest of the Ghee Hin members fled to the coast, their leader, So Ah-chiang, was captured by the Mantri at Teluk Kertang (Port Weld) and put to death. The leader of the Hai San side was Chung Keng Kwee (Ah Kwee).

[31]The Ghee Hin got reinforcements from Ujong Salang, Kedah, Province Wellesley (Saberang Kurau) and Larut, and the support of the Malay White Flag Society; they found a pretext in a trivial incident to attack their rivals. The Ghee Hin in Penang numbered about 25,000 to the Toh Peh Kong's 5,000.

[32]Originating in the case of Lee Ah-kun, representative in Larut of the Ghee Hin leader, Ho Ghi Sui. Lee was having an illicit love affair with the wife of a relative of the Hai San leader, Chung Ah-kwee; the pair were exposed by Hai San men and brutally murdered; attempts to settle the issue by monetary compensation failed. This time the Ghee Hin were well prepared, and bringing in 600 mercenaries via Krian, quickly drove the Hai San miners into Matang and out of the state.

[33]On the eve of their departure, the Hai San leaders appealed for British mediation as a ruse to cloak their intentions. At the same time they had the Mantri's steamer impounded by court order pending a trumped up debt case, thus preventing his effective intervention.

[34]Having shipped the Hai San back to Penang in March at his own expense but in boats provided by Ho Ghi Sui, the Mantri bargained with the Ghee Hin for the reopening of the mines in their sole possession at more favourable rates for himself.

[35]The reason given by the chiefs who elected Ismail for their decision was that they had waited in vain for the arrival of Abdullah during the requisite 30 days. In fact Abdullah dared not go upstream for his installation fearing the hostility of the Ulu chiefs. Nevertheless precedent shows that the presence of the new ruler at the funeral of his predecessor within a stipulated time was not obligatory. For a full discussion of the circumstances attending Ismail's election, see C.D. Cowan, 'Swettenham's Perak Journals', *J.M.B.R.A.S.*, Vol. 24, No. 4, 1952, introduction and notes, esp. pp. 58 and 17–20.

[36]The mission was headed by C.J. Irving, Auditor-General of the Straits Settlements. Irving was prejudiced against the Mantri, dismissed Ismail as 'an impracticable Malay of the old school', and recommended Abdullah.

[37]When the Mantri resumed his alliance with the Hai San; Abdullah had recently been incensed by the Mantri's refusal to lend him money.

[38]Krian and Kurau were rice-growing districts and an important source of Malay manpower. The Malay Red and White Flag societies had strong roots there. For this reason both Abdullah and the Mantri sought to establish a footing in the area; Abdullah was already there when the Mantri arrived.

[39]Tristram Charles Sawyer Speedy: described by Parkinson (op. cit.) as 'a slightly improbable character'; born 1836 in India; commissioned in Army, 1854; resigned in 1860; visited Abyssinia and New Zealand; took part in British expedition to Abyssinia in 1867; returned to Britain in charge of Ethiopian Emperor's son; married and three years as Deputy Supdt. Police, Oudh; arrived Penang as Deputy Suptd., 1871; promoted full Superintendent, 1872. Entered service of Mantri, 1873; appointed Asst. British Resident, Larut, 1874; resigned Perak service, 1877; more African adventures and took part in British Abyssinian expedition of 1884; died in England, 1910.

[40]These had been frequent since 1857, but as affairs in the tin states deteriorated they became more persistent. In 1872 there had been two major petitions from the merchants of Malacca and the Singapore Chambers of Commerce respectively. In 1873, 248 'Chinese merchants and traders—British subjects and inhabitants of Singapore, Penang and Malacca' sent another strong plea for British action in terms which suggested a European's inspiration.

[41]The meeting was attended by Anson, the Mantri, Raja Abdullah, Ho Ghee Sui (Ghee Hin), Chung Ah-kwee (Hai San), Foo Tye-sin (secretly pro-Hai San), Tengku Kudin (pro-Abdullah) and a British naval captain. The failure of Abdullah to secure an armistice in Larut was largely due to the failure of Ho Ghi Sui to back him up, probably because Ho considered the settlement gave the Hai San too great an advantage. Abdullah's failure prejudiced Anson against him and influenced the British decisions which followed.

[42]The vessel was H.M.S. *Midge*, which had been cruising off Larut, probably looking for trouble, when it was fired on by Ghee Hin junks. About 4,000 Ghee Hin were put to flight at the stockades and Matang itself was briefly occupied.

[43]Abdullah was arrested because he was using a vessel which the Mantri claimed before the courts was his.

[44]Raja Dris was a cousin of Abdullah; eventually (1887) became Sultan of Perak. He had at this time tin interests at Kampar and Batang Padang.

[45]Tan Kim Cheng/Ching: born 1829, son of Hokkien Tan Tock Seng; inherited his father's fortune and became one of the recognized Ghee Hin leaders in Singapore; had widespread business interests in Singapore, owned rice mills in Thailand and Saigon, and steamers; followed his father's generosity to public works and charities; played prominent part in public affairs; close associate of Read and Davidson; Thai consul-general in Straits Settlements and Malay States; died 1892.

[46]James Guthrie Davidson: born 1838; nephew of James Guthrie; arrived Singapore, 1861; former solicitor of Supreme Court of Scotland; joined as partner of legal firm of R.C. Woods; prominent in public affairs; British Resident, Selangor, 1874–5; British Resident, Perak, 1875–7; killed in Singapore road accident, 1891.

[47]In November and December there were eight major incidents of piracy involving Ghee Hin men off the Perak coast.

[48]By the end of 1873 the Ghee Hin had spent some $380,000 on the struggle while Raja Abdullah had raised loans amounting to $16,000 for the cause on his own account.

[49]At first Clarke was disposed to uphold the claims of Ismail; but Ismail's close links with the Mantri and Abdullah's strategic command of the lower reaches of the river and coast, apart from a favourable impression created when the two first met, were powerful counter-considerations.

[50]The main points of the agreement were: 1. both sides to disarm and dismantle their stockades; 2. commission of faction leaders and British officials to settle claims while Larut was to be placed under a British official; 3. faction leaders to pay $50,000 bond to keep the peace.

[51]Other provisions of the agreement were: all revenues to be collected and appointments made in the name of the Sultan; the cost of the Resident and his staff to be paid for by the state; the collection and control of all revenues to be 'regulated under the advice of the Resident'.

[52]In April 1874 when visited by Birch and Swettenham; in January 1875 when Birch convened a meeting of all the Perak chiefs for the purpose; in September 1875 when Governor Jervois visited Blanja.

[53]James Woodford Wheeler Birch: born 1830; joined the Commissioner of Roads Dept., Ceylon, 1846; writer in Ceylon civil service, 1852; Commissioner of Requests and Police Magistrate, 1853–6; Asst. Government Agent in various districts of Ceylon, 1856–66; Government Agent for Eastern Province, Ceylon, 1867; transferred to Straits Settlements as Colonial Secretary, 1870; assassinated in Perak, 1875.

[54]On the occasion of Birch convening a meeting of all the Perak chiefs at Blanja to get the regalia. Abdullah, on his way to attend, sent a letter in advance, saying: 'should you consent to my installation as Sultan, Perak will be given over to the English; for my words have caused me to be much indebted to them'. Quoted by Cowan, 'Swettenham's Journals', op. cit. p. 24. The meeting proved a failure.

[55]Debt slavery was a well established institution in Perak. Birch's tactless efforts to discourage it formed one of the most direct and bitter causes of friction between himself and the Perak chiefs.

[56]The governor, Clarke, told the mission to approach him through the Resident.

[57]Replaced Clarke in May 1875. Clarke was transferred on promotion to India to become a member of the governor-general's Council.

[58]Raja Yusof's support for the British dated from his visit to Penang and meeting with Clarke at the instance of Swettenham in June 1874. Convinced of British power, he knew his only chance of obtaining the sultanate lay with them.

[59]Abdullah only gave way when he was told that Yusof would be made Sultan if he did not.

[60]Jervois, hearing of trouble in Sungai Ujong, and expecting some from Raja Mahdi in Selangor, grossly overestimated his military needs.

[61]The Maharaja Lela, Dato Sagor, and some others were executed after trial. Ismail was exiled to Johore where he died at Scudai in 1889. Abdullah was allowed to return to Singapore as was also the Mantri in 1894, and died in Perak in 1922. In 1909, as part of the Anglo-Thai treaty of that year, Perak re-acquired the district of Ulu Perak which had been seized by the rajas of Reman during the course of the nineteenth century. For full details and background, see *Hulu Perak dalam Sejarah*, Y.M. Raja Razman, Y.B. Toh Muda Haji Meor Samsudin and Husain Mahmud, Ipoh, 1963.

[62]The post of Raja Muda was immediately disputed amongst the new ruler's sons as well as by one of his brothers. In the event, Sultan Mohamed outlived them all.

[63]Lukut started to develop as a tin mining centre under the control of Tengku Bongsu/Busu; in 1834, in retaliation against a raid and robbery by some Malays on a kongsi house, the Chinese miners rose up and killed every Malay in the district, including the Tengku; this in turn led to their own extermination or eviction. Today Lukut is part of Negri Sembilan; it was ceded in 1880 in exchange for Semenyih.

[64]Raja Ja'afar was a kinsman of the Bugis Yam Tuan Mudas of Riau.

[65]He imposed a flat 10 per cent duty on tin in place of the customary two-thirds. Juma'at's influence with Sultan Mohamed dated from 1839 when he saved the ruler from his Malacca creditors by guaranteeing the settlement of debts amounting to $169,000. In 1846 Juma'at assumed responsibility for all the losses the Sultan had incurred in mining in the Klang valley.

[66]Although Bugis themselves, the second generation chiefs of Selangor regarded the Bugis from Riau as outsiders and rivals.

[67]In fact there was no hereditary rule involved and the Sultan was fully entitled to make a fresh appointment.

[68]Kuala Lumpur itself sprang into existence as the landing point and store place for these mines. Abdullah and Juma'at raised $30,000 from two Malacca towkays and sent the first party of 87

miners from Lukut in 1857. Although of these only 17 survived the malaria, by 1859 fresh men had come and the mines flourished.

[69]The Kanching mines were opened by Abdul Samad around 1844, having been granted the fief of Ulu Selangor on marrying a daughter of Sultan Mohamed. By the late 1850s they had been nearly worked out, which was the principal cause of the friction with the new miners at Ampang.

[70]The friction between the Menangkabau and the Bugis had its origins in the conflicts of the eighteenth century.

[71]Actually he withdrew from Klang shortly before Raja Ismail started to invest it in 1869.

[72]The terms were that they received one-tenth of the revenues each.

[73]Arising out of an affray at Abdullah's custom house at Kuala Lumpur where a Batu Bahara man was killed. Abdullah refused redress and the Batu Bahara headman forthwith offered his services to Raja Mahdi.

[74]Including Read, Davidson, Tan Kim Cheng and others. They had a strong motive in backing Tengku Kudin in order to recoup their losses caused by Raja Mahdi's actions.

[75]Abdullah died at Malacca shortly after the loss of Klang in 1866.

[76]He sent another 250 of his Kedah men to Jugra. Raja Mahdi successfully appealed to Bangkok to cause the Sultan of Kedah to recall his subjects from intervening in another state.

[77]Yap Tek-loy: born, 1837, in Kwangtung Province, south China; was a Fei Chew Hokkien, son of poor peasants; left China for Malacca in 1854; worked as a coolie in Lukut mines, 1856-9; became pig-dealer and prospered; made Capitan China, Sungai Ujong, 1860; called to Kuala Lumpur to be manager of mines and assistant to Capitan China there, 1861; opened shop at Kuala Lumpur and married, 1865; became Capitan China, Kuala Lumpur, 1868; died in Kuala Lumpur, 1885. The rivalry between the Kanching and Kuala Lumpur miners came to a head in 1866 when the Kuala Lumpur miners took advantage of a quarrel amongst the Kanching leaders to have their own nominee elected as headman at Kanching; in 1869, the Kuala Lumpur nominee was murdered and a personal enemy of Ah-loy, called Chong Chong, took his place; later in the year Ah-loy was grateful for the strengthening of his position by being formally installed at Kuala Lumpur as Capitan China by Raja Mahdi; but in 1870, not long before Kudin recaptured Klang, Ah-loy had struck a severe blow at his enemies at Kanching; the luckless followers of Chong Chong and the defeated supporters of Raja Mahdi were thrown together in the Selangor basin, and made common cause; these circumstances drove Ah-loy and Kudin into each other's arms later the same year. Ah-loy first met Kudin at Jugra when on a visit to get the support of the Sultan in 1870.

[78]Raja Mahmud: son of Raja Berkat, Tengku Panglima Raja of Selangor; a born fighter, he acquired an awesome reputation; Swettenham wrote, 'he fought for no political reason, but for friendship's sake, and because he liked it'. Later, having been defeated in Selangor and Sungai Ujong, he served the British faithfully during the Perak War.

[79]Syed Mashhur: an adventurer of Arab descent from Pontianak. His quarrel with Kudin sprang from the death of his brother at Jugra for which he blamed the Sultan and the Viceroy. He deserted his post at Kuala Selangor and joined up with Chong Chong's Ghee Hins. He became the most formidable leader and fighter in Mahdi's coalition. After his defeat in Selangor, he took service with Raja Abdullah of Perak; he helped the British in the Perak War. In 1883 he returned to Selangor and became headman at Kerling.

[80]Notably Thomas Braddell, the Maharaja's private solicitor as well as Attorney-General of the Straits Settlements. Braddell persuaded Ord to leave Raja Mahdi alone in 1872.

[81]The Sumatrans had little to gain from Kudin's victory, which would mean less freedom, but they were also won over by the belief that the viceroy had lost British favour.

[82]Ah-loy had acquired the services of van Hagen, a Dutchman, and Cavalieri, an Italian, plus 80 sepoys. Fearing their predicament, the sepoy force had tried to break out and make its own way to Klang but was ambushed and decimated near Petaling. 64 were killed including both the Europeans.

[83]A Chinese junk from Penang was pirated with the loss of 34 lives. On receiving the complaint of its owner, a British naval search party located the pirated vessel at Kuala Selangor where it had been taken by the Chinese who had committed the crime.

[84]C.D. Cowan, Nineteenth Century Malaya, p. 88.

[85]Raja Bot and Raja Yahya were sons of Raja Juma'at and therefore nephews of the Sultan. Abdul Samad hoped to reduce the power of the viceroy by associating the Lukut rajas with him. Birch threatened to seize all the available tin in support of his ultimatum, which lay quite beyond his authority in dealing with the ruler of an independent state.

[86]Raja Mahdi immediately obtained the services of a Singapore lawyer to contest the legality of the British actions, and also the backing of the Maharaja of Johore and Thomas Braddell.

[87]Wan Ahmad was no admirer of Raja Mahdi who in 1870 had supported an abortive invasion of Pahang from Ulu Selangor by the sons of Wan Mutahir.

[88]The Sultan had been alienated by the viceroy's blockade of the Selangor coast to prevent supplies reaching the other side, and had petitioned for British intervention to restrain him.

[89]The concession including mining rights in Klang, Selangor and Bernam, with 5 per cent royalties dutiable on gross produce, and $3 per bahara exported for a period of ten years.

[90]The November piracy involved a Chinese vessel from Malacca. The second incident took place in December and the third was an attack on the Cape Rachado lighthouse by Selangor men in January.

[91]Including Tengku Kudin and two British observers, one of whom was Davidson.

[92]The trial of the Kuala Langat pirates was in fact a trial against Kudin's enemies in which he was one of the prosecutors himself. Swettenham later discovered that those tried and executed were not actually responsible for the deed 'though the punishment must have been deserved on general principles'. See Swettenham, *British Malaya*, p. 184.

[93]He was arrested and imprisoned at the height of the Perak troubles following the assassination of Birch for fear that he would start a fresh uprising in Selangor.

[94]Until they were transferred to the jurisdiction of the Colonial Office in London in 1867, the Straits Settlements were administered by the English East India Company and later the British Indian government from Calcutta; in fact, the Straits Settlements till 1867 were regarded as part of the British Indian Empire.

[95]In 1867 the Singapore Chamber of Commerce complained of the Raja's monopoly over cotton yarn, gambier, opium and tobacco. Ord protested to Kota Bahru with no effect, so he tried Bangkok—with success. Nevertheless while Weld was governor in Singapore (1880–7), he followed a policy of denying Thai suzerain rights and paid two visits to Trengganu in person in 1886 and 1887.

[96]The *Entente Cordiale* was the name given to the understanding (not a formal alliance) between Britain and France by which the two powers agreed to sink their differences in colonial matters and present a common front against the rising might of Germany.

[97]The complications arising from such activities have been well illustrated with regard to the attempts of a group of well-connected British speculators to float the Malay Railway and Works Construction Company by Chandran in 'Private Enterprise and British Policy in the Malay Peninsula', *J.M.B.R.A.S.*, Vol. 37, No. 2, 1964.

[98]Thailand was to receive one-tenth of the revenues of each state, but promised not to interfere in matters of internal administration unless there were disturbances.

[99]Kedah (21,000), Kelantan (50,000), Patani (54,000) and Trengganu (31,000), total 156,000, whereas Perak, Selangor, Johore, Pahang and the Menangkabau states combined amounted to some 139,000—figures taken from Newbold, *Political and statistical account of the British Settlements in the Straits of Malacca* (1839); quoted by Fisher, *South-East Asia*, p. 596. Figures for the Straits Settlements are not included here. At the time of British intervention in 1909, Trengganu's population alone was estimated at 154,000 (Wright and Reid, *The Malay Peninsula*, 1912), although the Sultan calculated it to be at 115,000 in 1905. See, J. de Vere Allen, 'The Ancien Regime in Trengganu', 1909–1919, *J.M.B.R.A.S.*, Vol. 41, No. 1, 1968.

[100]The Malay state of Patani has a long history; its queen created a great impression on the first Dutch and English traders to call there at the beginning of the seventeenth century. Like its neighbours, Patani experienced alternating periods of independence and Thai control. The sultanate's last bout of freedom came with the collapse of Thai power following the Burmese conquest of 1767 and it fought hard to preserve it against the resurgent power of the new Chakri dynasty at Bangkok. This struggle culminated in Patani's final subjection in the campaign of 1790–1. The seven principalities into which Patani was subsequently divided are Jala, Jering, Legih, Nong Chik, Reman, Patani and Sai. The principality of Reman became a source of trouble to Perak during the course of the nineteenth century.

[101]Its founder was Long Yunus (1775–94), a scion of the royal house of neighbouring Patani and with possible Bugis connexions. Prior to this Kelantan had been in its time subject to Majapahit and Malacca and divided between the Trengganu Malays and the Thais. Long Yunus himself was installed with Trengganu's aid. Kelantan broke away from Trengganu's suzerainty at the beginning of the nineteenth century.

[102]Raja Mohamad I (Sultan Mandul) (1800–35) died childless, leaving the throne to be contested by his relatives. The struggle became polarized around one of the late ruler's brothers, Long Zainal, raja of Banggul, and his clever nephew, Tuan Senik. Senik won, receiving the sup-

port of the Chao Phaya of Nakhorn Si Thammarat (the conqueror of Kedah). The Thais gave their support to Senik since the raja of Banggul had given assistance to the Kedah rebels in the uprising of 1831–2. When the second Kedah revolt of 1838 took place, mutual self-interest once again brought the Thais and Raja Senik's supporters together. For a fuller description of the background, refer to Skinner, 'The Civil War in Kelantan', Monograph II of *J.M.B.R.A.S.*, 1965.

[103]The founder of the present royal house of Trengganu was Tun Zainal Abidin, a half-brother of Sultan Abdul Jalil Riayat Shah of Johore who died in 1720. Zainal Abidin's successor was Mansor Shah who became the greatest of his line. He was installed in 1740 by Sultan Sulaiman of Johore, and although later on he followed an isolationist policy, Mansor spent the first 26 years of his reign combatting Bugis influence in the Riau Archipelago and the Straits of Malacca.

[104]The story goes that Mansor was invited by the Thais to join in on an attack on Ligor. Mansor's men arrived on the scene too late to take part in the fighting, but were all the same generously rewarded by the victorious Thais. Out of gratitude for this treatment, henceforward Mansor sent the 'bunga mas' to Bangkok. A less chivalrous interpretation of this story would be that Mansor recognized the reality of revived Thai power under the Chakri kings with the conquest of Ligor.

[105]Sultan Omar/Baginda Omar (1839–76), the second great ruler of Trengganu, had already failed in one bid for the throne in 1831 on the death of Sultan Abdullah (an uncle) and his short-lived successor, Sultan Daud; on that occasion he was ousted by another uncle, Sultan Mansor, and lived in exile in Kemaman and Riau. In 1839 he wrested the throne from Mansor's youthful and unpopular son, Sultan Mohamad Shah. He apparently did so with Thai approval, since Sultan Mohamad had compromised his position by showing a benevolent attitude towards the Kedah rebels of 1838. For a full discussion of the background, see Skinner, 'A Trengganu Leader of 1839', *J.S.E.A.H.*, Vol. 5, No. 1, 1964.

[106]Perhaps he did so to escape the wrath of Thailand or to escape responsibility for whatever might befall him with the British.

[107]Once the north-east monsoon set in, the East Coast would become virtually inaccessible by sea for six months, giving Mahmud plenty of time in which to achieve his objects on land without interference. With him at this time was Wan Ahmad, one of the main contestants in the Pahang Civil War.

[108]The British naval commander strongly resented his orders to bombard a defenceless seaport and was largely responsible for bringing the matter to the attention of the British public through questions in Parliament. Governor Cavenagh was officially censured for the action.

[109]Duff's first experience of Kelantan had been as a police officer in Clifford's party pursuing the Pahang rebels in 1895, which gave him his opportunity to gauge the economic possibilities of the state. Subsequently a district officer in Ulu Selangor, he resigned in January 1900 on medical grounds and returned to Britain in order to launch his Kelantan venture.

[110]Duff floated his Duff Development Syndicate in 1900 with the aid of six London businessmen and started with an initial outlay of £10,000.

[111]Duff described the ruler as 'gibbering' with terror, a description belied by his actions. Nevertheless, there is no doubt that the agents of the Chao Phaya of Songkhla were threatening to alienate a large portion of his state to Chinese interests.

[112]The litigation which followed the attempts of British officials to reduce the powers and scope of this concession lasted until 1930 and involved sums of over £1 million. For details of the whole story, see Rupert Emerson, *Malaysia*, Kuala Lumpur, 1964, pp. 255–62.

[113]Duff had already angered the Thais by evading the special commissioners sent to Kota Bahru to keep an eye on him. When news of his concession reached Bangkok, the immediate Thai reaction was to denounce it completely. Yet within one month the Thai Foreign Minister conceded that the issuing of land rights was in the hands of the Kelantan ruler. Meanwhile the British Foreign Office had been gently slipping from a position of an outright refusal to give Duff its support to one of silently recognizing Duff's claims whilst encouraging Thai sovereign rights.

[114]Reports of a Russian visit to Ujong Salang (Phuket) in 1885, of French schemes to build a canal across the isthmus of Kra in 1893, and of German interest in Langkawi (1899–1900) were topped by Duff's threat to establish the headquarters of his company at St. Petersburg (modern Leningrad) or Paris if he failed to get British backing.

[115]Namely W.A. Graham and Thomson as Resident-Commissioner and Adviser respectively. Neither knew Malay though both were fluent Thai speakers, and both inclined to the Thai

point of view. A vivid account of conditions in Kelantan in his time is to be found in Graham's annual reports and in his book, *Kelantan, a State of the Malay Peninsula*.

[116]The Sultan agreed to maintain Malay or Indian troops for the defence of the Peninsula should gross revenues reach $100,000 a year.

[117]Starting with the murder of a police sergeant by To' Janggut at Pasir Puteh. Pasir Puteh itself was then sacked and for some days the whole district was in anarchy. Order was eventually restored with the arrival of reinforcements from Singapore. In the fighting which followed To' Janggut was killed.

[118]Mindful of the Duff episode, the agreement stated that no concession of land of more than 3,000 acres or of mining land exceeding 500 acres should be granted to anyone except a native of Trengganu without British consent. In fact in 1909, the most important of the extant eleven concessions was the Bondi concession of the East Asiatic Company (largely Danish controlled) in Kemaman district.

[119]On his accession Zainal Abidin had to permit the distribution of all main river districts amongst powerful relatives as chiefs, remaining with only the Trengganu river and vicinity as his own fief. However, as Allen (op. cit.) points out, the revenue from each district was so meagre that no single chief could hope to accumulate undue wealth or power, and the young ruler was also careful to see that adjacent districts did not fall under one man. The Thais made themselves felt through the presence of personal representatives of King Chulalongkorn throughout the four-month long installation celebrations in 1881.

[120]For evidence of the Sultan's marriage diplomacy, refer to Allen, *The Ancien Regime*, especially pp. 35-9. Regarding the lapse of titles as they fell vacant, the rulers of Johore and Kedah were carrying out the same practice with the same purpose during this period.

[121]Described by Graham, the (British) Thai adviser in Kelantan, as being 'ridden with holy men' it is true that Trengganu contained a large and influential population of *syeds* and *hajis*, whose importance was enhanced by the abolition of the post of penghulu in the villages by an earlier ruler. Reformist Wahabbite influences were probably introduced into the state through the medium of the sizeable Arab colony at Kuala Trengganu and through the royal family's close connexions with Riau. For more details, refer Allen, op. cit.

[122]Setting up a Cabinet (Jema'ah Mentri) of eight to twelve ministers, and a State Council (Jema'ah Meshuarat Negeri). Cabinet posts could only be held by Muslim subjects of the ruler, who appointed both those and the members of the State Council. The Cabinet advised the Sultan on the appointment of the latter, and its approval was needed for all decisions of the Sultan and the Raja Muda. The Sultan held a suspensive veto of one year on all decisions of the Cabinet.

[123]The Sultan set out on the Haj in 1913 but was unable to get beyond Cairo because of ill-health. The cost of his pilgrimage amounted to $70,000.

[124]British officials were naturally not well disposed to the young prince who so clearly entertained few sympathies for them. Conlay described him as weak and lazy, as well as being 'excessively addicted to women and the use of aphrodisiacs'. Although by no means as bad as painted, the Raja Muda (aged 21 years in 1909) was barely literate and his influence appears to have been confined to the younger set of the Trengganu nobility.

[125]In this war, Britain together with France, Italy, Russia and later on the United States of America found themselves ranged against Germany, Austria-Hungary and the doyen of Muslim powers, the Ottoman Sultanate of Turkey. Turkish participation in the war on the side against Britain caused ripples of unrest amongst Britain's Muslim subjects, particularly in India. The British fear was of a popular outbreak assuming the proportions of a *jihad* in Trengganu and spreading amongst the Malay population of the other Peninsula states.

[126]The most serious charge involved the district of Kemaman which had been run more or less independently by Abdul Rahman Ishak (Enche Drahman), a former *budak raja* who had been put in charge of Kemaman and Kijal in 1885 by Zainal Abidin for his part in slaying Tengku Long, who had been molesting the Sultan's sister. Under his hand, Kemaman had been administered firmly but also somewhat haphazardly and arbitrarily, and certainly not in a manner consonant with British ideas of organization and progress. The other charges concerned a rape case where police were involved, the state of Trengganu gaol, concessions to Japanese and the question of debt slavery. In the event the first three issues became the subject of the Bucknill Commission's enquiries. In 1921, Abdul Rahman, now retired from his Kemaman post, was created Dato Sri Lela di-Raja by Sultan Sulaiman. He died at the age of 83 in 1938. For the background of Kemaman and Abdul Rahman, see Sulong bin Zainal, 'Dato Sri Lela di-Raja', *Malaysia in History*, Vol. 12, No. 1, 1968.

[127]The Commission was headed by the Chief Justice of the Straits Settlements, Sir John Bucknill,

and comprised two other members, accompanied by a professor of medicine from the King Edward VII College, Singapore, and the Commissioner of Lands and Mines, Johore.

[128]The first act of Sultan Mohamad on his accession had been to increase his emoluments to $9,500 a year from the $6,000 enjoyed by his father.

[129]Whilst he was in office, the British had harboured their doubts about Haji Ngah and his influence on affairs, but now they declared him to be 'loyal' and his dismissal unwarranted.

[130]Quoted by Chan Su-ming, 'Kelantan and Trengganu', *J.M.B.R.A.S.*, Vol. 38, No. 1, 1965, p. 191.

[131]The trouble had its origins in 1925 when Lebai Abdul Rahman and 27 followers refused to obtain official sanction to plant hill rice as required under new forest regulations. They later, however, obeyed a court order that year to desist from planting, and did not plant again until 1927. In March 1928 Lebai Abdul Rahman was fined for defying the regulations. His movement began one month later. For details of the disturbance see Dato Seri Lela di-Raja, 'The Ulu Trengganu Disturbance, May 1928', (diary extracts), *Malaysia in History*, Vol. 12, No. 1, 1968.

BALI AND THE GREAT EAST

In the rest of the archipelago Dutch authority was finally established almost everywhere during the last quarter of the nineteenth century and the first decade of the twentieth.

BALI AND LOMBOK

The most serious resistance came from Bali and Lombok where the Dutch only succeeded in overcoming opposition to their rule at a high cost in human lives. Both islands were under Balinese control although the population of Lombok is largely made up of the Sasaks, a people who have embraced Islam. The Balinese had a long and strong tradition of independence, evidenced by their retaining their Hindu beliefs and forms of social organization when the rest of the world around them had accepted Islam. The habitable parts of both islands were thickly populated and depended for their welfare upon an elaborate irrigation system built up over generations, which in turn helped to preserve rigidly the traditional forms of society.

Bali was originally under the sway of the rulers of Central Java, and after the downfall of Majapahit[a] was linked with the last surviving Hindu kingdom in east Java—Balambangan. In 1639 when Sultan Agong of Mataram[b] extinguished this ancient state, its princes fled to Bali and there successfully resisted all Javanese encroachments. For the next two-and-a-half centuries the Balinese were largely left to themselves. In 1692 they overran Lombok. By the nineteenth century the Balinese were split up into nine warring principalities.[1] They were self-sufficient and had little to offer the outside world except slaves for which a good market was to be found in Batavia.[2] They were also the terror of mariners who passed along their shores for they spared no one who was unfortunate enough to be shipwrecked there.

The nineteenth century brought changes. The British ended the slave trade when they occupied Java between 1812 and 1816. In 1826 the Dutch made the first of

[a]Reference p. 71.
[b]Refer p. 72.

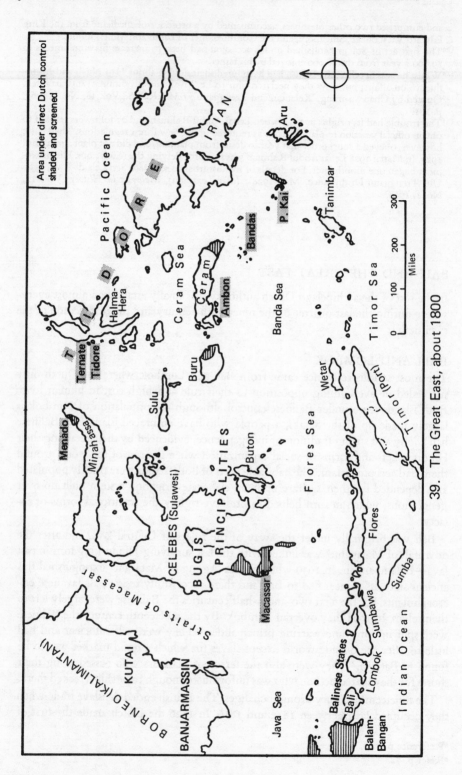

39. The Great East, about 1800

their attempts to bring the Balinese under closer supervision but it was a failure.[3] However, in 1839 they tried again, largely prompted by fears of British and other European competition and of possible British intervention.[4] In that year they set up a factory at Kota in the principality of Badung and appointed a commissioner, Huuskus Koopman, to conclude treaties with all the rulers on the island. Koopman exploited the hostility between the Lombok state of Mataram and the Balinese principalities to secure recognition of Dutch suzerainty from both.[5] Besides re-cognizing Dutch overlordship the Balinese rulers also agreed in these treaties to restrict the practice of shipwrecking along their coasts, but when they realized the duplicity of Koopman's tactics, they made no attempt to observe these engage-ments. An incident of shipwrecking in 1845 gave the Dutch the pretext they wanted for further intervention. In 1846 they sent an expedition against Buleleng and Karangasem, building a fort at Buleleng and forcing both states to renew their agreements, pay tribute, receive a Dutch representative, send embassies once in every three years and dismantle their defences. As soon as the Dutch withdrew, the agreements became a dead letter, and the Raja of Buleleng who had already made one appeal to the British in 1846 made another in 1847, although to no avail. The failure of the first expedition to achieve any lasting results called for a second in 1848, which being too small and hastily prepared was defeated and forced to with-draw. This necessitated a third expedition the following year which was led by the veteran Dutch warrior, Colonel Michiels,[a] and had the support of 4,000 fighting men from Lombok. Buleleng, whose ruler was killed in the fighting, was occupied and then handed over to Bangli, while Jembrana which had been conquered by Buleleng had its independence restored. Karangasem was also occupied but in a surprise attack on the Dutch column moving on Klungkung, Michiels himself was killed. Not withstanding this setback, the Dutch completed their nominal subjuga-tion of the island. Karangasem was placed under Mataram of Lombok as a reward for Mataram's aid, and all the Balinese rajas were forced to sign new treaties ack-nowledging Dutch overlordship, prohibiting piracy, slave-trading and ship-wrecking, and engaging not to allow Europeans to settle on the island without Dutch consent.

If Dutch policy had been inclined to annexation at this period, these events would surely have marked the end of Balinese independence; but in fact the islanders were left to go their own way for another generation, although the Dutch now had a foot in their camp. In 1854 as a consequence of Buleleng's resistance against her subjection to Bangli, the ruler of Bangli handed the territory over to the Dutch who then administered it through a member of the old ruling family. Two years later when the Raja of Jembrana was deposed by his people, the Dutch also took over. In the next two decades there were further incidents leading to Dutch inter-vention[6] but nothing of consequence, and even the setting up on paper of a Resi-dency of Bali and Lombok under a Dutch official in 1881 only had practical effect in Buleleng and Jembrana.

The Dutch conquest of Lombok and annexation of Bali
The events which led to the final extinction of Balinese independence began in the

[a]Refer p. 156.

1890s with the Dutch conquest of Lombok. In 1891 the Sasaks of Lombok rose up in rebellion against their oppressive Balinese rulers. Although the movement had been ruthlessly crushed by 1892 a Sasak deputation arrived in Batavia imploring Dutch assistance. The Dutch in response sent an envoy to mediate at Mataram but the Raja refused to receive him. The Dutch next protested against the purchase of two vessels in Singapore by the Raja which then flew the Mataram colours.[7] Dutch warships sailed into Ampenan Bay and seized the two ships but a second attempt by a Dutch official to come to terms with the ruler failed. Dutch preoccupations elsewhere (in Flores and Acheh) prevented further action by them for the next eighteen months. But in June 1894 they sent a third mission to Mataram, demanding an official apology, the surrender of the recalcitrant raja, and the supervision of the fulfilment of these conditions to be in the hands of the Dutch resident. The Raja of Mataram asked for time to consider and the mission returned to Batavia empty-handed. The following month a Dutch expeditionary force commanded by General Vetter arrived in Ampenan Bay. The general delivered a 48-hour ultimatum for a new treaty, indemnity and fulfilment of the earlier conditions. Receiving no answer within the time limit, the troops landed and quickly occupied Mataram itself. However, in a sudden counter-attack at Chakranegara, some miles beyond, the Balinese caused the Dutch to fall back and abandon the capital for the coast with the loss of over a hundred men including General van Ham, the second-in-command. Reinforcements arrived from Java at the beginning of September. The Raja was taken prisoner in November to be sent to exile in Batavia, and the Crown Prince committed suicide[8] soon afterwards. By August 1895 when the Dutch formally proclaimed the annexation of the island all resistance was at an end.

The annexation of Lombok should have been the writing on the wall for the princes of the island of Bali itself. Karangasem, as a consequence of the annexation, also came under direct Dutch control and in 1899 neighbouring Gianjar, threatened

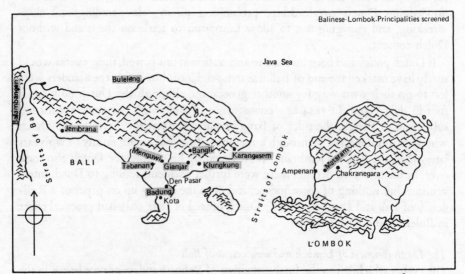

40. Map of Bali and Lombok, illustrating the extension of Dutch power

by Bangli, voluntarily placed itself under the Dutch flag. In 1900 the Dutch repulsed attempts by the rulers of both Bangli and Klungkung to regain control of Karangasem. The last phase began in 1904 when a shipwrecking incident provoked a fresh crisis, this time involving the richest of all the principalities, Badung. The Raja of Badung refused to pay the 7,500 guilders fine the Dutch imposed, so the next year they started to blockade his coastline. In 1906, Badung and Tabanan which had come to its aid still remaining defiant, the Dutch sent a strong expedition to subdue the two states. The Dutch troops landed at Den Pasar, the capital of Badung, in September, and took the town; Tabanan was soon overrun. The Balinese princes put up a brave struggle against hopeless odds, and then like their cousins in Sulu at about the same time[a] added horror to tragedy by enacting the rites of *puputan* as their last gesture of defiance.[9] After this the Dutch had complete control of the island. Buleleng and Jembrana already formed one residency. Now the remaining six states were brought together to form a second administrative division.[10] In 1908 a last bloody uprising took place in Klungkung against Dutch authority and was crushed. Bali's resistance was over.

THE SUBJUGATION OF THE BUGIS OF CELEBES

The next most serious centre of resistance to the spread of Dutch power was in south Celebes. Since the downfall of Macassar in the 1660s[b] the principalities of the region had all nominally subscribed to the Bongaya Contract.[c] But in fact these Bugis states were left largely to themselves until the nineteenth century. Chief amongst them was Boni, whose rulers, the Aru Palaka,[11] at first enjoyed the favour of the Dutch as their allies against the Gowa Sultanate. By the second quarter of the eighteenth century this attitude had changed. The Bugis of south Celebes resented Dutch monopolistic practices and followed the lead of Boni in opposing them. In 1739 Macassar itself was attacked by a Boni force and although the besiegers were driven off, Boni was not subjugated.

Throughout the nineteenth century Boni was the most powerful of the Bugis principalities and dominated their politics by challenging European pretensions and by seeking to spread its own control. Boni's rulers resisted the British takeover in 1812 and the Dutch comeback in 1824. In that year the Dutch governor, van der Capellen, arrived at Macassar to revive the Bongaya Contract and to secure the acquiescence of the Bugis princes. The Aru Palaka of Boni counter-demanded Dutch recognition of his authority over neighbouring states. Two smaller principalities, Tarnete and Supa, failed to send any emissaries to Macassar at all and repelled a small Dutch force sent against them later the same year. Encouraged by this demonstration of Dutch weakness Boni itself invaded Dutch territory in 1825. The invasion was thrown back but the Dutch failed once more to subjugate the state.[12] The next Dutch attempt to assert their suzerainty over the Bugis principalities came in 1858. Alarmed by British moves in Borneo, the Dutch rejected out of hand fresh demands from Boni's ruler for recognition of Boni's sovereignty over its neighbours, and sent a punitive expedition to avenge the insult of flying the Dutch flag

[a]Refer p. 216.
[b]Refer pp. 60–1.
[c]Refer p. 61.

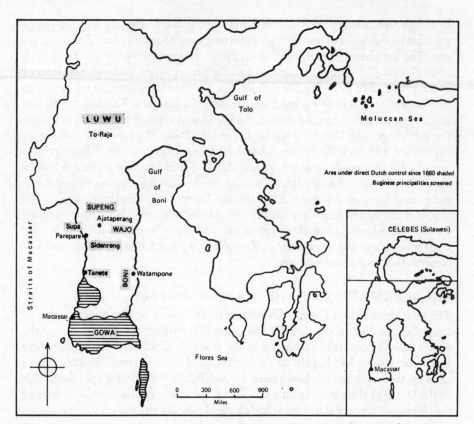

41. Dutch activities in the Celebes (Sulawesi) in the nineteenth century

upside down on Boni vessels. The expedition was a failure but a second one succeeded with the help of a Boni prince who coveted the throne and was put on it in 1859. At the same time the rulers of Wajo, Supeng and Luwu declined to enter into new agreements with the Dutch and the Dutch did not force the issue.[13] Dutch reluctance to assume greater responsibilities at this period ensured that their authority remained purely nominal.

The final crisis came in the 1890s. Although the Dutch intervened in a succession dispute in Boni in 1895 to put their own nominee on the throne, he proved sufficiently independent of them to resume the traditional Boni policy of asserting its hegemony over its neighbours. In 1896 Boni assisted Luwu against To-raja raids and annexed To-raja territory. In 1897 Boni attacked Wajo and was only forced to withdraw in 1899 as a result of Dutch response to Wajo appeals. Nevertheless the next year Wajo was attacked again and two years later Boni was putting pressure on Luwu and raiding the coasts of Flores. These conflicts gave the Dutch the opportunity they wanted to intervene. In order to stop the fighting and control the region they occupied the port of Parepare which was a source of smuggled arms to the warring states and also a source of evasion of the customs at Macassar. The principalities of Sidenreng, Gowa and Supeng then made war on the Dutch, joined also by the federation of Ajataperang—all encouraged by the Imam of Boni who, inspired by the Achinese, was the mastermind behind the scenes. Systematic campaigning soon brought about their defeat. The Dutch then turned their attention to Boni itself and in 1905 attacked and captured its capital, Watampone. The Imam fled, to be caught sometime later in Wajo. The Raja of Gowa was killed in a skirmish in 1906. All resistance was over by 1908.

THE LESSER SUNDAS AND IRIAN BARAT

The Lesser Sundas had been only fitfully touched by outside imperialisms until the second half of the nineteenth century when they, too, became caught up in the general movement of European expansion. Most of the islands submitted to Dutch authority during the 1880s and 1890s, although some had contacts reaching back to the seventeenth century;[14] Sumbawa in 1875, Dompa and Bima in 1880. The people of Flores whose resistance had caused Roman Catholic missionaries to seek Dutch help as early as 1859 maintained their hostility in the face of Dutch pressure in the 1880s and were not systematically brought under control until 1907. The complete occupation of Ceram took place in 1904.

As for Irian Barat (New Guinea), this sparsely populated region was nominally part of the domains of the Sultans of Tidore. Fearful of British and French pretensions, in 1828 the Dutch formally assumed possession and set up a post in Triton Bay (Fort du Bus). However this settlement was abandoned in 1836 because of its lack of economic value, its unhealthiness and its openness to pirate raids. For the next fifty years the Dutch contented themselves with sending warships on occasional visits as demonstrations of their sovereignty. But when the British and the Germans established themselves at the other end of the island in the 1880s,[15] the Dutch decided further action was necessary. In 1898 they started negotiating with the Sultan of Tidore for the formal relinquishment of his claims over the territory and set up a skeleton administration of their own.[16] In 1905 an Anglo-Dutch Treaty demarcated the frontiers between the two empires on the island. The limits of the Dutch East Indies had been rounded off.

---

[1] Namely: Badung, Bangli, Buleleng, Gianjar, Jembrana, Karangasem, Klungkung, Menguwi, and Tabanan. Klungkung enjoyed the highest prestige as its rulers claimed descent from a Majapahit prince. On Lombok, after the Balinese conquest, there were initially four states—Mataram, Pangutan, Pagasangan and Singasari. After 1838 Mataram started to unify the island under its control.

[2] In 1778 there were reportedly 1,300 Balinese slaves in Batavia.

[3] A Dutch official was posted in Badung but he was withdrawn in 1831.

[4] Anglo-Dutch relations had deteriorated over the question of Dutch tariff policy and British trade (Anglo-Dutch Treaty of 1824 provisions). Furthermore a number of foreign traders including a Singapore businessman were successfully developing a rice export trade with China in exchange for copper cash.

[5] The Rajas of Buleleng, Karangasem and Klungkung signed the treaties against verbal assurances of Dutch help against Mataram in 1841–2, while later Koopman used the threat of the Balinese to get the Raja of Mataram's signature. The Dutch factory at Kota proving uneconomic was withdrawn in 1844.

[6] In 1858 and again in 1868 the Dutch intervened in civil wars in Buleleng; and exiled the regents of Jembrana (in 1866) and of Buleleng (in 1872) for oppressive practices, to Banyuwangi and Padang respectively.

[7] Thereby implying Mataram's absolute sovereignty.

[8] The episode of the suicide of the Lombok prince has been described as follows: 'The King had surrendered, but one of his sons, a cripple, walked out with all his relations, dressed in gorge-

ous garments, bedecked with all their jewelry, and with their swords and lances attacked the Dutch army, only to find the death they courted. Those who were not killed in the fight were afterwards found to have also killed themselves'. Quoted by Sir Frank Swettenham, *British Malaya*, p. 110; This form of mass suicide involving the ruler, his family and his followers, known as 'puputan', was employed by the Raja of Badung at the cost of 400 lives.

[9] See above.

[10] Namely: Badung, Bangli, Gianjar, Karangasem, Klungkung and Tabanan. The ninth state, Menguwi, had been subjugated by Gianjar in 1893.

[11] This is the title of the office, not a personal name.

[12] In fact, they did not make the attempt. The outbreak of the Java War imposed too great a strain on their resources.

[13] But Luwu's Raja changed his mind and signed in 1860.

[14] For example, Timor (both Portuguese and Dutch); Sumbawa, signatory to the Bongaya Contract since 1674.

[15] The British over South-East New Guinea in 1884, and the Germans over North-East New Guinea (Papua) in 1885.

[16] The Sultan of Tidore was himself a vassal of the Dutch and had little say in the matter. For a full discussion of the validity of Tidore's sovereignty and the Dutch assumption of it, see Robert C. Bone, 'The International Status of West New Guinea until 1884'. *J.S.E.A.H.*, Vol. V, No. 2, 1964.

The bombardment of Palembang, 1821

the Chinese were induced to offer no foraging and mincy to a minimum of time labour of their Batavia Residency. Money was indicated in respect of the realization which but our power and over them was hardly on the subject and, to and position.

5. The Downfall of the Malaysian World: the Pattern of British and Dutch Policies

As the last resistance guttered out in the Gayo Highlands of Acheh or in the little known interiors of Celebes and the Sundas at the beginning of the twentieth century, the recasting of the political shape of Island South-East Asia was virtually complete. The peoples of the archipelago now found themselves, either directly or indirectly, under the yoke of Holland and Britain. The countries of the Malay Peninsula, the provinces of the Brunai sultanate in North Borneo and the off-shore islands of Penang, Singapore and Labuan were all under the British flag. Dutch authority was acknowledged from Sabang to Merauke, from the northernmost tip of Sumatra to the unexplored jungle peaks of West Irian, 2,500 miles away to the east, casting the outlines of modern Indonesia. Although the subjugation and division of the archipelago by two distant European powers took place during the course of the nineteenth century, the fate of the region had been settled years before. By 1700 the Dutch had already secured the mastery over the trade routes which formed the basis of power and empire in the islands. Their domination of Java gave them the key to the maritime highways of commerce throughout the islands; their conquest of Malacca (in 1641) sealed the fates of Mataram and Acheh as commercial powers; their control of Macassar and Bantam destroyed the last real centres of open trade in the region. While Dutch power was by no means ubiquitous or absolute, it was sufficiently strong to prevent the rise of any serious competitor from amongst the Malaysian powers. As a result, though they survived, the Malaysian empires of yesteryear withered. Brunai, Johore, Acheh—deprived of their monopolies and access to trade—all decayed within a generation. The sultanates of the Sulu archipelago—hemmed in between the Dutch south and the Spanish north —were stunted at growth. Thrown back onto their own subsistence economies, the sea empires were further pulled down by the feuds of their impoverished aristocracies, whose principal sources of revenue had been so much reduced or had disappeared altogether. Political instability, always latent, became endemic during the nineteenth century. Meanwhile the overwhelming commercial domination of the West was accelerated by the rise of Penang and Singapore during the first quarter of the new century. Old centres of power either declined and disintegrated more rapidly still or made a temporary revival and a shallow profit in the shadow of the new ports. Acheh and Siak, for example, were able to benefit for a couple of generations in this way. But the general fate was like that of Brunai or Sulu, whose ruling classes were forced to rely on smuggling and piracy in order to maintain a semblance of their former positions. Piracy was indeed the scourge of the Malaysian world, but this piracy meant more than robbery on the high seas; it had political implications—it represented the only practicable way of life for many of the inhabitants of the shores of the Straits of Malacca and of the China and Java seas. It also symbolized a kind of resistance against the Western monopolists. In this way, old states fragmented and their fortunes were directed by the activities of self-seeking individuals.

The basis of European domination lay in technical superiority. This superiority first made itself apparent when the Portuguese reduced Malacca with their handful of ships in 1511 and subsequently maintained themselves there ringed by a far more populous hostile world, until their turn came and they were ousted by the rival and far better-equipped power of the Dutch East India Company. The Dutch pre-eminence in spite of their small numbers was also secured because of this technological superiority in ships and guns. If this had been true in the seventeenth and eighteenth centuries, how much more true was it in the nineteenth century when the advance in scientific knowledge and the rise of the Industrial Age gave the Westerners an irresistible superiority all over the globe. Their new resources of power enabled them to humble the proud rulers of such ancient and peopled civilizations as those of India and China; a Brunai sultan could not be expected to quibble before the muzzles of a British gunboat nor the Balinese to repel a well-armed Dutch invasion by gestures of magic sacrifice. Nor was there any real opportunity for any Malaysian state to fight back against the colonialists with their own methods or weapons, once they were established; many attempts to do so were made but they inevitably failed because the Westerners had the vital command of the sea and controlled the way back to Europe. The most that a Malaysian leader could hope to do was to play off one of the European powers against another. Such tactics were tried out by Acheh, Macassar and Bantam in their day, as well as by the Johore Malays and the Bugis. All of them failed. Indeed, one of the only reasons why the resistance against the Europeans was prolonged at all was because of the limitations of the Westerners' own resources. The long drawn-out Padri Wars in west Sumatra were largely because the Dutch were fully occupied in Java at the time, and in Java itself Dipo Negoro's campaign lasted as long as it did since the Dutch faced severe economic difficulties at that period. The long Achinese war and even the Pahang rebellion dragged on because the colonial powers did not consider an all-out effort economically justifiable. In the long run these episodes of gallant resistance were doomed to failure. In the prevailing circumstances of the nineteenth century, the Europeans possessed power which made them invincible. It was only when the knowledge and techniques of the industrialized West became exportable to Asia that it was possible for Asians themselves to benefit and turn these things to their own advantage. Therefore it is clear in the last analysis that the course of events in Island South-East Asia was really beyond the control of the inhabitants of the archipelago themselves. All they could do was to respond to the new circumstances; they could hardly direct them. For a hundred years the political fate of the region and its division between Holland and Britain rested in the hands of the Dutch and British policy-makers themselves.

The Malaysian World and the Anglo-Dutch Treaty of 1824

The most outstanding consequence of the rise of Western imperialism in the archipelago was the dividing of the Malaysian world between Holland and Britain, ulti-

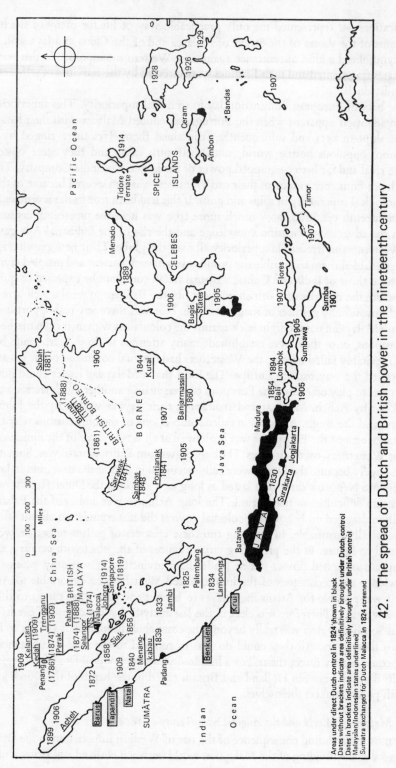

Areas under direct Dutch control in 1824 shown in black
Dates without brackets indicate area definitively brought under Dutch control
Dates in brackets indicate area definitively brought under British control
Malaysian/Indonesian states underlined
Sumatra exchanged for Dutch Malacca in 1824 screened

42.   The spread of Dutch and British power in the nineteenth century

mately leading to the creation of the three nation states of Indonesia, Malaysia and Singapore that we have today.

The foundations of this division were laid by the Anglo-Dutch Treaty of 1824 which was signed in London and was very largely the outcome of purely European considerations. By this treaty the Dutch withdrew from their settlement in Malacca which they handed over to Britain, and at the same time surrendered to the British all their political rights and commercial privileges in the Peninsula. They also recognized the legality of the British occupation of Singapore. The British for their part withdrew from their settlements at Benkulen and its dependencies[1] along the Sumatran west coast and gave up all their claims and rights on that island. In addition the British also undertook not to form any new settlements on the Karimun islands or 'on any other islands south of the Straits of Singapore'. These arrangements brought about a general separation of British and Dutch interests and had the effect of bringing to an end British political control in Sumatra and that of the Dutch in the Peninsula. This was fortified by the provision that neither power would attempt to interfere by founding new settlements or concluding new treaties with any of the principalities situated in the other's sphere of influence. An exception, however, was made of Acheh whose independence the Dutch agreed to respect. Another important article of the treaty was designed to keep out any third colonial power, for it was stated that none of the ceded territories 'should be at any time transferred to any other power. In case of the said possessions being abandoned by one of the Present Contracting Parties, the right of occupation thereof shall immediately pass to the other.' The treaty also included important provisions regarding commerce and for joint action to overcome the pirate problem. Although the effect of the treaty was to make the Malay Peninsula a preserve of the British and the archipelago one for the Dutch, the island of Borneo was not mentioned,[2] a fact which led to considerable diplomatic friction between the two powers in the middle of the century as a consequence of the activities of James Brooke in Sarawak. The formation of the protectorate of British North Borneo in the 1880s revived the issue, and the boundary between what had become British and Dutch Borneo was not finally settled until 1912.[a] Meanwhile with regard to Acheh, the British and Dutch signed a fresh agreement in 1871 which gave the Dutch a free hand there in return for certain concessions to the British in West Africa and the West Indies.

The factors which brought about the signing of the Treaty of 1824 are closely related to the political background in Europe where broadly speaking, in the aftermath of the French Revolution and Napoleonic wars, it was in the British interest to see the revival of a stable and friendly Holland while the Dutch needed British goodwill and support to further their recovery. The prospects for this friendship, however, were threatened by the existence of the 200 year-old rivalry of the two powers in the archipelago. At the beginning of this rivalry the Dutch gained the upper hand and the British found themselves all but shut out from the trade of the region. However during the eighteenth century as Dutch power declined British interests began to revive, eventually leading to the foundation of their settlement on Penang island in 1786. The reassertion of British power in Malaysian waters, marked by their occupation of Penang, reflected the emergence of powerful new factors which were during the course of the next century to affect the whole of Island South-East

[a]Refer p. 195.

Asia. One of these was the rapidly growing volume of trade between the West and China. Britain was the principal trader and this trade was the monopoly of the English East India Company.[3] In particular it was the tea trade which was becoming of major importance. During the 1780s the imports of tea to Britain —a Company monopoly—increased fourfold. This in turn led to a growth in the India-China trade too because the Indian trade got round the problem of paying for Chinese goods without using silver. Bengal opium and Coromandel piece-goods found a ready market at Canton, and moreover these goods could also be exchanged in Malaysian countries either for Spanish dollars[4] or for other goods in demand in the Chinese market. Another factor which ultimately was to overshadow everything else was the mounting pressure of the Industrial Revolution already well under way in Britain. Not only was there a demand for Eastern goods; there was also a growing concern for a market in which to dispose of the mass-produced articles of the West. A third factor was strategic, the need for a naval base on the eastern side of the Bay of Bengal in order to preserve British mastery of the seas to protect Coromandel coast during the monsoon seasons. All these things made it very important for the British to find some suitable site for a base in Island South-East Asia which could serve as a point from which to protect the British run to China as well as to safeguard their east coast Indian possessions, and to provide a centre for local trade and a place to repair and refit ships. As it was, the only existing British station at Benkulen on the Sumatran west coast was too far off the normal trade routes and the alternatives were a choice between expensive Dutch-controlled harbours or Malaysian ports like Acheh where the welcome was uncertain and facilities were missing. Before Penang became the final choice, the search for a base had been going on for some time. Attempts were made to set up bases off Cochin-China and on Balambangan off Borneo, and missions were sent to investigate the possibilities of Acheh, Riau, Ujong Salang, the Sunda Straits, the Nicobars and the Andamans, but none proved fruitful.

The foundation of Penang ushered in a new phase in Anglo-Dutch rivalry and between 1786 and 1824 the relations between the two powers in the archipelago came to crisis point. The British were able to take advantage of the French Revolutionary and Napoleonic Wars in Europe to occupy all Dutch possessions in South-East Asia.[6] Although they were restored to Holland in or after 1816, this interval gave the British their opportunity to establish a commercial foothold throughout the region. This was one of the principal concerns of the Dutch on their return. It was a question of the British championing free trade (which they could afford to do) against the Dutch who badly needed protectionist policies to enable their recovery. Accordingly after 1816 considerable friction developed between the Dutch and British authorities in the archipelago as each side jockeyed for the most favourable position for its interests. This friction was considerably enhanced by the activities of Thomas Stamford Raffles, who had a burning hatred for the Dutch and was fired by the idea of founding a latter-day Majapahit under British auspices to replace the Dutch hegemony. In fact, ever since his arrival in Malaysia in 1805, his whole career had been dedicated to this goal. After his efforts to supplant Dutch influence by British on a permanent basis throughout the island world during his governorship in Java had been undone by the restoration of that island to Dutch rule, Raffles now devoted all his energies to an attempt to forestall a resurrection of the

Dutch monopoly system which in his view would not only be bad for British trade but would also have baneful results for the inhabitants of the region. The antidote lay in founding a new centre of British influence and trade in the region which would be situated in the heart of the Dutch monopoly and be able to pierce it. Penang, from this point of view, had proved a failure. The result of all this was the foundation of Singapore which was to become his memorial. Elsewhere Raffles' efforts were frustrated and his schemes for British protectorates in Borneo, Sulu and the Sundas, and anti-Dutch leagues with the princes of Sumatra all came to nought. Such was the South-East Asian background against which the British and Dutch governments, more alive to their metropolitan interests, negotiated and bargained in Europe for over three years, finally producing the Treaty of 1824. The realities of the political situation in Europe produced the settlement; the settlement was of the greatest moment for Island South-East Asia.

The evolution of British and Dutch Policies in Island South-East Asia after 1824
Although the Treaty staked, as it were, the British and Dutch claims in the region, both powers were slow to follow them up. For the next fifty years the British pursued what is usually described as a policy of non-intervention with regard to the Malaysian countries within its sphere of influence. What this meant in practice was that the British authorities in the Straits Settlements[7] avoided as far as possible acquiring more territory, entering into fresh commitments or undertaking new responsibilities in the Peninsula states. However, the Peninsula could not be ignored and intimate contacts between the states and the British colony inevitably developed. Furthermore in 1826 the British felt obliged to delimit the sphere of Thai interest in the Peninsula by signing a treaty in Bangkok (Burney's Treaty). Although this Treaty came about as much through questions of trade and British relations with Burma as for concern about the Straits Settlements and the Peninsula states, it nevertheless became the keystone for checking Thai encroachments and provided the justification of forceful methods to restrain Thai pressure on occasion.[a] In the meanwhile, as the century wore on, the Malay rulers of the Peninsula inevitably turned more and more to the government of the Straits Settlements for help, protection and advice. Whatever the official policy, the realities of British power cast their long shadows over the Peninsula.

This static policy was very unpopular amongst those British subjects, Asian and European, who lived and traded in the Straits Settlements themselves. Firstly, the Company was upbraided for being pro-Thai; then, as the tin-fields were opened and anarchy spread, the interested merchants and chambers of commerce accused the Company of neglecting British interests in the Peninsula as well as the security of the Straits Settlements, while rival colonial powers were establishing themselves in the region. In fact there was some force in this second argument. As the Dutch extended their control over the east coast ports of Sumatra and tightened their hold on the port-states of Borneo and Celebes, Straits trade was affected.[8] The foundation of Hong Kong in 1841 deprived Singapore of its rôle as the chief collecting centre for the China trade, while the activities of the French who started laying the foundations of their Indo-Chinese Empire in the early 1860s reduced the island's area of trade still further.

[a]Refer pp. 272 and 294-5.

British policy, however, remained unchanged until the 1870s. One of the principal reasons for this was the fact that the Straits Settlements (until 1867) were ruled
from Calcutta. As such they were regarded as the outposts of an empire (the British
Indian Empire), not as Raffles would have wished or as the local residents believed,
the centre of a new one. Calcutta's interest and stake in the Straits Settlements
waned still further after 1833 when the Company's monopoly of the China trade
was abolished;[9] with this, from the commercial angle, the Settlements virtually
lost their *raison d'être*, although they still retained their immense strategic value.
This in the end proved to be the most decisive point.

In 1867, as the result of local agitation,[10] the control of the Straits Settlements was
transferred from the India Office to that of the Colonial Office. The significance of
the change and the reason why it was desired were that this gave British subjects in
the Straits Settlements themselves a much greater influence in the evolution of
policy.[11] However the transfer brought about no immediate changes; in fact, the
first governor (Sir Harry Ord) was instructed to adhere rigidly to the old principles
of 'non-intervention'. But the increasing seriousness of the disorders in Selangor
and Perak and their repercussions in Penang, Malacca and Singapore forced the
British authorities to reconsider their position. Ord's successor, Sir Andrew Clarke,
accordingly came armed with instructions to 'report' on what action might be
desirable to settle in the affairs of the Malay states. As we have seen, in the event
Clarke acted first and reported afterwards. Within twelve months of his arrival
British agents had been appointed in the three principal tin states of the Peninsula's
west coast. In so far as Clarke actually exceeded his instructions and precipitated the
new policy, the action of the 'man on the spot' can be said to have been the immediate cause for British intervention in 1874. Local opinion in the Straits Settlements was overwhelmingly behind him and he was able to persuade the Colonial
Office in London to acquiesce. However although it may appear that the 'man on
the spot' had initiated a new policy by presenting London with a *fait accompli*, it is
also clear from the very instructions that he was given that the British government
was already contemplating the action which Clarke put into effect.

Indeed the decision to intervene or the upholding of that decision once intervention had taken place was taken in London by the British Cabinet[12] or by a Cabinet
Minister with the approval of the Cabinet. The evidence points to the fact[13] that
this decision was influenced far more by considerations of imperial strategy than by
the shrill cries of the investors in the Straits Settlements. Throughout the development of British policy towards Island South-East Asia the strategic importance of
the Straits of Malacca had never been lost sight of, nor did the China trade lose its
prime importance. After 1869 when the Suez Canal was opened, shortening and
cheapening the trade route between Europe and the Far East, the rivalry among
the European colonial powers, old and new, in their quest for trade and markets intensified. France, Germany (and America) were all potential threats as far as Britain
was concerned. The French were the most obvious danger, established in South
Vietnam and Cambodia and menacing Thailand. The American and German
threats were more insidious and less visible, not possessing colonies (at the time)
but with their commercial houses in all centres of importance and their enterprising
fortune-hunting nationals everywhere. The Americans had demonstrated an in-

terest in both North Borneo and North Sumatra[a] but it was the Germans who were taken the most seriously. A new and fast rising power, Germany already posed a severe threat to Britain's long-established commercial predominance in Far Eastern markets. German enterprise was well represented in Singapore and German activities in the region had not gone unnoticed.[14] The British were determined that no rival power should be able to take advantage of the breakdown of government in the Malay States in order to secure a foothold in any one of them, thus threatening the life-line to China.

Similar considerations dominated in the development of British policy towards Borneo. The original establishment of British influence on the island by James Brooke had been entirely on his own initiative, and although he was convinced that British power should be promoted there, London for long remained unpersuaded about the advantages. However the acquisition of Labuan as a Crown Colony in 1846 was sanctioned because of its supposed usefulness as a coaling station on the fast-developing China trade route, as well as a handy base from which to check piracy and to keep an eye on Brunai. (In fact, it proved a failure from all these points of view.) The decision taken in the 1880s, by which time British ideas about colonies and their worth had undergone a radical change,[15] to place Sarawak, the British North Borneo's Company's concessions and Brunai itself under British protection was the express outcome of fear of German intentions, as Germany was actively acquiring possessions in East New Guinea and the Pacific at the same period.

In other words, the British forward movement in Island South-East Asia, although prompted by local conditions and circumstances, was a response to much more general considerations which involved Britain's interests and future as a world imperial and trading power.[16]

The same, although on a more limited scale, can be said of the evolution of Dutch policy in Island South-East Asia during the same period. At first, in exploiting their legacy, the Dutch were held up by its vastness which lay quite beyond their resources at the time. For the first couple of decades after 1824 the Dutch were satisfied to organize the financing of their recovery from their tribulations in Europe[17] by concentrating on the exploitation of Java and developing the Culture System,[b] that lifebelt of empire. As for the rest of the islands, the Dutch were content with a holding operation, sufficient to maintain their claims but little more. Their chief concern was to prevent any other colonial power from establishing a foothold in this preserve. Although the Treaty of 1824 with Britain seemed to remove the British threat, it was the activities of free-lance British imperialists and adventurers like James Brooke, Erskine Murray or Wilson that caused them most worry. The presence of James Brooke in Sarawak and his successful intervention into Brunai politics stimulated the launching of the Dutch forward movement in Borneo in the middle of the century by creating a paper administration for the whole island (except Brunai itself) and by the conclusion of hundreds of agreements with Bornean chiefs. Dutch action in Sumatra was precipitated by parallel circumstances—Raffles' intrigues with the Menangkabaus on the west coast, and Wilson's schemes on the east coast.[c]

[a]Refer pp. 179–80; 200, note 79; 228 and 230–1.
[b]See Book II.
[c]Refer pp. 153 and 249–50.

By the third quarter of the nineteenth century changed conditions demanded the launching of a more complete and systematic subjugation of the archipelago. By this time the Dutch had fully recovered from the disasters at the century's beginning and at the same time were faced with increasing pressure from rival colonial powers (other than Britain). Achinese tactics in soliciting support from the French, the Turks, the Italians and the Americans aroused the Dutch to the dangers of their position and provoked their campaign to subdue the state. Fear of similar circumstances arising elsewhere prompted the continuation of the policy once begun. Because of its scope and the sharp resistance often encountered, the completion of the process of stamping Dutch authority throughout the islands took over thirty years. During this phase the Dutch received the approval of the British in their actions, because British interests had less to fear from little Holland as a colonial neighbour than from the presence of a major colonial world power.

In this way the foundations of modern Malaysia and Indonesia were laid.

---

[1]Stretching from Tapanuli in the north to Krui in the south and including *inter alia* Manna, Moko, Priaman and Natal.

[2]The omission of Borneo was intentional. Its inclusion would have raised a whole host of problems which both powers were anxious to avoid at the time. See Tarling, *Anglo-Dutch Rivalry in the Malay World*, Ch. 5.

[3]The English East India Company was originally formed in 1600 by a group of London merchants who obtained a Charter by an Act of the English Parliament granting them the sole right amongst British subjects to trade with India and further East. As the Company's dominions increased, the Charter was amended to include powers of sovereignty and jurisdiction as well. By the nineteenth century the Company in Britain faced the growing opposition of those who wanted to open up Britain's eastern trade to free enterprise.

[4]The Spanish dollar was the generally accepted unit of currency throughout the Far East; based on the gold and silver from Mexico and Peru which was shipped to Manila. 'Dollar' is derived from the Austrian 'Thaler'.

[5]The British found that in order to maintain naval mastery over the Bay of Bengal and the Coromandel coast of India during the adverse season of the north-east monsoon, which made its harbours unusable, they needed a base further eastwards. In particular British experience during the Seven Years War (1756–63) and the American War of Independence (1776–83) when French admirals based on Mauritius either threatened or captured British posts in Madras Presidency drove the point home. However, to what extent naval considerations influenced Calcutta's decisions is a moot point. Although quite clearly the Directors of the East India Company hoped to assure the future of the settlement as a paying proposition by persuading the British Admiralty to establish a base there, the Admiralty was still looking for an alternative site even after the settlement had been founded. Penang proved useful during the Napoleonic Wars for assembling the forces to invade Java but as early as 1807 the Admiralty had decided against making the island a naval base.

[6]Although they occupied strategic centres like Malacca early in the war, the British did not take the decision to occupy Java until Holland itself was formally annexed as part of France by Napoleon in 1810.

[7]Singapore, Malacca and Penang were formed into the administrative unit of the Straits Settlements in 1826, initially as a Presidency subject to the general control of the Governor-General of India, then in 1830 as a Residency under the control of the Governor and Council of Bengal. Singapore became the capital of the Straits Settlements in 1832.

[8]One of the chief sources of Anglo-Dutch friction during this period arose from the tariffs imposed by the Dutch on British textiles and other goods entering Javanese and other Dutch controlled ports.

[9]This was the result of the campaign for throwing open Britain's eastern trade to all British subjects. The Company lost its monopoly over Indian trade when the Charter was renewed in 1813; the Charter of 1833 deprived the Company of its last monopoly and thereafter till its abolition in 1858 it was little more than a holding organization for the administration of British interests in India.

[10]This agitation, conducted amongst the European and Chinese merchant communities in the Settlements, came to a head in 1855 when a public meeting attended by practically every European resident in Singapore, resolved to end the Indian connexion. This led in turn to the Petition of 1857 which listed a whole catalogue of grievances, the most immediate of which were the attempts of the Calcutta authorities to impose port dues in the Settlements and to introduce the Indian rupee as local currency. For a full discussion of the background, see Mills, op.cit.

[11]Through the agency of pressure groups in London representing commercial interests in the Straits Settlements, who were able to lobby and petition British members of parliament and get at the Colonial Office through them with far greater ease than they could reach the Supreme Government in Calcutta. One such pressure group was formed by the Old Singaporeans, composed of British merchants and officials who had lived in Singapore. Amongst these was the distinguished English writer on the archipelago and erstwhile diplomat, John Crawfurd.

[12]An important change in the government of Britain took place in February 1874 when the ruling Liberal Party was ousted in a general election by its rivals, the Tories. The Tory Party, led by Disraeli, was closely identified with imperialism while the Liberals under Gladstone eschewed it. However, Clarke's instructions were issued by the outgoing Liberal Colonial Secretary, Lord Kimberley, and Clarke's actions were confirmed by the new Tory Minister, Lord Carnarvon.

[13]For a full discussion of the British political background, see Cowan, *Nineteenth Century Malaya*, especially Chapter 4; and Parkinson, *British Intervention in Malaya*.

[14]Before 1867 there were only three German firms in Singapore; by 1871 there were ten. In 1870 a Prussian gunboat informed the Singapore authorities of a projected survey of Endau and neighbouring off-shore islands as a site for a future coaling station, but its commander was warned off. In 1871 the 38 states which constitued a loose German Confederation were welded into a united nation by Bismarck. By the end of the century this new power had emerged as Britain's most serious competitor in commerce and was offering an important challenge to British naval hegemony.

[15]For the first half of the nineteenth century liberal opinion held that the acquisition and administration of colonial territories was an unnecessary encumbrance to trade; off-shore islands which could serve as *points d'appui* (such as Penang, Labuan, and Hong Kong) were much preferable. However the proliferation of British trading interests all over the globe, the growing threat provided by rival colonial powers and the increasing complications of local politics encouraged the evolution of a new imperialist philosophy.

[16]However, the last phase of British expansion in the Malay Peninsula (i.e. into Kedah and Perlis, Kelantan and Trengganu) was considerably influenced by the developing prospects of the rubber plantation industry.

[17]In the first place Holland was exhausted and her economy in ruins as the result of the occupation of her homeland by France and of her colonies by the British during the course of the Revolutionary and Napoleonic Wars (1793–1815). At the peace settlement of Vienna which followed Holland was joined to Belgium to form the Kingdom of the Netherlands but in 1830 the Belgians began a separatist revolt which resulted in a war lasting nine years and their eventual breakaway.

10. ISLAND SOUTH-EAST ASIA: THE ADVANCE OF WESTERN IMPERIALISM

	Sumatra	Malaya	Java	Borneo	Great East
1511		Portuguese capture Malacca			
1530–1574					Portuguese domination on Ternate
1578–1663					Portuguese-Spanish presence centred on Tidore
1605					Ambon annexed by the Dutch

	Sumatra	Malaya	Java	Borneo	Great East
1607					Dutch established on Ternate
1619			Foundation of Batavia		
1621					Conquest of the South Moluccas by J.P. Coen
1641		Dutch capture Portuguese Malacca			
1649	Beginning of Dutch influence at Palembang				
1653					Dutch annex East Ceram. West Ceram annexed (1647)
1663	Painan Contract. Beginning of Dutch influence on West Coast				
1667					Tidore accepts Dutch suzerainty
1669					The Bongaya Contract. Dutch annex Macassar
1677			Trunojoyo's rebellion. Dutch acquire Krawang & part of Priangan		
1679			Mataram cedes Semarang and Cheribon. Bantam placed under Dutch protection		
1684	British move to West coast (Benkulen)				
1705			Dutch acquire rest of Priangan and East Madura (First Java War). Dutch acquire all coastal districts		
1741					
1746			Tegal and Pekalongan ceded to the Dutch		
1777			Dutch conquest of Balambangan		
1786		British occupy Penang			
1800		British acquire Province Wellesley			
1811–1816			British occupation of Java		
1819		British occupy Singapore			
1824	Anglo-Dutch Treaty: British and Dutch define spheres of influence in region				
	Dutch take over British possessions in West Sumatra	British take over Malacca			
1825	Dutch control over Palembang established				
1830			Banyumas and other parts of Central Java annexed by Dutch		
1834	Dutch control extended over Jambi and Lampongs.				

	Sumatra	Malaya	Java	Borneo	Great East
1838	End of Padri Wars. Dutch supreme in Menangkabau. Dutch control extended over Indragiri				
1841				Brooke sets up rule in Sarawak	
1844–1850				Kutai and Bornean East coast under Dutch control	
1846				Labuan ceded to Britain	
1853				Brooke acquired Rejang Basin. Dutch control over Sambas & Pontianak	
1856					North Bali under Dutch control
1857	Siak under Dutch control				
1859–1863				Banjarmassin conquered by Dutch	
1861				Brooke acquired Oya and Muka	
1852–1865	Deli, Asahan, etc. under Dutch control				
1871–1907	Achinese War				
1874–1875		Perak, Selangor and Sungai Ujong brought brought under British control			
1878				Dent-Overbeck concession in North Borneo. Brooke acquires Baram	
1888		Pahang brought under British protection		British Protectorate over Brunai, North Borneo and Sarawak	
1905	Jambi interior subdued				
1906					Bali subjugated
1907	Batak lands subjugated				Bugis states subjugated
1909		Kedah, Kelantan, Trengganu and Perlis transferred to Britain			

BOOKS AND ARTICLES FOR FURTHER READING: MALAYSIA, SINGAPORE AND INDONESIA

Books

Bastin, J. and Roolvink R. (ed), *Malayan and Indonesian Studies*, Clarendon Press, Oxford, 1964.

Bastin, J., *Essays on Indonesian and Malaysian History*, Donald Moore, Singapore, 1961.

Bonney, R., *Kedah, 1771-1821: The Search for Security and Independence*, Oxford University Press, Kuala Lumpur, 1971.

Buckley, C.B., *An Anecdotal History of Old Times in Singapore*, reprinted, University of Malaya Press, Kuala Lumpur, 1965.

Clodd, H.P., *Malaya's First British Pioneer*, Luzac, London, 1948.

de la Costa, H., *The Jesuits in the Philippines, 1581-1768*, Harvard University Press, Cambridge, Mass. 1961.

—*Readings in Philippine History*, Bookmark, Manila, 1965.

Cowan, C.D., *Nineteenth Century Malaya*, Oxford University Press, London, 1961.

Emerson, R., *Malaysia*, reprinted, University of Malaya Press, Kuala Lumpur, 1964.

Fisher, C.A., *South-East Asia: A Social, Economic and Political Geography*, Methuen, London, 1964.

Grunder, Carel A. and Livezey, W.E., *The Philippines and the United States*, University of Oklahoma, Norman, 1951.

Hall, D.G.E., *A History of South-East Asia* (3rd edition), Macmillan, London, 1968.

Harrison, B., *South-East Asia: A Short History* (2nd edition), Macmillan, London, 1963.

Irwin, G., *Nineteenth Century Borneo*, Donald Moore, Singapore, 1955.

Khoo Kay Kim, *The Western Malay States, 1850-1873: The Effects of Commercial Development on Malay Politics*, Oxford University Press, Kuala Lumpur, 1972.

Leur, J.C. van., *Indonesian Trade and Society*, Van Hoeve, The Hague, 1955.

Mansoer, M.D. *et al.*, *Sedjarah Minangkabau*, Bhratara, Jakarta, 1970.

Parkinson, C.N., *British Intervention in Malaya, 1867-1877*, University of Malaya Press, Singapore, 1960.

Reid, Anthony, *The Contest for North Sumatra: Acheh, the Netherlands and Britain, 1858-1898*, Oxford University Press, Kuala Lumpur, 1969.

Robequain, C., *Malaya, Indonesia, Borneo and the Philippines*, Longmans Green, London, 1958.

Runciman, S., *The White Rajahs*, Cambridge University Press, Cambridge, 1960.

Sanusi Pane, *Sedjarah Indonesia* (2 vols), PPKPPK, Djakarta, 1955.

Saleeby, N.M., *The History of Sulu*, Bureau of Printing, Manila, 1908.

Schrieke, B., *Indonesian Sociological Studies* (2 vols), Van Hoeve, The Hague, 1955.

Sheppard, M.C.ff., *A Short History of Negri Sembilan*, Donald Moore, Singapore, 1965.

Swettenham, F. W., *British Malaya* (2nd edition), George Allen & Unwin, London, 1948.

Tarling, N., *Anglo-Dutch Rivalry in the Malay World, 1780-1824*, Queensland University Press, 1962.

—*Britain, the Brookes and Brunei*, Oxford University Press, Kuala Lumpur, 1971.

—*Piracy and Politics in the Malay World*, Donald Moore, Singapore, 1963.

—*British Policy in the Malay Peninsula and Archipelago, 1824-71*, reprinted, Oxford University Press, Kuala Lumpur, 1969.

Tregonning, K., *A History of Modern Sabah*, University of Malaya Press, Singapore, 1965.

Winstedt, R.O., *A History of Malaya*, Marican, Singapore, 1962.

Wong Choon San, *A Gallery of Chinese Kapitans*, Dewan Bahasa, Singapore, 1964.

Wurtzburg, C.E., *Raffles of the Eastern Isles*, Hodder & Stoughton, London, 1954.

Zaide, G.F., *Philippine Political and Cultural History* (2 vols), P.E.C., Manila, 1957.

Articles

Allen, J de V., 'The Ancient Regime in Trengganu, 1909–1919', *JMBRAS*, XLI (1), 1968.

—'The Elephant and the Mousedeer—A New Version: Anglo-Kedah Relations, 1905–1915', *JMBRAS*, XLI (1), 1968.

Allen, J. de V., 'Two Imperialists', *JMBRAS*, XXXVII (1), 1964.

Bassett, D.K., 'British Commercial and Strategic Interests in the Malay Peninsula during the late Eighteenth Century', in *Malayan and Indonesian Studies*.

—'The Portuguese in Malaya', *JHSUM* I (3), 1962–3.

Bastin, J., 'Problems of Personality and the Reinterpretation of Modern Malayan History' in *Malayan and Indonesian Studies*.

—'Raffles and British Policy in the Indian Archipelago, 1811–16', *JMBRAS*, XXVII (1), 1947.

Black, I.D., 'The ending of Brunei Rule in Sabah, 1878–1902', *JMBRAS*, XLI (2), 1968.

Bonney, R., 'Francis Light and Penang', *JMBRAS*, XXXVIII (1), 1965.

Cesar Abdul Majid, 'Political and Historical Notes on the Old Sulu Sultanate', *JMBRAS*, XXXVIII (1), 1965.

Chan Su-ming, 'Kelantan and Trengganu', *JMBRAS*, XXXVII (1), 1965.

Chandran, J., 'Private Enterprise and British Policy in the Malay Peninsula', *JMBRAS*, XXXVII (2), 1964.

de la Costa, H., 'Mohammad Alimuddin I, Sultan of Sulu', *JMBRAS*, XXXVIII (1), 1965.

Cowan, C.D., 'Swettenham's Perak Journals', *JMBRAS*, XXIV (4), 1952.

Gammans, L.D., 'The State of Lukut', *JMBRAS*, XII (3), 1924.

Gibson-Hill, C.A., 'Documents relating to John Clunies Ross, Alexander Hare, etc.', *JMBRAS*, XXV (4/5), 1952.

—'Raffles, Acheh and the Order of the Golden Sword', *JMBRAS*, XXIX (1), 1956.

Gullick, J.M., 'Capt. Speedy of Larut', *JMBRAS*, XXVI (3), 1953.

—'Sungai Ujong', *JMBRAS*, XXII (2), 1949.

Hughes-Hallett, H.R., 'A Sketch of the History of Brunei', *JMBRAS*, XVIII (2), 1940.

Khoo Kay Kim, 'J.W.W. Birch: A Victorian Moralist in Perak's Augean Stable?', *JHSUM*, IV, 1965–6.

—'The Origin of British Administration in Malaya', *JMBRAS*, XXXIX (1), 1966.

Leys, Peter 'Observations of the Brunei Political System, 1883–85', *JMBRAS*, XLI (2), 1968.

Linehan, W., 'A History of Pahang', *JMBRAS*, XIV (2), 1934.

Middlebrook, S.M., 'Yap Ah Loy', 1837–1885', *JMBRAS*, XXIV (2), 1951.

Mills, Lennox, 'British Malaya, 1824–67', *JMBRAS*, XXXIII (3), 1960.

Rentse, Anker, 'History of Kelantan', *JMBRAS*, XII, 1934.

Sankaran, R., 'Prelude to the British Forward Movement of 1909', *Peninjau Sejarah*, 1 (2), 1966.

Sheppard, M.C. ff., 'A Short History of Trengganu', *JMBRAS*, XXII (3), 1949.

Sinclair, Keith, 'The British Advance in Johore, 1885–1914', *JMBRAS*, XL (1), 1967.

Skinner, Cyril, 'A Kedah Letter of 1839', in *Malayan and Indonesian Studies.*

—'A Trengganu Leader of 1839', *JSEAH*, V (1), 1964.

—'The Civil War in Kelantan in 1839', *JMBRAS*, Monograph II.

—'Abdullah's Voyage to the East Coast, seen through contemporary eyes', *JMBRAS*, XXXIX (2), 1966.

Stubbs, R.E., 'Two Colonial Office Memoranda on the History of Brunei', *JMBRAS*, XLI (2), 1968.

Tan, Lily, 'A Glimpse into the Brunei Sultanate, 1830–1850', *JHSUM*, V, 1966/7.

Thio, Eunice, 'The Extension of British Control to Pahang', *JMBRAS*, XXX (1), 1957.

—'British Policy towards Johore; from advice to control', *JMBRAS*, XL (1), 1967.

Tregonning, K.G., 'The Mat Salleh Revolt', *JMBRAS*, XXIX (1), 1956.

Turnbull, C.M., 'The Origins of British Control in the Malay States before Colonial Rule' in *Malayan and Indonesian Studies.*

Winstedt, R.O., 'A History of Johore', *JMBRAS*, XII (3), 1934.

—'Notes on the History of Kedah', *JMBRAS*, XIV (3), 1936.

—'A History of Negri Sembilan', *JMBRAS*, XII (2), 1934.

—'A History of Selangor', *JMBRAS*, XIII (3), 1935.

—and Wilkinson, R.J., 'A History of Perak', *JMBRAS*, XII (1), 1934.

Note

JHSUM   Journal of the Historical Society of the University of Malaya, Kuala Lumpur.

JMBRAS   Journal of the Malayan/Malaysian Branch, Royal Asiatic Society, Singapore.

JSEAH   Journal of South-East Asian History, Singapore.

The village of Majajay, Central Luzon

The Philippines

THE Philippines are obviously part and parcel of Island South-East Asia yet have always lived aside from it. Geographically, economically and ethnically, the islands are one with the rest of the archipelago, but historically and culturally they are not. The Filipinos are basically of Malaysian/Indonesian stock, but they are Malaysians who have always lived just beyond the fringe, and have missed the great cultural influences which shaped the lives of their cousins in the other islands. Although there is evidence of contacts with Hindu traders, Hindu-Buddhist civilization never made an impression in the Philippines. Commercial contacts with China date from the dawn of history without carrying with them the impress of Chinese culture. And as Islam advanced from the south, it was stopped in its tracks by the arrival of the Christian Spaniards. As a result, the first really effective cultural influence from outside was brought by the Spaniards from the West, and it is this more than anything else which sets the Filipinos apart from their neighbours in South-East Asia today. From the sixteenth century onwards they became westernized to a degree unknown to any of the other peoples in the region. This was primarily because the culture of the islands had barely got beyond the tribal stage when the Spaniards came on to the scene, and the inhabitants had therefore nothing substantial of their own to fall back on with which to resist the cultural pressure of the West. At the same time, it must also be recognized that Spanish culture, and for that matter Christianity, as they evolved in a Filipino environment, acquired some unique characteristics of their own. One part of the Philippines, nevertheless, escaped the westernizing and Christian influences which engulfed the rest, namely the Muslim south comprising the greater part of Mindanao and the Sulu archipelago. In a cultural sense these regions have much more in common with the peoples of Malaysia and Indonesia than they do with their compatriots, but their historical development has always been oriented towards the north, even if in a rather negative way. The struggle between Manila and the Muslim south is one of the basic themes in Filipino history. The Philippines might be said to have been colonized twice. The first was the Spanish colonization which was contemporaneous with the activities of the Dutch East India Company on Java and in the Indonesian islands but lasted for hundred years longer, and the second was the American colonization which started at the end of the nineteenth century. The first colonization laid the foundations of the modern Philippines. The impact of Spain was far greater than that of Holland because the Spaniards were painting on an empty canvas whereas the Dutch had to make their mark on an intricate backcloth of Hindu and Muslim cultures. The rôle of the Roman Catholic missionaries during the Spanish period was very important as well and was one of the *raisons d'être* for the Spanish presence, whereas the Dutch were preoccupied with the more mundane business of buying and selling. The 300 years of Spanish tutelage made the Filipinos into a nation and gave them the substance to resist the second colonization which took place with the coming of the United States of America. The American conquest of the Philippines had many parallels to the forward movement of the Dutch in Indonesia, the British expansion into Burma and the French campaigns in Vietnam during the latter half of the nineteenth century. They were fighting a nation, and the pattern of events which followed brought the Philippines much closer in line with her neighbours in South-East Asia.

BEFORE THE COMING OF THE WEST

THE Republic of the Philippines was proclaimed in a glittering ceremony before some 300,000 people on the Luneta, Manila, on 4 July 1946, and so became the first state in South-East Asia to achieve its independence from a Western power.

The Republic is a unique creation of colonial rule. Indonesia and Malaysia can be considered as products of the colonial period in that these two nations were fashioned arbitrarily out of peoples of the same basic stock in order to suit the interests of rival imperialist powers. Britain and Holland divided the Malaysian world between them. The Philippines, on the other hand, can be considered the creation of Western imperialism in totally the opposite sense. The people of the Philippines owe their unity, nationality and sense of identity to the moulding influences of Spanish and American colonial rule. One could go so far as to say that until Villalobos gave the islands their name the Philippines did not exist.[1]

This is not to suggest, however, that the Filipinos of today have no cultural identity or heritage of their own, for as we shall see, they have. Living in the same environment and coming very largely from the same basic racial stock, the peoples of the Philippines had evolved a distinctive culture and way of life long before the arrival of the European colonizers; furthermore, this culture has blended with the influences brought by Spain and the United States to give the Philippines Republic its uniqueness amongst South-East Asian states today. At the same time, what made the Philippines different four hundred years ago was the fact that, politically speaking, its peoples had barely evolved beyond the tribal stage. There was no such thing as a Filipino nation.

The physical and racial background
The reasons for this lack of political development prior to Spanish rule are not hard to find. Nature did not fashion the islands to serve as the crucible of a nation. The 115,000 odd square miles that make up the Philippines are broken up into a host of over 7,000 islands, of which, nevertheless, only eleven are of economic interest and size.[2] In addition the inhabitable islands offer limited space for settlement. The largest plain in the Philippines is the Central Plain of Luzon which stretches for about 150 miles northwards from Manila and has an average breadth of 40 miles. Apart from this and the Bacolod Plain on Negros, the interiors of Luzon and of the other islands are cut up by rugged mountains and dense equatorial rain-forest, isolating settlements from one another. As was the case throughout the Malaysian world, the peoples of the Philippines found the best means of communication were by water. Such an environment naturally led to the formation and growth of small, self-sufficient communities, broke up streams of migrants into isolated pools of settlement, and discouraged the evolution of more complex political structures.

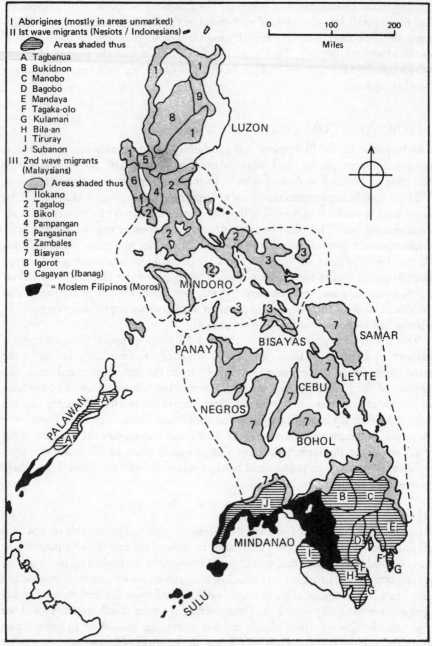

43. Philippines, shewing ethnic groups

These factors also account for the fragmentation of the Filipinos into an estimated 87 major ethnographic groups and as many different languages and dialects.[3] Behind this confusing prolixity of tribe and tongue may be discerned three main racial strains. The earliest, represented by the aborigines, known as Negritos or

Itas, are to be found today in reduced numbers in the mountain fastnesses of Sierra Madre and Zambales in Luzon[4] and in the remote jungles of the Visayas and Mindoro. They probably do not exceed 50,000 at the present time. Five times as numerous but forming a small fraction of the whole population, is the second strain, Nesiot in character but confusingly labelled 'Indonesian'.[5] They seem to represent the first wave of migrants to the Island after the aborigines, settling between 2,000 and 1,000 B.C. Today they are also chiefly settled in the interiors of the islands throughout the archipelago; they are associated with the introduction of farming. The overwhelming majority of modern Filipinos belong to the third strain, who represent the most recent waves of immigrants of basically Mongoloid, Malaysian stock. Out of a total population of about $19\frac{1}{4}$ millions (1948 census), the Malaysian element accounts for some 15 millions. The Malaysian Filipinos themselves may be sub-divided between the pagans who mainly represent the earliest immigrants, the Christians who make up the great majority, and the Muslims who are confined to the south—Mindanao, Palawan and the Sulu archipelago.[6]

The manner of the Malaysian migration was similar to the others into the Philippines and those elsewhere in Island South-East Asia. From around the beginning of the Christian era, in small groups dispersed over a large area during a prolonged period of time, they sailed in and settled down—sometimes by force, sometimes by peaceful means—in the lowlands, bringing about the withdrawal of the older inhabitants into the hills. The story of the ten Bornean Dato's who bought the island of Panay from its Negrito owners neatly symbolizes the whole process.[7] By the middle of the thirteenth century, when this event is supposed to have taken place, the peoples of the islands were to be found in their present homelands.

Filipino 'barangays' and the advent of Islam and Christianity

When the Portuguese and the Spaniards arrived in the Philippines during the course of the next century, the highest political unit they encountered was the Barangay. 'Barangay'[8] was the name applied to a community of people numbering from between thirty to one hundred families, related to one another by blood ties, and living together under the control of one chief. It could be that two or three barangays lived together, forming a village or small town, but in that case the chiefs treated each other as equals and the individual communities each went their own way—combining only in matters of mutual concern such as defence from outside attack. There are only three known examples of barangays which were considerably larger in size—Cebu, Manila and Vigan, and only in Manila did the barangay chief have attributes resembling those of a monarchical ruler. There were also cases of barangay confederations, such as the famous Madya-as Confederation of Panay,[9] and it is possible that under the influence of spreading Islam during the first half of the sixteenth century a trend to larger political units was developing. However, as far as most of the inhabitants of the Philippines were concerned they lived in scattered settlements or barangays under the rule of petty, independent chiefs.

According to tradition, an Arab missionary made his first converts in Sulu in 1380.[a] This event marks the arrival of Islam in the Philippines and the introduction

[a]Refer p. 216, note 3.

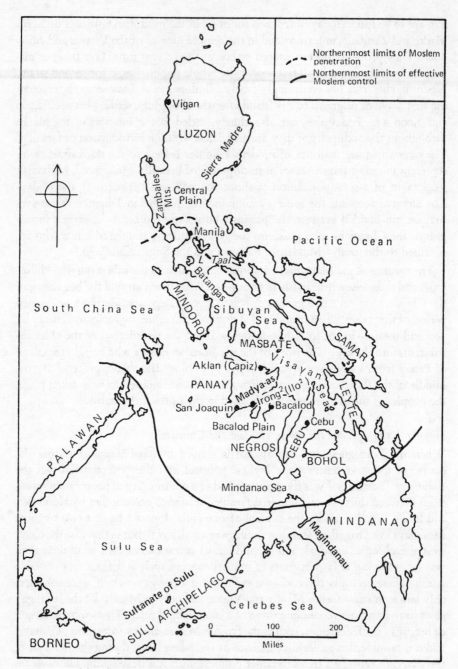

44. Philippines before the coming of the Spaniards

Legend on map:
- - - Northernmost limits of Moslem penetration
——— Northernmost limits of effective Moslem control

of a new element into the society and culture of the Islands. Islam was to prove to be a great unifying force which triumphed by virtue of new weapons, and a superior social organization wedded to a simple but effective creed.[10] It brought about the creation of the Sultanate of Sulu in the middle of the fifteenth century and the establishment of a second Muslim power in Mindanao, the Magindanau confederacy, on the eve of the sixteenth century. Meanwhile Islam continued to spread northwards and by the time the first Europeans arrived, petty Muslim states had already been established on Cebu, in Central Luzon around Manila Bay, and elsewhere. The advent of the Spaniards signified the introduction of a second but rival unifying force into the Philippines, because they came as the evangelizers of Christianity. The Spaniards arrived just in time to prevent the Muslim proselytization of Luzon and the northern islands but too late to dislodge the hold of Islam in the south. The result was that the Philippines we know today was moulded and unified by Spanish Christianity, while Mindanao, Sulu and Palawan ceased to form part of Philippine history until the American conquest at the beginning of the present century.[11]

[1]The Philippines were given their name in honour of King Philip II of Spain by Ruy Lopez de Villalobos, leader of the fourth Spanish expedition to the islands. Originally he gave the name to only one particular island (Leyte or Samar) where he had received good treatment; then the term came to be used for the whole archipelago. Magellan had called the Philippines the archipelago of St. Lazarus on his arrival in 1521.
[2]Namely Luzon and Mindanao which between them comprise 67 per cent of the total area; Samar, Negros, Palawan, Panay, Mindoro, Leyte, Cebu, Bohol and Masbate. About 880 islands in the archipelago are inhabited.
[3]However, the language picture can be simplified in general terms as follows: Tagalog—7 million; Bisayan tongues—8.5 million. Tagalog is the official national language and the most widely spoken; English (those speaking—7 million) is also widely used. On Luzon there are six main languages, viz. Tagalog, Ilocano, Bicol, Pangasinan, Pampangan, Ibanag (Cagayan); in the Bisayas there are three, viz. Samareno (Samar-Leyte), Hiligaynon (Panay and East Negros), and Cebuano.
[4]Ita—Tagalog term for 'people of the hills'. They are also found on Mindanao.
[5]Included in this group are the Kalinga, Gaddang and Apayao of north Luzon; the pagans of Mindoro and the Bisayas; the Tagbanua of Palawan; the Bukidnon, Manobo, Bagobo, Mandaya, Isamal, Tagaka-olo, Kulaman, Bila-an, Tiruray, Subanon and Bajau of Mindanao.
[6]The pagans include Bontok, Ifugao (collectively known as Igorot or 'mountain people') and Tinggian of north Luzon; the Christian Filipinos are chiefly divided between the Tagalog ('river men'), Bisayan, Ilocano, Bicol, Cagayan, Pampangan, Pangasinan and Zambales.
[7]According to tradition the ten dato's led by Dato Puteh landed at San Joaquin on Panay with their families, retainers etc. to escape the tyranny of Sultan Makatunaw, ruler of Brunai. Subsequently they negotiated with the negrito rulers of the island, King Marikudo and Queen Maniwangtiwan, at their village of Sinugbuhan on the Andona river who traded the lowlands of Panay for a gold saduk (wide-brimmed hat) and a long gold necklace. Seven dato's stayed to settle in Panay; the other three travelled to Lake Taal and settled in Batangas. Dato' Puteh eventually returned to Borneo.
[8]The term 'barangay' derives from the name of the sailing vessels in which the Malaysian migrants arrived. These vessels could carry from 30 to 100 families.
[9]The Madya-as Confederation consisted of the three main districts of Hantik (Antique), Aklan (Capiz) and Irong-irong (Iloilo), and was under the lordship of Dato' Sumakwel at the time of the Spanish advent. It possessed its own code of written law.
[10]The Malaysian immigrants who brought the religion never came in sufficient numbers to enable its spread by any other means.
[11]That is, viewing the Philippines in terms of the political entity forged by the Spaniards from their headquarters in Manila.

THE SPANISH CONQUEST

The Spanish conquest of the Philippines got under way properly speaking in 1565 when an expedition led by Miguel Lopez de Legazpi landed in the Visayas and eventually set up its headquarters on the island of Cebu. From this centre Spanish authority spread out over the neighbouring islands. In 1571 Legazpi captured Manila which from then onwards was the capital of the Spanish Philippines. By the end of the century the greater part of the inhabitable islands (apart from the Muslim south) was under at least the nominal control of the King of Spain.

Legazpi was by no means the first European or even the first Spaniard to come to the shores of the Philippines. The first known European to do so was the Portuguese sailor, Francisco Serrano (Serrao) who was shipwrecked on Mindanao in 1512.[1] The next visitor was Ferdinand Magellan who arrived by design and not accident in the Visayas in March 1521, authorized by Charles I of Spain to find the Pacific route to the Moluccas and empowered to annex any new lands discovered.[2] He arrived with three ships after an epic crossing of the Pacific Ocean which was accomplished with great hardship after a voyage of three months and twenty days. After having made the first of many Spanish-Filipino blood-pacts[3] with the chief of the little island of Limasawa, just south of Leyte and having declared that island a Spanish possession in front of a small group of incredulous inhabitants, he sailed on to Cebu with the guidance of the Limasawa chief. On Cebu he met Humabon who was probably one of the most powerful chiefs in all the islands at that time. Humabon demanded tribute but on being advised by a visiting Thai trader about the efficacy of European firearms, he dropped this demand and entered into a blood-compact with his guest instead. Within a week relations between the Cebuans of Humabon and the Spaniards had become so good that the Filipinos (800 of them, including Humabon himself) embraced Christianity. Then Magellan overplayed his hand. He tried to boost the Spanish position by attempting to secure the recognition of Humabon as overlord of all the neighbouring tribes, together with an attempt to win new converts for Christianity at the same time. Several chiefs indeed submitted but Lapulapu, ruler of Mactan, the island opposite Cebu, refused all advances. Magellan then took sides in a quarrel between Lapulapu and another Mactan chief, giving his support to Lapulapu's opponent. In the battle which followed,[4] the Spaniards were defeated and Magellan himself was killed. The Cebuans then seized this opportunity to get rid of their unwelcome guests and attempted to massacre them at a feast. The survivors fled Cebu and the Philippines. They made their way to Brunai, and from there to the Moluccas, and one of the surviving vessels, the *Victoria*, sailed westwards to complete the first circumnavigation of the globe by man.[5] However, from the immediately practical point of view in the Philippines, Magellan's expedition had been a failure.

Between 1521 and Legazpi's expedition, there were four more attempts by Spain to found a colony in the Philippines. In 1525 King Charles I put Juan Garcia Jofre de Loaisa in charge of an expedition consisting of seven ships and 450 men to follow up the exploits of Magellan. From the time it crossed the Atlantic it met with repeated disaster and achieved nothing.[6] Another expedition led by Sebastian Cabot[7] sailed from Seville in 1526 but never got beyond the River Plate in South America. A third expedition fitted out in Mexico in 1527 and put under the command of Alvaro de Saavreda, who had orders to investigate the fate of the previous two and carried a letter of apology to the chief of Cebu, failed to reach its destination in the Philippines and ended up in the hands of the Portuguese. In 1543 an expedition under Ruy Lopez de Villalobos succeeded in reaching the Philippines. Villalobos

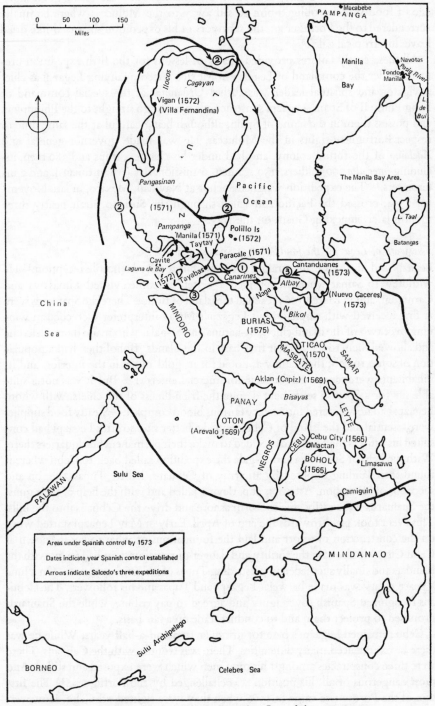

45. Philippines, illustrating the Spanish conquest

had orders to found a colony and spread Christianity, but local hostility and shortage of food supplies obliged him to sail away to the Moluccas where he finally
surrendered to the Portuguese; 'the survivors of his expedition dispersed like dried
leaves in a tropical gale'.[8]

All these costly failures provided plenty of lessons for the fifth expedition prepared under the command of Legazpi in Mexico. Accompanying Legazpi as chief
navigator and spiritual leader was Father Urdaneta[9] at the special command of
King Philip II of Spain. Legazpi's instructions were to go straight to the Philippines
and possess them in the name of Spain, although being careful at the same time to
respect Portuguese rights in the Moluccas. He was made governor-general and
Adelanto of the future colony, and had under his charge 4 ships and 380 men, including *inter alia* 200 soldiers, 150 seamen, 6 missionaries (Augustinians), and 2 interpreters.[10] The expedition weighed anchor at Navidad, Mexico, in late November 1564, crossed the Pacific and sailed through the Surigao Strait nearly three
months later, annexing Guam on the way.

The work of Legazpi; the foundation of Spanish power

Legazpi and his ships made straight for Cebu but received a hostile reception.[11] He
withdrew to Samar where he received a better welcome, visited Limasawa and
Camiguin, and in March 1565 reached the island of Bohol. There the Spaniards were
at first received with suspicion but Legazpi's Malay interpreter succeeded in winning over two of the island chiefs, Si-katuna and Si-gala, who made them welcome
and allowed them to set up their first base in the islands. Bohol then had a population of some 10,000; the island was noted for its gold mines in the interior, and its
inhabitants were renowned for their commercial enterprise. But it was not a suitable site for a Spanish settlement despite the friendliness of the chiefs, with whom
Legazpi had now entered into a very famous blood compact.[12] Steady food supplies
were essential and the island of Cebu seemed a better site, so after Legazpi had consulted his officers the Spaniards decided to make their permanent headquarters there.
With the help of Si-katuna and Si-gala the expedition sailed back to Cebu where it
found their landing opposed by an army of Cebuans, led by Tupas, the son and
successor of Humabon. Attempts at parleying failed and with the help of their guns,
the Spaniards were easily able to storm ashore and drive the Cebuans into the hills.
This event took place towards the end of April. Early in May Legazpi started work
on the construction of a fort and laid the foundations of what today is known as
Cebu City. He also saw the futility and danger of remaining on bad terms with the
islanders and finally succeeded in persuading Tupas of his good intentions. On 4 June
a peace treaty was made between Legazpi and Tupas and his followers. The Cebuans recognized Spanish sovereignty and agreed to pay tribute, while the Spaniards
promised to protect them and to conduct trade on a fair basis.

Cebu remained Legazpi's base for just over two-and-a-half years. While he was
there he experienced many difficulties. There was trouble with the Cebuans. There
were three conspiracies amongst his own men which were exposed and stifled. And
most dangerous of all, his position was challenged by the Portuguese.[13] The first
sign of the Portuguese came in 1566 when they were sighted off Cebu. However,
nothing further happened until the following year when an ultimatum arrived in
July from the Portuguese governor of the Moluccas, reminding the Spaniards that

they had no right to be there. This was followed up by another reminder in September. Just over a year later, on 30 September 1568, the attack itself came. A fleet of nine big ships under the command of Gonzalo de Pereira, the governor in person, supported by numerous Moluccas war perahu, appeared off Cebu. But the bombardment which followed was ineffective, attempts to land were repulsed, and a three-month blockade ended in the new year because of sickness amongst the Portuguese crews.

Had the Portuguese attack succeeded, there might never have been a Spanish Philippines. This experience and the constant difficulty of obtaining food supplies convinced Legazpi that he should move his headquarters further north. Accordingly, early in 1569, leaving a garrison behind at Cebu, Legazpi and the main party sailed to Panay and formed a new settlement there.[14] But Panay was merely a halting place on the way to a far more attractive goal still further to the north—Manila. Manila was already the most important centre in the Philippines, easily defensible, with a good harbour on sheltered Manila Bay and adjacent to the rich rice-growing plain of Central Luzon. Its ruler was Raja Sulaiman and its people were new converts to Islam. Across the river Pasig at Tondo was the court of Raja Matanda, (Raja Lakan-dula)—the 'old king', and uncle of Sulaiman. What the relationship was between these two has never been clearly established.[15] Raja Sulaiman, who was also a son-in-law of the Sultan of Brunai, appears to have been the acknowledged overlord of a number of barangays around Manila, and it is clear that with the adoption of Islam a new concept of kingship was emerging.

In May 1570 Legazpi sent an expedition under his Master-of-Camp, Martin de Goiti, and another of his lieutenants, Juan de Salcedo, to investigate things at Manila and if possible to bring it under subjection. The Manila princes received Goiti well, concluded a pact of friendship and consummated the traditional blood compact. But their attitude changed when they discovered Goiti required their submission and their tribute. An unpremeditated incident[16] led to fighting, and after a fierce battle Sulaiman and his forces fled from the scene leaving behind a hundred dead, eighty prisoners, several artillery pieces, gold and other booty. Then Goiti withdrew for the Spaniards were not prepared to hold the town, the typhoon season was near and Raja Sulaiman might counter-attack. The expedition returned to Panay where the reports of what had occurred and of the situation there decided Legazpi to make Manila his capital the following year. So in May 1571 a second expedition, this time under Legazpi himself, anchored off Manila. It consisted of 27 vessels, 280 Spaniards and several hundred Bisayan auxiliaries. Off Cavite the expedition was met by Raja Matanda who was submissive. But Raja Sulaiman spurned all approaches[17] and as they advanced, he retreated across the Pasig river, leaving Manila in flames and the landing of the Spaniards unopposed. Legazpi landed and took possession of Manila on 19 May. A fortnight later Raja Sulaiman launched a counter-attack by land and sea. At Navotas, near Manila, he had gathered his forces, supplemented by those of the Dato's of Hagonoy and Macabele and by the barangays of Pampanga. At sea, Raja Sulaiman led a force down the northern shores of the Bay of Manila which met and clashed with the Spanish flotilla under Goiti in the Bankusay Channel. In the ensuing action, Sulaiman and 300 of his warriors were killed; a number of his relations were taken prisoner. This battle of 3 June marked the end of the struggle for Manila; it was now securely in Spanish hands.

On 24 June 1571, Legazpi established a city government and proclaimed Manila to be the capital of the Spanish Philippines.

During the space of the next two years, the Spaniards succeeded in making themselves the masters of most of the accessible parts of Luzon. This was largely the work of one man, Juan de Salcedo, aided at the beginning by Martin de Goiti.[18] Goiti's contribution was with the support of Raja Matanda to reduce the chiefs of Central Luzon during the course of 1571. Most of this was accomplished by diplomacy rather than by arms,[19] and the Spaniards referred officially to the 'pacification' rather than the conquest of the country. Nevertheless, the 'pacification' tended to become a somewhat forceful affair, leaving the peasants of the countryside with little choice between accepting Spanish authority and paying tribute on the spot on the one hand, and losing their crops and their property and quite probably their lives on the other. Salcedo went further afield. In August 1571 this young commander left Manila with a force of 200 men (half of whom were Spaniards and the rest local auxiliaries) and one Augustinian missionary, and moved inland towards Laguna de Bay. The chieftaincies of Cainta and Taytay were overcome, the lands of modern Laguna province penetrated and the gold mines of Paracale in Camarines Norte discovered. By the end of this expedition, Salcedo had added over 24,000 subjects to the kingdom of Spain. In the next year, with 45 Spanish soldiers Salcedo made an expedition of conquest and discovery to the north. Capturing several piratical vessels on the way, Salcedo subdued the barangays of Ilocos and founded the town of Villa Fernandina (Vigan), rounded the north of Luzon, exploring the coast and estuary of Cagayan, and returned by way of the Polillo Islands and Tayabas to Manila. In 1573 Salcedo undertook a third expedition, this time accompanied by 120 Spanish soldiers. His objective was Bicolandia which was successfully 'pacified', with a town and garrison of 80 established at Libon in Albay under the command of Capt. Pedro de Chavez.[20] This became the nucleus of Spanish power in this region. Salcedo also brought the island of Catanduanes under his control during this campaign. In the meantime, in Manila on 20 August 1572, Legazpi himself had died of heart failure at the age of sixty-seven.

With the death of Legazpi and the conclusion of the campaigns of Salcedo, the first stage of the Spanish conquest and of the creation of the nation of the Philippines was completed. There were now four main Spanish settlements in the islands apart from their headquarters in Manila. These were at Cebu and Panay in the Visayas, in Bicolandia at Nueva Caceres (Naga) and Villa Fernandina (Vigan) in the north. A population of over half a million islanders—Tagalog, Bicols, Ilocos, Pampangans, Pangasinans, Bisayans, but not yet Filipinos—had been brought under Spanish rule. But large areas were still left unsubjected, particularly in the wild, mountainous regions of northern Luzon and in the south where Mindanao, Palawan, and the Sulu archipelago remained under the firm grasp of Muslim principalities.

The rôle of the Christian missionaries

All this had been accomplished with barely more than 300 Spanish soldiers, although they had enjoyed the support of much larger numbers of locally-raised auxiliaries. Clearly whatever their martial qualities might have been, the Spaniards did not succeed in establishing their dominion by virtue of the prowess of this small

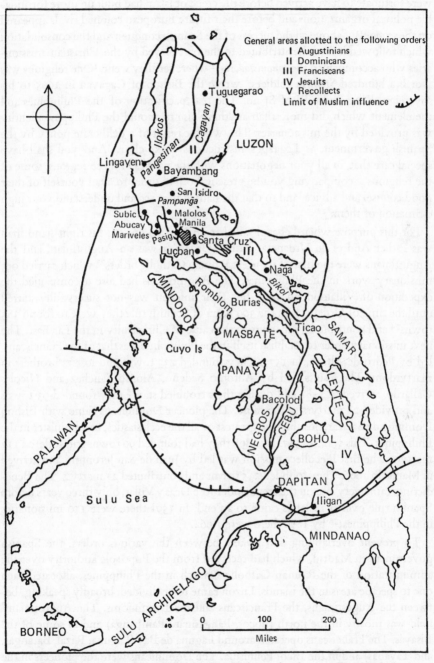

General areas allotted to the following orders
I Augustinians
II Dominicans
III Franciscans
IV Jesuits
V Recollects
Limit of Muslim influence

LUZON
Tuguegarao
Ilokos
Cagayan
Lingayen
Pangasinan
Bayambang
San Isidro
Pampanga
Malolos
Subic
Abucay
Manila
Mariveles
Pasig
Santa Cruz
Lucban
Naga
Bikol
MINDORO
Romblon
Burias
Masbate
Cuyo Is
Ticao
SAMAR
LEYTE
PANAY
Bacolod
NEGROS
CEBU
BOHOL
PALAWAN
Sulu Sea
DAPITAN
Iligan
MINDANAO
SULU ARCHIPELAGO
BORNEO

0   100   200
Miles

46. The role of the Christian missionaries in the Philippines

band of warriors alone. They were aided by the fact that the inhabitants of the islands could not offer anything more than small-scale, localized resistance. They were fortunate to have arrived before the creed of Islam had built up more formidable political organizations and before their future European colonial rivals appeared on the scene. But above all the success of the Spanish conquest and the consolidation which followed it must be attributed to the part played by the Christian missionaries who accompanied the *conquistadores*[21] wherever they went. 'One religious was worth a hundred Spanish soldiers,' wrote the Bishop of Cagayan in 1605 to his sovereign, King Philip III of Spain. The real pacification of the Philippines and the element which did more than anything else to mould the Philippine identity was provided by the missionaries. This was the result of a deliberate policy by the Spanish government, as Legazpi's instructions make clear. 'And you shall have special care that, in all your negotiations with the natives in those regions, some of the religious accompanying you be present, both in order to avail yourself of their good counsel and advice, and so that the natives may see and understand your high estimation of them.'[22]

For this purpose when Legazpi sailed from Mexico in 1564 his right-hand man was Father Andres de Urdaneta. Father Urdaneta was an Augustinian, and the Augustinians were the first of six great Roman Catholic orders[23] which carried out missionary work in the Philippines. The Augustinians had also accompanied the expedition of Villalobos in 1543 but their mission was not successfully started until the time of Urdaneta. In the 300 years of Spanish rule they were to found 385 towns[24] and contribute 57 martyrs to the cause of Christianity in the Far East. The next missionary order to establish itself in the Philippines was that of the Franciscans, led by Pedro de Alfaro, in 1577. They founded 233 towns and lost 72 brothers in martyrdom. The Jesuits, led by Antonio Sedeño, Alonso Sanchez and Nicolas Gallardo, arrived in 1581 and during their troubled stay[25] they founded 93 towns and provided 28 martyrs to the cause. The pioneer Dominicans came with Bishop Domingo de Salazar, possibly the greatest of all the ecclesiastics, to administer in the Philippines. This was in 1587. By 1898 they had founded 90 towns and suffered 112 martyrs. The first Recollect mission was led by Juan de San Jeronimo and arrived in Manila in 1606. They founded 235 towns and contributed 24 martyrs. The Benedictines came very late on the scene under Josè Deas y Villar, only three years before Spanish rule over the islands came to an end. In 1591 there were 140 missionaries in the Philippines;[26] by 1876 there were 1,962.

To prevent overlapping and rivalry between the various orders, the Spanish government in Madrid, which had received from the Pope sole authority over the administration of the Roman Catholic Church in the Philippines, allocated each one to specific areas in the islands. Luzon came to be divided, broadly speaking, between the Augustinians, the Franciscans and the Dominicans. The Augustinians' field was mostly in the north (Ilocos, Pangasinan, Pampanga) and in some of the Bisayas. The Franciscans operated around Laguna de Bay (Laguna, Rizal, Batangas, and Tayabas) and in the Bicol Peninsula. The Dominicans were the pioneers in the Cagayan valley and the surrounding region and concentrated their main effort there. They were also active in parts of Pangasinan. The Jesuits and Recollects shared between them the rest of the Bisayas and Mindanao.[27] These allocations were not immutable. In 1607, for example, the Augustinians gave place to the Recollects in Bataan and Zambales. On the banishment of the Jesuits from the Philippines in 1768, the Recollects took over their stations in Mindanao.

The first task and achievement of the missionaries was to spread Christianity and to convert the islanders. In this they were strikingly successful and by the end of Spanish rule there were over six million Roman Catholic Filipinos, and the Philippines had become the only Christian nation in Asia. Christianity was the cement that made the Filipinos into a nation, although it should be understood that it did not make them into little Spaniards. The practice of Christianity in the Philippines blended with deeper-laid Filipino beliefs to give the religion local characteristics of its own.[28] In order to proselytize, the missionaries had to leave the centres of Spanish power and go out and live amongst the people. While the few thousand Spanish colonists who lived by trade were found concentrated in and around Manila, the missionaries and a handful of Spanish officials lived in isolated outposts all round the islands. To make Christians out of the islanders also meant to change their social and economic way of life. The object was to resettle the scattered, shifting Filipino farmer in a compact village, dominated by the church, where he could be instructed in the articles of the new faith, acquire a rudimentary education and learn new skills. Although the amount of social and economic development was strictly limited, this programme was carried out with far-reaching results. Out of the centres founded by the missionaries grew most of the modern towns of the Philippines today. Malolos, Lingayen, San Isidro (Pampanga) were amongst the many towns founded by the Augustinians; Santa Cruz (Laguna), Lucban and Naga by the Franciscans; Dapitan and Iligan by the Jesuits; Abucay, Bayambang, Tuguegarao by the Dominicans; Mariveles, Subic, Bacolod by the Recollects—to list but a few. The missionaries were also the builders of roads, bridges, irrigation canals and dams and other public works.[a] They introduced new plants from Mexico and Europe[29] as well as new industries. They provided for social welfare by running orphanages and hospitals and were the only source of education, which went, however, up to university level. Through the missionaries, Spanish became the *lingua franca* of the archipelago.

The result of all this was that by the nineteenth century, the population of the Philippines had advanced from being a motley collection of communities lacking any political coherence to a state of being 'more civilized, more independent, and richer than any other European colony in Asia, and even in the whole Orient'.[30] Whether that observation may be considered wholly accurate or not, the fact remains that the Christian missionaries had welded the peoples of the islands into a nation.

The frontiers of the Spanish Philippines

However, the conquest of the islands was not complete in 1575 and it can be argued that it was not finally completed until the nineteenth century.[31] There were two fronts; in the north it was against the inhabitants of the mountain province of north-west Luzon, and in the south it was against the Moros,[32] the Spanish term for the Muslims of Mindanao and the Sulu archipelago. Between the two lay the heartland of Spanish power, centred on the great plain of Luzon and extending

[a]See Book II.

northwards up to Pangasinan and Ilocos and south through the Bicol Peninsula to the Bisayas. In fact, except for Central Luzon itself, this wide area was loosely held, and one important factor which contributed to the Spanish success in maintaining their authority over its inhabitants lay in their rôle of protectors against the raids and ravages of both the mountain peoples on the lowlands of Luzon and the Moros on the island coasts of the Bisayas.

Until the middle of the nineteenth century the Spaniards did not succeed in bringing the frontier regions under their control. In the north, spurred by dreams of gold and by the need to curb the head-hunting raids on the lowland farmers, the Manila government for over a century tried to reduce the region by means of military expeditions, but they all failed[33] in the face of the uncompromising hostility they encountered and the demands made on Spanish resources by the threats which came from other directions, especially those posed by the Moros and the Dutch.[a] Under the governorship of Manuel de Leon (1669-77), some kind of solution was found by creating a buffer zone between the mountainous country and the lowlands. In this zone the inhabitants were exempted from tribute and the missions established there were protected by small garrisons.[34] This system worked fairly satisfactorily until the nineteenth century when improvements in communications and the abandonment of all attempts at proselytization created conditions where the subjection of the mountain peoples became more practicable.

The struggle with the Muslim south

In the south, the struggle with the Moros was tougher, more bitter and more prolonged.[b] There were two main centres of Moro power, one set in the mountain island girdle of the Sulu archipelago with its headquarters on the island of Jolo, and the other called Magindanau situated on the great marshy plain of the Pulangi river.[35] This conflict between the Spaniards and the Muslims of the south was not brought about by political or economic factors alone. It was also a war of faiths, for the Spaniards, as we have seen, came not merely to trade but also to convert, and the Muslims were their traditional enemies.[c] The first skirmishes in what developed into a protracted war of three centuries took place during the time of Legazpi.[36] The first real declaration of war might be said to have come in 1578 when Esteban Rodriguez de Figueroa appeared with a Spanish squadron before Jolo and conquered it. Sultan Pangiran signed a treaty of vassalage which he tore up as soon as the Spaniards sailed away. An expedition sent by Figueroa the following year to crush the chiefs of Magindanau, however, was a failure. These two episodes were the start of the see-saw struggle. Spanish expeditions against the Muslim strongholds were answered by devastating raids along the unprotected and unprotectable shores of northern Mindanao, the Bisayas and even Luzon. Between 1578 and 1876 the Spaniards mounted sixteen major assaults on Jolo alone but only on three occasions did they succeed in occupying the city.[37] At the same time nearly as many expeditions were launched against Magindanau but all attempts to establish a settlement there were failures until the close of the nineteenth century.

[a]See p. 350.
[b]Refer pp. 204 et seq.
[c]Refer p. 16.

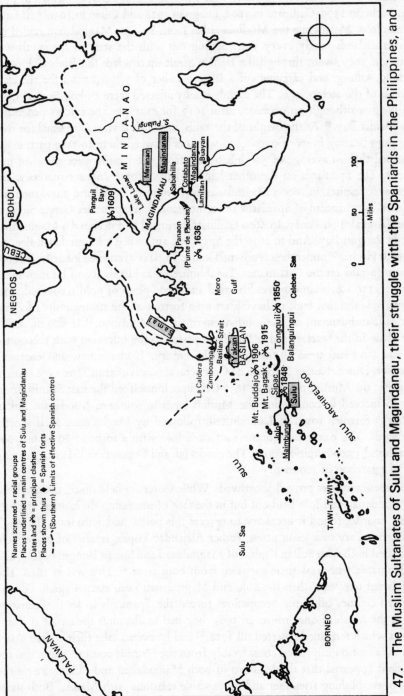

47. The Muslim Sultanates of Sulu and Magindanau, their struggle with the Spaniards in the Philippines, and the American conquest

For the first fifty years the advantage seemed to lay with the Moros. Figueroa was killed during a second abortive expedition to subjugate Magindanau in 1596. Juan Pacho in 1599, Gallinato in 1602, Luego in 1628 and Olaso in 1630[38] all failed to take Jolo. Meanwhile the Muslims either from Sulu or Magindanau raided the southern islands nearly every year. Setting out with the start of the south-west monsoon, they swept through the Basilan Strait up towards the Bisayas, looting, burning, killing, and carrying off a large number of unfortunates for the slave markets of the archipelago. The islands chiefly affected were Bohol, Samar, Leyte and Negros although on occasion, as in 1617 for example, the raiders penetrated into Manila Bay.[39] At the height of the raids, in which it was quite usual for over fifty ships bearing hosts of over 2,000 warriors between them to take part, it was reckoned that an average of 500 inhabitants from the islands were snatched into slavery. The Spaniards on the other hand did have some counter-successes, and there were respites. In 1600 a Magindanau force of some 60 sail and 3,000 men was repulsed by a handful of Spaniards and a thousand Bisayans under Garcia Sierra at Oton (Arevalo) on Panay. In 1609 Gallinato surprised and defeated a Magindanau fleet in Panguil Bay. And in 1636 the Spaniards ambushed a Magindanau fleet off Punte de Flechas[40] under their renowned leader Tagal as it returned loaded with booty from a raid on the Calamianes. Tagal himself was killed, 300 of his men made prisoner, 120 Christian captives liberated and 6,000 pesos of gold recovered. This victory was the first fruit of having set up a fortress at the strategic site of Zamboanga (Sambuangan) on the south-western tip of Mindanao.[41] It also marked a new phase in the warfare as the Spaniards passed to the offensive with success for the first (and last) time till the nineteenth century. Under a new and energetic governor, Don Sebastian Hurtado de Corcuera, successive campaigns were launched against the Muslim powers. In 1637 Corcuera himself led the first Spanish force ever to succeed in conquering the Muslim bases in southern Mindanao. Sultan Kudrat's[a] fortified town of Lamitan fell, followed by Magindanau itself shortly afterwards. The next year Corcuera attacked Jolo with a force of 80 vessels, 600 Spanish and 3,000 Filipino troops. The citadel fell and Corcuera sailed away, leaving behind a garrison of 400 men.

But these victories proved shortlived. While Corcuera held office, the garrisons in Magindanau and Jolo held out but in the face of increasing difficulties. His successor, Fajardo, found it necessary to reverse this policy and withdraw. Through the intermediary of a Jesuit priest, Father Alejandro Lopez, treaties of peace were negotiated both with Sultan Kudrat of Magindanau and Sultan Bongsu of Jolo, and the Spaniards withdrew their garrisons from both areas.[42] This was in 1646. The truce lasted ten years, then the Sulu and Magindanau raids started again. For the next half century other pre-occupations forced the Spaniards to let the initiative pass to the Muslims once more. In 1663 they had to abandon their post at Zamboanga which remained deserted till 1718,[43] and let events take their course. After 1718 the situation improved considerably from the Spanish point of view, and for a while it appeared that the Muslims of both Magindanau and Sulu were on the point of establishing friendlier and more stable relations with Manila. Both states

[a]Refer p. 206.

had evolved into clearly-defined monarchies under rulers who seemed interested in reform and in advances in knowledge. A treaty was signed between Sulu and Manila in 1725. A more effective one came into being in 1737 which some years later was also subscribed to by the Sultan of Magindanau. In 1747 both rulers went so far as to grant permission for Christian missionaries to establish themselves in their domains. The ruler of Sulu, Sultan Alimuddin I even came to Manila in 1749 and became a convert to Christianity.[a] But these tendencies aroused strong opposition at home and by the time the British occupied Manila (1762-4), the situation had reverted to one of the normal hostility.

The subjugation of the South

For the remainder of the eighteenth century the old pattern reasserted itself, although the Muslim raids increased in daring and intensity. They were no longer confined to the Bisayas and southern Luzon but regularly reached to the north and often penetrated Manila Bay, while from time to time groups of raiders set up bases on the island of Mindoro.[44] The losses incurred were tremendous and the cost of counter-measures excessive; between 1778 and 1793 alone the Manila government expended over 1.5 million pesos in largely fruitless attempts to defeat the Muslim menace. These activities continued during the first decades of the nineteenth century. Typical was the kidnapping in 1823 of the Provincial of the Recollects[45] together with the friar accompanying him on a tour of the islands by the Sulus; their release was secured only after a ransom of 10,000 pesos had been paid by the Order. Retaliatory raids had no lasting effects. Subsequent efforts to reorganize the naval bureau in Manila carried out by Pascual Enrile and the creation of a fleet of cruisers especially to deal with the marauders helped to contain later raids. In 1836 Governor Salazar ordered a ban on the sale of firearms and ammunition to countries 'hostile to Spain' and the following year succeeded in negotiating a commercial treaty with the Sultan of Sulu, hoping thereby to win him over to more peaceful ways. But Spanish tactics changed once more under Camba, his successor, who declared that the signing of such treaties was 'of no use in bringing any permanent or substantial advantage to Spanish navigation and commerce'.

In fact all Spanish efforts against the Moros were to remain ineffectual until the technical innovations of the nineteenth century came to their rescue. In 1843 the Spanish government purchased four steam gunboats from Britain. This spelt the doom of the Muslim sultanates in the south. Alarmed by the increasing activity of other colonial powers,[b][46] Governor Narciso Claveria sent his new steamships to destroy the fortifications of Balanguingui in 1848, bombarding and capturing Sipac, the main Balanini stronghold on the island in the process. His successor, Governor Antonio de Urbiztondo, destroyed Muslim bases on Tonquil in 1850 and three years later he launched a massive assault on Jolo itself. The capital was captured and the Sultan was forced to sign a treaty acknowledging Spanish overlordship, forbidding relations with other foreign powers, and placing himself and his ministers on a salaried basis from Manila. But the treaty was not effective. Finally, at the beginning of the 1870s, a determined campaign was launched to bring the whole of

[a]Refer pp. 208 et seq.
[b]Refer p. 213.

the Sulu archipelago under Spanish control. Its culminating point came in February 1876, when a strong force of steam gunboats carrying 9,000 men arrived off Jolo under the command of Admiral Jose Malcampo and attacked the capital. The Sultan withdrew and continued the fight inland, but in the middle of the next year he surrendered, signing a treaty accepting Spanish sovereignty.[47] But this was not the end of Sulu resistance which now took the form of guerrilla warfare, and the Sulus went on fighting until they were finally subdued by the Americans at the beginning of the present century.[a]

As for Magindanau, Spanish campaigns to bring this whole region under their control began in earnest in the 1880s. With the aid of modern field artillery and warships they were able to establish a series of coastal forts on Magindanau territory but all attempts to reduce the interior failed. Once again it was left to the Americans to complete the process of subjugating the Muslims of Magindanau to western rule. So in fact the Spaniards never succeeded in subduing the Muslim south, still less in assimilating it. This has been a factor of the greatest importance even down to the present day.[b]

External threats to the Spanish Philippines

One reason that contributed to the Spanish failure to deal with the Muslim south was the fact that they were seriously challenged by other enemies, particularly during the first two hundred years of their rule. The first of these challenges came from the Portuguese who all but nipped the Spanish colony in the bud,[c] but the Union of the Crowns in 1580 brought providential release.[48] The most serious challenge, however, came from the Dutch who for fifty years appeared to hold the life of the colony in their hands. Between 1600 and 1647 the Dutch made nine major attacks on the Philippines.[49] All were beaten off by dint of heroic effort against usually unfavourable odds but also at tremendous cost in terms of the human and material resources of the islands. The Chinese threat also loomed in fearful Spanish minds several times, resulting in dreadful massacres[50] but it materialized in reality only once when the Chinese outlaw and pirate, Lim Ah-hong, nearly captured Manila in 1574, only three years after the Spanish occupation. With difficulty were his forces and following driven into abandoning the Philippines by the end of the year. In the event, the only nation before the United States of America to succeed in capturing Manila from the Spaniards was Britain. In September 1762, during the course of the Seven Years War,[51] a British fleet of 13 ships with 6,830 men on board suddenly appeared in Manila Bay. After a ten-day struggle the city fell and a British occupation of two years followed. Although this was a brief interlude in the story of Spanish rule, it had very far-reaching effects.[d]

Revolts against Spain: the resistance of the old order

The long drawn-out struggle against outside foes presents two features. In the first place most of it (apart from the war with the Moros) was confined to the first cen-

[a]Refer pp. 215–16 and see pp. 379–80.
[b]See Book II.
[c]Refer pp. 340–1.
[d]See Book II.

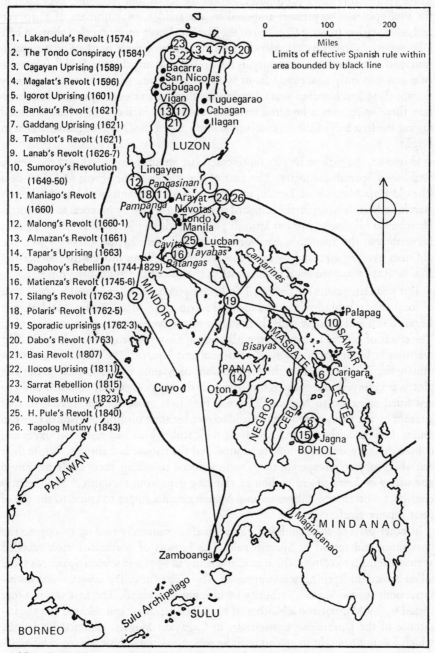

1. Lakan-dula's Revolt (1574)
2. The Tondo Conspiracy (1584)
3. Cagayan Uprising (1589)
4. Magalat's Revolt (1596)
5. Igorot Uprising (1601)
6. Bankau's Revolt (1621)
7. Gaddang Uprising (1621)
8. Tamblot's Revolt (1621)
9. Lanab's Revolt (1626-7)
10. Sumoroy's Revolution
    (1649-50)
11. Maniago's Revolt
    (1660)
12. Malong's Revolt (1660-1)
13. Almazan's Revolt (1661)
14. Tapar's Uprising (1663)
15. Dagohoy's Rebellion (1744-1829)
16. Matienza's Revolt (1745-6)
17. Silang's Revolt (1762-3)
18. Polaris' Revolt (1762-5)
19. Sporadic uprisings (1762-3)
20. Dabo's Revolt (1763)
21. Basi Revolt (1807)
22. Ilocos Uprising (1811)
23. Sarrat Rebellion (1815)
24. Novales Mutiny (1823)
25. H. Pule's Revolt (1840)
26. Tagolog Mutiny (1843)

0   100   200
        Miles
Limits of effective Spanish rule within
area bounded by black line

48.   Rebellions against Spanish rule in the Philippines, 1571–1896

tury of Spanish rule, and secondly it imposed a great strain on the island's burgeoning economy in the most formative years of Spanish colonial administration.
These two factors had a profound effect on the social and economic evolution of
the Philippines. The pressure imposed by the sudden establishment of European
and other settlers (mostly Chinese) in the islands, almost immediately followed by a
long series of attacks by outsiders, placed almost intolerable burdens on a population used to a subsistence economy. It is therefore not surprising to find that Spanish
rule was not only challenged from without but from within as well, especially
during these first hundred years. During the three centuries of Spanish administration there were over a hundred serious revolts—the majority of which occurred
during the first half of the seventeenth century when the Dutch offensive was at its
height.

However, the earliest revolts represented last attempts to overthrow the newly
established Spanish authority. The first of them all was the revolt of Lakan-dula
(the old Raja Matanda of Tondo) in 1574, who took advantage of Lim Ah-hong's
assault on Manila to set up the standard of rebellion at nearby Navotas to the north.
He rebelled because of broken Spanish pledges and the ill-treatment of his people.
Nevertheless, the Spaniards, hard-pressed as they were by the Chinese, won the
old man over by gifts and by fair promises, the rebellious movement faded away
and the Raja remained loyal till his death at the end of the following year.[52]

Ten years later came the famous Tondo conspiracy which involved a whole host
of local chiefs, behind whom the moving spirits were Magat Salamat and Martin
Legazpi, son and nephew of Raja Matanda respectively. It was a far-ranging plot.
The chiefs of central Luzon and the islanders of Cuyo were implicated, while help
was sought from places as far off as Brunai and Japan.[53] The plan was to exter-
minate the Spaniards before the fortifications of Manila were completed. But the
plot was betrayed, the conspirators arrested, the ringleaders put to death and the
rest fined or exiled to Mexico. This was definitely an aristocratic revolt, the last
attempt by the former lords of the land to recover their birthright. Spanish rule had
diminished the authority and power of the datos which had rested on slaves and
tribute. Slavery was no longer permitted and the tribute had shrunk. While their
erstwhile subjects prospered, they 'were reduced to selling their lands piecemeal
and sitting in their half-empty houses, thinking dangerous thoughts'.[a] Significantly
enough, no one in the villages around Manila raised a finger to come to the aid of
their former chiefs.

In other parts of the islands individual chiefs occasionally rose up to oppose the
imposition and spread of Spanish rule. The Igorots of northern Luzon rebelled
against attempts to convert them to Christianity in 1601 and several Spaniards were
killed before the uprising was suppressed. The Cagayan valley saw two serious in-
surrections against Spanish authority by unsubmissive chiefs. The first was in 1596,
stirred up by Magalat and a brother of his. Once captured and released (on the insistence of the Dominican missionaries in Cagayan) Magalat resumed his revolt,
which was not brought to an end until he was murdered in his house by a hired as-
sassin. Later, in the 1620s, two 'haughty' chiefs, Miguel Lanab and Alabahan, in the
Cagayan valley in the 1620s defied Spanish authority and pillaged Roman Catholic

[a]H. de la Costa, S.J., The Jesuits in the Philippines, 1581–1768, p. 112.

missions there, and were only suppressed after a strong expedition had been sent in 1627. One of the last and most tragic of this kind of revolt was led by Bankau, the aged chief of Limasawa who had been one of the first to welcome Legazpi in 1565. Now a Christian convert living in Leyte, in his old age Bankaw apostasized[54] and with the aid of his son and of a pagan priest called Pagali, incited the people of Carigara in the north of the island to revolt. The rebellion spread over the whole island but was crushed after spirited resistance by a force of some hundreds of Cebuans and a handful of Spanish arquebusiers.[55] Both Bankaw and Pagali died in the fighting. This uprising took place in 1621.

The seventeenth century: Sumoroy's rebellion

The rebellions of the seventeenth century had their roots in social and economic causes and were mostly the direct consequence of the fierce struggle between Spain and Holland. The first example of this kind of revolt was provided by the restless Cagayan valley in 1621[56] when Felipe Cutabay and Gabriel Dayag aroused the people throughout the Gaddang settlements to rise up and burn and pillage missions and churches. However, very largely through the efforts of Brother Pedro de Santo Tomas, the rebels were persuaded to return to their homes without further bloodshed. They gave as their reason for rebellion that they 'were weary of the oppressions of the Spaniards', which in this case referred to the exactions of soldiers and missionaries.

A much more serious uprising took place in Samar in the middle of 1649. It started when the commander of the local garrison militia, Juan Ponce Sumoroy—described as 'daring, intelligent and dependable'[57]—at Palapag assassinated the unpopular Spanish curate of the town. The incident quickly fanned into rebellion and its sparks ignited outbreaks in the islands ranging from northern Mindanao to the Camarines. In Samar itself Sumoroy inflicted several defeats on the avenging Spanish forces before he withdrew to a redoubt in the hills. Eventually, after a year of resistance, his mountain stronghold was stormed in July 1650 and Sumoroy was killed by his own supporters in a desperate attempt to bargain for their own lives.

Sumoroy had his private reasons for resentment but his defiance echoed a public grievance. Governor Fajardo wanted to relieve the Tagalog population around Manila from his incessant demands for labour in the shipyards for ships to meet the Dutch attacks, and ordered his officials in the Bisayas to recruit men from that region to work at Cavite. The order was unpopular; Cavite was far from Bisayan homes, the labour poorly rewarded and the chances of ever getting back again uncertain. The missionaries in the Bisayas sensed and sympathized with these local feelings and warned Manila of the dangers of implementing the scheme. But Governor Fajardo, who had never set foot in the outer provinces and regarded the missionaries' warnings as yet another example of clerical obstruction[58] paid no heed. The widespread support for Sumoroy was the result.

The seventeenth century: other uprisings

Ten years later came a fresh rash of revolts, basically brought about by the same factors. The most serious of these was led by Francisco Maniago and had its centre in the ricelands of Pampanga. It began in October 1660 as a mutiny of labourers who had been drafted for felling timber to build the ships needed to defend Manila.

The mutineers began by burning their own homes and declaring their intention to fight for their rights and for their liberty. They set up camp at Bacolod and closed the mouths of the rivers with stakes so as to interrupt the coastal trade with Manila. In the meantime Maniago sent letters to Pangasinan and Ilocos urging the people there to rise up and make common cause. Finally the rebels sent a deputation to Manila itself to meet the governor and place before him their grievances.[59] Maniago's revolt was a serious affair. Pampanga was a well-developed province, socially well-organized and numbering amongst its inhabitants many old soldiers who were thoroughly familiar with Spanish methods of warfare. Maniago himself was a village headman and a former master-of-camp in the royal Spanish Army.[60] However, the governor, Manrique de Lara, was equal to the situation. Firstly, he quickly sealed the one road leading south from Pampanga to Manila by despatching a cavalry squadron to Arayat; he then proceeded to win over its powerful chief, Macapagal, a descendant of Lakan-dula of Tondo, thereby weakening the united front of his opponents. Seeing his position thus restricted, Maniago now sent his deputation to Manila which the Spaniards kept talking there until the governor had assembled his forces and was ready to strike. Lara then sent small punitive expeditions into the disaffected districts, granted an amnesty to the main body of rebels, settled outstanding moneys due to the Pampangans and arrested and executed the ringleaders. The revolt was at an end.

The Maniago affair produced its repercussions in Pangasinan and Ilocos. At the end of 1660, at Lingayen, a Filipino master-of-camp called Andres Malong, started a rebellion. The local alcalde-mayor[61] was killed and the movement spread throughout the province. Malong had himself proclaimed king of Pangasinan and appointed his henchmen as generals and high officials. Sending messages to the surrounding provinces, Malong then sent one force of 6,000 men into Pampanga under the command of one of his generals, Melchor de Vera, another force of 3,000 into Ilocos and Cagayan under Gumpamos, and retained the remaining 2,000 in Pangasinan itself. This dividing of his forces was Malong's mistake. They were unable to stand up to the weight of the two Spanish armies sent against them. In 1661 all the rebels were tracked down in the mountains where they had fled, and were captured and executed.

Meanwhile in January 1661, inspired by the uprisings in Pampanga and Pangasinan, Pedro Almazan, supported by two other local leaders—Juan Magsanop and Gaspar Cristobal—proclaimed himself King of Ilocos. The rebellion had its centre at San Nicolas and Bacarra but was crushed by troops made up of Spaniards and loyal Filipinos.

The background to the seventeenth century uprisings

Many of the underlying grievances which led to these uprisings were expressed by Maniago's deputation from Pampanga. Forced labour and requisitions of materials—whether rice, timber or other provisions—to meet the needs of the ships and garrisons of the Spanish Philippines formed the two main items of complaint. The government needed labour in the forests, labour for transportation[62] and labour in the shipyards. It needed oarsmen and auxiliary soldiers. The labourers received wages but they were paid at a low rate, and from funds raised in the district or *encomienda*[63] from which they came. The system of requisitions created even greater burdens. The government was entitled to requisition foodstuffs, for instance, at rates well below the market price. Not only that, but usually the government bought on credit and in this way mounted up huge debts to the villages. In 1660 the revolting Pampangans were owed by the government 200,000 pesos, of which they made the reasonable demand that the government settle with an immediate instalment of 14,000 pesos only.

Another factor was corruption and peculation on the part of local officials. Provincial officials, from the governor of the province downwards received meagre salaries, but they expected to make this good out of the perquisites of office. Local officials often levied their own taxes and imposed their own duties on local produce, or even, as was the case with the Governor Gonzalez Ronquillo de Peñalosa,[64] engaged in private trade wholesale, adding tremendously to the burdens of the peasant in the countryside. These factors and the needs of the ever-growing non-food-producing residents of Manila created a situation where the basic necessities were scarce and their prices high. The usual Filipino response in these conditions was to run away to the hills where possible in order to escape the labour drafts of the governments or its demand for taxes. Only in cases of sheer desperation did they resort to rebellion.

The eighteenth century: anti-Christian movements and the repercussions of the British occupation of Manila

After the lifting of the Dutch threat, the situation eased somewhat and for the next hundred years rebellions reflecting agrarian distress did not occur any more. The one exception to this occurred in the years 1745–6 when a series of risings took place in the provinces around Manila—Bulacan, Batangas, Laguna, Cavite and Rizal. The first incidents took place in September 1745 with the burning of ranches and convents. The movement spread but was quite easily suppressed by government troops, and Matienza and others of its ringleaders were captured and shot. This unrest had its roots in a specific cause—the maladministration of mission lands. In the areas affected, the Jesuits, Dominicans, Augustinians and Recollects operated between them some twenty large cattle ranches—ten of which (in Bulacan and Batangas) were run by the Jesuits. Over the passage of time the friars had allowed their managers to usurp peasant land and to charge exorbitant rents. The peasantry found that not only had they lost their lands but also their fishing rights, free access to the jungle for jungle produce and free pasture. This matter was first raised in 1609 in a petition from Miguel Banal, a descendant of Raja Sulaiman. After the troubles of the 1740s the matter was brought before the Spanish King who subsequently appointed a commission to go into the matter.

One of the most singular uprisings against Spanish rule began on the island of Bohol in 1744 and was not brought to an end until 1829, three-quarters of a century later. The instigator of the revolt was one Francisco Dagohoy, who did so on purely personal grounds.[65] It spread 'over the whole island like a tropical typhoon',[66] and had strong anti-clerical undertones. Dagohoy took to the hills with 3,000 followers and established his own government there where it remained impregnable against the successive expeditions sent against it. The movement continued even after Dagohoy's death, and by the 1820s when the final determined attempts to crush the rebels were made, their number had multiplied to over 20,000. An expedition sent out on the orders of Governor Mariano Ricaforte in 1827 achieved some local successes but did not quell the rebellion. A second expedition sent out the following year succeeded in ending the movement after a hard twelve-month campaign. The great majority of the rebels were granted an amnesty and re-settled in various places in the lowlands.

Resistance against Spanish rule periodically expressed itself as a still more direct reaction against Christian missionary activities. To a large extent, Bankau's revolt of 1621[a] falls into this category as does Tamblot's revolt on Bohol which broke out earlier the same year and in fact helped to precipitate Bankau's uprising.[b] Outstanding amongst other anti-Christian uprisings were the Igorot rising of 1601,[c] Tapar's uprising on Panay in 1663, a rebellion in Ilocos Norte in 1811, the revolt of Hermano Pule in Tayabas in 1840, and the mutiny of the Tagalog regiment in 1843 which was in fact an echo of the Hermano Pule affair.[67]

The British seizure of Manila in 1762, and the humilation for Spanish arms and authority which this signified, provided the signal for a small host of new uprisings in districts which had remained dormant for three generations. The most spectacular of these was that raised by Diego Silang in Ilocos.[68] His first move came after the fall of Manila to the British in October 1762, when he approached the Spanish authorities in Vigan to demand the abolition of the tribute on the grounds that the Spaniards had failed to protect the islands against a foreign invasion. For his pains he was imprisoned but he was not inside for long as friends secured his early release. He then presented four demands[69] including one for his own appointment as commander-in-chief of an Ilocan army to fight the British. These demands were naturally rejected. So, on 14 December 1762, he raised the standard of revolt in Vigan. Spanish officials were harried out of the city, forced labour and tribute were declared abolished, and with Vigan as its base the movement spread to Pangasinan and to Cagayan. Spanish counter-attacks against Vigan failed and the Bishop of Nueva Segovia's force of Spaniards and Filipinos was defeated at Cabugao. In May 1763 the British sent messages to Silang offering aid and protection against the Spanish governor, Simon de Anda, who was successfully resisting the spread of British control over the islands.[70] Silang accepted this offer but before anything could come of it, he was assassinated in his own house by a *mestizo* in Spanish pay. However, the struggle was carried on by his wife, Gabriela, and by his uncle, Nicolas Cariño, who took command of the rebel forces and inflicted more reverses on Spanish arms. Finally they themselves were defeated at Cabugao. Cariño was killed and Gabriela fled to the mountains near Abta to recruit new forces. But her attempt to retake Vigan was repulsed and she and her followers became the quarry of the forces of Manuel de Arza, the Spanish Lieut.-Governor of Northern Luzon. Hunted down and captured, she was executed along with other leaders of the rebellion in Vigan in September 1763.

A similar movement sprang up at the same time in Pangasinan, led by Juan de la

[a]Refer p. 353.
[b]See p. 366, note 54.
[c]Refer p. 352.

Cruz Palaris.[71] Arguing on similar lines to Silang in November 1762, Palaris presented five demands[72] to the Spanish authorities in Binalatongan, which were rejected on the spot. He immediately stirred up a revolt which quickly spread to the principal towns in the province. Pangasinan remained in his hands for the next twelve months. However, after de Arza had completed his campaign in Ilocos he was free to deal with the southern rebellion. Palaris suffered his first reverse in December 1763, and was defeated decisively shortly afterwards. He and his supporters were hounded into isolated retreats during the course of 1764 and he was finally captured, after being betrayed by his own sister, in January 1765. As was the way with all rebels, he and his principal supporters were executed.[73]

The British occupation of Manila produced smaller-scale repercussions elsewhere —in Batangas, Tayabas, Cavite, Camarines, Samar, Panay, Cebu and Zamboanga. Spanish officials and priests were expelled or killed. But these were isolated and sporadic incidents, more the outcome of local resentments than a general movement.[74] Simon de Anda with the Spaniards and the loyal Filipinos under his control was soon able to bring them to nothing. The last of the movements engendered by the fall of Manila broke out in the Cagayan Valley at Iligan in February 1763. There the local inhabitants declared their independence and the revolt spread to Cabagan and Tuguegarao under the leadership of Dabo and Juan Marayac. Nevertheless Manuel de Arza succeeded in suppressing this uprising as well and its leaders paid the inevitable death penalty.

The ending of this wave of revolt marked the close of this particular form of resistance to Spanish rule. Great political, social and economic changes which took place in the Philippines and the Spanish world outside during the course of the next fifty years created an entirely different set of conditions, producing outbreaks of a very different character which formed the prelude to the emergence of a Filipino nationalist movement.[75]

The Spanish impact: 1600–1800

The catalogue of revolt and resistance against Spanish rule appears at first sight a long and formidable one, but on analysis it can be seen that these movements were confined in general to well defined periods and reflected specific circumstances. For many generations many parts of the Philippines enjoyed peace and security. Indeed in retrospect what is most striking about the pattern of resistance to Spanish rule is that prior to the nineteenth century it was so limited and so unsuccessful. None of the major uprisings before those of the 1760s ever seriously threatened the continuation of Spanish power in the islands.

The most obvious explanation for the futility of these rebellions lies in the absence of any sense of unity or community amongst the islanders during this period. They were not yet Filipinos. The Spaniards were able to treat each revolt as a localized affair and with a handful of European troops and a large number of auxiliaries drawn from other provinces in the islands were easily able to subdue it. They were able to play one ethnic group off against another. The clergy and the missionaries also played an important part. More often than not, they acted as intermediaries between the government and the people, frequently acted as delegates to represent

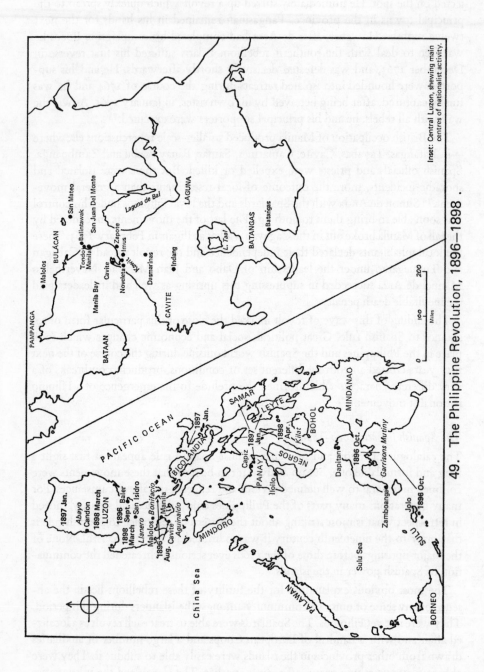

49. The Philippine Revolution, 1896–1898.

Inset: Central Luzon, shewing main centres of nationalist activity.

the people's grievances and even from the highest places defended the population from the worst abuses of authority.[76]

The Spanish regime also brought into being two classes of Filipinos which were eventually to form the spearhead of the nationalist movement but which in the beginning had a stake in the existing order. These were firstly the native constabulary, modelled on Spanish lines, led by Filipino officers who were given training in Europe and fought in every campaign, distinguishing themselves by their bravery and loyalty. Secondly there was the governing class, the *principales*, the descendants of the ancient aristocracy of the Philippines who played a key rôle in the local administration of the Spanish régime. It was not until the nineteenth century, when economic expansion brought the Philippines into closer contact with the outside world and helped to create a new Filipino middle-class which found its progress blocked by a heavy Spanish officialdom and ruling *élite*, that nationalism began to develop and Spanish rule was faced with its first effective challenge from within.

The outbreak of the Revolution of 1896

The story of the origins of that nationalist movement and its development belongs to another chapter.[a] Here we are only concerned with the fact that it led to the Philippines Revolution of 1896 and from this followed a series of events which culminated in the rule of Spain being replaced by that of the United States of America. The imposition of American control was stoutly resisted by Filipino nationalists but after a three years struggle, which was to prove a source of inspiration to other South-East Asian nationalists,[b] they had to admit defeat.

The Philippines Revolution began on 26 August 1896. At that moment the new Federated Malay States had been in existence for barely two months,[c] the Achinese were in the third decade of their epic struggle against the Dutch,[d] and De Tham, the last of the Vietnamese to resist the French conquest of that country, was still holding out in the mountains near the Chinese frontier.[e] By 1896, the Filipino nationalist movement was nearing maturity, and it was now in the hands of a secret nationalist society, the Katipunan,[f] whose leaders were convinced that nationalist aims could only be achieved by the violent overthrow of Spanish authority. As they were laying their plans for revolution, Spanish officials suddenly got wind of the movement,[77] and on 19 August 1896, laid bare the secrets of the whole organization. Andres Bonifacio,[78] Emilio Jacinto and other leaders fled Manila forthwith, making for the surrounding hills. From there, at Balintawak one week later, they uttered the 'cry of Balintawak', proclaiming the existence of the Revolution.[79]

Although no one could know this at the time, the writ of Spanish rule had only three more years to run, and at the end of that time they were not in sight of crushing the movement started by Bonifacio and his friends. After its proclamation, the movement soon spread. On 30 August the first clash between the nationalists and the Spanish authorities took place at San Juan del Monte, just outside Manila, when Bonifacio and Jacinto led an unsuccessful attempt to capture the magazine there.

[a]See Book III.
[b]See Book III.
[c]See Book II.
[d]Refer p. 232 et seq.
[e]See p. 457.
[f]See Book III.

On the same day the Spanish governor, Ramon Blanco, proclaimed a state of siege in Manila and all the surrounding provinces. The next days, weeks and months brought in reports of risings all over the islands. On 31 August Aguinaldo rose up in Cavite; on 2 September 2,000 nationalists led by Mariano Llanero attacked San Isidro in Nueva Ecija; in October the Filipino garrisons in Mindanao and Sulu mutinied. In November the nationalists won their first successes, repulsing Spanish troops under Blanco at Noveleta and other Spanish regulars at Binakayan, Cavite. Early in the new year, the revolution spread to Ilocos, Bicolandia, all over Central Luzon and throughout the Bisayas.

The Spaniards responded by a policy of terror which had the opposite of the desired effect. The first martyrs to the cause of Filipino nationalism—fifty-seven of them—were shot on the Luneta on 31 August. Many more were to follow.[80] One of the victims was Jose Rizal, the greatest nationalist leader of them all, who, having been in Spanish hands for four years[81] was tried for 'rebellion, sedition and illicit association' at the beginning of December and shot at dawn in Manila on 30 December. The execution of Rizal, a moderate, won many people over to the cause of the nationalists. Meanwhile the shootings continued and over a thousand Filipinos were sent into exile to serve their time in Guam, Fernando Po and other Spanish penal settlements.

The rise of Emilio Aguinaldo

Once the Revolution was under way, it became necessary for the nationalists to organize themselves, establish a firm leadership and decide on a clear cut policy and programme. As things stood the Revolution was being organized and controlled by the Katipunan. The Katipunan had been founded by Andres Bonifacio and up till the time of the outbreak of the Revolution he had been its undisputed leader. Now, under the stress of war, other figures began to emerge. One of these was Emilio Aguinaldo[82] who, at the end of October, issued from his birthplace of Kawit a manifesto urging the adoption of an American-type government for the Philippines. Successful in the field, his popularity rose, while that of Bonifacio who was not such a good general as politician, started to wane.

The rivalry between the two men developed over the question of the future of the movement. As far as Bonifacio was concerned the existing Katipunan organization was sufficient for the needs of the nationalists. Aguinaldo thought that a new revolutionary government should be set up. Both sides attracted to themselves supporters who came to form two rival groups within the Katipunan. Those supporting Bonifacio became known as the Magdiwang faction and the supporters of Aguinaldo as the Magdalo faction.[83] In order to resolve the differences between them and decide the proper course of action for the future, an assembly of the nationalists met at Imus at the end of 1896. The only decision reached was that another assembly should be held early in the new year. The second assembly met at Tejeros, San Francisco de Malabon, in March 1897. Although Aguinaldo himself was not present as he was engaged on the battlefield, the Tejeros Assembly resulted in a triumph for him and his faction. After a stormy meeting, it was decided to set up a new revolutionary government with Aguinaldo as its president.[84] The defeated Andres Bonifacio was elected Secretary of the Interior, but even this choice was disputed. After the Assembly was over, Bonifacio left with some loyal supporters with the apparent intention of setting up a new government of his own. But he was overtaken at Limbon, Indang, by Aguinaldo's men. In the skirmish which followed, Bonifacio was wounded and one of his brothers killed. He was made prisoner and put on trial in early May. He was found guilty of sedition and was executed on 10 May, although this was not apparently Aguinaldo's original desire.[85]

The Biacnabato Republic

This quarrel was a bad beginning for the Revolution. Some nationalists lost their enthusiasm and it weakened the nationalist effort as a whole. Emilio Aguinaldo, however, was now undisputed leader and was to remain so until his eventual capture by the Americans five years later. In November 1897 the revolutionary government, now established in the fastnesses of Biacnabato, proclaimed the foundation of an independent Republic of the Philippines. Known today as the Republic of Biacnabato, it was based on a constitution written by Isabelo Artacho and Felix Ferrer which closely followed the Cuban constitution of 1895.[86] Aguinaldo was elected President. Tagalog was made the official language.

The revolutionaries found themselves in the mountain retreat of Biacnabato since during the course of 1897 the Spaniards had gained the upper hand in the fighting and had recovered control over much of the lowland districts around Manila. Under General Camilo de Polavieja, who took over as governor from Blanco in December the preceding year, a vigorous campaign against the nationalists had been launched. In February three brigades marched on Laguna and Batangas, another into the mountains north and east of Manila into what is today Rizal province, while Polavieja himself led the main force against the centre of the nationalist movement under Aguinaldo in Cavite. After fierce resistance in which some of the flower of the nationalist leadership was lost,[87] Polavieja had with the capture of San Francisco de Malabon in the first week of April regained control of over more than half of Cavite province. But when his request for more reinforcements from Spain was turned down on account of the Cuban troubles,[a] Polavieja, weary and disappointed, resigned.

His place was taken by General Fernando Primo de Rivera on 15 April 1897, who resumed the campaign and by June all of Cavite was in his hands. At this juncture Aguinaldo and his followers fled to the hills, joining forces with those of General Miguel de Malvar[b] on the way. At first they made their headquarters near San Mateo but later, in July, made Biacnabato their main base. However the new opponent of the nationalists, Primo de Rivera, was subtler than his predecessors and more aware of the intractability of the problem which he faced. 'I can take Biacnabato. Any military man can take it. But I cannot answer that I could crush the rebellion', he told the Spanish Cortes (Parliament) in June. In August he sent Pedro A. Paterno, a well-known Manila lawyer, to the nationalist stronghold,[88] beginning a series of negotiations which culminated in the Pact of Biacnabato at the end of the year. Meanwhile, however, fighting resumed after a lull of three months, with the nationalists launching raids in all of the provinces around Manila.

[a]See p. 369.
[b]See p. 377.

The Pact of Biacnabato and its breakdown

The Pact of Biacnabato was signed by Aguinaldo and the Spanish authorities on 14 and 15 December.[89] In the first place Primo de Rivera agreed to pay 800,000 pesos to 'those in arms' and to allow Aguinaldo and his companions to go into voluntary exile in Hong Kong. Half that sum would be paid as Aguinaldo's party left Biacnabato, 200,000 pesos more when the number of arms surrendered exceeded 700, and the remainder when the general amnesty was proclaimed. The amnesty was to apply to all who laid down their arms. In addition, Spain agreed to pay 1,700,000 pesos (including the 800,000 already mentioned) to compensate for the damage done in the fighting, the money being devoted to reconstruction. In accordance with this agreement, on 27 December 1897, Aguinaldo and 25 companions sailed from Manila to their exile in Hong Kong.

The Pact of Biacnabato was not kept. Spain paid only 600,000 pesos out of the total indemnity promised; the amnesty was not observed—many who surrendered their arms were arrested and imprisoned, but not all surrendered their arms. Primo de Rivera never made any attempt to carry through the programme of reforms which, according to Aguinaldo,[90] he had promised to do, and the Filipinos continued to plot the overthrow of Spanish rule. In Hong Kong Aguinaldo's first act was to perpetuate the revolutionary government by forming the 'Hong Kong Junta' and by then enlarging it into the 'Supreme Council of the Nation'. And with his friends he waited and followed closely all fresh developments in the Philippines.

The failure of the Pact of Biacnabato was simply because neither party was interested in maintaining it. On the other hand, the Pact served the purposes of both sides. Cooped up in Biacnabato with diminishing resources, the nationalists realized that they were in a very weak position and that if they tried to resist much longer, they might ultimately have to surrender on far less favourable terms; the proffered compensation meant funds with which to buy arms. On the other hand, Primo de Rivera wanted to have the leaders of the movement removed outside the country from where they would find it much more difficult to organize trouble.

However, the advantage lay with the nationalists. Although Aguinaldo and his companions were in Hong Kong, they were shortly to get the opportunity to use their exile to establish contacts with other countries which would have been impossible had they still been in the Philippines. One of these contacts, with a local representative of the United States of America, was to lead to Aguinaldo's triumphant return within six months. At the same time nationalists in the islands themselves did not remain quiescent. On 7 March 1898 nationalist activity flared up in Zambales. On the 25th the town of Candon in Ilocos Sur was seized by Isobelo Abayo and his men, while in an affray in Manila Spanish soldiers massacred a group of Bisayans. This provoked a new uprising in Cebu at the beginning of April led by Leon Kilat. A pharmacist stirred up fresh risings in the districts around Manila and in Central Luzon, General Francisco Makabulos set up a provisional revolutionary government with a constitution written by him 'until the general government of the Republic of these Islands shall again be established'. On the 24th of the same month, Spain declared war on the United States.

[1]Serrano was a member of Albuquerque's expedition of 1511 which captured Malacca. He was on a mission to the Moluccas to gain an opening for Portuguese trade there; he died later in the same year during a second shipwreck whilst trying to return to Malacca.

[2]Ferdinand Magellan (Portuguese—Fernao Magalhaes; Spanish—Fernando de Magallanes) born 1480 at Sabrosa, near Oporto, Portugal, son of a minor noblemen; 1493, sent to the royal court at Lisbon, educated in military science and navigation; 1505, sailed to the East with Almeida's expedition; 1509, with de Sequiera at Malacca, promoted to Captain of Troops by Albuquerque; 1511, took part in the conquest of Malacca; 1521, returned to Lisbon and lived at the court; 1513, served with Portuguese expedition against Morocco, wounded at Battle of Azimur; 1517, renouncing Portuguese nationality, went to Spain to get backing for his scheme to find a western route to the Moluccas; 1518, commissioned by King Charles I of Spain to take the western route. By the agreement signed between the Spanish monarch and Magellan, the costs were to be borne by the king while Magellan and his partner, Ruy de Faleiro, were to receive 5 per cent of the revenues obtained from the lands they discovered. Magellan left the estuary of the Guadalquivir river in September 1519 with 5 ships and 265 men on board.

[3]The Blood Compact, kaseh2 or sandugo was a traditional Filipino rite by which friendship was sealed. Blood drawn from a slight wound on the left arm was mixed in a common cup of wine which both parties then partook of, thus becoming blood brothers.

[4]Magellan landed with a force of 60 Spaniards and 1,000 Cebuans on the shores of Mactan to support Lapulapu's enemy, Zula. They were defeated on the beach where they landed.

[5]Of the three surviving vessels in Magellan's fleet, one had to be destroyed at Bohol because there were not enough crewmen, and the second was forced to give up the attempt to return across the Pacific because of springing a leak and sailed back to surrender to the Portuguese in the Moluccas; four survivors from this vessel eventually reached Spain in 1522.

[6]Three ships were lost before reaching the Straits of Magellan; a fourth was forced to make for Mexico. Loaisa himself died at sea in the middle of the Pacific, and his three successors also died—the last of them poisoned by his own men on Tidore. The survivors established themselves on Tidore and allying themselves with local chiefs fought the Portuguese garrison there until they were relieved by Saavreda's expedition in 1528.

[7]Son of the famous explorer, John Cabot, and chief pilot to the King of Spain.

[8]Zaide, Philippines Political and Cultural History, Vol. I, p. 137. Villalobos himself died on the island of Ambon in 1546 with the celebrated Francis Xavier at his death bed.

[9]Miguel Lopez de Legazpi: 1504, born of noble family at Zuburraja, Guipuzcoa, Spain; educated in law and military science; 1528, went to Mexico, practised law and entered public service as (a) councillor in Mexico City (b) chief scrivener and (c) magistrate; appointed commander of the fifth expedition on the recommendation of Father Urdaneta.

Father Andres de Urdaneta: 1498, born of noble parents at Villafranca, Guipuzcoa, Spain; educated in philosophy and theosophy; joined Spanish army, fought in Italy and Germany, promoted Captain of the Troops; 1525, joined the Loaisa Expedition, returning after 10 years in the Moluccas to Spain in 1536; 1542, entered Augustinian monastery in Mexico City; 1552, ordained priest; 1559, offered command of the fifth expedition but declined in favour of Legazpi, his countryman; 1565, pioneered return Manila-Mexico route; rejoined the monastery in Mexico City; 1568, died.

[10]One ship deserted the expedition barely a week after leaving port.

[11]Legazpi's landing party was attacked and one man killed. The Cebuan hostility was due to recent Portuguese raids.

[12]Immortalized by a painting of the nineteenth century Filipino painter and nationalist, Juan Luna, depicting Rizal as Katuna.

[13]The Portuguese with justification maintained that the Philippines lay on their side of the demarcation line laid down by the Treaty of Tordesillas (1494) which divided the Spanish and Portuguese Empires. The line was fixed under this agreement at 370 leagues west of the Cape Verde Islands; all lands to the west of that line falling to Spain and all lands to the east to Portugal. In 1529 the position was clarified and confirmed by the Treaty of Zaragoza whereby for 350,000 decats Spain renounced her claims to the Moluccas and recognized a new demarcation line running north-south 297½ leagues east of the Moluccas. Thus the Philippines clearly lay inside the Portuguese sphere. For this reason Urdaneta had been 'highly displeased' when the unsealing of Legazpi's instructions on the high seas revealed their purpose to colonize the Philippines; he advocated merely rescuing Spanish captives in the area and trying New Guinea instead, but Legazpi insisted that royal orders must be complied with.

[14]According to Zaide (op. cit.) this new settlement was at Capiz on the Panay river; de la Costa (The Jesuits in the Philippines, 1581-1768) places it at Arevalo (Filipino-Ortong/Spanish-Oton) near Iloilo. From the new base parties were sent to bring Masbate, Ticao and Burias under Spanish control.

[15]According to Filipino historians Tondo and Manila formed one unit; according to the Spaniards they were distinct from one another.

[16]According to the Spaniards the incident occurred when Sulaiman misinterpreted the firing of a Spanish cannon which was signalling their ships in the Bay as the signal for an assault on his position. In the tense atmosphere prevalent only a spark was necessary to ignite the conflict. In the meantime Juan de Salcedo went to explore Lake Taal and clashed with local inhabitants at Pansipit river. He later rejoined Goiti in Manila Bay.

[17]Sulaiman is reputed to have replied to Legazpi's envoys as follows: 'Not until the sun is cut in two, not until I seek the hatred instead of the love of woman, will I be the friend of a Castila (Spaniard).' Quoted by Sir John Bowring, *A Visit to the Philippine Isles*, p. 166.

[18]Juan de Salcedo: 1549, born of noble parents and a grandson of Legazpi in Mexico; educated in chivalry and military science; 1567, arrived in Cebu with reinforcements for Legazpi; awarded an *encomienda* in the Ilocos for his subsequent campaign of pacification—see text below; died of fever aged 27 shortly after returning from the defence of Manila against Lim Ah-hong's assault.

Martin de Goiti; one of the most prominent members of Legazpi's expedition; troop captain; 1567, appointed Master of Camp; 1574, killed in action defending Manila from the assault of Lim Ah-hong.

[19]For example, Kasiki, the ruler of Pangasinan, at first defied the Spaniards but eventually submitted on the advice of Raja Lakan-dula.

[20]Later, on the orders of Governor Sande (1575–80), Chavez also founded the town of Nueva Caceres (Naga).

[21]Conquerors; a term originally applied to the Spanish commanders responsible for the conquest of Mexico and Peru.

[22]Quoted by Zaide, op. cit. p. 159, n. 6. In addition, the Spanish Crown granted the missionaries free passage, a stipend of 100 pesos and 2.5 bushels of rice a year. The Crown also allocated territory to the missionaries and confirmed all appointments.

[23]These orders are organizations of monks who, with the sanction of the Pope, live according to certain rules and disciplines laid down by their founders. The 'Augustinians' is thus the name given to all those orders—there are three main branches including the Augustinian Recollects—which follow the 'Rule of St. Augustine'; one of these, the Augustinian Hermits or Friars, arose out of the need to co-ordinate and regularize the various hermit communities living in Italy during the twelfth century. This order was created by papal authority about 1125 with its rules based on the precepts laid down by St. Augustine, Bishop of Hippo (396–430), in North Africa. The Jesuits or Society of Jesus was founded by St. Ignatius de Loyola, a Spaniard, in 1540. The Jesuits developed into one of the most powerful and influential orders, which was one reason why they suffered persecution later on, and it was especially associated with teaching and the efforts of the Roman Catholic Church to combat heresy (Protestant). The Dominican order was founded by St. Dominic between 1215 and 1220 with papal approval; the order was particularly designed for missionary work the world over and was bound by the vows of poverty, collectively and individually. The Franciscan order was created by St. Francis of Assisi, with papal sanction, in 1209, and was confirmed in 1223; it is identified in particular with the service of the poor. The Benedictine order arose out of the monks' fraternities which followed the rules prescribed by St. Benedict of Nursia (c. 480–540). The movement was formalized and received its name in the fourteenth century.

[24]Settled and permanent centres of population focused on a church, school, public square (plaza) and government buildings and quarters in place of the scattered and shifting Filipino settlements of before. Examples of such settlements which have grown into busy urban communities today are Bacolod (Recollect), Bayambang (Dominican), Iligan (Jesuit), Naga (Franciscan) and Pasig (Augustinian).

[25]The Jesuits were the best organized and best disciplined of all the Catholic orders in the Philippines and indeed in the world. Fear of their great influence and prestige, reinforced by the fact that they were directly controlled from Rome, led to a campaign against them in the increasingly nationalist-minded Roman Catholic monarchies of Europe during the eighteenth century. The Jesuits were expelled from Portugal in 1759, from France in 1764, from Spain in 1767 and formally dissolved by Pope Clement XIV in 1772. The effect of the Spanish expulsion reached the Philippines the following year when all Jesuit missionaries were ordered to leave. The Jesuits were restored in the nineteenth century and permitted to re-enter the Philippines in 1859.

[26]In 1591 the 140 consisted of 79 Augustinians, 42 Franciscans and 9 Dominicans; in 1898, there were 346 Augustinians, 327 Recollects, 233 Dominicans, 107 Franciscans, 42 Jesuits, 16 Capuchins and 6 Benedictines.

[27]Jesuits—Cebu, Leyte, Samar, Bohol and later Mindanao; Recollects—Mindoro, Masbate, Ticao, Burias, Romblon, Cuyo, Palawan, Negros and part of Mindanao.

[28]Most outstanding of which is the emphasis on ritual and emotional content with which Filipinos approach Christianity—the rôle of the *fiesta*, and the absorption of pre-Christian susperstitions and beliefs, especially those regarding the spirit world. For a full discussion of the interrelationship between Spanish and Filipino cultures, see Phelan, op. cit.

[29]Including Indian corn, tobacco, cotton, wheat, amongst others.

[30]From *Lucon et Mindanao: Extraits d'un journal de voyage dans l'Extreme Orient* by the Duke of Alencon, published in 1870. Quoted by Zaide, op. cit. p. 203.

[31]'The military phase of Spain's conquest of the Philippines must be thought of as a continuum, a movement which began in 1565 and one which was reaching its completion in 1898,' Phelan, op. cit. p. 136 *et seq.*

[32]Moro is a term originally used by the Spaniards of the Muslim invaders of the Iberian Peninsula who came from Morocco in North Africa; it was later applied by the Spaniards and the Portuguese to Muslims in general and to the Muslim inhabitants of Mindanao and the Sulu archipelago in particular. The Filipino Muslims fall into five main regional groups, viz. Magindanau (Cotabatu), Yakan (Basilan), Maranau (Lake Lanao), Samal (Zamboanga and south Mindanao) and Sulu (Sulu Archipelago).

[33]The major expeditions of 1591, 1608, 1635, and 1663.

[34]Tribute was a kind of annual headtax imposed on every Filipino family by the Spanish authorities from the time of Legazpi till it was lifted in 1884. In 1681 Spanish attempts to move thousands of Sambals from their mountain cave and huts in retaliation for their constant raids on the lowlands, and to resettle them on land opened by the Dominicans, provoked a serious rebellion which lasted for three years. This was the only occasion when such serious resistance was offered by the mountain peoples to the new Spanish policy.

[35]Called by the Spaniards Rio Grande (Great River).

[36]In 1569 off Cebu when Legazpi sent a small force to drive off Muslim raiders attacking coastal villages in the Bisayas.

[37]Namely in 1578, 1638-46, and 1853. See below.

[38]1599, Pacho repulsed at Jolo; 1602, Gallinato withdrew after laying a 3-month siege; 1628 Luego with over 100 Spanish and 1,000 Filipino troops failed to take Jolo citadel; 1630. Olaso with a fleet of 70 vessels, 350 Spanish and 2,500 Filipino troops failed to carry the Jolo citadel.

[39]Taking advantage of Spanish expeditions against the Dutch, a Sulu fleet destroyed the shipyard at Pantao in Camarines, burned Cavite and carried away 400 captives.

[40]Arrow Point, so named by the Spaniards after the arrows embedded in the cliff face; called Panaon by the Filipinos, it was regarded as a sacred place and passing fleets discharged a flight of arrows to obtain portents of their luck. If their fortune was to be good, the arrows found their mark and stuck; if not, the prospects were bad.

[41]All raiders returning down the coasts on the west side of the archipelago had to pass by Zamboanga to reach their home bases; the Spaniards also built a fort at La Caldera nearby.

[42]In fact, the Spaniards had already withdrawn from their outposts at Sabanilla (Polloc Harbour) and Buayan in Magindanau after suffering a severe reverse there in 1642.

[43]The Spaniards withdrew as a result of the fear of an attack from the Chinese freebooter, Cheng Ch'ng Keng (Koxinga) who had made himself master of Formosa in the early 1660s. The Formosan threat never materialized.

[44]In a particularly daring raid in 1769, the men of Sulu captured some fishing boats and plundered Malate, all within the full sights of Manila's cannons.

[45]The head of the Augustinian Recollect missionary organization in the Philippines.

[46]Both the French and the British had attempted to open up relations with the Sultan of Sulu during the 1840s: refer to pp. 210 and 213.

[47]The Sultan had by this time created a great problem for the future by signing away his rights in North Borneo to a German speculator called von Overbeck only six months previously. Refer to p. 131.

[48]In 1578 King Sebastian of Portugal perished in a campaign in Morocco without leaving any direct heir. Philip II of Spain laid claim to the vacant throne and established his rights there in 1580. The union of the crowns lasted until 1640.

The first Portuguese attack was made on Cebu in 1568 and the second came at the same place two years later. On both occasions the Portuguese assault was repulsed and their attempts at blockade failed for lack of sufficient supplies for themselves.

[49]In 1600, 1609-10, 1616, 1617, 1618, 1621-2, 1624, 1646 and 1647. The three most spectacular occasions were (a) in 1609-10, when the Spanish Philippines were threatened by a Dutch fleet of 13 ships and 3,000 men led by Admiral Wittert. The Dutch were defeated and Wittert

himself killed at the First Battle of Playa Honda; (b) in 1621–2, when Manila Bay was block-aded by an Anglo-Dutch force; (c) in 1646, when between March and October four separate Dutch attacks were decisively defeated by a defence which consisted of two old galleons recommissioned for service. These seemingly miraculous naval victories over superior adversaries led to the inauguration of an annual festival of thanksgiving held every October called the Naval de Manila, which is still celebrated to this day.

⁵⁰In 1603, 1639, 1662, 1686, 1762, and 1819. On all these occasions except for the last one the Chinese were also involved in an uprising against the Spanish administration. Decrees ex-pelling all Chinese from the Philippines were promulgated in 1596, 1686, 1744, 1755 and 1769 without, however, appreciably affecting the growth of the Chinese population from 150 in 1571 to 100,000 by 1896.

⁵¹The Seven Years War (1756–63) was one of a series of national and dynastic wars between the great powers of Europe during the seventeenth and eighteenth centuries. During these con-flicts Britain and France were always on opposing sides and so therefore were Britain and Spain since the rulers of France and Spain represented different branches of the same dynasty (Bourbon).

⁵²The old raja's complaints concerned the failure of the Spaniards to live up to their under-takings to exempt his men from tribute and forced labour when they had conquered Manila. Once mollified by Spanish gifts and renewed assurances, he proved his own good faith by helping in the attack on Lim Ah Hong in Pangasinan in 1575. When he died later in the same year, he had become a Christian convert. Reputedly one of his sons subsequently joined the Augustinian Order to become the first Filipino friar.

⁵³Martin Legazpi was also a son-in-law of the Sultan of Brunai, which explains why the con-spirators were able to count on the support of the Brunai Malays. The Japanese were involved through a Christian Japanese living in Manila who came to an understanding with a Japanese sea-captain called Joan Gayo to bring men and weapons from Japan. Legazpi was to be made king while the Japanese were to receive half the tribute collected as their reward.

⁵⁴Bankaw had been influenced by another rebellion which broke out on neighbouring Bohol. The Bohol revolt was led by a Filipino pagan priest called Tamblot and was directed against the presence of Jesuit missionaries on the island. This movement was finally crushed in 1622.

⁵⁵Soldiers using the arquebus, a primitive type of portable gun supported on a tripod by a hook or forked rest.

⁵⁶Apart from the two political rebellions noted above, the Cagayan valley had also been the scene of a serious uprising in 1589, directed in particular against the collectors of tribute.

⁵⁷De la Costa, *The Jesuits in the Philippines*, op. cit. p. 411. Sumoroy was appointed garrison commander, having won official favour by his daring scouting missions at sea whereby he was able to give ample warning of impending Dutch attacks. He fell foul of the Spanish curate as the result of his adultery; his mistress was sent to another village on the orders of the priest. Sumoroy took advantage of the unpopularity of the curate engendered by the latters' duty to arrange for the forced labour for Cavite to pay off his personal scores.

⁵⁸The relations between the officials of the Roman Catholic Church and those of the Spanish State as represented by the Governor and his officers were often far from cordial. At issue were questions of policy and of status. The conflict had reached an unprecedented pitch during the governorship of Diego Fajardo's predecessor, Hurtado de Corcuera (1653–44), who had gone so far as to exile Hernando Guerrero, Archbishop of Manila (1635–41), from the city to Mariveles.

⁵⁹Amongst the grievances which the Pampangans presented to the governor were (a) the gover-nment owed them for supplies and services rendered; (b) the local Spanish officials did not observe the royal decrees issued for the protection of the people; (c) itinerant workers were liable to forced labour; (d) goods were requisitioned without payment; (e) Pampangans were forced to work for private individuals instead of for the government; (f) when sick they were still made to work overtime; (g) illegal taxes and tolls were demanded of them; (h)they were obliged to pay excess tribute. For a full list and discussion of Pampangan grievances, see de la Costa, *Readings in Philippine History*, op. cit. p. 57.

⁶⁰Master-of-camp was the highest official post a Filipino could hope to obtain in the Royal Spanish Army.

⁶¹Alcalde-mayor was the title of the official in charge of an *alcaldia* or province; appointed by and responsible to the governor-general and exercising executive, judicial and tribute-collect-ing functions.

⁶²What this might involve is shown by the instance cited by de la Costa (*The Jesuits in the Philip-pines*, op. cit. p. 344) about the labour required to haul the mast of a galleon from the moun-tains of Laguna to the Lake of Bai during the time of Governor de Silva (1607–16): it took 6,000 labourers three months to do so—they were paid 40 rials (a pittance) a month by *their*

own villages, and had to provide for themselves out of that sum. Many died, others fled to the hills while others committed suicide.

[63]An *encomienda* was a piece of land or territory 'entrusted' (Spanish-*encomendado*) to the conquistadores and other colonizers under certain conditions and for specific periods of time. The duties of the encomendero included the maintenance of law and order, the provision of protection and aid to the inhabitants, the indoctrination of Christianity and the collection of tribute.

[64]Ronquillo's operations were so extensive that the Spanish colonists petitioned Madrid for some form of restraint on the Governor for 'no one else in the Philippines would be able to make an honest peso and the colony would be swiftly driven to rack and ruin.'; quoted by de la Costa, *Readings in Philippine History*, op. cit. p. 18. A council to restrict the powers of the Governor-General was set up in Manila in 1583 as a consequence; it was called the *Audiencia*.

[65]Arising out of an incident in which Dagohoy's brother, a Christian constable who had been killed whilst attempting to capture an apostate, was denied a Christian burial by the Jesuit curate of Inabangan, Father Gaspar Morales; the curate who had originally given the constable the task of making the arrest justified himself on the grounds that the dead man had infringed Church laws by duelling. Exasperated, Dagohoy killed Morales. At the same time, the Jesuit curate of Jagna was also assassinated.

[66]Zaide, op. cit. Vol I., p. 355.

[67]Tapar's Rising: led by a Visayan mystic called Tapar who founded a new religious sect based on a modified form of Christianity at Oton, Panay; attempts to suppress the movement provoked the rebellion. The Ilocos Norte revolt centred on the attempt to drive out the friars and establish a new religion based on the idolatry of a god called Lungao. Hermano Pule alias Apolinario de la Cruz, a Tagalog, rose up in 1840 because the Spanish ecclesiastical authorities refused to recognize the Cofradia de San José, a reformist religious body which he had founded at Lucban; he proclaimed a war in defence of religious liberty and was declared king of the Tagalogs. A Spanish attack led by Ortega, Governor of Tayabas, was repulsed and Ortega himself killed but later in the same year Hermano Pule was defeated, made prisoner and executed. The Tagalog Mutiny of 1843 was largely engineered by soldiers whose homes were in Tayabas.

[68]Diego Silang; an Ilocano born in 1730 in Pangasinan; brought up and educated by a Spanish friar at Vigan; on voyage to Manila was shipwrecked and became a prisoner of the Negritos; ransomed by a Recollect missionary, he returned to Vigan; became government courier between Vigan and Manila, thereby making a wide circle of Spanish and Filipino contacts and acquaintances.

[69]Silang also demanded; (a) the dismissal of the Spanish official (Antonio Zabala, Alcalde-mayor of Vigan) responsible for his imprisonment; (b) the appointment of his own nominee in his stead; (c) the expulsion of all Spaniards and *mestizos* (half-castes) from Ilocos.

[70]Simon de Anda, a member of the *Audiencia* of Manila, escaped from the city as the British entered Bulacan: he then set up a provisional government of the Philippines with himself as governor, defied the British and campaigned actively to put down the rash of revolts throughout the country. He maintained his position until Spanish authority was restored in 1764: subsequently in Spain he was made a Counsellor of Castile and granted an annual pension in recognition of his services by King Charles III of Spain.

[71]Juan de la Cruz Palaris alias Pantaleon Perez; 1735, born at Binalatongan, Pangasinan; father was a local official (*cabeza de barangay*).

[72]These demands included; (a) the suspension of tribute until Manila was restored to the Spaniards; (b) the tribute already collected but not yet despatched to be returned; (c) dismissal of Spanish officials, including that of governor of the province; (d) appointment of a local resident as master-of-camp; (e) local government to be placed in Filipino hands.

[73]According to (not altogether reliable) missionary sources, 10,000 Pangasinan Filipinos died during the course of the uprising as opposed to 70 Spaniards and 140 loyal Filipinos.

[74]These also included incidents where the Filipinos displayed their loyalty to Spain and resisted the British invaders. Such was the case at Pagsanjan in Laguna where the Filipino officials in the town overthrew the Spanish alcalde-mayor who obeyed orders from Manila *not* to resist the British.

[75]For example, the Basi revolt of 1807 in Ilocos where the people rose up against the wine monopoly imposed in 1786—*basi* is the name of a wine brewed from sugar-cane; the Sarrat Rebellion of 1815 in Ilocos Norte, where 1,500 Filipinos rose up in revolt on hearing that the liberal constitution for Spain promulgated during the Napoleonic Wars at Cadiz in Spain had been abrogated; the Novales Mutiny of 1823, when a *mestizo* army officer used his troops to seize control of Manila. All these movements sprang from specific grievances, economic and political, clearly linked with the changing times. The Novales Mutiny had its roots in the Mexican breakaway from Spain in 1821 and the subsequent discrimination in the Royal Army

against Spaniards of Mexican origin.

[76]In part, this was a reflexion of the power struggle between church and state in the Philippines. Perhaps the most celebrated champion of Filipino rights against official misrule was Domingo de Salazar, Archbishop of Manila (1581–94) who amongst other things in 1582 drew up a great memorial in defence of Filipino interests and succeeded in bringing about the establishment of the *Audiencia* of Manila. (Also see note 58).

[77]The Spanish authorities had heard from various sources of the clandestine activities of the Katipunan. The vital information came from a Katipunan member called Teodoro Patno who worked on the Manila paper, *Diario de Manila*; persuaded by his sister, he confessed the secrets and plans of the organization to an Augustinian priest who immediately informed the authorities. This took place on the evening of 19 August 1896.

[78]Andres Bonifacio; 1863, born in Tondo, the son of a tailor; orphaned at 14, made a living as a peddler, then as a courier for a couple of foreign firms in Manila; self-educated, inspired by the lessons of the French Revolution; he founded the Katipunan in 1892. For the background of the nationalist movement and other nationalist leaders, see Book III.

[79]The 'cry' was uttered in the hills of Balintawak, a few miles north of Manila where, at an impassioned meeting of his supporters, Bonifacio tore up his *cedula* (certificate/permit) in pieces and got his audience to do likewise, shouting 'Long Live Philippine Independence!'.

[80]On 13 September the '13 martyrs of Cavite'; on 4 January 1897, 12 Bicolandia patriots—shot in Manila; on 23 March, the '19 martyrs of Aklan' shot at Capiz etc.

[81]Actually Rizal was arrested on board a ship in the Suez Canal on the orders of the Manila government, whilst on his way to join the Spanish Army engaged in the Cuban Revolution as a surgeon; he had obtained permission to leave his exile in Dapitan, Mindanao, for this purpose. He was then brought back to the Philippines to face his trial and execution. In fact, although the Spanish authorities were convinced of his complicity in the Filipino uprising, Rizal did not support it at all but believed it to be premature. For his life and contribution to Filipino nationalism, see Book III.

[82]Emilio Aguinaldo; 1869, born at Kawit, Cavite, of middle-class parents (his father was a *capitan municipal*); educated at the College of San Juan de Letran, Manila, till his father's death; entered into farming and business to support his family; 1895, joined the Katipunan; elected *capitan municipal* of Kawit in the same year.

[83]Magdiwang and Magdalo—names of two local councils which declared themselves provincial bodies after the nationalist victories in early November. Aguinaldo's supporters had their headquarters at San Francisco de Malabon and both assemblies were held in territory dominated by them.

[84]Others elected included Mariano Trias as Vice-President, Artemio Ricarte as Captain-General, Emiliano Riego de Dios as Director of War.

[85]Aguinaldo at first commuted the sentence to one of solitary confinement but later yielded to the pressure of some of his lieutenants who felt that Bonifacio's continued survival would harm morale and disrupt the Revolution. In fact, the execution had the reverse effect to that desired: 'This tragic event dampened the general enthusiasm for the revolutionary cause. It hastened the collapse of the insurrection in Cavite because many.... went home in disgust.' Mabini, one of the Filipino leaders, in his memoirs *Revolucion, II*: quoted by de la Costa, *Readings in Philippine History*, op. cit. p. 238.

[86]The government was vested in a Supreme Council comprising a President, Vice-President and four Secretaries (Foreign Relations, War, Interior, Treasury). The Supreme Council could 'give orders with the force of law, impose or collect taxes, and supervise and direct military operations'. The executive power lay in the hands of the President or Vice-President. The Constitution included a Bill of Rights, and set up a Supreme Court of Grace and Justice.

[87]Including *inter alia* Edilberto Evangelista, a brilliant young engineer, at Zapote Bridge in February and the youthful college graduate commander, Flaviano Yengko, in March at Perez Dasmariñas. Aguinaldo's elder brother, Crispulo, was killed in action some three weeks later.

[88]Primo de Rivera had already sent a couple of Spaniards to contact Aguinaldo in March, but without success.

[89]The Pact consisted of three documents: the first entitled 'Programme' dealt with Aguinaldo's exile; the second entitled 'Act of Agreement' dealt with the general amnesty; the third, which was signed separately on the second day, was concerned with the indemnity.

[90]Aguinaldo claimed that Primo de Rivera agreed to expel the religious orders, restore Philippine representation in the Spanish Cortes (Parliament), establish equality before the law for Spaniard and Filipino alike, revise property rights and taxes in the Filipino favour and guarantee the basic freedoms. He also claimed that Primo de Rivera did not wish to have these promises written into the Pact as this would be embarrassing to the Spanish government.

THE AMERICAN CONQUEST

The Intrusion of the United States

The outbreak of the Spanish–American War in 1898 had nothing to do with the Philippines. Instead the issue centred on another island, Cuba, in the West Indies, also in the throes of a nationalist struggle for independence from Spanish rule. The Cuban crisis started with the uprising of February 1895 and soon provoked public attention in the United States because of the traditional antipathy of the Americans to colonialism (particularly colonialism in the Western hemisphere), and also because of the substantial American investments in the sugar-plantation industry there.[1] American public opinion was further aroused by the harsh, repressive measures employed during 1896 by the Spanish commander, General Valeriano Weyler, against the Cuban patriots, so much so that President Cleveland was constrained to protest to the Spanish government 'in the name of humanity'. Tension between Spain and the United States increased greatly at the beginning of 1898 with the 'policastro' scandal and came virtually to breaking point when the U.S. battleship *Maine* blew up in Havana harbour with the loss of 260 American lives.[2] At the beginning of April, President McKinley asked Congress for guidance; Congress replied a week later in the form of four resolutions; three demanding the independence of Cuba and authorizing the use of force. The fourth, the famous Teller amendment which was to twist many a liberal American conscience later on, disclaimed 'any disposition or intention to exercise sovereignty, jurisdiction or control' over Cuba and pledged the withdrawal of the United States once independence and a firm government had been established. Five days after Congress had passed these resolutions, the Spanish government in Madrid, exasperated by this American interference, issued its declaration of war.

The Philippines was very soon affected by these developments. An American naval squadron under the command of Commodore Dewey, which had been sheltering at Hong Kong in anticipation of these events,[a] sailed for the Philippines as soon as news of the declaration of war was received. At dawn on 1 May 1898 the American squadron steamed into Manila Bay and proceeded to blow the entire Spanish fleet out of the water. By midday it was all over. The Spanish fleet in Eastern waters had been destroyed and 381 Spanish sailors had been killed or wounded. The Americans did not lose one single man.[3] In this way the Battle of Manila Bay heralded the entrance onto the South-East Asian stage of the United States as a colonial power.

However, the Americans were not yet prepared for a campaign of conquest on land. Dewey demanded the surrender of Manila which was rejected by the Spanish governor, Basilio Augustin. So he could do nothing but wait until the expeditionary force which was now being feverishly recruited in California was ready. It was not until 30 June that the first American army contingent arrived in the Philippines under the command of Brigadier-General Thomas M. Anderson, having taken Guam en route. A second contingent under Brigadier-General Francis M. Greene arrived in mid-July, having taken Wake Island on the way. The third contingent under Brigadier-General Arthur MacArthur arrived at the end of the same month. The total American forces, which were under the overall command of

[a] See p. 382.

Major-General Wesley E. Merritt, numbered 11,000. Against them in the Philippines were 35,000 Spanish troops, of whom 13,000 were concentrated in Manila itself. However, the Americans had as allies 12,000 Filipino nationalists organized under the command of Emilio Aguinaldo.

The return of Aguinaldo and the formation of the Malolos Republic

Naturally Aguinaldo and his friends in exile followed the developing crisis between Spain and the United States with the keenest attention. When war broke out, Aguinaldo was actually in Singapore. Whilst there, through H.W. Bray, a British businessman well disposed to the Filipino leaders and who could speak Spanish, he was contacted by the American Consul-General, W.E. Spencer-Pratt, who discussed with him the possibilities of Filipino-U.S. co-operation against Spain. But Pratt declared that he could not discuss the political future when Aguinaldo asked him for American help to establish Filipino independence. Nevertheless the Americans were clearly interested in gaining Filipino support and Aguinaldo rushed back to Hong Kong to contact Dewey who, having been informed of the Singapore conversations, invited the Filipino nationalist leader to meet him.[4] When Aguinaldo arrived, he found that Dewey had already sailed to his victory in Manila Bay. Waiting in Hong Kong, Aguinaldo had further talks with the Americans, this time dealing with Rounseville Wildman, the U.S. consul there, who promised to purchase arms for the Filipinos. Meanwhile Dewey, hearing of Aguinaldo's return to Hong Kong, sent the cutter *McCulloch* from Manila Bay to carry the Filipino leader back to the Philippines. On 19 May 1898 Aguinaldo landed at Cavite to renew his country's struggle for independence at the behest of the Americans.

Once back, Aguinaldo wasted no time. He carried with him a draft constitution, the work of Mariano Ponce whilst in Hong Kong, for a federal Philippines Republic. But he was advised that the moment was not opportune to proclaim it and so as a provisional measure, he declared the creation of a Dictatorship at Cavite on 24th May, five days after his arrival. The next step was the formal proclamation of Filipino independence. This took place at Kawit, Cavite, on 12 June 1898 with a solemn ceremony at which an 'Act of the Declaration of Independence' (inspired by the American model) was signed by 98 people, the Filipino national anthem sung and the Filipino flag unfurled for the first time.[5] An ominous shadow over the event was cast by the absence of Commodore Dewey, now the chief American representative in the Philippines, who declined the invitation on the grounds that it was 'mail day' and he would be busy with the fleet.

The proclamation of independence was followed by a whole stream of decrees which set up—at least on paper[6]—the structure of a functioning administration. With the lawyer Apolinario Mabini[7] as his adviser and right-hand man, Aguinaldo issued proclamations reconstituting municipal and provincial government, setting up a committee in Hong Kong to obtain recognition for the Republic from the important powers[8] and providing for the convening of a congress to give the republic a constitution. On 23 June on the further advice of Mabini, Aguinaldo sagely revised the style of his régime from that of 'dictatorship' to one of 'revolutionary government' (with his own position restyled President) in a proclamation which declared his aim to be 'to struggle for the independence of the Philippines, until all nations, including Spain, shall expressly recognise it, and also to prepare the country for the establishment of a real republic'.

On 15 July 1898, the first cabinet of the revolutionary government took their oaths of office.[9] Two months later, the nationalists held their first congress at Barasoian church, Malolos. The original members numbered 85 but this rose later to 110. They represented a fair cross-section of the burgeoning Filipino middle class, the largest element being formed by lawyers (around about 40), with 16 doctors, 5 pharmacists, 2 engineers, 1 priest and the rest, merchants and wealthy farmers. Some had been elected but most were appointed. After the Congress was opened by Aguinaldo who spoke in Tagalog and Spanish, the body got down to electing its officials, and then divided itself into committees to carry out its functions.[10] At the end of the month, they ratified the declaration of independence; in October they sanctioned the floating of a domestic loan of 20 million pesos; and in November they produced a constitution.

The constitution of the Malolos Republic was drawn up by Felipe Calderon, a noted Filipino lawyer and social scientist who had been appointed the representative for Palawan by Aguinaldo. It was a liberal document consisting of a preamble, 14 titles and 101 articles. It laid down that there should be a 'popular, representative, alternative and responsible' government with legislative powers in the hands of an elected Assembly of Representatives and headed by an executive who could be the President himself, assisted by a Cabinet of seven Secretaries. The President was to be elected by the Assembly.[11] The constitution also provided for basic individual rights, the separation of Church from State[12] and a Supreme Court of Justice. Impressive on paper, the course of events never allowed the constitution to function in practice. It was approved by the Malolos Congress on 29 November 1898 and sent to Aguinaldo for signature. However, at first Aguinaldo, still guided by Mabini's advice, refused to sign on the grounds that the moment was inopportune and that the President should have more power. The ensuing deadlock was broken after both sides had compromised on their original positions. The Constitution was finally approved and on 21 January 1899 it was promulgated and formally inaugurated at the Barasoian Church when Aguinaldo took his oath of office as head of state. Less than a fortnight later the fledgling republic declared war on the United States of America and entered on its death struggle.

The collapse of the Spanish régime

Confrontation with the United States was the inevitable outcome of the collapse of Spanish rule. While Aguinaldo was fashioning the political structure of an independent Filipino state, the struggle with Spain went on. At the eleventh hour, the Spanish authorities tried to win over the Filipino nationalists with concessions. Three days after the Battle of Manila Bay, Governor Augustin ordered the creation of a Filipino Volunteer Militia to defend the country against the Americans, granting commissions to prominent Filipinos who at the first opportunity went over to Aguinaldo all the same. On the same day the governor decreed the setting up of a Consultative Assembly to be headed by Dr. Pedro Paterno. The Consultative Assembly held its first meeting on 28 May but although Augustin promised certain reforms it was clear from the beginning that none of the delegates were taking the business seriously. Within a fortnight the Assembly was adjourned *sine die*, having achieved nothing.

When all this was going on, Aguinaldo had already been active resuming the military struggle against the Spaniards. At the end of May, having received their first consignment of arms purchased through Wildman in Hong Kong,[13] his forces won their first success against the detachment of Spanish marines who had come to retrieve them. This was followed within a week by the defeat and capture of the Spanish General Garcia Peña who found himself and his men surrounded and cut off at Cavite. The new Volunteer Militia went over wholesale to the side of Aguinaldo. By 11 June the principal towns of Cavite had been captured, with the veteran Spanish general, Ricardo Monet, 'fleeing in terror' to Manila. By the end of the month, Aguinaldo's men controlled the greater part of Luzon outside Manila and had begun the investment of Manila itself. Soon, with its water supply cut and surrounded by 14 miles of trenches, the capital was in a state of siege. On 13 August by which time the Filipino forces had been added to by American regulars, Manila fell.[a]

After this the collapse of Spanish rule came swiftly and even painlessly. Having formally surrendered the city to the Americans, the new Spanish governor, General Diego de los Rios[14] transferred his headquarters to Iloilo in Panay, retracing the steps of Legazpi as it were. In December, facing heavy pressure from Bisayan patriots led by Delgado, the governor withdrew again, this time to Zamboanga (Sambuangan). Zamboanga was the last centre of Spanish authority in the Philippines. In May 1899, the Spanish civil administration and the garrison there made way for American troops. Only in isolated Baler, on Luzon's Pacific coast, did a Spanish garrison put up a spirited twelve-month resistance, finally surrendering to Aguinaldo's men on 2 June 1899.[15]

The breakdown in Filipino–United States relations

The elimination of Spain naturally brought to the fore the question of Filipino-U.S. relations and the problem of what the future was to be. Right from the very beginning there had been an element of doubt and unease in the relationships between the Americans and the nationalists. Aguinaldo, in his dealings with the American consular officials at Singapore and Hong Kong, had pressed for an American commitment on Filipino independence which neither man had been in a position to give. Subsequently Aguinaldo maintained that they and Commodore Dewey did in fact give him assurances that the United States of America would recognize Filipino independence, although this was denied by all three of them.[16] The truth is that the American government had not yet made up its mind what to do about the Philippines, with the result that, as one American historian has put it, 'If our handling of the Philippine problem during these months can be dignified by the term "policy", it may be summarized as one which sought the maximum of Filipino assistance with the minimum of American commitment'.[17]

From the nationalist point of view, American assistance was essential, and Filipino leaders could only hope for favourable circumstances and rely on American

[a]See p. 373.

good faith. Disturbing portents that this good faith was lacking accumulated as the weeks went by. There was Commodore Dewey's polite refusal to be present at the ceremonial proclamation of independence at Kawit in June. In July, General Anderson told Aguinaldo that he acknowledged the Filipino leader's military but not his civil authority. Much more serious was the manner in which Manila fell into American hands. Prior to the final assault on the city, Merritt, the American commander, came to a secret understanding with Fermin Jaudenes, the Spanish governor, according to which the capital would surrender after merely a token resistance, and by which Aguinaldo's Filipino troops would not be allowed in 'for fear that they might massacre the Spaniards in the city'. When this became known, the nationalists were outraged and it was only with difficulty that Aguinaldo prevented a clash from taking place between the Americans and his more impetuous followers.

After this incident Filipino-American relations steadily deteriorated. The day before Manila fell, the Spanish-American War came to an end with the signing of the cease-fire in Washington on 12 August.[18] This was followed by two months of negotiations between the two powers in order to come to a peace treaty. Felipe Agoncillo, Aguinaldo's representative in Paris where the Conference was being held, tried to get permission to appear before the Spanish and American delegates but this was refused. On 10 December the Peace Treaty was signed. Under its terms Spain ceded the Philippines, Guam and Puerto Rico to the United States and withdrew her sovereignty from Cuba. The future of the inhabitants of the ceded territories was to be determined by the Congress of the United States, and the United States was to pay to Spain the sum of $U.S. 20 million.[19] The nationalist reaction to all this was understandably one of extreme annoyance. Agoncillo in Paris filed an official protest and then went to the United States to join the growing forces of those who wished to oppose its ratification by the Senate.[a] However, after heated and nation-wide debates, the Senate did ratify the Treaty on 6 February 1899, by 57 votes to 27, that is by only 1 vote above the required two-thirds majority.[20]

Meanwhile back in the Philippines both sides had been preparing for the struggle which, it seemed, was inevitably going to take place. On 14 August General Merritt assumed formal responibility for the administration of the islands by proclaiming an American military occupation. American military rule was to last till 1901 when it was replaced by a civilian regime.[21] The next step came soon after the signing of the Peace Treaty in Paris but before its ratification by the American Congress. On 21 December 1898 President McKinley of the United States announced the American decision to retain the Philippines, whilst assuring the Filipinos that 'the mission of the United States is one of benevolent assimilation, substituting the mild sway of justice and right for arbitrary rule'.[22] However, General Otis, the new American military governor in Manila, correctly judged that these professions of good intent would not sound so well to nationalist ears and so delayed its publication till early in the new year. He also emasculated the text to make it sound more acceptable, but the U.S. army commander at Iloilo inadvertently published the original so that what President McKinley had actually said was soon known throughout the Philippines. The proclamation was predictably rejected by the nationalists. President

[a]See p. 382.

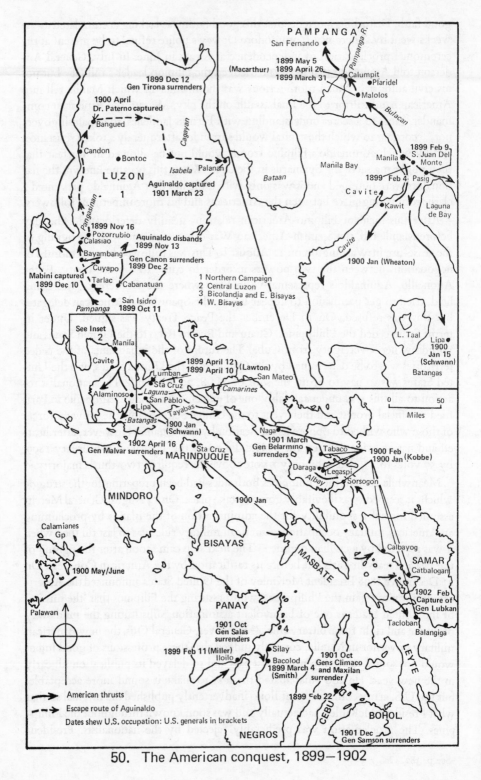

50. The American conquest, 1899–1902

Aguinaldo, in a counter-proclamation issued the following day, rejected the American claim to sovereignty, spoke of the Filipino role in the liberation of Manila and accused the American authorities of breaking their pledges. That night posters of the American proclamation were torn down in Manila streets and replaced by those of Aguinaldo.

A serious deadlock had now been reached. The Filipino nationalists with a proto-parliament at Malolos and a draft constitution awaiting the presidential signature were in no mood to surrender what was apparently within their grasp. The American government, on the other hand, had taken the decision to stay in the Philippines. On 7 January 1899, Dewey cabled Washington, advising the creation of 'a civilian commission composed of men skilled in diplomacy and statesmanship... to adjust differences'. Acting promptly, McKinley found out that Otis was in agreement and on 20 January appointed the First Philippines Commission under the chairmanship of Dr. Jacob Gould Schurman, the President of Cornell University.[23] The Commission was given three main tasks. It was to deliver a message of goodwill from the United States to the people of the Philippines. It was to investigate conditions there and it was to make recommendations as to the kind of government which should be established. Whether Aguinaldo and the men of Malolos would have been prepared to talk terms with this commission was never put to the test, because when Schurman and his colleagues arrived at Manila on 4 March the Philippines Republic had already been at war with the United States for one month.

The Philippine War of Independence
The incident which started the Philippine War of Independence took place at 8 p.m. on the night of 4 February 1899 at San Juan del Monte on the outskirts of Manila, when an American soldier shot dead a Filipino who failed to answer his challenge.[24] This was another of several such incidents which had been occurring during the previous few weeks but on this occasion more shots were fired on both sides until it became a general action. As soon as he heard the news of the fighting later that night, Aguinaldo issued a declaration of war. The war thus begun lasted on a large scale for two years and continued with spasmodic skirmishes right until 1904. It cost the United States the lives of over 4,200 of her troops and 600 million pesos worth of her treasure. 16,000 Filipinos were killed in action and another 20,000 died from the famine and plague which stalked in the wake of the fighting.

The main organized fighting was confined to the great central plain of Luzon, north of Manila, but General Otis's assumption that the war would be over once the Tagalog provinces were quelled proved to be mistaken. Organized fighting in Central Luzon lasted for the greater part of 1899. Initially it was centred in the immediate vicinity of Manila where the nationalists made an all-out attempt to take the city from within and from without between 22 and 24 February. But the Americans never lost the upper hand in the city, and in the meantime had already driven a wedge between north and south by driving across to Laguna de Bay, capturing Pasig on the 11th. Between February and April, the main nationalist forces fell back to the line of the Pampanga river. The Republic's first seat of government at Malolos fell on 31 March and Aguinaldo and his cabinet moved themselves northward to San Fernando behind the Pampanga. Three weeks later the Americans under General MacArthur forced the Bagbag river and entered Calumpit.

Shortly afterwards they crossed the Pampanga itself and on 5 May captured San Fernando.

A lull of several months followed, caused by the rains and the reorganization of the American forces.[25] The nationalists were able to use this breathing space to reconsider their position and the best tactics to follow. But at their new headquarters at San Isidro in Pangasinan serious dissensions broke out. A strong peace party emerged at a rump meeting of the Malolos Congress which voted in favour of attempting negotiations with the Americans. During April and May three attempts were made to come to terms with Otis and the Schurman Commission despite the opposition of Mabini and the obstruction of General Luna.[26] However they were all fruitless since Otis, suspecting the nationalists were merely playing for time, refused to compromise. The ranks of the nationalists were shaken even more profoundly in June by the assassination of General Luna.[27] Probably the best commander on the nationalist side, Luna's outspokenness and lack of diplomacy had alienated several of the other leaders including Paterno, Buencamino and Aguinaldo himself. Fearing for their own positions, they had him killed.[28]

The death of Luna destroyed the solidarity of the nationalists, and although Aguinaldo now took over personal command of the army, it was no longer possible to hold it together as before. This factor and the realization by Aguinaldo and the others that the next American offensive would probably prove irresistible determined a change of tactics. When the American offensive resumed at the beginning of October, the nationalist forces fell back rapidly. San Isidro fell on the 11th while Aguinaldo and the government moved first to Tarlac and then to Bayambang. There on 12 November Aguinaldo put into effect his decision to give up formal, organized resistance and to resort to guerrilla warfare. He disbanded the army and, dividing the country up into military zones, each under a guerrilla leader,[29] dispersed his forces.

The new tactics proved successful in prolonging the war by another two years. Although the principal centres of population quickly fell into American hands, the countryside remained wide open to the guerrillas who could always get all the supplies they needed and who could hardly be distinguished from the ordinary peasant. However, as organized resistance collapsed, many nationalist leaders surrendered or fell into American hands. Four days after the disbandment of the army, Felipe Buencamino[30] and Aguinaldo's son and mother were captured at Pozorrubio. In the following month General Fernando Canon surrendered at Cabanatuan (Nueva Ecija), Colonel Tirona gave himself up in Cagayan and Mabini was captured at Cuyapo. On Christmas Day, Aguinaldo's wife and sister were captured at Bontoc. Not everything went the American way. In a sharp skirmish at San Mateo in the same month, the American General Lawton met his death. Nevertheless, early in 1900 the rate of captured and surrendered leaders increased. The Americans now launched a series of campaigns to the south and within three months they had brought the whole of the island down to Albay and Sorsogon under their control.[31] Encouraged by their successes in July of that year they offered an amnesty to all Filipinos who had not violated the laws of war and would accept U.S. sovereignty. In addition, there was a 30 peso reward for every rifle—in good condition—which was handed in. The offer was for 90 days. A number of nationalists accepted these terms, but the hard core stayed firm. By the end of 1900, the main centres of guerrilla resistance were in Batangas (under General Malvar) and in Cebu, Bohol and Samar, while Aguinaldo himself was still at large.

The capture of Aguinaldo; the last days of the nationalist struggle

The capture of Aguinaldo in March 1901 was a severe blow to the nationalist cause. After he had given his orders to disband the army at Bayambang in November 1899, Aguinaldo fled northwards. Passing through Calasiao, Manaoag, Pozorrubio and Candon, he made his way through Ilocos and the Mountain Province to Isabela where at remote Palanan he set up his headquarters. For the first part of this journey the Americans were close on his heels, which gave rise to the epic stand at the Tirad Pass on 2 December 1899 when a small rearguard party of sixty picked riflemen, led by the 24-year-old General Gregorio del Pilar, held up an American force of some 300 men.[32] Aguinaldo's hide-out at Palanan remained undivined by the Americans for over a year. Then, early in 1901, they learned by chance of his whereabouts[33] and a small party led by five American officers made their way up the inhospitable Pacific coastline to Palanan, then achieving complete surprise captured Aguinaldo in his house. As prisoner he was treated well, and in April, apparently on his own volition, Aguinaldo issued his last proclamation accepting American sovereignty and advising his brother Filipinos to do the same.

Aguinaldo's capture did not mark the end of war, although by this time Filipino resistance had been reduced to a few isolated areas. From the depths of Batangas, General Miguel Malvar issued a call to Filipinos to continue the struggle. In September, Filipino guerrillas on Mariduque made prisoner a whole company of American soldiers from Santa Cruz. In the same month at Balangiga on Samar the guerrillas of General Lubkan killed 57 men of the American garrison there, the worst single setback the Americans suffered during the whole conflict.

However, the end was approaching. Generals Juan Climaco and Arcadio Maxilom surrendered on Cebu in October 1901 and Pedro Samson on Bohol followed suit two months later. This left two main centres of resistance—Samar and Batangas. General Lubkan defied the Americans on Samar till he was captured in February 1902. The American campaign on Samar was conducted by General Jacob H. Smith, or 'Hell-roaring Jake' as he was popularly known. His methods were so ruthless and savage that it gave rise to a public outcry in the United States, as a result of which Smith was recalled, court-martialled, found guilty and retired. The last Filipino general to surrender was Malvar in Batangas, but by 1902 even he saw the futility of further resistance and on 8 May of that year gave himself up to the American authorities. Shortly afterwards he made a proclamation, declaring all resistance to be at an end. And so it was to all intents and purposes. There were still some Filipinos who carried on the struggle after 1902, but their activities became virtually indistinguishable from ordinary brigandage, which was how they were regarded by the Philippine authorities. One after another they were rounded up, put on trial and executed.[34]

The reasons for the nationalists' failure

The defeat of the Filipino nationalists was to be expected in the conditions and circumstances prevailing at the time, a fact which a number of the protagonists themselves had realized right from the very beginning.[35] When the fighting started, the nationalist effectives probably numbered around 20,000, who were armed with a very varied assortment of weapons—Spanish, American, German; they possessed no artillery or cavalry to speak of, and there was hardly one military engineer in the whole of the nationalist forces. The 'generals' were brave and intelligent, fought magnificently and provided inspiring leadership; but no amount of these qualities could make up for youth and inexperience, almost a total lack of military training (there were a few exceptions), and the fact that their lieutenants were largely their own relatives and friends of the same calibre. Furthermore, the revolutionary struggle for independence did not have the whole-hearted support of all Filipinos. Many of the educated and wealthy upper classes either realized the futility of resistance, or thought that the Filipinos were not yet ready for independence, either[36] sincerely or for selfish reasons of their own. Nationalist morale was seriously weakened as the campaign went on. The murder of General Luna was a severe blow and the capture of Aguinaldo even greater.

On the other hand, the war might have been ended sooner had it not been mishandled on the American side at the outset. The vagaries of American policy before the time of McKinley's declaration assuming American sovereignty created an atmosphere of uncertainty and suspicion as well as effectively destroying Spanish authority without substituting that of its own.[37] In this way the forces of Aguinaldo were given time to concentrate and prepare themselves for the struggle. When the fighting broke out, the American commander, General Otis, consistently underestimated the strength of the resistance and his own needs, and whereas at first he stated he would require 35,000 troops, in the end he had to have twice that number.[38]

However, as American policy and intentions began to emerge more clearly as the Schurman Commission got down to work, an increasing number of Filipinos were won over to the new regime. The report of the Commission,[a] which was submitted to President McKinley in January 1900, while declaring that the Philippines was not yet ready for independence and that U.S. rule should continue, at the same time recommended that military rule should give way to civilian government as soon as possible and that representative institutions should be set up. In order to implement these recommendations, McKinley appointed a second Philippines Commission, this time under a Federal Judge, William Taft,[39] to hasten the transfer to civilian authority. It arrived in Manila in June 1900 and got straight to work. At the beginning of September, all legislative powers were transferred from the military governor to the Commission, and the final establishment of civilian as opposed to military authority was confirmed by the Spooner Amendment of March 1901.[40] On 4 July 1901, Judge Taft was officially inaugurated as the first American civil governor of the Philippines.

Certain sections of Filipino opinion had been so impressed with these developments that—with active American encouragement—they decided to form a political party supporting American sovereignty and ultimate statehood within the American Union. This was the Federal Party (*Partido Federal*) which was founded in Manila at the end of December 1900, by Dr. T.H. Pardo de Tavera and others.[b]

[a]See Book II.
[b]See Book III.

Other more nationalist parties made their first appearance during the course of 1902. The liberal policies pursued by Governor Taft had a most important effect in bringing about the general pacification of the country. On 4 July 1902, a few days after the passage of the Philippine Bill setting up an elective Philippine Assembly and extending the application of the American Bill of Rights to the Philippines,[a] President Theodore Roosevelt[41] issued an official statement declaring the War of Philippines' Independence to be at an end.

The incorporation of the Muslim South into the Philippine nation

Roosevelt's proclamation, however, only extended to the Christian regions of the Philippines. The Muslim South remained under military jurisdiction until 1913, during which time the Americans were engaged in a prolonged struggle to bring the region under their control. This episode may be regarded as the final act in the making of the modern nation of the Philippines, for during the Spanish period Manila had never succeeded in subjugating the south, let alone integrating it socially and politically with the rest of the archipelago. Only after the American conquest can Magindanau and Sulu truly be said to have become part of the Philippines of today.

The story of this last struggle is recounted more fully elsewhere.[b] Here an outline will suffice. American troops came to replace the Spanish garrisons in the region during the course of 1899. At first the whole area was treated as one military command, and its first commandant, General John C. Bates, succeeded in negotiating a treaty with Sultan Jamalul Kiram II of Sulu and four of his principal datos without difficulty. By this treaty, signed in August 1899, the Sultan and his chiefs acknowledged the American protectorate, promised to co-operate in the suppression of piracy and in the control of fire-arms, and to allow any slave who wished to buy his freedom to do so; in return, Sulu was guaranteed that its religion would not be interfered with and the Sultan with his principal chiefs would be paid salaries from Manila. However, the agreement did not work out satisfactorily. The Americans charged that the Sulu chiefs were happy to collect their emoluments but were not prepared to co-operate in maintaining peace and order. As a result of representations made by American officials on the spot,[42] Washington decided to abrogate the Bates Treaty, and the Sultan was informed accordingly, in March 1904. Jamalul Kiram then pointed out that with the agreement terminated, the position reverted to what it had been in 1899 under the Spaniards—whereby Sulu recognized Manila's overlordship but was not subject to Manila's interference in its internal affairs. Matters remained thus undefined for the next ten years during which time the sporadic acts of violence against Americans in the region intensified. Reckless acts of defiance had tragic consequences. Under various leaders, groups of Sulu men, women and children, strong in their religious hatred of Christians, defied death at the hands of the disciplined American soldiery. One of the worst such encounters was on the slopes of the extinct volcano of Bud Dajo on Jolo itself when 600 men with some women and children were killed in 1906. On a similar occasion in 1913 on Mount Bagsak, also on Jolo, another 300 perished.

[a]See Book II.
[b]Refer pp. 215–16.

Nevertheless by this time progress had been made in pacification and the Americans instituted ordinary civilian government for the first time. Under the first civilian governor of the province, Frank W. Carpenter, who went out of his way to win over the hostile datos by meeting with them and discussing their problems with them, a new agreement was reached in 1915 with the Sultan. By this, Jamalul Kiram abdicated from all political power, received a life pension of 12,000 pesos a year and was recognized as the spiritual leader of all Filipino Muslims. Meanwhile in Mindanao the Americans met with even more determined resistance, but, fragmented as it was, it represented more of a nuisance than a serious threat. It was many years before peace finally came to Moroland.

Spanish motives in the Philippines: trade and the Christian ideal
The Philippine experience is unique in several ways, not least in that both the Western powers that dominated the islands were motivated by a strong streak of idealism which has left irremovable traces on their political and cultural development. Spain was inspired by the Christian ideal; the United States by its own horror of colonialism and its faith in liberal democracy.

Three main motives brought the Spaniards to the Philippines. One was the obvious desire to win a share in the lucrative spice trade which had already been cornered by the Portuguese. Secondly, the Philippines were seen as the door which opened on to both China and Japan, great potential markets and sources of trade, and a vast field for missionary enterprise. Third was the desire to spread Christianity throughout the Philippines themselves. In the event, it was the third motive which was to prove the most constant and the most practicable. The Spaniards never succeeded in getting a share in the rich spice monopoly. It fell from the hands of the Portuguese into those of the Dutch, and as for the Philippines, they became a perpetual drain on the royal treasury. After some limited initial successes both Japan and China became closed to virtually all Christian missionary enterprise, and indeed to trade as well.[43] But as we have seen, the Spaniards did succeed in making the Philippines into a Christian nation.

The genuineness and reality of the religious motive should not be underestimated. The instructions of Legazpi which stated 'that the chief thing sought after by His Majesty is the increase of our Holy Catholic Faith and the salvation of the souls of these infidels', strongly reflected Dominican influence, in particular that of Francisco de Vitoria,[44] and the administrative arrangements made for the presence of the Roman Catholic Church in the Philippines[45] make it clear that these aims were meant to be carried out. More striking proof of the importance of the religious motive if not its paramountcy is afforded by the attitude of the court of Spain at the beginning of the seventeenth century, when it was under strong commercial pressure to abandon the Philippines altogether.[46] It was religious influence which prevented such a decision from being taken and which preserved the Philippines as 'an arsenal and warehouse of the Faith'. In fact, the Philippines administration could only be maintained by means of an annual subsidy from Mexico. The small merchant oligarchy of Manila may have waxed rich but the royal government of Spain supported an annual deficit which fluctuated between 85,000 and 338,000 pesos between 1572 and 1821,[47] and spent an estimated 400 million pesos in order to maintain both her sovereignty and the glory of the Catholic Faith in the islands.

U.S. motives in the Philippines: trade and the liberal ideal

The background to Spain's entry to the Philippines was an age of religious conflict, Christian against Muslim, Roman Catholic against the heretics of the Protestant Reformation.[a] The background to the arrival of the United States three centuries later was that of a young country which had freed itself from its colonial status and was wedded to the principles of the Rights of Man and of free enterprise. The idealistic liberalism of the Americans was at the same time tempered by a happy combination of political, strategic and economic self-interest which provided the reasons for their annexation of the Philippines at the turn of the nineteenth century. When the United States went to war with Spain in 1898, a strong imperialist, expansionist group was in existence amongst the ruling circles in the country. It had its strength in the Republican Party (although not all Republicans were of this persuasion) and its spokesman were such people as Theodore Roosevelt, Senator Cabot Lodge, the exponent of naval power, Admiral Mahan, and the publisher Randoph Hearst.—all of whom enjoyed the backing of business circles, jingoists[48] and military men. To them, in the words of Cabot Lodge, Manila was 'the great prize and the thing which will give us the Eastern trade', or as the financier, Frank Vanderlip, put it, the Philippines was the gateway to half the population of the world. Like the Spaniards before them, American businessmen valued the Philippines more as a gateway to the world of the Far East than for the islands themselves. To the strategist, however, the Philippines appeared as an invaluable *point d'appui* for American power and influence in the Far East, and Gage, Long and Day—all Cabinet members—wanted the islands for a naval base.

Then there was another consideration. What would happen to the Philippines if they were not retained by the United States? American public opinion would never tolerate their retention by the arbitrary rule of Spain. If left to themselves, it was doubtful whether the Filipinos would be able to prevent the spread of anarchy and this would only invite intervention from another imperialist power. Japan had already expressed her interest if the United States wanted a partner in running the islands. Germany was actively interested.[49] The other powers were watching each others moves carefully.[50] Britain let it be known that she would be happy if the United States took over.[51] To these arguments of trade, strategy and power politics were added those of religion. The religious press in the United States was almost unaminously in favour of annexation. The leading Roman Catholic prelates in the United States preferred an American presence to a Spanish one for the better educational opportunities this would offer. The Protestants[52] welcomed the chance to enter an entirely new field.

At the top of the imperialist coalition stood the President of the United States and leader of the Republican Party, William McKinley, whom Theodore Roosevelt once rather unkindly described as having 'no more backbone than a chocolate éclair',[b] and of whom the Spanish ambassador, Dupuy de Lome[c] said that he was 'weak and a bidder for the admiration of the crowd'. Be that as it may, McKinley had a good party man's instinct as to what would and what would not win votes,

[a]Refer pp. 14–15.
[b]Quoted by Grunder and Livezey, *The Philippines and the United States*, p. 30.

and although he was not keen on annexing distant territories, he knew that to return the Philippines to Spanish rule would be very unpopular in the United States.

The American decision to annex the Philippines

Before any final decision could be taken, however, both the Senate and the nation
would have to be consulted. The Senate had the constitutional duty to give its sanction to all acts of foreign policy[53] and therefore would have to ratify the peace treaty with Spain, and 1900 was an election year for the Presidency. Both the ratification and the election gave an opportunity to those opposed to the annexation to put
their case.

The anti-imperialist group, led by the 'silver-tongued' William Jennings Bryan,
leader of the Democratic Party and McKinley's opponent in the forthcoming presidential elections, contained some of the most distinguished figures in the United
States. Besides the Democrats it included prominent Republicans like the Senator
for Massachusetts, George Frisbie Hoare, Speaker of the House, Thomas B. Reed,
and Charles Francis Adams. Labour leader Samuel Gompers, educationist David
Star Jordan and other intellectuals like Jane Addams, E.L. Godkin and Carl Schurz,
and statesman Grover Cleveland opposed annexation. They had the backing of the
Democratic Party and that of the Anti-Imperialist League founded in Boston in June
1898. This opposition based its case on idealistic grounds. Imperialism was against
the American tradition. The United States had no right to take over the destiny of
others. It was contrary to the Constitution and against the spirit of the Rights of
Man contained in the Declaration of Independence. Annexation would bring with
it other disadvantages as well. Not only would the United States have to bear the
cost of subjugation but later might become involved in wars for the defence of the
annexed lands. Some prophetically pointed out that Asian competition might pose
a threat to both American labour and agriculture.

The great debate occupied the greater part of three years while the fate of the
Philippines was being worked out. But the imperialists had the advantage and were
able to shape events to suit their purposes. The first evidence of this lay in the mere
fact of the Battle of Manila Bay in 1898 and that Commodore Dewey had been on
hand at that particular time. This was the outcome of a manoeuvre which had its
origins in the previous year. In 1897 Theodore Roosevelt was appointed Assistant
Secretary to the Navy at the prompting of Cabot Lodge and against the better
judgement of McKinley who feared Roosevelt's irresponsibilities. Roosevelt was
well-known for his aggressive attitudes and in May 1896 had expressed his hope for a
war with Spain which would result in the United States getting 'a proper navy and
a good system of coast defence'. Once in office, he prepared for the possibility of
blockading and seizing Manila. His first success in this direction was to secure in
October the appointment of Commodore George Dewey as commander of the
Asiatic Squadron in place of the retiring Rear-Admiral McNair. Dewey's views
were similar to those of Roosevelt and his appointment was not popular with the
conservative-minded Navy Department.[54] Roosevelt's next move came in February 1898, when taking advantage of the temporary absence of his superior, Naval
Secretary Long, he ordered Dewey to Hong Kong to await developments.[55]

The *fait accompli* of Dewey's presence at Hong Kong and the subsequent destruction of the Spanish fleet in Manila Bay carried the annexationists further towards

their goal, although no final decisions had yet been taken. The next step was the signing of the peace treaty with Spain. Once again, although no official decision had yet been taken about the future of the islands, the government was manoeuvring itself into a position for getting a better option all the time. When the Spaniards made their first approaches for a ceasefire at the end of July, the United States' reply was that they would occupy and hold Manila—city, harbour and bay. One and a half months later the American delegates at the Paris Peace Conference were instructed that the United States wanted at least the island of Luzon. By 26 October, these demands had been increased to cover all the islands of the Philippines. By the time the Peace Treaty came before the Senate for ratification in January 1899, the country was to a large extent faced with a *fait accompli*.

As we have seen,[a] the ratification was carried by an effective majority of one.[56] This majority was obtained because at the last moment two wavering Senators convinced themselves that the outbreak of the fighting was the fault of the Filipinos. The defeated anti-imperialists now tried to make imperialism the key issue in the presidential elections in November of the same year. But the Republicans succeeded in turning the campaign on other issues[57] and it cannot be said that Bryan's decisive defeat at the polls was due to the question of imperialism. However, although they had failed to reverse official policy, the efforts of the anti-imperialists were not altogether in vain. The policy of the American administration in the Philippines had to make sure that its stewardship was justified. It can be truly said that no other imperialist power in South-East Asia worked so deliberately and conscientiously to prepare its subjects for their eventual independence.

[a]Refer p. 373.

[1]These amounted to over U.S. $50 million at the end of the century.

[2]The '*policastro*' scandal originated in the indiscretions of the Spanish Minister to Washington, Lopez de Lome, whose description of President McKinley as a '*policastro*' (cheap politician) became public knowledge. No evidence was ever discovered incriminating the Spanish authorities at Havana in the *Maine* disaster although it became popularly attributed to them in the U.S.A. The *Maine* incident took place in February.

[3]The result is not so surprising in view of the disparity in the forces involved: the U.S. fleet consisted of 7 vessels—4 modern armoured cruisers, 2 gunboats and a revenue cutter; the Spanish fleet comprised 7 ships including a wooden flagship with disabled engines, plus two armoured cruisers and two gunboats—all obsolete—with a total tonnage two-thirds that of the Americans ships. In addition the Spaniards possessed no torpedoes or mines.

[4]In meeting Aguinaldo in the first place, Pratt was acting on his own responsibility; likewise, Dewey's subsequent invitation to Aguinaldo to confer with him in Hong Kong was made without any prior reference to Washington.

[5]The national flag and the national anthem had both been created by the Filipino exiles in Hong Kong: amongst the 98 signatories was a U.S. colonel of artillery.

[6]Many critics have tended to regard the Malolos Republic as consisting of little more than its own constitutional documents, but a number of contemporary American observers felt that given a chance the Republic would have been viable. Refer to de la Costa, *Readings in Philippine History*, op. cit. pp. 244-5.

[7]Apolinario Mabini; 1864, born at Tanawan, Batangas, of humble origins; educated by Filipino priest-patriot, Father Valerio Malabanan, in Tawanan and at San Juan de Letran, Manila; obtained B.A. and later a law degree at the University of Santo Tomas, Manila; member of the Liga Filipina, arrested on the outbreak of the Revolution but released on account of his paralysis; became adviser of Aguinaldo in 1898; held high office under the Malolos Republic;

captured by the Americans in 1899, exiled to Guam in 1901; returned to the Philippines in 1903, died of cholera in the same year in Manila. Regarded as the brains of the Malolos Republic.

[8]In the event the nationalists only evinced a response from Japan where the Filipino envoys, Mariano Ponce and Faustino Lichano, were welcomed (though unofficially) by Prime-Minister Okuma, Ito Hirobumi and other leading statesmen in June 1898, and where the press was openly in their favour. Japanese veterans from the Sino-Japanese war (1894–5) volunteered for service in the Philippines and Ponce was easily able to purchase two shiploads of arms and ammunition. But the first consignment was shipwrecked and lost, and the second (which had been secured with the aid of Sun Yat Sen) was intercepted by the Americans and diverted to Formosa.

[9]The members included, apart from Aguinaldo himself, Mariano Trias as Secretary of Finance; Baldomero Aguinaldo as Secretary of War and Public Works; Llanero Ibarra as Secretary of the Interior. Ten days later Felipe Buencamino as Secretary of Promotion and Gregorio Araneta as Secretary of Justice were also appointed. Cayetano Arellano who was nominated Secretary for Foreign Affairs declined 'for he was not in sympathy with the Revolution'.

[10]That is, eight in all; viz. on congratulations; on messages; on internal regulations; on reception; on appropriations; on festivities; on style; to draft the constitution. As officials Pedro A. Paterno was elected President of the Congress, Benito Legarda its Vice-President and Gregorio Araneta and Pablo Ocampo its Secretaries. The Congress adopted the modified procedures of the Spanish Cortes.

[11]Joined by special representatives convened as a constituent assembly.

[12]This proved to be the most controversial issue: Calderon originally proposed the union of Church and State with Catholicism as the state religion; this was strongly opposed on grounds of democratic principle and resulted in a deadlock with Paterno refusing to give his casting vote. A second vote gave a majority of one to the separationists. The clause finally read 'That the state recognizes the freedom and equality of religion, as well as the separation of Church and State'. In the eyes of many nationalists the Church was too closely identified with colonial repression.

[13]Consisting of 2,000 Mauser rifles and 200,000 cartridges purchased by Wildman from Amoy and landed at Cavite with the connivance of the U.S. fleet.

[14]De los Rios succeeded Jaudenes as governor of the Philippines after the fall of Manila.

[15]In recognition of the valour of the Spanish garrison at Baler, Aguinaldo ordered their immediate release.

[16]The truth in this controversy will probably never be established: whatever the three American officials might have said, however, they could have been in no doubt about their own instructions. On 16 June, in reply to a cable from Pratt, the U.S. Secretary of State, William R. Day explicitly warned him 'to avoid unauthorised negotiations with Philippine insurgents', repudiated his authority to speak for Washington and urged no commitments to Aguinaldo which might lead the Filipinos 'to form hopes which it might not be practicable to gratify'.

[17]Grunder and Livezey, The Philippines and the United States, pp. 24–55.

[18]The cease-fire took place actually 23 hours before the final assault on Manila began but because Dewey had cut the cable lines between the Philippines and the outside world, news of this event did not arrive in time.

[19]As compensation for Spain's sacrifice, since this was a cheaper way of acquiring the Philippines than by renewing the war; it also provided a face-saving means of meeting the Spanish demand that the United States should assume responsibility for the Islands' Debt.

[20]The issue which decided the decisive votes of two wavering senators in favour of ratification was the outbreak of fighting between Aguinaldo's men and American troops near Manila— newspaper agency reports suggested that the Filipinos were at fault.

[21]The U.S. military governors of the Philippines were General Wesley Merritt, 14–29 August 1898; General Elwell S. Otis, 1898–1900; General Arthur MacArthur, 1900–11.

[22]Quoted by Zaide, op. cit. Vol. II, p. 313. At the same time, McKinley gave orders for the completion of the U.S. military occupation of the islands.

[23]The other four members of the Commission were Rear-Admiral George Dewey, Commander of the U.S. Asiatic Squadron; Major-General Elwell S. Otis, Military Governor of the Philippines; Charles Denby, formerly U.S. Minister to China for 15 years; Dr. Dean C. Worcester, Professor of Zoology at Michigan University, who had visited the Philippines twice previously on scientific expeditions.

[24]The shot was fired by a U.S. sentry; the Filipino may not have understood the challenge or perhaps a local commander, acting on his own initiative was planning an operation to force the U.S. lines back onto Manila.

[25]Many of the U.S. troops were State volunteers who were due for repatriation and had to be replaced by fresh reinforcements.

[26]In May when Paterno replaced Mabini as president of the Cabinet, he set up a peace committee of seven to negotiate 'an honourable peace' with the Schurmann Commission: Luna held up the delegates on their way to Manila and arrested them. A second committee of four set up by Paterno, however, did get through and discussed the U.S. terms in detail. The Filipinos failed to get satisfactory American assurances about the possible future for the insurgents in the U.S. Army and although they agreed to return after consulting Aguinaldo, the delegates never re-appeared.

[27]Antonio Luna; 1866, born at Binondo, Manila, of Ilocano parents; younger brother was the painter, Juan Luna; became a doctor of pharmacy; studied military science in Europe; at out-break of the Revolution rose to swift prominence as a military commander; responsible for reorganizing the Filipino forces after the fall of Malolos. Described as the best general the Filipinos had, he quarrelled with Aguinaldo and the other leaders over adopting guerrilla war-fare—which he opposed.

[28]He was killed by Aguinaldo's guards at Cabanatuan, Nueva Ecija, on 5 June 1899.

[29]The main regions of guerrilla activity were Laguna, Batangas, Samar, Cebu and Bohol.

[30]A member of Aguinaldo's Cabinet and one of the pioneers of Filipino nationalism.

[31]This, however, did not include all the inland areas.

[32]Del Pilar and 53 of his men died in this action, their position being lost when the Americans were shown an unknown path around the rear.

[33]By the fortuitous capture of Aguinaldo's messenger, Cecilio Segismundo, by the forces of General Funston in Nueva Ecija in January 1901. The expedition which subsequently set out consisted of 81 Macabebe scouts and 4 Tagalog, including one of Aguinaldo's former officers.

[34]The main leaders who carried on after 1901 were Mariano Noriel, a friend of Aguinaldo; Macario Sakay—a friend of Bonifacio who set up a Tagalog Republic in the mountains; Julian Montalon and Cornelio Felizardo—former officers under Mariano Trias; and Otoy, who led a gang on Samar. These men and their followers were labelled 'bandits' by the American autho-rities, and were known as *pujalones* in the Bisayas and as *tulisanes* in Luzon, which mean the same things.

[35]For instance, Colonel Arguelles, one of the emissaries sent by Paterno to negotiate with the Schurmann Commission in 1899 declared that the Filipinos were not capable of having self-government and that the nationalists were fighting for the honour of the army.

[36]Amongst these is to be numbered Rizal who regarded the Katipunan's plans for armed up-rising as premature. See de la Costa, *Readings in Philippine History*, op. cit. p. 236.

[37]One of the first American problems was the limitation placed upon their initative; the condi-tions of the cease-fire in August 1898 prohibited their troops from moving beyond Manila and Dewey rejected Spanish request for permission to reinforce their own garrisons in order to maintain law and order, fearing both a fresh outbreak of fighting against a strengthened enemy and of offending the Filipino nationalists.

[38]He started off with 21,000 under his command, of whom at least half were engaged in civilian duties, were sick or were stationed at Cavite and Iloilo.

[39]This all civilian body comprised besides Taft, a Tennessee judge called Luke E. Wright; a Vermont lawyer—Henry C. Ide; the Professor of Latin American History at the University of California—Bernard Moses; and Dean C. Worcester. Worcester was the only member of the Schurmann Commission willing to serve again. Its terms of reference were laid down in In-structions drafted by Taft and Elihu Root— the U.S. Secretary for War.

[40]This amendment, sponsored by John C. Spooner, Senator for Wisconsin, provided for the President to rule with the authority of Congress and not alone in his capacity as Commander-in-chief of the Armed Forces.

[41]McKinley had been re-elected for a second term in 1900 but was assassinated by a lunatic in 1901. Theodore Roosevelt, as Vice-President, automatically succeeded to the post.

[42]Notably Leonard Wood, governor of Moro Province in 1903, and before him General George W. Davis, military governor of Jolo and Mindanao in 1901. Also Dean Worcester, in Manila.

[43]In China where Dominicans (1631), Franciscans (1633), and Augustinians (1680) had succeed-ed in establishing themselves, the Manchu Emperor Kang Hsi (1662–1723) banned all Christ-ian missionaries in 1669, and again, effectively, after 1717, out of fear of their links with ag-gressive colonial powers. In Japan where Spanish missionaries were able to gain a footing in 1593, the Tokugawa dictator, Iemitsu, closed the country to missionaries and foreign traders for similar reasons in 1636.

[44]And also of Las Casas, another distinguished humanitarian Dominican. The royal instructions

to Legazpi 'could have been lifted almost verbatim from the lectures of the Dominican theologian, Francisco de Vitoria, delivered at the University of Salamanca', Phelan, *The Hispanization of the Philippines*, op. cit. p. 8. The Dominican ideal was pacification rather than conquest.

[45]In the Philippines as in other Spanish colonies and in Spain itself the Church and State were united: the civil authorities representing the king were bound to assist in the propagation of Christianity: the ecclesiastical authorities representing the Pope were bound to maintain the authority of the king. The salaries of Church officials and the expenses of the ecclesiastical administration were all borne by the State. In the towns the local curate also carried out civil functions and was in charge of health and charities, education, taxation, municipal budgets etc. 'In every friar in the Philippines the king had a Captain-General and a whole army'. Quoted by Zaide, op. cit. Vol. I, p. 206.

[46]From the merchants of Seville (in South Spain) who monopolized the trans-Atlantic carrying trade, as well as the textile interests of Andalucia as a whole—both groups feared the prospect of the competition of Chinese silks imported to Mexico and Peru via Manila.

[47]Till 1821 the Philippines was governed as a province of Mexico from where all the subventions came. The breakaway of Mexico from the Spanish Empire in that year led to the Philippines becoming a Crown Colony under the direct administration of Madrid.

[48]'Jingoists' meaning 'ultra-nationalists'.

[49]In fact a clash nearly took place between German warships and Dewey's fleet in Manila Bay soon after the destruction of the Spanish fleet in 1898. The Germans, along with the British, French and Japanese, had sent a squadron into the Bay to protect their interests; exasperated by the German defiance of his blockade measures, Dewey delivered an ultimatum to Von Diedrichs, the German commander. Faced with British support for Dewey's stand, the Germans finally acquiesced in the American blockade.

[50]Germany favoured Spain: the Russians feared the British would take advantage of U.S. moves to promote their own interests; the French were strictly neutral having ties with all parties; the British preferred American control to that of any of her European rivals.

[51]McKinley himself justified American annexation as follows: 'The truth is, I didn't want the Philippines, and when they came to us, as a gift from the gods, I didn't know what to do with them....' After having prayed to God for guidance; 'And one night late it came to me this way—I don't know how it was, but it came; 1. that we could not give them back to Spain—that would be cowardly and dishonourable; 2. that we could not turn them to France or Germany—that would be bad business and discreditable; 3. that we could not leave them to themselves —they were unfit for self-government and they would soon have anarchy and misrule over there worse than Spain's was; and 4. that there was nothing left for us to do but to take them all....' Quoted by Zaide, op. cit. Vol. II, pp. 223-4.

[52]With the exceptions of the Friends (Plymouth Brethren) and the Unitarians, two well-established Protestant groups who were strongly opposed to annexation on moral grounds.

[53]Specifically, no treaty and no declaration of war can be sanctioned by the President of the United States without getting the approval and ratification of the Senate.

[54]Roosevelt did this largely through the political influence of his friend, Redfield Proctor, Senator for Vermont.

[55]Roosevelt simply took advantage of a February afternoon which Long had taken off, leaving him in charge: the next day the dispositions of the Fleet had been altered, new stocks of ammunition ordered and Dewey's instructions sent out.

[56]That is, 57 to 27. The actual breakdown of senatorial attitudes at the beginning was: 34 annexationists against 29 anti-annexationists; 16 favoured annexation for a limited period only; 11 were undecided.

[57]The Republicans adroitly diverted public attention away from the Philippines problem to personalities, finance, monopolies, railway management and other domestic issues.

11. THE PHILIPPINES: CHRONOLOGY OF MAIN EVENTS

A. The Spanish Conquest

1512	Portuguese Francisco Serra(n)o in the Philippines
1521	Ferdinand Magellan in the Philippines
1525	The Loaisa expedition
1526	The Cabot expedition
1527	The Saavreda expedition
1542	The Villalobos expedition
1564	The Legazpi expedition leaves Mexico
1565	Legazpi arrives off Cebu (February);
	Legazpi on Bohol; the Legazpi-Katuna blood compact (March); Conquest of Cebu (April); Foundation of Cebu city (May); Pablo Hernandez' conspiracy (November)
1566	The Nunez conspiracy
1567	The Martin Hernandez conspiracy
1568	First Portuguese attack
1569	Legazpi moves headquarters to Panay; foundation of Capiz; Masbate, Ticao and Burias pacified; Albay reached
1570	First conquest of Manila (May); Second Portuguese attack on Cebu (October)
1571	Second conquest of Manila; made capital of Spanish Philippines (May); Central Luzon pacified (June); Cainta, Taytay, Laguna and Paracale pacified (August)
1572	Juan Salcedo's northern expedition (May–August)
1573	Juan Salcedo's southern expedition; the Bikols, Camarines and Cantanduanes pacified; Libon (in Albay) founded
1574	Chinese attack on Manila (Lim Ah-hong); Chinese withdrew to Pangasinan
1575	Chinese under Lim Ah-hong withdraw from Pangasinan and Philippines
1582	Japanese settlement at Cagayan destroyed
1600	First Dutch attack on the Philippines; first battle of Mariveles
1610	Second Dutch attack; first battle of Playa Honda
1616	Third Dutch attack
1617	Fourth Dutch attack; second battle of Playa Honda
1621–2	Anglo-Dutch blockade of Manila
1624	Third battle of Playa Honda
1646	Last Dutch attack; the 'Naval de Manila'
1647	The Albucay massacre
1762–4	British occupation of Manila

B. Revolts against Spanish Rule

1574	The revolt of Lakan-dula	Manila
1585	The first Pampanga revolt	Pampanga
1587–8	The Tondo conspiracy	Manila
1589	Uprisings in Cagayan and Ilocos	Cagayan, Ilocos
1596	Magalat's revolt	Cagayan
1601	The Igorot revolt	Ilocos
1621	The Gaddang revolt	Cagayan
1621–2	Bankaw's revolt	Leyte
	Tamblot's revolt	Bohol
1625–7	The first Cagayan revolt	Cagayan
1630	The Caraga revolt	Mindanao
1639	The Second Cagayan revolt	Cagayan
1643	Ladia's revolt	Bulacan
1649–50	Sumoroy's rebellion	Samar
1660–1	Maniago's revolt	Pampanga
	Malong's rebellion	Pangasinan
1661	The Ilocos revolt	Ilocos
1663	Tapar's revolt	Panay
1681–3	The Zambal revolt	Zambales
1744–1829	Dagoboy's rebellion	Bohol
1745–6	Uprisings in Central Luzon	Batangas, Bulucan, Cavite, Laguna, Rizal
1762–3	Silang's revolt	Ilocos
1762–4	Palaris revolt	Pangasinan
	General uprisings in Laguna, Batangas, Tayabas, Cavite, Samar, Panay, Cebu and Zamboanga	Mindanao
1763	Cagayan uprising	Cagayan
	Background of these revolts was the British occupation of Manila during the same period	
1807	The Basi revolt	Ilocos
1811	The Ilocos Norte uprising	Ilocos
1815	The Sarrat rebellion	Ilocos
1823	The Novales Mutiny	Manila
1828	Uprising of the Palmero brothers	Manila
1840–1	Revolt of Apario de la Cruz	Tayabas, Batangas
1843	Mutiny of Tagolog Regiment	Manila
1872	Cavite Mutiny	Cavite
1896	Start of the Philippine Revolution	Cavite

C. The Philippine War of Independence

1896	August	The 'cry of Balintawak'; start of Philippines Revolution
	December	Execution of Rizal
		The Imus Assembly
1897	March	The Tejeros Assembly; Aguinaldo leader of nationalist movement
	May	Death of Boniface
	July	Nationalists retreat to Biac-na-bato
	November	Creation of the Biac-na-bato Republic
	December	The Pact of Biac-na-bato; Aguinaldo and followers exiled to Hong Kong
1898	April	Start of Spanish-American War
	1 May	Battle of Manila Bay
	19 May	Aguinaldo returns to the Philippines
	28 May	Aguinaldo's men start the siege of Manila
	12 June	Aguinaldo declares Philippine independence at Kawit
	15 July	First Filipino cabinet appointed
	13 August	Americans enter Manila
		End of Spanish American War
	14 August	U.S. military occupation of the Philippines proclaimed
	15 September	Start of the Malolos Congress
	10 December	Treaty of Paris (USA and Spain)
	21 December	US President McKinley declares the annexation of the Philippines
1899	4 January	McKinley's Declaration published in the Philippines
	20 January	Schurmann Commission appointed
	21 January	Promulgation of the Malolos Constitution
	23 January	Inauguration of the Malolos Republic
	4 February	Aguinaldo declares war on the United States
	31 March	Malolos falls to the Americans
	4 April	American sovereignty over the Philippines formally proclaimed by the Schurmann Commission
	April–May	Filipino peace overtures rebuffed
	June	Death of General Luna
	October	New American offensive; San Isidro (provisional capital) falls.
	November	Aguinaldo switches to guerrilla warfare; regular forces disbanded
	December	Battle of Tirad Pass

1900	January–May	Pacification of South Luzon and Visayas completed
	March	Taft Commission appointed
	April	The Root Instructions issued
	August	Bates Treaty with Sulu
1901	March	The Spooner Amendment; civil government established in Philippines
	23 March	Aguinaldo captured
	4 July	Civil government inaugurated
	September	Massacre of Balangiga
1902	February	Resistance ends in Samar
	April	Surrender of Malvar, 'the last general'.
	4 July	State of Peace proclaimed throughout the Philippines

BOOKS AND ARTICLES FOR FURTHER READING: THE PHILIPPINES

Cady, J.F., *South-East Asia: Its Historical Development*, McGraw-Hill, New York, 1964.

Fisher, C.A., *South-East Asia: A Social, Economic and Political Geography*, Methuen, London, 1964.

Hall, D.G.E., *A History of South-East Asia*, (3rd edition), Macmillan, London, 1968.

Cesar Adib Majid, 'Political and Historical Notes on the Old Sulu Sultanate', *JMBRAS* Vol. 38, No. 1, 1965.

Corpuz, Onofre D., *The Philippines*, Prentice-Hall, New Jersey, 1965.

De la Costa H., *The Jesuits in the Philippines, 1581–1768*, Harvard, Cambridge,1961

—'Muhammad Alimuddin I, Sultan of Sulu', *JMBRAS*, Vol. 38, No. 1, 1965.

—*Readings in Philippine History*, Bookmark, Manila, 1965.

Grundy, Garel A., and Livezey, W.E., *The Philippines and the United States*, University of Oklahoma, Norman, 1951.

Phelan, J.L., *The Hispanization of the Philippines*, University of Wisconsin, Madison, 1959.

Saleeby, N.M., *The History of Sulu*, Bureau of Printing, Manila, 1908.

Zaide, G.F., *Philippine Political and Cultural History* (2 Vols.), P.E.C., Manila, 1957.

Part Two

MAINLAND SOUTH-EAST ASIA

THE world of Mainland South-East Asia bears much more coherence at first sight than does that of the islands. There is a much greater similarity in geographic conditions between the countries concerned, characterized by two basic elements—broad river plain and desolate, jungle-clad mountain range. There is racial diversity but each country tends to be firmly controlled by one particular race. There is a far greater degree of cultural unity to be found amongst the mainland nations than there is amongst the peoples of the archipelago. They are uniformly Buddhist (although the Vietnamese form is derived from China and not Ceylon), and in general they have been exposed to the same cultural influences in much the same kind of way. Politically speaking, too, the mainland monarchies enjoyed a far greater degree of stability than their contemporaries in Island South-East Asia. However, by the same token, the barriers between each state have been more rigid, and each has developed separately, evolving its own distinctive characteristics. This was well reflected during the course of the nineteenth century when the age of Western imperialism dawned. Each country responded to the European challenge in its own way and with different results. The Burmans reacted aggressively, the Laos passively. The Thais opened their doors to the West and accepted change; the Vietnamese tried to keep theirs closed and maintain their traditional ways. The story of each state and the development of its relations with the West has therefore to be told in its turn.

Burma

BURMA is a land of paradoxes. A cockpit of races, it developed into a one-race state. The Burmans are renowned for their gentle manners and quiet charm, but their rulers proved the most aggressive on the South-East Asian mainland. Linked with outside cultures since earliest times, yet it has been a country turned in upon itself. Essentially self-sufficient, the isolation and arrogance of Burma's kings brought national disaster in the course of the nineteenth century. In three successive stages the kingdom was swallowed up by the British. The moot point is to what extent this fate was unavoidable in view of Burma's proximity to British imperial power in India and to what extent it was the product of unwise and incautious policies pursued by Burma's monarchs. In this respect a comparison with the course of events in Thailand during the same period is interesting, and even more so a comparison between the characters and policies of the two rulers who reigned contemporaneously—Mindon in Mandalay and Mongkut in Bangkok. The reasons for Burma's downfall and the motives behind the final British annexation of the country are still matters upon which historians have yet to find agreement.

BURMA BEFORE THE BRITISH CONQUEST

THE independence of modern Burma was proclaimed at 4.20 in the morning of 4 January 1948.[1] In Rangoon, in the presence of Sir Hubert Rance, the retiring British governor, Sao Shwe Taik, the President-elect of Burma, and U Nu, the prime-minister and leader of the ruling Anti-Fascist People's Freedom League,[a] the British Union Jack was lowered and the flag of the new nation[2] was raised in its place. At the same time, similar ceremonies marking the moment of independence were taking place all over the country. With these celebrations 120 years of British rule in Burma were brought to an end.

The peoples of the Union of Burma

Under its new constitution,[b] independent Burma became a federation known as the Union of Burma consisting of Burma proper, Shan State, Kachin State, Kayah State and Karen State.[3] By this means the Burmese hoped to be able to meet the problems which resulted from their nation being the homeland of several different races. These races fall into three main groups: Mon-Khmer, Tibeto-Burmese and

[a]See Book III.
[b]See Book III.

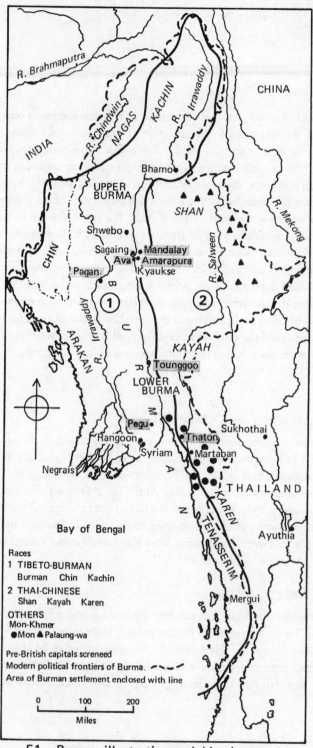

Races
1 TIBETO-BURMAN
   Burman Chin Kachin
2 THAI-CHINESE
   Shan Kayah Karen
OTHERS
   Mon-Khmer
   ● Mon ▲ Palaung-wa

Pre-British capitals screened
Modern political frontiers of Burma. ‒‒‒‒
Area of Burman settlement enclosed with line

0   100   200
        Miles

51. Burma, illustrating racial background

Thai-Chinese. According to the 1931 census, the total population of Burma was 14 millions[4] and was broken up as follows:

1. Tibeto-Burman	(a) Burman	9,627,196
	(b) Chin	348,994
	(c) Kachin	400,000
	(d) Lolo	93,224
	Total	10,470,414

2. Thai-Chinese	(a) Karen	1,367,673
	(b) Shan	1,037,406
	Total	2,405,080

3. Mon-Khmer	(a) Mon	336,728
	(b) Palaung-wa	176,382
	Total	513,110

4. Others:	Indians	1,017,825
	Chinese	193,594
	Indo-Burman	182,166
	Naga	70,000
	Eurasian	19,200
	European	11,651
	Total	1,494,436

From these figures it is clear that the great majority of the inhabitants of Burma are in fact of Tibeto-Burman stock, and of the Tibeto-Burmans nine-tenths are actual Burmans.[5] The Shans and the Karens form the largest minorities, having over a million people each. The Mon-Khmer group is numerically insignificant; its main importance is historical. The balance of the population is made up of the many tiny groupings of tribal people from the hills, and of recent immigrants such as the Chinese, Indians and Europeans.

The racial pattern of Burma emerges clearer still with a glance at the map. The Burmans occupy the lowlands on either side of the Irrawaddy in Upper, Central and Lower Burma. They also predominate in Arakan. The other races (apart from recent migrants) are all essentially hill peoples with the exception of the Mons. The Shans occupy the high land to the east and north-east. The Karen homeland also lies in the hills of the eastern frontier, especially in Tenasserim, although a considerable number of Karen have moved into the Irrawaddy Delta region within the last

century.[a] The more primitive tribes continue to live their isolated lives in the remote hills of north, north-east and north-west Burma.

Burman versus Mon

The story of Burma is to a very large extent the story of the struggle between the
three main racial groups; in particular, the struggle between the Burmans and the
Mons[6] and the Burmans and the Shans.

The Burman-Mon conflict began with the first contact between the settled,
civilized Mons of Lower Burma and the Burman invaders from the north, which
presumably took place some time during the course of the eighth and ninth centuries A.D. The Burmans gained the upper hand for the first time when King Anorata, the founder of the first Burman dynasty (at Pagan) conquered the Mon kingdom of Thaton[7] around 1057 and brought Lower Burma under his control. Perhaps, however, the real victory went to the Mons for they introduced Buddhism to
Anorata's court at Pagan and Mon culture and influence continued to be dominant
there for another hundred years. The Mons won back their independence in 1281
under the leadership of Wareru[8] who established the kingdom of Pegu. It was under this kingdom which lasted for two and a half centuries that the Shwe Dagon
Pagoda at Rangoon was completed in its present form and the first Europeans
opened their trade.[9]

The Mons lost their independence for the second and in effect the last time in
1541 when Pegu was conquered by the Burman ruler Tabinshweti, prince of
Tounggoo,[10] who thereby brought about the reunification of Lower with Upper
Burma. After this the story of the Burman-Mon struggle is of periodic Mon rebellions against Burman domination, all of which in the end were unsuccessful. The
one which came the nearest to success broke out in 1740[b] and encompassed the downfall of the Tounggoo dynasty itself. This rebellion reached its peak with the capture
of the dynasty's seat at Ava in 1752, but it was crushed very shortly afterwards. A
Burman chieftain from Moksobomyo[11] rose up against the Mons and defeated
them. He called himself Alaungpaya and became the founder of the Konbaung
dynasty which was to be the last line of Burman kings. In 1755 he captured Dagon
from the Mons and renamed it 'Rangoon' which means 'the end of strife'. In fact,
the strife came to an end some two years later with the fall of Pegu.

Other abortive rebellions followed during the second half of the eighteenth century but they were easily crushed.[12] The British relied over-heavily on Mon support when they invaded Lower Burma in 1824,[c] and they were disappointed. The
Mons did rebel against the Burmans when the British withdrew two years later;
once again they were ruthlessly suppressed. The Mon language was prohibited and
10,000 Mon refugees fled to British-occupied Tenasserim.[13] The last of the Mon rebellions took place in 1838.

Burman versus Shan

The Burmans had a still tougher time with the Shans, and they were fortunate that

[a]See Book III.
[b]See p. 397.
[c]See p. 406.

tribal jealousies prevented the Shan *sawbwas* (chiefs) from maintaining their unity. The Shans made their presence felt in Upper Burma during the declining years of the Pagan dynasty. They were able to rise to power in the chaos which followed the fall of Pagan to a Mongol army in 1287,[14] and in 1299 they sacked Pagan themselves, repelling a fresh Mongol invasion the following year.

For the next two and a half centuries (contemporaneously with the Mon kingdom of Pegu in the south), the Shans were the dominating force in Upper Burma. Shan sawbwas founded a number of principalities in the region at the beginning of the fourteenth century, of which those of Pinya and Sagaing were the most prominent. In 1365 Thadominbya, a Shan sawbwa, founded the kingdom of Ava which gained control over most of Upper Burma and kept it for the next 200 years. Most of that time was taken up with a struggle on two fronts—against the Burmans now centred on Tounggoo to the south, and against their own kinsmen, the Shan sawbwas of the hills who found it more profitable to keep their own independence and to supplement their livelihood by frequent raids on the lowlands. In fact in the end Ava was overthrown by a hill sawbwa in 1527.

The Shans of Ava adopted Burman culture just as the Burmans had adopted Mon culture before them. After the collapse of Ava in 1527 the Shans broke up into 'snarling' principalities with no semblance of unity at all. In these circumstances Bayinnaung, the successor of Tabinshweti who had conquered Pegu, was able to secure Ava for himself (in 1555) and in the following years to establish his overlordship over all the Shan states. From this time onwards, Burman domination over the Shans was secure, although as recently as 1883, under the weak rule of Thibaw,[a] the Shans attempted to throw off their allegiance to the Burman kings.

Another aspect of the Burman-Shan struggle was the long series of wars fought between Burma and Siam (Thailand). These resulted on two occasions in the subjugation of the kingdom of Ayuthia[15] but their outcome was quite inconclusive beyond bringing great hardship and devastation to the inhabitants and lands of Lower Burma.

The Konbaung Dynasty

The last of the Burman dynasties, that of the Konbaung kings, followed a short and tragic course. It ruled for 130 years before its final overthrow by British troops after a swift and easy campaign in 1885.

Under its founder, Alaungpaya, the dynasty seemed destined for greater things. Alaungpaya carved out a kingdom for himself from the chaos caused by the great Mon rebellion of 1740.[b] His successors[16] strengthened and enlarged the kingdom to an area never before attained, especially Bodawpaya (1781–1819) who, although he failed in his attempts to subdue the Thais, met with success in the north and overran Arakan and Assam instead. This was a fateful development because it brought the Burman kingdom into direct contact with the British in India, and under Bodawpaya's inexperienced grandson and successor, Bagyidaw (1819–38), a war broke out with the British which led to the first loss of Burmese territory by the Treaty of

[a]See pp. 416 et seq.
[b]Refer p. 396.

Yandabo.[a] From this time onwards (1826) Burma's future was overshadowed by the British presence, although this fact was either not apparent or was ignored by Burma's rulers. Kings Tharawaddy and Pagan, who followed Bagyidaw, certainly did not appreciate the nature of the British threat, and in 1852 Pagan found himself embroiled in a second war with the British which resulted in the loss of Lower Burma and in his own deposition.

The war of 1852 left Burma (or Ava, as it was more generally known) a weak, inland state, cut off from the sea by the British occupied provinces to the south and west. Its survival as an independent entity for the next thirty years was largely due to the sagacity of Pagan's successor, Mindon, who proved to be probably the most intelligent and capable of all the Konbaung kings. He was able to restore a measure of order and stability to his kingdom, and despite his limited knowledge and understanding of the outside world, he started to take the first steps to adapt Burma to the new situation which she faced. But weak government reappeared on his death. The new king, Thibaw, was largely the pawn of a court faction, pushed onto the throne by their machinations.[b] Against a background of rising anarchy and confusion, Thibaw's government became involved in a serious dispute with the British which became the occasion for the Third Anglo-Burmese War, the downfall of Thibaw and the final loss of Burma's independence. The British formally annexed Upper Burma on 1 January 1886.

The first Europeans in Burma

Although the British made themselves the masters of Burma during the course of the nineteenth century, they were not the first Europeans to have dealings with the country. The earliest European contacts with Burma date back to the fifteenth century when Burma was visited by two or three prospective traders, all of them Italians.[17] The first recorded of these was Nicolo di Conti of Venice who visited Burma in 1435. The first Englishman in Burma, a London merchant called Ralph Fitch, did not arrive till 150 years later. In the sixteenth century, which in terms of European expansion was the century of Spain and Portugal,[c] several free-lance Portuguese adventurers—half-trader, half-pirate—played important roles in local politics. One of them, Felipe de Brito, made himself master of Syriam for ten years and tried to set up a kingdom of his own in Lower Burma.[18] In the middle of the same century, a colony of Portuguese pirates established themselves in North Arakan near Chittagong, and for nearly a hundred years harried coastal shipping and conducted a profitable slave trade to the benefit of the ruler of Arakan and themselves. In the end they were suppressed by the Moghul viceroy of Bengal.[19]

During the seventeenth and eighteenth centuries, Syriam and several Tenasserim ports (in particular, Mergui) became centres for European free traders of all sorts— Portuguese, Dutch, French, English and others—while the Burman court up-country was content to let all Burma's external trade pass into the hands of foreigners. On the other hand, in the end the Dutch, English and French East India Companies all gave up their attempts to establish permanent factories in the country.[20] Anglo-

[a]See p. 406.
[b]See pp. 415–16.
[c]Refer p. 17.

French rivalry in India and on the Indian Ocean, and Burma's resources of teak, caused British and French interest in Burma to last throughout the eighteenth century, but with the establishment of the Konbaung dynasty under Alaungpaya these contacts were broken.[21] The poorly-supported attempts by the Europeans to found factories in Burma and their apparent inability to defend them no doubt was one major factor in the disastrous Burman failure to assess the true nature of the British threat during the course of the nineteenth century.

[1]This hour was chosen as being the most auspicious after consultation with the best astrologers in the land.

[2]Red and blue with six white stars for each of the component states in the Union.

[3]Karen State was actually constituted after independence. Refer to Book III.

[4]Estimated population in 1957 was 20 million. See Fisher, *South-East Asia*, op. cit. p. 468. The 1931 census is the last census with detailed figures for the whole country.

[5]'Burman' is used in this book to indicate people of Burman stock only: 'Burmese' is used according to the context to denote (a) the common nationality of all the indigenous racial groups in Burma as distinct from the Burmans themselves; (b) the language of the Burman.

[6]The Burman name for the Mon is Talaing—probably derived from 'Telingana', their supposed place of origin in India.

[7]Thaton is traditionally the first centre of Buddhism in Burma.

[8]Wareru was actually a Shan (Thai) from Sukhotai but he ruled in the Mon tradition with Mon followers. Pegu was the name by which Europeans used to refer to Burma commonly up till the nineteenth century.

[9]Namely, the Portuguese. Refer p. 398.

[10]Tounggoo was a principality founded *c.* 1347 by Thinhkaba who proclaimed himself king and built a palace there in the traditional style. Tounggoo itself originated around 1280 as a fortified village on a strategic spur which served as an outpost against slave-raiding Karens. After the fall of Pagan, Burman refugees from Shan rule made their home there.

[11]Meaning 'town of the hunter chief'; renamed Shwebo or 'town of the golden chief' by Alaungpaya.

[12]Notably in 1759, 1773, and 1783—occasioned by the heavy demands and losses incurred by the see-saw struggle of the Burman kings with their Thai adversaries of Ayuthia.

[13]The devastation of the 1826 rebellion was still obvious and commented upon by Burney on his way up to Ava in 1830. The Burmans had to give up their attempts to make the Mons pay the indemnity imposed by the British after the First Anglo-Burmese War of 1824-6.

[14]The Shan appear to have entered Burma during the thirteenth century. They founded the Ahom kingdom of Assam in 1229; the earliest historical evidence of their presence in Burma Proper dates to shortly before 1260 at Myangsaing in the Kyaukse District. The Mongol conquest of Pagan was part of the general attempt of the Mongol conquerors of China to assert their influence throughout South-East Asia. See also Java and Vietnam.

[15]Under Bayinnaung and Nandabayin, 1564-1586, and under Hsinbyushin, 1767-78.

[16]Naungdawggi (1760-3); Hsinbyushin (1763-76), the conqueror of Ayuthia; Singu (1776-81); Bodawpaya (1781-1819).

[17]Namely, Nicolo di Conti; Hieronimo de Santo Stefano of Genoa who was in Tenasserim and Pegu in 1496; and Ludovico di Varthema of Bologna who gave Europeans the first full description of these two places after a visit there in 1512.

[18]The first Portuguese to arrive in Burma was Ruy Nuñez d'Arcuna, sent by Albuquerque from Malacca in 1512 to report on trading conditions in Lower Burma. The first Portuguese trading station was opened at Martaban in 1519. In 1599 de Brito seized Syriam from the Arakanese whom he was supposed to be serving. He was overthrown and killed by Anaukpetlun in 1613. The Portuguese survivors of de Brito in Syriam were transported by the king to settle between the Chindwin and Mu rivers where they maintained their Catholic religion and provided gunners and guards for Burman courts for generations.

[19]The co-operation between the free Portuguese (they owed no allegiance to Goa) and the rulers of Arakan brought that state to the height of its power. Their downfall at the hands of Shayista Khan, the Moghul Viceroy of Bengal, also marked the rapid decline of Arakan itself.

[20]The Dutch maintained factories at Syriam and Ava between 1635 and 1679 but were not allowed to open one up at Bhamo; abandoned because they were not worthwhile. The English had a factory at Syriam for 10 years from 1647 but withdrew in face of the overwhelming

Dutch competition. The French were established at Mergui between 1660 and 1668, during which time their influence in Thailand was steadily increasing. At the end of the century the English sent two missions to Ava; the first in 1680 was designed to counteract French influence and was a failure; the second in 1695 resulted in the establishment of a dockyard at Syriam in that year. In other attempts to combat the French, the English made two abortive efforts to seize Negrais and Mergui in 1686 and 1687 respectively.

[21]The French also established a dockyard at Syriam in 1727. Both British and French establishments were destroyed during the great Mon Rebellion of the 1740s. The French attempted a come-back by supporting the Mons against the Burman counter-attack led by Alaungpaya between 1751 and 1756 but lost out as a consequence of his victory. The British supported Alaungpaya and obtained permission to settle on Negrais as a result in 1753. But in 1759 the settlement was destroyed and all its occupants massacred on the orders of the king who had been led to suspect British collusion in the Mon rebellion of that year. The Anglo-French struggle in India prevented either European power from taking any action to avenge these blows.

THE BRITISH CONQUEST

As has already been mentioned, the British conquest of Burma took place in three stages. After the first Anglo-Burmese War of 1824–6, they annexed the coastal provinces of Arakan and Tenasserim. As a result of the Second War of 1852, the British occupied the whole of the south (the region of Pegu, now known as Lower Burma) with its port of Rangoon. The remainder of the Burman kingdom was swallowed up by Britain after a short third war in 1885.

The origins of the First Anglo-Burmese War

The First Anglo-Burmese War arose out of incidents on the frontier between British India (Bengal) and Burma. Clashes took place at two points towards the end of 1823. In September of that year the Burmese overran the disputed island of Shahpuri in the mouth on the Naaf river on the Arakan-Bengal frontier, where the British had a small outpost. The British reoccupied the position but attempts to demarcate the frontier by negotiation afterwards proved a failure. A few months later the other clash took place, this time in Kachar State on the borders of Assam.[1] Kachar had already been declared a British protectorate in 1823 following earlier Burmese intrusions.[a] In February 1824 the Burmese invaded Kachar in strength and forced the British to make a fighting retreat. The resistance offered was sufficiently strong to cause the Burmese to abandon their offensive, but following these events the British authorities in Calcutta became thoroughly alarmed and declared war on Burma on 5 March.

These frontier clashes were the end result of the expansion of Burma under the Konbaung dynasty during the second half of the eighteenth century, particularly under king Bodawpaya. In 1784 Bodawpaya who has been described as probably the most powerful of all Burma's rulers[2] sent four divisions of his army totalling 30,000 men into Arakan at the instance of an Arakanese nobleman and conquered that distracted land.[3] Thereby Burma and British India became next-door neighbours for the first time, which led inevitably as the years went by to the creation of frontier problems. The main source of trouble arose over the question of the Arakanese refugees. Thousands poured across the border into British Indian territory

[a]See p. 405.

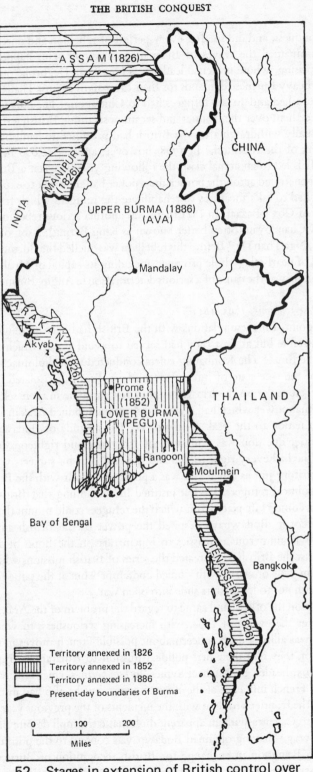

52. Stages in extension of British control over Burma

after the conquest, and did so after every period of rebellion and unrest in Arakan which accompanied the waves of Burman oppression.[4] This happened in 1794 when an uprising, whose principal leader was Nga Than De, broke out in reaction against the heavy Burmese demands for their campaigns against Thailand. This uprising was crushed and 50,000 refugees fled to Chittagong. The pursuing Burmese army chased them over the frontier and set up posts inside British territory. These were eventually withdrawn after the British had promised to hand over the three main leaders of the rebellion.[5] In 1798, however, another 10,000 fled to British territory. This led to an actual clash the following year between a Burmese force which had penetrated across the border and a police battalion sent to expel them, and the British had to take measures to rehabilitate the refugees which resulted in the foundation of Cox's Bazaar. In 1811 there was another serious rebellion in Arakan led by Nga Chan Byan (often better known as King Bering), a son of the former rebel leader, Nga Than De.[7] Before this rebellion was quelled the Burmese for a time lost control of nearly the whole province, including its capital of Mrohaung. Chan Byan's rebellion was the cause of a serious deterioration in Anglo-Burmese relations.

Anglo-Burmese relations, 1795–1811

Up to this point, Burmese relations with the British had been somewhat strained and unpredictable but at least they had served to avoid a war which neither side wanted at the time.[8] The Konbaung rulers conducted their diplomacy in sublime ignorance of the true state of international affairs. From the isolated seat of their power over 350 miles up the Irrawaddy they felt supreme in their self-sufficiency and in their manpower which had destroyed Ayuthia, subdued Arakan and brought the Burman nation to the peak of its power. The attitude of Bodawpaya to the Arakan frontier question was a mixture of arrogance and righteous indignation. He assumed he had every right to demand the return of his subjects who had fled to British territory just as much as it was a point of honour with the British not to hand over political refugees. He felt justified in demanding that British territory should not become a safe place from which the refugees could mount their counter-attacks. Moreover, Bodawpaya despised the power of the British authorities in Bengal and sent numerous embassies to Indian rajas in the hope of securing an alliance against the British.[9] He treated the series of British missions which reached his court from 1795 onwards with studied contempt[10] but at the same time he was shrewd enough not to let matters slide into open war.

The British on the other hand came to regard the problem of the Arakan frontier, especially after the events of 1794, with increasing seriousness, to which for the next decade was allied a deep concern about possible French moves in the region. For this reason they sent their first political mission to Amarapura, Bodawpaya's capital, in 1795, headed by Michael Symes. In fact Symes' chief task was to ward off suspected French influence at the Burman court, but he also had instructions to negotiate on the frontier problem with the incidents of the previous year in mind.[11] He returned to Calcutta with an apparent diplomatic triumph despite the obstacles placed in his way,[12] having obtained Bodawpaya's consent to the posting of a British Agent to Rangoon in exchange for British recognition of Burma's right to obtain the surrender of individual refugees. However, the experiences of Captain

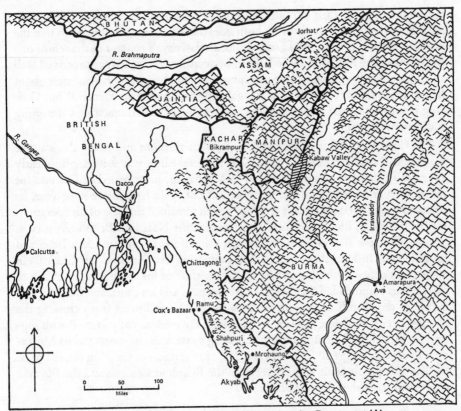

53. The background to the First Anglo-Burmese War

Cox who took up the appointment of British Agent at Rangoon the following year showed that some, at least, of Symes' optimism had been misplaced. After a two year sojourn at Rangoon which included a completely fruitless visit to Amarapura as well, Cox was withdrawn at his own request and to the obvious delight of the Burmese.

Cox's failure was no doubt due in part to his own tactlessness[13] but it was equally clear that Bodawpaya and his court were not out to solicit British goodwill. In March 1800, the Burmese *myo-wun* of Arakan pursued the frontier problem by sending an envoy to Calcutta to demand the expulsion of all Arakanese refugees from British territory, to which the British responded by agreeing to close the frontier. The governor renewed his demands in late 1801, adding the threat of war. This caused the British to send Symes to Amarapura once again. Bodawpaya nearly refused to receive the British envoy at all and subjected him to the usual round of humiliations as a demonstration of Burman authority,[14] but Symes' diplomacy won the day and enabled him to return for a second time with an apparent success in his hands. He bore a letter from the Burman King indicating a moderate stand over the frontier problem and permitting the re-establishment of a British Agent at Rangoon. For his part, Symes had guaranteed that the British would take measures to tighten their admittedly very lax control of the border. The bargain regarding the frontier was kept by both sides during the next few years so that the problem receded into the background; but Bodawpaya's consent to the return of a British Agent at Rangoon turned out to be worthless.[15] Bodawpaya received well an embassy led by Canning to Amarapura in 1809 to reassure the Burmese about British preparations in the Bay of Bengal designed against the French,[16] but Canning reported that the Burman ruler still dreamed of the conquest of Chittagong and Eastern Bengal.

The Chan Byan affair destroyed these tenuous relations and paved the way for the Anglo-Burmese conflict of 1824. When the rebellion was at its height in early 1811 with Chan Byan newly installed in Mrohaung, he appealed to Calcutta for recognition and protection. On being driven out again later in the same year, he returned to the safety of British territory which remained the base of his operations for the rest of his life. A Burmese army crossed the Naaf into British territory in pursuit while the British themselves made vain efforts to capture Chan Byan and his followers. In 1812 they succeeded in destroying his war-fleet, but Chan Byan eluded and defied both his pursuers up till the time of his death in 1815. None of these things commended themselves to Bodawpaya and his court, and the complete failure of the British to prevent Chan Byan and his followers from crossing the frontier after their defeat in 1811, coupled with the evidence of private British support for the rebels,[17] did not improve Canning's case when he journeyed to Amarapura to explain things in the same year. The 1811 mission of Canning proved to be the last direct diplomatic contact between the British in Calcutta and the Burman court until the end of the war of 1824–6.

Events leading to war: the Assam-Manipur problem

The Chan Byan affair convinced the Burman court of British duplicity and weakness, while the British grew increasingly suspicious as to Burman intentions. These suspicions were intensified with the extension of Burman interference to the frontier states of Manipur and Assam. Both these states were in a condition of chronic anarchy,[18] thereby creating circumstances which invited Burman attention. In 1813 Marjit Singh, a Manipuri prince engaged in a struggle with his brothers for the throne, turned to Amarapura for help. A Burman army was sent which after heavy fighting succeeded in installing Marjit Singh as ruler of Manipur. In return Bodawpaya obtained the cession of the Kabaw Valley for his kingdom. Marjit Singh's vanquished brothers fled into the neighbouring state of Kachar. In the case of Assam the Burmans had already intervened in 1805.[19] Now in 1816 a rebel governor (the Bar Phukan) sought British help to place his protégé, Chandrakant Singh, on the throne. Failing in his Calcutta mission, he was induced by Burman agents to turn to Amarapura where Bodawpaya lent a willing ear. So the following year a strong Burman force invaded Assam and placed the governor in power and Chandrakant Singh on the throne. As soon as the Burmans withdrew, however, the governor was assassinated and Chandrakant Singh deposed. In 1819 another Burman army re-entered the country, pillaged it and reinstated the raja; but as they withdrew once more trouble broke out again and Chandrakant Singh ended up a refugee in British territory.

These developments reproduced the same kind of problem which had bedevilled the Arakan frontier for so long. Refugees poured into neighbouring territories, pursued by Burmese forces spreading confusion and terror. At this juncture (1819), the experienced hand of Bodawpaya was removed by his death and his place was taken by his likeable but impetuous grandson, Bagyidaw, who was 38 years of age. By this time the royal Burmese armies had found a prestigious commander in Maha-bandula[20] who now set the pace of events. He first turned his attention to Manipur where Marjit Singh had ungratefully slighted the new Burman monarch by not attending his coronation. Manipur was invaded and laid waste while Marjit Singh himself and thousands of his subjects sought refuge in Kachar where they joined with their ruler's exiled brothers[a] to dominate the state. Kachar became a base for Manipuri attacks on the Burmese who occupied their homeland but when Burmese reinforcements arrived the Manipuri exiles turned their depredations on Kachar itself. In desperation the Raja of Kachar fled to Calcutta and implored British help both against the Burmese intruders and his unwelcome Manipuri guests. Bearing in mind the strategic passes of Kachar which formed the gateway into Bengal, in early 1823 the British in Calcutta declared that state and its mountainous neighbour Jaintia under British protection.[21]

In the meantime Maha-bandula had also dealt with Assam by occupying it on a permanent basis in 1820. Frontier friction quickly developed. Chandrakant Singh and other Assamese exiles organized raids against the Burmese in their homeland from their bases inside British territory, aided by a British adventurer called Bruce[22] who raised arms and men. In retaliation in 1821 Burmese troops entered British territory from where the raids emanated. In the middle of the next year, Maha-bandula sent an envoy to Calcutta to demand the extradition of the Assamese refugees.

Obtaining no satisfactory response in answer to this refugee problem from the British side, in 1823 Bagyidaw gave way to the mounting pressure around him to make war, capture Calcutta, bring back the British governor-general in chains of gold and march on to the conquest of England itself. Early in 1824 Maha-bandula launched a full-scale invasion of Kachar[23] and a few days later crossed the Arakanese frontier as well. As soon as the Burmese intention became clear, Calcutta issued its formal declaration of war.

The course of the war, 1824–6

The British campaign which followed the declaration of war in March 1824 was brilliant in its conception but wretched in its execution. Secretly, and achieving complete surprise, the British assembled an invasion force in the Andaman Islands and landed at Rangoon in early May. The main object was to relieve Burmese pressure on the Arakan frontier. This was completely achieved, to the great relief of Calcutta where near panic had been caused by the news of Maha-bandula's invasion of Chittagong and of the initial defeats suffered by the defending forces. But poor supply organization prevented the British troops from moving out of Rangoon so that they were caught by the rains and obliged to spend the rest of the year there. Lack of medical supplies and facilities then took its toll as thousands of troops suc-

[a]Refer p. 404.

cumbed to fever and dysentery, so much so that when Maha-bandula launched his counter-attack on Rangoon at the end of the rains in December, the British force had been reduced from 11,000 to 4,000 effectives. By the end of the campaign there were 15,000 casualties—most of them caused by sickness. Maha-bandula's attack was contained, and a few days later the British broke the Burmese siege of Rangoon by defeating them at Kokine, just outside. Meanwhile during the preceding months the principal ports of Tenasserim had been occupied, and in January 1825 the British took Mrohaung and spread their control over Arakan.

The British had counted heavily on a Mon uprising against the Burmans when they invaded Lower Burma. However, although the Mons and Karens[a] helped as suppliers, guides and informants, they did not do much until it was too late. During the dry season of 1825 the British forces pressed northwards and occupied Prome in April. However, the Burmese suffered their greatest loss with the death of Maha-bandula who was killed in action in the defence of Danubyu at the beginning of the same month. In Prome the British were once more confined by the rains. Meanwhile the Burmese opened up negotiations, and under cover of these attempted to recapture Prome by surprise in December but were foiled. In early January 1826 the British resumed their advance, and as they came to within a couple of days' march of Ava,[24] Bagyidaw sued for peace. The result was the Treaty of Yandabo which was signed on 24 February 1826.

The Treaty of Yandabo, 1826

This treaty imposed upon Burma an indemnity of £1 million or 10 million rupees for the cost of the war. Burma had to cede to the British East India Company her recent conquests of Manipur and Assam, together with the coastal provinces of Arakan and Tenasserim. A British Resident was to live at Ava, while a Burmese one was to be posted to Calcutta. Burma undertook not to make war on Thailand[b] nor to interfere on India's north-east frontier. A supplementary commercial treaty was to be negotiated at once.

Since the British did not go to war in 1824 primarily for conquest, they did not attempt to infringe on the sovereignty of Burma by the terms of the Treaty of Yandabo. Their annexation of the coastal provinces was basically for strategic reasons. Nevertheless the treaty was a very harsh one and a staggering blow to Burman pride and prestige. It undid the work of Alaungpaya and Bodawpaya and crippled the country with a heavy indemnity. The Burmese tried as far as they could to evade or reduce the demands of the treaty. They never appointed a representative to Calcutta; the commercial treaty negotiated by Crawfurd in 1826 proved worthless; and British attempts to establish a residency at the Burman capital, as we shall shortly see, broke down. In fact, after the deposition of Bagyidaw in 1837, the Burmese repudiated the treaty altogether. But the indemnity had to be paid—the last instalment was delivered in 1832—and despite all their efforts, the Burmese never succeeded in regaining either Arakan or Tenasserim.

The first Anglo-Burmese War was the 'fault' of the Burmese insofar as that it was they who provoked it, although their irritation with the British over the refugee

[a]See Book III.
[b]See pp. 498-19.

problem is understandable. More immediately it can be said that the falling of power into less experienced hands after the death of Bodawpaya was one of the major deciding factors in the outburst of Burmese aggression at the end of 1823. But the Burman kings had no way of judging the realities of the situation, or the nature and extent of British power and the world it represented. Their dealings with the British and other foreigners during previous years, particularly during the eighteenth century,[a] gave them no true indication of the power and resources which the Europeans possessed. Foreign attempts to open trade or found settlements had been feeble, while Burmese action against Europeans in the country had never brought about serious retaliation.[25]

More basically still, Burma had grown into a kingdom turned in upon itself. For nearly 200 years[26] the royal capitals of Burma had been sited far up the Irrawaddy and the court, already cut off by geography from easy access to the outside world, was in this way deprived of its only natural contact point with foreign peoples and influences. The devastating wars between Burma and Thailand which followed, and the age-old feud between Burman and Mon, helped to complete the isolation of Burman rulers and the introversion and self-sufficiency of the Burman court.[27] The result was that by the early nineteenth century Burma was unable to treat with the outside world on terms other than her own. This inability to see the world as it really was, was to reflect itself throughout the course of her unequal struggle with the British Empire.

The origins of the Second Anglo-Burmese War, 1852: the failure of Yandabo

The second war between Burma and the British, as was the case with the first, was not primarily brought about because of specific British designs against Burma. One of the most important factors leading to war was the complete failure of Burma's rulers to realize what they were up against and the dangers that they were courting in antagonizing their British neighbours. But as a result of the Treaty of Yandabo there were now new sources of friction which had not been present before 1826, and this friction came to a head at a moment when the British in India (for the time, at any rate) were remarkably free from other embarrassments and possessed in Dalhousie, as their chief, a man who was a convinced imperialist.

In the first place Bagyidaw and his court at Ava never drew any of the lessons they might have done from their defeat at the hands of the British, nor did they reconcile themselves to the terms of the treaty of Yandabo. As the effects of the war receded, so the old tactics and policies were revived. The losses which Bagyidaw felt keenest were those of Tenasserim and Arakan. Another source of friction was provided by the new frontiers, in particular the future of the Kabaw Valley.[b] Bagyidaw wanted the indemnity reduced and was reluctant, as Bodawpaya had been, to deal with a mere viceroy instead of with the King of England direct. Anglo-Burmese relations turned on these issues for the next few years without any satisfactory solution being found to any of them (besides that of the Kabaw Valley). Another consequence of the Treaty of Yandabo which led both to friction and increasing British involvement in Burmese affairs was the development of British trading

[a]Refer pp. 398-9.
[b]Refer p. 404 and see p. 425, note 66.

interests in the country. From their new acquisitions of Arakan and Tenasserim British commercial contacts grew and this British influence soon extended itself to Rangoon where a small, vigorous and raucous British trading community sprang up. The British traders of Rangoon were to provide the immediate cause of the Anglo-Burmese War of 1852.

Such was the background to the story of Anglo-Burmese relations from 1826 until 1840 when all direct diplomatic links between the two nations were broken. In September 1826, as a follow-up to Yandabo, John Crawfurd[28] appeared at Ava to negotiate the commercial treaty and to establish British representation there. His mission was a virtual failure. The Burman court treated the British envoy to all the veiled and studied insults of yore.[29] Crawfurd's draft treaty of twenty-two articles was whittled down to four, and when he returned to India, having refused to enter into discussions on the political aspects of the Treaty, he advised the British authorities there that to station a permanent representative at Ava would be a waste of time. So the political questions remained and the next year Bagyidaw sent envoys to Calcutta to open negotiations on them. Apart from the question of Arakan and Tenasserim, the most serious issue was that of the Kabaw Valley.[30] By 1829 it was clear that these problems could only be settled at the highest level and accordingly in 1830 the British sent Major Henry Burney[31] to Ava to attempt to find some permanent solution.

Burney proved to be a far more skilled diplomatist than Crawfurd and as a result was able to establish a permanent British representation at Ava which lasted for the next ten years. For the greater part of this time the British resident was Burney himself, but although he succeeded on getting on to very good terms with several members of the Hlutdaw and became a good friend of a number of the royal princes, he did not obtain the settlement of any problem other than that of the Kabaw Valley.[32]

The origins of the Second Anglo-Burmese War, 1852: internal instability
The ultimate failure of Burney's attempt to place Anglo-Burmese relations on a sound footing, the subsequent withdrawal of the British mission at Ava and the ending of direct Anglo-Burmese contacts in 1840 were largely brought about by the palace politics of the Burman court and Burney's own involvement in them. In 1831 Bagyidaw exhibited the first symptoms of the insanity which finally drove him off the throne. As a result a power struggle started to develop amongst his relatives for the succession. For a time it was evident that this was being won by the First Queen and her family, headed by her brother, the Minthagyi. In 1837 the crisis broke. One of Bagyidaw's brothers, the prince of Tharawaddy, decided that the time had come to forestall the Minthagyi's design, and so rose up in rebellion at Shwebo. Burney was immediately concerned since he was a friend of Tharawaddy and Tharawaddy now looked to him for support. However, Burney, as the diplomatic representative of a foreign power, declined to give any help and instead tried to leave the royal capital. But members of the court refused to let him go and he was forced to act as mediator for the safety of Ava. Burney successfully negotiated the peaceable surrender of the capital to Tharawaddy but once the triumphant rebel had gained control he ignored Burney's proviso that the traditional massacre of the

kinsmen should not take place. Five ministers had already been executed and members of the Minthagyi's family tortured before Burney intervened a second time to put an end to the slaughter.

Tharawaddy was infuriated by the foreigners' interference in palace matters, even though his own good faith was involved. Furthermore Tharawaddy did not feel himself bound by his predecessor's concessions under the Treaty of Yandabo and once on the throne repudiated the treaty entirely.[33] Tharawaddy's attitude stimulated the emergence of a new court faction which urged the retaking of the lost provinces by force of arms. Burney, fearing some incident at Amarapura (Tharawaddy's capital) which would make a new war inevitable, withdrew to Rangoon and advocated to India the use of force if need be against the new Burman ruler. Burney was recalled and his place taken by another British agent, but the Burman attitude had now become set and hostile so that in 1840 the mission to the court was closed and diplomatic relations brought to an end.[34]

Anglo-Burmese relations had thus reached a new peak of tension. The final factor which led to war twelve years later was the near-eclipse of royal authority. Not long after seizing the throne, Tharawaddy too became a victim of his family's streak of insanity and by 1845 had become so irresponsible that he had to be deprived of power. In the inevitable succession struggle which followed, the victor was one of his sons, the prince of Pagan. Pagan did not go mad, but he was unbalanced and completely careless about affairs of state. Having ruthlessly exterminated all possible royal rivals, he then ruled for the benefit of himself and his favourites,[35] passing the time in such pursuits as gambling, cockfighting and the pleasures of the harem. As a result, during his reign royal officials in the provinces were left undisturbed to rule as they pleased and to adopt whatever policies they chose provided that they remitted the stipulated provincial revenues to Amarapura. Men like Gaung-gyi, myo-wun of Tharawaddy, and Maung Ok, myo-wun of Pegu who actually precipitated the crisis which resulted in war with the British, became virtually as independent as the territorial chiefs of Perak and Selangor during the same period. It was against this background that a growing number of incidents involving British subjects and the Burman authorities in Lower Burma took place. Reports and complaints, justified and unjustified, started to flow to Calcutta from British merchants in Burma who yearned for security for their trade and urged the extension of British power. At Rangoon especially, where a number of British merchants were building up a trade, there was a series of incidents including cases of arrests and fines imposed on trumped up charges. A couple of these charges became the issue for war in 1852.

The outbreak of the Second Anglo-Burmese War and its conclusion

The trouble had started in the middle of the previous year. In July and August 1851, Maung Ok, myo-wun of Pegu and Rangoon—already notorious amongst the foreign community for his extortionate practices—imposed heavy fines on the captains of two British ships at Rangoon on charges of murder and embezzlement against them and their crews.[36] This action appeared to the local British community as something more than an attempt at enrichment at their expense but as a deliberate effort by the Burman authority to belittle them. When news of what had happened reached India, the British governor-general, Lord Dalhousie, reacted without delay by sending a small flotilla of three warships to Rangoon under the command of Commodore Lambert, deputy commander in-chief of the East India Company's naval forces. Lambert was instructed to present an ultimatum demanding the dismissal of Maung Ok and a full apology from the Burman authorities.

On delivery of the ultimatum Maung Ok was promptly dismissed, redress was promised and the Burmese themselves suggested the establishment of a British resident at Rangoon. At the same time troops were sent to reinforce Martaban and Bassein and the new myo-wun brought with him considerable forces to Rangoon. Furthermore Maung Ok's replacement turned out no better as far as the British were concerned than Maung Ok had been. He belonged to the anti-British faction at Pagan's court and on arrival embarked on a policy of obdurate non-co-operation. A delegation sent by Lambert to meet the new myo-wun and discuss compensation was rudely rebuffed.[37] In retaliation the 'combustible Commodore'[38] blockaded Rangoon, destroyed all Burmese shipping in sight, silenced the shore batteries and sailed back to Calcutta. It was now January 1852. The following month the British reappeared with a fresh ultimatum. This time they demanded an indemnity of one million rupees to cover the costs of their war preparations, and gave Pagan up till 1 April to make his reply. No answer was received by that date and so without further ado Dalhousie ordered an invasion of Lower Burma, landing British troops at Martaban and Rangoon in a gesture designed to force the Burmese to accept his terms.

However Pagan and his court were not prepared to be treated in this way. No doubt relying on the rains, fever and his own inaccessibility to do the work for him, Pagan refused to negotiate and so hostilities continued. In May the British took Bassein, in October Prome and in November Pegu. At Pegu they also successfully withstood a strong Burmese counter-attack. The efficiency of the British operations contrasted strongly with what had happened during the first Anglo-Burmese War 25 years before. Meanwhile Dalhousie proposed to London the annexation of Lower Burma—he had his eye on Rangoon as a second Singapore; London gave its approval and in December 1852 the annexation was unilaterally proclaimed.

The war went on[a] but organized resistance was fast coming to an end. By the end of the year the royal Burmese forces were showing signs of disaffection, centring on the person of the great Bandula's son whose failure to save Prome had placed his own life in danger. In the middle of the same month Mindon, a brother of Pagan who opposed the continuation of the war, fled from the royal palace at Amarapura to Shwebo where he was joined by his followers. This movement caused the withdrawal of troops from the front but did not prevent Mindon's triumph early in 1853 when he re-entered the capital, deposed (but did not execute) Pagan[39] and became king in his stead. The new ruler did not formally recognize the loss of Lower Burma although the war now officially came to an end. The first British Commissioner for Lower Burma, the diplomatic Phayre, did not attempt to make him do so.

This war has been described as 'Dalhousie's War', which refers not only to the promptness with which the governor-general acted and the efficient way in which

[a]See Book III.

it was conducted but also to the suggestion that he had planned it long in advance. Indeed in London, the radicals—in particular Richard Cobden—accused Dalhousie outright of unnecessary aggression.[40] Dalhousie's own reputation as an imperialist lent colour to the charge; during his administration in India he deliberately pursued a forward policy which resulted in the British annexation of nearly a dozen princely states, and he acted in the firm conviction that the extension of British rule was to the benefit of all concerned. However all the available evidence suggests that in the case of Burma Dalhousie, instead of looking for opportunities, merely exploited them as they arose.[a] It was Lambert, the man on the spot, who had been unnecessarily high-handed in the first place, and there is little doubt that the quarrel of 1852 could easily have been overcome with more tactful and perspicacious officials on either side. Nevertheless the Burmese were doubly unfortunate that their quarrel should have been with a man like Dalhousie and at a time when the absence of trouble in India gave the British a freer hand with which to act.[41]

The survival of Upper Burma: Mindon and the British

The Burmese defeat of 1852 converted the kingdom into what it had long been in spirit—an isolated inland state. Mindon's Burma was cut off from the outside world by the British occupation of the entire coastline and of the southern half of the country, and was dependent on British goodwill for its relations with other countries and the bulk of its foreign trade. Despite these most unfavourable circumstances the Burman monarchy maintained its independence for another generation before incidents arising out of an increasingly complex situation led to a British forward movement which swallowed up the entire country (1885).

Burma's survival as an independent entity for so long after 1852 was largely due to the policies of its new ruler, King Mindon, the tenth of his line and probably the wisest. A contemporary of King Mongkut (Rama IV) of Thailand and of Queen Victoria of Britain, Mindon had few illusions about the perilous situation in which his kingdom was now placed. Although he was no lover of the British he had opposed the war from the start and once it was over took care to maintain as good relations as possible with his powerful neighbour in the south. At the same time Mindon directed all his efforts towards strengthening the state by modernizing reforms and to asserting its independence by opening relations with other Western powers. The King did all he could to stimulate the economic development of the country. He introduced coinage by establishing a royal mint, remodelled the taxation system with the intention of replacing revenue from dues and services with revenues from trade; he encouraged industry by erecting factories[42] under Western management, and built up a fleet of river steamers of his own. He also sent young Burmans to study telegraphy in Rangoon and French and English overseas. With regard to foreign relations Mindon set out to do what the British increasingly tended to question his right to do—he despatched embassies and missions to the leading countries of the Western world and did his best to open up relations with them.[43] He paid most attention to France, popularly regarded as the traditional foe of Britain, and it was with the French that Burmese relations developed with the greatest degree of success.[b]

[a]See p. 534.
[b]See pp. 417-18.

In the pursuit of these policies Mindon was initally as successful as Mongkut of Thailand[b] in preventing a European takeover of his kingdom. At the same time, as his reign wore on increasingly serious problems arose in his relations with the British. Although the king took great pains to placate the British, by the end of his reign the issues at stake had reduced Anglo-Burmese relations even further, which paved the way for the Third Anglo-Burmese War and the annexation of Upper Burma.

The first of these problems arose out of Mindon's own refusal to accept the fact of the unilateral annexation of Pegu carried out by Dalhousie in 1852. Mindon at first adopted a friendly attitude towards the British in the hope that he might be able to persuade them to hand back the lost provinces. But a mission sent to Rangoon in 1854 with the intention of negotiating the retrocession met with a blank refusal from Dalhousie's representatives. Mindon was wiser than to make this the occasion for a new war but he obstinately refused to sign a peace treaty recognizing the annexation of Lower Burma or even to recognize the validity of the Treaty of Yandabo. As a result demarcation of the new frontier was difficult, leading to considerable friction until the British fixed the boundary line for themselves, while formal diplomatic relations remained unestablished for over a decade.

However Mindon saw the necessity for maintaining some form of contact with the British and so readily accepted Thomas Spears, a Scottish trader with a Burmese wife, who had long experience of the country, in the capacity of 'British Correspondent' at his capital. For ten years Spears acted as the unofficial link between the Burman court and Rangoon.[44] Mindon was also sufficiently encouraged by the good reception accorded to his embassy of 1854 to Rangoon to invite a return mission from the British. This was led by the patient and sympathetic Arthur Phayre,[45] and although the British in their turn failed to achieve their object (the negotiation of a treaty), good relations between the two powers were confirmed. In 1862 Phayre paid a second visit to the Burman court, now removed to Mandalay[46] with the object of securing a commercial treaty with the Burmese. This time Mindon gave way. He had been impressed by the consolidation of British power in the lost provinces[47] and he clearly saw the need to have a more clearly-defined relationship with his powerful neighbour. The resultant treaty signed that year consisted of a series of mutual concessions aimed at liberating and stimulating trade between Upper and Lower Burma.[48] More significantly still, it provided for the establishment of a British agent at Mandalay to represent British interests there and to smoothe over difficulties that might arise. But the treaty did not settle the question of the royal monopolies[49] and under the pressure of commercial interests in the south the British took up the matter again in 1867. In that year Phayre and his successor, Albert Fytche, negotiated a second commercial treaty with Mindon, giving the British virtually unrestricted access to Upper Burma and granting them extraterritorial rights in addition. Furthermore, also under British pressure, Mindon issued a proclamation suspending nearly all the royal monopolies for a period of ten years.[50] These two treaties were considered very satisfactory by the British government but they were to prove the sources of new friction which had a baleful influence on the subsequent development of Anglo-Burmese relations.

[a]See pp. 505 et seq.

The growth of Anglo-Burmese friction under Mindon

The most serious issues concerned the royal monopolies, the importation of fire-arms and perennial frontier problems. It was not long before Mindon discovered that he could not afford to suspend all his monopolies as he had promised, and to-wards the end of his reign he started to restore some of them. Amongst the revived monopolies was that over timber which was the item of trade which most con-cerned the merchants of Rangoon in British Burma. The question of the importa-tion of fire-arms arose out of a clause in the 1867 Treaty which stated that before such weapons could be imported through British Burma the permission of the Bri-tish Chief Commissioner of the province had to be obtained. On agreeing to this stipulation at the time, the Burmese delegates had supposed that as a general rule no objection would be made, but in practice they discovered that more often than not all importation of rifles and other guns was blocked. This provoked deep Burmese resentment.

Frontier problems also provided sources of constant friction. In the 1870s these were centred on the hills tracts of Western Karenni whose inhabitants had been gua-ranteed their independence by Dalhousie in the 1850s. But the hill tribesmen were slave-raiders and traders who found a market for Burmese and Shan slaves in the markets of Thailand and who were prone, often at the instigation of local Burmese officials, to make depredations on British territory. Furthermore the region was rich in teak forests. So when Mindon sent troops into Karenni in 1873 to try and bring the unruly tribesmen under some sort of control, his action became the sub-ject of a protest by the British on the grounds of Dalhousie's guarantee. The affair was settled by a British mission to Mandalay in 1875 led by Colonel Forsythe, the independence of the territory being recognized by both sides.[a] But the Forsythe mission created fresh problems of its own. On his return to India, Forsythe com-plained about the Burmese custom requiring all who wished an audience to appear barefooted in the presence of the King.[51] His complaint was taken up by the ag-gressive new viceroy, Lord Lytton[52] who forbade British diplomats to conform to this requirement. To this attitude Mindon reportedly declared, 'I did not fight to recover a province, but I will, sooner than yield on etiquette.'[b] Mindon's attitude might appear quixotic but there were limits to Burmese patience and pride. The 'Shoe Question', a matter of mere protocol, became a symbol of the great differ-ences in outlook between Burma and that of the Western world. In practical terms it meant that direct relations between the British and the court of Mandalay ceased to exist, for although a British Agent continued to live at the Burman capital for an-other four years, his refusal to conform to Burman protocol made Mindon inacces-sible. This breakdown in diplomatic contact led to a rapid deterioration in Anglo-Burmese relations so that when Mindon died in 1878 many old issues remained un-resolved while new ones mounted up.

Another aspect of Mindon's policies which led to increasing friction with Britain developed over the question of foreign relations. The British felt after their second war with Burma that they had a tacit right to supervise the kingdom's foreign rela-

[a]See Book III.
[b]Quoted by D.P. Singhal, *The Annexation of Upper Burma*, p. 29.

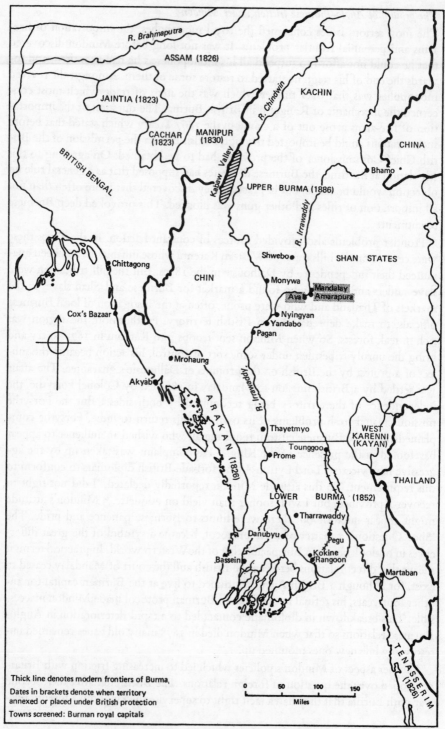

54. The three Anglo-Burmese Wars

Thick line denotes modern frontiers of Burma.

Dates in brackets denote when territory annexed or placed under British protection

Towns screened: Burman royal capitals

R. Brahmaputra

ASSAM (1826)

JAINTIA (1823)

CACHAR (1823)

MANIPUR (1830)

BRITISH BENGAL

Kabaw Valley

R. Chindwin

KACHIN

CHINA

Bhamo

UPPER BURMA (1886)

Chittagong

CHIN

SHAN STATES

Shwebo

Monywa

Mandalay

Ava

Amarapura

Cox's Bazaar

Nyingyan

Yandabo

Pagan

Mrohaung

Akyab

ARAKAN (1826)

R. Irrawaddy

Thayetmyo

WEST KARENNI (KAYAN)

Tounggoo

Prome

THAILAND

LOWER BURMA (1852)

Tharrawaddy

Danubyu

Pegu

Kokine

Bassein

Rangoon

Martaban

TENASSERIM (1826)

0   50   100   150

Miles

tions. Mindon, on the other hand, anxious to demonstrate his independence and to strengthen his position *vis-à-vis* the British by dealing directly with other foreign powers, sent out numerous embassies abroad and encouraged European visitors to his royal capital. Burmese ambassadors appeared in the United States in 1857 and in France ten years later. In 1872 an embassy led by Mingyi U Gaung visited France again as well as Italy, concluding commercial agreements with both of them. In 1874 Mindon made approaches to Russia. But nothing rankled more than the British refusal to treat with him on terms of equality. The King of Thailand could correspond with Queen Victoria but the occupant of the Lion Throne had to be content to deal with Her Majesty's representative in India, the Viceroy. All attempts to establish a direct relationship with London were rebuffed.[53] When Mindon died in 1878 the relations of his country with the British were bad indeed and under his successor Thibaw they quickly degenerated to breaking point.

Internal weaknesses and the accession of King Thibaw
If Mindon tended to arouse British antagonism towards the end of his reign by his show of independence and by his determination to maintain Burmese rights, he was nevertheless considered by many at home to favour the foreigner too much. Only the King appeared to appreciate the nature of the European threat while his relatives, courtiers and ministers interpreted his conciliatory diplomacy with the British as attempts to sell out his kingdom. These feelings coupled with the traditional intrigues of the Burman court meant that the throne was never secure. In an attempt to bring about greater stability Mindon introduced a system of fixed salaries for his higher officers in place of the traditional feudal appanage and imposed a new household tax (the *thathameda*)[54] to raise the required revenue. But he failed to remove the greatest evil which afflicted the domestic politics of Burma—the absence of a clearly defined order of succession to the throne. The practice was for the reigning monarch to nominate his own successor or heir-apparent (*ein-she-min*). Inevitably this system created the jealousies, fractions and intrigues which have pockmarked the course of Burmese royal history. It also led to the well-established and horrific custom of eliminating all possible royal rivals on the accession of a new ruler. Such massacres took place with the accession of Bodawpaya, Tharawaddy, Pagan, and Thibaw.[55] Mindon was the exception to all this; he did not even go so far as to execute Pagan when he deposed him in 1853. But Mindon's attempt to overcome the problem of the succession by nominating one of his brothers as ein-she-min[56] early on in his reign did not work out either. In 1866 two of his sons—he had forty-eight altogether—attempted to seize the throne. The ein-she-min was assassinated as he presided over an emergency meeting of the royal council (*Hlutdaw*)[57] in Mandalay but Mindon himself, who was in the summer palace a few miles outside the city, escaped. By the end of the day he had re-entered Mandalay and the rebels had been driven out of the palace and the city. But the rebellion spread far and wide in the provinces and it was several months before the uprising was finally put down.[58]

This traumatic experience made Mindon reluctant to appoint another successor lest the same thing should happen again. This was a grievous mistake because it merely led to intrigue amongst Mindon's queens to secure the succession for their own progeny. In this way the Alenandaw Queen[59] worked her way up in Mindon's favours and after the death of the Chief Queen came to take her place. Now known as Sinpyumashin,[60] she used her position to advance the fortunes of her daughter, Supayalet. Supayalet had a lover, the learned but weak Thibaw-min, and now with the aid of the Kinwun Mingyi, the Taingda Mingyi and other well-placed palace officials manipulated the recognition of Thibaw as successor to the dying king.[61] As Mindon lay on his death bed, Sinpyumashin and her fellow-conspirators imprisoned their rivals or forced them into exile[62] and on 1 October 1878, when the old king breathed his last, Thibaw-min became the new ruler of Burma.

King Thibaw and the British

Thibaw was king of Burma for seven years. Although there were those who hoped that the accession of a new ruler would lead to an easing of Anglo-Burmese relations, these hopes were soon dashed to the ground. Thibaw himself was never little more than a puppet on the throne which he owed to the machinations of his mother-in-law, his ambitious wife and the faction led by Taingda Mingyi, the Captain of the Palace Guard. In the year following his accession Thibaw secured the elimination of his royal rivals in a butchery which reputedly took eighty lives. This ensured the absolute supremacy of the Taingda Mingyi-Sinpyumashin faction who now proceeded to reap the benefits of their *coup* by exploiting their authority to the full in order to enrich themselves. As a result royal authority quickly broke down throughout the kingdom. Corruption, with Taingda Mingyi himself setting the leading example, became rife and dacoity commonplace. In 1883 the Shan sawbwas rose up in rebellion.[a] The following year Chinese freebooters seized and looted Bhamo, Kachin tribesmen swooped down into the plains from the north and in Mandalay itself another atrocious massacre was perpetrated.[63]

Against this background of growing anarchy all the old issues at stake between the Burmese and the British were revived leading to the final deterioration in relations. These relations had already taken a serious turn for the worse in 1879 when, at the height of the royal massacres, the British Residency at Mandalay was withdrawn. This move was occasioned by the death of the incumbent British Agent, Shaw, but had been actively pressed for by British officials in the south for some time in the hope that the British withdrawal would further provoke the domestic crisis and provide grounds for intervention.[64] Friction also mounted with recurrent incidents involving the ships of the powerful Irrawaddy Flotilla Company and with the escape of two royal pretenders to British territory where they became the centres of private intrigue aimed at their restoration.[65] In the following year (1880) the friction was further increased by the revival of the issues concerning the royal monopolies and the importation of fire-arms, as well as with the outbreak of fresh trouble along the Anglo-Burmese frontier. The monopolies issue arose out of Thibaw's desperate need for more revenue. In 1881 the cotton monopoly was reestablished while those over cutch and salt were contemplated. This provoked rigorous protests from the British prompted by the business community of Rangoon, to which pressure Thibaw's government finally submitted by revoking the monopolies early the next year. At the same time the fire-arms question again rank-

[a]See Book III.

led as British permission to import new weapons made urgent by the insurgency in the country was once more withheld. And the frontier problem flared up with local Burmese raids into Manipur.[66]

Whatever its shortcomings, the royal government of Burma was fully aware of the dangers inherent in a situation where friction with the British continued unabated. Indeed the first Burmese reaction to the withdrawal of the British Residency in 1879 had been to despatch an envoy to the British Viceroy of India, pleading for a resumption of the relations 'between the two great dominions and countries'. But the mission was not permitted by the British to get beyond the border at Thayetmyo and after a seven months' wait there returned to Mandalay empty-handed.[67]

The cancellation of the royal monopolies under heavy British pressure together with the problems of the Manipuri frontier, where towards the end of 1881 the British had started to fix the boundary line unilaterally, prompted the despatch of a sizeable Burmese mission to Simla[68] which left Mandalay in the middle of 1882. The mission's purpose was to regulate Anglo-Burmese relations afresh and to negotiate a new treaty settling outstanding issues. The Burmese delegation proposed a treaty of 43 articles which would have permitted the re-establishment of certain royal monopolies, provided for other fixed duties, abolished British control over the importation of fire-arms and granted Thibaw's government the right to direct representation in London (as the King of Thailand had). This last demand was the one at which the British Indian government baulked most but a compromise formula was found by which two treaties were to be concluded—a general one of friendship in the name of Queen Victoria, and a second one specifically related to questions of trade signed by the Viceroy of India.[69] However, before anything came of this, the Burmese envoys received instructions to break off negotiations and return home, possibly because Mandalay wanted to bargain for better terms. Thereafter, although the Burmese subsequently submitted two other treaty drafts,[70] neither was deemed satisfactory by the British and thus relations remained distant and unsettled.

King Thibaw and the French

The failure of these attempts to reach a satisfactory understanding with the British led Thibaw's government to take the steps which probably determined its fate. Mindon's policy of seeking to establish relations with other European powers as a foil to British pretensions was revived. In May 1883 a high-powered Burmese embassy led by four ministers left for Europe. It visited Rome where an inconclusive commercial agreement was signed and then with active French encouragement arrived in Paris. The negotiations and agreements which followed became the subject of the greatest heartburning to the British.

As we have seen,[a] French contacts with Burma had been revived during the reign of Mindon. In 1856 a French embassy arrived at Amarapura in return for one sent by Mindon two years earlier. In the same year a French missionary society established itself at Bhamo.[71] In 1859 another group of Frenchmen arrived in Upper

[a]Refer p. 412.

Burma, including technicians and artisans for service there. In 1872 the ambassadors of Mindon in Paris signed a commercial treaty with France but this turned out to be a dead letter.[72] Thibaw's embassy, however, produced results. It stayed in Paris for two years and in the end signed a new commercial treaty with France.[73] This was followed by the arrival in Mandalay in June of 1885 of a French consul called Haas. Within a month he had persuaded Thibaw to sign a fresh Franco-Burmese agreement which, amongst other things, gave the French a concession to build a railway from Mandalay to Tounggoo[74] and provided for the setting up of a state bank of Burma with French capital. On top of all this the Nyaung Ok prince[a] was now spending his exile in the French Indian settlement of Pondicherry.

These developments caused the British government considerable alarm and led to diplomatic representations in Paris. Then suddenly the French backed down. They had gone to war with China over the status of Annam[b] at the start of the year and things were not going so well as expected. The French government fell and in September, Freycinet, the new French prime-minister, repudiated Haas's Mandalay agreement. The following month the over-zealous consul was recalled from Mandalay forever.

By this time the British merchant community in Lower Burma was up in arms. The increasing number of incidents involving British subjects in Thibaw's disorderly domains, the hindrance to trade and the French threat all added fuel to the flames of those who burned to see the absorption by Britain of the independent Burman state. At a 'notorious' meeting held in Rangoon in 1884,[75] the European merchants gathered there openly demanded annexation, a demand which was repeated early the next year and which received the official backing of the Rangoon Chamber of Commerce. Perhaps with some more justification the Irrawaddy Flotilla Company complained of the prevalent state of insecurity and of the need for firm action. It was against this background that the government of Thibaw became involved in a serious dispute with the Bombay-Burman Trading Corporation, a British firm dealing in teak based on Rangoon. This quarrel provided the British with the pretext for making war.

The case of the Bombay-Burmah Trading Corporation and the outbreak of the Third Anglo-Burmese War

The Bombay-Burmah Trading Corporation had held a valuable concession over the rich teak forests of Ningyan for the previous twenty years and the lease had just been renewed in 1884. The Company waxed rich on this concession but was peculiarly susceptible to Burmese pressure since the source of its wealth lay within the Burmese frontier. The dispute arose over an accusation that was made in late 1884 to the effect that the Company had bribed the myo-wun of Ningyan to accept less than the proper royalty due on the timber exported. The Company was also accused of failing to pay dues on all its exports and of not paying certain labourers their wages. The matter was brought before the Hlutdaw which imposed a heavy fine on the Company. There were probably some grounds for the allegations but also the probability of French intrigue behind the scenes.[76] The Company

[a] See note 62, p. 424.
[b] See pp. 455–6.

accepted the verdict but maintained that the fine imposed—2.3 million rupees—was excessive, and demanded arbitration. The Hlutdaw nevertheless imposed the fine in August 1885 and in September halted the trade in timber at the frontier until the first instalment of the fine was paid. The British started to mobilize for war, and on 19 October Calcutta sent an ultimatum to Mandalay. In the ultimatum the British demanded that the Burmese negotiate over the fine, accept a British Agent with guards to live at the royal capital and to have right of access to the King, and agree to British control over all Burma's foreign relations. The ultimatum gave Mandalay twenty days grace.

These British demands were tantamount to ending the independence of Burma. Thibaw's government prevaricated and played for time and at the beginning of November sent a reply which failed to satisfy the British. It stated that the Hlutdaw could not negotiate over the fine but that it was prepared to receive a petition regarding its amount.[77] The Hlutdaw was prepared to accept a British agent in Mandalay (it pointed out that the last British representative had left of his own accord) but failed to specify what his actual position would be. As for the question of British control over Burma's foreign relations, the Hlutdaw suggested that the matter be referred to the French, Italian and German governments with which Mandalay was in diplomatic contact so that a joint decision could be reached. This reply reached Rangoon on 9 November. The British regarded it as a virtual rejection of their ultimatum and Thibaw himself does not seem to have anticipated any other result, for two days previously he had caused a proclamation to be issued, warning his people of the impending conflict with the British and appealing for their whole-hearted support. But the royal court was not prepared for the swiftness with which the British now acted. On 14 November, a British invasion force under the command of General Prendergast and consisting of three infantry brigades with cavalry and naval support crossed the frontier and marched on Mandalay. The Burmese were shocked and offered hardly any resistance. The court was divided between those who realized only too well the futility of resistance against this powerful Western state[78] and those who preferred to fight whether for reasons of pride or out of ignorance. The army was unprepared, its commanders at cross-purposes. By the 28th Prendergast and his men had entered the royal capital and Thibaw made his submission. The defeated ruler and his queens were sent downstream to Rangoon and passed into an Indian exile.[79]

The annexation and subjugation of Upper Burma

The question now was what was to be done with Upper Burma. Three possibilities appeared to be open—to maintain Burma as a kind of buffer state with its external relations controlled by Britain, to place Burma under British protection with a British adviser at the court of a compliant Burman prince and government, and to annex the kingdom outright and make it part of British Burma. After due consideration and plenty of encouragement from interested parties,[80] the British government opted for annexation, and a proclamation to this effect was issued by the Viceroy of India on 1 January 1886. Annexation appeared to be the most effective way of eliminating rival foreign influences and it opened encouraging prospects of new trade links with China.[81]

The absence of determined Burmese resistance to the British invasion persuaded many British minds that in fact the Burmese welcomed the British take-over and that the disappearance of Thibaw's tyrannical monarchy would be popular in the country. This, however, was speedily proved not to be the case. The abolition of the monarchy came as a great shock to most Burmese and touched their pride. The result was the almost immediate outbreak of rebellion not only in Upper Burma but in the south as well. The royal army did not disband as ordered, but dispersed into the villages and forests and embarked upon local dacoity.[82] The movement spread rapidly in January 1886, affecting particularly Bhamo, the Chindwin valley and the Shan plateau. The following month, an uprising began in Lower Burma. It was led by former territorial chiefs and officials (*wun* and *myothugyi*), royal pretenders, bandit chiefs, and significantly enough Buddhist monks.[83] For two years every district in Upper Burma was involved. There was a complete breakdown in civil administration in the region and by the middle in 1887 the British had been obliged to draft into the country 40,500 Indian troops and police to restore and keep order. The British began to gain the upper hand during the second half of that year. By January 1888 the most formidable bands had been broken up and the principal leaders driven into hiding. Disaffection in Lower Burma continued into 1889, centred in the Thayetmo area, while in 1890 there were still 35,300 troops and police in the country, of whom 30,000 were in Upper Burma. The resistance of the hill peoples was not finally quelled until 1895.[84]

The roots of the Burmese resistance of 1886–90 lay in their own sense of national pride and tradition. They were outraged by the suppression of the monarchy by foreigners, as indeed several more percipient British officials had suspected they might be.[85] Feelings were in addition inflamed by the British treatment of the *thathanabaing*, who lost his official status, and the dismissal of the Taingda Mingyi with the disbandment of the Hlutdaw[86] early in 1886 served as the signal for overt revolt. Burmese feelings were further inflamed by the harsh British countermeasures which in effect began before active rebellion broke out.[87] Those found with loot or bearing arms were summarily shot, villages were burned and other suspects were publicly flogged. Finding that these methods were reacting against them, the British relaxed them in February 1886.

The resistance movement was bound to fail in the circumstances of the time. No Burman force could challenge the technical superiority of western arms nor the overwhelming preponderance of British power. The movement also lacked coherent leadership. Attacks were locally led and had no common goal. In the interest of security and order the trading classes soon came over to the British side. In Upper Burma the *Sangha*[88] started to work for the restoration of peace, and the construction of the Toungoo-Mandalay Railway absorbed a lot of would-be rebels. In Lower Burma the co-operation the British received from the Karens was an important factor in containing the Burman rebellion.[a]

In this way the proud dynasty of Alaungpaya was brought to an end. The British motives stand out more clearly in the contents of their October ultimatum than in the details of the issues at stake between the Bombay-Burmah Trading Corporation and Mandalay. These motives were governed by the ambitions and discontents of

[a]See Book III.

the thriving commercial interests in Lower Burma and by official fears of colonial rivals, above all France. Therefore it can be seen that as in 1852 the occasion for the Anglo-Burmese conflict was a dispute involving commercial interests. But the reasons which led to the war of 1885 were far more complex than those of 1852, and in contrast to the former occasion the British acted this time with the deliberate intention of gaining control over the remainder of the kingdom. Clearly questions of trade were uppermost in British minds, and in particular the threat to the prospects of that trade which French influence appeared to represent. Burma was a weak power brought through the rapid development of commerce into constant friction with the British in the south. Unable or unwilling to adapt herself to the realities of the new world she had been forced into contact with, it seemed inevitable that sooner or later she must forfeit her independence. The trading company dispute and France's entanglement in Tongking provided the British with an obvious opportunity to complete a process that—unconsciously—had been started in 1824.

On the other hand, as Furnivall has said, 'Burma was unfortunate in its kings'. This proved to be particularly true of Burma under the Konbaung dynasty whose serious internal weaknesses undermined its attempts to preserve its position. Thus the work of king Mindon was largely undone by the two basic flaws in the Burmese monarchy. These were the unbridled authority of the monarch and the absence of a fixed law of succession to the throne. The first meant that in the last analysis everything depended on the character of the king himself while the second opened the way for endless instability and intrigue. These essential weaknesses of the monarchy, together with its relative inaccessibility to the outside world[89] were important factors in Burma's failure to meet the challenge of the West.

[1]The outpost on Shahpuri had been set up by the British earlier in the same year to protect British subjects using the Naaf river who often found themselves fired upon by Burmese frontier guards; a force of 1,000 Burmese soldiers attacked the island and destroyed the post and its 13 occupants. In Kachar the first action took place at Dudpatli where 4 English officers and 155 sepoys were killed and wounded by an invading Burmese column.

[2]See G.E. Harvey's estimate, *History of Burma*, p. 293.

[3]Separated from the Irrawaddy Valley by a wall of hills Arakan had grown up as a separate Burman kingdom, particularly open to sea-borne influences from India. After the loss of Chittagong in 1666 to the Moghuls (refer note 19) and the suppression of the activities of the Portuguese freebooters which accompanied this, the kingdom fell into disunity and disorder. Hari, the Arakanese nobleman who sought Bodawpaya's intervention, was expressing a popular desire to be rid of the anarchy in the country. King Thamada, the last of his line, was easily defeated and died in honourable captivity at Amarapura a year later.

[4]When Bodawpaya's armies entered Arakan in 1784 they were often welcomed with music by whole villages who came out to greet them as liberators. But Burman methods were so rough and their demands so exacting that the population was goaded into rebellion. See Harvey, op. cit. p. 280.

[5]The British weakly accepted the Burman contention that they were mere dacoits, although they were in fact Arakanese noblemen; one of them managed to escape on his way to Amarapura; the other two defiantly died agonizing deaths at the Burman capital.

[6]Named after Hiram Cox, an official of the English East India Company put in charge of the refugees: the police party was driven off by the Burmese with considerable loss. Bodawpaya demanded the return of the refugees and threatened war, but nothing came of it.

[7]Nga Chan Byan was the most famous of the Arakanese rebels against Burman oppression: his family were the myosas of Sindin in Akyab district.

[8]Bodawpaya was too shrewd to seek an open clash with the British, whilst the British, on the other hand, between 1793 and 1815 were preoccupied with their struggle with Revolutionary and Napoleonic France and its implications for their position in India.

[9]The missions of 1807, 1808, 1813, 1818, 1820, and 1823 to North India, reaching Delhi and Lahore; however Burman moves were always forestalled by the establishment of British paramountcy.

[10]Both Symes and Cox were made to wait for months on an island in the Irrawaddy under miserable conditions. The Burman attitude is partly explained by their resentment at being asked to negotiate with a servant (in the form of the governor of British India) of the British king rather than directly through his own personal representative.

[11]Other objectives included obtaining a fixed tariff agreement for British subjects, guarantees for the proper treatment of vessels in distress and the posting of an English political agent at Rangoon. The possibilities for promoting British trade were of course always uppermost in British minds.

[12]Although permitted to look at the king, Symes was not granted an audience: he obtained his concessions only after threatening to withhold the presents he had brought.

[13]Cox, against his own instructions, attempted to insist on being treated as of ambassadorial status and unlike Symes refused to submit to Burman ceremonial.

[14]Despite the fact that Symes' second embassy had been furnished more impressively than ever, with the purpose of demonstrating to the Burman court the true measure of British power.

[15]Lt. John Canning was sent to Rangoon to take up the appointment in May 1803. He met with so many obstructions from local officials that he withdrew six months later.

[16]The British were making preparations against the French islands of Bourbon and Mauritius in the Indian Ocean and were also planning for the invasion of the French occupied island of Java.

[17]The British merchant community at Chittagong definitely favoured Chan Byan's cause and the Burman Viceroy of Arakan specifically cited Dr. McRae, the civil surgeon at the town, as being involved in the rebellion of 1811.

[18]Manipur had owned Burman suzerainty in Bayinnaung's day. During the second half of the seventeenth century and the first half of the eighteenth century its rulers were independent and made destructive raids on Burma. The Burman revenge came when Alaungpaya had established his dynasty. His raid of 1758 devastated the principality. Another devastating raid during the reign of Hsinbyushin took place in 1770, followed by a Burman occupation; the state was abandoned in 1782. Depopulated and impoverished, Manipur relapsed into a condition of impotent anarchy. The Ahom kingdom of Assam had sunk into decline during the latter half of the eighteenth century, riven by the strife between the Brahmins and the Moamarias, a minority sect who were opposed to Brahmin supremacy, and ruled over by an imbecile monarch, Gaurinath Singh (1780–94).

[19]At the request of one of the pretenders; the Burmese invaded twice in that year but withdrew on receiving bribes.

[20]Bandula; c. 1780 born at Ngapayin in Monyua district; attracted attention of King Bodawpaya as a youth at court who showed considerable temerity by assaulting a minister and given a military post in consequence; rose to distinction in the Assamese campaign as a commander in the field; 'a handsome man of fine presence', he was adored by his followers; traditionalist and aggressive but honest and willing to learn from experience; largely responsible for development of Burmese policy on the northern frontier under Bagyidaw. See Harvey, op. cit. pp. 300–1.

[21]During the reign of Singu, Burman armies exacted homage out of these two states and thereafter Burman kings claimed suzerainty over them; this suzerainty, however, had remained purely nominal.

[22]Born in India; Bruce raised 300 muskets and 2,000 men, mainly Sikhs and Hindustanis, for Chandrakant.

[23]The first shots were fired on 18 January at Bikrampur, just inside Kachar. This war was a popular one in Burma. See Harvey, op. cit. p. 363.

[24]The royal capital was moved from Amarapura to Ava in 1823.

[25]Furthermore their easy conquests of Arakan and Assam, their campaigns into the Menam Chao Phaya basin and down to Ujong Salang and above all their victory over the Chinese invaders of 1765–9 convinced Burma's rulers of their invincibility. As a Burman minister once told a British envoy: 'You do not realise. We have not yet met the race that can withstand us'. Quoted by Harvey, op. cit. p. 259.

[26]The royal capital was removed from Pegu in Lower Burma to Ava in 1635 during the reign of King Thalun of the Tounggoo dynasty.

[27]In this respect, the attitudes of the Burman court were very similar to those that prevailed at the court of the Manchu rulers of China at Peking in their dealings with the Westerners during the nineteenth century.

[28]John Crawfurd; born 1783; joined English East India Company's Bengal Medical Service, 1803; served in Penang, 1808–11; with Raffles in Java, 1811–17—including a period as Resi-

dent in Jogjakarta; 1822, sent as envoy to Thailand and Vietnam: 1823–6, Resident in Singapore; went on mission to Ava in 1826; retired, 1827; attempted to enter Parliament four times between 1832 and 1837 without success. In retirement he campaigned tirelessly for Straits trading interests and took a leading part in the agitation against the imposition of port dues and Indian currency on the Straits Settlements in the 1850s—at this period, he was head of the Old Singaporeans' Association in London. In 1820 he published his three volume *History of the Indian Archipelago*, and subsequently published accounts of his embassies to Thailand, Vietnam and Burma.

[29]He was received by the king on a *kodaw* day when vassals came to present their customary obeisance and homage; his presents were described as token of submission and as a plea for pardon.

[30]Originally ceded to Burma by Manipur in 1813, the territory was reoccupied by the Manipuris during the course of the First Anglo–Burmese War. An Anglo–Burmese boundary commission failed to agree and the British unilaterally fixed their own boundary line. However, in face of very strong Burmese representations the British agreed to withhold a final decision.

[31]Henry Burney; born *c.* 1790; appointed ensign in a regiment of the Bengal Native Infantry in 1809; took part in the conquest of Java. 1810–11; stationed at Penang, 1811–24—appointed Secretary to the governor of Penang, 1818; prior to 1825, went on several missions to Ligor and Kedah; headed embassy to Bangkok and negotiated treaty, 1825–6; appointed one of the commissioners for Tenasserim, 1828; British Resident at Ava, 1830–7; retired, 1838; in 1841, now a Lt.-Colonel, defended the Company's Kedah policy in London; 1842, the Company accepted his recommendations regarding the restoration of the Sultan of Kedah. He had a good command of Thai and Burmese.

[32]The valley was restored to Burma, largely on his advice.

[33]In so doing Tharawaddy was following normal Burman practice by which the new ruler did not hold himself bound by the acts of his predecessors.

[34]Burney was reprimanded for withdrawing by the British Indian government but his replacement, Colonel Benson, was completely ignored officially and assigned a residence liable to flooding during the monsoon season. He left on grounds of ill-health in 1839 and was soon followed by his deputy, who took over the post.

[35]One of these, Maung Baing Zat, the Muslim *myo-wun* of Amarapura, was allegedly responsible for the killing of 6,000 people before the king was forced by the inhabitants of the city to order his execution.

[36]All exactions on British vessels, apart from normal harbour dues, were supposed to have been waived by the terms of the Treaty of Yandabo.

[37]Not only was Lambert's delegation refused an interview, but the governor followed this up by complaining in a letter to the Commodore that his afternoon rest had been disturbed by a party of drunken British officers.

[38]Dalhousie's own phrase: Dalhousie laid the blame on Lambert for being too precipitate although basically he approved of his action.

[39]Pagan lived in retirement till his death from a smallpox epidemic in Mandalay in 1880.

[40]In a pamphlet on 'How Wars are got up in India....'

[41]The British position in India seemed at this particular juncture very secure; the Sikh problem had been settled with the definitive annexation of the Punjab in 1849 and no other strong autonomous Indian state was present to challenge the British hegemony. The Great Rebellion of 1867 was still undivined.

[42]For lac, cutch, sugar, cotton and silk piece goods, etc.

[43]During his reign no less than 15 missions were sent abroad. Amongst those was one to the U.S.A. in 1857 which achieved nothing; contacts were made *inter alia* with France, Germany, Italy and Russia. An Italian mission was at Mandalay in 1871.

[44]Spears was recommended for this task by Arthur Phayre and after some initial hesitation this was agreed to by Dalhousie.

[45]Arthur Purves Phayre; born 1812; commissioned into Bengal Native Infantry, 1828; posted to Mon police unit in Tenasserim, 1835; frontier district officer in Arakan, 1837–52; appointed a major on Dalhousie's staff, 1852; commissioner of Pegu, 1852–62; Chief Commissioner of British Burma, 1862–7. Owed rise to knowledge of Burmese and as a result of having attracted Dalhousie's attention. Published a pioneer history of Burma in 1883. On his first embassy to Mindon's court, Phayre was accompanied by Colonel Henry Yule who has left us with an invaluable record of the occasion.

[46]The capital was removed from Amarapura to Mandalay in 1857.

[47]In that year (1862) Tenasserim, Arakan and Pegu were brought together under one administration to form the province of British Burma.

[48]Principal terms—abolition of all customs on goods carried between Upper and Lower Burma

on the Irrawaddy; the British to put this into effect within one year; the Burmese could withdraw their dues over a longer period. All rice imports into Upper Burma were to be duty-free; all restrictions on traders' movements on the Irrawaddy were to be reduced.

⁴⁹By tradition the Burman monarch was the chief trader in the state. For such articles as cotton, wheat, palm-sugar, pickled tea, cutch, ivory and earth-oil, exports were in the hands of the king's own agents and licensees. The king also controlled the import trade, especially in rice and piece goods. Mindon used his monopolies to fetch artificially high prices for his exports—doubling, for example, the market value for earth-oil—and sent his royal agents to purchase commodities in Lower Burma and India at below market prices and with extended credit.

⁵⁰By the Treaty, Fytche got Mindon to promise to abandon all his monopolies save those over rubies, earth-oil and timber. Shortly afterwards the British threatened to reimpose the frontier dues which had been abolished by the 1862 Treaty. This caused Mindon to issue his proclamation announcing the abolition of the monopolies in question.

⁵¹Burman court etiquette required much more than the removal of shoes but it was relaxed for the British benefit. Hitherto the British had always shown themselves prepared to accept the Burman protocol on the shoe issue; even the British envoys who came to sign the treaty of Yandabo at Ava after the First Anglo-Burmese War conformed to the practice. The 'Shoe controversy' had its almost exact parallel in the 'kow-tow' question which bedevilled Anglo-Chinese relations at the time of the embassies of Lord Macartney and Lord Amherst, and similar attitudes were involved.

⁵²Lytton became Viceroy in 1876. A convinced imperialist, from the outset he favoured war and the annexation of Upper Burma.

⁵³For example the Burmese mission of 1872 visited England but was not permitted to have direct access to members of the British Cabinet. The British insisted that all diplomatic transactions be conducted through their government in India.

⁵⁴This tax was continued under British rule and acquired great unpopularity.

⁵⁵Known as 'the massacre of the kinsmen'; Thibaw's massacre in which 70 to 80 of his relatives died is the best known since it was subject to the greatest publicity; it was not therefore necessarily the worst.

⁵⁶Meaning heir-apparent or crown prince.

⁵⁷The meeting was called to discuss the rumours of rebellion which had already reached the *ein-she-min's* ears.

⁵⁸The rebellious princes escaped from Mandalay in the king's steamer and after plundering the countryside downstream, fled into British territory. One of them, the Myingon prince, subsequently tried to raise fresh rebellions in 1881 and 1882. The Padein prince, one of the late ein-she-min's sons, also rose up in rebellion, fearing that his chances for the throne had been destroyed. For a time he threatened Mandalay itself, and Mindon considered abdication, but the rebellion petered out and the Padein prince was captured and executed. This episode marked the only serious rebellion in Mindon's reign.

⁵⁹Or Queen of the Centre Palace; reputedly Mindon's favourite queen, she was a daughter of King Bagyidaw and half-sister to Mindon himself.

⁶⁰Meaning Mistress of the White Elephant; awarded by Mindon as a mark of honour in compensation for his refusal or inability to nominate her the new chief queen.

⁶¹The Kinwun Mingyi is the best known of Mindon's ministers; one of the four great ministers of state who made up the *Hlutdaw*. The Kinwun Mingyi was largely in charge of foreign affairs and had led two embassies to Europe. He spent most of his early life in a monastery. A measure of his ability was his survival as minister after Mindon's death, though his influence was diminished. He also survived Thibaw's downfall and served the British. The Kinwun Mingyi nearly lost his life in the attempted palace coup of 1866. The Taingda Mingyi was formerly a personal servant to Thibaw.

⁶²False orders summoning the royal princes to the palace were issued by the conspirators and they were arrested as they arrived. But the two most likely claimants, the Nyaung Yan prince and his brother, the Nyaung Ok prince, suspecting danger, fled and were eventually smuggled to safety in British Burma with the aid of Sladen, the British Resident at Mandalay.

⁶³In 1884 when around 300 prisoners were massacred on the pretext that they were attempting an uprising but in fact this was an effort on the part of the court to eliminate all possible support for the Myingon prince who was known to be plotting a rebellion.

⁶⁴Lytton remained in favour of the annexation of Upper Burma; a decisive consideration was the fate which overtook another isolated British embassy, the one at Kabul where the British envoy and his mission were massacred by a furious Afghan mob in September 1879.

⁶⁵The Nyaung Yan and Nyaung Ok princes (see above, note 62). Regarding the Irrawaddy Flotilla Company, in 1878 their ship, the *Yankeentoung*, had been boarded and interfered with

at Shwemyo and Myingyon by local officials; another incident took place at Shwemyo in 1879 and the Company's vessel *Yunnan* was detained at Salaymyo in 1880. The governor of Myingyon was dismissed as a consequence of the first incident; the detention of the *Yunnan* was justified on the grounds of local disturbances.

66The trouble centred on the Kabaw Valley which was restored to Burma in 1833. The new frontier had never been satisfactorily defined since that time.

67The Burman envoy even failed to obtain an interview with the British Chief Commissioner in Rangoon, as the British demanded 'specific and acceptable' proposals from the Burman side before any negotiations should begin.

68Used as the capital by the British during the hot season in India.

69By this device the British hoped to satisfy Burman pride without openly committing themselves to recognition of the Burman demand that they be treated on a basis of equality.

70The British objected to the inadequate clauses regarding the position and safety of the British Resident, the liberties of British subjects in Upper Burma, the maintenance of certain monopolies and the continued Burmese refusal to acknowledge the validity of the Treaty of Yandabo.

71The Société des Missions Etrangères which planned to use Bhamo as a base for the proselytization of Tibet.

72The treaty was never ratified by Mindon because he demanded a supplementary treaty providing for a defensive and offensive alliance betweeen the two states and the granting of facilities for the supply of arms. These proposals were rejected by the French who were not in a position to commit themselves so far at that time.

73The treaty, which was purely commercial in nature, provided for the rights of French subjects to live and trade in Upper Burma. The French did not secure any extra-territorial privileges.

74The proposed railway would link up with the British-built line from the south. France would loan £2.5 million at 7½ per cent interest and obtain a 70-year lease on the railway. Another £2.5 million was to be provided for the setting up of the State Bank. These loans were to be out of river-customs receipts. News of all this reached Rangoon through the Italian consul at Mandalay, Andreino.

75The chairman of this meeting was the local representative of a firm which had its eye on the ruby mines. See Furnivall, *Colonial Policy and Practice*, p. 84.

76The evidence suggests that Haas had assured the Burman court of French willingness to take over the Ningyan concession should the Bombay-Burmah Trading Company's contracts be cancelled.

77The Kinwun Mingyi offered to settle for a reduced fine of 100,000 to 200,000 rupees.

78Especially men like the Kinwun Mingyi who had travelled abroad and seen the reality of Western power for themselves.

79Thibaw died in exile in Bombay in 1916; Supayalat was later permitted to return to Burma and pass the rest of her days in Rangoon on a meagre pension.

80Such as The Liverpool General Brokers' Association and the London Chamber of Commerce.

81'Annexation of Burma has opened up a large and prosperous trade with those vast districts of China which hitherto we have been unable to reach.' Lord Salisbury, British prime-minister in the British parliament. Quoted by Singhal, *The Annexation of Upper Burma*, p. 85.

82One good reason for the Army's reaction was that they were without pay.

83Buddhist monks were to play a very prominent role in the evolution of Burmese nationalism. See Book III.

84The hill peoples—Shan, Chin and Kachin—were not fighting for the Burman monarchy but to assert their own independence. See Book III.

85Including Bernard, the Chief Commissioner of Lower Burma, who believed that while Thibaw should be dethroned, his place should be taken by another royal prince.

86The *Thathanabaing* was the head of the Buddhist hierarchy in Burma and enjoyed a specially privileged position in the realm, being in certain respects beyond the authority of the king himself. The Taingda Mingyi had at first proved indispensable to the British in establishing their authority, but at the first opportunity he was deported to India; later he was allowed back to Rangoon where he ended his days as a trader.

87The rôle of the Provost-Marshall, a high British army officer responsible for the execution of military justice during the period of military administration, who delighted in taking photographs of prisoners shortly before they were to be shot, became the subject of bitter criticism in *The Times* and of questions in the British parliament. An enquiry was held, the allegations proved correct, but although censured no serious action was taken against him. See Singhal, op. cit. p. 83.

88Name of the organization controlling the Buddhist monkhood.

89Compare Thailand where the capital was far more accessible and where Thai rulers were able to inform themselves far more accurately of the nature of the Western threat.

12. BURMA: CHRONOLOGY OF MAIN EVENTS

A. Before the British Period

ca.	800+–1057	Burmans enter Burma and are converted to Buddhism
	1057–1287	Period of Burman supremacy (Pagan)
	1287	Destructions of Pagan by Mongols
	1287–1539	Period of Shan ascendancy in Upper Burma; Mon rule in South
	1539–1752	Restoration of Burman supremacy under the Tounggoo dynasty
	1752–7	The Great Mon Rebellion
	1752	Foundation of the Konbaung dynasty of Alaungpaya
	1764–76	Burman domination of Thailand
	1765–9	Chinese invasions repelled
	1785	Conquest of Arakan
	1820	Annexation of Assam
	1821	Annexation of Manipur

B. The British Conquest

1435	First recorded European visitor in Burma (Nicolo di Conti)
1519	Portuguese open trading post at Martaban
1550–1660	Portuguese freebooters at Chittagong, Arakan
1587	Ralph Fytche of London in Burma
1599–1613	Felipe de Brito controls Syriam
1635–79	Dutch factories at Syriam and Ava; withdrawn as unprofitable
1647–57	English factory at Syriam; withdrawn because of Dutch competition
1660–88	French base in Mergui
1680	First English embassy to Burman court; a failure
1686	Abortive English attempt to seize Negrais
1687	Abortive English assault on Mergui
1695–1743	English dockyard at Syriam; yards destroyed during Mon Rebellion
1727–40	French dockyard at Syriam; destroyed by the Mons
1753–9	British settlement at Negrais; destroyed by Alaungpaya
1784–5	Bodawpaya's conquest of Arakan
1794	Nga Than De's rebellion against the Burmans in Arakan; start of refugee problem
1795	Syme's first embassy to Ava
1796–8	Hiram Cox resident at Rangoon; recalled

1798		Arakan rebellion; more refugees; negotiated settlement
1799		Arakan refugee problem; Anglo-Burman clash near Chittagong
1800		British close Arakan frontier to placate Burmans
1802		Syme's second embassy to Ava
1803		Canning at Rangoon as British agent; forced to withdraw
1809		Canning's first embassy to Ava
1811–15		The Chan Byan Revolt
1812		Canning's second embassy to Ava
1813		Burman raid on Manipur
1816		Burman intervention in Assam; ruler seeks Burman protection
1817		First Burman invasion of Assam
1819		Second Burman invasion of Assam
1820		Burman conquest and annexation of Assam; new refugee problem
1821		Burman conquest of Manipur; Kachar seeks British protection
1822		British place Kachar and Jaintia under their protection
1823	September	Bandula's ultimatum to the British; the Shahpuri affair
1824	February	Burmans start invasion of Kachar
	March	Calcutta declares war on Ava
1824–6		FIRST ANGLO-BURMESE WAR
1826		Treaty of Yandabo: British annex Arakan, Tenasserim; Assam and Manipur also ceded by Burma
		Crawfurd's mission to Amarapura; commercial treaty signed
1826–7		Mon rebellion in Lower Burma crushed
1830		Burney's embassy
1830–7		Burney as British representative at Amarapura
1833		Kabaw Valley dispute settled
1837		Deposition of Bagyidaw and accession of Tharawaddy; Burney withdraws to Rangoon
1840		British representation withdrawn from Amarapura
1846		Death of Tharawaddy; succeeded by Pagan
1851	July-December	British sea-captains fined; Lambert at Rangoon
1852		SECOND ANGLO-BURMESE WAR
		British unilaterally annex Lower Burma

1853		Pagan deposed; Mindon becomes king
1854		Mindon's embassy to Rangoon to seek retrocession of lost provinces
1854–61		Thomas Spears acts as unofficial agent of British at Amarapura
1855		Phayre's first embassy to Mindon
1856		French mission at Amarapura (in response to Mindon's embassy of 1854)
1859		Second French mission to Burman court
1861		French established in Cochin-China
1862		First Anglo-Burmese Commercial Treaty; British Resident at Mandalay
1862–72		British Representation at Mandalay
1863		Clement-Williams, British agent at Mandalay, explores Bhamo route
1867		Second Anglo-Burmese Commercial Treaty; British consulate at Bhamo
1867–8		Lagree-Garnier expedition up the Mekong
1868		Col. Sladen's mission to Panthay
1872		Mindon's second embassy to Europe; commercial treaties with Paris and Rome
1874		The Margary affair. Burmese mission to Russia
1875		The Forsythe Mission and the Shoe Question
1878		Death of Mindon; accession of king Thibaw
1879		Withdrawal of British mission from Mandalay
1882		Burmese mission to India to negotiate new relationship with Britain
1883		Outbreak of Shan Revolt
		Burman mission to France
1884		Bhamo sacked by Chinese bandits; Kachin tribesmen invade plains
		Start of Bombay-Burmah Trading Company dispute
1885	January	Franco-Burmese Commercial Treaty signed in Paris
	June	Arrival of French Consul Haas at Mandalay
	July	Supplementary Franco-Burmese commercial agreement
	August	Hlutdaw imposes fine on Bombay-Burmah Trading Company
	September	French government repudiates Haas' commercial agreement
		Burmese close timber traffic on frontier
		Haas recalled
	22 October	British ultimatum to Mandalay
	9 November	Burmese reply received in Rangoon

	14 November	British invade Upper Burma
		THIRD ANGLO-BURMESE WAR
	28 November	Mandalay captured
1886	1 January	British unilaterally annex Upper Burma
		Pacification of Upper Burma; rebellion in Lower Burma
1886–91		Pacification of Upper Burma; rebellion in Lower Burma

C. The Konbaung Dynasty and its Capitals

1. Alaungpaya	1752–60	
2. Naungdawgyi	1760–3	son of (1)
3. Hsinbyushin	1763–76	brother of (2)
4. Singu Min	1776–81	son of (3)
5. Maung Maung	1781	son of (4)
6. Bodawpaya	1781–1819	son of (1)
7. Bagyidaw	1819–38	grandson of (6)
8. Tharrawaddy	1838–46	brother of (7)
9. Pagan	1846–53	son of (8)
10. Mindon Min	1853–78	brother of (9)
11. Thibaw	1878–85	son of (10)

Royal capitals at:	Shwebo	1752–5
	Ava	1755–60
	Amarapura	1760–1823
	Ava	1823–37
	Amarapura	1837–60
	Mandalay	1860–85

BOOKS AND ARTICLES FOR FURTHER READING: BURMA

Cady, J.F., *South-East Asia: Its Historical Development*, McGraw-Hill, New York, 1964.

Fisher, C.A., *South-East Asia: A Social, Economic and Political Geography*, Methuen, London, 1964.

Hall, D.G.E., *A History of South-East Asia*, Macmillan, London, 1964.

Cady, J.F., *A History of Modern Burma*, Cornell University Press, New York, 1958.

Christian, J.L., *Modern Burma*, University of California Press, California, 1942.

Foucar, E.C., *They Reigned in Mandalay*, Dobson, London, 1946.

Furnivall, J.S., *Colonial Policy and Practice*, University Press, New York, 1956.

Hall, D.G.E., *Burma*, Hutchinson, University Library Press, London, 1950.

—*Europe and Burma*, Oxford University Press, London, 1945.

Harvey, G.E., *British Rule in Burma*, Faber and Faber, London, 1946.

—*History of Burma*, Longmans Green, London, 1925.

Phayre, Arthur, *A History of Burma*, Truebner, London, 1883.

Scott, J.G., *Burma from the Earliest Times to the Present Day*, T. Fisher Unwin Ltd., London, 1924.

Singhal, D.P., *The Annexation of Upper Burma*, Eastern Universities Press, Singapore, 1960..

Trager, Frank, N., *Burma: From Kingdom to Republic*, Pall Mall Press, London, 1966.

The southern gate of the Imperial Palace, Hué

IV VIETNAM (ANNAM)

Vietnam

Vietnam is the odd man out amongst the states of Mainland South-East Asia. Unlike its neighbours to the west, Vietnam followed the Chinese model in social organization, government and outlook, the only country in the region to have absorbed China's cultural influence. Vietnam was also remarkable in being the only country in South-East Asia (apart from the Philippines) to have acquired a sizeable Christian community amongst her population. Conquest, rebellion and civil war have cratered the course of Vietnamese history, in which the dominant themes have been the struggle for emancipation from China, the push southwards and the subsequent conflict between its northern and southern poles. Confucian conservatism and the problem of the Christian converts were the two principal items which led Vietnam into its disastrous confrontation with France in the nineteenth century. The persecution of French missionaries gave France the pretext for her first action against Vietnam, and the refusal of the court of Hué to learn from the evidence resulted in the second and final stage of the French conquest. As for the French, unlike those of their British and Dutch contemporaries, their motives in building a South-East Asian empire were a compound of religious idealism and a yearning for greater international prestige, by comparison with which the economic incentive appears to have been secondary.

THE VIETNAMESE BACKGROUND

The Emperor Bao Dai,[a] who on 11 March 1945 declared (under Japanese auspices) his country's independence from France was the direct descendant of a long line of rulers of the Nguyen dynasty who have played a major rôle in the history of Vietnam during the past four hundred years. Bao Dai's inheritance included all the territories occupied by the Vietnamese people, namely Tongking, Annam and Cochin-China, which had been united under the hand of his forbear, the Emperor Gia Long, at the beginning of the nineteenth century.

Unlike his fellow sovereigns and contemporary leaders in South-East Asia, Bao Dai was the heir to a Chinese instead of an Indian tradition, and ruled over a people who culturally as well as politically had been profoundly influenced by Chinese as opposed to Indian ideas. The influence of China on the country is the most outstanding feature of Vietnamese history and distinguishes the Vietnamese from the Thais, their neighbours to the west (who are basically of the same racial stock) and from the Cambodians, who are their neighbours in the south.

The origins of Vietnam: the Chinese legacy
The origins of the Vietnamese are obscure, but as a people the dawn of history

[a]See Book III.

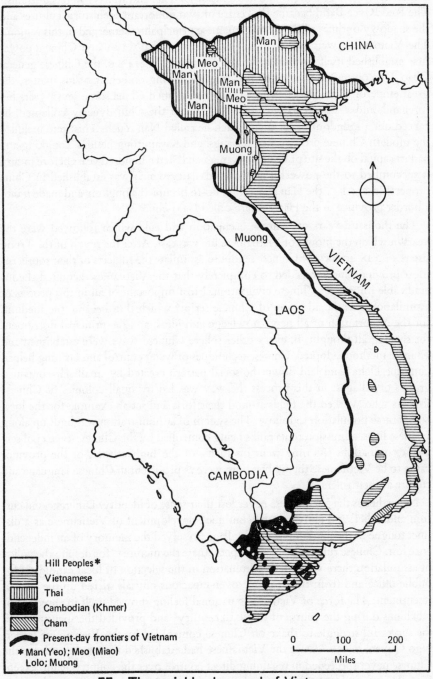

Hill Peoples *
Vietnamese
Thai
Cambodian (Khmer)
Cham
Present-day frontiers of Vietnam
* Man (Yeo); Meo (Miao)
  Lolo; Muong

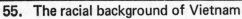

0   100   200

Miles

55. The racial background of Vietnam

found them living a tribal existence in the swamps and forests of the Red River Delta, representing in all probability a fusion of Thai and Malaysian racial strains.[1] The Red River Basin became the centre of two important prehistoric cultures and the shadowy outlines of the first Vietnamese principalities emerged in this region.[2] The Vietnamese were still living in a primitive, tribal way when Chinese power first established itself on the borders of Tongking. In 214 B.C. the Chinese general Chao T'o conquered the northern part of Tongking on behalf of his master, the great emperor Chin Shih Huang Ti who had unified China some seven years beforehand, and a few years later (208 B.C.) when the Chin dynasty collapsed, he carved out a kingdom of his own which he called Nan Yueh. This state included the modern Chinese provinces of Kwangsi and Kwangtung besides Tongking and had its capital on the site of Canton. Nan Yueh lasted a hundred years before in turn it succumbed to the powerful new Han dynasty which was established in China proper.[3] In 111 B.C. the Han general Lu Po-to occupied Tongking and made it into a border province of the Han Empire called Gaio-chi.[4]

The thousand years of Chinese occupation and rule which followed were the years in which the mould of Vietnamese life was cast. After the revolt of the Trung sisters in A.D. 40–44[5] the Chinese set out to assimilate the subjects of their southernmost province and succeeded so completely that the Vietnamese acquired the ineradicable impress of Chinese civilization. Most important of all in this process of assimilation was the adoption of Chinese script[6] which thus became the medium for the importation of all new knowledge and ideas, and the principal instrument for shaping all thought. In every other sphere Chinese ways were established and Chinese methods adopted. Chinese techniques of water control and farming helped tame the Delta[7] and laid down the social pattern created by small self-contained groups of villages; in this process the way was led by small colonies of Chinese soldiers who worked the fields around their forts and set an example for the local Vietnamese population to follow. The system of administration was built up along Chinese lines, admission to its ranks being controlled by the Chinese-type civil service examinations. As time went on many of the high officials of the province came to be Vietnamese themselves who were as proficient in Chinese language and culture as their rulers.

Nevertheless the Vietnamese never lost their sense of identity. Differences in custom and belief, and above all the continued development of Vietnamese as a distinct tongue in the market place and village preserved the memory of an independence lost. Chinese rule itself helped to perpetuate the memory, for despite the policy of assimilation there was still discrimination in the selection of local candidates for public office and from time to time over-rapacious officials stirred up the fires of resentment. The force of Vietnamese national feeling showed itself in three major rebellions during the course of the sixth century[8] and provided the mainspring in the successful struggle to shake off Chinese control led by the Vietnamese leader, Ngo Quyen, in 939.[9] Once the Vietnamese had established their independence the Chinese never succeeded in regaining direct control over the country again, except for a short period between 1406 and 1428 when the Ming dynasty took advantage of a dynastic upheaval to reassert its authority.[10] On the other hand, the rulers of independent Vietnam were never foolish enough to overlook the immediate and

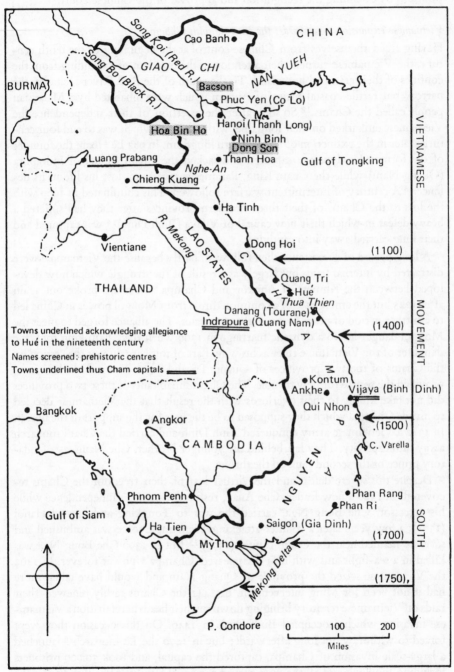

56. Vietnam: historical background

overwhelming presence of Chinese power and made sure of confirming their own positions by obtaining the recognition and approval of the Chinese court.[11]

Vietnamese expansion southwards: the struggle with Champa

Having freed themselves from Chinese control at the beginning of the tenth century, the Vietnamese turned their attention to the problem of expanding from the confines of their cramped homeland. To the south of the Red River Delta lay the narrow but fertile coastal plains of Annam which were inhabited by a Malaysian people called the Chams.[12] So soon after the assertion of their independence the Vietnamese embarked on their long duel with Champa which was to end four centuries later in the extinction of the southern kingdom. In 982 Le Hoan, the founder of the former Le dynasty, captured and sacked the Cham capital of Indrapura (Quang Nam) while the Cham King, Parameswaravarman, lost his life in its defence.[13] A century of intermittent warfare followed. This culminated in 1069 with the loss to the Chams of their three northern provinces after they had suffered a heavy defeat in which their new capital of Vijaya (Binh Dinh)[14] was captured and their king carried away into captivity.

A long period of coexistence then followed, partly because the Vietnamese were distracted by internal feuds but largely as a result of the struggle which now developed between the Khmers of Angkor and Champa.[a] Warfare broke out again after 1225 but the emergence of a common threat from Mongol power in China led to a further period of peace between the two states. The alliance forged to meet the Mongol danger led to a dynastic marriage in 1306 when the Cham king took the daughter of the Vietnamese ruler as his wife. Part of this bargain was the cession by the Chams of the two provinces of Quang Tri and Thua Tien which, however, provided the source for new trouble. The Cham inhabitants of these two provinces did not take kindly to their overlords with the result that the Vietnamese decided to invade Champa which they supposed to be the base for the support of the unrest. In 1312 a Vietnamese army conquered Binh Dinh and carried the Cham monarch away into captivity. They left behind his younger brother, Che Nang, as a feudatory prince of the second rank on the throne.

Despite this severe defeat and the virtual loss of their freedom the Chams recovered. In 1326 a new leader, Che Anan, restored Champa's independence while his successor, Che Bong Nga, carried the war to Tongking and burned Hanoi (1371); a few years later a counter-attacking Vietnamese force was ambushed and severely mauled near the Cham capital (1377).[15] But in 1390 Che Bong Nga was killed in a sea-fight and with him disappeared Champa's power forever. In 1402 the Vietnamese seized the province of Quang Nam and would have taken more had it not been for Ming intervention. In 1441 the Chams rashly renewed their raids on Vietnamese territory bringing down on their heads in retaliation a Vietnamese invasion which reoccupied Binh Dinh in 1446. On this occasion they were forced to withdraw not long afterwards; but in 1470 the Le monarch[16] launched a large-scale invasion of Champa, captured the capital, and took 30,000 prisoners including the King and all the members of the royal family. After this disaster the area of the kingdom of Champa was confined to the coast and hinterland between

[a] See p. 469.

Cape Varella and the Mekong Delta. The independent existence of a Cham King and court were recognized by the Chinese up to 1543 and the Chams maintained a separate identity until 1720. In that year the last King of Champa and his followers fled before the inexorable advance of the Vietnamese into the jungles of the west.[17]

The Vietnamese conquest of Champa was not merely political. As the Chams yielded their lands, so Vietnamese colonist-farmers moved in and settled down in the newly-won territories. By 1500 the population of the coastline as far south as Qui Nhon was predominantly Vietnamese. Under the rule of the Nguyen Kings at Hué the movement continued, imperceptible at first, but 'like so many centres of infection', as Groslier puts it,[a] spreading ever southwards until it penetrated the Delta of the Mekong. This advance into the Mekong Delta inevitably brought the Vietnamese into contact with Cambodia which was already slipping under the shadow of Thai Ayuthia.[b] At first the Cambodians welcomed the Vietnamese as a useful counter-weight to the Thais and permitted Vietnamese settlers to found a new colony at Gia-Dinh (Saigon). Profiting from the struggle for power over Cambodia by 1700 the Vietnamese had formed three provinces in the mouths of the Mekong. By the middle of the eighteenth century their authority was firmly established in all the land south of Gia-Dinh up to the My Tho arm of the Delta. The process of colonization received an added impetus during the early part of the same century with the arrival of refugees from Mançhu China who were given permission by Hué to settle in the Delta region. One such group, led by Mac Cuu, settled in the Cambodian province of Ha Tien around 1700; other colonies sprang up at My Tho and Bien Hoa. These all eventually became absorbed by Vietnamese jurisdiction. As for Cambodia itself, by the beginning of the nineteenth century its kings were having recourse to the device of acknowledging the overlordship of both Hué and of the Thais in Bangkok.[c] In 1845 this position was formalized under an agreement signed by Thailand, Vietnam and Cambodia.

The partitioning of Vietnam: north versus south—Trinh versus Nguyen

However while the Vietnamese people gradually spread themselves the length of a coastline which stretched 1,200 miles from the delta of the Red river to that of the Mekong, the problem of maintaining political unity became insuperable. As a result during the first quarter of the sixteenth century there began a division of the country into two independent political units which was to last for the best part of 300 years. The origins of this split lay in the decline of the Le dynasty which by 1500 had fallen into the hands of a series of ineffectual debauchee rulers. These circumstances provided the opportunity for an ambitious general called Mac Dang Dung[19] to seize power and usurp the throne (1527). But neither Dang Dung nor his successors were able to eliminate entirely the supporters of the former (Le) dynasty. In 1532 another general, Nguyen Kim, who was a member of a well-established and powerful family from Thanh Hoa province raised the standard of a Le pretender in the neighbouring mountains. The next year he succeeded in driving the usurpers out of Nghe An and Thanh Hoa provinces and in bringing about the

[a]Bernard Groslier, *Art of the World: Indo-China*, p. 4.
[b]See p. 470.
[c]See p. 471.

restoration of the Le rulers. However he died before he could continue his campaign and recover Tongking itself.[20]

Nguyen Kim laid the foundations of the fortunes of his house but before the dynasty could consolidate its position or bring the whole country under its control, it was challenged by the rise of a rival family, the Trinh. With the restoration of the Le monarchs, Nguyen Kim had secured for himself the key position of mayor of the palace. On his death he was succeeded in his post at Tay Do[21] by his very able son-in-law, Trinh Kiem. Under Trinh Kiem's capable management, Trinh now replaced Nguyen. This development was challenged by two of Nguyen Kim's sons. Trinh Kiem was able to procure the assassination of the elder of the two but Nguyen Hoang, the other son, escaped his grasp by obtaining the governorship of the difficult newly-acquired Cham provinces in the south.[22] Perhaps Trinh Kiem was counting on Nguyen Hoang's failure and eclipse in his difficult task of pacification, but to the contrary Nguyen Hoang showed skill and statesmanship and by bringing the provinces firmly under his control was able to build up his power. In 1600, having crushed a Cham uprising in Ninh Binh, Nguyen Hoang felt strong enough to sever all links with the Trinh in the north.

In the meantime Trinh Kiem's successor, Trinh Tong,[23] drove the effete Mac dynasty out of Hanoi in 1592 and thereby brought the greater part of Tongking under his control. With this, therefore, Vietnam was now divided politically between two families, both of whom claimed to be ruling in the name of the Le dynasty. Of the two, the Trinh dynasty appeared to be in the better position with their power based on the rich Tongking Red river basin and with the traditional throne in their possession. The centre of Nguyen power was in the province of Quang Tri where Nguyen Hoang had been able to build up his followers as Trinh Tong campaigned in the north. While Nguyen Hoang stayed alive no open hostilities took place between the rival families but fighting broke out soon after his death. The struggle began when Nguyen Phuc-Nguyen (alias Sai Vuong), Nguyen Hoang's successor, refused to hand over the revenues of Thanh Hoa and Quang Nam provinces to the Trinh in Hanoi in 1620. A bitter see-saw contest ensued which went on for the next fifty years and confirmed the political division of the country. The Trinh dynasty continued to rule over Tongking from Hanoi while the Nguyen at Hué ruled over what the Europeans came to call Annam and over the ever-expanding territories of the south known as Cochin-China.[24] The partitioning of Vietnam was symbolized by the construction of a fortified wall which divided the plains north of Dong Hoi.

The reunification of Vietnam: the Tay Son rebellion and the rôle of Nguyen Anh
The partitioning of Vietnam was brought to an end in 1802. The reunification was brought about by a scion of the Nguyen dynasty called Nguyen (Phuc-) Anh who in that year proclaimed himself Emperor of Vietnam with the reign title of Gia Long.[25]

Nguyen Anh's success in reuniting the country came about after a long struggle which began with disaster for his family and himself. In 1773 three brothers with the name of Nguyen but of no connexion with the Hué dynasty, took advantage of the weakness and intrigue at the Nguyen court to rise up in rebellion. The Tay Son[26] revolt which began in the neighbourhood of An Khe on the borders of Binh

Dinh and Kontum provinces quickly gained adherents. The plight of the Nguyen rulers was worsened when the Trinh took the opportunity to launch an invasion from the north early the next year. By the end of 1775 Hué was in the hands of Trinh Sam and the south was largely in the hands of the Tay Son rebels. Nguyen Phuc Thuan, the Hué ruler who had been a puppet in the hands of his minister, was dead. The fortunes of the Nguyen dynasty were now at their lowest ebb. The Tay Son rebels extended their control; in 1777 they captured Saigon for the second time[27] and although their attempts to drive the Trinh from Hué itself failed, they succeeded in checking the Trinh advance further south. Van Nhac, the eldest of the brothers, now proclaimed himself emperor.[28]

Meanwhile the survivors of the Nguyen dynasty were hunted down and only Nguyen Anh, a youth of fifteen, managed to escape. Twenty-five years of strife and privation lay ahead for the fugitive prince. During the course of the fluctuating struggle which ensued in the south, Saigon changed hands four times and Nguyen Anh was thrice a fugitive and an exile before he finally recaptured the port in 1788.[29] In that year the Tay Son brothers completed their conquest of Tongking, destroying the power of the Trinh and driving the last puppet emperor of the Le dynasty, Man Hoang De, into a Chinese exile, followed by Van Hué, the youngest and ablest of them proclaiming himself the new emperor. The outcome of these developments was that while the Mekong Delta was now securely back in the hands of the Nguyen dynasty, Tongking was held by the Tay Son rebels. Fourteen more years of bitter struggle followed before the Tay Son supporters were finally overcome, but the fortunes of war flowed steadily in Nguyen Anh's favour. By the end of 1789 he had succeeded in reducing systematically the whole of Cochin-China. In 1792 the Tay Son fleet was annihilated off Qui Nhon and in the same year, Van Hué died at Hanoi,[30] depriving the rebels of their most effective leader. His sons carried on the struggle but were unable to prevent the fall of the key fortress of Qui Nhon in 1799.[31] After changing hands twice Hué itself fell to Nguyen Anh's forces in 1801 and there Nguyen Anh proclaimed himself King of Annam. Exactly one year later, as his troops were engaged in the final phase against the Tay Son in Tongking, Nguyen Anh caused a second proclamation to be read, styling him as Emperor of all Vietnam, with the reign title of Gia Long. Just over one month after this Hanoi fell to his forces, the Tay Son movement was finally vanquished and the reality of his claims established.

One of the factors that contributed to Gia Long's spectacular achievements was the help which he received from European sources. Since the end of 1788 he had been receiving aid from Frenchmen, obtained through the good offices of a remarkable French missionary called Pigneau de Béhaine.[32] Pigneau had spent over twenty years in Cambodia and Cochin-China when he met the emperor as a boy-prince refugee from the Tay Son. From this first contact ripened a friendship which culminated in the sending of a Nguyen embassy to Paris and the signing of a treaty of alliance with the French court.[33] As a result French officers and men of fortune organized his armies, gave him a modern navy and constructed a powerful system of forts which assisted in the pacification of the country.[34] Pigneau himself, who died during the investment of Qui Nhon in 1799[35] towered above them all, a fully ordained Catholic bishop who excelled as an administrator and as a leader in war. After his death, when Nguyen Anh paid him the highest honours in person, several of his French followers stayed on to receive mandarin status and to serve the monarch during the rest of his reign.[a] So French intervention, albeit on a small scale, helped to re-establish the dynasty of Gia Long and to bring about the reunification of the country. Yet barely eighty years later men of the same nation reduced his descendants to the status of puppet kings and made parts of his empire their own.

[a] See p. 444.

[1]Originally the Vietnamese were part of common Thai stock; they acquired their distinctiveness as the result of cross-breeding with Malaysian/Indonesian tribal groups. In 1955 the indigenous population of Vietnam was reckoned as follows: Vietnamese—22,750,000; hill peoples—1,200,000; Thais—825,000; Cambodian (Khmer)—480,000; Cham—40,000. See Fisher, South-East Asia, op. cit., p. 559. The hill peoples include the Man (Yao), Meo (Miao)—who live exclusively above the 3,000 ft. contour—Lolo and Muong in the north; in the centre and south they are known as Moi to the Vietnamese, as Penong to the Cambodians and as Kha to the Thais (all collective terms meaning 'savage') and have close cultural affinities with the Dayaks of the Bornean interior. The Thai have been broken up into distinct groups as a result of the broken and rugged terrain of the interior; viz. Thai Dam (Black Thai), Thai Khao (White Thai), Tho, Lu, Nung and Nhang.

[2]The prehistoric cultures take their names from the places where their artefacts have been found in the greatest abundance—namely at Hoa Binh, which is identified with the Mesolithic Age, and at Dong Son which is identified with the use of iron and bronze. Other important finds have been found at Bac Son in the same region. Regarding early Vietnamese principalities, there were two legendary states—Chia-quy and Van-long—followed by a third historically identifiable one called Au Lac which flourished in the third century B.C. and had its capital at Phuc Yen (Co Loa).

[3]After the collapse of the Chin dynasty, its place in north China was quickly taken by a general called Liu Pang who founded the Han Dynasty in 202 B.C. Han power was spread to the south during the reign of the Emperor Wu Ti (140–87 B.C.).

[4]During the time of the Chinese T'ang dynasty (A.D. 618–907), they renamed Giao Chi as An Nam or 'pacified South'; the term 'Viet Nam' meaning 'distant South' was officially adopted by the Gia Long Emperor in 1802.

[5]Namely Trung Trac and Trung Nhi. The consequence of their rebellion was the introduction of Chinese forms of administration in place of the feudal system permitted hitherto.

[6]Until the thirteenth century purely Chinese ideographs were used. Later modifications were made, but in the seventeenth century Roman Catholic missionaries introduced a romanized form of writing called 'qu'oc nga' which is now in standard use.

[7]This was vital since the Song Koi (Red River) tends to flood during the the wet season while constant sedimentation has raised the level of the river bed. The Chinese began the complex system of bunds which were still inadequate to contain the flood waters when the French took over in 1885.

[8]In A.D. 544–47, 592 and 600–2.

[9]Taking advantage of the confusion in China following the collapse of the T'ang dynasty in 907 Ngo founded a line of rulers who exercised a nominal sway until 968 although in fact the country was split up amongst warring chiefs. The Ngo dynasty was followed by that of Dinh (968–80), the Former Le (980–1009), Li (1010–1225) and Tran (1225–1400). During the thirteenth century Vietnam was subjected to severe Mongol pressure; Hanoi was sacked three times (1257, 1285 and 1287) but the Mongols failed to establish a permanent foothold in the country owing to the intensity of the Vietnamese resistance.

[10]The throne of the Tran dynasty was usurped in 1400 by a rebellious general. Members of the dispossessed dynasty appealed for Chinese help to which the Ming Emperor Yung Lo responded by sending an army to their aid. As before, Chinese attempts to assimilate the Vietnamese merely provoked resentment which found expression in a rebellion led by Le Loi, a wealthy landowner from Thanh Hoa, in 1418. Le became the founder of the second Le dynasty after he had triumphed over the Chinese in 1427.

[11]For example, Le Loi's first measure after establishing his throne was to send an embassy to Peking offering his submission. Fear of Chinese disapproval was one good reason why the powerful Trinh and Nguyen families did not depose the Le emperors long after the real power had slipped from their hands.

[12]The Chams are a people of Malaysian stock who first emerge in history as the Lin Yi of the Chinese chronicles. According to the latter, the kingdom of Champa was founded in A.D. 192 by a Cham official called Chu Lien during the declining years of the Later Han Dynasty in China.

[13]Le Hoan's invasion was the result of Cham provocation; they had imprisoned one of his envoys who had come to announce his accession to power.

[14]The Chams moved their capital to Binh Dinh in 988 as a consequence of the disaster of 982.

[15]After the Cham capture of Hanoi in 1371, the Ming Emperor ordered their attacks to cease; the Chams thereupon stopped their attacks by land but raided Vietnamese shipping on the pretext of suppressing piracy, sending the booty to China.

[16]Le Thanh Ton (1460–97), probably the greatest ruler this dynasty produced.

[17]There are roughly 120,000 Cham survivors today, of whom only 40,000 are to be found within the frontiers of Vietnam near Phan Ri, west of Phan Rang. The rest are in Cambodia.

[18]Mac Cuu, a Chinese refugee from his homeland after the final downfall of the Ming dynasty to the Manchus, created a nucleus for Chinese and Vietnamese colonists in Ha Tien at the beginning of the eighteenth century. When his settlement was attacked by the Cambodians in 1715 he fled to Hué. With Nguyen military help, Mac Cuu returned to Ha Tien as governor. Under his son, Mac Thien Tu, who was confirmed as governor in his stead when he died in 1735, Ha Tien developed into a prosperous vietnamized province of Hué's empire.

[19]'An ambitious mandarin... who had made and unmade kings since 1519, ordered the reigning monarch, Le Hoang De Chuan, to commit suicide and usurped the throne.' Hall, *History of South-East Asia*, op. cit. p. 188. Although he formally abdicated in favour of his son in 1529, he retained the real power in his hands until his death in 1541.

[20]He was assassinated.

[21]To become the capital of the Trinh family, where in the name of the Le monarchs they controlled Thanh Hoa, Nghe An and Ha Tinh provinces. The Mac family still ruled in Hanoi.

[22]Nguyen Hoang offered to withdraw from the court on condition that he was granted the governorship of Quang Tri, Thua Thien and Quang Nam.

[23]Trinh Tong came to power on the death of his father in 1570. The Mac dynasty fled to Cao Banh where they maintained an independent existence with Chinese backing until 1677. The Trinh made Hanoi their capital in 1593.

[24]Today and ever since the French conquest Cochin China refers specifically to the provinces of the Mekong Delta; during the eighteenth century the name was applied by Westerners to all the domains of the Nguyen dynasty of Hué, thereby embracing what is now known as Annam. According to Alastair Lamb (*British Missions to Cochin China 1778–1822*, *J.M.B.R.A.S.*, Vol. 34, Nos. 3 & 4, 1961), the term originally came from the the Portuguese 'Cauchi China' which in turn was believed to derive from the Malay 'Kutchi China'; 'kutchi' is the Malay rendering of the Chinese Giao Chi, their term for Tongking. According to Hoang Van Chi (*From Colonialism to Communism*, p. 27), Cochin China is a corruption of Ke Chien, the seventeenth century capital of the Nguyen in Quang Nam province, which was pronounced by foreign traders as Cochin. China was added to distinguish it from the Indian port of Cochin.

[25]Gia Long derived his reign title from *Gia* Dinh, the old name for Saigon, and Thanh *Long*, the old name for Hanoi.

[26]The movement takes its name from the district of Tay Son near An Khe. In origin it was a peasant movement which received the backing of the merchant class, both groups alienated by Nguyen oppression.

[27]Van Lu had captured Saigon the previous year but was driven out again by Mac Thieu Tri of Ha Tien. After Saigon's second fall, Mac fled to Thailand.

[28]The three brothers were Nguyen Van Nhac who established himself at Hué; Nguyen Van Lu, the conqueror of Saigon; and the youngest and most brilliant of the three, Nguyen Van Hué who eventually captured Hanoi and was proclaimed Emperor Quang Trung.

[29]Saigon was captured by the Tay Son and regained by the Nguyen on four occasions as follows: 1776, 1777, 1781–2, 1784–8. Nguyen Anh was a refugee in 1777, 1781–2 and 1783–7.

[30]Already recognized by China as the Emperor Quang Trung; he was succeeded by his son who took the title of Quang Toan.

[31]However, Qui Nhon changed hands again later the same year and was not finally recaptured by Nguyen Anh's forces until 1801.

[32]Pierre-Joseph-Georges Pigneau; 1741, born at Béhaine in Aisne, France; trained as a missionary in the Paris Seminary; 1765, arrived at Ha Tien (Hon Dat), Cambodia, to take over the mission station there; 1768, imprisoned for three months for allegedly helping a refugee Thai prince; 1769, Ha Tien ravaged by Chinese and Cambodian pirates—fled to Malacca and Pondicherry; 1770, set up new seminary at Virampattnam, near Pondicherry; 1774, consecrated Bishop of Adran and designated Vicar-Apostolic to Cochin China, Cambodia and Tongking;

left for Macao *en route* to re-establish seminary at Ha Tien; 1775, reopened mission at Ha Tien:
    1777, met Nguyen Anh, a refugee from the Tay Son, for the first time; identified himself with
    the Nguyen cause; 1783, fled to Chantaburi, Thailand, after second Nguyen defeat.
[33]This treaty, signed at Versailles in 1787, laid down that France was to assist Nguyen Anh with
    1,200 infantry, 200 artillerymen and 250 kaffirs (Indian slave-troops); in return, France request-
    ed the cession of Pulau Condore and control over Da Nang (Tourane) harbour with com-
    mercial and shipbuilding facilities. In addition French subjects were to have exclusive rights of
    freedom to trade inside Vietnam with access to the interior on passports issued by the French
    commander at Da Nang. Local forces could be raised for the protection of the French esta-
    blishments but these could not be taken beyond the Straits of Malacca.
[34]In the event, the outbreak of the French Revolution in 1789 made the treaty inoperable. At
    Pondicherry on his way back to Vietnam, Pigneau failed to get the co-operation of the gover-
    nor, de Conway, who had been given secret discretionary powers by Paris and considered the
    whole affair too hazardous. Nevertheless Pigneau raised a private force of 360 men—100 from
    French officers serving in India, 125 from the crew of his ship and another 60 free-lance French
    adventurers from the Far East. He arrived back in Vietnam in 1789. Prominent amongst those
    Pigneau recruited were Dayot, Vannier, Chaigneau and de Forceaux who built up the Nguyen
    navy and Puymanel who was responsible for fortifications.
[35]According to Hall and Lancaster, he died of sickness shortly after the fall of Qui Nhon; accord-
    ing to Cady he died actually leading an assault during the siege.

THE FRENCH CONQUEST

The French subjugation of Vietnam took place in two stages. First of all they seized
the Mekong Delta in an operation which began in 1858 and was completed by
1864. Then in the 1880s they established their control over Tongking and converted
the rest of the country (Annam proper) into a French protectorate.

Vietnam and Christian missionaries

These events marked the first establishment of French colonial power in South-
East Asia, but French connexions with Vietnam and her neighbours had existed
since the early part of the seventeenth century when Alexander of Rhodes founded
a Roman Catholic Christian mission in Tongking.[1] Soon after this the powerful
Société des Missions Etrangères was established in Paris[2] and in 1662 set up its first
missionary headquarters at Ayuthia, then the capital of Thailand.[a] The following
year French missionaries of the *Société* entered Cambodia[b] and Vietnam and so
started the long line of dedicated Christians who lived out their lives in the country.
The presence of these Frenchmen in Vietnam naturally aroused the interest of
French governments from time to time and led occasionally to projects for developing commercial and political relations.[3] But nothing came of these until the episode
of Pigneau de Béhaine. The missionaries and their converts were frequently subjected to persecution but in spite of this by 1750 the number of Vietnamese Christians was reckoned to stand at around 300,000 people. During the nineteenth century French missionary activities intensified, providing the government of Vietnam
with one of its main preoccupations and later on giving to the French government
a ready-made pretext for intervention.

Generally speaking these Christian missionaries never enjoyed the favour of the
rulers of Vietnam. In the first place they were foreigners, and Vietnamese offi-

[a]See p. 501.
[b]See p. 478, note 5.

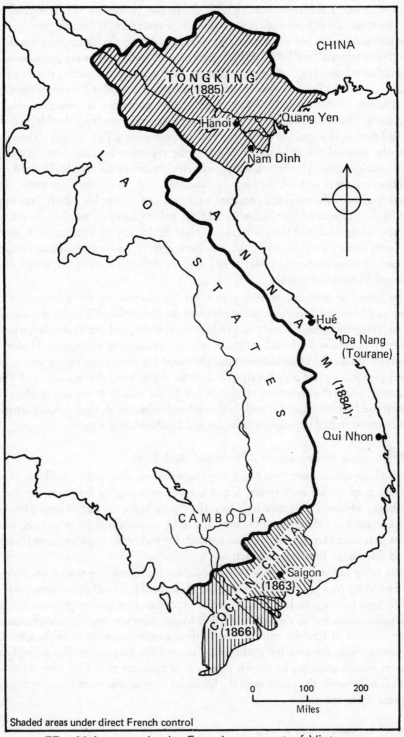

57. Main stages in the French conquest of Vietnam

cials were never able to determine what the precise connexion was between them and their unruly fellow-countrymen who came as traders. Whatever they knew of the connexion was not very reassuring. There had been the Cambodian episode of the 1590s when a handful of Spanish adventurers, with missionary acquiescence if not actual connivance, had come within an ace of making themselves the masters of that country.[a] In Thailand missionary influences had assisted in the rise of the Greek adventurer, Constantine Phaulkon, who all but succeeded in overthrowing the monarchy in favour of Louis XIV of France.[b] Even in China itself the Ching dynasty had seen fit to expel the Jesuits in 1721 for professing a dual loyalty. Then there was the internal threat to the stability of the régime which the activities of the missionaries posed. The French who came lived the life of the people. They adopted Vietnamese dress, learned the language and followed the country's customs. They quickly gained adherents and preached a religion and way of life which were opposed to the precepts of Confucianism and the cult of ancestor worship encouraged by the ruling class and the court. As a result the loyalty of Vietnamese Christian converts to the ruling dynasty quickly became suspect, and only too often Christian influences were connected with the endemic revolts against authority which pockmarked Vietnamese politics.

So from the moment of their arrival on Vietnamese soil the missionaries met with suspicion and with subsequent persecution. Alexander of Rhodes was expelled from Tongking within three years of his arrival there, and the Trinh dynasty consistently maintained a hostile attitude towards missionary enterprise. Under the Nguyen of Hué the same basic attitude prevailed but with them things were a little easier for some time if only because the Nguyen kings lived in expectation of European aid against their northern rivals.[4] When by the middle of the seventeenth century it had become clear that such help was not forthcoming, rigorous and frequent persecutions started throughout Annam and Cochin-China too.

The missionary problem under Gia Long and Minh Mang

As we have already seen, the Gia Long Emperor was somewhat beholden to missionary help for his own triumph and consequently during his reign the French Catholics obtained a greater influence than they had ever had before. However Gia Long did not lose sight of realities, and as he consolidated his power, he was at pains to restrict French influence and towards the end of his reign increasingly tended to discourage European contacts.[5]

Gia Long died in 1820 and was succeeded by his fourth son who took the reign title of Minh Mang. During his reign the traditional policy of isolationism was revived with full vigour. It coincided with a renewed phase of European commercial and political interest in Vietnam but Minh Mang, who was a devout Confucian and keen admirer of Chinese culture, saw in these and in the presence of the Christian minority inside the country nothing but danger for his régime. Accordingly the several French attempts to reopen commercial relations with Hué after 1820 met with failure[6] while the position of the Christian community in the country steadily became more precarious.

[a]See pp. 473 and 478, note 1.
[b]See pp. 502–3.

Although Minh Mang was determined to curb Christianity, he held his hand at first because of the influence of powerful mandarins like Le Van Duyet, the governor of Cochin-China, who were sympathetic towards the Christians, and because of the need to secure his own position. But the clandestine landing of a French missionary reported near Da Nang in 1825 provoked the first anti-Christian edict which declared that 'the perverse religion of the Europeans corrupts the heart of man'. The death of Le Van Duyet in 1833 was followed by the outbreak of a rebellion in the south led by his son, Le Van Khoi,[7] in which the Christians were believed to be implicated. The discovery of Father Marchand, a French missionary, in the rebel camp at Saigon when it was recaptured by Minh Mang's troops in 1835, confirmed these suspicions, and led to the wholesale persecution of Christians the length and breadth of the country. Decrees were issued that made Christianity illegal and its practice a crime punishable by death. All buildings used by Christians were to be demolished and all foreign Christian missionaries were summoned to the court at Hué where they were detained.[8] The following year the death penalty was extended to foreign missionaries discovered in the country[9] and all Vietnamese ports were closed to European shipping save Da Nang. Minh Mang's policy was in direct imitation of that being followed contemporaneously by the Chinese authorities in their dealings with the Westerners at Canton. However, the Chinese policy culminated in the outbreak of war with Britain in 1839[10] and Minh Mang, observing the consequences decided to tread more carefully in his own dealings with the European powers. In an attempt to secure some kind of recognition for his position and to show his willingness to trade, in 1840 Minh Mang sent embassies to Batavia, Paris and London. The embassy to France achieved nothing (not even a royal audience) owing to the understandably hostile intervention of the *Société*,[11] nor did the mission to Britain achieve anything concrete either. By the time they got back to Vietnam, Minh Mang was dead.

Reaction and foreign intervention under Thieu Tri
Minh Mang's successor was the Emperor Thieu Tri who reigned for the next seven years. He inherited the same problem as Minh Mang and shared the same prejudices but did not have the intelligence and flexibility to see or meet the dangers that he was courting. So after some initial hesitation brought about by British activities in South China, Thieu Tri, with the full support of his Confucian advisers, resumed the policy of persecution in 1842. A spate of arrests of foreign (mostly French) missionaries followed, generally resulting in imprisonment, but for the unfortunate one or two in death. The effect was to restrict missionary activity to Tongking where there was already a considerable Christian following and where the mandarins were more open to subornation. But on this occasion there was positive foreign counter-action. For the first time a French warship appeared off Da Nang in 1842 to demand the release of five missionaries condemned to death.[12] Yielding to threats, Thieu Tri handed over these men. In 1845 a similar operation was performed by another French warship at Da Nang, this time in order to rescue Mgr. Lefebvre, the Bishop-Apostolic of West Cochin-China who had been imprisoned. Once again Thieu Tri bowed before the threat of force and let the Bishop go.[13]

In 1847 the first clash of arms took place between the Vietnamese and the French. In March of that year a small French force anchored off Da Nang to secure the release of another missionary and to obtain guarantees for the safety of French nationals. During the negotiations that followed deadlock ensued and suspecting a plot to destroy them the French attacked the Vietnamese warships in the harbour, causing heavy loss of life, and silenced the harbour forts.[14] The French commander, realizing that he could not carry the issue any further, then sailed away, leaving the Christians of Vietnam to the fury of Thieu Tri and his court. The Emperor reacted wildly, ordering the killing of all Europeans on sight and placing a price on the head of all foreign missionaries.[15] These orders were not fully carried out but it is not surprising that a British trade mission which arrived at Da Nang later in the same year made no headway at all. Thieu Tri died ten days after its departure.

The worsening of foreign relations under Tu Duc

Thieu Tri was succeeded by Tu Duc, a pious and learned Confucian, who was fated to preside over the downfall of his empire. The events of Thieu Tri's short reign should have served as ample warning that Western powers should be handled with care but the warning was not heeded. Although the governors of Cochin-China and Tongking saw only too clearly the dangers ahead and were opposed to any policy which might provoke European intervention, the new emperor was too devout a Confucian and too influenced by the precepts of China to be able to hear.[16] He was surrounded at the court by the ruling *literati* class whose hatred of Christianity in particular and of foreigners in general confirmed him in his policy which was also deeply influenced by his mother.

Nevertheless at the beginning of his reign Tu Duc also hesitated. What clinched matters was the outbreak of·a new rebellion in Tongking in 1851 led by an elder brother, which appeared to have Christian support and raised the fear that European intervention might take place. Tu Duc determined on radical measures. All Christian communities were to be broken up and dispersed, their villages destroyed and their lands redistributed. Christians themselves were to be branded on their left cheeks and banished from their home districts. Many thousands of Christians died in the wave of persecution which followed, including two French missionaries.[17] The outbreak of a fresh rebellion in 1855 in Tongking in which the Christians were again implicated produced a new set of decrees aimed at extirpating all expressions of Christianity. Now all priests, Vietnamese and foreign, were placed under the death penalty and rewards were offered for their capture.

This anti-Christian policy failed at first to provoke more than a very weak response from the European power most concerned, namely France. In 1856 French warships again appeared off Da Nang, the heralds of an official embassy led by de Montigny, the French Consul-General to Thailand and Cambodia.[18] They bore a letter from de Montigny to the Emperor, offering a treaty of friendship, commerce and navigation with guarantees for the free practice of religion. The letter spoke of the final chance for friendship and hinted darkly at the possible consequences if this was not achieved. Two clashes occurred whilst negotiations were in progress, prompted by the French fear that measures were being prepared to attack them; on the second occasion the French destroyed the harbour forts and occupied the citadel. In the meantime, however, the Vietnamese government rejected the letter without ceremony. The French demand for religious toleration was considered inadmissible, affecting as it did the internal stability of the régime. It was too high a price to pay for the opening of trade. Soon after this the French vessels withdrew, being unable on account of shortage of supplies and of other commitments elsewhere to await the arrival of de Montigny himself who had been delayed at Kampot.[19] When de Montigny did come early in 1857, therefore, little could be done. There was already a deadlock and his own lack of escort gave him no means of applying pressure, and so the French envoy sailed off again after a brief stay, having accomplished nothing.

This episode convinced the court of Hué that there was not much to be feared from the French and the persecution of Christians in the country was intensified.[20] Three months after the departure of de Montigny, the Vietnamese arrested Mgr. Diaz, the Spanish bishop of Tongking, and in the following July he was executed at Nam Dinh.

The French and Spaniards intervene

This latest affront to Western Christendom came, although unknown to the Emperor Tu Duc, at a most inopportune moment. It confirmed the resolve which had been formulating for some time in French minds to turn the Vietnamese problem to their own advantage,[a] and it occurred at a period when powerful French forces were available in Eastern waters as a result of the crisis with China.[21]

At the end of August 1858, a combined Franco-Spanish force comprising 14 war vessels and some 3,000 men[22] emerged on the Da Nang horizon. Within 48 hours these forces had landed after a preliminary bombardment and occupied the town. The Vietnamese defenders were taken by surprise and could only offer token resistance with their eighteenth century cannon-ware. But once the enemy had landed, the Vietnamese were able to hold their own, reinforced by the effects of the tropical sun and disease on the invaders who were quite inadequately prepared for such things.[23] The French and Spanish forces soon discovered that they could not advance inland without more troops and supplies and in the meantime the Vietnamese rapidly built up a large army to bar the way to Hué. By November there were 7,000 to 8,000 Vietnamese troops in positions barely two miles from the European camp, and there they stayed, withstanding all attempts to dislodge them.

Faced with this impasse, the French commander, Admiral de Genouilly,[24] decided to switch his attack to the south which was the main source of the country's grain. Leaving behind a small garrison at Da Nang, he set sail in early February for Saigon with a detachment of five ships. There he launched an attack on the town and its defences and after a week's hard fighting Saigon fell into his hands. Large quantities of supplies fell into French hands, including a year's rice supply for the needs of 6,000 to 8,000 troops. More serious still was the fact that the rice harvest of the Mekong Delta was now lost to Hué. However, the invaders were hamstrung by limited numbers and scarcity of other supplies so that de Genouilly was forced to leave Saigon again in April, entrusting it to the care of a small garrison of hardly 1,000 men; he returned to Da Nang where despite some reinforcements the position remained exactly the same as before.

In May 1859 a big clash took place between the European forces at Da Nang and the Vietnamese who invested them. Although the issue was in favour of the in-

[a]See p. 535.

vaders, it was in no way decisive. Disease continued to take its toll, fresh developments in China removed all hopes of receiving more reinforcements and Tu Duc
showed no sign of giving way.[25] In June de Genouilly opened negotiations, demanding freedom of religion, freedom of trade and territorial concessions. Tu Duc
and his advisers saw no reason to move. In August de Genouilly's demands were
reduced to the creation of a French protectorate over Christians in Vietnam and to
the establishment of a consulate-general. Hué maintained its silence. Exasperated,
de Genouilly delivered an ultimatum which expired unanswered on 7 September.
A week later, after a French attempt to move on Hué had failed, the unpalatable
decision to evacuate Da Nang was taken. The process of withdrawal was started in
November under de Genouilly's successor, Admiral Page,[26] and it was completed
some four months later in March 1860. Tu Duc had won a great victory and felt he
could ignore the mild terms that Page now offered him.[27]

The loss of the southern provinces (Cochin-China)

However, the Franco-Spanish garrison at Saigon still held despite the immense
pressure that the Vietnamese put onto it. As soon as de Genouilly had left, Vietnamese irregulars started launching attacks on the beleaguered port but without
success. In mid-1860 the Vietnamese assembled a huge force of 12,000 men, made
up of regulars and volunteers, many of whom were drawn from the tough soldier-
colonists who farmed the Delta region. But the mere weight of numbers could
not overcome superior arms and when the French admiral Charner forced his way
up the Dong Nai river in February 1861, the heavily-outnumbered garrison was
still intact. Tu Duc failed to repeat the Da Nang success at Saigon. Saigon was easily
accessible from the sea and was easier to defend. When the China crisis was finally
settled,[28] the French were able to pour large reinforcements into the Delta. Charner
relieved the Saigon garrison after a three-week struggle which culminated in the
battle of Chi Hoa. The back of the main Vietnamese resistance was broken and the
area around Saigon was evacuated by them. In May My Tho was captured and in
the following month the bulk of the French forces which had served in China
arrived to help crush resistance in the Delta. In that month Gia Dinh province and
parts of Bien Hoa and Go Cong provinces were lost, and now Charner attempted
to reopen negotiations on the basis of the cession of these three provinces, freedom
for missionary activities and an indemnity for the costs of the war.

The French (and the Spaniards) had by this time indubitably got a foothold in
the south, but the court of Hué did not despair. Guerrilla fighting at which the
Vietnamese excelled now took the place of more formal resistance. In July Charner
declared the unilateral annexation of Saigon but when the greater part of the
French forces was withdrawn for repatriation a few months later the Vietnamese
launched an offensive which carried them into Cholon. Nevertheless the French
counter-attacked and by the first quarter of the new year (1862) had succeeded in
bringing the whole of Baria and Bien Hoa provinces into their hands, as well as the
islands in the mouth of the Delta together with the famous Pulau Condore.[29] With
the fall of the island fortress of Vinh Long in March, the most important and richest
rice-bearing regions of the Delta were lost to Hué, and faced with the outbreak of
yet another rebellion in the north led by a Christian-influenced pretender of the Le

58. The French conquest of Cochin-China, 1859—1866

dynasty, Tu Duc decided to exchange the methods of war for those of diplomacy, and sued for peace.[30]

Tu Duc's peace mission which made its first overtures in May 1862 was led by the able and astute Phan Thanh Giang.[31] However, confronted by the circumstances which prevailed in mid-1862, he was in a weak position and could do little but accept the French terms. These were harsh. Tu Duc was to cede to France the three eastern provinces of Cochin-China[32] as well as Pulau Condore, while the Europeans were to evacuate Vinh Long. The Catholic religion was to be fully tolerated in Vietnam. Da Nang, Ba Lat and Quang Yen were to be opened to French trade, and French shipping was to be allowed free passage up the Mekong to Cambodia, over which country Tu Duc was to renounce his suzerainty. An indemnity of 4 million piastres[33] was to be paid in instalments spaced out over a period of ten years. Most far-reaching of all, Article 4 of the proposed treaty forbade the cession of any Vietnamese territory to a third power without French consent, and should a third power intervene in Vietnamese affairs, Hué was to consult France. But at the same time, the French were not committed to helping Vietnam and retained full freedom of action.

These terms clearly placed Vietnam under the shadow of the French tricolour but Tu Duc and his court had no intention of honouring them if they could be evaded. Unable to prevent the Europeans from establishing a foothold in his country, the emperor now had recourse to diplomatic subterfuge and seized every opportunity to defend his far-compromised sovereignty. The unavoidable delay in having the treaty ratified provided him with his first chance. The ship carrying the treaty documents back to Europe was delayed by storms and during the interval Tu Duc refused to ratify the treaty on his side. Furthermore Tu Duc's envoys tried to exploit Franco-Spanish differences,[34] demanding Spanish help in suppressing the Tongking troubles as the price for ratification. But these tactics only served to bring the two European powers together again; in November 1862 the French and the Spaniards threatened to intervene on the side of the Tongking rebels if the treaty were not ratified within a month of its return from France. The outbreak of fresh resistance in the Delta in December stiffened Tu Duc's attitude but the arrival of more French reinforcements from China in February of the next year brought this to an end, although guerrilla activity continued in Bien Hoa and along the Cambodian border. Fear of French intervention in the north, however, proved to be the determining factor, and rather than risk this taking place Tu Duc finally ratified the treaty in April 1863.

However Tu Duc still had not given up hope of recovering the three Delta provinces. Soon after the ratification, he sent an embassy to France, led by Phan Thanh Giang, in order to secure its revision. The embassy was very nearly successful. Tu Duc offered to acknowledge a French protectorate over all six provinces of Cochin-China, to grant full commercial access to Annam and to pay an indemnity of a quarter of a million francs or annual tribute if only the French would hand back their title to the three annexed provinces.[35] It was a tempting offer, particularly as Cochin-China appeared far from pacified, and the French ruler, Napoleon III, sent a naval lieutenant called Aubaret to Hué where the revised treaty was actually signed in June 1864. But the following year Napoleon changed his mind, giving way to the strong opposition to this new policy which had been aroused in French governing circles,[a] and he repudiated the 1864 agreement in favour of the original one of 1862.

[a]See p. 537.

All the same the end had not been reached yet. Guerrilla resistance was still rife around Saigon, and much of it was succoured by help from the Vietnamese-held provinces in the west of the Delta, namely Vinh Long, Chau Doc and Ha Tien. The French were convinced that these activities had the clandestine support of the Hué court[36] even though Tu Duc went so far as to appoint the familiar Phan as governor of the three western provinces in an attempt to allay French suspicions. Phan's appointment produced no change in the situation and so the French governor, Admiral de la Grandière,[37] sent his troops into the region and demanded the cession of the three provinces. Phan Thanh Giang was coerced into accepting the French occupation but preferred suicide to a French asylum. Tu Duc had no choice but to accept this new extension of French control but he refused to make formal cession of the territory.[38]

Franco-Vietnamese relations, 1864–74: the Tongking affair of 1873–75
The first stage of French expansion in Vietnam was now over and nearly 20 years were to elapse before the second and final stage was begun. During these years Tu Duc was still on the throne but he failed to find any solution to his problem. It was no longer a question of tolerating or not tolerating French Roman Catholic missionaries but how to restrain and limit the commercial imperialism of a great European power. Unfortunately Tu Duc and his court continued to look for their solutions to the example set by their ancient neighbour and traditional overlord, China, whose rulers were persisting in their suicidal policy of evasion and obstruction in their dealings with the Western states. Tu Duc's immediate problem, nevertheless, concerned Tongking which ever since the French occupation of the south had been in a state of perpetual rebellion and unrest. During this period the situation passed beyond Hué's control as the result of an influx of refugees and insurgents from China itself.[39] An appeal to the Chinese viceroy at Canton for assistance to restore the situation evoked a response but the Chinese troops sent merely deserted and joined in the general pillage.

This disturbed state of affairs provided a permanent temptation to the French who had begun to develop a keen interest in the possibilities of the Red river (Song Koi) as a new trade route into the Chinese interior,[40] and who were at the same time equally as anxious to wring out of Hué the formal cession of the whole of Cochin-China. In 1873 a crisis blew up in Hanoi as a result of the activities of a French trader and adventurer called Dupuis. Finding his way barred from proceeding upstream with some merchandise,[41] in May of that year Dupuis took the law into his own hands, occupied a part of Hanoi with a small force of Chinese and Filipino followers, and appealed to the French in Saigon for help. Two months later the Emperor also addressed an appeal to Saigon for help—but in this case, for help to expel Dupuis whose presence and activities, as Hué pointed out, violated existing treaty arrangements. Governor Dupré's response was to accede to Tu Duc's request, and for that purpose he sent a small task force at the end of October under the command of a strong-headed, ambitious and forceful naval lieutenant called Francis Garnier.[42] However, Dupré's intention was not only to arbitrate and secure the removal of Dupuis. His instructions to Garnier mentioned placing the 'commerce in opening up the country and its river to all nations under the protection of France'. Furthermore his choice of Garnier, well known for his imperialist views,

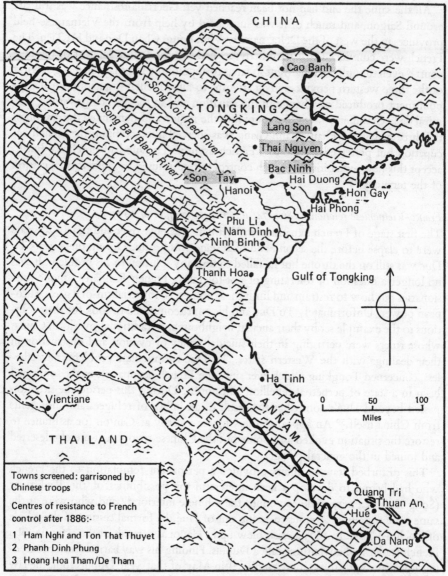

CHINA

2 • Cao Banh

3

TONGKING

Song Koi (Red River)

Song Ba (Black River)

Lang Son •

• Thai Nguyen

Bac Ninh

Son Tay •
Hanoi •

Hai Duong

• Hon Gay

Hai Phong

Phu Li •
Nam Dinh •
Ninh Binh •

Thanh Hoa •

Gulf of Tongking

1

L A O S   S T A T E S

A
N
N
A
M

• Ha Tinh

0   50   100
Miles

• Vientiane

THAILAND

Towns screened: garrisoned by
Chinese troops

Centres of resistance to French
control after 1886:-

1 Ham Nghi and Ton That Thuyet
2 Phanh Dinh Phung
3 Hoang Hoa Tham/De Tham

• Quang Tri
• Thuan An
• Hué

• Da Nang

59. The French conquest of Tongking and the occupation of Annam,
1874–1886

to carry out the mission suggested that the governor had other more ambitious schemes in mind.

The Vietnamese at Hanoi on the other hand naturally regarded Garnier's one and only function to be the removal of Dupuis and this quickly became the main point at issue after the French leader's arrival there on 5 November. Garnier was out to pick a quarrel, which was not a hard thing to do,[43] and on the 17th he provocatively and unilaterally declared the Red river open to the commerce of all nations. The Vietnamese authorities in the city began to make preparations for a fight which led to an ultimatum from Garnier two days later, forbidding further military preparations. The ultimatum was ignored and the following day (20 November) Garnier's men seized the citadel of Hanoi. Then with local support (largely Christian) Garnier proceeded to storm and occupy five strongholds in the Red river Delta—Hai Phong, Hai Duong, Ninh Binh, Nam Dinh and Phu Li. By the end of the month the administration of Lower Tongking was in his hands. At the court of Hué despair and resignation reigned, but the mandarins of Tongking decided to call in those roving Chinese bands of pirates and marauders known to the French as the Black Flags.[44] In mid-December the Black Flags started to lay siege to Hanoi, and Garnier himself was killed whilst leading a sortie against them on the 21st of the month.

If events had gone far beyond the control or desires of Hué, they also had exceeded the wishes of Saigon and Paris. Dupré had been given explicit instructions from France not to get involved in hostilities in Tongking[45] and yet this had happened. In early December he sent Philastre, an inspector of native affairs, to Hanoi to restrain Garnier and to sign a new treaty with Tu Duc. By the time Philastre reached Hanoi, Garnier was dead. Acting on his own initiative Philastre repudiated all agreements made locally since Garnier's arrival, condemned French aggression and ordered the immediate evacuation of all French-held forts and the seizure of Dupuis' vessels. He then went on to Hué where he negotiated a treaty of 'peace, friendship and perpetual alliance' with Tu Duc which was signed on 15 March, 1874. On paper the treaty represented a great triumph for France. The Emperor recognized French sovereignty over the six provinces of Cochin-China; he agreed to accept a French Resident together with armed escort, who would hold the Vietnamese rank of Minister; Qui Nhon, Hai Phong, Da Nang and Hanoi were to be opened to French trade with a French consul at each, also with suitable protection. In addition, French ships were to be granted most-favoured nation treatment, French officers were to hold key posts in the Vietnamese customs, the navigation of the Red river was to be free up to Yunnan, and Christians in the country were to be granted complete religious freedom. In return for these very considerable concessions France recognized the complete independence of Vietnam with regard to any foreign power (i.e. China) but this was qualified by the clause by which Tu Duc undertook 'to conform his foreign policy to that of France and to change nothing in his present diplomatic relations'. France also agreed to defend Vietnam against aggression but only on request. All outstanding sums of the 1862 indemnity were cancelled and the French undertook to supply gunboats, arms and instructors to deal with the Black Flags.

Franco-Vietnamese relations, 1875–84: the second Tongking crisis

When Tu Duc signed this treaty he had no intention of abiding by it. He misread Philastre's mission at Hanoi and the evacuation which followed it as a sign of French weakness and mistook what was in fact a reprieve for a retreat. Accordingly he resumed his policy of persecuting Christians, whose disloyalty in Tongking had contributed greatly to Garnier's success there, and adopted an attitude of evasion and obstruction when it came to implementing the terms of the treaty. Most decisive of all, in spite of his promise 'to conform to the foreign policy of France', Tu Duc now hastened to place himself under Chinese protection.

The Christian persecutions in Tongking began as the French withdrew, and were all the more intense as a result of the widespread popular resentment of the traitorous way in which the Vietnamese Christians had just behaved. Fourteen Christian villages went up in flames the day the French pulled out of Nam Dinh; the number of villages destroyed in this way soon swelled to several hundreds. At the same time those who had helped Garnier and the French were punished. An estimated 20,000 people were massacred and 70,000 more were made homeless.

Meanwhile the French consular officials who came to take up their new posts found themselves subjected to the 'greatest indignities'. The new French consul at Hanoi tried for two years to exercise the right conferred by the treaty of free commercial access up the Red river without any success. Elsewhere the French consuls found that all attempts to secure their exclusive jurisdiction over foreigners, as provided for by Philastre's treaty, were frustrated.

In 1876 Tu Duc made his first approach to China when he revived the traditional tribute which signified China's overlordship.[46] Four years later another tribute-bearing mission was sent, bearing along with it this time a request for Chinese assistance against the ever-increasing insurgency in Tongking. Peking responded swiftly and in the same year (1880) sent regular soldiers to garrison key centres such as Lang Son, Cao Banh, Thai Nguyen and Bac Ninh. However the same insurgents whom Tu Duc and the Hué court now regarded as a useful foil by which to frustrate French commercial designs and to obtain Chinese assistance also provided the French themselves with their chief excuse for further intervention. When the news of the presence of Chinese troops reached Saigon, the first French reaction was to strengthen their garrison at Hanoi. In April 1882 a French naval force commanded by Captain Henri Rivière sailed up to Hanoi with reinforcements. Shortly afterwards Rivière launched an attack and seized control of the city, using as a pretext Garnier's excuse of the need to forestall a Vietnamese plot against his men.[47] Events then followed a very similar pattern to those of 1873-4. The Vietnamese turned to guerrilla tactics and Tu Duc called in the aid of the Black Flags who had already suffered from the French assault. The French, in the meantime, extended the area of their control around Hanoi to include Nam Dinh and in March 1883 the anthracite mines at Hon Gay. In the same month the Black Flags closed in on Hanoi and laid siege to it. Like Garnier before him Rivière was killed during a sortie which he led against the besiegers, but this time the French were in no mood for a retreat. The government of Paris was in the hands of Jules Ferry[48] who once observed that 'colonial policy is the daughter of an industrial policy'. He believed in the need for an assured market for the goods of an industrial power and so plans were laid for sending a strong force to Vietnam to establish French predominance there. While a expedition of 3,000 troops was being mobilized in Europe for service in the East, General Bouet was put in charge of the French forces at Hanoi, Admiral Courbet was placed in command of all naval forces and a civilian, Dr. Harmand, was designated Commissioner-General with the task of organizing a French protectorate over Tongking.

The establishment of the French Protectorate over Vietnam

In the midst of these events the aged Tu Duc died (July 1883), precipitating a succession crisis at Hué. Power now rested in the hands of a Council of Regents since Ung Chan, the designated heir who assumed the reign title of Duc-D'uc, was still a minor. The Council, as indeed also the Court, was divided as to the best policy to pursue with regard to the French in Tongking. The traditionalists were led by two of the regents, Ton That Thuyet and Nguyen Van Tuong. They wanted to maintain an inflexibly hostile line and on the third day of the new reign they seized power and deposed Duc D'uc who leaned towards the conciliatory faction.[49] In his stead they placed on the throne Hong Dat who took the reign title of Hiep Hoa. Whatever policy Hiep Hoa and his sponsors might have wished to follow remained an academic question since they had no control over the course of events; the initiative lay entirely in French hands. On 20 August 1883 Admiral Courbet arrived off Thuan An at the mouth of the Hué river with a substantial force. In the ensuing bombardment the defenders of the forts suffered such heavy losses that the Court sent a mandarin of ministerial rank to plead for an armistice. This was granted on condition that the Vietnamese surrendered all forts and war vessels in the Hué area and negotiated a new treaty at once. Dr. Harmand then set to work and 'at the point of the bayonet' the youthful Hiep Hoa emperor had to sign the document which to all intents and purposes ended the independence of his empire.

By the terms of the Harmand treaty which was signed on 25 August 1883, Vietnam recognized the French Protectorate and surrendered control of her foreign relations to France. All Vietnamese troops in Tongking were to be recalled while the French were to occupy all the forts on the Hué river and as many as were necessary in Tongking to preserve peace and order there. The French were to be specifically responsible for opening the Red river to commerce, for restoring peace in the region and for defending it. French Residents with protecting garrisons were to be appointed to all the chief towns with jurisdiction over the local Vietnamese authorities everywhere. The administration of customs was to be in French hands and all proceeds from customs dues to be retained by France until the indemnity to meet the costs of the French occupation had been paid. Finally Vietnam surrendered the southern coastal province of Binh Thuan, adjoining French Cochin-China, and all her warships to France.

Just under a year later this treaty was modified by a second agreement which became the definitive basis for French control over the country. Under this new treaty of 1884, Binh Thuan was returned to Vietnam but Tongking was separated from the administration of Hué to become ruled directly by France, although the Emperor retained nominal suzerainty. Annam proper was deemed a protectorate with the French right to occupy militarily any place in it. A French Resident-General was to be posted at Hué with the right of private audience with the Emperor.

The Franco-Chinese struggle

This time, as far as Hué was concerned, there was no means of escape from these treaty obligations. But a champion of the Vietnamese cause still remained. In 1881, with Vietnamese encouragement, China formally declared its overlordship over Tongking. Consequently when the action of Rivière and the events leading to the Harmand Treaty became known, the Chinese Minister at Paris immediately pro-

tested. His protests went unheeded, so China prepared for action, sending reinforcements into Tongking and placing orders for warships and ammunition in
Europe. The first open clash between French and Chinese troops took place in
December 1883, when the French captured Son Tay from its Chinese garrison.
Already the French were behaving as if they were the rulers of the land for, on
the orders of General Bouet, the defenders were treated as rebels and all the
prisoners were beheaded. In the first quarter of the next year (1884) French reinforcements advancing in three columns captured Bac Ninh, Thai Nguyen and
cleared the Black river region. Bac Ninh had also been garrisoned by Chinese
troops. In early May the French and the Chinese signed a draft convention at Tientsin. By the terms of the Convention China was to withdraw her troops from
Tongking and 'to respect in the present and in the future the treaties concluded or
to be concluded between France and the Court of Hué', France on her part was to
guarantee China's southern frontier, and if the occasion arose, to protect it.

The Convention of Tientsin represented a triumph for the peace party at Peking
led by the veteran statesman, Li Hung-chang, and for the moderates on the French
side. But misunderstandings quickly arose between the two parties regarding the
date of the withdrawal of the Chinese troops; apart from that, the Chinese were
not really happy to give up their position in Tongking and to expose their southern
frontier to the full blast of French commercial influence and interest. In June 1884
a serious clash took place between French and Chinese detachments at Bac Le in the
district of Lang Son, in which the French were worsted. China turned down French
demands for compensation and hostilities were resumed. In February 1885 French
forces took Lang Son and Courbet swept with his ships to the north, blockading
Formosa, bombarding Foochow and occupying the Pescadores. But no decisive
victory was gained by either side and as the war dragged on, it became an embarrassment to both. So negotiations were reopened which ended up in a peace protocol
at the end of March 1885. Just before the protocol was signed, the French suffered
another severe reverse at Lang Son, which caused them to abandon the town.[50] This
confirmed the French determination to bring the war to an end and in June the
protocol was confirmed by the Treaty of Tientsin. The treaty restored the Pescadores and the points occupied by the French in Formosa to China. The French
claims for an indemnity were abandoned. The other terms of the treaty were identical to those of the Convention signed the previous year.

The last struggles of old Vietnam

The treaty with China confirmed the loss of Vietnamese independence and the
establishment of French control but it did not mark the end of resistance inside
Vietnam itself. At Hué the young Hiep Hoa Emperor paid with his life in November
of that year,[51] for signing the treaty with Harmand. The regents Ton That Thuyet
and Nguyen Van Tuong then placed a 14-year-old boy on the throne, who is
known to history as the Kien Phuc Emperor.[52] But he was deposed (and probably
poisoned) in July the next year by the same men who had found another more
suitable figurehead in the person of his younger brother now put on the throne
with the title of Ham Nghi. The two regents brought about Ham Nghi's elevation with the support of all those conservative court officials and Confucian scholars
who were determined to resist the French encroachments to the bitter end.

In the meantime preparations had already been made for resistance inland and a headquarters chosen in a mountain stronghold in the hinterland of Quang Tri province. The moment of trial came very soon after Ham Nghi's accession. On 2 July 1885, General de Courcy, the new French Resident-General of Annam and Governor of Tongking, arrived to take up his post at Hué. He immediately caused offence by insisting on using an entrance into the city only permitted to the Emperor himself.[53] The Court planned a surprise attack by night on the French party within the coming week but the plot miscarried. Instead the Emperor and the Queen Mother, Ton That Thuyet,[54] and 5,000 troops fled from the capital to the mountains of Thanh Hoa and Ha Tinh which they made their base for future operations. The flight of the Court became the signal for a general massacre of Christians throughout the country, detested because of their association with the foreigners.

The resistance movement which now gathered in the hills comprised in the words of a French observer 'the partisans of the old régime represented by Thuyet and his young sovereign, and all the enemies of the prince we installed upon the throne, in other words, almost the whole of Annam'.[a] The prince referred to, put on the vacant throne at Hué by de Courcy, was a brother of Ham Nghi who took the title of Dong Khanh. He reigned for two years and was regarded as a usurper by most Vietnamese. Meanwhile Ham Nghi and his followers waged guerrilla warfare for three years before the Emperor was finally betrayed and fell into the hands of the French.[55] With the capture of Ham Nghi effective resistance came to an end save in the difficult country on the northern frontier where sporadic fighting still continued. In 1893 there was a sudden flare-up of guerrilla activity in this region, led by the scholar Phan Dinh-Phung. Amongst other things the betrayer of Ham Nghi was killed by the insurgents but after the death of Phan himself in 1895 the movement collapsed. Elsewhere in the upper reaches of the Red river French authority continued to be defied by a series of guerrilla bands, the most celebrated of which was that led by Hoang Hoa Tham (or de Tham). De Tham's base was in the Yen Tre, east of Thai Nguyen. He kept up his resistance until he was assassinated in 1913.[56]

These last efforts to defend or to restore the old régime could not be described as posing a serious threat to the French position but they nevertheless caused the French a lot of trouble, and kept alive the spirit of resistance which served as a source of inspiration to a new generation of Vietnamese nationalists.[b] For years the problem of the Tongking frontier defied French solution. After 1891, however, the whole region was placed under military control and a systematic method of pacification was adopted. The French sent agents to gather as much information as they could about the guerrilla bands, their movements and their feuds. At the same time the French set up garrisons at strategic villages and followed a deliberate policy of winning over the local community. Once a particular area was 'pacified', the garrisons were transferred to other districts and the process repeated. These methods brought success, and after 1894 when the Chinese signed an agreement on the policing of the frontier, the French rapidly gained the upper hand. By 1897 only De Tham's force remained.

[a]Capt. de Grosselin; quoted by Ellen Hammer, *The Struggle for Indochina*, p. 54.
[b]See Book III.

The downfall of the Nguyen dynasty of Vietnam within such a short period during the second half of the nineteenth century followed a pattern similar to that which marked the downfall of China during the same era, and it came about broadly for much the same reasons. The Emperor of Vietnam was, like his far more powerful peer, the Emperor of China, in theory an absolute monarch whose edict reached to all corners of the land. In practice he was insulated from the outside world by the protocol and tradition that surrounded him. The effectiveness of his authority was limited by the powerful officials who controlled the provinces while at court he was surrounded by men whose upbringing in the traditions of Confucianism did not equip them with a suitable outlook for coping with the intrusion of the Western world and whose personal ambitions and interests were best served by stifling the emergence of an active and well-informed sovereign. As a result the government of Vietnam, as represented by the court of Hué, had a totally distorted view of the outside world and little concept of the realities of power which the Europeans stood for. Gia Long and Minh Mang were perhaps more aware of these problems than either of their successors but even they missed the opportunities which were taken by the Chakri dynasty in Thailand.[a] Thieu Tri and Tu Duc pursued policies whose motives are understandable but which completely failed to meet the needs of the time. The disastrous Chinese pattern of evasion, subterfuge and defiance was imitated, provoking the inevitable reaction from a powerful European state and providing it with ready pretexts for intervention. Before the new techniques and inventions of the Industrial Revolution Vietnam much less a match than China was, and the completeness of her subjection was a reflexion of her size.

[a]See pp. 505 et seq.

[1]In 1627. His mission was short-lived, being expelled in 1630 by the Trinh who were jealous of the success of the Christian missionaries and feared their links with Western traders. The earliest missionary settlement in Vietnam was founded at Fai Fo by an Italian Jesuit called Francisco Busomi in 1615.

[2]The Société owes its foundation to Alexander of Rhodes who returned from the Far East in 1649. In 1653 he obtained approval from the body controlling Roman Catholic missionary endeavours (The Congregation for the Propagation of the Faith) at Rome to recruit a new missionary society from members of the French clergy for the purpose of providing missionaries and funds to train an indigenous Roman Catholic hierarchy in East Asia. His movement gained the support of and was organized along the lines suggested by Mgr. Francois Pallu of the University of Paris. The leading missionaries were to be designated by Rome as Vicars-Apostolic, holding the rank of bishop and the titles of extinct sees under the direct authority of the Pope. A training school or seminary was set up in Paris in 1663.

[3]The most notable of these was that of Pierre Poivre, a former missionary of the Société, who in 1749–50 went to Vietnam as representative of the French East India Company and successfully negotiated a treaty with Hué. However, the ruler (Nguyen Phuc Khoat) was antagonized by the abduction of an interpreter, the project fell through and all 27 Roman Catholic missionaries in the country were expelled into the bargain.

[4]In particular of that of the Portuguese who were the sworn enemies of the Trinh.

[5]The British made three attempts during Gia Long's time to open up trading relations with Vietnam, namely in 1793, 1803 and 1804. None bore any fruit and they created a bad name for themselves when in 1812 an English sloop at Da Nang threatened the use of force in a trading dispute. As for the French, after Pigneau's death and Nguyen Anh's consolidation of power, their influence declined rapidly and by 1802 only four of the Bishop's original followers remained (Vannier, Chaigneau, Forsanz and Dr. Despiau). In 1818 a French embassy led by de

Kergariou landed at Da Nang but was not regarded as official nor allowed to proceed to Hué to have an audience with the Emperor. However, the Vietnamese did not discourage trading contacts conducted on a small scale.

[6]Minh Mang's accession occurred just at the time that the French had determined on a new effort to develop relations with Vietnam. For this reason Chaigneau who had returned to France in 1819 came back as Consul and Agent for France in 1820. But the following year Minh Mang rejected a proffered French treaty and refused to recognize Chaigneau's position as Consul. In 1822 he ignored a visiting French frigate at Da Nang. Other French attempts to develop treaty relations in 1825, 1826, 1827 and 1831 were likewise rebuffed. The British sent a mission led by Crawfurd in 1822, the major result of which seems to have been to convince Minh Mang of the wisdom of keeping them and therefore all Europeans at arm's length. U.S. probes in 1820, 1832 and 1836 also produced no results. The last of Pigneau's followers and French mandarins, Chaigneau and Vannier, left Vietnam for good in 1824. For a full discussion of the development of Vietnamese-Western relations under Gia Long and Minh Mang, see Lamb, op. cit.

[7]Le Van Khoi was an adopted son. The occasion of the revolt was the desecration of Van Duyet's tomb on the orders of Minh Mang himself, but underlying was the Emperor's desire to consolidate his position against the wealthy and far too independent-minded governor of the south.

[8]They were summoned on the pretext that their services were needed as translators and interpreters, and once arrived they were refused permission to return to their own districts.

[9]Between 1833 and 1840 at least 10 foreign missionaries were executed, including Marchand, six other Frenchmen and three Spaniards.

[10]The First Anglo-Chinese War or Opium War of 1839–42 marks a turning point in the history of the Western powers in the Far East. As a result of the war China was forced to abandon her centuries-old policy of seclusion and to open her doors freely to Western trade, thereby ushering in a new era which saw the rapid spread of Western influences and the complete decay of traditional Asian society.

[11]The *Société* had been suppressed in 1792 as a consequence of the French Revolution and was permanently re-established by the Restoration Monarchy in 1819.

[12]Namely Fathers Miche (later of Cambodian fame), Duclos, Berneaux, Galy and Charrier.

[13]Lefébvre, undaunted by his banishment, re-entered the country with Duclos in 1846 by bribing the frontier guards. The two were soon arrested, however, and imprisoned. Lefébvre died of illness at Saigon in 1846; before his second entry, Lefébvre was in Singapore where he allegedly rejected a British offer to send him back if he would await the outcome of British negotiations over freedom of worship and missionary activities in Vietnam.

[14]The French force consisted of two warships under the command of Cdr. Lapierre and Capt. Rigault de Genouilly: they justified their demands on the basis that the Emperor of China by the Treaty of Whampoa with France (1844) had already made similar concessions. The ensuing deadlock was over the question as to where the imperial reply should be received—on board or on shore. The Vietnamese actually tried to fire the French ships and capture their officers.

[15]He also had all the European furniture in his palace destroyed.

[16]The attitude of the Emperor and his Confucian advisers at court is well exemplified by their rejection on eight occasions between 1853 and 1871 of reform proposals put before them by Nguyen Truong To, the first Vietnamese scholar to visit Europe.

[17]Namely Fathers Schoeffer and Bonnard.

[18]Louis Charles de Montigny had had a colourful career prior to his present appointment; born in German exile in 1805, he had fought for the Greeks during their struggle for independence (1821–30) and accompanied the Lagrené mission to China of 1843–5. Since 1848 he had represented French interests in Shanghai first as Vice-Consul, then Consul, during which time he had taken an active part fighting the Taiping rebels; in 1856 he was appointed the head of a mission to negotiate commercial treaties with Thailand, Cambodia and Vietnam.

[19]By the delaying tactics of the Thais who wished to prevent King Ang Duong of Cambodia from entering into any direct treaty relations with France.

[20]Between 1853 and 1857 it is reckoned that 95 missionaries and priests lost their lives; 44 in the south (6 Europeans) and 51 in Tongking (8 Europeans).

[21]In 1856 France joined with Britain in a second assault on China. Known as the second Anglo-Chinese War or the Arrow War, its object was to force the Chinese to remove all the obstacles which still impeded Western trading activities in their country. In 1858 peace negotiations resulted in the Treaty of Tientsin but fighting broke out afresh later the same year and the war was finally brought to an end in 1860 with the signing of the Convention of Peking.

[22]The Spanish contribution consisted of one steam warship, 450 Spanish Filipinos plus another 300–400 recruited by the French themselves. 500 Spanish reinforcements arrived later at Da Nang.

[23]Apart from the ravages of cholera, dysentery, scurvy and heat prostration from 'the murderous sun', the Europeans were hindered by their inability to navigate the bar at the mouth of the river, the the absence of small craft and transport for the big guns and the failure of the local Christians to rise up in their favour. Another problem was the open disagreement between de Genouilly and the religious interest represented by Bishop Péllerin. The Bishop, with his eyes on the Christian population there, favoured a diversionary attack on Tongking which de Genouilly rejected as unfeasible. Ultimately Péllerin was forced to withdraw from the expedition.

[24]Rigault de Genouilly; French naval officer; first in eastern waters as captain of a corvette on the Lagrené mission to China, 1843–5; one of the commanders at the bombardment of Da Nang, 1847; promoted to Admiral; appointed commander of the French naval forces in China waters, 1857; and *ipso facto* in command of operations in China and Vietnam between 1857 and 1859; 1867, appointed Minister of Marine and the Colonies.

[25]Cholera and typhus continued rampant; by July monthly deaths averaged 100; not only the resumption of hostilities in China but the outbreak of the Franco-Austrian War in Europe in May 1859, precluded the arrival of more reinforcements.

[26]Page took over from de Genouilly in October 1859.

[27]These terms included (a) a French protectorate over 'harmless' missionaries; (b) the establishment of three consulates, including one at Ba Lat; (c) French control of the port dues at Saigon for 20 years in lieu of indemnity; (d) the privilege of sending a French chargé d'affaires once every three years to Hué.

[28]With the Anglo-French occupation of Peking and the signing of the Convention there.

[29]Because of its strategic importance, Pulau Condore became a bone of contention between the British and the French from the seventeenth century onwards. In 1702 the British founded a settlement there, thereby forestalling the French who had similar plans. But it was destroyed three years later when the Macassarese garrison revolted and massacred their officers. By the treaty made with France by Pigneau on behalf of Nguyen Anh in 1787, the French were to occupy the island.

[30]This rebellion had long been feared; it received the usual element of Christian support and its leaders made a direct appeal to the French for help which reactivated Hué's worst fears. The French clerical interest and the Spaniards urged French intervention there but Bonard, like de Genouilly before him, considered the undertaking too risky.

[31]Phan Than Giang was the dean of Vietnam's mandarins and controlled the rice-rich provinces of the Mekong Delta.

[32]Bien Hoa, Gia Dinh and My Tho.

[33]Half of this eventually went to Spain which was all she gained out of the whole affair.

[34]The Spaniards and the French were at loggerheads over Tongking policy. Since the Spaniards had joined the French to avenge the death of Mgr. Diaz, they felt that intervention in the north was the proper course of action.

[35]The French, however, were to be allowed to retain direct control over Saigon, Cholon, and Cap St. Jacques.

[36]In fact the resistance enjoyed popular support both from within the areas affected and from the regions of Go Cong and the Pleine des Joncs.

[37]Benoit de la Grandière was the fifth of the Admiral-Governors of French Cochin China (1863–7); his predecessors were de Genouilly (1859); Page (1859–61); Charner (1861); Bonard (1861–3).

[38]Donald Lancaster (*The Emancipation of Indo-China*, p. 41) quotes a telling excerpt from an edict of the Emperor Tu Duc promulgated at this time: 'There have never been so many disastrous events as in our times; there have never been such great misfortunes as have happened this year.... Above me I fear the decrees of Heaven, and when I look beneath me, compassion for the people weighs on me day and night. I tremble and blush at one and the same time while I assume without faltering all the odium for these misfortunes, so that the people shall bear no part of the responsibility. But before atonement can be made fresh calamities assail us. Truly one does not know what to say, or what to do in order to help the subjects of this kingdom.'

[39]Conditions in the south of China had been disturbed for years as a result of the Taiping Rebellion (1848–64) and the Muslim Panthay Rebellion (1856–73) in Yunnan. The collapse of these movements led to insurgent refugees pouring into Tongking, joined by professional pirates and the like, as well as by supporters of the defunct Le dynasty.

[40]An expedition led by Doudart de Lagrée and Francis Garnier in 1868-7 up the Mekong demonstrated the unsuitability of that route. See p. 538.

[41]Jean Dupuis had been operating in the Far East with his headquarters at Hankow since 1860. It was at Hankow that he first met Garnier on the last stages of his Mekong expedition in 1868 and subsequently became interested in the opening of the Red river route. He reached Yunnan-fu (Kun Ming) by this way for the first time in 1868-9. On a second visit in 1871 he came to an arrangement with Marshal Ma, the Chinese military commander suppressing the Panthay uprising, to get arms and ammunition in return for tin and other commodities. Returning to France for the supplies he failed to get official backing for his enterprise. In November 1872 he was back at Hanoi with a small force of two gunboats and two other vessels and despite the disapproval of the Tongking authorities made his way up to Yunnan. He had returned to Hanoi again by May 1873 with a cargo of copper for sale in exchange for salt. Since salt was a monopoly of the Tongking mandarinate, they refused to allow Dupuis to proceed upstream: thereupon Dupuis occupied part of Hanoi with the aid of some 150 Chinese and Filipino followers.

[42]Francis Garnier first came to South-East Asia as a naval lieutenant on the staff of Admiral Charner's expedition in the China War (1859-60); took part in the relief of Saigon in 1861; on half-pay appointed District Officer for Cholon, 1863; served as member of the Agricultural and Industrial Development Committee for Cochin China; 1865, acted as Inspector of Indigenous Affairs; 1866-8, co-leader with Doudart de Lagrée of expedition up the Mekong; 1872, published his excellent and comprehensive *Voyage d'Exploration en Indo-Chine...*, resigned naval commission and returned to the Far East; 1873, explored the Yangtse Kiang as far as Chung King; called back to Saigon by Dupré. Described as 'the adventurer-imperialist *par excellence*' by J.F. Cady (*The Roots of French Imperialism in Eastern Asia*, p. 281). The force led by Garnier consisted of 188 French and 24 Cochin-Chinese troops.

[43]Garnier made issue over the quarters assigned to him and his men, demanding that they be quartered in the citadel, which the Hanoi authorities understandably were not prepared to allow.

[44]They got their name from the colour of their standards. The Black Flags were the most prominent of several rival groups.

[45]In reply to one of Dupré's despatches about developments in Indo-China, Paris telegraphed orders on 8 September to avoid all entanglements. France was at a very low ebb after her defeat by the Prussians in the war of 1870-71, and neither the Prime Minister, de Broglie, nor the Foreign Minister, de Remusat, were prepared to consider intervention.

[46]The Emperor Gia Long continued the traditional policy of Vietnamese rulers in acknowledging China's overlordship in 1803 shortly after he had completed the reunification of the country. Chinese recognition was on the basis of tribute every two years and homage every four, but during the course of the nineteenth century this had fallen into abeyance.

[47]He objected to the arrival of Vietnamese reinforcements and the carrying out of repairs to the citadel.

[48]Jules Ferry who was identified with a policy of imperialist expansion was twice Prime Minister of France—from 1880 to 1881 when the decision to reduce Vietnam to the status of a French protectorate was first taken, and from 1883 to 1884 during which period this programme was completed.

[49]Duc D'uc was disposed of by being immured in a pavilion and left to die of hunger and thirst.

[50]The French commander, General de Negrier, was ambushed and wounded whilst on cavalry reconnaissance outside the town; his second-in-command, on taking over, decided to evacuate, precipitating a panic amongst the troops, many of whom abandoned their weapons and equipment and took to the hills. This episode merely added to the embarrassment of Ferry's ministry, whose China campaign was alienating other European powers because of its interference with their trade and whose stock at home was falling rapidly as a result of such reverses. In fact the news of the Lang Son disaster caused the fall of the ministry.

[51]He was bludgeoned to death with wooden stakes.

[52]But he was old enough to be aware of the perils of the position and had to be dragged from underneath a bed to be placed upon the throne.

[53]The central arch of the ceremonial 'Bull Gate' into the imperial city. The court were prepared to let de Courcy himself go through but not the escort.

[54]The Co-Regent, Nguyen Van Tuong, stayed behind at Hué.

[55]Ham Nghi was exiled to Algeria where he died in the 1940s. Ton That Thuyet fled to China.

[56]Another rebellion was led by Bai Chay between 1885 and 1889.

13. VIETNAM: CHRONOLOGY OF MAIN EVENTS

A. Before the establishment of French Power

B.C. 208–111	Nan-yueh: state founded by Ch' in general in Tongking and Kwangtung
111–A.D. 939	Chinese domination—border province of Giao Chi
A.D. 939	Restoration of Vietnamese independence (Dai-co-viet under Ngo dynasty)
968–980	The Dinh dynasty
980–1009	The Former Le dynasty
1010–1225	The Li dynasty
1225–1400	The Tran dynasty
1400–7	The Ho dynasty
1407–28	Chinese interregnum
1428–1527 (–1786)	The Le dynasty
1527	Throne usurped by the Mac family
1532	Le pretender proclaimed by Nguyen Kim
1540	China recognizes Mac rulers in Tongking and Le ruler to the South
1620–1802	VIETNAM DIVIDED BETWEEN THE NGUYEN AND TRINH DYNASTIES

B. The Reunification of Vietnam and the French Conquest

1615	First Christian mission settlement (Jesuit) at Fai-fo
1659	Foundation of Société des Missions Etrangères in Paris
1663	First missionaries from the Société enter Vietnam
1767	Establishment of Société's headquarters at Ha-tien
1773–1802	The Tay-son revolt
1777	Nguyen Anh flees to Ha-tien; meets Pigneau de Behaine
1784	Vietnamese mission to France with Pigneau de Behaine
1788	Tayson rebels defeat Trinh; take over the north
1788–9	Reconquest of Cochin-China with French aid
1792	Death of Van Huey, rebel emperor at Hanoi
1799	Qui-nhon captured by Nguyen Anh; death of Pigneau de Behaine
1801	Hué captured by Nguyen Anh
1802	Nguyen Anh proclaimed emperor of Victnam as Gia-long
1820	Death of the Gia-long Emperor; accession of Minh-mang

1826	Minh Mang rejects consular relations with France
1833	Death of pro-Christian governor of Cochin-China, Le Van-duyet
	Rebellion in Cochin-China; start of active persecution of Christians and missionaries
1836	All ports save Da-nang closed to foreign shipping (Western)
1840	Embassy to Europe;
	Death of Minh Mang; accession of the emperor Thieu Tri
1841	Anti-Christian persecutions resumed
1842	First French naval demonstration off Da-nang in support of missionaries
1847	French bombard Da-nang
	Death of Thieu-tri; accession of the Emperor Tu Duc
1848	Revolution in France; coming to power of Louis Napoleon
1851	Rebellion in Tongking; renewal of anti-Christian persecutions
1855	Second rebellion in Tongking; anti-Christian persecutions intensified
1856	Second French bombardment of Da-nang
1857	De Montigny's abortive visit to Da-nang;
	Execution of Mgr. Diaz, Bishop Apostolic of Tongking
1858–63	FIRST STAGE OF FRENCH CONQUEST; the occupation of Cochin-China
1858	Franco-Spanish force seizes Da-nang
1859	French under de Genouilly capture Saigon
1860–1	French besieged at Saigon; Da-nang evacuated (1860)
1861	Saigon relieved; first governor appointed
1861–2	Subjugation of eastern provinces of Cochin-China
1862	Franco-Viet Treaty; rebellion in Tongking; guerrilla warfare in Delta
1863	Vietnamese embassy to France to re-negotiate treaty
1865	1862 Treaty ratified by Louis Napoleon
1866–7	Lagrée-Garnier expedition up the Mekong
1867	French unilaterally annex western provinces of Cochin-China
1868–9	Jean Dupuis explores Red River route to Yunnan
1873	Depuis seizes part of Hanoi; he and Hué appeal to Saigon
	Garnier at Hanoi; killed
1874	The Philastre Treaty with Hué; renewed persecutions of Christians as French evacuate Hanoi

1876		Tu-duc renews homage to China
1877+		Growing anarchy in Tongking; influx of Chinese bandits, refugees, etc.
1880		Tu-duc appeals for Chinese help in Tongking; entry of regular Chinese forces; proclaimed protectorate over Tongking (1881)
1882		French force under Rivière sent to Hanoi to protect French interests
1883	March	French extend control over Tongking; Rivière killed as Hanoi besieged
	May	French parliament votes war credits
	August	French forces attack Hué; Vietnamese back down
		The Harmand Treaty
	December	Start of Sino-French hostilities in Tongking
		SECOND STAGE OF FRENCH CONQUEST; annexation of Tongking and protectorate over Annam
1884	Jan–May	French and Chinese fighting in Tongking
	May	Convention of Tientsin
	June	Revised treaty with Hué establishing French protectorate
		Renewed Sino-French fighting
1885	March	French defeat at Langson
	June	Peace Treaty of Tiensin; end of Sino-French hostilities
	July	Convention of Hué
1885–8		Ham Nghi's revolt
1888–95		Phan Dinh-Phung's rebellion
1893–1913		De Tham's rebellion

C. The Nguyen Dynasty

1. Nguyen Kim	died 1545	
11. Nguyen-Phuc-Anh	1802–20	Gia-Long
12.	1820–40	Minh Mang
13.	1840–7	Thieu-Tri
14.	1847–83	Tu-Duc
15. Ung Chan	1883	Duc-D'uc
16. Hong Dat	1883	Hiep-Hoa
17.	1883–4	Kien-Phuc
18.	1884–8	Ham-Nghi
19.	1886–8*	Dong-Khanh
20.	1888–1907*	Thanh-Thai

* placed on throne by the French

BOOKS AND ARTICLES FOR FURTHER READING: VIETNAM

Cady, J.F., *South-East Asia: Its Historical Development*, McGraw-Hill, New York, 1964.

Fisher, C.A., *South-East Asia: A Social, Economic and Political Geography*, Methuen, London, 1964.

Hall, D.G.E., *A History of South-East Asia*, 3rd ed., Macmillan, London, 1968.

Buttinger, J., *The Smaller Dragon: A Political History of Vietnam*, Praeger, New York, 1958.

Cady, J.F., *The Roots of French Imperialism in Eastern Asia*, Cornell University Press, Ithaca, 1954.

Coedès, G., *Angkor: An Introduction*, Oxford University Press, Hong Kong, 1963.

Fall, Bernard, *The Two Vietnams: A Political and Military Analysis*, Praeger, New York, 1964.

Hammer, Ellen, *The Struggle for Indochina*, Stanford University Press, California, 1954.

Hoang Van Chi, *From Colonialism to Communism*, Praeger, New York, 1964.

Lamb, Alistair, 'British Missions to Cochin China: 1778-1822', *JMBRAS*, Vol. 34, No. 3/4 Singapore, 1961.

Tarling, N., 'British Relations with Vietnam', *JMBRAS*, Vol. 39, No. 1, Singapore, 1966.

Worshipper before Buddha, Angkor Wat, Angkor

V CAMBODIA

Cambodia

Cambodia in the nineteenth century was a pygmy amongst the powers. The most ancient kingdom in the whole of South-East Asia, its ancient glories vanished, it had been reduced by mid-century to the status of a buffer state between Vietnam and Thailand, admitting the overlordship of both. The substitution of Vietnamese with French authority in the Mekong Delta inevitably meant the subjection of Cambodia to France in the fullness of time. The only remarkable thing was the courage of the resistance exhibited in the face of hopeless odds by the Cambodians before they finally succumbed.

THE CAMBODIAN BACKGROUND

When King Norodom Sihanouk proclaimed the independence of Cambodia in March 1944[1] he was reasserting his rights to the oldest throne in South-East Asia. The independence he sought was from France which had ruled over his country for the best part of eighty years. But even before the French protectorate had been established Cambodia's independence had been a very shadowy affair for generations, and its rulers the pawns in the contest between the Thais and the Vietnamese for supremacy over their domains.

Early Cambodia and the rise of Fu Nan
Originally a gulf of the sea, when the waters receded Cambodia was left a basin with a great natural reservoir known as the Tonlé Sap[2] in its middle and was dominated by the powerful Mekong which flows through it to the ocean. The Mekong enters the China Sea through a large delta which today is part of Cochin-China, a province of Vietnam, but which formerly was part of Cambodia proper.

The facts of Cambodian life have been shaped by this great river and by the Tonlé Sap which, acting like an appendix, absorbs its overflow. Between June and September every year the river floods, fed by the melting snows of the distant Tibetan peaks and soaked in the south-west monsoons. The delta region is inundated by its waters which carry with them fresh deposits of fertile loam, while the sudden excess flows back into the Tonlé Sap causing it to expand four times its normal size. The rise and decline of Cambodian civilization has turned on the problem of controlling and harnessing these waters.

The Cambodians or Khmers[3] have been the inhabitants of this region since the dawn of history. Of Malaysian stock they settled in the area during the period of the great Malaysian migrations southwards and by the beginning of the Christian era were firmly established in the country which covers Cambodia proper, Cochin-China and part of the Menam Chao Phaya basin today. Three factors have shaped their history; firstly Cambodia's position at an important staging point on the an-

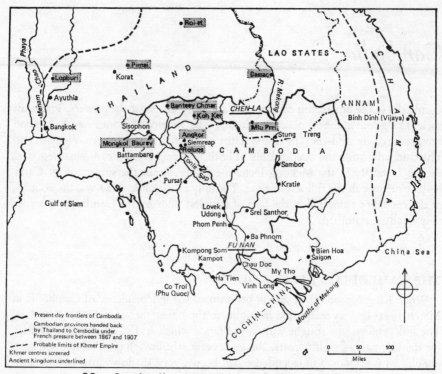

60. Cambodia: general historical background

cient route between east and west, China and India; secondly, the problem of water-control; and thirdly their struggle against the twin pressures of Thai and Vietnamese which developed subsequently on either flank.

The earliest phase of Cambodian civilization is associated with the rise of Fu Nan,[4] the first great empire of South-East Asia. Not much is known of this pioneer state which flourished between the first and fourth centuries A.D., but its power at its greatest extent appears to have covered all that is present-day Cambodia and Cochin-China, and to have stretched over the Menam Basin and across the Gulf of Siam to the isthmus of Kra and the northern part of the Malay Peninsula. Fu Nan played a very important part in the development of Cambodia. Its centre lay in the Mekong Delta where it brought Cambodians into contact with the great cultures of China and India, especially that of India. Not only did the Indians introduce their beliefs and ideas but also their techniques including the very important art of irrigation[5] which was to provide the necessary economic base for the expanding empire. The techniques of water-control acquired during the period of Fu Nan were to provide the foundations on which the power and prosperity of the Khmer Empire of Angkor that followed were built.

The Civilization of Angkor

Around the beginning of the seventh century the Fu Nan Empire came to an end, succumbing to the rebellion of a vassal state.[6] Two hundred years of division and confusion followed, out of which arose the great Empire of Angkor. The period of Angkor was the greatest one in Cambodian history. The new centre of power was no longer situated in the Delta but inland around the northern end of the Tonlé Sap. Its founder was Jayavarnam II who built his first capital in the region of Hariharalaya (modern Roluos) around 800. There followed a period of some four centuries under a succession of Khmer kings who made their capitals in the Angkor district which grew into the centre of an immensely wealthy and powerful state. These rulers have left their mark in the form of great temple mausoleums which are certainly the most impressive remains to be found in South-East Asia and of which the greatest of them all, the Angkor Wat, represents the largest religious edifice built by man.[7] The construction of these great buildings reflected a high degree of social organization and political power which made itself felt over all of the Mekong and Menam Chao Phaya basins and penetrated into the adjacent regions as well. Their principal neighbours to the east were the Chams[a] with whom there was a constant state of warfare,[8] while to the west were the Mons[b] who in the Menam Chao Phaya basin at least were obliged to submit to Khmer overlordship. As late as the thirteenth century the Chinese were still writing of the kings of Angkor as the mightiest and wealthiest monarchs in all South-East Asia.[9]

The economic basis for this power lay in the complex system of water-control which was developed in the Angkor district. The rulers of Angkor, inheriting the techniques of irrigation from their predecessors of Delta Fu Nan, created a vast and intricate system of reservoirs and canals which served both to store the water during the dry season and control it during the floods, thus enabling the growth and sustenance of a large population. Eventually the area covered by these waterworks and brought under padi cultivation covered some 12.5 million acres, divided up into square fields which could produce two, three or even four harvests a year.

The whole system on which the power and prosperity of Angkor depended could only be maintained by the existence of strong social sanctions. These were provided by the cult of the god-king whose divinity rested on his position as organizer of the water-works, the guarantor of the fertility of the land, the guardian against the adverse circumstances of nature and man. The intricate culture of Angkor depended on this god-king and the elaborate hierarchy around him whose maintenance ate up the energies of the people. But during the twelfth century important changes started to take place which completely undermined this civilization. A new form of Buddhism penetrated the country[10] and was adopted by peasant and ruler alike. It destroyed the concept of the god-king; Angkor's rulers ceased to believe in it themselves and as it disappeared, so did the sanctions which compelled the upkeep of the complex socio-economic system. The great irrigation system fell into neglect and decay and with it production declined. At the same time the intensively cultivated land showed signs of exhaustion. Parallel to this came the thrust of the Thais[c] down into the Menam Chao Phaya Basin and along the upper reaches of the Mekong. With failing resources and declining population the Khmer kings found themselves engaged in a costly struggle against the new invaders, with thousands dying in the Thai raids or being carried away into captivity. Ultimately the

[a]Refer pp. 436–7 and 441, note 12.
[b]Refer pp. 395–6.
[c]See pp. 485–6.

turn of Angkor itself came. In 1431, after a seven month siege, the great city was captured by the Thais.[11]

The fall of Angkor was not the end of the kingdom of Cambodia but it marked the end of the great period of Cambodian history. The Cambodians fled from the shadow of their great cities and moved back towards the Mekong Delta to resume a more primitive existence.[12] In the meantime, the Thais wrecked the water system of Angkor and allowed this part of Cambodia to revert to jungle or desert.

The rise of the Thais and the Vietnamese challenge

The rest of the story of Cambodia up till the establishment of the French protectorate in 1863 is filled with the endless struggle against the Thais, and later against the Vietnamese as well in order to preserve Cambodian independence. For the first one and a half centuries after the abandonment of Angkor the Cambodians on the whole managed to hold off the Thai pressure and on occasion carried the war into the heart of Thai territory.[13] However, in 1593, under a brilliant young leader called Naresuen,[a] the Thais decisively defeated their main enemies, the Burmese, and then launched a powerful invasion of Cambodia, capturing the capital of Lovek early the next year. From this time onwards Cambodia lay under the shadow of Thai power, and indeed as far as the Thais themselves were concerned it was regarded as a vassal state.

Thai overlordship, however, was frequently challenged both by the Cambodians themselves and by the growing presence of the Vietnamese to the east. Vietnamese adventurers, traders and outlaws had been moving down the long China Sea coastline past Cape Padaran and into the Mekong Delta for decades. By the early part of the seventeenth century Vietnamese influence was sufficiently established for Cambodia's rulers to turn to them as a source of help against the Thai menace. In 1618 the newly-crowned king Chetta II who was married to a Vietnamese princess, declared his independence of Thai suzerainty and during the course of his reign permitted the settlement of a Vietnamese colony at Saigon. This initiated a long contest between the Thais and Vietnamese for the control of Cambodia. The instability of Cambodian domestic politics, where dissensions amongst members of the royal house and the ambitions of territorial chiefs made civil war and rebellion endemic, gave plenty of opportunities for both sides to interfere and try and establish their advantage. Succession disputes in 1675 led to direct Thai and Vietnamese intervention on opposing sides which gave rise to a prolonged civil war lasting till 1691.[14] The first quarter of the eighteenth century was taken up by a similar struggle and Thai-Vietnamese rivalry led to fresh intervention in the 1760s and 1780s. On the whole the Thais succeeded in keeping their title to the overlordship of Cambodia, and· by 1794 when they restored the 27-year-old Ang Eng[15] to the throne, the Thai claim seemed to be indisputably established.

The Thai-Vietnamese struggle in the nineteenth century; the compromise of 1845

Nevertheless Vietnamese power had been steadily growing. During the course of the eighteenth century the Vietnamese had converted the sparsely-populated

[a]See p. 498.

swamps of the Cambodian territories in the Mekong Delta into their own well-farmed and regularly administered provinces.[a] In 1806, the year in which Ang Eng's successor, Ang Chan, was formally invested as the new Cambodian king by the Thais in Bangkok,[16] the Tay Son rebellion was brought to an end in Vietnam[b] and the country reunified under the rule of the victorious Nguyen dynasty. Ang Chan's ministers[17] thereupon embarked on the wise policy of paying homage to both Bangkok and Hué which was gratifying enough to the Vietnamese but galling to the Thais. The Thais then seized the opportunity provided by a quarrel between Ang Chan and a younger brother in 1811 to support Ang Chan's opponent and reassert their influence.[18] But Ang Chan appealed to the Vietnamese who responded in such strength that the Thais discreetly withdrew. From 1813 for the next seventeen years there was a period of Vietnamese ascendancy. Ang Chan was restored to his capital, Udong, and was guarded by a Vietnamese garrison posted at Phnom Penh.[19]

In 1831, encouraged by their successful campaign against the Laotian state of Vientiane,[c] the Thais launched a new invasion of Cambodia under the command of the victorious general, Phaya Bo Din. They swept through the country, defeating the Cambodians at Kompong Chhnong, occupying Phnom Penh and Chaudoc, and reaching as far as Vinh Long in the Delta where Ang Chan had taken refuge. But as the Thais advanced eastwards Cambodian resistance stiffened, cutting off Thai supplies and ambushing the Thai columns. At Vinh Long itself the Thais lost a whole flotilla bearing their supplies, and were forced to withdraw. The following year Ang Chan with the backing of 15,000 Vietnamese troops re-entered his capital of Udong in triumph. A large Vietnamese garrison stayed behind.

Barely twelve months later, in 1833, Ang Chan died and the Vietnamese made a determined bid to extinguish Cambodian independence altogether and to absorb the country. Through the intervention of Ong Kham Mang, the Vietnamese garrison commander at Udong,[20] the two younger brothers of the late king, Ang Eng and Ang Duong, were excluded from the succession and their 20-year-old sister, Ang Mey, was placed on the throne in their stead. The young queen was soon made to realize that she was a figurehead and that the real power lay with the Vietnamese. In the same year the administration was completely reorganized; the country was redivided into 33 provinces, all with new names and attached to Cochin-China. Alongside this the Vietnamese built fifty forts at strategic points throughout the country. Popular unrest developed. In 1835 two brothers from Kompong Som raised a rebellion but were defeated. In the years that followed similar outbreaks occurred which were watched with sympathetic eyes by Ang Eng and Ang Duong from their Thai exile in Battambang province.

In 1840, however, Ang Eng was captured by the Vietnamese and exiled to Hué. This was followed the next year by the banishment of Queen Ang Mey herself, together with other members of the royal family and her ministers, to the same place. The exiling of the royal family became the signal for a national uprising. The length and breadth of the country Cambodians set upon and killed all the Vietnam-

[a] Refer p. 437.
[b] Refer pp. 438-9.
[c] See pp. 493-4 and 499.

ese they could lay their hands on, while the great territorial chiefs met in secret con-
clave and resolved to call for Thai help to restore Ang Duong to the throne. Bangkok was only too happy to take this new opportunity and sent an army to install
the pretender under the command of the now aging Phaya Bo Din. A long, tough
and inconclusive struggle ensued between the Thais and the Vietnamese with the
result that both sides were sufficiently exhausted to agree to a compromise. Accordingly in 1845 Ang Duong was recognized as king of Cambodia by both Bangkok
and Hué on the understanding that he acknowledged the suzerainty of both powers.
At the same time Thai and Vietnamese troops were to be withdrawn from Cambodian soil although the Thai occupation (since 1814) of Stung Treng, Tonlé Repu
and Mlu Prei was confirmed. With this Cambodia was formally established as a
buffer state, leaving her rulers to rely on their wits to preserve the country's future
integrity. This was the position when Cambodia was confronted by the French
nearly twenty years later.

[1] This was done with Japanese inspiration, as they were occupying the country at the time.
[2] Meaning 'The Great Lake'.
[3] Khmer is the vernacular name for Cambodian.
[4] Fu Nan is the Chinese transcription of the Khmer word 'phnom' which means hill. What the
actual inhabitants of Fu Nan called their state is not known.
[5] Introduced by the Tamils who had acquired their knowledge and experience in irrigating
the parched lands of South India.
[6] Namely Chen La, a Khmer state centred on the Bassac (Champassak) region of the middle
Mekong; the rise of Chen La is associated with the general pattern of the slow migration of
people southwards. As the population of Chen La increased as a result of this steady immigration from the north, it rose to a position to challenge and finally to overwhelm Fu Nan.
[7] The most notable buildings are the Angkor Wat itself, constructed during the reign of King
Suryavarnam II (1113–50) on a site covering nearly a whole square mile; the Angkor Thom
and Bayon built during the reign of Jayavarnam VII (1181–1219). These great monuments
were designed to symbolize the centre of the Khmer universe, to act as the focus for the cult of
the god-king in life and to serve as his tomb in death. See Hall, *History of South-East Asia*, op.
cit. Ch. 5.
[8] Jayavarnam II beat off Cham attacks in the ninth century; Suryavarnam II made a determined
effort to conquer Champa during the first half of the twelfth century and succeeded in occupying the country for four years. In 1177 a Cham force raided and pillaged Angkor. Jayavarnam
VII conquered Champa and held it for 17 years before making a voluntary withdrawal (1203–
20).
[9] See the description by Chou Ta-kuan, a member of an embassy sent by Timur Khan, the
Mongol ruler of China in 1296–7, who wrote a glowing account of Angkor's power and
splendour.
[10] Namely Hinayana or Theravada Buddhism which had already penetrated Lower Burma and
the Menam Chao Phaya basin from Ceylon. More closely related to the original doctrines of
Buddhism, Theravada Buddhism stressed poverty and simplicity.
[11] Angkor's fall was more due to treachery than the weakness of its defences; after the death of
the king during the siege two ministers and two Buddhist monks defected to the Thais. After
a short Thai occupation, the Khmers re-established their independence, but in 1432 Angkor
was abandoned for a site remoter from Thai attacks.
[12] The new ruler first moved to Basan, in Srei Santhor province, and then to Phnom Penh in
1234. Subsequently all Cambodian capitals were centred in this region—at Lovek, Udong and
Phnom Penh itself.
[13] Especially during the reign of Ang Chan (1516–66) who, taking advantage of Thai dynastic
troubles and Burmese attacks, invaded the Menam Chao Phaya basin and reached the walls
of Ayuthia (1564).
[14] During the course of this struggle Chinese refugees from Manchu persecution settled in the
Mekong Delta at My Tho and Bien Hoa; the Cambodian ruler had to appeal for Vietnamese

help in order to control them and subsequently gave Hué the title to two provinces in the region around Saigon.

[15]Ang Eng ascended the throne in 1779 at the age of 15. He was deposed after quarrelling with some of his powerful ministers and fled to Bangkok. There he received education and in 1794, having been installed as king of Cambodia in the Thai capital, he was escorted back to Phnom Penh and reinstated with Thai aid. In return the Thais 'silently' occupied Mongkolbaurey, Sisophon and Korat and were allowed to occupy and garrison Battambang and Siem Reap.

[16]Ang Eng died in 1796; he left behind a four year old son, Ang Chan, who was taken by the Thais to Bangkok while a regency was set up in Cambodia.

[17]In 1803, after his return to Cambodia, the ministers forming the Regency Council sent a complimentary mission to Hué. In 1805 they requested permission to pay annual homage and in 1807 sent an envoy with the task of securing the formal investment of Cambodia as vassal of the Vietnamese emperor. After 1807 the Cambodians sent embassies every year to Hué.

[18]The younger brother, Ang Sugnon, demanded to be appointed Obbarac (Uparat or Second King) and to be awarded the fief that went with it. Denied this, he fled to Pursat and appealed for Thai aid.

[19]A Thai army forced Ang Chan to take refuge in Saigon in 1812. In 1814 the Thais retaliated against Vietnamese assistance by occupying the Korat basin, Stung Treng, Tonlé Sap and Melou Prei.

[20]Acting on orders from Hué.

THE FRENCH ASCENDANCY

With devastating suddenness in 1863 Cambodia was brought face to face with French power and forced to accept French protection. This development was the direct outcome of the French occupation of Cochin-China which had begun in 1859,[a] but although sudden it was not unexpected. For the second time in her history Cambodia fell into the clutches of a Western power.

The first occasion had taken place nearly 300 years previously when the kingdom fell briefly into the hands of a group of Portuguese and Spanish adventurers, who enjoyed the support of the Spanish authorities in Manila. Taking advantage of the current threat of a Thai invasion and of internal disunity, the Europeans succeeded in putting their own nominee on the throne, but the triumph was shortlived[1]. The net result was to make the Cambodians extremely chary of Western influence and from the time of Sri Suriapur (Boromoraja IV),[2] European traders were denied access to the country. However this prohibition was also shortlived for Western traders again appeared during the reign of King Ponya To (1625–30). These traders were Dutch and Portuguese and for the next two decades these two rival races unsettled the politics of Cambodia with their intrigues and struggle for influence. In this rivalry the Dutch gained the upper hand[3] but towards the end of the century their interest and that of other European traders waned[4] while local feeling did not encourage them. By the nineteenth century Cambodia had sunk into obscurity as far as the colonial powers of the West were concerned, and the only Western influence in the country was represented by a handful of French Roman Catholic missionaries.[5]

The establishment of the French Protectorate

The revival of the Western threat in the shape of the French took place at the beginning of the 1860s. The ruler at that time was Ang Duong's son and successor, Si

[a]Refer pp. 448–51.

Votei, who had come to the throne in 1860 at the age of twenty-nine and had taken the title of Norodom. Right from the start of his reign Norodom was faced by the problem of the French who had started on the conquest of Cochin-China the previous year. Cambodia's involvement was at first only indirect as the French quarrel was with the Vietnamese but its implications for the future were obvious. The first complications began in March 1861, when the French commander, Admiral Charner, sought Norodom's assistance in crushing the Vietnamese resistance in the Delta, guaranteeing at the same time the integrity and independence of Cambodia. But Norodom, fearful of the Thais and doubtful of the French, replied that the king of Thailand was his protector, and declined to give any help. The French admiral was displeased but Norodom's attention was turned to more immediate problems when his youngest brother, Si Votha, rose up in rebellion against him later in the same year in an attempt to gain possession of the throne. Si Votha enjoyed considerable support in the country and when two of his lieutenants, Suang Saur and Rama Yuthea, defeated the royal troops, the King fled to Bangkok (August 1861). Ram Yuthea occupied Udong, the capital, on behalf of Si Votha, and Admiral Charner demonstrated his resentment at Norodom's failure to co-operate by sending a small group of officers to assist the rebels.

Nevertheless French influences were at work on both sides. As we have just noted, long before the arrival of French gunboats off the mouths of the Mekong French influence had been represented by Roman Catholic missionaries. The celebrated Pigneau de Béhaine had arrived in Cambodia at the start of his career,[a] in 1765. In the early 1840s when the *Société des Missions Etrangères* re-established itself in Indo-China, the vicariate of Cambodia was taken up by Monsignor Miche. Miche had been in the country[6] ever since and no doubt seeing himself as a nineteenth century Pigneau de Béhaine used his influence to orientate Cambodia's rulers towards France. Miche was probably behind Ang Duong's alleged attempt to secure a French alliance in 1854 which resulted in the abortive visit of the French envoy, de Montigny, to Kampot two years later.[7] Now in 1861 he was determined to win over Norodom by bringing about his restoration to the throne. Accordingly he despatched a message to the French consul at Bangkok, requesting French backing to Norodom's plea for Thai assistance. At the same time within Cambodia itself Miche played a decisive part in quashing the rebellion. He entered into a league with the Queen Grandmother and other notables who succeeded in forcing Rama Yuthea and his rebel supporters to leave Udong, then used the presence of a French gunboat sent upstream at his request to protect the missionaries at Phnom Penh, to force Rama Yuthea to pay a fine and make good his escape into the jungle. Miche also persuaded the French officers despatched by Charner to help Si Votha to abandon their mission. A few months later—in March 1862—Norodom re-entered his capital without opposition[8] after landing from a Thai steamer at Kampot, and took up the reins of government once more. He was also accompanied by a Thai Resident.

However, the French problem still remained and soon reasserted itself. In September of the same year, Charner's successor as governor of Cochin-China, Ad-

[a]Refer p. 439 and p. 441, note 32.

miral Bonard, arrived at Udong to pay a visit and press French claims to suzerainty over Cambodia.[9] He got no further than doing just that but he returned to Saigon alarmed by the obvious strength of Thai influence at the capital. By now Miche was working behind the scenes to persuade Norodom of the desirability of accepting French protection. To strengthen the Bishop's hand, Bonard sent up to Udong early in 1863 a capable and energetic young officer on his staff called Doudart de Lagrée, who was instructed to carry out a geological survey and to promote French influence. He reported back that 'the king of Siam is more powerful in Udong than the king of Cambodia himself'. This report prompted further French action. Bernard's successor, Admiral de la Grandière, arrived in July 1863 in order to clinch matters before it was too late. A month later, acting on his own initiative,[10] de la Grandière signed on behalf of France a treaty negotiated by Miche which 'transformed' Vietnam's right of suzerainty over Cambodia, held since 1807, into a French protectorate.

By the terms of this treaty France gained exclusive control over Cambodia's foreign relations and over the right to install foreign consulates in the country. A French Resident was to live at the Cambodian capital and a Cambodian representative was to stay in Saigon. The treaty also granted reciprocal freedom of travel and rights of property ownership to the residents of both Cambodia and Cochin-China and granted to French merchants the right to exploit Cambodian forests, to French missionaries the right to preach and teach, and ceded to France a small piece of land in the vicinity of Phnom Penh.

The Franco-Thai contest for Cambodia

Norodom had so far been obliged to yield to the force of circumstances but neither he nor the Thais intended to accept this situation. His hand was strengthened by the fact that the treaty had yet to be ratified by the French government in Europe who did not even know of its existence. So the king profited from the time that must elapse before the treaty was confirmed to reinsure his position with Bangkok and if possible to play one side off against the other. The Thais (with British backing) protested against the treaty and not long afterwards Norodom signed a secret agreement with Thailand which not only confirmed Cambodia's vassalage to Bangkok but stipulated that Norodom was in fact the Thai viceroy. The agreement also made it clear that Thailand was responsible for Cambodia's defence and internal security. To establish his position still further King Mongkut announced that he intended to pay a visit to Cambodia in person to confer the vice-regal crown.

De la Grandière protested against all these proceedings and Mongkut compromised by summoning Norodom to Bangkok for his coronation instead. Despite French protests, Norodom went ahead with his preparations for the journey to Bangkok, which led Doudart into decisive action to stop the king. He called for forces from Saigon and in the meantime sent his own detachment of marines into the royal palace and had the French flag raised in its grounds. This and the arrival of the reinforcements[11] caused King Norodom to turn back. A month later, in April 1864, the treaty duly ratified arrived back from Paris and Norodom was left with no choice but to ratify it himself. The final ratification took place on 17 April.

The Treaty of 1864 defined the new status of Cambodia but it did not settle the dispute over suzerainty which now existed between France and Thailand. The Thais had one card up their sleeve in that they still possessed the regalia which Norodom had carried with him on his original flight to Bangkok in 1861. In June 1864 King Mongkut agreed to hand back the regalia to Cambodia provided that Norodom was crowned by both Thai and French representives. This was agreed to but when the ceremony actually took place Doudart refused to allow the Thai delegate to perform his part in the crowning. The Thai envoy returned to Bangkok the next day, after having formally restated Thailand's claim to suzerainty and her right to the occupation of the three western provinces.[12] Norodom, now a virtual prisoner of the French, paid a state visit to Saigon towards the end of the year.

Norodom and the Thais made one more attempt to re-establish their former relationship. In April 1865 the King, accompanied by a protesting Doudart went to Kampot in order to receive Mongkut. What the actual purpose of this meeting was to be is not clear but in any case the Thai monarch did not appear. Two years after this the Thais and the French came to an agreement over Cambodia. By the treaty signed in 1867 Thailand recognized the French protectorate over the country and renounced all her own claims to suzerainty. France, on behalf of Cambodia, gave up all claims over the provinces of Battambang, Siem Reap and Sisophon.[a] King Norodom, this time with the active encouragement of Doudart de Lagrée, protested, but in vain. The treaty was negotiated between the Thais and the French consul at Bangkok.[b] The reason for Thailand's surrender in the dispute lay in her fear of antagonizing France at a moment when British influence in the region was apparently on the move.[13]

The Franco-Cambodian Agreement of 1884 and Si Votha's second revolt

Although French influence in Cambodia was now established beyond any shadow of doubt, effective French control was not really brought about until the late 1870s, and the final extinction of Cambodian independence might be said to have come with the Agreement of 1884. Prior to 1867 much of France's energies were taken up with her schemes in Mexico[14] as well as by the resistance of the Vietnamese in Cochin-China.[c] In 1870 the Franco-Prussian War broke out and crippled the French for the next five years.[15] In the meantime King Norodom showed a marked reluctance to follow the advice proffered him by French officials. Certain reforms were in western eyes indispensable and certain actions taken by the king met with hearty French disapproval.[16] In 1877 the king was obliged to put his hand to decrees abolishing slavery, restricting gambling, providing alternatives to forced labour and giving the French Resident right of access to the Cambodian Council of Ministers. But in the French view, despite these impositions, Norodom still retained more freedom of action than was desirable, and still maintained his reluctance to follow the French way of doing things.

No doubt the interests of either party were contradictory and the French, exasperated, decided—being the more powerful of the two—to put an end to the

[a]See p. 519.
[b]See pp. 509-11.
[c]Refer p. 451.

existing situation. In June 1884 the governor of Cochin-China, Charles Thomson, suddenly arrived at Phnom Penh by steamboat with an escort of a hundred armed guards. On arrival he sent an officer into the royal presence to demand Norodom's signature to a new convention. Norodom refused. This was followed by a threat to deport the king to Algeria on the very boat which had brought the French governor. Norodom climbed down and signed away his birthright for ever. By the Convention of 1884 the king agreed to accept whatever reforms in the administration which the French might consider necessary. The French Resident-General (*Resident-Supérieur*) was given the right of private and personal audience with the king, and he was entitled to override or ignore the wishes of the Council of Ministers if he chose. The expenses of the Protectorate were to be provided for in the Cambodian budget. Each province was to be placed under a French official (called Resident) with general powers to supervise the work of the Cambodian hierarchy and their councils, and with direct authority to collect land revenue, customs duties and indirect taxes. The French officials were also to be responsible for the preservation of law and order and for the maintenance of public works. Fire-arms could only be imported into the country through the French authorities. In return for all this, the king was provided with a fixed civil list, and was permitted to retain his court ceremonial and other royal prerogatives. Essentially the Agreement of 1884 was little different from those agreements which the British imposed upon the rulers of the Malay States during the previous decade—except in the terminology.

The Convention of 1884 brought Si Votha back to the scene. He had never been wholeheartedly pursued by Norodom and now he became the focus of a widespread movement of protest and revolt against the new agreement. Popular feelings had already been aroused by some of the earlier decrees which Norodom had been made to sign, in particular those relating to the ending of the capitation tax on the Vietnamese and the imposition of duties on opium and alcohol. The rebellion broke out in January 1885, with the massacre of some of the Vietnamese escorts provided for the new French Residents. It quickly spread and for eighteen months the initiative lay in rebel hands. After 1886 Si Votha became a hunted man but he eluded capture until depleted of all resources he was forced to give himself up in 1892. The rebellion cost many lives on both sides. Cambodian losses are reckoned to have stood at around 10,000 people; the French also suffered heavy casualties although, like the British in Burma, their losses were more often due to fever and ill-health than the action of the Cambodian resistance.

In this manner Cambodian independence came to an end. Her resistance was gallant but futile and her fate under the circumstances ineluctable. However, Cambodia's decline did not start in the nineteenth century. It might be said to have begun with the forsaking of Angkor, for only the economic basis which made the Angkor Empire possible could have sustained the Cambodians as a great power. As it was, they became increasingly wedged in between the two powerful peoples who moved in on their flanks. The Thai conquest of 1595 marked the real end for Cambodia, for that after its rulers were obliged to seek a *modus vivendi* between Thai and Vietnamese power. Internal feuds and instability created by lack of a firm economic base and a disintegrated social system could offer no means of standing up to the overwhelming preponderance of French power.

[1]This episode centred on the personalities of a Portuguese adventurer called Diego Veloso and the Spaniards Blas Ruiz de Hernan Gonzales and Gregorio Vargas. Veloso secured great influence at the Cambodian court, was 'adopted' by King Chettha I (1574–95) and became leader of the palace guard. After many vicissitudes and adventures, in 1595 Veloso together with Blas Ruiz and Vargas, persuaded Manila of the feasibility of getting control over Cambodia and converting the king and people to Christianity. By the time these plans were made, Cambodia was in Thai hands. The expedition led by Juan Juares Gallinato and some Dominican friars was dispersed by a storm but Veloso and Blas Ruiz were able to take advantage of the confused state in which Cambodian politics now stood as a result of the Thai conquest to depose Prah Rama, a usurper, and place one of the late King Chettha's sons on the throne in his stead. The new king, Ponya Tan, was a puppet in the hands of the Europeans, but the position of Veloso and his group remained precarious in the extreme. A small expedition sent from Manila in 1598 to strengthen their hand was also dispersed by storm and the following year the small European clique was overthrown in a rebellion led by a Malay leader (who bore the title of Laksamana).

[2]Sri Suriapur was restored with Thai help around 1600 after the Laksamana's rebellion. Throughout his reign he remained a loyal vassal of Ayuthia. He abdicated in favour of his son in 1618.

[3]During the reign of Thupdey Chan (1642–59) the Dutch warned the Cambodian court of the dangers of Portuguese influence but a Dutch naval visit of 1645 was badly rebuffed. In 1653, however, the Cambodians came to terms with the Dutch whose influence in Thailand was also considerable at the time; a commercial treaty was signed giving the Dutch exclusive advantages.

[4]Notably that of the British who established a factory at Lovek in 1654 but were forced to abandon it as the result of a Vietnamese invasion in 1659.

[5]French missionaries of the *Société des Missions Etrangères* had been established in Cambodia since the late seventeenth century. In 1765 the *Société*'s seminary at Bangkok was transferred to Ha Tien as a result of the Burmese attacks on Ayuthia; Ha Tien was also the scene of much of the activity of the celebrated French bishop, Pigneau de Béhaine.

[6]Miche had originally worked in Vietnam where he was arrested in February 1842 during the Emperor Thieu Tri's first wave of anti-Christian persecutions. Sentenced to death, he was released as a result of French naval intervention. See p. 445.

[7]King Ang Duong, at Miche's instigation, is supposed to have sought French support through the French consul in Singapore. Miche was no doubt anxious to foster relations with France but whether Ang Duong actually made this move is not certain. Nevertheless Miche and de Montigny did draft a Franco-Cambodian treaty on the lines of the one recently concluded with Thailand. The treaty would have made Roman Catholicism one of the established religions of Cambodia and would have provided for the cession of the island of Co Trol (Vietnamese—Phu Quoc; Thai—Kol Duat) to France 'as a guarantee of admiration' and as a safeguard against Vietnamese attack. De Montigny's visit to Kampot was a complete failure as two Thai commissioners from Bangkok were present throughout to foil any French advances.

[8]In the final pacification, Norodom's second brother, Ang Sor, the Obbarac (Uparat), played an important part.

[9]The French, with the encouragement of Miche, based their claims on the argument that their occupation of the Delta made them the heirs to Hué's suzerainty in the South.

[10]Since the French admiral had already exceeded his instructions—he was authorized only 'to take soundings' in Cambodia—it was agreed that the treaty should be kept secret until it had been ratified by Paris. But Norodom did not succeed (and probably did not wish to anyway) in keeping the secret for long. Its contents were soon known in Bangkok.

[11]Consisting of three gunboats and 100 marines sent upstream from Saigon.

[12]Battambang, Sisophon and Siem Reap. Confirmed in Thai possession by the 1867 Treaty, in 1907 Battambang and Siem Reap were handed back to Cambodia in a territorial adjustment with Thailand. In 1940 the Japanese rewarded the Thais for their co-operation by re-annexing the provinces to Thailand.

[13]The British had already forcibly restrained a Thai advance in the north-east Malay Peninsula states of Trengganu and Pahang (the bombardment of Kuala Trengganu 1862) and were strengthening their hand in Burma (treaties of 1862 and 1867). Another source of concern to the Thais was the progress of a rebellion in Cambodia led by a holy man calling himself Pa' Kombo (Pu Koma), which had broken out in 1866. Centred on the Middle Mekong and engendering wide popular support, the rebels had killed the governors of Sambor and Kratié and were building a stronghold at Choeuté'al-Phlos in Kanchhor. In June a royal army was defeated at Ba Phnom. Mongkut feared lest he should be associated in French minds with the

movement, thereby providing them with a pretext to make fresh demands. The rebellion was brought to an end in 1867.

[14]In pursuit of his policy of championing Roman Catholicism, Louis Napoleon of France had allowed himself to be drawn into an improbable scheme for establishing a new French protected Catholic empire in Mexico. The whole operation ended within five years in humiliating failure.

[15]In this war the French were defeated and Louis Napoleon's regime collapsed. The country was saddled with a large indemnity and a German occupation until it was paid. Out of the French defeat were born the Third French Republic (which lasted till 1940) and a united German Empire.

[16]Particularly concerning his fiscal policy. In 1863 the royal capital had been transferred from Udong to Phnom Penh, causing great expense. To make ends meet the King, against French advice, imposed a head tax, restored customs posts that had been abandoned inside the country and farmed out opium.

14. CAMBODIA

A. Chronology of Main Events

A.D.	100–550	The Empire of FU NAN
	550	Fu Nan conquered by Chen-la
	802	Foundation of ANGKOR by Jayavarnam II
	1190	Introduction of Theravada/Hinayana Buddhism
	1313	Start of Thai attacks on Angkor
	1432	Angkor abandoned by the Khmers/Cambodians
	1553	Arrival of Portuguese Dominican missionaries
	1594	Thai conquest; start of Thai claims to suzerainty
	1596–9	The Spanish episode
	1602	First Dutch traders in Cambodia
	1603	Thai overlordship re-established
	1618	Cambodians reassert independence
	1654	English factory in Cambodia
	1659	Cambodians acknowledge overlordship of Hué
	1679–1749	Cambodians lose Mekong Delta to the Vietnamese
	1700–1812	Cambodia cockpit for power struggle between Thais and Vietnamese
	1794	Thais install Ang Eng on throne in Cambodia; occupy Battambang and Siemreap
	1802	Thais install Ang Chan II on throne of Cambodia
	1803	Ang Chan sends mission of homage to Hué
	1807	Cambodia formally under Hué's protection
	1812–13	Thais and Vietnamese intervene in palace dispute; Ang Chan restored with Vietnamese help; Vietnamese garrison at Phnom Penh

1831		Thai invasion; Ang Chan flees for Vietnamese help
1833		Ang Chan restored by Vietnamese; start of Vietnamese policy of assimilation
1834		Queen Ang Mey put on throne by Vietnamese
1835		Rebellion at Kompong Som crushed by Vietnamese
1841		Queen Ang Mey deposed by Vietnamese; outbreak of general revolt; Thai intervention
1845		Thai-Vietnamese compromise; Ang Duong recognized as Cambodian king under joint protection of the two powers
1856		Montigny's mission at Kampot
1860		Death of Ang Duong; accession of Ang Votey as Norodom
1861		Si Votha's revolt; Norodom flees to Bangkok
		French establish their power at Saigon
1862		Norodom restored in Cambodia with Thai help; mission of Doudart de Lagrée to Udong
1863	April	Doudart de Lagrée takes up post as French Resident in Cambodia
	July	De la Grandière visits Cambodia
	August	Treaty accepting French protectorate over Cambodia
1864	March	French prevent Norodom's departure for Bangkok
	June	Norodom crowned king of Cambodia under French auspices
1866		Pu Kombo' revolt
1867		Franco-Thai agreement recognizing French protectorate over Cambodia
1877		French tighten control over Cambodian government
1884		French impose new convention on King Norodom
1885–92		Si Votha's second rebellion
1907		Battambang and Siemreap handed back to Cambodia as result of Franco-Thai Treaty

B. Cambodian Rulers in the Nineteenth Century

1779–96	Eng Eng	supported by Thais
1796–1806	Thai Regency	
1806–34	Ang Chan (II)	installed by Thais; supported by Hue
1834–41	Ang Mey (queen)	imposed by Vietnamese
1841–59	Ang Duong	compromise candidate recognized by both sides
1860–1904	Norodom	

BOOKS AND ARTICLES FOR FURTHER READING: CAMBODIA

Cady, J.F., *South-East Asia: Its Historical Development*, McGraw-Hill, New York, 1964.

Dauphin-Meunier, A., *Le Cambodge*, Nouvelles Editions Latines, Paris, 1965.

Fisher, C.A., *South-East Asia: A Social, Economic and Political Geography*, Methuen, London, 1964.

Hall, D.G.E., *A History of South-East Asia* (3rd ed.), Macmillan, London, 1968.

Cady, J.F., *The Roots of French Imperialism in Eastern Asia*, Cornell, Ithaca, 1954.

Coedès, G., *Angkor: An Introduction*, Oxford University Press, Hong Kong, 1963.

Groslier, B., *Indochina*, Methuen, London, 1962.

Ghosh M., *A History of Cambodia*, T. K. Gupta, Saigon, 1960.

Moffat A.L., *Mongkut, King of Siam*, Cornell, Ithaca, 1961.

Wat Benjamobophit, Bangkok, built by King Chulalongkorn in 1900

VI THE THAI STATES: THAILAND AND LAOS

Thailand and Laos

Thailand's success in preserving her independence during the nineteenth century when all her neighbours were losing theirs is the most outstanding feature of her modern history. There is no doubt that a combination of favourable circumstances helped to make this possible, not least amongst which was the colonial rivalry of the French and British on the mainland. But Thailand's own background should also be taken into account. Probably the most stable and best-administered state in all South-East Asia, the Thais accepted the lead of a vigorous monarchy through the centuries of their struggle with the Burmese. They had survived several national disasters and had maintained their traditions. The Thais also had a longer experience of dealings with Europeans than any other people on the mainland. They had permitted Western traders to do business in their country ever since the arrival of the first Portuguese early in the sixteenth century and they had successfully coped with a French bid to take over the kingdom in the middle of the seventeenth. Circumstances made Thailand's rulers practical men, aware of the realities of the outside world, and never was this more important or more clearly demonstrated than during the reigns of Mongkut and Chulalongkorn during the nineteenth century. Thailand was the only South-East Asian state to open its doors voluntarily to the West. This did not save the country from losing outlying territories to Western imperialism, but the wise, compromising policies of her kings saved her from greater disaster.

Laos is nominally a Thai state, having a bare majority of Thai as opposed to non-Thai inhabitants. It is also hardly a credible state, strung along the banks of the Mekong, more divided than united by nature. Although it could boast proud historical antecedents in the once powerful kingdom of Lang Chang, by the beginning of the nineteenth century it was already broken up into a patchwork of principalities, a number of which fell more under the influence of Hué than Bangkok. Its occupation by the French during the last decades of the nineteenth century was largely the work of one man, who reassembled the broken fragments of the Laotian polity. Bangkok's ineffectual attempts to prevent the French advance brought about Thailand's closest confrontation with the West.

THE THAI BACKGROUND

Stretching in an arc from the valley of the Upper Brahmaputra in the west to the low hills of the Chinese border in the east live some thirty-five million Thais. Politically speaking the bulk of this Thai population is to be found within the confines of the kingdom of Thailand itself[1] which is centred on the basin of the Menam Chao Phaya.[2] Another independent state which is also predominantly Thai[3] is the riverine kingdom of Laos. Elsewhere the Thais are the subjects of other masters—in

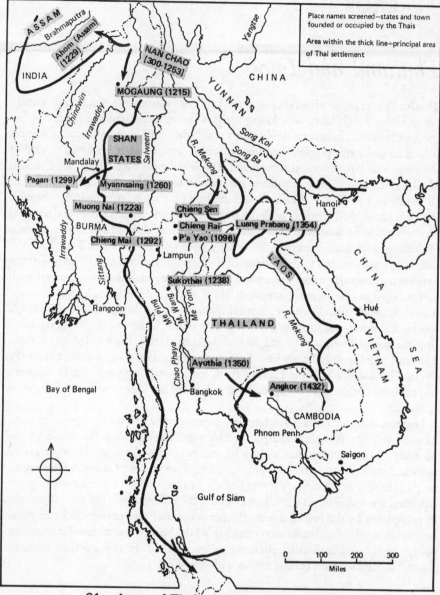

61. Areas of Thai migration and settlement

Assam they fall under the Indian government; in Burma the Shan states[a] form part of the Burmese Union; approximately half a million Thais live in various parts of Vietnam, and another million in south China. But whatever their political circumstance, all Thais share a common identity. Not only do they have a common background and origin and speak the same language, but by and large they follow the same agricultural life and share Buddhist and animist beliefs.

[a]Refer pp. 396–7.

In this section we are only concerned with those Thais who enjoy a separate political identity, namely the Thai populations of Laos and Thailand itself; the story of the other branches of the Thai family is covered in the sections dealing with the countries in which they find their homes.

As South-East Asian states both Laos and Thailand are unique. Laos has emerged after a period of French tutelage as the revival of a kingdom which disintegrated during the course of the eighteenth century. Thailand is the only country in the whole region to have retained its political independence during the hey-day of Western imperialism.

Thai origins and the great migration to the south

As states both Laos and Thailand are of comparatively recent origin, neither of them possessing a history which goes back further than the fourteenth century. This underlines the fact that the Thai peoples themselves are comparative new-comers to South-East Asia. Along with the Vietnamese to whom they appear to be closely related, the starting point of the Thais seems to have been somewhere in south-west China. The first Thai state which can be identified is that of Nan Chao[4] which was based in modern Yunnan. It flourished from the fourth till the thirteenth century when it was overrun and destroyed by the Mongols in 1253. During that period it came to exercise considerable influence and was an important factor in the power struggle between the Tibetans and the Chinese.[5] At the same time the Thais were strongly influenced by Chinese culture. Thai methods of war, diplomacy and trade all followed the Chinese pattern, their literature and writing (like that of the Japanese, Koreans and Vietnamese) were in the Chinese characters, and they follow-ed the Chinese (Mahayanist) form of Buddhism. In the centuries which followed all this was to change and Indian influences replaced those of the Chinese. However, in the Thai language, architecture and culture of today these Chinese foundations are still clearly discernible.

The changes in Thai culture and outlook which took place came about as a result of the great migration southwards. As was the case with the Vietnamese, from the dawn of their history the Thais suffered from the inexorable pressures of Chinese power and advance. The state of Nan Chao itself represented a Thai shift to the west from their original homelands. Its fall to the Mongols in 1253 accelerated a process which had already begun several centuries earlier. In the pattern of the Malaysian peoples who had preceded them, small groups of settlers moved down from the Yunnan tableland and followed the routes of its watershed. This led them down the Irrawaddy, some branching up the Chindwin into Assam while others settled in the Shan highlands; yet others followed the Mekong to form the nucleus of the Thai population along its banks and the heights dominating them today. Some found their way down the various streams of the Menam Chao Phaya into the Menam basin itself. This migration never assumed the proportions of a mass movement. Rather it was a steady process of infiltration where small bands of Thais would settle down amongst the more civilized Khmer, Mon and Burmese populations already established in the region. Their numbers imperceptibly but surely increased until the point came when they outnumbered the masters of the land they were living on. Then came the seizure of power, with the overthrow of the local ruler by a Thai leader and the reversal of the rôles. The first small Thai principalities began to appear in South-East Asia during the eleventh and twelfth centuries.[6] Evidence of the growing Thai presence is provided by chronicles[7] and even from the *bas-reliefs* of Angkor where Thais are depicted acting as scouts for a Khmer army.[8]

The rise of the first Thai states

During the thirteenth century the political power of the Thais began to become firmly entrenched. The Shan states of Mogaung (1215), Muong Nai (1223) and the Ahom dynasty of Assam (1229) all came into being during the first half of that century. The Mongol invasions together with the fall of Nan Chao and of the great Burman empire of Pagan[a] which accompanied them in the latter part of the same century stimulated the foundation of many more such principalities, especially in Burma.

Amongst these new states were two which were destined to play a great part in subsequent Thai history—Chieng Mai and Sukhothai. Chieng Mai was founded by Mang-rai, a Thai chief from Chieng Sen[9] who carved himself a kingdom out of the ancient Mon state of Lampun (or Haripunjàya). Chieng Mai was to have a turbulent and chequered history before it finally became part of the Bangkok monarchy[10] but it established itself as the capital of the north and became recognized (and is still to this very day) as the centre and stronghold of conservative Thai traditions.

The rôle of Sukhothai, however, was to prove of even greater significance. Formerly a province of the Khmer empire of Angkor,[b] its Khmer governor was overthrown in a revolt led by two Thai chiefs[11] who then declared their independence. One of them, Phaya Rang, became Sukhothai's first king but remains a semi-mythical figure. The foundation of Sukhothai took place in 1238. Nearly fifty years later one of his sons, who became king with the title of Ram Kam Heng, extended the kingdom, bringing the Mons of the Menam basin under his control as well as the inhabitants of the greater part of the Upper Mekong. Ram Kam Heng's conquests did not outlive him long but their effects helped mould the Thailand of today to such as extent that people refer to Sukhothai not only as the first historical kingdom but as the cradle of Thai civilization. During the century of Sukhothai's supremacy, the Mons came to influence their Thai conquerors in the Menam basin much as they had done the Burman rulers of Pagan. This influence was reflected in art and architecture, language and religion. Theravada Buddhism (as opposed to Mahayana Buddhism) became adopted as the religion of the people; bronze casting, pottery making and new styles of architecture were acquired and the Thais took over an Indian script for their alphabet.[12] The outlines of the Indianized culture of Thailand today were defined during the period of Sukhothai, and as a result Thais regard Sukhothai in the same way that the Malays consider Malacca as the classical period of their culture and civilization.[13]

Nevertheless politically Sukhothai was not destined to be the progenitor of the two Thai kingdoms of today. Their foundations were laid within a decade of one another over a hundred years later. In 1350 a Thai chief from Chieng Sen who took

[a]Refer p. 396.
[b]Refer p. 469.

the title of Rama Thibodi founded the kingdom of Ayuthia in the heart of the Menam basin. Three years later, another Thai chief of ancient lineage called Fa Ngum laid the foundations of the kingdom of Lang Chang (Luang Prabang).

[1] Until 1939 the official name for Thailand was Prathet Sayam or Siam and the inhabitants were known as Siamese. In 1939 the official name was changed to Prathet Thai and has remained such ever since (except for a short period from 1946 to 1949). In this book the terms Thai and Thailand have been used throughout for purposes of simplicity.

[2] With a population of approximately 25.5 million—preliminary report, 1960 census. See Fisher, *South-East Asia*, op. cit. p. 484.

[3] The indigenous racial composition of Laos by 1955 estimates is: Thais—800,000; Hill Peoples —600,000; Vietnamese—50,000. The Hill Peoples are made up of Kha (Moi/Penong), Meo/ Miao, Man/Yao, Muong and Lolo. 'The peoples of Laos are distributed about their country in a distinctive pattern in which altitude is the indicator,' Dommen, *Conflict In Laos*, p. 3. The Thai element can be divided between the Lao who live mostly in the valley of the Central Mekong along either bank of the river, and the various Thai tribal groupings mostly found in the valleys of northern Laos, especially around Muong Sing and near Dien Bien Phu; the main tribes are Thai Dam (Black Thai), Thai Khao (White Thai); Thai Deng (Red Thai), Thai Neua, Thai Phong and Phon Thai. The main distinction between the tribal Thais and the Lao is that the former are not Buddhists. The Kha (Lao word for 'slave') covers 60 distinct tribal groups of basic Mon-Khmer (Malaysian) stock and are found in all mountainous areas but especially in the south and on Bolovens Plateau. The Meo are the Gurkhas of Laos, a warrior race occupying the higher crests and ridges and who normally never settle below 3,000 feet; they are most numerous in Chieng Kuang province and also in Luang Prabang, Sam Neua, Phong Saly and Nam Tha. The Man/Yao appear to be related to the Meo. The Muong and Lolo are found interspersed with the Kha.

[4] Our earliest information about Nan Chao and about the Thais is all derived from Chinese sources.

[5] Two great Nan Chao rulers made their mark—Ko Lo Feng who overran the valley of the Upper Irrawaddy between 757 and 763, and his grandson and successor, I Mou Hsun who expanded Nan Chao's territory and also accepted Chinese overlordship. Later rulers during the ninth century conquered Lower Burma, raided Tongking and Annam and invaded China itself on two occasions.

[6] For example, the small state of Pha Yao in 1096 at the junction of the Me Ping and Me Wang north of Raheng (Tak).

[7] The earliest evidence of the Thai presence in the Indo-Chinese Peninsula comes from an eleventh century Cham inscription which mentions prisoners of war from 'Sayam'.

[8] The presence of these Thai mercenaries in the Khmer army illustrates the manner in which the Thai infiltration took place and their influence grew.

[9] Or Lau Na.

[10] In 1775 when it was reconquered from Burma by Phaya Tak Sin.

[11] Significantly enough, they were formerly both officials in charge of townships under Khmer control.

[12] The script adopted was the one used by the Mon of the Menam Chao Phaya basin; known as the Sukodaya script the earliest extant examples come from Sukhotai itself on an inscription dated 1292.

[13] This parallel can be carried further in that both peoples adopted a new culture on an older basis; the Malays embraced Islam which was superimposed on Hinduism, and the Thais Hindu-Buddhism which overlaid Chinese foundations.

THE LAO STATES

The story of Fa Ngum affords a classic illustration of the manner of Thai infiltration southwards and the subsequent seizure of political power. Fa Ngum was the chief of the small Thai principality of Muong Swa, in the region of modern Luang Prabang. He was the grandson of the last of the rulers of Muong Swa mentioned in the chronicles and claimed descent from the legendary Khun Barom. Khun Barom

The Library, Vat Sisaket, Laos

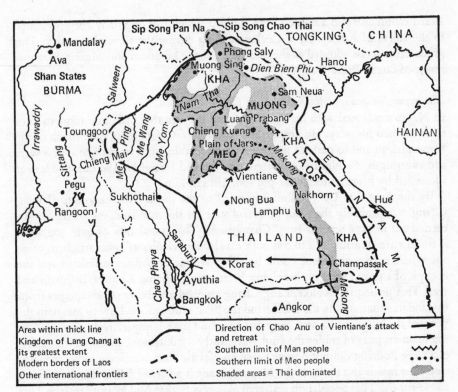

62. Laos, illustrating historical and ethnic background

was allegedly a prince from Yunnan who had been sent to direct the Thai migration to the south. According to the legend, he appeared on the banks of the Mekong on a white elephant, accompanied by a host of functionaries, pages, musicians, maids of honour and the like. Khun Barom also brought with him regalia for his own coronation and for the coronations of his seven sons who were predestined to rule over all the Thai principalities in South-East Asia.

Whatever its credibility this story symbolizes the manner in which the Thai occupation of the Upper Mekong took place during the period between the eighth and thirteenth centuries. By 1200 the Thais along the Upper Mekong were probably under the aegis of the Khmers of Angkor and some time later under that of Sukhothai. Significantly Fa Ngum of the illustrious background enters history as an exile from his state, living in Angkor and being instructed by learned Buddhist monks. When he came of age, he was married to a daughter of the Khmer ruler and was then provided with military support to win his claims to Muong Swa. No doubt the Khmer intention was to reassert their influence in the Upper Mekong which had fallen under the sway of aggressive Thai marauders but for Fa Ngum it was the opportunity to create an empire of his own. He set out in 1352 and within two years had occupied Vientiane and brought the Lao chiefs of the Upper Mekong under his control. Fa Ngum thereupon declared himself King of Lang Chang.[1] However, this did not lead to a complete rupture with Angkor. In 1358 Fa Ngum sent to the Khmers for help in propagating Theravada Buddhism amongst his own subjects. As a result a party of Buddhist monks arrived at Muong Swa complete with the sacred canon and also a statue of the Buddha which had originally been presented to the rulers of Angkor by a Ceylonese King during the eleventh century. This statue came to be adopted as the palladium of the kingdom and Muong Swa was renamed Luang Prabang.[2]

The expansion and consolidation of Lang Chang

Fa Ngum continued with his conquests until the area that makes up modern Laos today owned his sway. His empire also spread into Chieng Mai, over much of the Korat plateau and to parts of northern Cambodia. In 1373, tired of countless wars and campaigns, Fa Ngum's ministers rose up and forced his abdication. He was succeeded by his seventeen-year-old son, Un Hu Eun.

By the time that Un Hu Eun succeeded to the throne, the kingdom of Lang Chang was probably the most powerful state on the mainland. As a male census carried out in 1376 reveals, Lang Chang had a Thai population of over 300,000;[3] it could raise an army of 150,000 with cavalry and elephants' units attached. In an age where manpower alone could be a decisive factor and the mainland was the cockpit of a power struggle involving Vietnamese, Chams, Khmers, Burmans and rival Thai principalities alike, Lang Chang enjoyed a number of advantages from this and its situation. On the other hand the basic problem was how to maintain the unity of the kingdom. Lang Chang was an inland state, comparatively remote from the main avenues of trade; the land was mostly mountainous and even the capital of Luang Prabang did not possess a rich and fertile plain which could be its mainstay. The rapids and rocks of the Mekong made it a barrier rather than a unifying factor for the Thai population scattered along its banks. And in any case, the Thai or Lao population did not in fact amount to more than 50 per cent of the whole.[4]

During the forty years of his reign Un Hu Eun attempted to grapple with this problem and succeeded in laying down the basis on which the kingdom was organized and on which it was to survive for the next 300 years. The first step was the taking of the male census of 1376 already referred to. This became the basis for organizing a permanent standing army controlled from the capital, which was supported by 20,000 auxiliaries.[5] In addition to this militia units were created under the command of regional governors known as *Chao Muong*. The governors were key figures. They were in fact territorial chiefs of the areas they administered; they maintained the militia out of their own revenues and submitted half of the local crops as tribute every third year. Although they were appointed by the king,[6] these officials tended increasingly to become hereditary. As for the royal succession itself, no law of primogeniture obtained; the king's successor was selected from amongst the members of the royal family by a council of chiefs convened by the *Maha Upahat* or viceroy.

Un Hu Eun made other important contributions to his kingdom. He encouraged the study of Buddhism by building temples, monasteries and schools. He married a Thai princess from Ayuthia and his system of administration came to be much influenced by the practice of that kingdom. Lang Chang's control over the routes between Annam and the Menam basin stimulated its trade.

The disintegration of Lang Chang

Nevertheless the kingdom's basic problem of internal unity was never resolved.

The absence of a strong hand at the centre resulted in an inevitable trend towards regionalism. This and the pressure of foreign invasion proved to be the undoing of Lang Chang, so much so that an observer writing in 1964 could say: 'Laos is less a nation state than a multiplicity of feudal societies. The family clan is all important'.[a] The wonder is that the rulers of Luang Prabang ever succeeded in creating a united kingdom at all.

In fact, the unity of Lang Chang was maintained until the Burman incursions under Bayinnaung during the second half of the sixteenth century.[b] Bayinnaung never actually succeeded in annexing Lang Chang himself although he was able to occupy Luang Prabang in 1565, but as a result of his invasion the Burmans put themselves in a position to exploit the internal dissensions amongst the Laotian ruling class and assert their own supremacy for the next generation. It was not until 1592 that Burman suzerainty was shaken off and the unity of Lang Chang was restored.[7]

Lang Chang continued to survive as a united kingdom for another century.[8] For a considerable part of that time the kingdom was under the hand of Suligna Vongsa the last strong ruler that Lang Chang was to know.[9] He reigned for 57 years and succeeded in restoring much of the prosperity, power and influence of the Laotians. But on his death in 1694, the throne was usurped by his chief minister, Tian Thala.[10] In 1700 Tian Thala himself was overthrown and killed by Nantharath, the governor of Nakhorn. These events led directly to the partitioning and disintegration of the kingdom. Rival claimants now struck to oust the new usurper. One of these, Sai Ong·Hué,[11] marched on Vientiane at the head of an army of Vietnamese soldiers, seized the city, killing Nantharath, and sent his half-brother, Thao Long, to take Luang Prabang. Seven years later, two other claimants, grandsons of Suligna Vongsa,[12] advanced on Luang Prabang with a force of 6,000 men raised in the Sip Song Pan Na,[13] defeated Thao Long and captured the capital. Kit Sarat, one of the victorious pair, was proclaimed king, and then demanded the recognition of his title to all the land north of the Nam Thuong from Sai Ong Hué in Vientiane. Sai Ong Hué, who was preoccupied by the restiveness of his southern domains, had little choice but to give way. In this manner the kingdom of Lang Chang split into two to form the separate and mutually hostile states of Luang Prabang and Vientiane.

But the disintegration of Laos was not yet complete. In 1708 the ancient principality of Chieng Kuang (Xieng Khouang) or Tranh Ninh[14] took the occasion of Kit Sarat's proclamation as king to reassert its own independence of Vientiane, and five years later a number of small territories along the Middle Mekong also broke away from the rule of Sai Ong Hué to create a principality of their own known as Champassak under their leader, Chao Sri Sisamut.[15] The Laotian states were not brought together again under a single administration until they all fell under French control towards the end of the nineteenth century.

The divided Lao: the fate of Chieng Kuang
Once disunified the Laotian states were completely unable to avoid falling under the influence of their far more powerful neighbours, in particular the Thais of Ayu-

---

[a]J. Dommen, *Conflict in Laos*, p. 17.
[b]See p. 498.

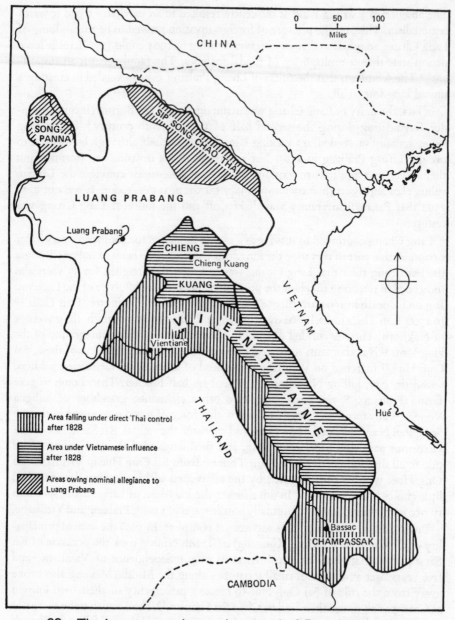

63. The Lao states prior to the spread of French control

thia and the Vietnamese. The existence of mutual rivalries and jealousies amongst the Lao princes themselves did nothing to help their position.

The weakest of these states[16] was Chieng Kuang which oscillated between Vientiane and Luang Prabang, Hué and Ayuthia. Unable to play off its enemies against one another, in 1832 Chieng Kuang came under Vietnamese domination. Hué first emerged as the champion of Chieng Kuang against the demands of Vientiane during the eighteenth century.[17] After this the rulers of Chieng Kuang tried their best to maintain a wary line between the two. But this act proved no longer possible after 1830 when Chao Anu, the king of Vientiane himself, turned up in Chieng Kuang as a refugee from the Thais of Bangkok. Bangkok now demanded that the refugee ruler be handed over to them. To surrender the king to the Thais would antagonize Hué which had given its backing to Vientiane; not to surrender him would be to invite a Thai invasion. To Chao Noi, the king of Chieng Kuang, the latter possibility appeared to present the more immediate danger, so he handed Chao Anu over to the Thais. An enraged Hué summoned Chao Noi to the Vietnamese capital to give an explanation, a summons which no amount of costly gifts could postpone. In 1832 a Vietnamese force descended on Chieng Kuang, arrested the king and carried him back to Hué where he was publicly executed some weeks later.

Chieng Kuang now became part of the Vietnamese empire but in the 1850s the brutal policy of the Vietnamese who aimed at assimilating the hardy mountaineers to Vietnamese civilization provoked a rebellion during which the Vietnamese governor was killed.[18] Order was eventually restored and the eldest son of Chao Noi was reinstated as 'an imperial mandatory prince.' After this Chieng Kuang remained a tributary province of Hué but Vietnamese influence visibly weakened as they became more involved with the French threat. Bangkok took advantage of the vacuum which this created to try and restore its own influence. Matters were at this ambiguous stage when the French began to take an interest in the country.

The divided Lao: the downfall of Vientiane

Chieng Kuang fell under the yoke of Vietnam as a direct consequence of the conquest and annexation of Vientiane by the Thais of Bangkok in 1828. The loss of Vientiane's independence came after a century of careful policies pursued by Sai Ong Hué's successors. For the greater part of the eighteenth century, Vientiane sheltered behind a Burman alliance. When this policy failed with the decline of Burman power after 1760,[a] the rulers of Vientiane were forced to submit to the suzerainty of Bangkok.[19] However in 1805 there came to the throne Chao Anu (Anurath), 'a man of outstanding ability', whose ambition was to shake off his country's tutelage to the Thai rulers of the Menam basin. He matured his plans secretly and carefully, strengthening his own hold over the country and building up contacts with his neighbours. At the beginning of his reign he sent tokens of allegiance to the Emperor Gia Long in Vietnam.[20] In 1820 he attempted (unsuccessfully) to form an alliance with his arch-rivals in Luang Prabang against the Thais of Bangkok. Then in 1826 he struck. Putting his trust in rumours—which proved false—that the British were about to attack Thailand from the sea,[21] he launched a three-pronged invasion by land. His advance scouts reached as far as Saraburi, some 80 miles from Bangkok itself, before stiffening Thai resistance checked his drive. Then his forces were thrown back on Korat which not long after was retaken by a large army under the command of General Phaya Bo Din. Early next year a seven-day battle at Nong Bua Lamphu opened the way to the Thais for the crossing of the Mekong and the break-up of Chao Anu's forces. He fled to Hué where he was well

[a]See pp. 498-9.

received by the Emperor Minh Mang, but an attempt in 1828 to restore his king-dom with the aid of Vietnamese troops ended in complete failure.

After this second débâcle Chao Anu threw himself on the mercy of Chieng Kuang with the results that we have already seen. Vientiane's last king became a prisoner of state in 1831 and died four years later in captivity in Bangkok. Mean-while Vientiane was systematically despoiled and the inhabitants of whole districts were removed to repopulate areas in Thailand previously devastated by the Bur-mans.[22]

The divided Lao: the story of Luang Prabang

Luang Prabang was the strongest of the successor states to Lang Chang, the one most successful in maintaining its autonomy and the one which forms the nucleus of the state of Laos today.[23] During the eighteenth century after the partition, Luang Prabang's kings naturally followed the opposite course to that pursued by Vientiane which meant that they relied on the Thais in Ayuthia against the Bur-man threat. This policy resulted in a Burman conquest in 1753 and another incur-sion in the 1770s, but the policy reached its fulfilment with the triumph of Phaya Tak Sin in establishing Thai suzerainty over Vientiane in 1778. Phaya Tak Sin's victory, however, also meant that from this time onwards Luang Prabang fell un-der the shadow of Bangkok's power. When Vientiane was annexed in 1828 during the reign of King Mantha Thuruth, the king started sending tribute to Hué to counteract Bangkok's influence.[24] This led the Thais on his death in 1836 to re-affirm their overlordship by sending a high-ranking official to the ruler's cremation at Luang Prabang where he publicly proclaimed Bangkok's suzerain rights. The point was driven home still further by Bangkok delaying the installation of the new king for three years and then conducting the formal installation at Luang Pra-bang themselves. The rulers of Luang Prabang made no further attempts to escape Bangkok's overlordship; in fact, events in the second half of the century made them turn to Bangkok for protection.

---

[1]Meaning literally 'kingdom of the million elephants'.
[2]Meaning literally 'town of the statue'.
[3]Hence Un Hu Eun's other name or title of Sam Sen Thai or 'the lord of 300,000 Thais'.
[4]The 1376 census also reveals an adult male non-Thai population of some 400,000.
[5]These auxiliaries served as a supply corps. The army proper was divided into infantry, cavalry and elephant corps.
[6]The chao muong were selected by the king or by a council of notables from (usually) the mem-bers of the family of the previous incumbent.
[7]After a period of confusion and anarchy during which the Burmese placed two of Lang Chang's rulers on the throne, the abbots of leading monasteries in the kingdom secured the return of Nokeo Khoman, the son of a former king, from his Burmese captivity, to become the king. On his return to Luang Prabang in 1592 he formally declared Lang Chang's inde-pendence of Burma.
[8]Save for the period 1623–37 when the throne was contested between five claimants.
[9]Suligna-vongsa seized power in 1637 thereby putting to an end the prolonged civil war. During his reign Lang Chang was visited by Europeans for the first time. A Jesuit, Father Giovanni Maria Leria, tried for five years to run a mission at Luang Prabang (1642–7). In 1641, a Dutch merchant and traveller, Gerrit van Wuysthoff, was at the capital of Suligna-vongsa and has left behind a vivid description of an opulent court and a pleasure-loving people.
[10]When Suligna-vongsa died there was no living son to succeed him. His only son and heir had

been executed on his own orders for seducing the wife of a court official—testimony to the sternness of the ruler's make-up.

[11]Sai On Hué was a nephew of Suligna-vongsa, being the son of the late ruler's eldest brother, Sam P'u, who had been defeated in the contest for the throne in 1637. Sai Ong Hué had spent a life of exile in Vietnam.

[12]Namely Kit Sarat and Intha Som, who were minors at the time of their grandfather's death.

[13]Sip Song Pan Na or 'the 12,000 rice-fields'—a region on the Upper Mekong overlapping the modern boundaries of Laos, Burma and China. In the early days of Thai migration the districts in this region formed a semi-autonomous and loose confederation of their own.

[14]Tranh Ninh was the Vietnamese name for this Thai principality centred on the Plain of Jars. Chieng Kuang paid homage to the restored kingdom of Lang Chang in the 1590s. During the reign of Suligna-vongsa a feud between the two states developed over the refusal of Chieng Kuang's ruler to give his daughter in marriage to Suligna-vongsa. This resulted in Lang Chang's conquest of Chieng Kuang in 1652 which ultimately drove the principality into the arms of the Vietnamese.

[15]Chao Sri Sisamut, another scion of the royal house of Lang Chang, reigned till 1747. He maintained close relations with Thailand and Cambodia. Champassak occupied the territory of the ancient state of Chen La which had destroyed the empire of Fu Nan.

[16]This is not to take into account Champassak which was virtually always a vassal of Bangkok; it was permanently weakened by the feuds amongst its ruling class which provided frequent opportunities for Bangkok's intervention.

[17]In the 1750s, King Chom P'u refused to pay homage to Vientiane, thereby incurring first an invasion and then his own kidnapping in Vientiane itself. On both occasions the Vietnamese intervened and forced King Ong Long of Vientiane to back down.

[18]The Vietnamese went to the lengths of demanding conformity in architecture and dress; the rebellion was stirred up by agents from Thailand.

[19]Despite the eclipse of Burmese power in the Thai lands after the rise of Phaya Tak Sin, King Ong Bun (Siribunyasen) of Vientiane maintained his Burmese connections. In 1778, using some minor frontier disturbances as an excuse, Phaya Tak Sin sent General Chulalok to subdue both Champassak and Vientiane. After a four month siege Vientiane fell, the king fled east and the country was placed under Thai military government. In 1782 when the Chakri dynasty has been established at Bangkok, King Ong Bun made his submission and was allowed to return to Vientiane although his son was installed as king by the Thais. At the time of their invasion of 1778, the Thais seized and carried back to Bangkok the Prabang and the Emerald Buddha, two ancient symbols of Lang Chang. They remain in Bangkok to this day.

[20]Symbolic of this tightening grip was the foundation of the temple of Sisaket (Wat Sisaket) which became the place for receiving the homage of his feudatories. Chao Anu also took advantage of a Kha revolt in Champassak to intervene and then get Bangkok's acquiescence to one of his sons being appointed governor there. As for the tribute to Hué it was sent in 1804, in 1808 (after a reminder), 1811–12, 1814 and in 1817.

[21]These rumours arose in connexion with the impending embassy of Henry Burney and were probably originated by the Dutch. Although they had no foundation in fact, they were taken sufficiently seriously for Chao Anu to justify his advance on Bangkok as a measure to protect the Thai capital against the expected Anglo-Burmese attack.

[22]Especially the Korat Plateau.

[23]The present king of Laos is a member and direct descendant of the Luang Prabang line of rulers.

[24]Two missions were sent, the first in 1831 and the second in 1833. However, the Thais had the upper hand, keeping one of Mantha-thuruth's sons who had been nominated his successor a virtual hostage in Bangkok until his father's death.

THAILAND

If Sukhothai may be regarded as the cradle of Thai civilization, the Ayuthia monarchy saw the development and consolidation of Thai power. Its founder, Rama Thibodi,[1] another descendant of the princes of Chieng Sen, married the daughter of the Mon ruler of U Thong. When the Mon king died, Rama Thibodi succeeded him. A powerful ruler, Rama Thibodi soon forced the pious King of Sukhothai, Lu Thai,[2] to acknowledge his authority. Then, faced with a cholera outbreak at U

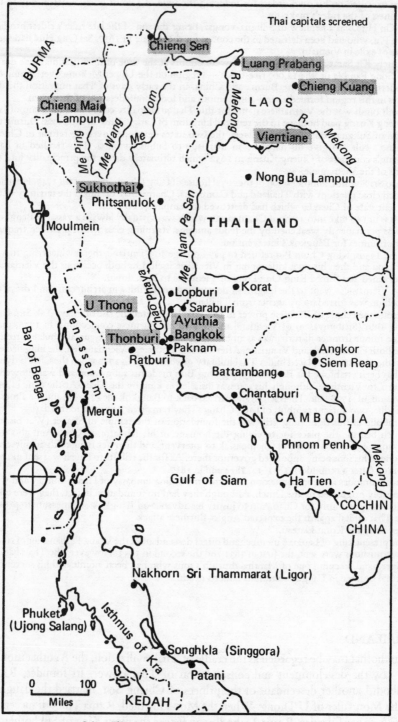

64. Thailand: historical background

Thong, Rama Thibodi evacuated his capital and moved 50 miles to the south-east to found a new city on an island in the Menam Chao Phaya at a place called Dvaravati Sri Ayuthia. There in 1350 Rama Thibodi had himself crowned king. Ayuthia was to remain the capital of Thailand for four centuries until its capture and sack by the Burmans in 1767. After that disaster the present dynasty of Thai kings made their headquarters further down the river at Bangkok which is the capital of Thailand today.

The rise of Ayuthia

Under Rama Thibodi and his successors the new kingdom expanded to control the whole of the Menam Chao Phaya basin and struggled to extend its influence over its neighbours at all four points of the compass. Sukhothai was reduced to vassaldom in 1378 and finally incorporated in the kingdom of Ayuthia sixty years later. Thai influence pressed down the shores of the Malay Peninsula and was only checked by Chinese-protected Malacca.[3] To the east, Angkor was captured in 1432, leading to its abandonment by the Cambodians who transferred the centre of their power further east.[a] A long see-saw struggle followed which finally resulted in Cambodia being overrun and placed under Ayuthia's tutelage in 1594. But until the nineteenth century Thai power was not able to expand beyond these limits. Their way to the north was barred by the powerful kingdom of Lang Chang.[b] To the east they were confronted by the rising power of Vietnam which with increasing success disputed their hegemony over Cambodia.[c] Most dangerous of all, in the west stood the Burmans who were to engage the Thai rulers in a life-and-death struggle which lasted for three centuries. A pawn in this latter struggle was the ancient Thai state of Chieng Mai whose feud with Ayuthia dated from the 1380s.[4]

Under the Ayuthia monarchy Thailand became the best organized state in Mainland South-East Asia. The conquest of Angkor in 1432 had very important consequences for the development of the Thai kingdom. The influence of the host of high Khmer officials borne away as captives from that city found itself reflected in the new concept of monarchy which now grew up in Ayuthia. The paternal traditions of Thai royalty, as evinced by Sukhothai and derived from a tribal past, where kingship was identified with prowess in battle, the preservation of old traditions, the rôle of supreme arbiter and the patronage of Buddhism, gave way to the new idea of absolutism. The Ayuthia king became 'The Lord of Life' with the attributes of a Brahamanic king-god. His actions now lay beyond challenge and he was regarded as supreme in all fields. He was no longer the arbiter between men and men but the intermediary between mankind and the gods. On him depended the success of the harvest and the fertility of the soil.

Under the new order grew up an elaborate bureaucracy, the foundations of which were laid down during the reign of the energetic monarch Parama Trailokanat (Trailok) in the middle of the fifteenth century. Trailok's intention was to centralize the administration and in this way reduce the feudal propensities of his provincial governors.[5] Government was divided into two sectors, civil and military.

[a]Refer p. 470.
[b]Refer p. 470.
[c]Refer pp. 470-1.

The civil administration was organized into five departments of which the most important was the ministry of the interior, headed by the chief minister himself. The ministry of local government was responsible for the city and province of Ayuthia; the ministry of finance was also in charge of foreign trade; the ministry of agriculture was responsible for cultivation and land tenure, and the ministry of the royal household dealt with palace affairs and royal justice. The military administration under an official called the Kalahom (Galah Hom) was also departmentalized.

With Trailok the social structure of the country was also re-defined. What were known as the *Sakdi Na* grades were regulated. These grades indicated the social status of a person and determined the amount of land that such a status was entitled to; it also determined the emoluments to be received and the punishments to which the holder was liable.[6] These official gradings symbolized a major social development under the Ayuthia monarchy. The close family and tribal ties of earlier days were over and had been replaced by a new class system which distinguished between an aristocracy of officials and the mass of the peasant and trading population. The distinctions, however, were not rigid, for the history of Ayuthia is full of instances of talented commoners rising to positions of rank and importance; nor was there great social distress because land was plentiful and the official limit on land holdings high. Thus the bulk of the people lived as self-sufficient farmers, grouped in small village communities over the great Menam Chao Phaya basin. They were liable to military service, forced labour and taxation[7] which on paper might appear oppressive but which in practice were light. The history of the Ayuthia monarchy is peppered with civil strife but the strife represented the feuds of the aristocracy. In startling contrast to most of its neighbours, peasant uprisings were virtually unknown.

The struggle with Burma and the foundation of the Chakri dynasty

The effective political and social organization of the Ayuthia monarchy goes a long way to explain why Thailand survived as an independent state. This independence was threatened on many occasions throughout its 500-year history. The most serious challenge prior to the nineteenth century came from the Burmans who between 1650 and 1800 launched no fewer than fourteen major invasions of the country.[8] Most of these were successfully beaten off but on two occasions Thailand was actually overrun and subjected to Burman control. The first Burman conquest under Bayinnaung[a] in 1569[9] brought to an end the dynasty established by Rama Thibodi. But fifteen years later the Thais found a new leader and champion in Narasuen, who not only drove the Burman invader out and restored Thailand's independence but also extended Ayuthia's suzerainty over Cambodia.[b] The second conquest came with the invasion of 1767, led by King Hsinbyushin.[c] This marked the end of the fourth dynasty of kings to rule from Ayuthia[10] and the end of Ayuthia as the capital of Thailand. This time the Thai recovery was led by a general of mixed Thai-Chinese ancestry called Phaya Tak Sin. He soon drove the Burmans out of Ayuthia but made his new capital at Thonburi, some forty miles downstream. However the Burman threat still remained and Thailand itself had fragmented between four would-be masters.[11]

[a]Refer p. 397.
[b]Refer p. 470.
[c]Refer p. 399, note 16.

It took Phaya Tak Sin fourteen years of hard fighting to restore the situation. By 1782 after ceaseless and brilliant campaigning he had completed the fundamental task of reuniting the country, but the strain had turned his mind and believing himself to be a new incarnation of the Buddha he went insane. This prompted an attempted palace revolution which was taken advantage of by Chulalok, one of Phaya Tak Sin's most successful generals, to break off a campaign in Cambodia to return to Thonburi and seize power.[12] The hapless Phaya Tak Sin was killed and Chulalok proclaimed himself king in his stead. Chulalok was the founder of the present Chakri dynasty, and he moved across the river from Thonburi to make his capital at Bangkok.

Soon after its establishment the Chakri dynasty faced another Burman invasion, this time led by Bodawpaya.[a] But the Burmans were heavily defeated in 1785 and two more attempts (one in 1787 and the other in 1797) failed equally as disastrously.[13] After this the Burman menace receded. Fighting and border raids continued, mostly centred on the isthmus of Kra. With the outbreak of the Anglo-Burmese War of 1824–6[b] and the subsequent British occupation of Tenasserim, it disappeared altogether.

In the meantime the new rulers of Bangkok sought to revive the traditions and power of the monarchy. Chulalok, now styled Rama I, set out very consciously to restore all that had been lost in the disaster of 1767 for with the Burman sack of Ayuthia the art, records and treasures of two centuries had been consigned to the flames. The new monarch's coronation ritual was based on careful research into the traditional rites which had been observed for generations at Ayuthia. The whole of the Buddhist canon, lost in those years, was painstakingly re-edited, and in 1805, the laws of the land were completely recodified.[14]

At the same time the new dynasty worked to restore Thailand's influence over her neighbours. Vientiane had already been brought under Thai control in 1778 by Phaya Tak Sin;[c] in 1828, as a result of Chao Anu's rebellion,[d] that state was completely annexed. As a consequence of this, Luang Prabang fell more securely into the Thai orbit. To the east, Cambodia was brought back under Thai suzerainty towards the end of the century,[e] but there and in the Laotian states Bangkok was to find itself increasingly checked by the power of newly reunited Vietnam.[f] By the middle of the nineteenth century Cambodia had fallen under the joint protection of the two powers,[g] while in Laos Luang Prabang was under Bangkok's influence and Chieng Kuang under that of Hué.[h] To the south, provoked by Burman intrigue, the Thais resumed their traditional pressure on the Malay states. Suspicious of Burman influence and dissatisfied by the attitude of its ruler, the governor of Ligor overran Kedah in 1821 and actively intrigued for the extension of Thai influence

[a]Refer p. 397.
[b]Refer pp. 405–6.
[c]Refer p. 493.
[d]Refer pp. 493–4.
[e]Refer p. 470.
[f]Refer pp. 470–1.
[g]Refer p. 472.
[h]Refer pp. 492–4.

into Perak and Selangor as well,[a] while pressure was also brought to bear on the north-east coast states of Kelantan and Trengganu.[b] However these moves in the south met with a sudden check. The check came from the newly-established influence of Britain from the island base of Penang.[c] In this way Thailand was brought face to face with the problem which was to pose the greatest threat to her independence in her whole history—the problem of European imperialism.

[a]Refer pp. 270–2.
[b]Refer pp. 292–4.
[c]Refer pp. 106–7.

[1]Reigned from 1350 till 1369. He was responsible for the promulgation of the first written code of laws in Thailand.
[2]Lu Thai was a son of Rama Kam Heng and the fourth of his line.
[3]Malacca originally paid homage to the Thais but secured the protection of China as a result of the visit of the Ming admirals, Yin Ch'ing in 1403 and Cheng Ho in 1409.
[4]The Thais of Ayuthia intervened unsuccessfully in a succession dispute in Chieng Mai in 1387. Intermittent warfare between the two states in which Lang Chang and Burma were also involved continued throughout the sixteenth century until Chieng Mai fell under the control of Phra Naret (Naresuen) in 1595. Chieng Mai subsequently was in Burman hands from 1615 for nearly a hundred years. Chieng Mai reasserted its independence in 1717 but was reconquered by Burma under Hsinbyushin in 1764. The principality was finally brought under the Thai monarchy in 1775 when Phaya Tak Sin drove out the Burman occupiers.
[5]Nevertheless, despite this centralization provincial officials retained much of their independent feudal traits, being virtually hereditary and as a result left with wide discretionary powers of their own.
[6]The amount of land a person was entitled to varied from 4,000 acres for a Chao Phaya to 10 acres for the lowest class.
[7]In theory a man was liable to do six months forced labour a year if so required, but there were many exceptions to this—members of the royal family, officials, monks, women, slaves and foreign minority groups. Those who were liable could often substitute payment in cash or kind.
[8]In 1548, 1564, 1569, 1584, 1586, 1593, 1618, 1661, 1760, 1764, 1767, 1785, 1787 and 1797.
[9]Bayinnaung had already taken Ayuthia in 1564 but his vassal regime had been overthrown.
[10]The second dynasty founded by Naresuen of Sukhotai was usurped by Prasat Thong in 1630; Prasat Thong's line was ended by Phra Phet Raja in 1688.
[11]The governor of Nakhorn Si Thammarat who styled himself King Mu Si Kah; the governor of Phitsanulok who proclaimed himself King Ruang; a Buddhist monk called Ruan who proclaimed the theocratic state of Fang, and Korat which was in the hands of a son of King Boromokot (Maha Tammaraja II, 1733–58). The Burmese were occupying Ratburi.
[12]Chao Phaya Chakri or Phaya Phuttha Yot Fa Chulalok had distinguished himself in the campaign to recapture Chieng Mai in 1775, commanded the invasion of Champassak and Vientiane in 1778 and was currently engaged in Cambodia. When in 1781 he heard news of the deposition of Phaya Tak Sin by a palace official called Phaya Sankhaburi, he ordered Phaya Suriya, the governor of Korat, to suppress the movement, and returned himself in triumph back to the capital the following year.
[13]One result of these reverses was to divert Burmese attention increasingly to the opportunities awaiting on their northern frontiers, leading in turn to their involvement with the British.
[14]It has been reckoned that barely one ninth of the royal records survived the sacking of Ayuthia in 1767.

THAILAND AND THE EUROPEANS

The Thais were not new to the threat from the West nor were the British the first European people with whom they had had dealings. In common with most other

South-East Asian states, the first contact the Thais made with the Europeans was with the Portuguese. In 1512 the Portuguese Duarte Fernandez arrived at Ayuthia during the reign of Rama Thibodi II to announce the capture of Malacca by Albuquerque.[a] Subsequently the Portuguese were permitted to trade at Ayuthia, Mergui, Tenasserim, Patani and Nakhorn Si Thammarat. Their numbers were never great enough to pose a serious threat. They introduced fire-arms, cannons, up-to-date fortifications and a small Eurasian population.

Dutch traders and French missionaries

The Portuguese were followed by the Dutch who obtained permission to open a factory at Patani in 1602 and another one at Ayuthia itself in 1608. From the very start the Dutch were much more powerfully represented. In 1617 they gained a virtual monopoly over the export of hides and in 1632 their influence increased greatly as the result of the help they gave King Prasat Thong in suppressing a Japanese uprising.[1] The Dutch conquest of Malacca in 1641[b] further enhanced Dutch influence and prestige and made them more truculent in their attitude towards the government of Ayuthia. Twice within the fifteen years that followed tension flared up between the Thai authorities and the Dutch merchants, culminating in the threat of a Dutch blockade of the Menam Chao Phaya.[2]

These developments convinced King Narai, who came to the throne in 1657, that he must seek to encourage other European traders as a counterbalance to the Dutch. In 1661 the English East India Company reopened their factory at Ayuthia[3] with the direct encouragement of the king. Three years later Narai equally enthusiastically welcomed the foundation of a Roman Catholic Seminary at his capital, run by the Apostolic Vicars, Lambert and Pallu, of the French *Société des Missions Etrangères*.[4] The missionaries in question won this concession in return for helping to strengthen the fortifications of Ayuthia against an anticipated Dutch assault. The Dutch reacted to this growth of rival European influence by blockading the mouths of the Chao Phaya later in the same year. Ayuthia was unable to stand up to this form of pressure and had to give way to Dutch demands for a treaty. This new agreement confirmed the existing Dutch monopoly over the trade in hides, established a virtual monopoly over the sea-borne trade between Ayuthia and China; and granted the Dutch several extra-territorial privileges into the bargain. But the Dutch success also increased Narai's determination to find some counter-weight to their influence and pressure.

The king's encouragement of the French missionaries led them to believe that there was a serious chance of converting him, and through him the people of Thailand, to Christianity. With this in mind, Mgr. Pallu, whilst on a return visit to Europe, persuaded officials in France that the attempt should be made, and in 1673 returned to Ayuthia with letters from Louis XIV of France[5] proposing the opening of diplomatic relations. Seven years later Narai sent an official embassy to France, asking for French aid. The embassy never reached its destination, being shipwrecked and totally lost off Madagascar. But in the same year (1680) the first French ship to appear in Thai waters anchored at Ayuthia to do trade.

[a]Refer p. 43.
[b]Refer p. 48.

The episode of Constantine Phaulkon

At this juncture a new figure stepped onto the stage. This was Constantine Phaul-kon, a Greek who had come to Thailand in the service of the English East India Company and who was to have a very great influence on the course of events that followed.[6] In 1680 he entered into the service of the Ayuthia government as an in-terpreter for the ministry of finance. He displayed such skill and ability that within two years he had been promoted to the post of Superintendent of Trade. Within a very short time after this Phaulkon was one of the most influential persons at the court of King Narai and held the ear of the king himself.

Phaulkon shrewdly identified his own advancement with the policy of opposing Dutch influence. At first he was inclined to advise Narai to look for English support, but the general ineffectiveness of the English establishment at the capital and a per-sonal quarrel between Phaulkon and the principal English factor[7] led him to res-pond to the much more earnest overtures of the French. By this time the *Société* in Ayuthia was actively campaigning for a French effort to convert Narai and the Thais to Christianity. Through Phaulkon's influence, Narai despatched a second embassy to France in 1684. This time the mission reached its destination. It was well received and the French missionaries who accompanied it won over the Versailles Court[8] to the practicability of the scheme for conversion. Further negotiations followed both in Thailand and in France during which Phaulkon secretly commit-ted himself to a scheme which involved the arrival of a large group of missionaries in the Thai kingdom. Once arrived, they would be appointed by Phaulkon to the governorships of provinces, towns and fortresses throughout the kingdom, while their safety would be assured by the presence of 'two good colonies' of French troops. Phaulkon also agreed that Singgora (Songkla) should be occupied by a French garrison on the pretext of deterring the Dutch.

In 1687 the scheme got under way. On 1 March a squadron of six French war-ships with 1,600 soldiers on board under the command of Marshal Desfarges, set sail from the French west coast port of Brest. Accompanying the expedition was the Jesuit priest, Father Tachard,[9] who had played a leading part in the previous nego-tiations. Six months later the expedition arrived in Thai waters but Desfarges an-nounced on disembarkation a significant change of plan. Instead of stationing a French garrison at Singgora which was considered to be too far away, French troops were to occupy Bangkok instead, while another detachment was to be sent to Mergui which the French wanted to hold because of its commercial value. Phaulkon, who by this time had been created a count of France and had been awarded the order of St. Michael, decided to give way to these moves.[10] He had little choice. The French had arrived and had orders to use force if necessary; the Thai court would not like it but it was too late to turn back. So from now on Phaulkon identified himself wholly with the French cause. Desfarges and his men occupied Bangkok which they strongly fortified. A hundred and twenty men un-der Dubruant went to Mergui. A treaty was negotiated granting extra-territorial privileges to all the subjects of Louis XIV in Thailand, permission to build trading posts wherever suitable and the cession of all islands within ten miles radius of Mer-gui. In order to keep out the Dutch Thailand had all but lost its sovereignty to France.

The downfall of Phaulkon and its aftermath

The inevitable Thai reaction was not long in coming. Phaulkon quarrelled with the French missionaries at Ayuthia,[11] thereby causing dissensions in the French camp. Then early in 1688 King Narai fell seriously ill at Lopburi. Phaya Phet Raja, master of the royal elephants at Ayuthia, took this opportunity to stage a *coup d' état* and have himself appointed Regent. His action received widespread support in the country. In May Phaulkon was arrested and two months later publicly executed. The French forces found themselves beleagured at Ayuthia and Mergui. Desfarges succeeded in negotiating for the evacuation of his men to Pondicherry in September, but had to leave behind him his two sons and the Roman Catholic bishops as hostages. Dubruant in Mergui had to fight his way out and only after suffering heavy losses managed to escape to his ships and sail for India. Desfarges made a foolish attempt to reassert French influence the following year by seizing Phuket[12] but this only resulted in a revival of the persecution of the Frenchmen left behind at Ayuthia, many of whom lost their lives. Father Tachard went to the capital to make peace while Desfarges withdrew once more back to India. The persecutions stopped and the missionaries were allowed to resume their work, but all Father Tachard's attempts to open fresh negotiations were without effect.

Today it seems unlikely that the French of Louis XIV would have been able to maintain their foothold in Thailand during the seventeenth century, even if their plans had been successful, when the difficulty and slowness of communications, the resources and the political circumstances of the time are borne in mind. But the narrowness of their escape was burned into the Thai consciousness. Phaya Phet Raja, now king,[13] continued the policy of keeping his relations with European states to an absolute minimum, and this policy was strictly adhered to by those who followed him for another one and a half centuries.[14]

The development of Anglo-Thai relations: the missions of Crawfurd and Burney

The establishment of a British colony on the Kedah island of Penang, four years after the foundation of the Chakri dynasty in Bangkok, signified the re-emergence of the European threat.[a] Within the next generation British power in the Malay Peninsula was enlarged by the occupation of Singapore and the acquisition of Malacca (1824).[b] In the same year that they acquired Malacca, the British also made war on Burma.[c] By the treaty of Yandabo which followed they not only annexed Arakan and Assam but also occupied Tenasserim, giving them a long common frontier with the Thais. In the 1850s the British extended their control over the whole of Lower Burma;[d] in the 1870s they brought the most important states of the Malay Peninsula under their rule[e] and in 1885 overran and annexed the rump of the Burman kingdom of Ava.[f] Meanwhile, with disconcerting suddenness the French advanced into Vietnam. Cochin-China was seized in the 1860s and Cam-

[a]Refer pp. 106–7.
[b]Refer pp. 119–21.
[c]Refer p. 405.
[d]Refer p. 410.
[e]Refer p. 279 and pp. 288–90.
[f]Refer pp. 419–20.

bodia fell under French influence at the same time.[a] Twenty years later, the remainder of Vietnam disappeared equally as swiftly beneath the French tricolour.[b]

Needless to say these developments were regarded with the greatest apprehension in Bangkok which was at the same time powerless to prevent them. Until the accession of Phaya Chom Klao (Rama IV or Mongkut) in 1851, the policy of the Chakri rulers was to keep the Europeans at a distance. Mongkut reversed this policy and he and his successors endeavoured to adapt the country to the new conditions created by the impact of the Western powers.

The renewal of Western pressures first came during the reign of Rama II (1809–24) whose talents were more literary than political.[15] These pressures were the result of the British occupation of Penang which brought them into close relations with Kedah, a state regarded by Bangkok as its vassal. The arrival of letters and presents from the British authorities on Penang in 1818 and 1819 indicated that they were anxious to reach an accomodation over the issues which were developing between the two powers.[16] But the court of Rama II remained profoundly suspicious of British intentions and in 1821 ordered the subjugation of Kedah[c] in order to secure the Thai grip on that state. The conquest of Kedah stirred the British to renewed efforts. In the same year the British governor sent a private Singapore trader called Morgan to Bangkok to report on conditions there and to try and allay Thai fears. In 1822 they followed this up by sending a full diplomatic mission led by the scholar administrator John Crawfurd,[17] in order to negotiate a treaty. The embassy had a poor reception and eventually withdrew without having achieved any of its purposes beyond that of learning much more about a country of which there was a profound ignorance in the West.[18] The negotiations with Crawfurd were in the hands of the Phra Klang (the Minister of Finance) who was at that time Prince Krom Chiat, shortly to become king as Rama III. The prince was a man of conservative disposition. Steeped in the traditions of the court and deeply religious, he tended to regard all foreigners with the utmost suspicion. Every effort was made to belittle the status of the visitors and Crawfurd's position was not strengthened by the fact that he did not come as the accredited representative of the King of England but merely as the envoy of the British governor-general in India. Like the Konbaung kings of Burma, the Thai court was not prepared to abase itself by negotiating at this level. Furthermore it was also apparent that the Phra Klang and his associates would stand to lose considerably should they make the concessions which the British sought.[19] The outcome was that Crawfurd had to go away contented with a vague promise that the (unknown) duties levied on British merchants would not be increased and that the Thai authorities would always assist these traders with their 'benevolent exertions'. With regard to Penang and the question of the Sultan of Kedah, the Thais would not make any concessions; not only did they refuse to restore the Malay ruler but they demanded that the allowance the British made to him for the cession of Penang be paid to their nominee instead!

When a second British embassy headed by an East India Company official called Henry Burney[20] arrived at the end of 1825 Krom Chiat was on the throne as Phaya

[a] Refer pp. 473–5.
[b] Refer p. 455.
[c] Refer p. 107.

Nang Klao (Rama III). The Thai attitude remained the same but circumstances had changed, and as a result the king was prepared to make guarded concessions. His main preoccupation was the British war with Burma that had begun the previous year. British troops were in Tenasserim and the nature of British intentions was far from clear. Furthermore the British authorities in Penang had put considerable pressure on the governor of Ligor and had prevented him from carrying out his plans for bringing Perak and Selangor under Thai control.[a] British intentions, in fact, turned out to be primarily commercial but the Thais were more anxious to reach a political settlement in the Malay Peninsula and avoid provoking Britain on the Tenasserim border than to make trading concessions in Bangkòk. The result was a treaty signed in 1826 whose most important clause confirmed Thailand's possession of Kedah[21] and guaranteed the independence and integrity of Perak and Selangor.[b] The commercial clauses were only a degree less vague than the undertakings given to Crawfurd three years previously.[22]

Thailand's new course under King Mongkut

This treaty was the only one of consequence made with a European power during the reign of Phra Nang Klao, and its implementation was in direct ratio to the amount of pressure applied by the British to see that it was carried out.[23] In 1833 the United States envoy, Roberts, succeeded in gaining an agreement concerning the status of U.S. citizens in the country but its effect was negligible. In 1850 both the British and the Americans made new attempts to secure more favourable trading arrangements but met with complete failure.[24]

However European elements were infiltrating into the country. Since the 1830s Western missionaries had again been permitted to carry on their activities and small but influential groups of European and American merchants and businessmen had established themselves in the Thai capital. By the middle of the century, when Phra Nang Klao died (1851), they represented a problem which could no longer be ignored. Phra Nang Klao's place was taken by his younger half-brother, Phra Chom Klao or Mongkut, who ascended the throne as Rama IV.

If Burma was unfortunate in her kings, and the emperors of Vietnam, purblind to change, led their country to disaster, Thailand was blessed with great good fortune in the characters of the two rulers who guided her fortunes for the next sixty years. King Mongkut was able to perceive the nature of the European danger and to change the outlook of his countrymen sufficiently to be able to meet it. His son, Chulalongkorn, laid the foundations of the modernization of the country which enabled Thailand to survive as an independent state into the twentieth century.

Mongkut should by right have succeeded to the throne on the death of his father, Rama II, in 1824. However, he was only twenty years of age at the time and was in a monastery[25] doing his period of noviciary. A powerful faction at Court decided to place his elder half-brother (who was not of a royal mother) on the throne in his stead, probably feeling that a more experienced hand was needed at the top. So Mongkut elected to continue his monastery life and in fact followed it till the day of his accession 27 years later. These years in the monastery were put to good effect.

[a]Refer pp. 271–2.
[b]Refer p. 108 and pp. 271–2.

He became a keen Buddhist scholar and won renown for his knowledge of the Pali scriptures.[26] His researches led him to the conviction that reforms were necessary in Buddhist organization, that the essential message of Buddhism was being obscured by meaningless rites and formulae. In 1837 he was appointed abbot of the Wat Pawaraniwesa in Bangkok and there launched a new sect known as the *Dharma-yutiakka*.[27] Meanwhile his quest for knowledge and the truth led him to seek the acquaintance of some of the European missionaries who were the standard-bearers of their religion at Bangkok. His first contact was with the French missionary bishop, Pallégoix, from whom he learned Latin, mathematics and astronomy. Later he learned English from some American missionaries[28] and acquired a knowledge of geography, physics and chemistry. It was this unique liberal educational background which enabled Mongkut to appreciate the problems facing Thailand when he came to the throne.

The Bowring Treaty of 1855

When Mongkut acceded to the throne in 1851,[29] European imperialism was making great strides in Asia. Apart from the developments already noted in South-East Asia itself, the European impact was being felt in neighbouring regions. India now lay firmly under British control[30] and even the great and ancient civilization of China had already suffered one humiliating defeat at the hands of the West and was on the eve of receiving another.[31]

Mongkut already knew that it was futile to resist Western pressure so he decided to yield where it was necessary and to gain as much time as possible to learn western techniques and to adapt his country to the new world lapping at its doorstep. Therefore when early in his reign he received requests from the British for a reopening of the negotiations on trade which had foundered in 1850, he readily responded and personally paved the way for a new British mission by entering into direct correspondence with the British authorities concerned. When the mission, headed by Sir John Bowring,[32] arrived in Bangkok in March 1855, it encountered a very changed atmosphere. It was received, for want of precedent, by the protocol which governed Louis XIV's first embassy in 1685, and within one month of discussions starting the treaty was ready for signing.

The British obtained virtually all that they came for. The treaty, which consisted of twelve articles, established a system of fixed tariffs on imports and exports,[33] permitted British residents at Bangkok to rent or buy land near the capital, exempted them from arbitrary taxes and tolls, and provided for the posting of a British consul at Bangkok (as soon as British trade reached ten ships a year) with powers of civil and criminal jurisdiction over all British subjects in the country. A supplementary convention was signed with Britain the following year to cover points omitted in the original negotiations, including *inter alia* the organization of a customs service.[34] It has been pointed out that the British obtained these pleasing results partly through cajolery and the employment of veiled threats,[35] but the fact remains that from the outset Mongkut had determined on a concessionary policy towards the European powers, and that the British embassy provided him with his first opportunity to put it into practice. Indeed, even before the arrival of the Bowring mission, the king had started on a tariff reform policy of his own.

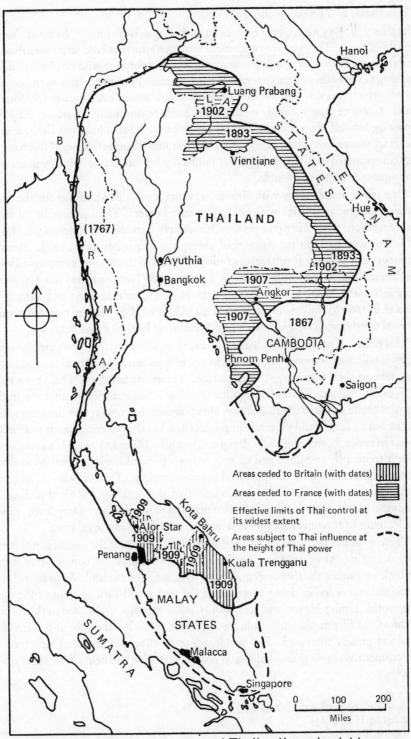

65. The extent of Thai power and Thailand's territorial losses to
the British and French during the nineteenth century

The evolution of Thai policy after 1855

The treaty of 1855 has rightly been described as 'epoch-making'.[a] As far as the internal politics of Thailand are concerned, it marked the first bold step towards modernization, the first success of the small nucleus of reformers who now surrounded the king at the helm of state.[36] It represented a serious drop in revenue to the government which had surrendered its monopolies, and was an even greater loss for the great officers of state through whose hands trade traditionally passed. As Sir John Bowring himself observed, the Treaty 'involved a total revolution in all the financial machinery of the government'.[b] Great economic changes followed[c] but Mongkut compensated the Thai ruling class politically by interfering with their ancient prerogatives as little as possible.

One result of the treaty with Britain was that it provided a model for the concluding of similar treaties with other Western powers. The opening up of such treaty relations with other powers was deliberately pursued by Mongkut who hoped in this way to avert the dangers of giving too much advantage to the British. Consequently a spate of such treaties followed. In 1856 treaties were concluded with the United States and with France.[37] Treaties with Denmark and the Hanseatic League[38] came in 1858, with Portugal in 1859, Holland in 1860 and Prussia in 1862.[39] In 1868 Mongkut commissioned his old friend, Bowring, to negotiate commercial treaties with Belgium, Italy and Sweden on behalf of Thailand.

This policy of opening the doors of Thailand to Western trade was complemented by a policy of inviting Westerners to come in as teachers, instructors and advisers, who in their turn played an important rôle in educating the Thai aristocracy in Western ways and attitudes. In addition king Mongkut tried to alter the traditional attitude towards the monarchy. He abolished the custom that the king's face might not be seen[40] and whereas his predecessor left the palace precincts only once a year in order to visit one of the Bangkok temples, Mongkut made it a practice to appear frequently in public and to visit various parts of his kingdom. As another step in this direction, the king revived the ancient right of direct petition. In addition, Mongkut stimulated the development of shipbuilding and the building of roads and canals. He introduced the first printing press into the country, encouraged the learning of foreign languages and in 1860 established the royal mint.

These steps did not amount to a radical westernization of the country, nor were they meant to. At heart, Mongkut himself was probably too conservative in his outlook to initiate the thoroughgoing westernization of the land. What he did aim to do and succeeded in doing was to alter the traditional Thai concept of the outside world. Under his son and successor, Chulalongkorn, who came to the throne at the age of fifteen, the same policies were continued, but the pace of modernization was greatly increased. The whole administrative and financial structure of government was reorganized along Western lines with the help of Western advisers.[d]

[a]Hall, *History of South-East Asia*, p. 633.
[b]Quoted by Hall, p. 633.
[c]See Book II.
[d]See Book III.

Thailand and the problem of the British in Malaya

Mongkut and Chulalongkorn dealt and effectively coped with the problem of handling the Europeans who came to live and trade within the boundaries of the kingdom proper during the course of their reigns but they were still confronted by the problems raised by Western pressure on Thailand's dependencies.

As we have already seen, the first crisis in this respect was raised by the British occupation of Penang which endangered the Thai position in the northern Malay states. Burney's Treaty of 1826 together with certain subsidiary arrangements in the Malay Peninsula itself[a] helped to solve that problem, at least as far as the west coast Malay states were concerned. But in the 1860s a new crisis developed over Trengganu and Pahang where growing British commercial interest clashed with Bangkok's desire to strengthen and extend its influence. Bangkok decided to take advantage of civil war in Pahang and the presence of Mahmud, the ex-Sultan of Lingga and pretender to the throne of Johore, in the Thai capital to bring the recalcitrant Sultan of Trengganu to heel and promote their influence in Pahang.[b] This provoked a strong reaction in Singapore where the Chambers of Commerce were concerned for their fast developing trade with these two states. Ultimately the British governor, Cavenagh, sent a couple of gunboats to Kuala Trengganu to deter the Thai presence there. The Trengganu capital was bombarded without achieving any obvious immediate effects but Mongkut heeded the warning and withdrew all his support from the Malay pretenders.

After this incident there were no further conflicts or incidents springing from Anglo-Thai relations in the Malay Peninsula for the rest of the century. Within the first decade of the twentieth century negotiations took place between Britain and Thailand for the transfer of suzerainty over the four northern Malay states from Bangkok to London. This was finalized with the signing of the Anglo-Thai Treaty of 1909 at Bangkok.[41c]

The Cambodian problem

However, the most serious threat did not come from the British to the south or west, but from the French who in the same decade as the bombardment of Kuala Trengganu were laying the foundations of their Indo-Chinese Empire.[d] As soon as the French had established themselves in the Mekong Delta, they set out to challenge the Thai position in Cambodia.[e] A visit to the Cambodian capital in 1862 by the French governor of Cochin-China for that purpose was followed by the appointment of a French Resident and by the signing of a treaty which placed the country under French protection the next year. Mongkut, with British encouragement, protested against these proceedings and hastened to make use of the gap between the signing of the treaty and its ratification to make a secret treaty of his own with the Cambodians. Under this secret agreement King Norodom of Cambodia acknowledged Bangkok's responsibility for the defence and internal security of Cambodia and allowed himself to be regarded as the viceroy of the Thai king.

[a]Refer pp. 108 and 270-2.
[b]Refer pp. 294-5.
[c]See pp. 519-20.
[d]Refer pp. 448-51.
[e]Refer pp. 475-6.

Next Mongkut, who had the advantage of possessing the Cambodian royal regalia[a] announced his intention of going to Udong to install his viceroy in person. It
was now the French turn to protest and so Mongkut modified his position by inviting Norodom to hold his coronation in Bangkok instead. But when in March
1864 the Cambodian king started out on his journey to the Thai capital, he was
forcibly detained by a detachment of French troops. The following month the
treaty of protection arrived having been duly ratified in Paris, and Norodom had
little choice but to follow suit. Meanwhile negotiations went on in Bangkok and in
July 1864 Mongkut accepted a compromise whereby he agreed to hand over the
royal regalia on condition that both the Thai and French representatives should
have a part in the coronation ceremony. In the event, however, the French Resident in Cambodia refused to permit the Thai representatives to act their rôle at the
coronation, and discomfited they left for home the following day, after having
reiterated Bangkok's claims to suzerainty.

The next development was the arrival in Bangkok of a new French consul, Gabriel Aubaret,[42] who was also the French *charge d'affaires* at the court of Hué. Shortly after his arrival he learned of Mongkut's secret treaty with Norodom (through a
report in a Singapore newspaper), and immediately demanded redress. Mongkut
agreed to reopen negotiations over the status of Cambodia. In April 1865 a draft
treaty was agreed upon between the French consul and the Thai government, by
which, in return for the annulment of the secret agreement of 1863 and Thai recognition of the French protectorate over Cambodia, the French acknowledged the
right of Cambodia to pay tribute to Thailand if she so desired and agreed to the
Cambodian royal princes being educated in Bangkok. Nevertheless this treaty,
which bore a striking resemblance to the Kedah clauses in Burney's Treaty[b] of 1826,
was considered by the Paris government to be too favourable to the Thais when it
arrived in France for ratification. Accordingly Aubaret was instructed to hold further negotiations, which were begun in 1866. An attempt by Mongkut in the inte-
rim to hold a conference with Norodom at Kampot never materialized.[43]

The new negotiations over Cambodia started in June and had reached a deadlock
by December. This was to a large extent due to the crudeness of Aubaret, about
whose manners and methods the Thai government formally protested to the French
governor in Saigon. Furthermore, realizing that he was going to be forced to make
more far-reaching concessions, Mongkut decided that less loss of face would be
involved by making them in direct negotiation with the French government in
Europe rather than with the French consul in Bangkok. So in January 1867 the
Thais announced that they were going to transfer the negotiations to France. In his
instructions to his envoys, Mongkut told them that they should be prepared 'to make
sacrifices, so as to bring the whole unpleasant business to a close'. The king added
that he did not want to rely on British support if this could be avoided[44] but he was
insistent that Aubaret should be removed from his post at Bangkok. 'If you fail to
get Aubaret removed, then you may cross over to Britain and ask for whatever
assistance that you may think fit....'[c]

[a]Refer p. 476.
[b]Refer p. 108 and p. 505.
[c]Quoted by A.L. Moffat, *Mongkut, King of Siam*, p. 124.

The Paris negotiations produced a new treaty which was signed in July 1867. By its terms Thailand renounced her secret agreement of 1863 with Cambodia and recognized the French protectorate. She also waived all her rights to overlordship over the state and agreed to the Mekong and its tributaries being opened up to French vessels. France, on behalf of Cambodia, gave up in return all claims to the provinces of Battambang, Siemreap and Sisophon. King Norodom, who protested against this treaty in vain, was at no time consulted during these negotiations.

Thus, in the closing years of his reign, King Mongkut was forced to accept a reduction in the area of Thai influence. He did so philosophically. 'Since we are now being constantly abused by the French because we will not allow ourselves to be placed under their domination like the Cambodians, it is for us to decide what to do; whether to swim up-river to make friends with the crocodile or to swim out to sea and hang on to the whale.... It is sufficient for us to keep ourselves within our house and home; it may be necessary for us to forego some of our former power and influence'.[a] The truth and realism of these remarks were borne out during the long reign of Mongkut's successor, Chulalongkorn (Rama V), who in his turn had to make important concessions to the Western powers in order to preserve the integrity of his homeland.

The origins of the Laotian problem

The French occupation of the Mekong Delta and the establishment of their protectorate over Cambodia obviously threatened Thailand's position in the Laotian states. France had based her claims to suzerainty over Cambodia on the basis that she had acquired them from Vietnam. Similar arguments could lead to the establishment of French influence over Chieng Kuang,[b] already part of the Vietnamese empire, and over Luang Prabang[c] which had sent tokens of submission to Hué in the 1830s.

Signs of French interest in the Mekong were not long in forthcoming. In 1866 Tiantha Khoman, the king of Luang Prabang, found himself playing host to a party of ten Frenchmen headed by Doudart de Lagrée and Francis Garnier,[d] who were on their way upstream to explore its possibilities as a trade route to China.[45] The King received them well but nothing came of the expedition. It passed into Yunnan and returned down the Yangtse Kiang, persuaded that the rapids of the Middle Mekong made that river impracticable as a trade route.[46] Consequently French eyes turned onto the possibilities of the Red river route which proved to be far more promising,[e] and the Laotian states were left undisturbed by French designs for another twenty years.

The French seizure of Tongking and the creation of a protectorate over Hué itself in 1883 brought the whole problem of the future of the Lao states to the fore once again, and Thailand reacted swiftly to forestall a possible French advance. The Thais had a ready-made pretext for intervention. In the middle of the 1860s bands of refugees, army deserters and plain bandits, fleeing from the upheavals brought

[a]Quoted by Moffat, p. 124.
[b]Refer p. 493.
[c]Refer p. 494.
[d]See p. 538.
[e]Refer p. 451 and see p. 538.

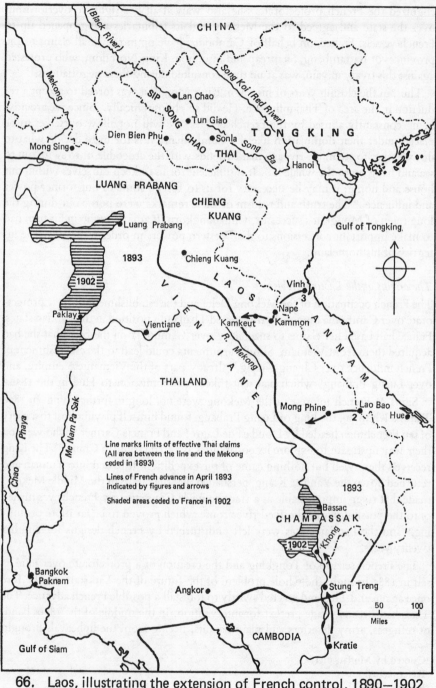

Line marks limits of effective Thai claims
(All area between the line and the Mekong
ceded in 1893)

Lines of French advance in April 1893
indicated by figures and arrows

Shaded areas ceded to France in 1902

66. Laos, illustrating the extension of French control, 1890–1902

about in south China by the Panthay and Taiping rebellions started moving into Tongking.[a] These infiltrators were divided amongst themselves and were known to the French who had dealings with them by the colour of the flags they used for their banners. To the Thais they were simply known as the Ho, which is the Thai term for Chinese. In 1871 one group of these marauders, the Red Flags, who numbered around 2,000, were driven from the Black River valley by their rivals, the Yellow Flags, and took refuge in Chieng Kuang. There the combined forces of Hué, Luang Prabang and Chieng Kuang itself failed to crush the invaders who proceeded to capture both Chieng Kam and Chieng Kuang. The following year, Un Kham, newly installed by Bangkok as the king of Luang Prabang[47] appealed for Thai help. A Thai army was despatched, and joining with local forces succeeded in driving the Ho back to their stronghold at Tung Chieng Kam. Having secured a vague recognition of their suzerainty the Thai troops then withdrew. But the problem of the Ho was unresolved, and after the Thai departure there was increasing disorder in the Twelve Thai principalities (cantons) or Sip-song Chao Thai, around Dien Bien Phu, which Luang Prabang was quite unable to control.[48]

The establishment of the French protectorate over Vietnam spurred Bangkok on to new efforts. In 1883 Chulalongkorn sent a mixed force of Laos and Thais to storm the Ho strongholds but it was badly defeated. In 1885 a second expedition under the command of general Chao Mun Vai Voronat was sent to occupy all the country north-east of Luang Prabang up to the basin of the Black river (the Plain of Jars). On his arrival at Luang Prabang Vai Voronat appointed two Thai commissioners to superintend the administration of the kingdom alongside the aging King Un Kham. This action led the French to assert formally Hué's claims to overlordship in the area.[49] A warning note was issued to Bangkok to which the Thais replied that they had sent their forces to defend the region against the Ho. France then proposed the setting up of a joint commission to examine the boundaries of Luang Prabang and discussions were opened which resulted in a provisional agreement between the two countries signed in May 1886. This agreement sanctioned the setting up of the boundary commission and permitted the creation of a French vice-consulate at Luang Prabang itself.

Auguste Pavie and the spread of French influence in the Lao states

This seemingly innocuous agreement was to pave the way for the loss of Bangkok's influence over the Lao states if for no other reason than for the personality and character of the man appointed to become the first French vice-consul at Luang Prabang. His name was Auguste Pavie.[50] His instructions were quite simple. He was to explore the routes connecting the Upper Mekong with Tongking and to hold himself in readiness to join the proposed boundary commission. But Pavie had already made up his own mind that the land east of the Mekong should fall to France.

The Thais were not at all happy about the presence of a Frenchman in Luang Prabang, least of all of this particular Frenchman who had already won such a reputation for winning local hearts.[51] Bangkok's first concern was to have the situation in

[a]Refer p. 451.

the Lao states firmly under control before the vice-consul arrived, so that he should have no chance of fishing in troubled waters. For this reason Pavie was held up in Bangkok for six months before he could get his permit to travel to the north, while Vai Voronat tried desperately but unsuccessfully to crush the Ho stronghold at Tung Chieng Kam. Finally Pavie could be delayed no longer and in December 1886 he left Bangkok for Luang Prabang, accompanied by eight Cambodian bodyguards and two servants. He arrived at Luang Prabang in February where he received a frigidly polite reception from the Thai commissioners there. In the same month Vai Voronat declared the region to be pacified and returned to Bangkok a few weeks later with the Maha Upahat, two of Un Kham's sons and a number of hostages from the Twelve Cantons. The Thai officials left behind at Luang Prabang successfully prevented Pavie from establishing contact with the Court and managed to cut down his dealings with the local public to a minimum. Pavie thereupon proceeded to carry out his commission to explore the routes eastward into Tongking.

With the departure of Vai Voronat for Bangkok and Pavie for the east, Deo Van Tri, a leader from the disaffected Twelve Cantons, rose up in rebellion[52] and threatened the town of Luang Prabang itself. Pavie, on Thai advice, abandoned his expedition and returned to the capital. In June Luang Prabang was sacked by Deo Van Tri. The Thai commissioners fled the town in good time, leaving behind the old king who was only able to make good his escape to Pak Lay because of the aid given by Pavie himself. Pavie seized this opportune moment to point out the deficiencies of Bangkok's powers of protection and to persuade the ruler of Luang Prabang that he would be far more secure under France. King Un Kham was won over and agreed to accept a French protectorate over his country.

The Thais had now completely lost the initiative. They had proved themselves unable to control the Ho or to protect the inhabitants of Luang Prabang while the wily Pavie had won over the king himself. Chulalongkorn countered by inviting King Un Kham to Bangkok where he was received with great honour. In 1888 Vai Voronat, who had by now been elevated to the rank of Phaya Surrisak, reoccupied the country and in January 1889, in the presence of the Thai commander-in-chief and Pavie, the king was reinstated in his ancient capital.

These gestures, however, could not disguise the fact that the real pacification of northern Laos was brought about not by the Thais but by the French, in fact largely by Pavie himself singlehanded. As a result of the 1887 debacle, Bangkok took steps to form the boundary commission which was to consist of three Thais and three Frenchmen. Pavie was appointed as one of the members. Early in 1888 he went to the Twelve Cantons and at Tun Giao met the commander of the French forces in Upper Tongking, Colonel Pernot, who was engaged in pacifying the area.[a] The two men agreed that the Twelve Cantons should be annexed to the French empire[53] and Pavie then set out to bring about their submission by persuasive rather than violent means. At the same time French military outposts were set up at Lai Chau, Son La and Van Bu. In March Pavie returned to Luang Prabang to announce to the Phaya Surrisak the progress that he had made and the French intention to annex the Twelve Cantons, on the grounds of their former allegiance to Vietnam. After a visit to Hanoi where Pavie was instructed to organize the administration of

[a]Refer p. 457.

the territories about to be annexed and to investigate affairs in the region of the Middle Mekong, he returned to the Twelve Cantons and received the submission of the Black Flags there in October. Two months later at a ceremony held near Dien Bien Phu, Phaya Surrisak on behalf of the Thai government formally surrendered the Twelve Cantons to France.

After witnessing the reinstatement of King Un Kham at Luang Prabang in January 1889, the next month Pavie started out for the Middle Mekong region of Kam Keut and Kam Mon which after the destruction of Vientiane in 1828[a] had been annexed by Vietnam. Here the Thais were making another attempt to forestall the French advance to the Mekong by infiltrating the area themselves. Pavie confined himself to warning the local Thai officials that they were trespassing on a French protectorate and to advising them not to interfere with the newly-established French military outpost at Napé. In June, feeling that nothing more could be achieved without support from Paris, Pavie went back on leave to France.

Thus, by the turn of 1890 Thailand had been forced to make certain concessions in the Lao states. Chieng Kuang was indisputably under French protection and so now were the Twelve Cantons of northern Luang Prabang. The position of Luang Prabang itself was still ambiguous. In a moment of stress King Un Kham had indicated his willingness to be placed under French protection but Bangkok still continued to dominate his capital and his court. And further south in the provinces of the Middle Mekong, Bangkok was determined to dispute the French claims to suzerainty.

The growth of crisis on the Middle Mekong

Nevertheless within the next three years Thailand was forced to give way completely. After a serious confrontation which took place at Pak Nam, guarding the approaches to Bangkok, in 1893 Chulalongkorn was obliged to sign a treaty with France by which Thailand surrendered all her claims to the territory on the east bank of the Mekong.

The originator of these developments was still to a remarkable degree one man, Auguste Pavie. When on leave in Europe during the second half of 1889, Pavie spent his time organizing a large-scale scientific expedition to study the Lao states. It was aimed not only to explore the geography of the region but 'to investigate land and river routes, create trading depots, examine commercial procedures, and produce a definitive statement on the nature and products of the Mekong basin'. In other words Pavie was intent on making out a case for the annexation of the Mekong provinces by France.

The mission arrived in Indo-China and got down to work at the beginning of 1890. It divided into groups, each group being responsible for investigating a particular part of the country. One group went to Chieng Kuang, another to Kam Mon, and a third to Stung Treng. Pavie himself worked north-east of Luang Prabang and added to France's political influence in this region by receiving the submission of Deo Van Tri[54] in April of the same year. None of this activity was viewed with favour in Bangkok and when Pavie appeared in the Thai capital in October in an attempt to open fresh negotiations on the subject of the Lao states the government

[a]Refer pp. 493–4.

politely but firmly rejected all his overtures. Predictably the reports of the groups working in the Middle Mekong revealed signs of growing Thai infiltration and Pavie reacted by urging the French governor in Saigon to erect frontier posts to check 'the Siamese invasion'. Then in January 1891 he disappeared again in the direction of the Sip Song Pan Na and the Chinese frontier.[55]

By this time Chulalongkorn's government was beginning to lose its patience. On the haziest of pretexts and with the most shadowy of claims Pavie and his followers were busy laying the foundations of French influence in the Lao states. Thailand started to call up its reserves; stocks of weapons were built up and new forts and strongpoints erected along the Mekong. Pavie, who all along was a convinced imperialist, sensed on hearing reports of these moves that the showdown was coming and abandoning his activities in northern Laos, returned to make his way back to Paris. When in Bangkok en route, the Thai government this time offered to discuss matters but now Pavie himself refused and continued on his journey back to Europe intent on getting full backing for his policies. He carried with him the whole-hearted support of the French authorities in Tongking who during the previous six months had also come to the conclusion that the moment was ripe for a bold forward policy.

The announcement made in Paris in February 1892 that Pavie was to be the holder of the new post of Resident-minister at Bangkok[56] indicated that the French government had been completely won over to his ideas. It also hardened the resolve of Chulalongkorn and his ministers to resist the French pressure that was clearly going to be put upon them. Pavie arrived at Bangkok in June. Within a month he had organized semi-political and semi-commercial posts at Udene, Bassac and Stung Treng. All efforts at negotiation between the Thai and the French broke down and Bangkok intensified its occupation of the provinces of the Middle Mekong.

The Pak Nam incident, 1893

The situation was now getting out of control, as Pavie, no doubt, intended that it should. In September 1892 a number of incidents started to take place in the disputed areas which involved Thai and French officials. Two French agents at Udene were expelled by the Thai authorities without any reason being given. Massie, the French agent at Luang Prabang, abandoned the place in despair at Thai obstruction and died on the way in circumstances which at first aroused suspicion. And in the Kam Mon district, Grosgurin, a French police inspector, was killed in a skirmish with some Thais whilst withdrawing from an outpost in the Middle Mekong.[57] These incidents provided the French with the pretexts they needed for taking unilateral action to annex the eastern bank of the Mekong. While public opinion was being deliberately inflamed in France itself, the Paris government instructed its governor-general in Indo-China in February 1893 to take 'energetic action on the Siamese frontier' if immediate reparations were not obtained from Bangkok. A month later Pavie was formally instructed by Paris to lay claim to all territory lying on the eastern bank of the Mekong.

These claims were rejected outright by Prince Dewawongsa[58] who nevertheless offered to negotiate. Pavie insisted on the French claims and took steps to see that they were secured. Early in April three French columns advanced from Vietnam into the Lao states. The southern column under Captain Thoreaux moved from Kratié and seized Stung Treng and shortly after the island of Khong. Another column advanced in the centre from Lao Bao onto Muong Phiné while to the north the third column advanced from Vinh into the Kam Mon region. This invasion inevitably provoked a whole rash of new incidents, of which the most serious took placed at Khong where the force under Captain Thoreaux was attacked, some of his Vietnamese soldiers killed and he himself made prisoner. At first Bangkok denied responsibility for the incident, blaming it onto unruly tribesmen; later, however, the government maintained that the attack was justified. All the same under British pressure, the Thais then gave way to Pavie's demand that Thoreaux be handed over. The French continued to apply the pressure. At the beginning of July, Pavie informed the Thai government that two French warships would be arriving on 13 July at Pak Nam which guarded the approaches to Bangkok and requested that pilots be furnished to conduct them upstream to the capital. The Thais pointed out that no foreign warships could proceed beyond Pak Nam to the capital without the express consent of their government, as was laid down in the Franco-Thai Treaty of 1856.[a] Pavie replied that one of the warships would proceed up to Bangkok, whether there was opposition or not. The Thais prepared to block the river.

Chulalongkorn now found himself in the very position of direct confrontation with a European power that he and his father before him had consistently sought to avoid. Apart from abject surrender, only two courses seemed to be open—offer to negotiate once more or get the support of another power. Prince Dewawongsa tried both. He declared himself prepared ready to negotiate at any time, and he appealed to Britain for help.

At this juncture British policy was to avoid a showdown with France over Thailand by persuading the Thais to give way to French demands. Nevertheless Britain issued a warning to the French government that she should be kept fully informed of all developments, in particular of naval movements. The French assured Britain and Prince Dewawongsa that their boats would not proceed above the bar at Pak Nam. However, when the two French gunboats did make their appearance off Pak Nam, on 13 July as scheduled, they at once attempted to make their way upstream.[59] The Thai gunners in the Pak Nam forts opened fire and an engagement in which both sides suffered casualties, ensued for the next twenty minutes. Then, having forced the bar, the two vessels sailed up to Bangkok.

The Franco-Thai Agreement of 1893

Prince Dewawongsa rose to this occasion by congratulating the captains of the two ships concerned on their hazardous exploit and also agreed on the spot to Paris's demand that all Thai troops be withdrawn from the eastern bank of the Mekong. In spite of this the French were not satisfied that they had got their way and on 20 July Pavie was instructed to hand over an ultimatum which contained three points. Firstly, all territories claimed by Thailand on the eastern bank of the Mekong, including Luang Prabang, were to be ceded to France. Secondly, Thailand was to pay an indemnity of 3 million francs for the damage and casualties sustained by the French at Pak Nam. Thirdly, the officers responsible for ordering the Pak Nam forts

[a]Refer p. 508.

to open fire and those responsible for the death of Grosgurin were to be punished.

The Thai government accepted the second and third stipulations but wished to compromise on the first. Pavie refused to bargain and fixed 26 July as the date for the expiry of the ultimatum. On the 25th, no reply having been received, the French started to blockade the Menam Chao Phaya; the blockade lasted till 3 August. Meanwhile on the 27th, Chulalongkorn accepted all the terms of the ultimatum unconditionally.

But this was still not the end of the matter. The French now presented some additional demands, including the French occupation of Chantabun until the Thais had completed the evacuation of the east bank, the Thai withdrawal of her forces for twenty-five kilometres from the west bank of the Mekong, and the evacuation by the Thais of the provinces of Battambang and Siemreap. These fresh terms delayed the treaty negotiations but finally, and once again reluctantly following British advice, Chulalongkorn gave way. The treaty was signed on 3 October.[60]

The Mong Sing Incident and the Anglo-French Agreement of 1896

Understandably enough the government of Chulalongkorn was bitterly critical of the British failure to lend more positive support at the moment of crisis, but ultimately it was the British concern that Thailand should not fall into French hands[61] and that the two rival colonial empires should not share a common frontier which preserved and guaranteed Thai independence. As it was, the British only acquiesced in the Franco-Thai Agreement of 1893 on the understanding that the independence of Thailand itself would be respected and that a buffer state would be set up to separate the British-ruled Shan states in Burma from the French-protected Lao states. After 1893 British efforts were directed to the formation of this buffer state and very soon a Buffer State Commission consisting of J.G. Scott on the British side[62] and Pavie on the French was formed.

The two commissioners agreed to meet at Mong Sing, the capital of the Shan state of Keng Cheng, which was in the heart of the area designated for the proposed buffer state between the two empires. However, Keng Cheng itself was the subject of controversy. The British recognized it as one of the Shan states whose allegiance they acquired when they conquered Upper Burma in 1886.[a] The French claimed it formed part of Laos by virtue of being on the eastern bank of the Mekong, as provided for by the Franco-Thai Agreement of 1893. The *myosa*[63] of Keng Cheng was in a quandary as to what to do or as to whose authority to acknowledge when his visitors arrived. Doubtless the diplomatic thing to have done would have been to raise the flags of both parties but in actuality he hoisted the French and then wisely, as Scott remarked later, fled. Of the two commissioners, Scott was the first to arrive at Mong Sing and therefore to find the French flag flying. He hauled it down and put the Union Jack up in its place. Pavie arrived a week later to find Scott already installed and the British flag flying. The meeting was a deadlock from the very start.

This little incident which marked the end of the idea of a Buffer State swelled quickly into international proportions and brought Britain and France, in that prickly era of European nationalism, to the brink of war with one another. In the

[a] Refer p. 420.

end, however, it resulted in a treaty between the two powers which became something like a charter for Thailand's independence. Signed in 1896, the treaty made the Mekong the dividing line between the British and French empires in South-East Asia and thus incorporated Keng Cheng into Laos. More important from the Thai point of view, France and Britain categorically guaranteed the independence of the Menam Chao Phaya valley and agreed not to seek exclusive advantages in Thailand.

The last of Thailand's concessions to the West

The heartland of Thailand was thus safeguarded but the guarantees did not run to the peripheral areas of dispute such as the Korat Plateau or the Malay Peninsula. Having settled the problems of their own rivalry, Britain and France could now deal with Bangkok separately and settle outstanding issues in their own spheres of interest without fear of arousing the opposition of the other party.

So in the first decade of the twentieth century Thailand was called upon to make her last sacrifices. In 1902 France added some west bank territory on the Mekong opposite Luang Prabang and in Champassak. In 1904, by a major agreement, Thailand formally renounced her sovereignty over Luang Prabang and agreed to the setting up of a joint commission to settle the Cambodian frontier, while France agreed to evacuate Chantabun (occupied since 1893) and to reduce her privileges regarding her Asian subjects in Thailand itself.[64] In 1907, Thailand surrendered the Cambodian provinces of Siemreap and Battambang in return for some other frontier adjustments in her favour. At the same time France gave up her jurisdiction over French Asians in the country.

In making these later territorial concessions, Chulalongkorn was not sacrificing any of his country's vital interests. Granted the fact of the establishment of French power in Cambodia and Laos, it was a matter of resolving the minor details of confusion and friction along the common frontier. On the other hand, the Thai King was also pursuing a deliberate policy of trying to re-establish Thailand's legal sovereignty.[65] The same considerations guided his dealings with the British during the same period.

The series of agreements concluded with Britain after 1896 which culminated in the Bangkok Treaty of 1909 were all connected with the Malay States. During the course of the nineteenth century Britain had clearly become the paramount power in the Peninsula. After 1895 all the Malay States were under British control, directly or indirectly, except those occupied by Thailand in the north. As far as Bangkok was concerned her Malay dependencies were a source of loss rather than profit. In 1897 and again in 1902 discussions took place regarding the status of those states and ended with the understanding that they remained under Thai control provided that no third power should obtain concessions in them injurious to British interests. In 1904 by when Anglo-French rivalry had been converted into friendship,[66] serious talks were held on the future of the northern Malay States. The growth of the rubber industry and the question of the Bangkok-Penang railway added point to these new discussions. The outcome was the Treaty of 1909 whereby Thailand surrendered her sovereign rights over Kelantan, Kedah, Perlis and Trengganu and made certain other important concessions guaranteeing the future of British interests in the Isthmus of Kra.[67] In return Britain surrendered in principle all her extra-territorial rights in Thailand,[68] and granted a loan of four million pounds for the construction of the railway between Prai and Bangkok.

The cession of these four northern Malay states was the last territorial concession made by Thailand to a Western power.

Thailand's survival as an independent state during the peak period of Western imperialism and its gradual transformation into a modern nation was a great achievement. Three major factors were involved. The first and most obvious was the part played by the ruling Chakri dynasty itself. The quiet policies of the early monarchs restored the power and stability of the kingdom after the upheavals of the last half of the eighteenth century. The Thais owe even more to the fourth and fifth rulers of the dynasty who had the intelligence, courage and skill to perceive the nature of the world evolving around them and to reorientate the attitude of their own subjects to the realities of the nineteenth century. The second equally obvious factor is the rôle of geographical and political circumstance. The centre of Thai life and politics, whether at Ayuthia or Bangkok, was never far from the main currents of change which swept by from the outside world. The historical experience of the Thais and their long dealings with European traders made them more conscious of the dangers and possibilities involved. The development of Anglo-French rivalry in mainland South-East Asia during the second half of the nineteenth century provided the Thais with the opportunity to steer between the two. The third factor, and by no means the least significant, was the stability of Thailand and of the Thai monarchy. Centuries of warfare with the Burmans had developed a keen sense of national consciousness amongst the Thais. The leadership of the monarchy in this long struggle and the compactness, ease of communication and unity of the Menam Chao Phaya basin reinforced this national solidarity. These factors and the growth of a well-organized administration gave to the Thai kings more truly effective power than any of their fellow sovereigns in neighbouring lands. King Mongkut was able to reverse national policy in the middle of the nineteenth century, hurting many vested interests in the process, because his authority was undisputed. He was not hemmed in by a narrow clique of conservative advisers as were the emperors at Hué, nor faced with the entrenched opposition of over-mighty subjects as faced Mindon in Mandalay. A fortunate combination of these various factors accounts for Thailand's survival as an independent state.

[1]King Prasat Thong (1630–56) had usurped the throne with the help of Yamada, the leader of the flourishing Japanese community in Ayuthia. Then Yamada tried to exploit the situation to his own advantage by overthrowing Prasat Thong. He was killed in the attempt and after a bloody struggle the Japanese community was massacred in 1632.

[2]In 1649 and 1654. The 1649 tension originated in the Thai refusal to entertain certain commercial demands put forward by the Dutch; the Thais retaliated to Dutch pressure by besieging the Dutch factory and threatening its occupants with death. The 1654 crisis arose from the Dutch refusal to co-operate with the Thais in crushing the rebellious vassal of Singgora (Songkla).

[3]The English East India Company had set up its first factory at Ayuthia in 1612 but it was closed down ten years later, largely owing to Dutch competition.

[4]Lambert de la Motte and Francois Pallu were the first bishops-apostolic to be designated (1658) to open up missionary activities in the Far East on behalf of the *Société*. They arrived in Thailand in 1662. The seminary was at Ayuthia from 1667 till 1765 when it was moved to

Hon Dat (Ha Tien) in Cambodia as a consequence of the Burmese invasions. For more details regarding the *Société* and its activities in the Far East, refer to p. 442.

[5]Louis XIV of France (1643–1715), the Sun King, was perhaps the greatest of all the Bourbon monarchs, who succeeded during his long reign in making his court into the political and intellectual centre of Europe.

[6]Phaulkon or Constantine Hiérarchy; c. 1648, born in Cephalonia, Greece, the son of an inn-keeper; ran away from home to become a cabin-boy on an English ship; 1670, accompanied George White, an English private trader, to India and thence, in the service of White and his partner to trade at Ayuthia. For a good discussion and description of the background to this whole episode, see Collis, *Siamese White*.

[7]Phaulkon's quarrel was with Potts who, as chief factor for the English Company at Ayuthia, was responsible for all English trade there. Potts who was an incompetent drunkard became embittered when Phaulkon wisely denied him the opportunities for trade and profit which he offered to more reliable people.

[8]Especially Father Vachet who took the lead in urging the practicability of converting the court of King Narai to Christianity; he also succeeded in getting Jesuit backing.

[9]Father Tachard had accompanied the embassy led by the Chevalier de Chaumont to Ayuthia in 1685 to negotiate the arrangements for French missionary activity on a large scale in Thailand. He played a leading part in the negotiations with Phaulkon. On his second arrival, in Thailand, he was destined to play a key rôle as intermediary in the events which followed the fall of Phaulkon.

[10]It was one of Father Tachard's tasks to inform Phaulkon of the change of plan and to secure his acceptance of it.

[11]With Bishop Laneau, head of the *Société*'s mission at Ayuthia, who objected to the Jesuits' demands for priority put forward by Phaulkon.

[12]Ujong Salang or Junk Ceylon.

[13]Phra Narai died in August 1686, barely a month after Phaulkon's execution; whether as a result of his illness or at the behest of Phra Pet Raja himself will probably never be known.

[14]The Dutch appear to have been the only exception. They had remained scrupulously aloof throughout the whole Phaulkon episode and with the destruction of French and English influence at Ayuthia, they were able to negotiate a fresh treaty in 1688 which largely restored their former commercial privileges, especially those regarding hides and tin.

[15]Described as 'one of the great Siamese poets', he produced new texts of the Ramakian (Ramayana) and other Hindu-Thai classics.

[16]These centred on problems arising out of Thai relations with Kedah, (in particular the British desire to get formal Thai acquiescence in their occupation of Penang) and the British desire to develop trade, particularly in teak, at Bangkok.

[17]The same Crawfurd who led missions to Ava and Hué. For his background, refer to Burma, Section (b), note 28. The present mission left Calcutta in November 1821; was at Bangkok from March to July 1822 and in Vietnam from August to October the same year.

[18]In 1818, Crawfurd published his *Journal of an Embassy… to the Courts of Siam and Cochin-China* which embodied all this information.

[19]The British mission was most keenly opposed by the Muslim Indian merchant community at Bangkok, who were long established there and held a dominating position in the country's export trade. It was not difficult for them to persuade the Phra Klang that the profits of his monopoly, the proceeds of the exorbitant duties and the gifts which his position entitled him to, would all be jeopardized if the British demands for a fixed tariff, etc. were acceded to.

[20]Henry Burney later became British Resident at Ava. For details of his career, refer Burma, Section (b), note 31.

[21]The Thais reciprocated by recognizing the British ownership of Penang and guaranteeing of food supplies. However, the problem of Kedah kept recurring for the next couple of decades and was not really settled until the Thais reinstated the Sultan as their vassal in the 1840s.

[22]The commercial clauses stated that British merchants were only to pay 'the customary duties' and were to be free to buy and sell without any opposition from Thai officials including the Phra Klang himself. Fullerton, Governor of Penang, commented, 'They appear to be advantageous but so little faith do I repose in their fulfillment that I scarcely think it worthwhile to enter into any serious discussion regarding them.' The systematic manner these stipulations were evaded in practice afterwards at Bangkok by Thai officials appears to justify Fullerton's remarks, but there was nevertheless some expansion in trade.

[23]The British put pressure in the Malay Peninsula to see that the Thai guarantees regarding the

integrity of the Malay states were kept, as is illustrated by British pressure in Perak immediately after the signing of the treaty and their action in bombarding Kuala Trengganu in the 1860s.

[24]The British mission was led by James Brooke of Sarawak fame. Amongst the reasons for Brooke's failure were the rumours about his having lost favour with the British government arising out of the commission of enquiry held over his anti-piratical measures and incidental but untoward matters such as that his letters were two years out of date and signed by the Foreign Secretary Palmerston and not Queen Victoria and that his vessel ran aground in the Menam Chao Phaya and had to have assistance to be refloated. The American mission led by Joseph Balestier, the first American consul to be posted to Singapore, who 'succeeded only in making a bad impression' by his aggressive behaviour, was equally unsuccessful and on arrival at Bangkok he did not even succeed in obtaining a royal audience. Both Brooke and Balestier advocated the use of force to make the Thais open their country to Western trade.

[25]In Thailand as in other Buddhist countries every male Buddhist is supposed to do a period in a monastery as a monk.

[26]In recognition of this, his brother (Rama III) nominated him head of the Board of Pali Examinations.

[27]Or Dhammayutta. What in effect was a reform movement, the sect aimed consciously at cleaning Buddhism of all the accretions of custom and at promoting purely the basic, original Buddhist doctrines as given in the sacred scriptures. The sect was officially recognized during the reign of Chulalongkorn.

[28]Namely Rev. Jesse Caswell, D.E. Bradley and Dr. House.

[29]Phra Nang Klao (Rama III) wanted his eldest son to succeed but gave way to the pressure in favour of Mongkut on condition that his brother, Prince Itsarat Rangsan, should be appointed Uparat (Second King). Itsarat, who had a perfect command of English, exercized considerable influence behind the scenes during Mongkut's reign.

[30]Britain was clearly the paramount power in India by 1850 although in 1857 her authority was to be rudely challenged by the outbreak of a serious rebellion (the Indian Mutiny).

[31]The defeat of China during the First Anglo–Chinese War (1839–42); the Second Anglo–Chinese War broke out in 1856 and was concluded by the humiliating Convention of Peking in 1860.

[32]John Bowring had had a very varied career before his appointment as governor of Hong Kong in 1854, which was his position when he led the British mission to Bangkok. Well travelled, a linguist and economist, he had also taken an active part in politics in England, being secretary for some years to the radical Jeremy Bentham and sitting as a liberal member of parliament. Despite his liberal views (or perhaps because of them) he was largely responsible for Britain's second war with China which began in 1856.

[33]A limited duty was payable on goods imported by British merchants up to 3 per cent *ad valorem*: opium could be imported duty-free although subject to certain controls: exports were to be subject to duty according to a fixed tariff.

[34]The supplementary convention was negotiated by Bowring's chief adviser and interpreter, Harry Parkes, 'after difficulty'. It also provided for the duty-free export of gold and rice, the abolition of the government monopoly over coconut-oil and the right of foreigners to acquire living quarters and warehouses.

[35]Cady (*The Roots of French Imperialism in East Asia*, pp. 143 and 148) points out that 'Bowring did not depend entirely on his own powers of persuasion or even on the formidable personality of Harry Parkes,' but also exploited the presence of the gunboat, H.M.S. *Rattler*, anchored in the river off Bangkok 'which could deliver frequent 21 gun salutes with the maximum psychological effect.' Bowring also at one point threatened to delay his departure when negotiations had got held up. According to Cady also, Parkes' 'angry, bullying negotiations' in 1856 greatly alienated the Thais. No doubt the recent British moves in Burma (the war of 1852 and the annexation of Pegu) served as a potent warning to Mongkut of what could happen if misunderstandings arose. However, a measure of the confidence that Mongkut acquired in Bowring is demonstrated by the fact that he subsequently commissioned the British diplomat to conclude treaties on his behalf with certain other European states.

[36]Including the chief minister (Kralahom), Chao Phaya Sri Suriyawongsa.

[37]The treaty with France was negotiated by de Montigny and with the United States by Townsend Harris who later made his name as the first American ambassador to Japan. The two treaties were substantially the same as the British one, although the French obtained religious concessions as well.

[38]The Hanseatic League was the name given to an association of North German ports which formed part of the loose Germanic Confederacy prior to 1866.

[39]Prussia was the largest of the 39 German states (excluding Austria) which made up the Germanic Confederacy created by the Congress of Vienna in 1815. Under the leadership of Count Bismarck, Prussia led the way towards the creation of a united German Empire with the king of Prussia as the German Emperor. The process was completed with the defeat of France in 1871. In other words in the 1850s, Germany as a nation did not exist.

[40]This was in line with Mongkut's general policy of emphasizing the Buddhistic qualities of the monarchy where the king is regarded as a man and a human being, and of discarding the semi-divine attributes of kingship typical of Hindu tradition and exemplified by the prohibition on looking at the monarch.

[41]The agreement did not include the ancient Malay state of Patani which still remains as part of Thailand. For more on Patani's background, refer note 100, Pt. I, 4 (c).

[42]Aubaret originally came to South-East Asia as a naval lieutenant on Admiral Bonard's staff in 1861; back in Paris he supported the proposals of Tu Duc's embassy in 1863 and was sent to Hué to sign the revised treaty; in 1864 appointed French charge d'affaires at Hué and consul at Bangkok.

[43]The reason why Mongkut did not appear is not known.

[44]Although Mongkut had secured the services of Bowring in order to conclude treaties with certain European powers, their content and aim were strictly commercial.

[45]An earlier French visitor had been the naturalist and explorer, Henri Mouhot, in 1861. It was through the publication of Mouhot's account of his travels in the French journal 'Tour du Monde' in 1863 and of his book in English, 'Travels in the Central Parts of Indo-China (Siam), Cambodia and Laos during 1858-60' the following year that the remains of the Khmer civilization of Angkor were brought to the attention of the Western world. Not long after his visit to Luang Prabang Mouhot died of fever at Ban Naphao, a village nearby.

[46]Doudart de Lagrée died en route at Tong Thuen, Yunnan, in the region of the Upper Yangtse.

[47]King Tiantha Khoman died in 1869.

[48]The Sip Song Chao Thai or the 12 Thai Cantons, like the Sip Song Pan Na further to the West, was a region composed of a loose confederation of chieftaincies which were supposed to owe allegiance to Luang Prabang but were generally left to themselves. Today Sip Song Chao Thai lies within the frontiers of North Vietnam in Tongking along the south bank of the Song Ba (Black River) centred on Dien Bien Phu.

[49]Based on the fact that in the 1830s Luang Prabang had sent tribute to Hué (see section on Luang Prabang, note 4), while Chiang Kuang had definitely fallen under Vietnamese control.

[50]Auguste Pavie; like so many other French empire-builders in South-East Asia, Pavie first arrived as an officer in the marines; 1868, transferred to Postal and Telegraphic Dept. of Cochin-China; 1871, stationed at Kampot; 1880, in charge of the construction of the telegraph line between Cambodia and Bangkok; also busy doing surveys of Cambodia. First attracted official attention by his researches into ancient Khmer civilization, also his work on flora and fauna—work read by governor Le Myre de Vilers (1879-82); 1885, returned to France with a group of young Cambodians to found school for colonial peoples; 1886, appointed through Le Myre's influence as Vice-Consul at Luang Prabang. First mission in Laos lasted from 1887 till 1889; returned to France and then came back on second mission, 1890-1; reported back to Paris and appointed Minister-Resident at Bangkok in 1892; played leading part in the Paknam incident and subsequent developments; served in Laos till retirement in 1895. Published 'Mission Pavie en Indo-Chine, 1879-95' in ten volumes between 1898 and 1918.

[51]Regarded by Frenchmen as the creator of modern Laos, he had 'a kindly nature and simple ways' which endeared him to Cambodians and Laotians. He was also 'a doer, forever clambering into his pirogue for a quick trip upstream to look into some local situation. He travelled from Luang Prabang to Hanoi, to Bangkok, to Saigon, and to most of the river junctions and outposts in between. He would sit down with his small retinue in a village headman's house and exchange tales over a jug of stiff choum, or rice wine, sucked through long straws, and the next day he would be off on the trail again, over mountain passes and through steaming valleys. In this way he won over the tribal leaders and could show the French tricolour in regions two weeks' march from any sizable town.' Arthur J. Dommen., op. cit. p. 10.

[52]Deo Van Tri (Vietnamese name) alias Kam Um (Lao name) was the eldest son of Kam Sinh, chief of Muong Lai (Lai Chao), the most powerful of the White Thai chieftains in Sip Song Chao Thai. Although a close friend of King Un Kham, to whom he had entrusted the education of his sons, Kam Sinh refused to acknowledge either Thai or French overlordship. When Vai Voronat retaliated by making his sons in Luang Prabang hostages, Kam Sinh ordered Kam Um (Van Tri) to threaten Luang Prabang. Raising a force of 600 Black Flags, Kam Um did just that.

[53]Annexation was favoured by the French military authorities in Tongking on strategic grounds,

being a necessary measure to bring the Chinese and Vietnamese resistance and tribal insurgency to an end.

[54]By now Kam Um (Van Tri) was the paramount chief at Lai Chao.

[55]He went there to survey and study local conditions, joined by Kam Um (Van Tri).

[56]He was to act as *chargé d'affaires* with the rank of Consul-General; the French consulate at Bangkok was raised to the status of a legation at the same time.

[57]According to the French version, Grosgurin was attacked and murdered by Thais as he was leading a frontier garrison back to the Mekong from an abandoned outpost. Subsequent investigation has shown, however, that it was the Thais who were attacked by Grosgurin's party. The incident was given the fullest publicity in France with a view to rousing popular support for the annexationist policy of the government.

[58]Prince Dewawongsa was one of the first products Mongkut and Chulalongkorn's policy to create a western-educated and oriented aristocracy. The Prince was the first foreign minister to be conversant with several European languages. He handled the whole of the situation during the crucial days as Chulalongkorn 'had been in a state of collapse throughout the crisis' (Hall, op. cit. p. 660).

[59]It is possible that the French commanders had not received the latest orders prohibiting them from doing so.

[60]However, only after a second French ultimatum had been delivered.

[61]Britain had a dominating interest in Thailand's export trade. See note 27, next section.

[62]James George Scott was a British journalist who had covered French operations in Tongking. Later he was to make his career in the British Burma administration and became associated in particular with the Shan States.

[63]Burman title for territorial chief.

[64]According to the principles of extra-territorial jurisdiction, Europeans in Thailand were exempt from Thai courts and Thai justice since these differed in basis and standard so greatly from European concepts. Instead Europeans were tried in their own courts according to their own laws. This privilege had unilaterally been extended to cover the non-European (Cambodian, Burmese, Indian, Chinese etc.) subjects of the colonial powers to whom these considerations did not necessarily apply.

[65]To secure the abolition of the extra-territorial privileges enjoyed by the Western powers which in reality constituted an infringement on Thai sovereignty.

[66]The growing rivalries between the great European powers divided them into two rival groups. Fear of the rising might of Germany, united since 1871, led Britain and France to sink their traditional differences and come to an understanding for diplomatic and even military co-operation. Known as the *Entente Cordiale* (The Friendly Understanding), it took effect from diplomatic exchanges between the two governments in Europe in 1904 regarding British and French colonial policies and ambitions in North Africa.

[67]'The Siamese government shall not cede or lease, directly or indirectly, to any foreign government, any territory situated in the Malay Peninsula south of the southern boundary of the Mouthon, or Rajaburi, or in any of the islands adjacent to the said territory; also that within the limits above mentioned a right to establish or lease any coaling station, to build or own any construction or repairing docks or to occupy exclusively any harbours the occupation of which would be likely to be prejudicial to British interests from a strategic point of view, should not be granted to any foreign government or party.'

[68]The British gave up all their extra-territorial rights of jurisdiction over their non-European subjects in Thailand with immediate effect and agreed to withdraw their other extra-territorial rights altogether as soon as the codification of the Thai laws in all subjects had been completed.

15. THE THAI STATES: CHRONOLOGY OF MAIN EVENTS

A. Main Periods

A.D. 679–1253	Nan chao		
1000–1300	Period of Thai migration and settlement in Menam Chao Phaya basin and adjacent areas		
1238–1350	The Sukhothai period	1353–1707	Lang Chang
1350–1767	The Ayuthia Monarchy	1707	Lang Chang divided between Luang Prabang and Vientiane
1782	The Chakri dynasty	1828	Destruction of Vientiane
1851	Start of modernization		

B. The Laotian States

1353	Foundation of the kingdom of Lang Chang by Fa Ngum
1582–91	Inter-regnum
1591–1707	Restoration of national unity
1707	Division of Lang Chang between Luang Prabang and Vientiane

	Luang Prabang	Vientiane	Chieng Kuang (Tran Ninh)
1707	Beginning as separate kingdom	Establishment of kingdom by Sai Ong-hue	Chieng Kuang attempts to assert independence of Vientiane
1713		Attempts to control Bassac failed	
1757–60			Chieng Kuang invaded by Vientiane; saved by Vietnam
1778		Thai general Chulalok (Chakri) conquers Vientiane	
1782		Thais install Chao Nan as king in Vientiane	
1787–91	Civil War		
1792		Chao Nan deposed by Thais for intervening in Luang Prabang	
1805		Accession of Chao Anuruth	
1819		Extension of Vientiane's influence over the Bassac region	

	Luang Prabang	Vientiene	Chieng Kuang (Tran Ninh)
1826		Chao Anuruth launched invasion of Thailand	
1828		Chao Anuruth at Hué seeking help	
1831	Luang Prabang sends tribute to Hué	Chao Anuruth handed over to the Thais by ruler of Chieng Kuang	
1832			Chieng Kuang annexed by Vietnam
1833	Second tribute-bearing mission to Hué		
1839	King Suka-seum officially installed by Bangkok		
1850			Revolt against the Vietnamese
1851	Accession of king Tiantha-khoman		
1855			Chieng Kuang royal house restored as vassals of Hué; also paid tribute to Luang Prabang
1861	French explorer Mouhot at court of Tiantha-khoman		
1867	Tiantha-khoman receives Lagrée-Garnier mission		
1869	Accession of king Un-kham		
1871+	First Thai campaign against the Red Flags		Start of Red Flag incursions (see Luang Prabang)
1883	Second Thai campaign against the Red Flags		
1885	Third Thai campaign against the Red Flags; Thai commissioners at Luang Prabang		
1886	Provisional Franco-Thai agreement on Laos		
1887	French consulate at Luang Prabang, Pavie the first consul; Deo Van Tri's revolt		

	Luang Prabang	Vientiene	Chieng Kuang (Tran Ninh)
1888	France annexes Sipsong Chu Thai		
1893	Paknam Incident; Franco-Thai treaty regarding Laos		
1904	Franco-Thai Convention over Luang Prabang renouncing Thai sovereignty		

C. The Thai-Burmese Wars

	Thai	Burman
1356–1420	Thai raids on Burma. Martaban seized	
1548		Tabinshwetl besieges Ayuthia
1564–93		First period of Burman domination. Ayuthia captured, 1569. Bayyinaung, Nandabayin
1593+	Thai recovery under Naresuen. Burmans expelled. Chiengmai conquered (1595)	
1618		Anaukpetlun captures Chiengmai
1661–2	Thai-Burman wars	
1760–76		Second period of Burman domination. Ayuthia captured, 1767. Alaungpaya. Hsinbyushin**
1768–82	Thai recovery under Phaya Tak Sin; new capital at Thonburi, later Bangkok	
1785–97	Chakri dynasty consolidated	Last Burman offensives; defeated Bodawpaya

** Burman raids reached Chiengmai, Vientiane and Luang Prabang

D. Thai-Relations with the West

1512	Arrival of the first Portuguese
	Portuguese opened factories at Ayuthia, Mergui, Patani and Nakhorn Sri Thammarat
1602	First Dutch contacts; factory opened at Patani and at Ayuthia (1608)
1612–22	English factories at Ayuthia and Patani; withdrawn because of Dutch rivalry
1632	Japanese uprising; Dutch aid the court
1649	Thai-Dutch tension; Dutch factory at Ayuthia besieged
1654	Second Thai-Dutch crisis; Dutch naval demonstration
1661–84	English factory re-established at Ayuthia
1664	Société des Missions Etrangères sets up its headquarters at Ayuthia
	Dutch blockade the Menam Chao Phya and obtain concessions
1682–8	The Phaulkon episode
1688	Dutch reopen factory at Ayuthia and sign new treaty
1786	British occupy the Kedah island of Penang
1800	Sultan of Kedah cedes Province Wellesley to the British
1818	British approaches to Bangkok for better trading conditions
1821	Thai conquest of Kedah
1822	Crawfurd's embassy to Bangkok
1826	Burney's embassy to Bangkok; Anglo-Thai treaty regarding Northern Malay States
1833	American treaty with Thailand about US subjects there
1850	James Brooke and Ballestiers' missions to Bangkok
1851	Accession of King Mongkut
1855	Bowring's Treaty opening Thailand to British trade
1856–70	Thailand concludes commercial treaties with USA, Holland, France, Portugal, Denmark, German states, Italy, Norway, Sweden and others
1863–7	Cambodian crisis; Thailand recognizes French protectorate over Cambodia (1867)
1886–93	Laotian crisis
1893	Paknam Incident. Franco-Thai Treaty on Laos
1895	The Mong Sing incident
1896	Anglo-French Agreement regarding Thailand's integrity
1897	Secret Anglo-Thai Agreement regarding Northern Malaya
1904	Franco-Thai Agreement on Cambodian frontier
	Anglo-Thai Agreement about advisers in Northern Malay States
1907	Thailand hands Siemreap and Battambang to French Cambodia
1909	Anglo-Thai Treaty; Thailand relinquishes suzerainty over Kedah, Perlis, Kelantan and Trengganu to Britain

E. The Rulers of the Chakri Dynasty

1. Rama Thibodi (Chulalok)	Rama I		1782–1809
2. Isara Sunthorn	Rama II	son of (1)	1809–24
3. Nang Klao	Rama III	son of (2)	1824–51
4. Mongkut	Rama IV	brother of (3)	1851–68
5. Chulalongkorn	Rama V	son of (4)	1868–1910
6. Vajiravudh	Rama VI	son of (5)	1910–25
7. Prajadhipok	Rama VII	brother of (6)	1925–35
8. Ananda Mahidol	Rama VIII	nephew of (7)	1935–46
9. Bumipon Adulet	Rama IX	brother of (8)	1946–

F. Pavie and Laos

1883		French Protectorate established over Hué
		Defeat of Thai-Lao expedition against the Red Flags in Chieng Kuang
1885		Thai troops occupy Luang Prabang and Chieng Kuang; French protests
1886		Provisional Franco-Thai agreement; French vice-consulate to be set up at Luang Prabang and Boundary Commission to be appointed
1887		Pavie at Luang Prabang as French vice-consul
		Luang Prabang seized by Deo Van Tri; king escapes with Pavie
		Boundary Commission appointed; Pavie a member
1888		Pavie organizes submission of Sip-song Chu Thai to France; Bangkok accedes
1889		King Un-kham reinstated at Luang Prabang in presence of Thais and Pavie
		Pavie returns to France to organize expedition to Lao states
1890–1		Pavie returns to Laos at head of scientific expedition; spreads French influence
1891		Pavie returns to France to get government backing
1891–2		Deterioration in Thai-French relations. French posts established in Middle Mekong
1892		The Grosgurin incident
		Pavie made French Resident-Minister at Bangkok
1893	April	French military columns invade Lao states
	July	The Paknam Incident
	October	Thai-French settlement
1895		Pavie one of the parties involved in the Mong Sing incident

BOOKS AND ARTICLES FOR FURTHER READING:

THAILAND AND LAOS

Cady, J.F., *South-East Asia: Its Historical Development*, McGraw-Hill, New York, 1964.

Fisher, C.A., *South-East Asia: A Social, Economic and Political Geography*, Methuen, London, 1964.

Hall, D.G.E., *A History of South-East Asia*, 3rd ed., Macmillan, London, 1968.

Cady, J.F., *The Roots of French Imperialism in Eastern Asia*, Cornell University Press, Ithaca, 1954.

Collis Maurice, *Siamese White*, Faber and Faber, London, 1951.

Dommen, Arthur J., *Conflict in Laos*, Pall Mall Press, London, 1964.

Hutchinson, E.W., *European Adventurers in Siam in the Seventeenth Century*, Royal Asiatic Society, London, 1940.

Lancaster, D., *The Emancipation of French Indo-China*, Oxford University Press, London, 1961.

LeBar F.M., and Suddard, A., (ed.) *Laos: Its People, its Society, its Culture*, Taplinger, New York, 1960.

Moffat, A.L., *Mongkut ,King of Siam*, Cornell University Press, Ithaca, 1961.

Nuchterlein, D.E., *Thailand and the Struggle for South-east Asia*, Cornell University Press, Ithaca, 1965.

Riggs, F.W., *Thailand: The Modernization of a Bureaucratic Policy*, East-West Centre Press, Honolulu, 1966.

Thompson, V., *French Indo-China*, Allen and Unwin, London, 1937.

Wilson, D.A., *Politics in Thailand*, Cornell University Press, Ithaca, 1952.

Wood, R., *History of Thailand*, T. Fisher Unwin Ltd., London, 1926.

Wyatt, D.K., 'Siam and Laos, 1767–1827', *JSEAH*, Vol. 4, No. 2, Singapore,1963.

Burma: King Thibaw made a prisoner of the British

The Pattern of British and French Policies

In retrospect it is clear that the fate which overwhelmed the mainland monarchies of South-East Asia during the course of the nineteenth century was basically ineluctable. Not one of them possessed the organization, techniques or resources required to stand up to the incursions of the industrialized powers of the West, and even though their political systems tended to be more developed and coherent than those which prevailed in Island South-East Asia, the peoples of the mainland were ultimately as much at the mercy of outside forces as were their neighbours in the Malaysian archipelago. Because these forces did not make themselves felt effectively until the century was well under way, they succumbed later to the Western impact. But in effect the destinies of the mainland states during the nineteenth century were determined by the policies of two major Western powers and the relationships between them in just the same way as had happened in the archipelago. The fate of Malaysia-Indonesia had been settled by the British and the Dutch. The fate of the mainland lay in the hands of Britain and France. It has already been observed that the rivalry between Britain and France goes back to the roots of their national pasts; it originated in Europe and was transferred to the continents of America and Asia to be fought out there, with the British gaining the upper hand by the end of the eighteenth century. But during the nineteenth century circumstances had changed. The traditional emnity between the two nations died away after the downfall of Napoleon in 1815 and was gradually replaced by increasing friendship and co-operation in Europe. Against this background, therefore, the main characteristic of the diplomatic relations between the two powers with regard to their conflicting colonial interests in South-East Asia was the attempt to find a way in which to accomodate each other and avoid a head-on collision.

The evolution of British policy in Burma

British power in Mainland South-East Asia established itself in Burma and from there tended to spread—economically at least—into the Menam Chao Phaya basin. The start of British intervention in Burma, however, during the first quarter of the century had little to do with direct commercial interest, still less with the French but arose, as we have seen, out of frontier friction between two powers of totally contrasted interests and ways of thought.[1]

The decision to annex Arakan taken after the First Anglo-Burmese War was itself a direct consequence of the factors that led to war and had not been contemplated previously. Together with the annexation of Manipur and Assam at the same time, it was obviously a step taken to prevent recurrence of the frontier troubles, although as always the British had a shrewd eye open to the possibilities for trade. The decision to occupy Tenasserim was orginally taken as a measure to serve as a bargaining counter for extracting commercial concessions from Thailand whose possession it had been forty years earlier. But the realization of the province's strategic value, coupled with the development of the teak industry and the disappointing results of Burney's mission at Bangkok[a] caused the British to change their minds and retain their acquisition.[2]

Britain's Second War with Burma likewise was no part of some long thought-out grand imperialist design. Its chief cause lay in the fact that the king of Burma was a heedless despot who had already shown traces of the strain of insanity which ran in his royal line, while in Calcutta the British governor-general was an avowed imperialist. For Dalhousie it was, as much as anything else, a question of prestige: 'The Government of India,' he explained, 'could never, consistently with its own safety, permit itself to stand for a single day in an attitude of inferiority towards a native power, and least of all towards the court of Ava.'[b] Nevertheless, a study of his official and private correspondence reveals that on this occasion Dalhousie had no wish to go to war with Burma or original intention to annex Burmese territory.[3] Once hostilities had begun, however, Dalhousie could not resist the opportunities offered to him, and with visions of founding a second Singapore in Rangoon, he unilaterally annexed Lower Burma. Up to this stage, fear of the French had played little part in British policy which was motivated primarily by considerations of strategy and trade.

The evolution of French policy in Indo-China

French colonial policy, as it evolved towards the states of Indo-China, was far more consciously deliberate in its origins than that of the British in Burma. It was dominated by two distinct, and at times, contradictory influences—religious and commercial. Up till the middle of the nineteenth century, the French stake in Vietnam, Cambodia and Thailand was almost entirely religious. France's missionary links with these kingdoms went right back to the seventeenth century[c] and formed the chief justification for the fantastic ventures undertaken by the court of Versailles in Thailand towards the end of the seventeenth century and in Vietnam towards the end of the eighteenth century.[4] Political developments in France during the first half of the nineteenth century led to an increase in Roman Catholic influence over the French government in Europe and to a revival of their missionary activities overseas.[5] The lead in all this in Indo-China was taken by the old-established Société des Missions Etrangères[d] which despite the increasing hostility of the Vietnamese régime persevered in its work. By 1840 Roman Catholic pressure had been able to establish the presumption that the French government was the protector of Roman Catholic missionary enterprise in South-East Asia, and Rome itself recognized the large rôle being carried out by the French missionaries by abolishing Portugal's ancient Right of Patronage in 1839[6] and assigning all the six vicariates of Indo-China together with several others in China itself to the French Society.[7] The sharpening persecutions of Christian missionaries and converts in Vietnam under the Emperors Thieu Tri and Tu Duc provided a ready weapon for Catholic interests to prod French governments with after 1840.

[a]Refer pp. 504–5.
[b]Quoted by Hall, History of South-East Asia, p. 578.
[c]Refer pp. 442–4; p. 478, note 5 and p. 501.
[d]Refer p. 458, note 2.

During the 1840s the first French naval demonstrations in protest against the anti-Christian persecutions took place along the Vietnamese coast and marked the increasing involvement of the French navy in the Indo-Chinese question. In the years that followed French naval commanders often played a decisive role in promoting a forward policy in Vietnam.[8] However, the main factor in setting France along the path of imperialist expansion in Indo-China sprang from the establishment of the régime of Louis Napoleon which from the very outset relied heavily on Roman Catholic support. In pursuit of this policy Louis Napoleon had taken the Pope himself under his protection in 1849,[9] became involved in a dispute with Russia over Roman Catholic rights in Jerusalem which led to the Crimean War in 1854, and in the 1860s was to attempt to create a new Catholic Empire in Mexico.

In the late 1850s he faced increasing pressure from the Catholic missionaries in Vietnam. As early as 1852 eight French bishops in the Far East appealed to the French emperor for greater steps for their protection. In 1857, as Mgr. Retord of Tongking pointed out, the action which had been taken—naval demonstrations off the coast with the occasional bombardments which were never followed up—only exposed the Christian population of Vietnam to worse reprisals after the French warships had departed.[10] The only remedy, it was urged, was for France to take strong action such as landing on Vietnamese soil and if necessary establishing a base there. Mgr. Retord, and other French missionaries, assured the French government that the oppressed Christian Vietnamese of Tongking were strongly separationist in feeling and would rise the moment France moved.

These views were fully endorsed by the French consul in China, Bourbolon, who advocated a policy of force by seizing Da Nang and region to secure the implementation of French demands which should include a treaty protecting the rights of missionaries, an indemnity of 1,800,000 francs and a series of commercial concessions. Bourbolon as a layman naturally stressed the commercial advantages that might follow any such action, but so did the missionaries. Mgr. Retord himself reported that Tongking possessed gold, silver, copper, coal and timber. Louis Napoleon responded to these appeals by setting up a commission to go into the whole question. In a report which was adopted by the government at the end of the same year (1857), the commission decided unanimously on the seizure of three towns in Annam in order to secure the desired ends and to place the Vietnamese ruler under the protection of France. The Emperor's decision to adopt this forward policy was taken against the advice of his Foreign Minister and owed much to the influence of another French prelate in the region, Mgr. Pellerin, the Vicar Apostolic of Upper Cochin-China, who was given the opportunity to air his views before the commission.[11]

The suitable time for putting the new policy into effect was dependent on the progress of affairs in China,[12] for by this time the Vietnamese question and that of Christian missionaries had become part of the whole issue of French policy in the Far East. A side attraction of the programme to intervene in Vietnam was that it would provide a means of escape from the preponderance of British initiative in the area.[13]

Having eventually seized the Delta region of the Mekong (1859–62),[a] French

[a]Refer pp. 448–50.

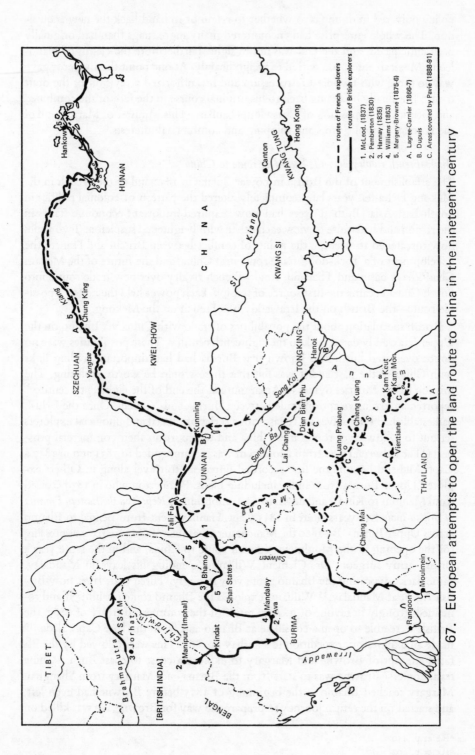

67. European attempts to open the land route to China in the nineteenth century

policy quivered in doubt as to whether to retain or to hand back the new acquisition. The whole enterprise had encountered many more snags than had originally been anticipated, and the end was not in sight. Furthermore the claims of Napoleon's Mexican enterprise started to weigh heavily. At one point the Emperor gave way to those who favoured retrocession and he authorized a revision of the draft treaty. But finally he swung back to his original course in the face of the combined and formidable opposition of Chasseloup-Laubart,[14] his Minister of Marine, and of the Roman Catholic press and shipping and commercial interests.[a]

Anglo-French rivalry over the back-door route to China

The establishment of the British in Lower Burma in 1852 and of the French in the Mekong Delta ten years later completely altered the pattern of colonial politics in South-East Asia. Both powers had now acquired important economic stakes in the region and had cause to view each other with heightened suspicion. Two issues now threatened to become the points of conflict between Britain and France; the development of a 'back-door' trade route into China, and the future of the Menam Chao Phaya basin and Thailand. Anglo-French rivalry over new trade routes into South China became the first source of tension. Each power held the key to a possible route—the British on the Irrawaddy, the French on the Mekong.

British speculation about the possibilities of trade with China via Bhamo on the Upper Irrawaddy dated back to the eighteenth century. These possibilities were no doubt overrated but it was known that Burma had had important trading links with China in the past and it was felt that these would be worth exploring. The mission led by Michael Symes to Amarapura at the end of the eighteenth century[b] reported an extensive cotton trade between Burma and Yunnan. Once the British had established themselves in Tenasserim a series of official and unofficial explorers set out to follow river routes into China and to report on their commercial prospects. The Salween route from Moulmein was recommended in 1831 and in 1837 a Capt. McLeod became the first recorded European to travel along it. Others explored Upper Burma from India, including Lieut. Pemberton who in 1830 crossed from Manipur to Kindat and down to Ava, publishing a *Report on the Eastern Frontier of British India* five years later. In 1835 Capt. Hannay went from Bengal to Bhamo across Upper Burma. By 1860 the Manchester Chamber of Commerce was pressing for the opening of the Moulmein-Yunnan route to China, and in the same year a British army surgeon, Dr. Clement Williams, spending his leave in Mandalay, came back advocating the Bhamo route very strongly. Three years later, now British Agent at Mandalay,[15] Williams explored the Bhamo route for himself and remained strongly in favour of it. As a result of the commercial treaty of 1867, the British were able to open a consulate at Bhamo and from this base Capt. Sladen[16] made an exploratory expedition to Panthay in 1868. This was followed by the ill-fated attempt of Browne and Margary to explore a coast to coast Burma-China trade route.[17] Browne was to start from the Burma end, Margary from Shanghai. Margary reached Bhamo at the beginning of 1875 before Browne had even left, and started on the return journey to prepare the way for Browne. He was killed on

[a]Refer p. 450.
[b]Refer p. 402.

the way by local Chinese resentful of rumoured schemes for building a railway through their territory. The closing of the Mandalay Residency shortly afterwards, the worsening of conditions in Thibaw's Burma, and doubts about the suitability of the route as a whole led to further projects being dropped for the time being.[a]

Just around the time that the British were setting up their consulate at Bhamo, the French were launching their first expedition up the Mekong. In 1866, an expedition under the joint leadership of Doudart de Lagrée and Francis Garnier left Saigon to explore the Mekong and to see its practicability for development as a trade route into Yunnan. The real inspirer of the expedition was Garnier, a born adventurer, explorer and imperialist,[b] consumed by a burning zeal to build up a French Empire in the East and extremely conscious of the advantageous position secured by Britain whom he regarded as France's most serious rival. The Lagrée-Garnier mission[18] drew disappointing conclusions. The Mekong was not suitable as a trade route. The same rapids that impeded Laotian unity impeded travel and trade. The important consequence of the mission was that it directed French attention to the Red river as an alternative route into South China.

The extension of French control over Tongking and Annam

The extension of French control over Tongking and the establishment of a French Protectorate over Annam were the inevitable corollaries of the foundation of French power to the south in the Mekong Delta. It was clear by the Franco-Vietnamese Treaty of 1862[c] that France henceforward intended to regard the domains of Hué as much part of her preserve as the British regarded Mindon's kingdom of Burma. The results of the Lagrée-Garnier exploration of the Mekong dramatically underlined the impractibility of that route as a source of new trade and the rising pitch of European imperial rivalries[19] during the last quarter of the nineteenth century ensured that sooner or later the French would move to round off their Indo-Chinese imperium.

The moves to bring Tongking under French control owed their direct inspiration to the vision and initiative of Frenchmen on the spot, amongst whom Francis Garnier stood out head and shoulders above the rest. Garnier was the exponent of the French version of manifest destiny. He believed that France's destiny lay in Indo-China where her civilizing influences could help regenerate Chinese culture which he greatly respected but whose conservatism he deplored. He admired and feared the success of the Anglo-Saxons in spreading their trade and influence in all quarters of the globe.[20] His views were well known in Paris and Saigon and his appointment as head of the mission sent to deal with the situation created by Dupuis in Tongking in 1873[d] showed that he enjoyed the sympathies of the highest placed French officials in the region. Like Clarke in Malaya at almost the same moment, Garnier exceeded his instructions and tried to present his home government with a *fait accompli*, but apart from the fact that he lost his own life in the attempt,[e] the

[a]Refer p. 416.
[b]Refer p. 461, note 42.
[c]Refer p. 450.
[d]Refer p. 453.
[e]Refer p. 453.

French government at that juncture was in no position to allow itself to get involved in a colonial adventure in South-East Asia. France was still recovering from the effects of her defeat at the hands of Prussia in 1871 and still had a German army of occupation on her soil.[21] So Philastre was sent to Hanoi and Hué to undo what Garnier had done without sacrificing French advantage. He was only successful on paper[22] and the extension of French power had to wait another ten years. But Garnier's martyrdom in the cause of French imperialism was not entirely in vain; he had succeeded in putting Tongking on the map in the minds of most Frenchmen.

By the 1880s the political picture in both South-East Asia and Europe had changed. In Tongking itself matters had gone from bad to worse with ever-growing anarchy, the intrusion of the Chinese and the obvious need to do something to protect French subjects and interests in the region. By this time too, the new French Republic[23] had consolidated itself and the need for France to compensate for her loss of prestige and territory in Europe was beginning to make itself felt. Imperialism became respectable and as was the case in Britain, all sorts of bodies and associations in France started to press for a forward movement in areas within the French sphere of interest.[24] On the wave of this nationalistic and imperialistic fervour Jules Ferry was swept to power for the first time in 1880 and with his Foreign Minister, de Freycinet[25] embarked on an expansionist policy. In July 1881 the French parliament voted credits for action in Tongking and early the following year Rivière received his instructions to secure French interests at Hanoi.[a] Ferry made no secret of his belief in the necessity for imperialist expansion. It was necessary for the national honour and prestige of France as a world power. France had a civilizing mission to fulfill and needed colonies and naval bases with which to fulfill it. The consequence was that while Rivière's expedition ran into the same difficulties that Garnier's had done, the reaction of the Paris government was quite different. The news of Rivière's death inspired the French deputies in Paris to vote supplementary credits for the despatch of a French army to Tongking and subsequently to give their support to the strong policy followed by Ferry towards China.[26]

The British annexation of Upper Burma

The increasing activities of French adventurers, empire builders and businessmen—so reminiscent of Britons of similar stamp who had secured remarkable triumphs in various quarters of the globe—in Tongking, Laos and Yunnan became a serious source of concern to the British after 1875. Their unease was not diminished by the foreign policy pursued by King Mindon and continued by his successor, King Thibaw, who tried to neutralize the threat posed by British power in Lower Burma by cultivating relations with other European states,[b] in particular France. These apprehensions reached their climax when after a Franco-Burmese treaty had been signed, despite British pressure on Paris, the new French consul, Haas, arrived in Mandalay and forthwith proceeded to obtain far-reaching economic concessions.[c] This, together with the rapid extension of French power in Indo-China within the

[a]Refer p. 454.
[b]Refer pp. 417-8.
[c]Refer p. 418.

previous decade[a] led the British to decide to take decisive action to bring Burma firmly under their control by the appointment of a British Resident at Mandalay and the taking over of Burma's external relations—by force if necessary. At the same time British pressure on Paris was resumed, this time to secure the withdrawal of Haas from Mandalay. France, now involved in a conflict with China over Tongking,[b] was not prepared to make an issue over Burma, and yielded to British demands. Shortly afterwards the Burmah-Bombay Trading Corporation's dispute with the Burman government came to the fore, and at the end of the year Britain made war on Burma.

There are two schools of thought amongst historians as to what was the most decisive factor in determining the British to annex Upper Burma. Hall, Furnivall and Cady all lay stress on the British fear of French intervention.[c] However, another recent study places more emphasis on the unremitting pressure of commercial interests whose ambitions and discontents led them to press for a forward policy.[d] The European and foreign Asian trading community which had grown up in Rangoon and Lower Burma after 1852 played a role analogous to that of their contemporaries in the Straits Settlements prior to British intervention in the Malay States. Rangoon itself[e] underwent rapid development as it became the chief port through which the rapidly expanding rice trade passed to its new overseas markets. As it became more established, the business community cast its eyes northwards and anticipated the benefits which could follow the extension of British rule there. From the businessman's point of view, things as they stood were far from satisfactory under Mindon and even less so under Thibaw. Mindon aimed to preserve his country's independence by strengthening his own authority and fostering its trade. His administrative reforms and his policy towards the Buddhist hierarchy[f] were aspects of the first intention, and his efforts to extend Burma's trade under his own auspices reflected the second. The system of royal monopolies which covered every important item of trade and the existence of numerous duties and tolls on the trade between Upper and Lower Burma were irksome in the extreme to the merchants of Rangoon. To aggravate the injury, the King's agents also appeared in Rangoon itself and in other Lower Burma ports to buy up rice and piece goods, nor did they hesitate to by-pass local merchants and deal directly with Calcutta or other overseas centres in order to obtain better bargains. Indeed Mindon went so far as to suggest that Bassein should be handed back to him as a port through which he could conduct his own trade.

The continued existence of the kingdom of Burma—resistant to Western encroachments under Mindon, too unstable for investment and enterprise under Thibaw—was therefore an unwelcome check to the commercial ambitions of the foreign traders in the South. By the 1880s the merchant community of Rangoon

[a]Refer pp. 448–51.
[b]Refer pp. 455–6.
[c]Hall, p. 606; Furnival *Colonial Policy and Practice*; pp. 68–70; Cady, *A History of Modern Burma*, p. 116 et seq.
[d]Singhal, *The Annexation of Upper Burma*, Chapter IV.
[e]See Book II.
[f]Refer p. 411.

was openly clamouring for annexation. A meeting which gave voice to this demand was held by the European merchants of Rangoon in October 1884,[a] and similar demands were repeated early the next year. The Rangoon Chamber of Commerc-demanded action, and the Irrawaddy Flotilla Company, which had cause for come plaint,[b] added its voice in a plea for security and protection for trading interests. These pressures did not come only from Rangoon. In March 1885 a deputation from the London Chamber of Commerce had an interview with the British Colonial Secretary on the same issue. The Chambers of Commerce of Calcutta and of Glasgow also voiced their views.

In the final analysis it is difficult to separate the motives. Although the French crisis had passed before war broke out, the possibility of fresh French intervention was clearly strong in official minds. Sladen favoured annexation and the suppression of the Burman monarchy as being the only sure way to remove the dangers of renewed French influence. This attitude had the wholehearted support of the commercial community in Lower Burma who were as anxious to preserve Upper Burma from French competition as they were to have unrestricted access to its timber and mineral resources, and control of the river route to China. The dispute with the Bombay-Burmah Trading Corporation proved a convenient pretext for action, but even this might not have got so far had Thibaw not been counting on French backing for his position at that time.

Anglo-French Rivalry: the final phase

With the whole of Burma in British hands and the whole of Vietnam and Cambodia under the French the area of potential conflict between the two colonial powers now centred on the Laotian states of the Mekong and on the heartland of Thailand itself. From this point onwards (after 1885) Britain's main concern was to protect her very considerable economic stake in Thailand,[27] and to prevent the British and French colonial empires from sharing a common frontier with all the possibilities for friction that this could engender. The French, on the other hand, wished to consolidate their hold on their new Indo-Chinese Empire, and through the exertions and activity of Auguste Pavie,[c] the French authorities in both Hanoi and Paris came to believe that this implied setting the French frontiers on the Mekong.

The immediate problem concerned the position of the Shan states which fell under British control as a result of the annexation of Upper Burma. Two of them, namely Keng Tung and Kiang Hung, had territory which stretched over to the eastern bank of the Mekong, thus falling in an area claimed by Luang Prabang which was already under strong French influence. The British plan was to create a neutral zone between British Burma and French Indo-China by handing over Keng Tung to Thailand and Kiang Hung to China.[28] In order to facilitate this, in 1889 a commission (the Ney-Elias Commission) was appointed to define the Thai-Burmese frontier.[29] In the meantime the French, also with an eye to the future, approached the British government in London with the idea that Thailand should

[a]Refer p. 418.
[b]Refer p. 418.
[c]Refer pp. 514–16.

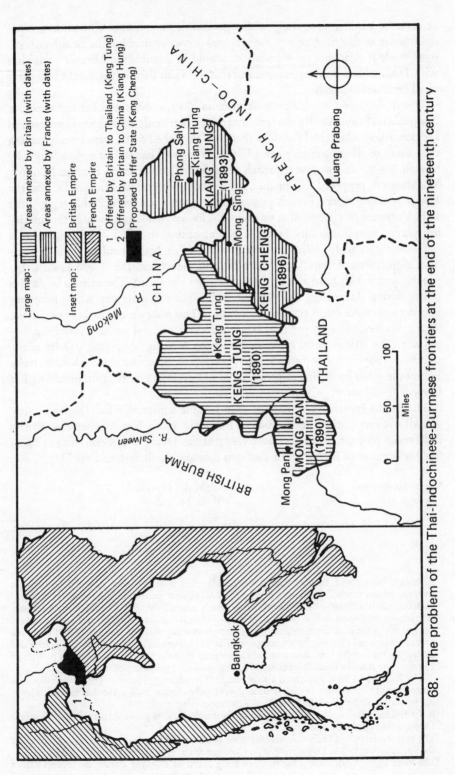

68. The problem of the Thai-Indochinese-Burmese frontiers at the end of the nineteenth century

be declared a buffer state along with a general demarcation of all frontiers. Since this fitted in with British policy, the proposal was welcomed but the British government made it clear that no negotiations would be possible until France's frontiers with Thailand had been settled first and that the Thais themselves should be a party to all decisions reached.

This diplomatic interchange took place in 1889 without any further measures being taken afterwards. By the time that the French made their second approach to London, the situation had radically changed. Now the French were openly staking their claim to all the territory east of the Mekong and had in fact gone a long way to realizing it.[a] In his new approach in early 1892 the French Foreign Minister, Waddington, proposed that neither power should extend its influence beyond the Upper Mekong. Since French power had not yet even reached this region, the British rejected this proposal as unrealistic. This led Waddington early the following year to reveal officially France's real intentions, to which the British gave a non-committal reply. What followed was the Pak Nam Incident,[b] the Franco-Thai Agreement of 1893,[c] the Mong Sing Incident[d] and the Anglo-French rapprochement which have already been discussed elsewhere. The essence of British policy during this period was to persuade the Thais to give way where necessary in order to avoid a direct rupture with France. This policy succeeded in as far as the Thai concessions of 1893 preserved their independence and possibly avoided a major war. The British naval movements off the Menam Chao Phaya Delta in the middle of 1893 probably dissuaded the French from undertaking any bolder stroke but on the other hand British pressure did not prevent France from obtaining her immediate objectives.

The Anglo-French Agreement of 1896 became a guarantee for Thailand's integrity but it also marked the division of Mainland South-East Asia between British and French power in much the same way that the Treaty of London of 1824 signified the division of Island South-East Asia between the British and the Dutch.

[a]Refer pp. 515–16.   [c]Refer pp. 517–18.
[b]Refer p. 516.   [d]Refer pp. 518–19.

[1]Although France and Britain warred with each other over a period of seven centuries, a struggle which reached its climax during the Napoleonic period, they have never engaged each other in hostilities since the time of Napoleon's downfall in 1815. Commercial and colonial frictions continued and on occasion provoked serious tensions (Paknam and Fashoda in the last quarter of the nineteenth century) but other more compelling factors emerged. France as a great power was in eclipse for a generation after 1815. Politically as liberal states, France and Britain found they had much in common contrasted with the outlooks of the other powers of Europe. The rise of a united Germany overshadowed all European politics after 1871.

The British had been concerned about possible French moves prior to the downfall of Napoleon in 1815. After that, French influence was barely a factor at all in the developments leading up to the outbreak of the First Anglo-Burmese War.

[2]If the Burmese had made a reasonable offer in the 1830s, it is possible that the British might have considered the deal.

[3]The whole question of Dalhousie's motives has been explored by Hall, op. cit. See in particular the introduction to The Dalhousie-Phayre Correspondence, 1852–56 by the same writer.

[4]The Phaulkon episode during the reign of King Narai of Thailand during the second half of

the seventeenth century and the Pigneau de Béhaine episode during Nguyen Anh's struggle for power in Vietnam during the last quarter of the eighteenth century.

[5] After the collapse of Napoleon's regime in 1814–15, the former Bourbon dynasty overthrown by the Revolution was restored, and with it a strong Roman Catholic revivalist movement took place. During the reign of Louis XVIII (1815–24) the *Société des Missions Etrangères* was re-established (1819), 'L'Oeuvre pour la Propagation de la Foi', a new missionary organization deriving most of its support from France was founded (1822), and the Paris Seminary for training missionaries reopened (1823). During the reign of Louis-Philippe (1830–48) France's rôle as protector of Roman Catholicism became established, a policy intensified under Louis Napoleon (1848–70).

[6] The Right of Patronage gave the King of Portugal the sole right to authorize, protect and control missionary activities on behalf of the Church in Rome in specific parts of the globe. The Right of Patronage had been granted to the Portuguese during the sixteenth century.

[7] The Chinese vicariates assigned to the *Société* were Chekiang and Kiangsi (1838); Hunan and Hupeh (north of the Wall) and Shangtung (1839); Yunnan (1843); Kweichow and Tibet (1846); Kwangsi (1849).

[8] The officers and men of the French navy were largely recruited from aristocratic families and rural areas where Roman Catholic loyalties were strongest. Naval commanders were appointed to govern Cochin-China for the first decade—Grenouilly, Page, Charner, Bonard, Grandière, Dupré—nearly all of whom were associated with expansionist instincts. Grenouilly was subsequently able to make his influence felt as Minister of Marine and the Colonies in 1867. Other naval men who played important roles in the development of French policy in Indo-China were Doudard de Lagrée, Garnier, Aubaret and Pavie.

[9] Louis Napoleon's régime depended for its existence on the support of the conservative interest, of whom the Roman Catholics formed a substantial part. He took the Pope under his protection in 1849 by sending French troops to Rome to put down the revolutionary movement there and enabling the Pope to return from his exile.

[10] This was demonstrated dramatically after de Montigny's abortive visit to Da Nang in 1857 which was followed by wholesale persecutions of Christians in Tongking and brought about the death of the Bishop-Apostolic there, Mgr. Diaz.

[11] Pellerin had actively concerned himself with canvassing for French government support and intervention; he offered his services as interpreter to the de Montigny mission of 1856–7 to Thailand, Cambodia and Vietnam, and after its failure at Da Nang returned to France where he appeared before the Paris commission.

[12] As part of Louis Napoleon's policy to champion Roman Catholicism and at the same time assert French influence and promote French interests in the Far East, the French had taken the pretext of missionary persecution in China to join in the Second Anglo-Chinese War on Britain's side.

[13] Vietnam was virtually the only region in the whole of the Far East where the British did not have well-established influence and interests.

[14] The Comte de Chasseloup-Laubat, as Minister of Marine (1860–7), resolved the hesitations of the Paris government regarding an expansionist policy in Indo-China by supporting it strongly. In 1865 he threatened to resign rather than accept a revised version of the 1862 treaty with Vietnam. He played an active part in retirement as President of the Paris Geographical Society to promote colonial policies and helped to launch the Lagrée-Garnier exploration of the Mekong, to which the Society contributed 25,000 francs.

[15] Appointed in 1862 as a result of Phayre's treaty with Mindon in that year.

[16] Capt. Edward Sladen was one of Williams' successors as British Resident at Mandalay. Later he became a vigorous advocate for the British annexation of Upper Burma on the grounds of forestalling French influence.

[17] Up the Yangtse Valley, following very much in the footsteps of Garnier who had arrived in Yunnan by way of the Mekong and made his way down to the China coast from there.

[18] The expedition, consisting of 10 Frenchmen (including *inter alia* 5 naval personnel of whom one was a botanist and another a geologist, and also a representative from the French Foreign Ministry) and a party of interpreters left Saigon in June 1866; held up on the Cambodian-Thai border for want of cash and proper passports, they explored Angkor; passed by the ruins of Vientiane and were received by King Tiantha Khoman at Luang Prabang; penetrated into Yunnan but refused permission to go beyond Ta Li Fu; Doudart de Lagrée succumbed to fatigue and died near Ta Li Fu; rest of party led by Garnier went across the Yunnan Plateau and down the Yangtse Kiang to Hankow.

[19] In particular the 1880s saw an intensification of these European rivalries which had already been stimulated by the shortening and cheapening of East-West communications with the

opening of the Suez Canal in 1869. The 'Scramble for Africa' took place in that decade, by which the vast continent was carved up between the various colonial powers. There was also increased German and French activity in the Far East and in the Pacific.

[20]Garnier admired the pertinacity with which the British people had pursued their overseas interests and deplored the parochial outlook of his fellow-countrymen in this regard; he felt that France had allowed her interests to be subordinated to those of the British in the Far East for too long and that to raise her prestige and influence, France must assert and establish herself in every important region in the globe. 'It is fairly obvious that Garnier fancied himself to be the heir and successor of Dupleix.' (Cady, *The Roots of French Imperialism in Eastern Asia*, p. 282.)

[21]The German army of occupation remained in certain parts of the country until the indemnity was paid in full.

[22]The Treaty of 1874 which he negotiated at Hué proved to be virtually a dead letter from the start.

[23]The Third French Republic was set up after the collapse of Louis Napoleon's régime in the 1870s but prior to 1880 it was by no means clear whether the republican form of government was acceptable to the majority of Frenchmen or not.

[24]Such organizations as the Paris Geographical Society, many other regional Geographical Societies, the Society of Colonial and Maritime Studies founded in 1878, all advocated French colonial expansion. Other bodies such as chambers of commerce, political and religious groups as well as books and articles in journals and learned magazines joined in this chorus at the end of the 1870s urging the annexation of Tongking and the spread of French trade in China. For more background see Cady, ibid. pp. 293-4.

[25]De Freycinet became prime minister for some six months in between Ferry's two ministries (between 1881 and 1883), and revived the expansionist programme in Tongking.

[26]However when Ferry's aggressive policy appeared to be failing with the prolonged and indecisive struggle with China he equally rapidly lost popularity, and with the news of the second reverse at Lang Son his ministry fell. By this time peace negotiations with the Chinese were already at a very advanced stage and the defeat clinched matters. Ferry's government was also aware of the grave animosity that his policies were creating amongst other European powers.

[27]It has been reckoned that by the end of the nineteenth century 90 per cent of Thailand's foreign trade was in British hands, while seven-eighths of that was concentrated in the Chao Phaya Menam basin.

[28]This scheme did not work out. China was not willing to accept Kiang Hung at first; Thailand was prepared to take Keng Tung but was too weak to defend it. In 1892 the British ceded Kiang Hung and Muong Lem to China on condition that they were not re-ceded to any third power; but after the Pak Nam incident and the Thai surrender to French demands, Peking handed over Kiang Hung to France. The British absorbed Keng Tung themselves in 1890.

[29]The Thais were invited to appoint commissioners of their own to join the commission but they did not do so; they accepted all the recommendations that the commission made.

16. MAINLAND SOUTH–EAST ASIA: THE ADVANCE OF WESTERN IMPERIALISM

	Burma	Thailand	Laos	Cambodia	Vietnam
1512	Beginnings of Portuguese relations with the countries of the region				
1550–1660	Portuguese free-booters in Arakan				
1596–9				Spanish interlude Blas Ruiz, Vargas, Veloso	
1599–1613	de Brito rules Syriam				
1602	Beginnings of Dutch and English relations with the countries of the region				
1682–8		The Phaulkon episode.			
1786		British occupy Penang.			
1800		British acquire Prov. Wellesley			
1824–6	First Anglo-Burmese War British annex Arakan & Tenasserim.				
1852	Second Anglo-Burmese War. British annex Lower Burma				
1859–62					French war with Vietnam. French annex East Cochin-China
1863–7				French place Cambodia under their protection	
1867					French annex West Cochin-China. French attempt to seize Tongking
1883–5					Sino-French War. French extend control over Tongking and Annam
1885	Third Anglo-Burmese War. British annex Upper Burma				
1893	Paknam Incident: Lao states fall under French rule. Anglo-French Treaty on integrity of Thailand				
1907			Luang Prabang and Champassak completely under French control	Batambang and Siemreap returned to French Cambodia	
1909	Anglo-Thai Treaty; Kedah, Perlis, Kelantan, Trengganu to British control				

Index